Marvin V. Blake

Why
Copyright © 2023 Marvin V. Blake

Library of Congress Control Number: 2023915138
Paperback: 979-8-9886071-4-4

"The whole commerce between master and slave is a perpetual exercise of the most boisterous passions; the most unremitting despotism on one part, and degrading submission on the other. Our children see this, and learn to imitate it, for man is an imitative animal—this quality is the germ of education in him. From his cradle to his grave, he is what he sees others do."

—Thomas Jefferson

****

"Freedom is never voluntarily given by the oppressor; it must be demanded by the oppressed."

—Martin Luther King Jr.

****

"You've got to be taught to hate and fear,
You've got to be taught from year to year,
It's got to be drummed in your dear little ear,
You've got to be carefully taught."

"You've got to be taught to be afraid,
Of peoples whose eyes are oddly made,
And people whose skin is a different shade
You've got to be carefully taught"

"You've got to be taught before it's too late
Before you are six, or seven, or eight
To hate all the people your relatives hate
You've got to be carefully taught"

—Oscar Hammerstein II

****

"Freedom is never voluntarily given by the oppressor; it must be demanded by the oppressed."

—Martin Luther King Jr.

****

"They made us many promises, more than I can remember. But they kept but one-they promised to take our land...and they took it."

—Chief Red Cloud

****

This novel is dedicated to, the three women,
who most influenced my life.

In the three ladies order of appearance:

Ruth Blake Ambrose, my mother who nurtured, loved and during very difficult times, kept the family together.

Miss Eleanor Dimmy, my seventh grade English teacher, who at Baltimore's Cherry Hill Jr. High, through an avalanche of books, opened my eyes to the vast world beyond the housing projects.

Linda Blake, my wife who from the very beginning, has been convinced that I could accomplish anything…and she continues to believe.

WHY!   WHY!   WHY!

Chapter 1
(1853)

Rosewood one of Virginia's grand plantations, is resplendent with its' vast acreage of the South's most important cash crop, King cotton!

Field after field, for as far as the eye can see, is awash with rows of the snow-white pellets — King cotton rules supreme!

The pristine fields of cotton plants, is the undisputed economic engine of the Southern way of life. A labor-intensive agrarian society, made economically feasible and possible, due to the legalized practice of human bondage, Slavery.

The living quarters of the eighty-three inhabitants of Rosewood, who ranged in age from 3 days, the youngest slave child, to that of 82 years, the age of Jeremiah, the father of Rufus, the Rosewood Master's, man-servant.

The living quarters of the eighty-three inhabitants of Rosewood, who ranged in age from three days, the youngest slave child, to that of eighty-two years, the age of Jeremiah, Rufus' father, consisted of; the "Big House", a magnificent three storied colonial structure that the slaves reverently referred to as; the *"Da Man's House"*; the modest neat, brick three room house of the overseer, and the multiple, one room, dirt floor, slave shacks.

This basic layout, the fields, the owner's mansion, the overseer's quarters, and the slave's quarters, was typical of the feudal, gentrified life style of the large plantations of the antebellum south.

****

The sky was a glorious azure blue, with scattered little puffs of fluffy white clouds. The sparse array of clouds did nothing to mediate the oppressive heat.

The relentless noonday sun literally baked the cotton fields, while making miserable the physical activities of the scores of inhabitants, both black and white, of the Rosewood Plantation.

Henry Billings, the six-foot-tall, strikingly handsome, aristocratic, some might say autocratic, distinguished, Master of Rosewood, seated at his massive antique oak wood desk, bellowed, "Rufus, where are my spectacles? Why in the hell is this ink well dry?"

5

"How many times do I have to remind you to tend to your duties? It's not like you're pulling your weight around here. You're not working in the fields anymore. Damn it boy, you're as lazy and shiftless as your Daddy was."

Rufus, a fifty-year-old black man, who walked and moved like an arthritic old man in his seventies, hastily responded, *"Scouse me Sir, let me fill that inkwell for ya"*.

"Massa Henry, I done worked in dem fields most of my life; from sunup to sundown since I be a youngin. Me, my pappy, my woman, an all my thirteen chillin, done worked in dem fields. "I powerful sorry rite now dat my back's ailing and I aint so spry no mo".

Henry Billings extremely intelligent, clever, business savvy twenty-eight-year-old, was the youngest son of Artimas Billings. Henry's father Artimas was himself, the son of one of the Virginia patriots that had fought in the American Revolutionary War.

Consistent with old world common law, custom, and tradition, Henry's older brother Robert had stood to inherit the Rosewood Plantation. Thus Artimas, for multiple reasons, foremost among them being, concerns for his youngest son's future, encouraged and pushed Henry, at an early age, to consider, the study, and the pursuit of a career in the law.

Artimas' plans to ensure the successful familial transfer of the ownership of his beloved Rosewood to his eldest son Robert would never come to past.

Artimas, his eldest son Robert, and his beloved wife Abigail, were all victims, killed during an outbreak of Typhus.

Upon Artimas' death, Henry had would become the Master of Rosewood.

Henry mumbling under his breath, but definitely loud enough to be heard by Rufus; "Sun goes down and all you niggers act as if the day's work is done, Jubilation Time. Hallelujah, time to eat, get drunk, and fornicate. "Where's Ruth, has she attended to Mistress Margaret's bedtime female needs yet"?

Without waiting for a response, Henry began to nimbly climb the ornate staircase leading to the three bedrooms, situated on the second floor of the mansion.

At the top of the staircase, Henry called out, "Peggy, are you decent? Can I come in?"

Margaret (Peggy) Billings, Mistress of Rosewood, was seated at her dressing table, rubbing her hands, arms and elbows, with a delicately scented lotion.

"Henry dear, is it necessary that you shout and raise your voice when you're speaking to Rufus? Rufus and his daddy have tended to this family; to your father and mother, to Robert, and to you and me for ages."

Peggy then took Henry's hand and gently placed it on to her abdomen, "God willing, Rufus or his boy will take care of our son's, soon to arrive brother or sister".

"Hell honey, you and Rufus both know I don't mean nothing by it. I guess I'm just frustrated from trying, in vain, to make sense of the ledger books. I can't reconcile what's notated in the books, with what I can plainly see. Our assets and the figures in this business ledger just don't make sense."

"This year's cotton crop is good. The cotton plants are flourishing, endless rows, of cotton, as far as the eye can see. Yet the numbers, the expense/profit ratio reflected in the ledgers, stubbornly remain in the red". "I tell you honey, something's just not right".

Peggy, with both hands supporting her obviously with-child belly, rose from the table, and gingerly walked to the bed, and in awkward stages, lay down under the sheet. "Henry, I don't understand". "What are you saying?" "Are you saying that we have money problems?" "How can that be?"

Henry walked over to the bed, bent down and kissed his wife's forehead, "It's nothing Sugar". "Don't fret and worry your pretty little head about it." "I'm sitting down with Lucas in the morning. We'll straighten it out".

Henry undressed, and slipped under the sheet, beside his wife. He leaned over and urgently kissed his wife, he then roughly squeezed her breast through her flannel nightgown.

Peggy initially, dutifully returned his kiss. When Henry touched her breast, she ended the kiss by turning her head to the side. Henry placed a hand on each of her cheeks; he put his mouth over her lips and attempted to insert his eager probing tongue into her mouth. "Henry, stop it"! "You know Dr. Sawyer said we shouldn't".

Dejected and frustrated, Henry groaned; "I know, I know. Hell, Peggy a man's got needs." "Its' been months since we made love".

Henry and Peggy Billings lay next to each other, rigid, side by side in the increasingly uncomfortable damp, bedding. Henry was on his back, eyes fixed on the ceiling.

After an interminable ten minutes, which to Henry, seemed like an eternity, Peggy begin to softly snore. Henry pulled back the sweat sodden sheet, stepped into his trousers and with boots in hand; he tiptoed quietly from the room.

****

Henry, trousers, shirt, hat and shoes in hand entered the large, still bustling kitchen, and sat down on one of the two chairs adjacent to the vegetable crib. Matilda the *"Big House"* cook, sat at a table shucking pea. Fanny a spirited, feiste, member of the house-slave contingency, was busy washing dishes, pots and pans.

Tilda was a rotund, robust portly middle-aged slave, whose complexion, reminded Henry of those delicious caramel candies that Peggy loved. Whenever Henry made a business trip to Richmond, he always returned to Rosewood with boxes of *"Tilda colored"*, caramels.

"Evenin Massa Henry you fixing to get yoself some fresh air?" Tilda, despite her differential subservient tone, exuded a distinctive air of competence, confidence and authority.

Henry sat in a vacant kitchen chair, and began to pull on his boots. Without looking up he growled, "Tilda, how many times do I have to tell you, where and when I'm going, on my own land is my business, and no business of yourn?"

Henry, tucking his shirt into his trousers, left the *"Big House"* slamming the kitchen door in his wake.

With the sound of the door still reverberating, Tilda folded her arms across her amble bosom, and commented; *"Air aint da only fresh thing dat man be afta"; "lawd knows chile, Massa Henry be gettin his nightly taste of dat fresh black pootang twix Ruthy's legs".*

Fanny threw her head back, and laughed. Still giggling she exclaimed, *"Ain't dat da truff; "White folks sho loves screwing us niggers".*

****

In addition to the *"Big House"*, Rosewood Plantation's living quarters consisted of eleven primary structures.

The Slave Quarters are located approximately 200 yards from the *"Big House"*. The Overseer's house is located approximately 120 yards from the outermost slave cabin, ¼ a mile's distance from the *"Big House"*.

Ten two room, wood and mud, dirt floor cabins, provided shelter for the Rosewood slaves. Three strategically placed communal outdoor privies, Out-houses, were used by the slave community.

Mistress Peggy's lady's maid Ruth, Matilda's daughter, was in her cabin in the process of tugging her eight-year-old son Jason, into bed.

Jason tall for his age, nearly as tall as his mother, was an inquisitive active boy, whose young body was beset with aching muscles from twelve hours of hauling cotton bags from the fields to the storage barn.

He was a strong boned handsome boy, who was relentlessly teased by his playmates. Jason was referred to by the kids, and by many adult slaves, as a "yeller-nigger".

A hurtful commonly used pejorative, bestowed upon that fraction of the slave population whose physical appearance strongly suggested mixed parentage. That is the individuals are the offspring of a slave women, and a white man.

"Momma, I can't get ta sleep", "arms sore"; "legs sore"; "back sore"; bones sore"; "Ise sore all over". "Hush boy", I'll rub ya down with some of this here leniment", honey you'se got to be quite now. Go to sleep boy. "Massa Henry be coming here directly".

Ruth has been described by men and women, black and white, as a breathtakingly, spectacular beauty. A diminutive five-foot two inch, one hundred-ten-pound, porcelain, ebony doll.

Ruth, at the age of twenty-five, was one of nature's finest accomplishments. She was truly a rare beauty. Born at Rosewood in 1828, the daughter of Matilda, now the Big House cook, and a White Man, most likely Henry's Father, Artimas Billings, Ruth indeed epitomized the recently described genetic concept called *"Hybrid Vigor"*.

Ruth affectionately, lightly slapped Jason's behind, *"der now boy—I'se done, get yoself some sleep." "Massa Henry be comin' ta visit directly".*

Ruth slowly, gingerly, pushed herself up from Jason's bed. She clasped her hands under her swollen belly, reached above her head and pulled over the sheet that divided the cabin. The extended sheet was intended to afford a modicum of privacy for both mother and son.

Still caressing her stomach, she mumbled, *"Shoo hope dis younin come out easy den dat boy done".* As Jason changed position in the bed, he heard the familiar sound of the cabin door opening, and the unmistakable voice of Henry Billings, Master of Rosewood.

Lying in the bed, tossing and turning, Jason's inability to fall asleep, was definitely heightened by the muffled distinctly coherent sounds emanating from his mother's side of the room.

The incessant loud, crackling sounds of the rustling cornhusks, that made up Ruth's bed; his mother's moans, *"Oh Massa that feel so good; that it, that it, right dere; ahh, ahh, feel so good; you so hard".* Jason heard Massa Henry's voice, "Damn right – I'm coming – I'm coming – Ahhhh, Oh Shiiit! And then the sounds of silence — muffled by heavy breathing.

Jason rolled over on to his stomach. Within minutes, he was fast asleep.

****

Henry walked into his large, formal dining room. His wife Peggy, and his six-year-old son Jesse, was each nibbling a biscuit, while waiting for him to arrive. Henry walked around the long table cleared his throat, and seated himself at the table.

"Morning Sugar", he then ruffled Jesse's head of sandy colored hair. Morning sprout". Tilda placed a huge smoking platter of ham, eggs, and grits before Henry.

"Moning Massa Henry", *"hopes youse good an' hungry"*. Henry ignoring the cook, grabbed a hot biscuit from the smoking pile on the table, "I don't have time for breakfast", "Tilda — would you have one of the stable boys… naw", snapping his fingers, "better yet tell that skittish boy, the one can't keep still, what's his name Tilda"?

Matilda rubbing her hands on her apron replied, *"Yassa, that one be Fannie's boy – Pee wee"*. "Tell Pee wee to find Mr. Prentess. Tell Prentess that I want to see him, now".

Henry's son, five-year-old Jesse Billings, heir to the Rosewood Plantation, excitedly, gleefully, jumped up from his chair and exclaimed "Daddy –can I go with Pee wee and fetch Mr. Prentess?

Henry smiled at his son, lovingly tousled his hair once again and said, "all right sprout, but make sure you're back in time for your lessons."

Henry slowly walked the short distance that separated the main house from the outer boundary of the slave quarters. He stopped momentarily, raised his hand to his forehead, shading his eyes, he turned slowly, his gaze made a full circle.

Henry's expression conveyed his unmistakable pride and affection for his beloved Rosewood Plantation. His facial expression abruptly changed to that of puzzlement and concern. Henry turned on his heel – walked back to the "Big House" and entered his office.

While impatiently awaiting the arrival of Lucas Prentiss, Rosewood' stern, many would say, sadistic Overseer, Henry reflected upon the past decade –
his time as the Master of Rosewood.

****

(1838 - 1853)

His peers regarded Henry's father Artimas, the man responsible for the development, the construction, and the sustained success of Rosewood, as a leading pillar of the community.

A staunch supporter of the South's "Peculiar Institution" Slavery, Artimas was an excellent example of the Southern Gentleman. Artimas represented the best of the South's Aristocratic Class. He and his peers occupied the very top rung of the "food-chain".

Artimas was a crafty, shrewd, individual. Intellectualy he recognized that the foundation, the underpinning, the very bedrock, of the South's economy, was totally dependent upon its ready access to abundant, unlimited free labor – Black Slaves.

Not surprisingly, politically Artimas, was an ardent vociferous advocate and supporter of the doctrine of "States Rights".

When Artimas' wife Abigail gave birth to a male child their youngest son –who they named Henry, the patriarch of Rosewood was bitterly disappointed.

Throughout this pregnancy, both Artimas and Abigail had talked about and hoped, for a daughter, a sweet little chubby pink baby girl.

For Artimas, she would be Daddy's little princess. His daughter to be loved, protected and if he had anything to do with it, to be spoiled rotten.

Abigail looked forward to having a white female around the plantation. Of gossiping about the neighbors, or just sharing "girl-talk."

She daydreamed of planning and throwing lavish balls with her daughter; to creating and hosting the Rosewood Cotillion, Southern Society's, preeminent Debutante Ball.

Abigail dreamt of her daughter's coming-out in Southern Society. She looked forward to the ultimate mother/daughter collaboration, the planning of, and the occasion of her daughter's wedding.

When he initially held his newborn son – the first words spoken from father to son were, "dammit – I got another boy"! "You shoudda been a girl".

Artimas' exclamation was not made because of any particular prejudice against sons; it was based upon the fact that his 5-year-old son Robert was the designated heir to Rosewood.

Artimas knew in his heart that the little wrinkled; squirming tyke in his arms was destined for a life of playing 2nd fiddle, as the potential future Master of Rosewood.

To Henry, growing up on the plantation was the most glorious, wonderful, time of his life. Everyone –whites and blacks – treated him as if he were a little prince.

While young Henry adored his parents – he loved and literally worshipped his big brother Robert. Henry relentlessly and persistently followed his big brother "Bobby", the young Massa, around the plantation.

Sometimes his tagging along was permitted. However more than likely, big brother Robert would shoo him away with dismissive gestures and deflating words; "Henry get outta here–you're always underfoot."

Henry when not compelled to study his ABC', history, and math, with his tutor, would continue to clandestinely follow his big brother about the plantation. As long as he could remember, Henry had emulated and imitated, the habits and the mannerisms his older brother Robert.

"Bobby" as his family and friends called him, looked and comported himself in a manner that, met the highest standards expected of the potential Master of Rosewood Plantation.

Young Master Robert had been raised by is father, to take very seriously his responsibility to protect and to care for Rosewood. His father Artimas, had since the boys' adolescence, daily, repeatedly, reminded Robert of his duty.

Artimas constantly lectured Robert, and he always tried to keep Robert apprised of the status of Rosewood's assets.

Day after day, year after year, Artimas could be heard relentlessly drumming into his son and heir's head, "Bobby, someday this place will be yourn".

"Always keep in mind son, the three most important thing we own are the land, the slaves, and the livestock. You've got to hold onto the land. "Cotton's what let's us keep the land. Land without niggers to work it – to plant, tend to, and bring in the cotton, ain't worth shit!"

"Niggers, like horses and mules are valuable animals. Work um; feed um; keep um warm; and let em rut. Works for your horses and your mules; and for most of your Niggers. Remember son, while Niggers ain't human like us, some Niggers can actually think!"

"A thinking Nigger, is a dangerous Nigger!"

"Yep a good horse and a good nigger – they both work best if you lay the right amount of lash to their behinds"

* ** *

Artimas was seated at his desk perusing, and then signing what appeared
to be the last page of a multi-paged document. Lewis Frazier, Artimas' long time
attorney, was placing the pages of the document before him.

With a loud sigh, Artimas replaced his pen into the ink well, he clasped his hands behind
his head and exclaimed "Okay – that's done".

"Lewis I've been thinking, you've been taking care of my legal affairs for more than
twenty years, long before both of my boys were born".

Lewis Frazier, Rosewood's Lawyer, was a short corpulent "fidgety", Southern
Gentleman. Despite Lewis' considerable girth, which undoubtedly contributed to his
propensity to copiously perspire, Lewis was a man who seemed to be in constant motion.

Lewis' most distinctive feature was his eyes. He had the most penetrating, piercing blue
eyes. When pleased or amused about something, his eyes would sparkle, and would give
one the impression that they were looking into a soothing tranquil pool of water.
However, when he became angry or resolute, Lewis' eyes would smolder, cloud over,
and darken.

Some said that if you were the target of his angry stare, it was like watching the coming
of a ferocious summer thunderstorm. "Mr. Billings, it's been my pleasure and my
extreme honor to have had the privilege of handling your legal and business affairs for so
long."

"Hopefully, the good lord willing, we'll be working together for another twenty years."
Artimas took a sip of his drink, smacked his lips and exclaimed; "now that's good
whiskey".

Artimas reached over and opened a beautifully carved cigar box. He offered a cigar to
his guest. Both men bit off the tip of their cigars. Lewis walked over to the fireplace,
stuck a stick into the open fire, held the extended burning stick to Artimas, and then lit
his cigar.

"Lewis took an appreciative drag on his cigar. "How are your boys sah?" Artimas took
another sip of his drink, took a long draw from his cigar, and blew out a large cloud of
smoke. Before responding, he studied the stokey in his hand; "Robert just turned twenty-
one last March, Henry will be sixteen come September."

Artimas placed his cigar in the heavy onyx ashtray on his desk. His eyes met those of the
lawyer; "Lewis, Henry's future is a problem."

Lewis arched a quizzical eyebrow; "problem sah–what do mean?" Whiskey bottle in hand, Artimas set down on the sofa beside Lewis; "Henry's been following Bobby around like a puppy dog ever since he could walk."

"Both of those boys know just about everything you need to know, to be Master of Rosewood. Problem is, there can only be one Master of Rosewood. Artimas paused, then emphatically proclaimed; "When I die, Robert becomes Master of Rosewood. Henry needs a profession".

"Lewis, I need you to let Henry study the law under you". "Hell, Lawyering ain't being Master of Rosewood, but I reckon it's a respectable enough living."

Since Rosewood accounted for more than 95% of Lewis' income, as Artimas expected, Lewis without any hesitation, enthusiastically responded, "why sure Mr. Billings, I'de be glad to teach Henry the Law".

The men shook hands. As Artimas walked Lewis to his buggy, he once again shook the Lawyer's hand and patted him on the back.

As Lewis' driver helped his master into the buggy, he noticed that despite his master's smile, his shirt collar was drenched with sweat, and his usually bright blue eyes, were dark and cloudy.

As Lewis' driver climbed up to his seat, he wearily shook his head and muttered under his breath; *"Ole lawdy we's in fo it now"*.

****

After informing his wife Abigail, of his decision to send Henry to Richmond to study law, Artimas met with his sons. Henry's immediate reaction to his father's decision for his future was that of genuine confusion, and out right anger.

He felt betrayed; he felt abandoned. All that he knew, the wealth of knowledge obtained over a lifetime (fifteen years), to young Henry an eternity, was his life at Rosewood.

His first breath, his first meal of sweet warm mother's milk, milk suckled reflexively by baby Henry from the breast of his *"Black Mammy"*.

His exploration and knowledge of the natural world; all of these things were a part of this world, the world of his beloved Rosewood.

Henry implored, begged, and pleaded with his father to reconsider. At first Henry spoke to his father calmly; then he shouted, he wept, he turned a mournful gaze towards his mother; all to no avail.

Artimas slammed his fist upon the desk, "Cut it out boy", "act like a man – not like a sniffling pup". "Face facts boy; when I pass on, Robert will become Master of Rosewood. "Where will that leave you? "We've got an Overseer".

"Boy you'd be about as useful around here, as tits on a bull. Me and your mother have given this a considerable amount of thought. I 've made up my mind. Henry, the law's the thing for you".

Henry, looked at his brother Robert, who quickly looked away, avoiding eye contact. He wiped his eyes with the back of his hand, and asked, "When do I have to go?" Artimas sat down, and lit a cigar; "Mr. Frazier will be expecting you in Richmond in two weeks".

****

Henry knocked on Robert's bedroom door, then without waiting for a reply, entered his brother's room. "Bobby did you know that they were fixing to send me away?"

Robert shook his head vigorously from side to side, "Squirt, believe me, this is the first time I heard of this. I was as surprised as you were".

Robert jumped from the bed, he placed a hand firmly on each of his brother's shoulders, looked deeply into eyes and said, "I can't imagine not having you here, always being underfoot."

"Damn, two weeks; that don't give us a hell of a lot of time." Henry detached himself from Robert's grip. He gave his big brother a quizzical look; "What are you talking about…time for what?"

"Well kid I wanted to wait until your birthday, but now's as good a time as any; "I'm gonna give you a special gift."

"It don't matter how many times in your life you do it, your first time happens only once;" Henry fixed Robert with a look of genuine curiosity; "First time for what…what are you talking bout Bobby?"

Robert affectionately begin to tousle his little brother's hair; "Your cherry boy, it's bout time you lose it." "Gonna get yourself some pussy, some choice poo-tang."

"I know you being sneaking 'round, peeking at the wenches cleaning themselves in the creek, jerking-off regularly—nothing wrong with that—perfectly natural; but you ain't never screwed a woman, have you?"

Henry's face turned a bright red. He lowered his head; he then sheepishly admitted that he was indeed, still a virgin.

Robert asked Henry if there was any particular female that he; "Wanted to screw?" Henry enthusiastically replied, "Sure I'd like to do it to Mistress Peggy."

Robert gave him a surprised incredulous stare. "Whoa, whoa, hang on there stud. Are you talkin' bout that sweet young daughter of our neighbor, Cap'n Martin? Cap'n Martin's 's precious, little blonde, baby girl, Ms. Margaret?"

Margaret (Peggy) Martin was the beautiful, blond-haired, seventeen-year-old, the youngest, daughter of Captain Joseph T. Martin.

The Martin family plantation was Rosewood's closest neighboring plantation.

"Cause if you're thinking you can get into Peggy's pants, or for that matter, screw any white female, other than one of the town's "white-trash" whores – between now, and you leaving in two weeks, forget it!"

"It just aint gonna happen. Quality white women require a heap of time courting, before it's proper to even hold their hands, to give'em a kiss.

"Listen up brother, time you learned the facts of Southern Life. In the South a White gentleman don't just screw around with a Southern Lady of quality."

"If you want to screw a Southern Lady, a lady of breeding, of quality, someone like a Miss Peggy Martin, you better be intending to marry her."

"Our Southern ladies need to be wooed, you gotta give 'em flowers, candy and such. That starts with talking to the lady's father and getting his permission to come a courting."

"You ain't got time for all of that shit…right? Boy what you need right now is some readily accessible pussy. Little brother, you don't need to get permission. What you need to get, is to get laid."

Robert asked his brother; "Henry, have you and Daddy talked about what goes on between a man and a woman? I mean how screwing makes babies?"

Henry gave his brother an incredulous, haughty stare; "Do you mean Sex?" - "Course I know; I've seen stallions mount mares in heat; bulls mount cows"; rosters and hens. I figured out long ago when I was just a kid, that that's what makes fowls, calves, and chicks… stands to reason, between people, it makes babies too".

"Look Henry, the way you should lose your "cherry" should be the same way that me, Daddy, and most of the white planters, lost ours. The same way that just about all slave owning Southern gentlemen do; you gotta pick yourself out a prime piece of "black ass", preferably, one that ain't been tapped too much before, and let'er rip."

16

The next morning, Henry excitedly woke up before the first roster crowed, which routinely announced the start of a new day. He awoke with a feeling of acute anticipation.

Feelings somewhat akin to what he used to experience as a child, looking forward to presents on Christmas mornings.

While lying in the bed, Henry's right hand, unconscientiously, found its' way to his daily morning, semi-erection. He gently squeezed his now pulsating member, he drew his hand away and thought; to himself, "no need to jack-off today, today I get to do it; do the real thing; today I become a man."

* *

Henry leapt from the bed, pulled the chamber pot from beneath the bed, and proceeded to relieve himself. While absently, wistfully stroking his now flaccid member, his mind began to drift. He remembered what he regarded, his years of shyness and disappointment with what he considered his failure to grow. Specifically, his disappointment was failure to grow "down there", and his failure to spout pubic, or facial hair.

Last year at the age of fourteen, Henry to his delight, began to exhibit definite signs of puberty. His pants no longer fit, his shirts were too tight, none of his cloths seemed to fit.

Seemingly from out of the blue, the tone of his voice deepened. Henry had grown a foot and eight inches in two months. Little patches of dark brown hair, miraculously, appeared under his arms, as well as "down there".

Suddenly from what to him seemed to have come straight out of the blue, what he and his brother called his "little pee-pee", had miraculously grown, and thickened.

"Little pee-pee" now, when at rest or, if standing at erect full attention, was now an impressive "member" of the masculine community. Henry took pride in the fact he could now proudly state that his "member", was nearly as big as that of his brother Robert's.

Henry quickly dressed, left his room and proceeded to pound on Robert's bedroom door. 'Bobby, are you up", hurry up, let's get going! Come on Bobby! Let's go!"

* *

The pungent smell of horse manure, mixed with the sweet flowery fragrance emitted by the magnolias in the garden, wafted on the early morning breeze, towards the stables.

When Henry and Robert left the *"Big House", in* route to the stable, they were greeted by at least a half dozen blacks, who were all engaged in various activities.

Those slaves who labored around the grounds, immediately adjacent to the *"Big House",* were either elderly, disabled, or they were children.

A chorus of, "Moning Massa Bob", moning Massa Henry", filled the air. Each greeting was mumbled by a slave, head bowed, his straw hat in hand, if he happened to own one, followed the brothers as they made their way to the stable.

As they approached the stable, the rhythmic clang, clang of a hammer, repeatedly striking an anvil, grew louder and louder. The clanging abruptly stopped when Henry and Robert entered the stable.

Standing before them, sledgehammer in hand, was a huge, heavily muscled, black as midnight, giant. *"Monin' Massas", how can I help ya?"* Robert answered; "Morning Sampson – me and Massa Henry will be needing our horses."

Sampson was the plantation's blacksmith/groom. Sampson had been smithing for as long as he could remember. Actually, it was shortly after his twelfth summer, when Massa Artimas noticed and commented on the size (height), of this awkward, gangly, skinny slave boy.

Artimas arranged for Sampson to train, to apprentice as a blacksmith, and to eventually acquire the skills of a master-smithy. That gangly, skinny slave boy was no more. Sampson, now thirty years old, stood six foot-three inches. He weighed two hundred and forty-five pounds, two hundred and forty-five pounds of rock-hard, solid.

Sampson turned and called out; *"Pee wee, wer'yu at boy?"* Pee wee, one of the older stable boys, had been raking up horse manure in one of the stalls; he shyly peeked around the stall and in a subdued tremulous voice, muttered; *"Yassa?"* Sampson lightly cuffed the boy behind the ear; *"you and Leroy Fetch the Massas' hosses";* "Gwine get — move yo lazy black asses"!

While waiting for "Pee wee and Leroy to return with the horses, Robert walked over to Sampson; "Looka here Henry", he walked over to the blacksmith – "Make a muscle boy", Sampson replied, *"Yassa Massa"*, and complied. Robert attempted to encircle Sampson' bulging right bicep with both of his hands — "this here is an example of prime nigger flesh."

The stable boys returned with the brothers' mounts. Henry and Robert took the reins from the young slaves. Satan, Robert's horse snorted, tugged at his reins, reared-up standing on his rear legs, with front legs pawing at the air. "Whoa, Satan, easy boy". The stallion settled down – four hoofs planted firmly on the ground.

Robert, gently stroking the horse's muzzle, looked over at Henry, and said, "this here's the finest, fastest piece of horse flesh in the county." "Ole Satan here's won every race he's ever run. Won all kinds of prize money."

Robert glanced around the stable, spotted "Pee wee, and bellowed, "come here nigger", "stand beside me." "Okay Henry, which of these critters is worth more to this plantation? This magnificent stallion, or this scrawny nigger?"

Henry gave Robert a quizzical, incredulous look, he responded; "Come on Bobby, let's get going." Robert said, "I'm serious, we ain't going no where till you answer my question. Which of these animals do you think is more valuable to Rosewood and why?"

Henry, put his foot in the stirrup, swung his leg over his horse's back, and replied; "Satan is." And I'll tell you why," "He's stronger, he's faster, besides, he can make us bundles of money racing and in stud fees." Robert mounted Satan.

As they rode from the barn, he turned to Henry and said firmly, "your answer, was the wrong answer little brother, "the nigger's the right answer." Henry looked up at his older brother, and before he could protest; Robert said with conviction – "Horse can't pick cotton."

As Robert and Henry rode through the endless rows of cotton plants, they observed the numerous slaves tending the crops. The slaves working the in fields were mostly male; ranging in age from their teens, to males slaves in their mid to late thirties. There was a scattering of female slaves. The morning sun was at an angle of approximate 30 degrees, above the eastern horizon.

Despite the early hour, the slaves were perspiring profusely, and constantly wiping their brow with dirty bandanas. The female slaves were attempting to keep the male slaves hydrated, by giving them ladled drinks of water. The females carried their water-buckets, "cooley-style."

Each female wore a collar resembling a yoke. Two poles, equidistance from the center of the device, cradling the water-bearer's neck, protruded from the yoke; one pole on the left the other, on the right.

Henry swung around in his saddle, "Bobby, why are we out here riding the fields? "You said that today was the day that you would help me loose my virginity." Robert chuckled; "Have some patience little brother, getting you laid is precisely what we're gonna do."

Robert shading his eyes, looking into the sun asked; "See them wenches out yonder, is there any of em that you'd like to fuck?" Henry frowned; "Watta you talking 'bout Bobby, I sure as hell don't intend to lay down with none of these dirty, sweaty stinking wenches."

Robert looked hurt; "Hey man, don't be silly, nobody intended fucking anyone of these gals til they got cleaned up."

"Bobby, since my first time ain't gonna be with a white lady, and its'gonna be with a nigger wench, I was kinda hoping that maybe I could do it to a virgin."

Robert grinned, clapped Henry on the back, "well I'll be damned, not only is little brother chomping at the bit to lose his cherry, you want to do it by busting some pick-a-ninny's black juicy cherry.

"Course Henry, you gotta realize, there ain't no such thing as a thirteen-year-old, black virgin, wench. Any black wench that's thirteen years old, been fucked, and fucked a plenty. Most of them been regularly fucked by some black bucks; or maybe fucked by Pa, Me, or by the overseer.

"For a first timer, deflowering a virgin can be tricky. No matter how hard your dick is…it ain't gonna go easy into a virgin pussy."

Henry was intently listening; concentrating on every word spewed forth by his older, presumably wiser, brother. Robert continued; "you gonna come up against a barrier… you gotta bust through that pussy boy; break open that black cherry; draw you some "blood." "You sure that's what you want for your first? "You fucking some young pickaninny-virgin? Be like the blind leading the blind".

Henry thoughts fixated on little ten-year-old Sadie, the daughter of Matilda, the "*Big–House*" Cook. For the past ten years or so, to Henry it seemed as though for all of his life, little Sadie and he had been constant companions, getting into mischief in the "*Big–House*", the two of them being constantly underfoot.

Henry fondly recalled the countless times that he and Sadie had gone swimming, in the creek, both of them, buckass –naked. Initially the children felt totally comfortable viewing their respective nakedness. Henry recalled, with a smile, the first time that he and Sadie, shucked off their clothes, and jumped into the creek together.

At the time, he was ten; Sadie was six. Kids being kids, Sadie was curious and asked; *"Massa Henry, what dat lil worm twix yu legs?"* Henry reached down with right hand, jiggled his shriveled penis; "This here is my pee-pee." "It always shrinks up a little when its'cold."

Sadie examined the region between her legs, then she commented; *"I'se ain't got none; momma say dat dis here"*, as she parted the labia of her vagina; *"be my honey-pot."*

Without uttering another word, no further explanations being needed or required, the two children, ducked their heads under water, and swam towards the fat frog seated on a leaf in the middle of the pond.

As the brothers leisurely rode back to the Big House, Henry's thoughts were of his childhood; growing up, exploring the vast acreage of the plantation.

Playing hide and go seek; climbing tress, learning to swim, all of the things that he experienced with his slave child-hood companion, Sadie.

Snapping out of his brief reverie, Henry looked over at Robert, and said emphatically; "Yes I'm sure. I'm positively certain."

****

"Sadie, afta you finish wid polishn' dem knifes and forks, dun yu forgets to pick us nuff corn, peas, tomatas, for the white folk's dinner, ya hear?"

"I hear's you momma." I ain't be foget'n." Sadie finished polishing the silverware. She meticulous placed each piece of silverware into its' appropriate slot, in its' teakwood, velvet lined case.

Sadie washed her hands, grabbed her basket, and literally skipped out of the kitchen. The screen door slammed behind her with a loud resounding bang. Matilda, Sadie's mother shouted out to her daughter's rapidly receding back; *"Sadie, ain't I done tol yu a hunnerd times, not ta slam dat door! Dat chile neva listen!"*

Sadie hurried from the *Big House,* on her way to the vegetable garden. She closed the gate that fenced in the spacious well-kept garden that supplied vegetables for the white residence of Rosewood.

Most of the vegetables consumed by the slaves, were either grown by slaves, whole cultivated small gardens of their own, or for those slaves that did not have gardens, vegetables were obtained by the bartering of goods and services amongst the slaves.

Sadie was bent over, humming to herself, rapidly picking vegetables from the garden when the Billings brothers rode pass the garden. "Bobby, I 'de like my first to be with her." "With who?" Henry reined in his horse, as did Robert, he turned in the saddle and pointed his finger, at the busy, industrious little slave girl, picking vegetables in the garden, "I want to do it to Sadie."
****

Immediately after finishing supper, Robert and Henry asked to be excused from the dining room table. Artimas, had noticed that throughout the family meal, his sons had been unusually fidgety, and restless. "What's your hurry boys?" "You've both been acting like you got ants in your pants."

Robert looked at his mother; "mother would you mind if Henry, Daddy and I retired to the study? We'd like to discuss some plantation business." Abigail responded with a dismissive wave of her hand; "certainly, all of my men-folk are excused. You all know how that business talk just bores me to tears."

Artimas ushered his two sons into his study, and closed the door. "All right boys, what the Hell is going on? Bobby?" "Well Pop, with Henry leaving for Richmond tomorrow, I just thought it was 'bout time that before he leaves for the big city, he, that he became a real-man." Artimas gave Robert a brief look of puzzlement. Then he smiled. "Ah ha, okay, okay now I take your meaning."

Artimas, with a broad smile – shaking his head from side to side; "Henry, I can't believe it. All this fine black pussy that we own, and you're still a virgin?" Both Artimas and Robert put a hand on Henry's shoulder.

"Bobby which one of the wenches are you gonna use?" "Now if you're asking for my advice, I highly recommend Pearl?" "That Pearly gal really knows how to pleasure a man."

"You got that right Pa; I know exactly what you mean. "When it comes to all manner of fuckin' and suckin', Pearly don't take a backseat…wait a minute that just ain't quite right, that gal Pearly likes for you to put your picker into any body orifice, including in her back-seat."

Both Artimas and Robert experienced a short spasm of uncontrollable laughter. "I was gonna have Pearly break him in – but can you believe it, Henry here wants a virgin he wants to bust two cherries at the same time, his and hern. He wants to bust some nigger-virgin cherry."

"Go on boys, get outta here; pick your-selfs out a wench – but remember you're handling valuable Billing's property!" "Don't do nothing that'll drop the value of our property."

Henry and Robert left the *Big-House;* entered Slave Row, and proceeded to Matilda's cabin. Matilda, and her eldest daughter Ruth, Sadie's deceased mother's, sister, were both at the mansion, cleaning up after dinner.

Henry knocked on the cabin door. Sadie, who had just finished sweeping the cabin's dirt-floor, answered, *"Who dat?" "I ain't 'llowed to open de dor…my momma an' granny ain't here."*

"It's me Sadie, Massa Henry, open the door." Sadie opened the door and stepped back into the room. Henry, followed by Robert entered. *"Evnin' Massa Bobby; evnin' massa Henry."* *"My momma an' sister ain't here."* *"What yu genlemen want?"*

Robert turned; he shut the door, picked-up the wooden board that secured the door, and slide it into place. Robert growled; "Nigger we didn't come here to see your momma or your sister."

Sadie stepped back behind the small table, placing the table between herself and the brothers. *"Massa Henry what yu here fo?"* Henry hesitated, saw the unabashed, stark fear, and terror in Sadie's eyes; "Bobby, I don't know about this; I've changed my mind…I don't think this is right. "Let's go."

Robert raced around the table and grabbed Sadie by the arm, Sadie stood stock-still, paralyzed with fear. "Whoa, wait a minute there little brother; what are you saying, what do you mean, you don't think it's right?"

"We've got every right – what's wrong with you boy?" "You're going to Richmond tomorrow to start studying the law. Are you sure that you're cut out to practice the law?"

Robert sneered; "I ain't no lawyer but I know that the law says that each and every Rosewood's niggers is our property! I know that that's the LAW!"

"We're within our rights as property owners, to do with our property what ever we want to do with, or to our property. Owning niggers is no different than owning hogs or cattle."

If you get a taste for veal, and want to butcher one of your baby cows, that's your right. If you want to whip your slowed down old slave, or you want to fuck your child slave, that's your right."

"Henry, I'm no lawyer, I don't know that much about the law." "But the law that I, and every other God Fearing Southern Christian man of property knows, is the absolute, fundamental law, we're within our rights as property owners, to do with our property whatever we want to do with, or to our property."

"Rosewood's nigger slaves are our property!" Robert tightened his grip on Sadie's arm; he dragged the screaming terrified girl across the room, and threw her onto the mattress, that served as the child's bed. Sadie attempted to get off of the mattress, she couldn't move. She was pinned down to the mattress by the weight of Robert's body.

Robert grabbed the top of Sadie's dress and twisted it in his fist. With one violent tug, the dress split. While still lying upon the screaming, squirming child, he maneuvered his body, and managed to pull the flimsy garment from beneath Sadie's twitching, writhing buttocks.

After several agonizing, minutes, Henry's revulsion, morphed into something altogether different and overpowering. His initial feelings of disgust and discomfort of the rape of Sadie by his brother Robert, in the fifteen-year-old Henry's body, had now been transformed into feelings of pure, animalistic lust.

Robert continued his incessant rapid thrusting into the ravished, bruised body of the moaning, crying, Sadie. Henry, now holding and stroking his engorged throbbing penis in his right hand, looked on. With one last deep penetration, Robert exclaimed "Ahaaa!" — and rolled off of Sadie.

He looked up a Henry, saw his brother caressing his penis; — Robert smiling, gave Henry a wink; "Okay boy—your turn." "I know sloppy seconds ain't what you had in mind for your first time—just remember though you coulda busted this wench yourself." Without a word, Henry knelt between Sadie's legs.

Sadie lay beneath him, limp, bleeding, unconscious; "Bobby she's all sticky and bloody down there." Robert replied, "Don't pay no mind to that—that's just black-cherry juice."

"Have at it boy." Without another word Henry positioned himself between Sadie's legs— abruptly, Sadie moaned and opened her eyes; she stared up at Henry; *"Massa Henry, please Don't hurt me no mo—Massa you'se my friend!"*

For a second Henry hesitated, and then an impassive smirk crossed his face. Henry clumsily, forcefully inserted his erect penis into Sadie.

Sadie screamed; she placed her fist into her mouth to muffle her screams, and bit down on her lower lip, drawing blood. Henry thrust his penis into the helpless girl, just once. He could not control the gushing-forth of his pent-up semen; He immediately groaned, ejaculated, and fell onto Sadie's again, limp, unconscious body.

Earlier that evening, when Robert and Henry first set foot onto slave-row street, practically the entire slave community knew that the two white Massas, were in their midst.

Sister Maybelle, slave row's "town crier", had spread the word. *"Somebody tell Pearl and Lizzie, dat dat randy Massa Robert, wid his lil bruda, Massa Henry, be down here, mo den likly, on da prowe fo some black pootang."*

The fact that some of Rosewood's white Massas were in slave row, after the conclusion of the workday, was not a particularly unusual event. As Sister Maybelle, so succinctly put it, they were *"mo den likly -- on da prowe fo some black pootang."*

When Robert and Henry went directly to Matilda's cabin, and entered, all of the inhabitants along Slave Row, raised quizzical eyebrows.

When the little girls first high-pitched pleading screams were heard coming from the cabin, Sampson, the giant blacksmith, along with two other male slaves, sprinted towards the cabin.

"Maybelle yelled; "wa you niggers doin'?" – Sampson shouted without breaking stride, *"don't ya hear dat chile a screamin' – she needin help – dats my baby in dere."*

Maybelle stepped in front of Sampson, blocking his path – *"Sampson -- yu fixin' to get yo' self kilt?" "Dat be white men, Massa Bobby and Massa Henry in dere wid dat chile."*

The three male slaves stopped in their tracks, and looked anxiously at the cabin, then at the gathering crowd. At that moment, three piteous screams emanated from the cabin.

Maybelle, weeping and wringing her hands; *"Lawd have mercy; wha da doin' ta dat chile."* A group of slaves, both male and female, looking-on in horror, took up positions surrounding Sampson, blocking his path to the cabin.

Sampson, visibly distressed and agitated, was rocking back and forth on the balls of his feet. The big man was holding his trembling left hand over his face. Silent tears of rage and frustration were streaming down his cheeks, from between his fingers.

This towering behemoth of a man, was crying. He was sporadically clenching and unclenching his massive right hand, into an awesome, lethal-looking fist. The tendons in Sampson's right forearm resembled taut ropes.

When the two brothers exited the cabin, the crowd of slaves that had gathered in front of Matilda's shack momentarily startled Robert.

Some of the slaves were mumbling and shuffling their feet in the dirt. The other slaves were standing meekly, heads bowed, eyes fixed upon the dirt path.

Robert quickly regained his composure, threw his arm around Henry's shoulder, and shouted, "Whatcha all looking at? You niggers best be getting outta our way."

An eerie, unnerving quite descended, and hung over the crowd. Silently the crowd of slaves began to thin. Heads bowed, they departed, making a path for the young Massas of Rosewood.

As the assemblage of slaves, slowly began to break-up, and to return to their cabins. Maybelle noted that Sampson was nowhere to be seen.

****

After Robert and Henry's departure, Maybelle, followed by several members of the crowd, rushed into the cabin. *"Lawd have mercy – da massas don kilt dis chile."*

Sadie lay on the bed; motionless legs spread apart; blood smeared across her thighs. Maybelle leaned over the little girl, put her head on the child's chest, and exclaimed; *"she barely breffing. Lucious, get ya black ass up ta da Big House; fetch Tilda and Roof! Wher's Mammy Esta? Somebody get Mammy Esta!"*

Matilda and Ruth burst into the cabin. Maybelle was rocking and trying to console, a thrashing, hysterical Sadie. Matilda hurried over to her daughter, picked her up and begin to rock her back and forth, chroning; *"Oh lawdy lawdy, my baby, my baby—who be hurtn' my baby?"*

Sadie sobbing and whimpering; *"momma, massa Bobby don hurt me bad."* *"Shh shh, hush baby; it gonna be alright...yu be fine."* *"Momma, why massa Henry hurt me...massa Henry my fren."* *Why momma, why?"*

"Yo fren, ther ther baby – ain't no such thing -- white and nigger don't be frens." *"No baby; he not yo fren; he be yo MASSA!"*

Maybelle shooed everyone from the cabin, she quietly closed the cabin door. Maybelle could hear Matilda trying to comfort the sobbing child. *"Hush, hush, child, momma's here"*. They last distinguishable voice that Maybelle heard was Sadie's weak imploring question; *"why momma; why!"*

Bright and early the next day, Artimas and Peggy Billings embraced and kissed their youngest son, as Henry departed Rosewood for Richmond, to study law.

****

Book#2

Chapter #1

To his family, Henry's departure from, Rosewood, was a momentous emotional, and as Artimas had forecast, a pragmatic event.

In addition to missing the companionship of a son and brother, Henry's leaving represented a 25% decrease, in the plantation's population of white men. However, his absence went largely unheralded, and unnoticed by the vast majority of the Rosewood slaves.

Henry's absence from Rosewood did not change the slave's regimented existence; they continued to labor six days a week, from sun-up to sundown.

The slaves reward for a lifetime of involuntary servitude (the enslavement of themselves and of their descendants into perpetuity on earth), was according to the slave preacher's emotional, lyrical oration—the promise of emancipation, freedom and equality in the after-life, in the *"Great Bye and Bye"*.

In fact, the prevailing opinion amongst the slaves regarding Henry's departure was – *"glad ta be shet of him; one les' white debel on da place."*

As far as the slaves were concerned, nothing had changed— *"da sun com up— we wuks our selfs til we's dead—da sun go down." "It dont make no neba mind"*

At least one notable exception to this general sentiment in the slave community was the thoughts and the sentiment held by Matilda.

Matilda, the "Big House" cook— as was her mother (father unknown) — was born at Rosewood—property of the Billings family. Matilda was a third generation, American-born black slave.

For the entirety of her life, being a slave was all she knew. A docile submissive life of servitude was what she knew, and was all that she expected from life. That this was the natural order of things, Matilda never questioned.

Matilda's mother, as did the mothers of all of the black babies born into slavery, did their best to instill in their offspring basic survival knowledge and skills. *"In dis ha worl'chile ya does ya work — "ya neber sass or tok bac ta da white folks."*

"Yu's bo'n a nigger-slave an' ya's gonna dies a nigger-slave." "Pray ta Jesus fo stren'th an sava'tion; he deliba yu and mak' it be all rite in heben."

****

The months, the seasons, the years, seven years to be precise, following Henry's absence from Rosewood, passed by relatively quickly. Robert, now twenty-nine years of age, had gradually, methodically assumed the role and the mantel of Master of Rosewood.

Artimas, the family patriarch, had willingly and gracefully "retired" from the daily plantation business matters, and had gladly turned over the reigns of the running the plantation, to Robert.

Artimas and his beloved, bejeweled, Abigail, were now enjoying after thirty plus years, the "fruits of their labor". The patriarch and matriarch of Rosewood were now living the leisurely life of the wealthy gentry.

The epitome of Southern Aristocracy. A society built upon, sustained, and made possible by "the peculiar southern institution," the enslavement of millions of black people.

Prior to, and as a condition of his retirement, Artimas and Abigail had relentlessly pressured Robert to marry, and thus to provide them with a grandson, a future Master of Rosewood.

Robert, after a world-wind courtship of Miss Margaret Martin, the daughter of Captain Martin, master of the neighboring Claremont Plantation, after numerous "trial-runs, and rehearsals, asked the Captain for permission to marry his daughter Margaret (Peggy).

Captain Martin, a graduate of the United States Military Academy (WestPoint), and a decorated veteran of the Mexican-American War, saw the union of his only child to the heir-apparent of Rosewood, as a godsend. An excellent match, as he saw it, a golden opportunity to, as he put it, to "kill two birds with one stone."

Captain Martin, a widower, had long since resigned himself in the knowledge that without a son, there would not be a Martin, coming after him to carry-on the Martin name.

While Peggy's marriage to Robert Billings would not solve his problem of the passing on of the Martin name, the marriage could accomplish two things that had lately, more and more become extremely worrisome to the Captain. Who would succeed him as Master of his beloved Claremont Plantation? And the problem of the impending demise of the Martin name.

The marriage of Peggy to the very "eligible" Robert Billings, the Captain hoped, would lead to the eventual merging of the two neighboring plantations. And although the children from this union, the Martins and the Billings, would not contribute to the immortality of the Martin name, it would at least ensure the extension of the Martin lineage.

As far as Margaret was concerned, Robert Billings was the most eligible bachelor in the county. The fact that he was both wealthy and handsome, was, as she confided to Celia, her slave lady's maid is; "frosting-on-the cake." For years she had subtlety flirted with Robert, and unbeknownst to him, spun an intricate web intended to "snag" him as her husband.

When Robert proposed, Margaret's demure response was; "Why Sir, you take me totally by surprise." "I am deeply honored—please give me a little time to consider your totally, unexpected proposal."

Ten days later, after what seemed to Robert, an interminable amount of time, and to Margaret, the appropriate length of time, Margaret shyly and coyly, agreed to become Mrs. Robert Billings, Mistress of Rosewood.

The wedding of Robert Billings and Margaret Martin, was the biggest, the grandest social event of the year. Everyone who was anyone, in Essex County Virginia, attended.

Young Henry along with his mentor, Lewis Frazier, Esq., were integral members of the grooms inner-circle. Henry was his brother Robert's "Best Man". The learned, esteemed Mr. Frazier, served as groom's man in the wedding party.

Additionally, Lewis provided invaluable legal services for the Billings Family. Lewis drew-up the legal documents that upon the death of Captain Martin, would merge the Rosewood and Claremont Plantations.

The reception following the wedding, was the most extravagant lavish-ball that anyone, black or white could remember.

During the height of the celebration, surrounded by well wishers, Robert and his brother Henry, found a somewhat secluded corner, and stood alone, puffing on huge cigars basking in the merriment and jubilation of their guests. Robert took a long draw from his, cigar, blew out a cloud of smoke, placed his hand on Henry's shoulder; "well little brother, I did it; I'm a married man."

Henry, who now stood two inches taller than his "Big-brother" spoke in a reverent, some might say, envious voice; "Bobby…you're probably the luckiest man on the planet."

Robert beamed, then did a double- take, looked Henry in the eye; "why thank you little brother…hold on a minute, do I detect a note of jealousy?" "Oh yeah—now I recall, baby brothers' got a great big crush on my brand-new blushing bride."

Henry's face turned a crimson shade of red. He lowered his head— "Cut it out Bobby."
"I have nothing but respect and sisterly affection for Peggy." "Don't be so vexed
Henry…ain't nothing wrong with you having a little harmless crush" "Hell boy that only
shows that you've got good taste in woman-folk."

After a week's worth of vacation, and the attending to semi-business affairs, Henry and
Lewis returned to Richmond.

Rosewood, with Robert at the helm, following Artimas' retirement, continued to enjoy
unprecedented prosperity due in large part, to the increasing demand for, and the soaring
price of cotton.

Two weeks following their first wedding anniversary, while the family sat back from the
dining room table, after enjoying one of Matilda's scrumptious dinners, Robert tapped his
fork against his crystal goblet.

He took Peggy's hand, and announced to his parents; "Momma and Daddy, you're about
to become grandparents—Peggy and I are gonna have a baby."

Abigail, tearing-up—dabbed at her eyes with her fine laced-linen napkin, and
exclaimed— "Oh my dear, that's such wonderful news…I'm delighted, our first
grandchild." Artimas pushed back his chair, walked to the other side of the table and
gave Robert a resounding slap on the back; "Way to go boy…I knew you had it in you."

Seven months later, Robert and Peggy gave birth to a healthy, noisy baby boy. Life at the
plantation for the two generations of white-Billings, was ideal, it was great.

The harvests were plentiful, the slaves docile and seemingly content. In addition to a
bumper crop of cotton, the last year had seen a 'bumper crop" of valuable, new- born
slaves. Life was wonderful. Then without warning tragedy struck Essex County.

Epidemic — Typhoid Fever came to Rosewood.

****

Following the rape of Sadie by the Billings brothers, Matilda's unquestioned life-long
acceptance of slavery, that is that the enslaved plight of blacks in America was "da
lawd's will", abruptly changed.

Matilda's metamorphosis from docile acceptance rapidly progressed from that of grief, to
rage, to anger. To a festering, all consuming hatred of the Billings Clan.

As a result of the physical, emotional, and mental assault perpetrated upon her by Robert
and Henry, Sadie ceased to be the spirited young, beautiful, innocent, pre-pubescent
child.

The creature that gradually developed in the days, weeks and months following the rape, was best be described, by the words of the slave population; *"dat chile don changed"*; *"huh don make no sense atall"; dat gal be touched in da head."*

Sadie had trouble sleeping. At night, she constantly tossed and turned; moaning and groaning incoherently, throughout the night.

The first week following the rape, Matilda set-up most nights, holding and rocking her daughter, until sheer exhaustion, resulted in both mother and daughter dozing off.

During the day Matilda doggedly continued to perform her work as "Big-House" cook.

Sadie had lapsed into a state of total "helplessness". She was no longer able to function. Any separation between mother and daughter would result in Sadie's instantaneous descent into wild hysterics.

She would scream, and scream, and scream for her mother. Those attempting to calm the frantic hysterical girl were themselves subjected to animalistic bites, kicks and scratches.

Matilda was literally forced to be with Sadie, at all times, night and day. When Matilda was working at the "Big- House, Sadie would hang on to her mother's apron, moaning and grunting. Making unintelligible wounded animal-like sounds.

At first, Ruth, Sadie's little sister Ruth, was totally perplexed and confused. She knew that the young massas had hurt Sadie. Hurt Sadie real bad. What she couldn't understand was why, after weeks and months, following the attack, what seemed to her, like forever, her big sister no longer smiled; did not talk to her; would not play with her.

When Ruth asked her mother; *"momma wha's wrong wid Sadie?" "Why she don talk no mo?" "Why she won't let you be?"* Matilda would pick Ruth up in her arms, while the tormented teenaged Sadie clung to her apron; *"Baby de lawd woks in mystery ways"; "He don lef Sadie body here, and don took huh mind and huh soul to glory."*

Two months after the brutal attack of Sadie, by the Billings brothers, it appeared to all; slaves and white-folks alike, that; Matilda, with the passage of time, had gotten over her grief.

Although Matilda never smiled, her sweet, docile, stoic, disposition had returned.

Sampson, Matilda's man, and Sadie's father, and Fannie, Matilda's assistant saw that with each passing day, it was becoming more and more obvious, that physically and emotionally, Matilda was barely holding on.

****

The Billings family; Artimas, Abigail, Robert and Margaret were seated for breakfast, around the huge dining room table. Artimas, surveying his growing family buttered a hot biscuit, and then took a bite. He frowned, gave a surprised critical glance at the biscuit, and bellowed; "Tilda, Tilda; where in hell's my coffee?"

Fannie, sterling silver coffee pot in hand, burst through the dining room door. *"Massa I'se sorry; "here da coffee"; "food be here directly."* Robert, busily tucking his napkin beneath his chin, asked, "Who the hell are you?"— "Where's Tilda?"

Fannie, pouring coffee into Margaret's fine porcelain china cup, responded; *"Ise Fannie Massa—Tilda feelin' right poorly" "she be mighty sick dis moan'n...couden even get out da bed."*

Abigail dabbed at speck of jam at the corner of her mouth. She smiled at her husband, "Well I do declare Artimas, I believe that this is the first time since we've been married —thirty years now—that Tilda hasn't prepared and served our meal".

Robert glared at Fannie, and asked, "What's wrong with Tilda?" "When will she resume her duties?" Fannie bowed her head and mumbled; *"Massa, I don't rightly know" "Yestaday—Sunday, she say she got da mos terrible achy head—she be burnin up." "Touchin her head be lik touchin da stove."*

Artimas filled the ensuing silence; "Alright Bobby, that's enough gabbing, let's let Fannie finish getting our breakfast." "I'm sure that nigger conjure woman— Mammy Ester's taking good care of Tilda."

Matilda could not remember ever feeling this sick. For the past week, she had been experiencing variety of irritating ailments. It started with a lingering headache and a persistently dripping, bloody-nose.

She initially ascribed these, minor, annoying symptoms to her lack of sleep, following the rape of Sadie, and a bone numbing weariness, that seemed to pervade every bone in her body.

The constant twenty-four hour per day, care of Sadie, in addition to keeping up with her regular work, was taking its physical and mental toll, on Matilda.

Just last week, while she was toiling in the kitchen, getting together the *"fixings"* to make a batch of *"Special Brownies"*, for Massa Bobby, she had inexplicably begun to sweat profusely, she became light-headed, dizzy.

The jar of spices that she held, slipped from her sweaty hands, and shattered on the floor. Sadie, who had been clinging to Matilda's apron, begin to cry. Matilda's head begin to spin. She grabbed the edge of the table for support, to keep from falling.

Fannie, who had been seated at the table removing the husk from an ear of corn, jumped up; *"Tilda is you alrite?"* Fannie leaned down to pick up a piece of the broken glass from the shattered spice jar; *"what dat smell?"*

Matilda sat down and leaned back in her chair. Her hand fluttered as she placed it between her heaving breasts, and gasped; *"lawdy, lawdy, my heart bout ta bus from my ches...gimme a minit gal."*

Fannie's eyes bulged, she was visibly concerned; *"Tilda, is ya alrite? ...does you wants me ta fetch Mammy Esta?"* Matilda scooped up Sadie and loving whispered in the girl's ear; *"it be alrite baby...momma's here."* She turned her gaze to Fannie; *"Naw gal...ain't no need fa Mammy Esta...I be fine, I be alrite."*

Matilda was not *"alrite"*, Matilda was seriously ill.

* *

Mammy Ester was attending to Matilda. She lay tossing and turning, thrashing and babbling incoherently, on her foul-fecal smelling, sweat soaked bed.

Mammy Ester was attempting to restrain Matilda; *"She be burn'n up...she got da nervus feber sur nuff."*

Ruth stood in the corner, weeping, and frightened attempting to calm her big sister Sadie. *"Mammy Esta"*, is momma gonna get betta?" *"Will she be alrite?"* *"Chile, I don't ritely know"*, *"dis here be da slow feber."* *"All's we can do now baby is ta keep her cool an' wait"*— *"it up to da lawd now."*

For three weeks Matilda was bedridden. She was delirious, in and out of consciousness. Her temperature continued to rise. She experienced frequent episodic, spasms of diarrhea. Matilda was unable to control her bowels.

Mammy Ester and/or Ruth were constantly at her bedside, ensuring that a cool cloth was maintained on Matilda's feverish brow, that her soiled bed linen was changed.

After being bed-ridden and delirious for fifteen days, at noon on day sixteen, Matilda lay still in her bed, breathing regularly— "Mammy Ester put her gnarled, wrinkled hand on Matilda's brow— *"praise da lawd; da feber done broke."*

Matilda opened her eyes and whispered *"Wher Sadie at; wher's my baby?"* Ruth sat down on her mother's bed; *"howse you feelin' momma"* ..." *"Ise been so worried—so scared."*

Matilda looked pass Ruth, then her gaze came back to Ruth; this time in a much stronger voice she asked; *"Wher Sadie; wher yo sister? Wher's my baby?"*

Ruth took her mother's hands, *"Momma, Sadie dead."* Matilda's eyes were blank. She stared at nothing. Her incomprehensive gaze flickered from Ruth to Mammy Ester.

Then flames appeared in her eyes, flames that exceeded the hottest of the recent fevers, Matilda screamed *"Noooo da done kilt my baby!"*

****

Sadie, as a little girl, had been an extraordinary tomboy. She could outrun, climb faster, "chuck" a stone further than most of the boys her age. It was Sadie's athletic-prowess that first caught the eye of young—a very young Massa Henry.

Frequently when ten-year-old Henry was unceremoniously shooed away by his older brother Robert for "being under-foot", Henry would wonder over—stand apart from—and watch the slave kids play.

One of their favorite past-times, especially during the hot summer Sundays, was splashing and frolicking in the creek.

The creek, was a ribbon of shallow water which bi-sected the southwest, lower sixty acres of Rosewood. Somebody or more accurately, sombodies had in the past, by blocking with shrubs and bushes, the flow of creek-water, had created an eight to ten-foot-deep swimming-hole.

Young Massa Henry had become fascinated with one particular little pick-a-ninny girl, who literally swam like a fish, and dived like a rock, barely making a ripple in the still water, Matilda's daughter Sadie.

When Henry had first described Sadie's aquatic skills to his brother Robert, he had exclaimed, "Bobby when that skinny little pick-a-ninny girl, dived in the swimming-hole from the branch of that big oak, branch must be at least ten feet high, when she hit the water, her arms and hands straight as an arrow, out in front; not a splash!"

Young Massa Henry, and the "little pick-a-ninny girl" Sadie, became child-hood friends and confidants.

During Matilda's bedridden incapacitation, Sadie's depression deepened, and had become all consuming. In the absence of Matilda's constant, warm, maternal reassuring presence, Sadie felt completely alone and abandoned.

Although her little sister Ruth, did her best to see to Sadie's needs, during Matilda's illness, Sadie's depression deepened, she became manic.

On the fourteenth night of Matilda's confinement to bed, Ruth was seated on Matilda's bed, following Mammy Ester's instructions, to keep applying cold wet rags to her mother's feverish brow, Sadie walked over to the bed; *"Ise hungry momma—I want's my momma."*

Ruth, replacing the now warm old comprise with a fresh cold rag, did not look at Sadie, her attention was fixated on her sick mother; *"Not now Sadie, I'se busy wid momma".* *"I'll get yu somp-un ta eat inna minut."*

Sadie turned and left the cabin. The night was clear and cool. A full moon lit her path. Sadie walked aimlessly through the woods towards the swimming hole.

As she walked, she muttered, over and over; *"Momma, why Massa Henry hurt me…Massa Henry my fren. Why Massa Henry don hurt me so bad? Why momma, why?"*

When Sadie reached the swimming-hole, without hesitation, she simply walked in. As she waded through the water, the water gradually covered her head.

Reflexively Sadie held her breath; she instinctively bobbed to the surface treading water for several moments; she did not attempt to swim; her arms became increasingly heavy as the minutes passed; when her lungs were bursting for air from her exertion, she opened her mouth, swallowed a mouthful of the warm water, and sputtered *"Why?"*

Sadie sank to the bottom of the swimming hole.

****

Typhoid Fever—The Epidemic, was devastating to the inhabitants of Rosewood. The fever swept through Rosewood, like the biblical plague described in the Old Testament. Mammy Ester, the "Conjure-woman", administered to the needs of the many slaves that, as she said; *"don tok'n sick wid da feber."*

Dr. Sawyer, the town's white-doctor, was summoned to Rosewood to attend to the plantation's sick white population. Both of the health-care providers, the white physician, and the black Conjure woman, worked tirelessly, incessantly, to doctor and nurse the increasing number of feverishly sick Rosewood residents.

Henry, seated at his desk in his Richmond Office, was busy opening, scanning, and reading the morning's legal correspondence.

After having finished reading the third letter dealing with property disputes, Henry noticed a pale blue envelope, addressed to him, written in the familiar hand of his mother, Abigail. He reached for the envelope, sat back into his chair, and began to read:

My Dear Henry,

June 8, 1837

I hope this letter finds you in good health. Unfortunately, I write to inform you that both your father and your brother's, health is far from good.

As you have no doubt heard, Rosewood has been hard-hit by the Fever. Henry, your father and your brother, are both desperately ill.

I truly fear for their lives. If I ask Dr. Sawyer when and if they will recover, he answers in vague terms.

Dr. Sawyer has quarantined the plantation. Until the epidemic subsides, no one is allowed to either enter, or to leave Rosewood.

Yesterday both your father and Robert were burning up with fever. They were delirious.

I'm truly in fear for their lives.

Pray for us.

Love,

Mother

Henry let the letter drop from his hand. It landed at his feet. Henry reached for a piece of stationary. He scribbled a hasty note to his mentor:

Lewis, family emergency, I most leave for Rosewood immediately!

Henry

****

Despite the Herculean-efforts of Dr. Sawyer, and the house-slaves who dutifully followed the doctor's treatment instructions, neither of the Massas of Rosewood survived.

Artimas and Robert, father and son, both succumbed to the fever. By some quirk of fate, some say perhaps providence, all of the female members of the household, Abigail, and Peggy survived.

Matilda was the primary house-slave that administered to the nursing-care of the gravely ill Massas, Robert and old Massa Artimas. She saw to it that the doctor's instructions were meticulously followed. Cool cloths were constantly being applied to the Massas feverish bodies.

Matilda saw to it, that they were made as comfortable as possible. As soon as they were soiled, the bed sheets were changed.

Dr. Sawyer's treatment plan was to try to control the fever, and to replace the fluids that the patients were losing, through profuse sweating and constant diarrhea.

Of the many nursing instructions issued by the doctor, for the care of Robert and Artimas, Matilda was especially judicious and adamant in seeing to it that the patients were nourished. That following Dr. Sawyer's instructions, the patients consumed lots of fluids.

Matilda was especially judicious in seeing to it that, the broth that the doctor insisted, if necessary, be "force-feed" to Robert and Artimas, was personally prepared by her.

Matilda made it her personal commitment to ensure that the prescribed broth be especially "tasty", with the addition to the broth, of her very "special-spices."

* *

Henry arrived in town, at dusk. He frantically attempted to arrange for transportation to Rosewood Plantation.

None of the local livery establishments would agree to take Henry, and his luggage to Rosewood.

Word of the particularly virulent epidemic at Rosewood, had spread through out the county. Henry offered to double, to triple their normal rate. No one was willing to break the quarantine.

Henry, anxious to get to his father and his brother's bedside, sought to make arrangements to rent a horse and buggy, to transport him and his luggage to Rosewood.

Due to the uncertain status, as to the length of the quarantine, none of the merchants would enter into a rental agreement with Henry.

Out of desperation Henry, made arrangements to store his luggage, and was forced to purchase a horse.

The merchant that sold Henry the horse had strongly urged Henry to at least, wait until morning, before attempting to reach Rosewood.

After a hastily gulped down sandwich, and a mug of beer, Henry mounted his newly acquired, horse and set out for Rosewood.

A horse and buggy normally accomplished traveling the distance between the town and Rosewood, during the daylight, on well-traveled roads, in approximately ninety minutes.

Henry had chosen, not only to travel after sunset, he had decided to make time by taking short cuts. To make off trail departures, through the woods often through tangled underbrush.

Henry had been riding at a steady gallop. Despite his staying on the well- traveled horse and buggy roads for the most part, he was making good time.

Henry was about a quarter mile from Rosewood, when he decided that he could cut his remaining travel time in half, by cutting through the woods that surrounding Rosewood.

Henry was very familiar with this particular wooded area, a stretch of woodland on the perimeter of Claremont, Captain Martin's Plantation.
Unfortunately, for Henry, his horse was in, unknown terrain.

Henry sat relaxed in the saddle. He knew that shortly, very shortly he would be within the borders of Rosewood. Henry's mind was fixated on recalling his mother's letter.

His horse, jumped over a fallen tree limb, misjudged the width of the limb, stumbled and threw Henry from the saddle.

Henry knew he was falling. His immediate thought was to avoid falling under the horse. Of having the full weight of the horse come crashing down on his unprotected body.

He freed his feet from the stirrups, and was propelled over the horse's head. Henry's head struck a rock. Henry was knocked unconscientious. Henry lay still, motionless on the ground.

Sampson, Rosewood's gigantic blacksmith, was returning to his cabin.

After the evening meal, and after most of the slaves had gone to bed, as had become his habit, Sampson had been aimlessly foraging in the woods.

Now and then he would find a piece of wood, suitable for carving. More often then not he would just wonder in the woods, beneath the stars, berating himself for not having intervened when his daughter Sadie was being raped.

Sampson was consumed with guilt, for not having saved Sadie.

Sampson and Matilda had been "seeing" each other for more then twenty years. Everyone in the slave community knew that "Massa Artimas wen he horny, com a tippin' ta Tilda", other wise Tilda be Sampson's woman".

Artimas was aware of Sampson and Matilda's relationship. However, he reasoned, as long as Sampson made himself invisible, when he, the Massa was having his way with Matilda, he concluded that the potential products, especially the birth of strong young bucks and wenches, that resulted from the mating of Sampson and Matilda, was sound business practice.

While Sampson hated sharing the woman he loved with the Massa, both he and Matilda accepted it, as did the entire slave community, as a fact of life, the degradation that a black man had to endure, to survive in the South.

After Sadie's death, Sampson had been lapsing into prolonged periods of melancholy, of deep depression. Although speculation as to who was Sadie's real "Pappy", persisted as an item of gossip within the slave community, it was never ever even hinted at, in the big man's presence.

To Sampson, Sadie was, and would always be, his *"baby gal"*.

****

That horrible night when the young Massas were brutally raping Sadie, and he impotently just stood by not — as it appeared to everyone — prevented by the shear number of his fellow slaves holding him, as much as being prevented by decades of indoctrinated subservience.

That night, that horrible night, when he failed to respond to his baby's piteous cries for help was by far, the worst night of his life.

****

Sampson heard the horse's frightened whinnies. He heard a man's voice shouting "whoa…whoa", then thrashing sounds in the brush, and the thud of a body hitting the ground.

Sampson ran to the fallen rider, intending to give assistance. As he approached the scene, he saw the horse, trembling, standing next to an unconscious white man lying motionless, facedown, bleeding on the ground.

Sampson hurried over to the man, turned him over. He recognized immediately, that the injured man was Massa Henry.

Sampson was rapidly blinking his eyes, and then he froze. The compassion and empathy that he had been feeling for the unconscious man, had been instantly transformed to unbridled, all consuming, hatred.

Sampson looked down at the face that had haunted him, each and every night, since that horrible night. The hated face of the animal that had tortured, raped, and ultimately murdered his baby.

Sampson calmly, ran his hands along Henry's right leg as though he was checking for fractures. Apparently satisfied that the leg was intact, Sampson stood. He picked up a heavy fallen tree branch, raised it over his head, and murmured; *"Des be fo my baby…dis be fo Sadie".*

Sampson swung the heavy branch, with all of his strength down on Henry's leg.

The large bone in Henry's thigh shattered, splintered. Henry screamed, and once again slipped into unconsienciousness. One jagged edge of the splintered bone, protruded from the skin just above Henry's knee.

Blood was gushing from the wound. Sampson casually reached down and picked up a sturdy tree limp, and snapped it over his knee. He then used his pocketknife to cut the pants from Henry's uninjured leg.

Sampson cut a two-foot strip of cloth from the pants. He tied the cloth above Henry's shattered femur. He placed the tree limb inside the knot, and twisted with all of his enormous strength.

The gushing blood flow became a trickle, which slowly seeped from the wound, then stopped. Sampson picked Henry up from the ground, and laid him across his horse's saddle. Then he gathered the reins, and began to lead the horse back towards the plantation.

****

Finally, after his last patient's fever had subsided, and the dead had been buried, Dr. Sawyer determined that the Rosewood-Fever Epidemic had run its' course. In his capacity as the county's Chief Medical Officer, Dr. Sawyer, officially lifted the quarantine of the Rosewood Plantation.

Dr. Sawyer was busy packing his medical supplies and instruments. His intent was to return to town as soon as possible. He planned to leave Rosewood, first thing in the morning. As he was closing his medical bag, his attention was drawn to some sort of commotion in the yard.

Fifteen feet from the porch of the Big House, Sampson began to run, shouting, *"help, help... It's Massa Henry, he bad hurt. Ise needs Doc Sawyer, help, help!"* Dr. Sawyer and Rufus ran down the steps.

Henry's face was deathly pale. His breathing was rapid and shallow. Henry had lost a great deal of blood. Dr. Sawyer, medical bag in hand, raced to Henry.

Sampson had gently placed Henry on the ground. The doctor clamped and sutured Henry's femoral artery. He cleaned fragments of bone from the wound, approximated the ends of the fractured bone, and immobilized the leg by encasing it in three pieces of oak.

Sampson, the plantation's blacksmith and master craftsman, constructed a wooden cast for Henry's leg, which Dr. Sawyer cushioned with goose down.

Dr. Sawyer had no doubt that Sampson's actions had saved Henry's life. The doctor was absolutely convinced, that had the giant blacksmith not fashioned and applied that tourniquet, Henry would have bleed to death.

As to Henry's eventual recovery, Dr. Sawyer attributed that to a combination of his youth, the grace of God, and just plain, blind good luck.

After two months, Dr. Sawyer removed Henry's wooden cast. Following six weeks of rehabilitation on crutches, and finally with the aid of a cane, Henry was able to once again, walk. His stiff leg would not allow him to ever again, sit a horse.

****

During the epidemic, Lucas Prentiss, the plantation's—at-best—mediocre overseer, despite the depleted sick slave work force, attempted to work the fields, as usual.

Lucas' supervisory style was simple. His intent was to accomplish the same amount of work, with far fewer slaves, by increasing the individual field-hand's productivity.

His means and method of increasing the individual slave's productivity, was generally that which was applied by most slave owners. As Lucas frequently stated, "handling niggers", was simple, "best way to get good-work outta a nigger is by the generous application of the lash."

Lucas firmly believed that the "smartest nigger, weren't no smarter than a child." And as his own momma had repeatedly quoted from the good book, to Lucas and to his eight siblings, "Spare the rod—you spoil the child."

****

The constant relentless, merciless whipping of the already sick field hands, many of whom were weakened by fever, instead of maintaining the fields, had the opposite effect. Rosewood's once pristine cotton fields were rapidly, going to ruin.

When Henry Billings was finally up to assuming his responsibilities as the new Master of Rosewood, he found his beloved home, in a state of chaos.

Almost the entire slave population, at some point, had been bed-ridden, and unable to work. Six of the bed-ridden slaves did not survive the epidemic.

Consequently, the formerly pristine cotton-fields had become overgrown with grass and weeds. The cotton plants at an alarming rate were steadily losing the battle with the weeds, for the soil's nutrients.

****

Henry, with a vengeance, threw all of his considerable energy and talent, into the daunting task of the saving, and the restoration of Rosewood.

It had been two years since he had last seen his grief-stricken mother. The loss of his father and brother during the recent epidemic was devastating. Henry had loved and worshipped both men.

As much as the lost of Artimas and Robert, affected Henry, the loss of her husband and eldest son, filled his mother Abigail, with what she described as an intolerable grief, an unrelenting ache deep within the very marrow of her bones.

Like her mother-in-law, Peggy too had lost to the epidemic, the two most important men in her life, her husband Robert, and Captain Martin, her beloved father.

For her entire life, Peggy had had a strong man to fend for her, to protect her, a man to depend upon. The widow Margaret (*Peggy*) Billings, the now single mother of four-year old heir to Rosewood, Jesse Billings, Peggy Billings, the Mistress of Claremont Plantation, felt abandoned, adrift, lost.

Henry and his business-mentor, Lewis Frazier, concluded that Rosewood's survival required that they immediately maximize the plantation's capital, capital needed to restore the cotton fields.

This was accomplished by divesting themselves of non-essential "livestock". High on the list of non-essential livestock, were Artimas' stable of sporting racehorses, and a few valuable slave artisans, the slave artisans.

High up on the list of valuable slaves to be sold for instant cash, were Matilda, the finest cook and pastry chef in the county, and Sampson, the plantation's blacksmith, carpenter, and leather craftsman.

Matilda and Sampson were sold.
****

At Peggy's request, Henry, with the assistance of his mentor Lewis Frazier, was meticulously, examining the Claremont Plantation's books and ledgers.

Their audit of the Claremont books revealed that Captain Martin's, lavish, flamboyant life-style, far exceeded the plantation's assets. Claremont was heavily in debt, and on the brink of foreclosure.

Henry was seated on his plush sofa, sipping a glass of lemonade. Rufus, now one of the oldest Rosewood slaves, entered the study and stood beside his master, holding a fresh filled glass of the sweet beverage.

Lewis was at Henry's desk, shifting through a box that contained voluminous documents, past due bills, current bills, and bills that would soon be coming due.

The contents of the box, more than attested to the woeful financial state of the Claremont Plantation.

Lewis sighed and looked across the room towards Henry; "This is a mess." "Looks like ole Captain Martin died just about in the nick of time."

Henry put down his glass—turned towards Lewis and asked; "what do you mean—how bad is it?"

Lewis raised both of his hands. Each hand was stuffed with papers. "The notes of indebtedness suggest to me, that any day now, the bankers and the creditors, with the sheriff in-tow, will come-a-knocking on Ms. Margaret's door."

Henry, lost in thought, unconscientiously picked up his second glass of lemonade, took a long sip, and pondered. Events and circumstances had changed drastically, and it seemed to him, for the worst during his protracted time away from Rosewood.

Through the passing years, he had dutifully visited the plantation, wanting to be with the family and to celebrate holidays and special family occasions.

That the quality of the lifestyle at Rosewood, had declined, was undeniable. He sipped his lemonade, and mumbled; "Hell even the lemonade was different—it lacks that unique tangy-flavor that the drinks Matilda use to make, had had."

Lewis put down the papers, placed his elbows on the desk, clasped his hands together, forming a steeple; "Henry, if Claremont and its' assets are sold at auction—in this depressed economy—Miss Margaret would be lucky to get ten cents on the dollar!"

He leaned over and smiled at his protégé. "Hell man, if I were you, I'd kill two birds with one stone; I'd just marry the lady, sell off most of the Claremont niggers; use that money to placate the vultures, and merge the adjacent Claremont fields with those of Rosewood.

That would solve both of your problems. And to boot man, no offense intended, if I may say so, Ms. Margaret is the finest looking white woman in the county, bar-none."

In bed, Henry lay contemplating Lewis' suggested solution to his and to Peggy's dilemma. At first Henry had dismissed Lewis' tongue-in-cheek suggestion, as just that. Humorous banter-something half-heartedly said in jest.

When recalling the conversation, his first reaction was that to pursue Lewis' suggested course of action, would be "cold, grass, calculating, and manipulative. However, the more he thought about it, the more it made sense.

Henry even as a child growing up had always thought of Peggy as the most beautiful desirable girl in the world. And while he knew in his heart, growing up as a smitten teenager that, if his handsome older brother Robert chose to court her, neither he nor any of the other area bachelors, stood a chance at winning the heart of the beautiful Margaret Martin.

The more he thought about the solution, proffered fleetingly and half-heartedly, by Lewis in passing, the more he was inclined to admit that it made a lot of sense. Of course, none of it would be possible, if Peggy was not so inclined.

Each passing grief-filled day that Peggy mourned the untimely deaths of the two most important men in her life, her husband and her father, Margaret (Peggy) Billings, experienced a steady, resolute, emotional shift.

When Robert and her father the Captain, both became victims of the epidemic, Peggy felt loss, totally alone and abandoned.

For her entire life, Peggy had been *"taken-care of"*. Looked after by strong by men. First by her father, then by her husband, Robert.
****

Peggy was by no stretch of the imagination, stupid. In fact, Peggy's intelligence was well above that of most of the male plantation masters.

Her familiarity and knowledge of western literature and poetry was substantial. Peggy could hold her own, and indeed often lead, discussions dealing with the works of such old-world geniuses as, Shakespeare, Michelangelo, Beethoven, Mozart.

Peggy's dilemma was that she was profoundly, almost totally, ignorant of business, more specifically, the business of running a plantation.

Her lack of exposure to the pragmatic business vicissitudes, needed to learn how to manage a large plantation, were directly the result of her gender.

Being a female raised in the prevailing Southern Plantation-Culture, did not include a lady being exposed to business affairs.

The female children of the planter gentry-class were raised under the philosophy that girls, and women were to be placed on a pedestal.

That they are fragile, porcelain doll like creatures to be cherished and literally, worshipped.

In essence Southern womanhood was fastidiously protected. Females were not to be exposed to, or to be knowledgeable of such serious, by definition, masculine things, as agriculture, business, or the workings of the marketplace.

Southern belles of the planters-caste were to be "seen and not heard." Southern ladies were treated as if they were beautiful ornaments.

Raised to marry the white gentlemen, and to bear white children, who would in-turn repeat the cycle. Thus, ensuring the growth and perpetuation of the Southern Aristocracy.

Peggy Billings, the widowed mistress of Rosewood, and the orphaned mistress of Claremont, was at a complete loss. She did not have the slightest idea as to the running of a plantation.

Peggy had quickly come to what she considered the inevitable conclusion, the only logical conclusion that her "Southern-belle— protected rearing had prepared her for, Peggy needed a husband.

She, the Rosewood, and the Claremont Plantations, needed to find the right man to assume the mantle of Plantation Master.

* *

Henry could not deny that his attraction towards, and his feelings for Peggy had never really totally, died. True, for the sake of propriety, decency and his love of his brother Robert, he had suppressed and buried his deep-seated amorous feelings for his sister-in-law.

When Robert and Peggy's son Jesse was born, Henry could not deny that he experienced mixed feelings. His rational mind swelled with the love of an uncle for his nephew.

Yet Henry had to admit, if only to himself, that subconscientiously, he fantasized that Peggy should have been his wife, and his nephew Jesse should have been his biological son.

For two solid months following his recovery from the accident, with his cane, now accepted as a permanent, third leg, Henry's demeanor towards Peggy gradually changed from that of a brother towards his sister-in-law, to that of a man definitely attracted to a beautiful, available woman.

On Sunday May 13, 1855, Henry Billings and Margaret Martin Billings were married.

Henry, in league with, and influenced by the unrelenting, pragmatic advice generously voiced by his mentor Lewis Fraiser, had successfully, executed a campaign which wooed, pursued, and chased Peggy Martin, Billings.

The plan was flawless, and strategically well executed. Henry James Billings, wooed, pursued, and chased Peggy Martin, Billings, until SHE (Margaret *Peggy* Martin Billings), caught HIM.

****

Lucas Prentiss, Rosewood Plantation's overseer knocked firmly on the office door. Henry, with a start, lifted his right leg from the hassock, upon which it rested, and placed it uncomfortably on the floor.

He grumbled a single terse word; "Enter". The overseer, Lucas Prentess, hat in hand opened the door, "Morning Mister Billings", you wanted to see me suh?"

"Have a seat Lucas. Lucas I need your help. I've been having a great deal of difficulty in making sense of these ledgers. The gross quantity of bales of our cotton crop, that is bales per acre, is good. The crop yield appears to be consistent and proportional, to our crop of niggers."

"The number that puzzles and alarms me, is the most important number—the bottom-line."

Lucas sat uneasily on the edge of his seat, his hat in-hand, "I don't know what you mean Mr. Billings—what exactly is that bottom line talk?"

Henry reached across his desk and removed a fragrant cigar from the humidor on his desk. He held the cigar beneath his nose and took a long appreciative sniff.

Henry sat back relaxed in his chair, twirled the stocky between his thumbs; "Simply put Lucas the amount of profit that Rosewood is making, after you allow for the cost of running the place—your salary; and hell, the cost of feeding the livestock, including the niggers, the profit, what's left over is no where near what it was when my father and brother, were the Masters of Rosewood."

Henry rose from his chair, with his cane in hand, limped over to the fireplace, awkwardly bent over and removed a sliver of wood from the flames, and lit his cigar.

Henry took a long draw, inhaled and blew-out a huge cloud of blue smoke; "The variable, that is the crop yield minus the expenses are pretty much the same. It's only the bottom line, the profit margin that's noticeably different."

"Lucas, do you have an explanation for these anomalies?"

While Lucas wasn't familiar with the word anomalies, he was quite familiar with the jest of his employer's, implicit accusation.

For years now, Lucas had been skimming small amounts of money, "A little bit of cream from the top." Small little things such as "short-counting" the number of bales of cotton—selling and pocketing the difference—renting out the labor of especially skilled slaves such as Sampson and Matilda—even resorting to the pimping of some of the wenches—preferably the promiscuous ones like Pearl—to the young white men of the neighboring farms.

During Henry's father's time as Master of Richmond, Lucas' entrepreneurial enterprises had been sanctioned and condoned, with the explicit understanding that 2/3 of the illicit money went to the plantation.

And that the family would have complete deniability of any hint of impropriety associated with prostitution, in the event that those activities lead to scandal.

Artimas and Robert listed the prostitution monies in the ledgers, under the column labeled, miscellaneous. The remaining 1/3 went to Lucas.

Following the deaths of Artimas and Robert, these monies, legal and illegal, had ceased to be incorporated in Rosewood revenue stream, Lucas, for the past several years, had been the sole recipient of these "*miscellaneous-side monies.*"

Lucas, absent mindedly reached into his trousers and removed a soiled rag. He dapped at the perspiration that had begun to accumulate on his brow, his mind began to race, *"Damnation, this here young Mister Henry ain't nobody's fool."*

"I can't for the life of me put my finger on the reason for the short-fall." "You can rest your mind; I'll look into it—and fix it right away suh"

Henry took a long drag from his cigar, exhaled a long stream of aromatic smoke, stared at Lucas with his steely blue-eyes, and remarked; "I have every confidence that you will get to the bottom of this, and will move swiftly to rectify the situation."

Before Lucas could respond, Rufus, Henry's Man Servant, closely followed by his wife's maid Ruth, burst into the office. *"Massa Henry, Missy Peggy send me; she screaming and moaning something awful."* Ruth, gasping for breath, nudged the old man aside— *"Massa, the Mistress water done broke — "she bout to birf dat baby."*

Henry pivoted from the fireplace; he began to issue a rapid stream of orders. In a firm commanding voice, he instructed Lucas to immediately give Pee wee, one of the stable boys, a travel pass.

"Have Pee wee take a buggy to town and fetch Dr. Sawyer." He dispatched Rufus to "fetch Mammy Ester, that old Conjure Woman." Henry limping as fast as he could, followed Ruth, up the stairs.

****

Peggy sat slumped, exhausted in the bedroom's rocking chair. Her sweat-drenched nightgown clung to her like a sodden shroud.

For the past two days and nights, Peggy had been experiencing occasional, periodic, irregular contractions. The first contraction had occurred two nights ago and had awakened Peggy.

Peggy had rolled-over in bed, and was not surprised to find that Henry's side of the bed, was empty. Henry's absence from their marital bed was of no particular surprise.

Three weeks after they were married, Peggy became aware and accustomed to, her husband's habit of, once she fell asleep, quietly gathering his cloths and leaving their bed. In fact, these patterned departures were especially predictable, if for any reason she had declined his amorous advances.

Peggy knew of Henry's, as she described it *"dalliances"* with her maid, Ruth. Henry's demeanor when he was around Ruth, coupled with the little snippets of slave-gossip amongst the house-slaves, that she occasionally overheard, solidified her suspicions, Henry was sleeping with her personal maid, Ruth.

Peggy pragmatically and intellectually, acknowledged and accepted Henry's relationship with Ruth, as well, just a matter of fact. It was common knowledge that the Southern-Aristocratic, way-of-life, allowed for and embraced the practice.

A way of life that Peggy, all things considered, —as did most Southern White Ladies— lived and enjoyed.

Peggy's knowledge of her husband's extra-curricular sexual activities with Ruth, in no way affected her genuine affection for Ruth—her slave. As far as Peggy was concerned, Henry was within his rights as the Master, and that Ruth's participation, was her duty as the slave.

Henry, dragging his right leg behind, trailed by a lumbering very pregnant Ruth, ascended the staircase. Henry was attempting, but failing, to take the stairs two at-a-time.

He burst into the bedroom. Henry limped over to his wife's side; "How you feeling Sugar?" Peggy looked up into the face of her husband, then down to her swollen belly; "I'm alright, honey, though I must admit, I have had better days."

Peggy's face became contorted by a spasm of pain. She gasped between shallow breathes; "Has anyone gone for Dr. Sawyer?"

Before she or Henry could speak, Mammy Ester, followed by Rufus, came into the room. *"Wat yall doing har? Landsakes...lok lik a Sunday go to meetin' up in here."*

Mammy Ester went over to Peggy; *"How ya feelin' missy... how close da cramps?"* Peggy's facial muscles relaxed, still she continued to squeeze Henry's hand; "The pains have been coming about every half hour or so."

Mammy Ester turned and spoke to Henry: *"Massa we need to git des peeples outta dis room. I needs ta zimen da Mistress."* Henry leaned over, kissed Peggy on the forehead, and motioned by waving his arms that everyone should leave.

Mammy Ester reached for Ruth; *"You stay gal. I'll be needing a han wid my zimanin."*

His head turned towards the bedroom, Henry tightly gripped the banister, and slowly, haltingly, descended the stairs. Rufus led Henry into the parlor. *"Massa Henry...sit yoself down, I'll git you a whiskey an' water."*

Henry broke away from Rufus grip; "Where's the doctor…Rufus did that boy get back yet with Dr. Sawyer?"

"Please Massa Henry, sit yo self down…Doc Sawyer on da way…he be here soon. Mistress Margaret being token good care of…Mammy Esta done birfded hunnerds of babies."

Mammy Ester, walked into the parlor, she was drying her wet hands on her apron. "What's happening Mammy Ester…how's Mistress Margaret… is she allright?"

"She be doin' fine Massa Henry…it be a while yet foo dat baby come-out. You best be gon'n bout ya bizzness…ain't nuttin you can do but wait. Dat baby come when da lawd want it ta come."

Little six-year-old Jesse, ran crying into the parlor, jumped up onto Henry's lap, and between gasping breaths blurted; "Pa I'm scared, Pee wee and Doc Sawyer just rode up in the buggy. Pee wee said that he fetched Doc Sawyer for Mommy. Is Mommy all right…is mommy sick?"

Henry hugged Jesse to his chest. "Mommy's fine Jesse — hey guess what pal, mommy's going to give you a brand-new little brother."

This revelation had an instantaneous calming effect on the little boy. He gave a puzzled look to his father, a broad grin began to light-up his face, wiping the tears from his cheeks, he excitedly exclaimed; "really Pa? "really…where is he, where's my little brother?

Henry looked lovingly into his son's eyes, and once again hugged him to his chest, "Remember when Mommy and I let you put your hand on Mommy's swollen stomach…Remember how surprised you were when you thought that her tummy had kicked your hand?"

"We told you then that that was your little brother growing inside her tummy. "Dr. Sawyer is here to help your baby-brother leave mommy's tummy."

Dr. Sawyer, entered the parlor, "evening Henry", he took-in at a glance, the small group of people gathered in the room, Rosewood's white-ruling family members, and three of their most trusted house-slaves.

His eyes sought-out, and found Mammy Ester; "Mammy, how's your Mistress…how far along is she?"

Mammy Ester, prior to her being sold to the Billings of Rosewood, and during her time at Rosewood, had delivered scores of slave babies. She had "*helped*" many a white doctor deliver white babies.

Mammy walked over to the doctor; "*Mistress Margaret doin just fine…she got a while yet*". Mammy skillfully maneuvered Dr. Sawyer so that their backs were to the group, she spread her thumb and index finger approximately an inch apart; "*She be open bout dat much.*"

Dr. Sawyer turned to face Henry, "Sounds like we gotta a while yet…I'll see my patient now." Dr. Sawyer and Mammy Ester climbed the stairs, he quietly knocked on the bedroom door, without waiting for an answer, he entered the bedroom.

Peggy, attended to by Mammy Ester and by Ruth, for the remainder of the night was kept relatively comfortable. Dr. Sawyer spent the night down-stairs in the parlor, smoking cigars and sipping drinks with the nervous, apprehensive expectant father.

He had left instructions with Mammy Ester to; "Come get me if Mistress Margaret begins to bleed, or when the cramps start to come fast."

Mammy Ester acknowledged that she understood his instructions by mumbling; "*Yassah Massa Docta…I sur nuff come get cha ifin any dem things happen.*"

As soon as the doctor closed the door, and his foot-steps could be heard descending the stair-case, Mammy Ester turned to Ruth; "*dam-fool white man—I done birfed mo babies den dat ole cracka got hairs on he head.*"

Peggy feigning sleep, overheard Mammy's comments, but had the good sense to act as if she had not.

Dr. Sawyer was well aware of, and to himself, grudgingly respected Mammy Ester's medical skills. She had more than earned his respect, when they had worked, shoulder to shoulder, during the "Great Typhoid Epidemic".

Dr. Sawyer went downstairs to join Henry. He knew that his patient was in very good hands.

Dr. Sawyer spent the night downstairs in the parlor, smoking cigars and sipping drinks with the nervous, apprehensive expectant father.

At sunrise the following morning, both Henry and Dr. Sawyer sat drowsing at opposite ends of the sofa. Ruth gently shook Dr. Sawyer; "*Doc, Mammy say yo should com now— Mistress Margaret be open all da way, and ready to push out da baby.*"

Dr. Sawyer leaned over intending to awaken Henry, who had slouched down, at his end of the sofa. The Master of Rosewood and soon to be new father, was gently snoring, Henry was fast asleep.

The doctor hesitated, withdrew his hand, turned towards Ruth and put his finger to his lips; "let's let him sleep." Dr. Sawyer and Ruth climbed the stairs and joined Mammy Ester.

At 9:36 AM, Henry was awakened from his alcohol-induced slumber by the distinct sound of a crying infant. For a brief moment he was disoriented, confused. As the crying persisted, his head began to clear.

Henry raced up the stairs, two steps at-a-time. When he burst into the bedroom, he saw his beloved wife Peggy, lying in the bed, cooing and rocking, what he thought was the most beautiful, pink, blue-eyed, baby in the world.

Peggy smiled at her husband; "Henry, come and say hello to your daughter, Rebecca Elizabeth Billings, your daughter. The baby, continued to announce her own arrival utilizing, as Dr. Sawyer put it, "a very impressive pair of lungs."

When Henry and Dr. Sawyer returned to the parlor, Henry walked over to the shelves of books, lining one of the walls. He reached in between two of the books, his hand returned with an unopened box of Cuban cigars.

Henry cut the seal, opened the lid and offered the box to the doctor; "I've been waiting for a special occasion to open these".

Dr. Sawyer reached into the box and removed a cigar. He held it to his nose and gave an appreciative sigh; "I can't think of any occasion that would be more special than this."

After the doctor left, Henry went over to the shelves that were lined with his "special" books. He removed a thick black book. The book's pages were edged in gold leaf. On the spine of the book, in gold lettering, bore two words, "The Holy Bible".

Henry opened the "Billings Family Bible", to the second page. The page depicted the "Billing's Family Tree. His heart filled with pride; Henry amended the page:

THE BILLINGS FAMILY

William Billings _____ Dorothy Jenkins Billings
(1771 - 1818)   (1780 - 1833)

Children: 1) Artimas; 2) Lucille; 3) Mary

Artimas Billings _____ Abigail Smithson Billings
(1795 - 1845)   (1802 - 1845)

Children: 1) Robert; 2) Henry

Robert Billings _____Margaret Martin Billings
  (1815 - 1845)   (1823 -
                        Children 1) Jesse

Henry Billings _____Margaret Martin Billings
(1820 -   (1823 -

Children 1) Rebecca - July 19, 1852

Three days after Rebecca's birth, Ruth went into labor. She was attended to by Mammy Ester, and by Fannie. Ruth gave birth to a beautiful, healthy, caramel-complexioned-baby girl.

Ruth named her daughter, Mandy. The next day, while serving the family breakfast, Fannie told Master Henry that; *"las nite, Roof had dun dropped a baby gal." "She name da baby, Mandy."* Henry grunted and asked Jesse to pass the biscuits.

Later that afternoon, while seated at his desk, Henry pulled a blue ledger from the shelf in the bookcase behind his head. He opened the book, dipped his pen into the ink-well, and made under the column; Slave-Property,
the following entry:

> July 22, 1852 – Born, one nigger wench;
>
> Name: Mandy
> Mother-Ruth
> Father-Unknown.

****

Prior to the birth of his daughter, Henry Billings, Master of Rosewood, had been considered amongst his peers, as the perfect example of the Southern gentry.

He was young, successful, happy and content. And indeed, the perceived image, for the most part, was entirely accurate. Henry was a true son of the South.

Henry was a verbose, enthusiastic, staunch proponent and supporter of the Southern way of life, a way of life which mandated that he believe in, and advocate for the continuation, and the expansion of the "South's Peculiar Institution", Slavery.

Henry truly loved his wife, and his heir apparent son (biologic-nephew), Jesse. He could not imagine anyone or any thing, entering his life that could possibly, enhance his blissful state of contentment.

Henry was wrong. From the very first moment that he looked into his daughter's sparkling baby-blue eyes; he was hooked. When *Becky* smiled, and those cute little dimples, in each of her pudgy little cheeks appeared, he was hooked. When Henry felt the pressure, she exerted with her chubby little hand, when she enthusiastically squeezed his thumb, he was hooked.

Henry was hooked, completely captivated by his baby girl. Henry Billings experienced an overwhelming emotion. An emotion that he thought could not, and would not, ever occur. Henry fell head-over-heels in love with a female other than Peggy.

Rebecca Elizabeth Billings, or as her father would forever think of her as, "Becky", his little princess, completely captured Henry's heart.

****

Peggy was thrilled that the baby was a girl. Although she had never admitted it, not even to herself, she had always lurking below the surface, buried in the recesses of her mind, thought there was the possibility that a boy, might have diminished the genuine love and affection, that Henry felt for their son Jesse.

Peggy literally and emotionally, immediately within hours of the baby's birth, took Rebecca to her breast.

As Dr. Sawyer had noted at her birth, Rebecca was born in possession of "a very impressive pair of lungs." Within hours, following Rebecca's first meal at her breast, Peggy lay in bed, gingerly massaging her sore nipple.

Peggy came to the realization that baby-Rebecca, in addition to healthy lungs, baby-Rebecca was also born with a very impressive, hard-sucking reflex.

Rebecca was an especially active newborn. She was an alert constantly smiling, squirming, bundle of perpetual motion.

To Peggy, the baby's appetite was enormous. More often then not, Becky's incessant cries were cries of hunger. With that thought in mind, as the baby furiously waved her tiny knotted fists, and cried at the top of her still developing lungs, Peggy–resolutely biting her lower lip–dutifully presented one of her painfully sore nipples, to the baby.

Henry noticed with increasing alarm, Peggy's obvious pain and discomfort, when she breast-feeds the baby.

At night, Peggy would lie in the bed on her back. Her usual sleeping position was either on her side, or an alternating combination, of her side and her stomach.

Peggy would groan in pain, and recoil from him, if he intentionally, or inadvertently, touched her breast. Growing increasingly concerned, Henry sent for Dr. Sawyer.

When Dr. Sawyer arrived at the plantation, he drove his buggy directly to the stable. Before he could hand the reins to a stable-boy, Henry–breathing heavily, with Pee wee, having notified the Massa of the Doctor's arrival, close at his heels, arrived to greet the doctor.

Henry extended his hand toward the doctor. The men shook hands; "Thanks for coming Doc. "I'm really worried about Peggy…she" Dr. Sawyer held up his hand; "Hold on Henry, it's perfectly normal for a woman who delivered a baby just a week ago, to be a bit out of sorts.

"I've seen new mothers with crazy mood-swings, I've seen mild to severe depression in women, for months after delivery. It passes, you've got to be patient...give her a little time."

As the two men walked towards the Big House, Henry was vigorously shaking his head from side to side; "That's not it Doc...when Peggy's with the baby, she's happy...she's all smiles, both of them–gushing and cooing–she really loves the baby."

Dr. Sawyer's expression changed he looked quizzically at Henry; "What's wrong, what's the trouble Henry?"

Henry visibly uncomfortable, stammered; "It's her–her, he hesitated...then blurted it out–"its' her breasts. Doc–whenever she feeds the baby–you know puts the baby to her chest, Peggy's face turns red, she bites her lip...she's obviously in pain. When I ask what's wrong, she says it's nothing–she's just that she's somewhat sore." "I'm really worried Doc."

Dr. Sawyer asked; "Where is she?" Does she know that you sent for me?" Henry glanced down, then sheepishly responded; "That's just it Doc, when I told her that I was going to send for you, she said no, don't... she was adamant...she said that the soreness would pass." "I didn't tell her that you were coming."

"I would really appreciate it if you'd say that you were in the neighborhood and you just decided to drop in."

Dr. Sawyer thought to himself, here before me stands Henry Billings, one of the most powerful and wealthiest men in Essex County, Master of one of the richest plantations in the state of Virginia, owner of and lord and master of almost one hundred slaves. This enormously powerful man is afraid that I'll tell his wife that he sent for me.

"No problem Henry, I'll tell Margaret just that...that I just happened to be in the neighborhood."

Dr. Sawyer climbed the stairs, and softly rapped on the Master bedroom door. Peggy's Seamstress/Maid, Ruth tentatively partially opened the door.

She recognized the doctor, turned and announced; *"Mistress Margaret, it doc Saw'r."* Without waiting for permission to enter, Dr. Sawyer pushed pass Ruth.

Peggy was setting up in bed, in obvious discomfort, nursing the baby.
Peggy's attempted smile was abruptly turned into a grimace, when Baby-Rebecca gave an aggressive tug on her nipple. "Ooh, ouch...hello Doctor, to what do I owe this unexpected, pleasure of your company?"

"Afternoon Margaret, I was on my way home from the Baxter's farm, their young'un fell from a tree, broke his wrist." Thought I'd stop in on my way back to town; see how you and baby-Rebecca's are getting along."

Dr. Sawyer approached the bed, leaned over Peggy, and noticed that the area surrounding the nipple of her left breast, which baby-Rebecca held firmly between her lips, was red and swollen.

Dr. Sawyer gently, but firmly removed the suckling baby from Peggy's breast. Baby-Rebecca gurgled, then let out a resounding cry of protest.
Dr. Sawyer handed the baby to Ruth. He then turned his attention to Peggy.

He instructed Peggy to untie, and pull down from her shoulders, her nightgown. She complied exposing her two red swollen breasts. He gently touched Peggy's left breast. Peggy moaned — in obvious discomfort — "Ooh."

The doctor then gently grasped her nipple between his thumb and forefinger, and exerted slight pressure. Peggy, at first groaned, gritted her teeth, then she screamed in pain. Dr. Sawyer removed his hand. "How long have you been experiencing discomfort, nursing the baby?" Peggy, wiping tears from her eyes, gingerly and slowly, retied the nightgown over her shoulders.

Peggy folded her hands in her lap, she looked up, her eyes pleading; "They became tender and started to hurt after the second day of breast-feeding."

Dr. Sawyer sat down on the bed, took Peggy's hand in his, and looked directly into her eyes; "Margaret there's a sure-fire, easy way to stop the pain." Peggy looked up expectantly, with hope in her eyes. "What can I do, Rebecca's a good baby. "I thank god that she's been blessed with a good, healthy, appetite."

Peggy wiped a tear from her cheek. "I won't ever see her go hungry.
I don't want to switch her to cow's milk."

"Dr. Sawyer, I have complete faith in your medical judgment. I took it to heart when you said that in your experience, most infants thrived better, on their mother's milk."

Doctor Sawyer took Peggy's hand in his; "As I said Margaret, there's a sure-fire, easy way to stop the pain." He looked over at Ruth whole was comforting the fidgety baby; Looks like Ruth over there is bursting with milk. I guarantee that Ruth has enough milk for Rebecca, with plenty left over for her pick-a-ninny."

****

Following Dr. Sawyer's visit, the residents and the house-slaves of the "Big House", became increasingly accustomed to the sight of a "high yeller gal, Ruth, sitting in a chair, nursing one or two babies.

Sometimes she would have the white, blond blue-eyed, Rebecca nursing at her breast, while at other times, Ruth had her curly haired, caramel complexioned infant, Mandy contently receiving nourishment at her breast.

But as the two infants became more and more in tune to each other's moods, they began to experience hunger pangs at the same time. When one was hungry, they both were hungry.

The sight of Ruth sitting at the kitchen table, nursing two babies at the same time, simultaneously, together, became commonplace.

As she sat at the table, with the white, blond, blue-eyed, Rebecca, happily nursing at her left breast, while Mandy, her light-brown-eyed brown haired, beauty, was contently nursing at the other.

Ruth chuckled; *"I swear Fannie, dis here Chile"* she nodded towards Rebecca, *"she be jus lik her daddy, Massa Henry. Dey boff liks to suck on my lef tit, more den da do da rite one. Now dis one,"* nodding her head towards Mandy, *"she taks afta her mommy. Ya cant be to fussy, don mak no neva mind which tit, good food be good food."*

****

While Peggy was aware of Henry's regular nocturnal visits to Ruth's Cabin, these tryst that Peggy dismissed as Henry's "dalliances" with Ruth, were not considered to be uncommon.

These so-called "dalliances" between the Master and his female slaves, had for centuries, been accepted as a fact of life in Southern Society.

The unspoken doctrine, the belief that the MASTER has the right to do with his slaves as he wishes, was fostered, believed, and practiced in the South.

This philosophy had been firmly ingrained, drummed into Peggy's psyche both overtly and sub-conscientiously.

Despite these long-held beliefs, she could not help reflecting on the irony of Henry depositing "life creating liquids-semen", into Ruth. And now ironically, Ruth her maid, her husband's "black piece of tail", was routinely delivering "life sustaining liquid, breast-milk", into the body of her baby, Rebecca.

Peggy was fully aware of the possibility, no of the probability, that Henry had fathered both Rebecca and Ruth's pick-a-ninny, Mandy.

However, the thought that the girls were sisters (half-sisters), was so foreign to her Southern up bringing, that honestly, the thought had never entered Peggy's mind.

To entertain such a radical thought, that Rebecca and Mandy could be sisters, Peggy would have had to acknowledge that black slaves, which is the classification that the laws of the state of Virginia ascribed to Ruth and her baby Mandy, that slaves, are in fact, people.

That black slaves are, members of the same species as is she; as are her children Jesse and Rebecca; as is her husband Henry, and for that matter, that black slaves belonged to the same species as did all of the members of the White race.

The fact that Peggy did not hold Henry's infidelity against Ruth, was not entirely surprising. In order to experience the normal human emotion of jealousy, Peggy and the South's white-population at large, would have had to recognize the inhumanity and the immorality of slavery.

Since all black slaves, and by extension in Peggy's case, since Ruth was considered, and legally regarded as less then human, the human emotion of jealousy towards a fellow human being, just did not apply.

For Peggy to be jealous of Ruth would undermine Peggy's life-long belief in the validity and the morality of the Southern way of life. For these "dalliances", as Peggy called them, these acts to be deemed immoral, society would have to regard Ruth, or for that matter any of the thousands of female black slaves, that were routinely forced to submit to the white-master's sexual demands, as being human.

Regarded and treated as human beings, not treated as sub-humans, not as animals, not as livestock, not treated as property to be callously used and abused.

Because of her upbringing, the dogma, the philosophy that she had been taught, and had seeped and been pounded into her head since child-hood, would not allow Peggy to even entertain the idea, that the two girls, Rebecca and Mandy, shared any human, familial, kinship.

* *

That there existed a special bond – that grew and intensified as the years passed – between the girls, was evident to all. As toddlers, the girls were inseparable.

When they were toddlers, Ruth was under strict orders to ensure that Mandy was in Rebecca's room, when Rebecca awoke. Ruth was not allowed to take Mandy home, until Rebecca had gone to sleep.

To those who observed and interacted with the hyperactive toddlers on a regular basis, the two young girls seemed to be closer to each other than "sisters".

The color of their skin, not withstanding, Rebecca and Mandy, bore a remarkable physical resemblance to each other, as well as a resemblance to Rebecca's father, Henry.

The resemblance became all the more, pronounced, when they smiled or laughed at some mutually amusing event. Their faces beamed with merriment, each cherubic face displaying "the cutest" little dimples.

****

Henry and Peggy were seated at the dining-room table. Jesse and Rebecca had long since left the room. Fannie and Rufus were upstairs, assisting the children in preparing them for bed.

Over the years, Henry had repeatedly discussed with Peggy, his feelings as to whether or not, the closeness of the girls, was in Rebecca's best interest.

Henry placed his coffee cup in its' saucer. He gazed across the table, at Peggy. Their eyes met and locked. Henry removed his napkin from his neck, neatly folded the napkin and began to speak; "I'm telling you Sugar, I think Becky's around that little nigger wench Mandy, far too much. The two of them talk-a-like, they even sound the same, hell, they're together so much, they're beginning to look alike."

The girls grew like healthy-strong, wild weeds. During their "Reign of Terror"; the terrible-two's, which, Rebecca and Mandy extended to include the terrible-three's, four's, and five's, the hyperactive tykes were literally, inseparable.

The house slaves, when speaking of the two mischievous girls, who seemed to manage to "get into everything", would often lament; *"dem two's lik two peas inna pod; lik grits n gravy" "Iffin ya sees one, da otta ain't fer behin."*

The Billings' decision to indulge and placate Rebecca's insistence that Mandy be Rebecca's ever-present playmate, for Mandy, had a few unanticipated results. Since infancy, the vast majority of Mandy's time was spent in the company of Rebecca, and by extension, with Rebecca's parents.

Therefore, it was only natural that the environmental factors that led to the development of Rebecca's speech patterns, the sounds and consistent exposures to the speech and language of others, affected both Rebecca and Mandy's speech and language development.

In addition to Mandy's constant exposure to the words, sounds, *inflections*, and pronunciations of the "Billings' World", Mandy was equally, exposed to the words, sounds, *inflections*, and pronunciations of her mother's world, the "World of the Black Slave." As a result, Mandy for all intents and purposes, had been raised and grown up, bilingual.

Mandy had an uncanny way of flawlessly switching, between her two native languages. When speaking to Rebecca, Mandy's English, speech pattern, intonation, and pronunciation was exactly identical to that of Rebecca's.

However, when she spoke to her mother, to Rufus, to Fannie, to Pee wee, to any of the slaves, or to whites other than Rebecca, without thinking, Mandy's words, her dialect, became the words, the dialect used by, and understood in the slave community.

Words and speech patterns that the whites interpreted, and considered validation of the slave's ignorance and stupidity.

Although Rebecca had not yet, been taught the rules, the laws, and the morality of interaction between slaves and whites in the South, Mandy on the other hand, had.

****

For Ruth, the long day had finally ended. She had completed her seamstress duties, by finally putting the finishing touches to a beautiful satin evening gown for Mistress Margaret. That particular project had begun over four months ago.

Ruth had seen to the Mistress' bedtime preparation needs, had said her goodnights to both the Mistress and to baby Rebecca, and then she had scooped up the half asleep, drowsy Mandy, and left the "Big House".

When she entered her cabin on slave row—barely able to support her daughter's weight—she pulled aside the curtain that bisected the cabin.
As she anticipated, Jason was already in bed, and the spread on Mandy's bed, had been turned down.

Ruth smiled and turned her gaze towards the small table adjacent to the fireplace, and noticed the dirty plate and drinking glass. She shook her head a wearily muttered; *"Thank da lawd fo Pearly."*

Although Pearly possessed, a well-deserved reputation among the slaves as a "sporting-woman", Pearly had found the time to see to it that Jason had eaten. Ruth reflected, that in Pearly, one could not have a more loyal friend.

Ruth sat on the edge of Mandy's bed, and gently, slowly began to remove the little girls' cloths. Mandy stirred and murmured; "Mommy, Becky and I will be starting school soon."

Ruth grasped Mandy firmly by the shoulders, and gave her a violent shake. *"Mandy yo cut out dat tawk rite now!"* *"Stop doin' dat white tawk rite now...you har me!"*

Mandy, now fully awake, begin to whimper and stammer; "Mama, Ise sawry...wa I ment—me an Missy Becca be startn' scol directly."

Ruth, with tears of frustration streaming down her face; *I dun tol yo a hunnert times, yo gawn git yo self kilt.* *"Lawd help us chile, yo got ta stop dat white tawk!"*

"Niggers hear dat tawk, dey says yo uppity, puttin' on airs, thnk yo betta den da res of us. White fok hear dat tawk, specialy tawk bout nigger goin' ta scol—yo be whipped and sold 'way frm here licky de split!"

"Baby it be agin da law, ita crime, ta lern a nigger ta reed or to rite!" Ruth pulled Mandy to her breast. She was overcome with tears of frustration, and fear for her child's safety. Mandy begin to cry. Between sobs she tried to console her mother; "Mama Ise sawry, plees mama, plees dun cry."

****

The next morning, Peggy clothed in gardening apparel, which included a large sunbonnet and long linen gloves, was concentrating on pruning the rose bushes in her garden. As she leaned over, without warning, her basket was knocked from her hand. Flustered, she looked around to determine the cause of the turmoil.

At her feet, sat Rebecca, out of breath, grinning from ear to ear; "Mommy, Mommy, can Mandy sit with us in class? Peggy picked up her basket and her pruning shears.

At a glance, she quickly took in her immediate surroundings. At her feet, pulling on her skirts, looking up at her, with a beseeching, cherubic smile, was her bright-eyed Becky, her precocious little girl.

Mandy, who Peggy often thought of as Becky's shadow, stood back, a little to the right of Rebecca. Mandy was clutching Rebecca's stuffed rag doll, *"Patty"*.

Mandy and Rebecca, to all who regularly observed the two of them together, appeared to be so close that "they might as well be connected at the hip".

Mandy, even at the tender age of 6, knew enough to act reserved and submissive, *"stayed in her place,"* when she and Rebecca were in the company of white-folks.

Flustered, Peggy removed a kerchief from her basket and slowly waved the linen, fanning her face; "Heavens Becky, where did you come from? How often do I have to tell you, that you're not to play in the garden?"

Rebecca looked down at her feet, and said sheepishly; "We're not playing in this old garden. Mandy, Patty, and I, — *"Patty"* was Becky's rag doll—we were having tea when we saw you over here, in the garden."

Peggy put her pruning shears into her basket. She put her handkerchief to her lips, moistened the fabric, then gently wiped a smudge of dirt from Rebecca's forehead. "There now, we can't have you looking like a little pick-a-ninny, now can we." Rebecca persisted; "Mommy when can Mandy sit with us in class?"

Peggy picked Rebecca up into her arms. She turned her back to Mandy, and spoke; "Becky, Mandy cannot join us during our classes. I've told you time and time again, Mandy is not like you and me. Mandy is a slave. We would get into serious trouble if we let her into our classroom. Besides honey, it would be cruel to let Mandy in class. Like I've repeatedly told you, slaves are not capable of learning".

Still holding Rebecca in her arms, Peggy turned to face Mandy; "Mandy, I want you to go find Ruth. Tell her that I will be up to change my clothing shortly — give *"Patty"* back to Miss Rebecca".

Mandy, eyes lowered to the ground, extended her arm, doll in hand, upward towards Rebecca.

"Yassum Misstress —I gwine tell my mammy rite away." Rebecca reluctantly accepted the doll.

As Mandy hurriedly walked from the garden towards the Big House, Peggy turned her attention to Rebecca. "Sweetheart, Mandy will never be taught—not by me or for that matter, by anyone else."

Rebecca began to squirm in her mother's arms. Peggy put her on the ground. Rebecca gave Peggy a look of abject bewilderment, she asked; "Why mommy, why?"

Before Peggy could respond, she noticed that two grizzled, tobacco chewing, white-men, where riding up the path. Pee wee, one of the Rosewood stable boys, his hands tied together, trotted and stumbled behind the horse of one of the tobacco chewing men.

The two riders dismounted at the stable. Peggy pulled Rebecca to her skirts, obstructing the little girl's vision from the scene unfolding at the stable.

****

Pee wee exhausted, and bleeding profusely from his mouth and nose, collapsed into the dirt. One of the two slave-catchers handed the rope binding Pee wee, to Lucas Prentiss the plantation's overseer.

"Mornin' Lucas, we catched this here runaway nigger for you. He says he's one of yourn. Me and Jake will be haven' our money now."

Lucas looked with disgust, and annoyance, at the slave groveling at his feet. He accepted the rope. Lucas counted out a sum, handed a wad of crumbled bills, to the slave-catcher, and then replaced the remainder of the bills into his pants pocket.

Lucas viciously yanked on the rope, which was biting into Pee wee's wrist. The rope was tinged with blood. "What the hell was you doing on the road boy...was you running?"

Pee wee, in obvious anguish lay moaning in the dirt, *"Please Massa Lucas, I ain't no runaway—I'se jus been wid my gal las' nite, ova at da Turmon Place...I dint wake up dis monin...I ober sleeped...I ain't no runaway."*

Lucas pointed to two burly slaves, "you boys drag this nigger inside." Pee wee did not resist. Peggy saw the heavy stable doors close.

The slave-catchers remounted, turned their horses' heads, and slowly, and at a walk, rode towards Rosewood's gates.

As they approached Peggy's garden, both men removed their hats. The slave-catcher who had accepted payment from Lucas, spit out a stream of tobacco juice; "Mornin' mame, sure is a nice day for pickin' flowers".

Peggy, clutching Rebecca to her skirt, did not reply. She acknowledged, the man's greeting with a nod.

Peggy abandoned her gardening apparatus; she took Becky by the hand. And walking rapidly, almost running, proceeded to half drag her daughter to the Big House.

* *

Peggy entered the house through the kitchen door. Fannie was stoking the fire in the large fireplace. She looked up in surprise when Mistress' Margaret and Becky, unceremoniously burst through the door. Fannie dropped the poker into the hearth, and alarmed, hurried over to her Mistress.

"Lan'sakes Mistress Margaret, whas' wrong?" Peggy attempting to catch her breath, put her free hand to her breast, she gently pushed Rebecca towards Fannie. "We're alright Fannie... do you know where Master Henry is?"

Fannie protectively, enfolded the confused child into the shelter of her amble bosom. *"Master Henry jus' now, gwine ta da stable. Yu wants I sends som one ta fetch him?"* For a moment Peggy looked flustered, she then quickly regained her composure;

"No no...don't bother him. Fannie give Miss Rebecca a cookie and a glass of milk. I'll wait for the Master's return, in his study."

Fannie seated Becky at the table. Her first instinct was to ask about Mandy's whereabouts, for rarely, at this time of day, were the girls apart.

She quickly discarded the thought. *"Yessum, wen he com...I tell da Master you in da study waitin' on him."*

* *

Mandy with Ruth, her mother in tow, entered the garden. The garden gate, which was always kept closed, ostensibly a barrier to small herbivores—rabbits, squirrels, etc. — was unlatched and ajar.

Ruth let go of Mandy's hand; *"Chile, wha fo you dun drag me out here fo? Mistress Margaret ain' here."* Mandy looked around confused; *"Da Mistress was here mammy...she sen' me ta fetch you."*

In the corner of her eye, Mandy spotted Becky's doll *"Patty"*, lying on the ground. She ran over and picked up the doll. Mandy showed the doll to her mother. *"See mammy, da was here lik I sayd."* Ruth with a sense of foreboding grabbed Mandy's hand and begin to run towards the Big House.

When Ruth pushed through the kitchen door, her frantic petrified glance, when she noticed Rebecca, calmly sitting at the kitchen table, a large cookie in one hand, and a tall glass of milk in the other, was somewhat assuaged.

Her first thought when she saw the deserted garden, and Rebecca's favorite doll in the dirt, was that something awful had befallen the Mistress, and to Rebecca. *"Fannie wha happen', wher da Mistress...why Mistress Becky down here eatn' cookeys?"*

Fannie hurried over to Ruth; *"Calm yoself gal...da Mistress in da Master's study."* *"She com a rushn' in here wid lil Missy Becca."*

Mandy ambled over to the table were Rebecca was working on her third cookie. Mandy squeezed onto Rebecca's chair, and helped herself to one of the cookies.

Between bites, she asked Rebecca; "What happened...can I have some of your milk?" Rebecca handed Mandy her glass. While Mandy was gulping down the milk, Rebecca slide down from the chair, grabbed Mandy's hand.

Rebecca put her finger to her lips, signaling for Mandy to remain silent. The two girls walked quietly to the door, and slowly left the house.

Their departure went unnoticed by Ruth and Fannie, who were animatedly engaged in hushed conversation.

The girls ran from the house. They found refuge in the garden. Both girls were out of breath. Mandy was the first to speak; "Becky, what's happening...why are we running?"

Rebecca recounted the arrival of the two strange men on horseback who were leading Pee wee—lurching and stumbling, hands bound by rope—trailing behind the horsemen, to the stable.

Mandy stood wide-eyed, transfixed by Rebecca's recounting of the incident. She and Rebecca, at the same instant, looked in the direction of the closed stable doors.

Mandy whispered; "What do you think they're doing?" "Why did they tie-up Pee wee." Rebecca held *Patty*, her rag-doll up to her chest. "How should I know...Pee wee, probably did something bad."

Inexplicably, a chilling feeling of dread, swept over Mandy. For her entire life, tales of cruelty inflicted by whites on slaves, had been drummed into her head by her mother, and by members of the slave community.

The fact that she had spent most of her life in the Big House, as Rebecca's companion, had prevented her witnessing the routine welding of the whip by the overseer, on the backs of the slaves working in the fields.

Mandy frowned; "Do you think Master Lucas is going to whip Pee wee?" Rebecca gave Mandy an incredulous look, "Don't be silly…my Daddy says that we don't whip our slaves."

"Daddy and Mister Prentiss are probably giving Pee wee a good scolding for breaking the rules. Come on silly, let's go take a look."

Mandy, lead by Rebecca, ran around to the back of the stable. The girls located a separation in the wood planking on the stable's wall. They both peered into the opening.

At first, they could only make-out shadows, as their eyes adjusted from the bright sunlight to the subdued lighting of the stable. Gradually the activity in the stable came into focus.

Henry Billings was questioning his overseer, Lucas Prentiss; "What exactly did the boy have to say for himself…is he a runner?" Lucas replied; "Says that las night he snuck over to the Thurmond's place to see his gal Claudia."

"Said he and Claudia had been sparking each other when she was one of ours, here at Rosewood, and that they was getting ready to be hitched afore you sold her to the Thurmonds."

"Claims he been sneaking over there at night regular, and always returns afore daybreak. "He says that this mornin' they both overslept — says he was comin' back home when he was caught by the slave-catchers. I paid the catchers $30.00, and sent for you."

Henry reached into his pocket, pulled out a large row of "greenbacks", peeled of $30.00, which he handed to Lucas.

The girl's attention was suddenly diverted, when almost in unison, they each shifted their gaze to the source of an anguished moan emanating from the center of the building.

Pee wee, naked to the waist, was being strung-up, suspended by his wrist from one of the joists that supported the hayloft. His feet were about ten inches from the dirt floor. The muscles of the young slave's arms and rib- cage were quivering spasmodically.

Pee wee's hair was matted with blood, his lips were swollen and his right eye was bruised and closed. Two burly male slaves were securing the ropes that bore Pee wee's weight, to an adjacent stall.

Henry and Lucas walked over to the moaning — "strung-up by the wrist"— slave. Henry placed his hand on Pee wee's waist and slowly rotated the tortured slave, so that slave and Master, were facing each other.

Henry, his face inches from Pee wee's, growled; "How about it boy…are you a runner?" Pee wee lifted his head and looked at Henry, he forced open his swollen eye focused on Henry; *"Massa Henry, I ain't no runna…Ise comin' bak…comin' home when dem mens catched an beat me!"* *"Ise jus comin bak home from seein' my gal Claudy."*

Henry looked deeply into Pee wee's pleading left eye, Pee wee's right eye was swollen shut. In addition to the pleading, and the terror evident in the slave's frightened stare, Henry saw and believed that Pee wee was telling the absolute, unvarnished, truth.

Henry reasoned that in the past on numerous occasions, he had sent Pee wee — albeit with the mandated pass in hand — on errands to neighboring plantations, and frequently into town. Pee wee had always promptly returned to Rosewood.

Henry walked away from the moaning slave. He motioned for Lucas to come to him. Henry, with his hands massaging his face, spoke to the overseer; "I believe him. But the fact still remains that he did leave the place without permission. Let's give him fifteen lashes. I'll lay-on five, you do five, and pick one of these boys to give the last five."

Henry went back to Pee wee. Without a word, he rolled up the sleeve of his shirt, took the whip from Lucas, stepped back and delivered a resounding blow to Pee wee's back. Pee wee emitted a bone-chilling, animalistic scream. The horses in the stable reacted by whinnying loudly, and began to kick their hoofs against the walls of their stalls.

The stable boys scurried to calm the horses. Pee wee pleaded; *"Please Massa, I'se a good nigger…won't runnin'…please, please Massa."* Henry, ignoring Pee wee's pleas, deliberately straightened the whip, and administered the second lashing.

Rebecca and Mandy watched through opening in the wall, as the scene in the stable unfolded. At first the girls stood transfixed as Henry began to whip Pee wee. As the whip rose for the second blow, then tore into Pee wee's flesh, Mandy almost in unison with Pee wee, began to scream and scream.

She then pivoted on her heel and ran, crying, tears streaming from her eyes, towards the Big House. Rebecca's reaction was one of shock and disbelief. Her brain could not reconcile the horror of what she had just witnessed, with her image of, and her love for her father.

Mandy's screams and her headlong flight jolted Rebecca into motion. She turned, unwittingly dropped her doll, and ran as fast as she could, attempting to catch Mandy.

In addition to the anticipated scream from Pee wee, Henry heard, what sounded to him, the scream of a child. He looked in the direction of where he thought the sound had come, and saw the spot where the sunlight entered the stable.

"What in hell was that? He handed the whip to Lucas. Here, you finish up for me." As he walked towards the door, he rolled down his sleeve, turned his head; "Lucas, give him thirteen more, then let him down."

When Henry emerged into the sunlight, he walked slowly, deliberately, to the side of the stable. He located, the spot where there was an opening. He bent over and peered into the stable.

When his eyes adjusted, he was able to clearly make out what was going on in the stable. He saw Pee wee hanging from the beam. He saw and heard his overseer Lucas, cursing, and whipping Pee wee.

As Henry examined the ground, he noticed his daughter's favorite doll, "*Patty*", lying in the dirt.

When Henry arrived at the Big House, he walked directly to the master bedroom. There he found Rebecca sobbing in her mother's arms. Peggy, rocking Becky to and fro, looked up as Henry entered the room.

She motioned to Henry that he should not speak. Henry stood motionless, at the entrance to the bedroom door. Gradually, Becky's sobs diminished. Becky, exhausted, fell asleep in her mother's arms.

Peggy, with Becky in her arms, walked over to the bed, and gently placed their daughter onto the bed. Peggy turned towards Henry, placed the index finger of her right hand to her lips; "shhh." She took her husband by the hand, lead him from the room, and quietly shut the door behind them.

Together Henry and Peggy descended the stairs that lead to his study. Rufus appeared, "*Massa Henry, Mistress, Margaret, can I getcha sompum'?*" Henry shook his head and waved Rufus away. He then firmly closed the study doors, walked over to the sofa, and wearily, he sat down.

Peggy turned angrily; "Henry, what did you do?" Before he could respond, Peggy rushed on; "First Mandy comes running into the kitchen, screaming hysterically, and crying…mammy, mammy, I wants my mammy."

"Ruth was in the middle of taking my measurements for a new dress, that she's making for me. Ruth was so startled; she actually stuck me with a pin. She was mortified…she couldn't stop apologizing."

"I shooed her and told her to go to her child. Before I could get dressed, Rebecca burst into our bedroom, beside herself, crying, mama, oh mama, Daddy's got Pee wee tied up, and he's whipping him...he's whipping Pee wee."

"Henry, what have you done?" Have you lost your mind?" "Why in the world would you whip Pee wee, for that matter, why would you whip any of the niggers in front of Becky?"

"Calm down Peggy. It wasn't like that." He then explained to Peggy, what he called the Pee wee incident. As she listened to Henry's recounting of the details, she made but one interruption; "Pee wee, a runner, that's ridiculous, preposterous. I don't believe it for a minute."

Henry agreed with Peggy. He admitted that he believed Pee wee's story. "You believed him…then why did you whip him?" Henry explained that while Pee wee was technically, not attempting to run away, he was off the property without a pass.

"Sugar, if we let that go unpunished, it'll be taken by some of our nigger-bucks, that we don't enforce the rules, the law. You know, there's a lot of truth in that old saying; give a nigger an inch, next thing you know, they'll be taking a mile."

Peggy sat back on the sofa; her temper somewhat mollified. "Why did you whip Pee wee in front of Becky? Rebecca and Mandy were both traumatized, they were hysterical."

"Whipping a slave in front of Rebecca, for goodness sakes Henry, what on earth were you thinking?"

Henry stood and started to pace back and forth; "We were in the stable with the door closed." I had no way of knowing that Rebecca — and her perpetual shadow, Mandy — were watching. They were peeking through separated slates, openings in the stable walls."

Peggy interlaced the fingers of both hands, and folded her hands onto her lap. She looked up at Henry; "Well what's done is done. What this does point out though, is that you were right. We need to have a serious sit-down talk with Becky."

Henry removed a long cigar from the humidor on the end table. "I totally agree." We've got to set boundaries. Becky's eight years old now...it's time she grows-up."

"Peggy, I think that the two of us, her mother and her father, have to sit-down with Rebecca, and once and for all, we have to fully explain to her, her responsibilities as a leading lady of the South."

"This unnatural bond that she has forged with Mandy, has got to be broken. Sure, it was cute when they were babies, I've even heard some white-folks say when they were toddlers, "how adorable" the two of them together were".

Henry pointed his cigar at Peggy; "This coddling and tip-toeing around Rebecca's sensibilities, has got to stop! Rebecca's got to face reality. She's has got to come to grips with the fact that the only proper and permissible relationship between her and Mandy, can only be that of Mistress and Slave".

"Rebecca's has to acknowledge, and accept the fact that Mandy is her slave, Mandy is her property." Henry reached for Peggy's hands, "Tomorrow, for her own good, you and I have got to sit down with Becky, and have this talk."

The following day, Henry and Peggy sat Rebecca down in the study, for "the talk". Rebecca sat listening attentively. At the conclusion of "the talk",

Henry reemphasized just how important it was that she understood. "The only proper and permissible relationship between you and Mandy, can only be that of Mistress and Slave."

Henry, in the sternest voice that he could muster, asked; "Rebecca, it's important that you understand. Do you understand?"

Rebecca acknowledged that yes, she indeed understood. She then requested and was granted by her father and her mother, permission to leave.

When Rebecca left the study, she saw, as expected, Mandy seated in the corridor. Mandy rose, and after she assured herself that she and Rebecca were alone, she spoke; "Hi Becky, what was that all about?"

Rebecca smiled, hugged Mandy and replied. "Nothing, nothing at all. Come on, I'll race to the creek."

****

Henry and Peggy were relaxing, lingering at the dining room table, leisurely sipping their coffee. As usual, after the conclusion of the family meal, their two teenagers, Jesse, 17, and Rebecca, 13, had asked to be excused, and had each, bolted from the table

Henry patted his stomach, burped and asked; "When's that Yankee school-teacher, that we hired…what's her name again, due to arrive?" Peggy answered, "Eleanor Leary, her name is Miss Eleanor Leary." She folded her linen napkin, and placed on to her lap.

"Miss Leary is due to arrive at Rosewood, in two weeks. Henry we've had this discussion over and over." We agreed that it's time for Becky, and Jesse for that matter, to be exposed to formal education, exposed to the classics, and to science by a trained, qualified, professional, educator."

Henry picked up his coffee cup, took a sip, replaced the cup in its' saucer; he then retrieved the precisely folded napkin from his knee, and blotted his lips; "I know, I know, Miss Leary huh."

"That's not what's bothering me." "I'm in complete agreement…it's time the Becky, not so much Jesse, for Becky to be taught by a college prepared teacher, preferably by a refined, cultured college prepared, Southern lady."

Henry sipped his coffee. "I know that you think that I'm "beating a dead horse". Frankly honey, to be truthful, despite our many talks with Becky, you know that the issue of putting and keeping, Mandy in her place, over the years, hasn't really changed."

"Oh, don't misunderstand me, when Becky thinks that we're around, watching, or listening, she attempts to play the role of Mistress. I can tell that it's an act. I know that girl. I can tell that her heart's not in it."

I for one, am still bothered about the dangerous, unnatural bond that I fear, still seems to exists, which over the years, may have even grown stronger, between Becky and Mandy."

"It's time for us to put an end to that nonsense." Peggy looked genuinely puzzled at her husband; "Henry, I don't understand, what exactly is bothering you?" Henry frowned. He appeared to be collecting his thoughts.

"It's those two girls, they're always together. Being constantly together as babies is one thing…I guess Becky like every little girl, needed to have baby-dolls and such; have toys, to play with…but by God, now their 13 years old."

"Being life long best friends with a nigger is against the laws of nature. It's blasphemous; it's impossible, impractical, and downright illegal. It's against God's and Virginia's law."

"I know we've been saying this over and over, time and time again. At the risk of being accused of perpetual redundancy, for the umpteenth time, for our daughter's sake, for Becky's sake, we have got to put an end to this silly "friendship" nonsense!"

Peggy remained silent. Not having heard an objection from his wife, Henry, continued; "Ever since we told Becky about that teacher coming, Miss…what's her name again?" Peggy responded; "Miss Leary…her name is Eleanor Leary." "Right, Miss Leary…ever since we told Becky that she would be starting to take lessons from this Yankee college graduate, Miss Leary, she's been bubbling over with excitement. I hope that this Yankee Liberal Arts Professor, manages to live up to Becky's expectations."

"Even at the age of 13, I know she's still a child, but Sugar, I truly think, for her own sake, that now's the time for her to learn to behave like a Southerner. She needs to know and to accept the fact that that nigger-gal Mandy is not, and can never be her friend. Mandy is her slave. Mandy is her property!"

****

Since she had began to talk, and to understand, Mandy had been taught by her mother, and by the entire Rosewood slave community, the "rules", the fundamental rules drummed into the heads of each and every child born into bondage.

Rules whose strict adherences to are vital for the slave's very survival.

Survival in the Southern Society committed to, and governed by the promulgation, the adherence to, rules and laws that foster and support the South's "Peculiar Institution", Slavery.

Ruth, more so then most slave mothers, had been particularly fastidious in seeing to it that Mandy was well versed and aware of the *"slave's rules of survival."* Ruth's zealous emphasis of the rules, of the absolute necessity to adhere to and abide by the rules, was—in large-part—due to Mandy's unique relationship with the white child, Mistress Rebecca Billings.

It was obvious to all who interacted with the girls, blacks and whites, slave and master, that with each passing day, each passing year, the bond between Mandy and Rebecca had grown stronger and stronger.

Over the years, Mandy was compelled to sit through unending lectures from her mother, all with the same recurring message; *"Lis'n honey, don' matta how Missy Becca laff an grin wid yo, youse got ta always 'member baby, she not yo frien. She be yo Massa."*

This is the message that Ruth had been, for the past thirteen years, repeatedly drilling into Mandy's psyche.

****

As the family was about to conclude its' morning meal, Jesse wiped his mouth with his napkin, placed it beside his plate, and asked his father to be excused. "Pa I've got to get going...gotta meet Mister Prentiss, we gotta break-in three new field-hands today." Rebecca jumped down from her chair, and hurried towards the door.

Henry caught her by the arm; "hold on young lady...your mother and I want to have a talk with you." Rebecca impatiently, placed her hand on her father's, leaned over, and kissed his cheek. She employed this tactic whenever she needed to "calm him down". However, her next statement, completely, totally, neutralized her ploy; "Daddy I'm going be late, Mandy's waiting for me. She'll be upset if I keep her waiting."

Henry jammed his lit cigar into the residual grits, remaining on his half-empty plate. He fixed his daughter with a steely, withering glare; "Damn it Rebecca...you — own — Mandy! Mandy's your slave! She is not your friend...she is not your equal! When are you going to get that through that cute little head? Who the hell cares if a slave is upset?!

Peggy admonished her husband; "Henry, you will not use profanity when speaking to our daughter."

Rebecca thought, to herself, "Oh, oh, I'm in real trouble. Daddy's calling me Rebecca, and mother's referring to me as their daughter."

Peggy motioned for Becky to join her. "Come here sweetheart, come sit next to me." Rebecca did as her mother asked.

"Becky this is your home, Rosewood Plantation is your home." Rosewood provides for, and is the home for more then one hundred individuals."

"There's me, there's you, your brother, your father, and Mr. Prentiss our overseer. "We are the white people of Rosewood...we are the ruling class."

Peggy placed her hands onto Rebecca's chair, she slide the chair so that she was looking directly at Rebecca. She bent over and placed her hands-on Rebecca's thighs. Peggy looked deeply and searchingly into her daughter's eyes.

When she was satisfied that she had Rebecca's full attention, she continued; "Mandy, her mother Ruth, Fannie, Pee wee, and all of the rest — the babies, the children and the grown-ups — they are all, each and everyone of them, the property of our family, the Billings Family." "They are our black slaves, our property."

"Rebecca honey, the South's way of life, our family's way of life, is dependent upon those slaves. We all, the blacks, as well as whites, are dependant upon the preservation of slavery."

"Miss Leary will be arriving soon. Miss Leary was raised in the North. She attended school in the North. And she undoubtedly, has been subjected to vast quantities of Northern, Anti-Slavery propaganda."

"Up North, they depict us as monsters. Do you think that we're monsters? Do you think that I'm a monster? Do you think that your father's a monster? And despite that when you were growing up, you frequently called your brother one, do you really think that Jesse's a monster? Well honey, do you?"

Rebecca momentarily dropped her gaze. She then once again met her mothers stare; "No mother I don't think that we're monsters?" Peggy straightened and sat back, she sighed, "good".

"While Miss Leary is with us, it's important, at least it's important to me, that Miss Leary gets to see the South, through our eyes. That she gets to understand and see slavery as we do. That she comes to appreciate that the South, is indeed a Benevolent Slave Holding Society."

Henry had sat quietly, intently watching Becky's reaction to Peggy's attempt to communicate to their daughter, what Henry considered, were the essential facts of life in the South.

Henry spoke in a soothing, he thought comforting, monotone; "Becky do you understand what we're saying?" Rebecca was clearly not wholly convinced.

In a subdued, steady voice she answered her father; "Daddy, of course I'm aware that Pee wee and Fannie are slaves. I've always known that all of the black people are slaves." But Mandy, Mandy is...

Henry held up his hand; "Hold it, stop right there...the black people? That's precisely the problem. Becky, you really truly do not understand. Once and for all Becky, get it through your head, the blacks, the slaves are not people! The slaves are property, our property."

"Just as the horses are our property, the mules are our property, the pigs and chickens, the slaves are our property."

"Mandy is a slave. Mandy is your slave. Mandy is your property. Mandy is not your friend. She does not have the right to be upset with you. Mandy — your slave Mandy — has no rights!"

Peggy patted Rebecca's hand; "Sweetheart, any day now, Miss Leary will be arriving. I know how excited you've been. I can only imagine, the pretexts you plan to use to have Mandy sit with you in class. Becky, Mandy will not, and cannot, be with you for your lessons with Miss Leary."

Rebecca withdrew her hand from beneath her mother's. She opened her mouth to speak. Before she could utter a word, Henry, with all of the power and authority vested in him as Rebecca's father, and as Master of Rosewood spoke. "Becky, even if it were possible for them to learn, which it is not, teaching niggers, to read and write, is unwise, immoral, and its' against the law."

****

When Rebecca finally joined Mandy at the girl's favorite reclusive hideaway, Mandy was sitting under the shade of a huge sprawling, oak tree, in the shady the meadow, just below the creek.

Mandy rose from the grassy carpet, beaming, obviously pleased upon Rebecca's arrival; "Becky, I've been sitting here forever waiting for you; what took you so long?"

Before Rebecca could respond, Mandy breathlessly continued; "I've been busting to tell you; My mama says that she heard from Atlas, that that school teacher, Miss Leary, will be here in a day or two. We'll be starting school soon. I can hardly wait."

Instead of the anticipated excitement, she had expected from Rebecca, Becky's reaction was the complete opposite. Her life-long friend appeared to be depressed, saddened by the very news that they had both been so anxiously awaiting.

"Becky, Becky, what's wrong?" Rebecca wiped a tear from her eye with the back of her hand. "Oh Mandy, its' awful, mother and daddy say that we can't attend Miss Leary's classes together. They said that because you're a slave, it's against the law for you to read and write. They kept repeating over and over, that you're a slave. That we can never be friends."

Mandy, stood stark still beside Rebecca, petrified, as if she were frozen. That day had finally arrived. That day, the day that her mother Ruth, had predicted was here. Ruth and Fannie had warned her, admonishing that her relationship with Rebecca, would someday drastically change.

As she stood there stunned, immobile, disbelieving, she could hear her mother's voice; *"Mandy honey, I knows you think Missy Becca your frien...lawd kno da way you two always wit one anotha, together all da time...it no wonda you feels dat way."* *"Lisen ta me honey, it ain gonna stay lik dat. Missy Becca white! You is black! You is a slave chile."*

When Mandy protested, exclaiming "Momma, I'm not black, I'm brown. Becky and I are truly, best friends." Ruth would become frantic, moaning and crying; *"Mandy, how many time I done toll you, yous gotta stop dat talk soundin lik you white. It gonna get you whip'd. If dem white folks think you uppity, you gets yoself sold fo sure. Oh lawd, my poo baby, my chile gonna get hurt real bad".*

Frequently, Ruth would ask her best friend Fannie, to *"help me talk som sense into dis po chile...fo her own good. Help me make her unnerstan dat dis her bein' friends wid Missy Becca...jus can' be."* *"Sho da Massa and Mistress let you be round Missy when yu'll babies, dat help ta keep der baby, Missy Becca happy an quite; but yu'll aint babies no mo. Yu'll grow'n up fast."*

"Soon Missy Becca gonna haf her white frens. Dem white girls be goin to parties an dances an such, aint no place for a nigger-wench. Mayhaps Missy Becca let you be her maid." *"Honey you is a slave, don't matter if you be black, brown or high yeller...you is a black slave!"*

Mandy sank down in the grass beside her life-long playmate. "I guess we won't be being taught together by Miss Leary." Tears begin to stream down the cheeks of both girls. They clung to each other, two minor, innocent, casualties of the South's *"Peculiar Institution"*.

****

Becky and Mandy continued to visit their favorite spot, the large oak in the meadow. The girls would unceremoniously, plop down on the ground. They would sit facing each other, shaded by the sprawling, leafy branches of the large oak.

For the past two months, the anticipated arrival of Miss Leary, and the excitement of the types of subjects, and classes that the girls thought that they would be taking together, had been the major topics of discussion.

The girls, after Rebecca's devastating announcement several days ago, that it was against the law, for Mandy to be taught, that to merely teach her to read and write, was a criminal offense, continued to visit their sanctuary, to sit in the shade at their retreat, and to cry and cry, missing what they now knew, could never be.

They would bemoan the unfairness of the law. At their last pilgrimage, Rebecca proposed a plan to circumvent, the law. "Mandy, I will learn everything that Miss Leary teaches. I will be attentive, and studious. I will then teach to you, all that I have learned.

I promise you, my word of honor, that you won't miss a thing...everything she teaches me, I promise, I'll teach to you."

****

Pee wee brought the carriage to a complete stop, at the steps of the "Big House", he climbed down from the shiny family carriage, opened the carriage door, pulled down the folding steps, and extended his hand to the carriage's occupant.

From the interior of the carriage, first emerged a petite, gloved hand, and followed by a pastel colored parasol. Miss Eleanor Leary emerged from the carriage.

Eleanor Leary, the Yankee teacher, at a glance, looked to be a diminutive classic example of what one would expect of a Southern Belle.

She stood in the hot afternoon sun. Five foot five inches tall, she wore a fashionable gray dress, discretely buttoned to the neck, gray calfskin boots, which accented perfectly, the symmetry of her dainty feet.

Her hair was reddish, chestnut brown, parted down the middle, drawn back into soft folds on each side of her face.

Small, delicate gold earrings, dangled from her ears. Her hairdo accented and flattered her pale, round, oval face.

Peggy was genuinely surprised by the good-looks of the educator standing before them. The self-assured, handsome, mature woman standing before them was not at all, what she and Henry had envisioned.

In fact, in the months since they had committed to the hiring of Miss Leary, Henry and Peggy, when speaking of Miss Leary, had assigned to her, what they thought — surmised from the reading of her correspondence —various descriptive adjectives. "The spinster, the old maid school marm," are a few terms that they so liberally applied to the then, unseen, Miss Eleanor Leary.

Henry and Peggy stood on the porch, like bookends, surrounding their offspring, Rebecca and Jesse. The Billings family was dressed as if they were about to attend Sunday Services. Peggy mused; "Thank god we dressed."

Miss Leary scanned the Rosewood people assembled before her. Her first thought was that they resembled military troops awaiting inspection.

Eleanor's astute analytic mind quickly accessed and categorized the Billings family, standing respectfully, before her.

Immediately behind the family, in crisp fresh livery, she surmised, were a few of the key, house-slaves. The stout pitch-black middle-aged woman, with the starched snow-white apron, was undoubtedly the cook.

Next to the cook, stood a beautiful, statuesque, caramel-colored Negris, probably Mrs. Billings' personal maid. The strikingly attractive Negress was wearing a simple; yet at one time obviously, expensive dress, probably a hand-me-down from the Mistress.

Standing beside and holding the hand of the maid, was an alert pre-teenage girl, her daughter, Eleanor thought.

Henry stepped down from the porch and extended his hand towards Eleanor; "Welcome to Rosewood Miss Leary." Eleanor fluttered a lace handkerchief, as she shaded her eyes from the sun. She delicately accepted Henry's hand. "Mr. Billings, I am so very happy to finally make your acquaintance."

Henry, lightly holding Miss Leary's hand, led the teacher up the steps, leading to the porch. "Miss Leary I would like to introduce you to my family; my wife Margaret, my son Jesse, and our daughter Rebecca."

Miss Leary shook the hand of each Billings' family member. When she reached Rebecca, a broad smile spread across her face... "Miss Rebecca Billings I've been so looking forward to meeting, and to teaching you."

Eleanor had a fleeting thought, as she once again glanced at the maid's daughter. The maid's daughter was the caramel colored, brown eyed, curly black-haired, spitting image of this beautiful blond, blue-eyed beauty, the daughter, her pupil, Rebecca Billings.

Rebecca looked to her mother, with an expression of surprise and curiosity, evident in her bright blue eyes. "Your mother's letters conveyed a most accurate portrait of Rosewood's second lady."

Henry gave instructions to Pee wee and Atlas, to take Miss Leary's luggage to her room.

Peggy stepped forward and extended her hand; "Come have a seat in the parlor Miss Leary. You must be exhausted. How was the train ride? Quite dusty and thirsty, I would expect."

****

The family sat on the sofa. Eleanor observed that their seating arrangements exactly mirrored the group's alignment on the porch. The father Henry sat at one end of the plush, horsehair, sofa, the mother Margaret, at the other.

The Billings' children, sat between their parents. The teen-aged son Jesse sat uncomfortably, squirming, beside his father. Rebecca the daughter, sat beside her mother. Eleanor concluded that Henry and Margaret Billings, were innately protective parents.

Eleanor was seated in a comfortable armchair facing the sofa. Ruth, followed by Fannie, entered the room. Ruth was carrying a sterling silver tray containing, five large drinking glasses, and a stack of neatly folded, embroidered cloth napkins.

Ruth walked to the sofa; each occupant of the sofa removed a glass, and a napkin. Fannie trailed behind Ruth, exactly four steps behind. Fannie carried a sterling silver tray, which contained a large pitcher of lemonade, and a plate of cookies.

Fannie filled each glass, with lemonade. Ruth followed by Fannie, trays in hand, moved behind Miss Leary, to an inconspicuous corner of the room.

With the exception of Jesse, all of the seated occupants of the parlor took polite, discrete sips from their glasses. Jesse downed his drink in one huge gulp.

Margaret looked at her son in shock, and disbelief. "Jesse, where are your manners?" "Sorry Mom, Dad, Miss Leary, I have to leave. Today's the day that me and Lucas are overseeing the planting of our southwest fields.

As Henry was about to protest, Miss Leary raised her hand. "It's quite all right Mr. Billings. Believe me, I understand, having been raised on a farm, I understand completely."

Jesse rose from his seat, and as if by magic, Ruth was by his side, tray extended to receive his empty glass. Jesse placed his glass on to the tray.

Jesse bolted for the door. Miss Leary turned in her seat; by the way Jesse; "Lucas and me, is the correct sentence structure." Jesse stopped in mid-stride; he looked quizzically at Miss Leary.

Henry, with a broad grin on his face, slapped his thigh; "Touché Miss Leary." He raised his glass and nodded in the direction of Miss Leary; "Welcome to Rosewood, welcome to our home."

■■

Once Miss Leary had excused herself, and retired to her room, Becky ran from the parlor, in search of Mandy.

Mandy was in the kitchen, helping Fannie and her mother, wash, dry, and put away the "white-folk-company", silver-ware and glasses. Ruth was washing the glasses. Mandy was drying. And Fannie was polishing the sterling silver serving trays.

As Becky entered the kitchen, she heard Fannie; *"Dat teecha...Miss Lee'ree sho is a looka! an smart. "Did ya see how she done sit rite Massa Jesse's white talk?"*

Ruth turned to answer Fannie; *"Sho did; she sho nuff smart; sprise me wen she done spoke rite up; don't look lik no fighta; she look lik a lil white doll-baby." "Mandy, ya bes be carful wid dem glasses an dat dere diss."*

"Mistress an Massa hav us skin'd iffin we breaks um." Mandy was being exceedingly careful, in her handling of the family's expensive crystal glasses and the china. *"Yessum mama, I'se bein' careful...ain't nuttin gwine slip from dese hans."*

Becky burst into the kitchen. Mandy, Mandy, we've loss most of the day. Let's go! Mandy was in the process of folding the dishtowel, she looked to her mother, eyes pleading. Ruth sighed, snatched the towel from Mandy's hands; *"Git; you chillin don go gittin' in no trabul now yull here me!"*

Becky and Mandy ran out of the kitchen; Fannie shouted; *"Don slam dat doo!"* As the screen door "banged" loudly behind them.

****

Becky and Mandy ran, hand in hand to their favorite spot, the large oak in the meadow. The girls unceremoniously, plopped down on the ground. They sat facing each other, shaded by the sprawling, leafy branches of the large oak.

For the past two months, the anticipated arrival of Miss Leary, and the excitement of speculating as to the types of subjects, and classes that the girls thought that they would be taking together, had been the major topics of discussion of their young, girlish conversations.

Mandy was bursting with questions; however, Rebecca was the first to speak. "Mandy why is it that when you speak to Ruth and to Fannie, you speak in nigger talk?"

Mandy silently, looked down at the ground, plucked a blade of grass from nature's velvety green carpet, she examined the blade for several seconds; "My mother does not like to hear me speak "white-folks" talk."

Rebecca gave her an incredulous look; "Why in the world would Ruth object to your speaking English correctly?" Mandy removed the grass from between her lips; "Mother constantly reminds me that I'm a slave." She says that my speaking like white-folk, will get me into trouble, hurt me, makes me look stand-offish."

"Black folks will think that I'm putting on airs — they think, that I think, that I'm better then them. White folk, she says, if they hear me speaking "white", will think that I'm a trouble maker."

"I explained to mama that when I hear her speak, I innately, with out thinking, understand what she's saying, and I can repeat, exactly what she said, in perfect "white-folk" talk. I can do the same thing when we talk."

"What ever you say to me in "white-folk" talk, I can tell mama, Fannie, or for that matter, any slave, what you said, what you meant, in what we slave consider, perfect "nigger-talk."

Mandy feeling that she had adequately answered Becky's question, hastily, launched, in rapid succession, a series of questions concerning the arrival of Miss Eleanor Leary.

"What's she like? — When do you start classes? — Will Jesse be taught with you?" Mandy was at first puzzled by Rebecca's silence. "Come on Becky, answer me…what's wrong? Why won't you answer me?"

Rebecca sighed. "Nothing's wrong, I was just thinking about how splendid it would have been if we were both being taught together."

****

Eleanor O'Leary was the first live-born child, of Sean and Molly O'Leary. Molly, before the live birth of Eleanor, had previously miscarried a child. Three years following the birth of Eleanor, and two subsequent heart-wrenching pregnancies that terminated in miscarriages, a son Patrick was born, followed the next year with the birth of the baby, Timothy.

Sean O'Leary, Eleanor's father was the son of itinerant, Irish potato farmers. Sean's family, like his parents, and grandparents, were dependent upon the crops they grew, and the largesse of their landlords.

During the height of the Irish Potato Famine, Sean due to the pandemic potato blight was finding it increasingly difficult, to raise an edible crop, in the depleted Irish soil.

In order to prevent his family from starving, the Sean O'Leary Family fled Ireland and immigrated to America.

Sean his wife Molly, their thirteen-year-old daughter Eleanor, and their two toddler sons, Patrick, and baby Timothy landed in the American port city of New York.

Sean would rise each day before the crack of dawn, collect from Molly, his meager lunch, which he would hastily stuff into a kerchief in his pocket, and would then hurry to the docks, looking and praying for work.

If he was both lucky and aggressive enough, Sean might secure a favorable position in that days long lines of men hoping to be selected for a day's work.

Working as longshoremen, the monotonous, loading and unloading of cargo from ships, was hard, tedious, back breaking manual labor. Sean was accustomed to hard work.

He was not accustomed to boring work. Sean O'Leary as was his father, and his father's father, was a farmer. A man accustomed to tilling the soil, and reaping the rewards of his labor.

On those days that Sean, competing with the hordes of fellow immigrant-Irishmen for limited jobs on the docks, was fortunate enough to be plucked out of the long lines of men begging for work, he would work from sunup, to sundown, off loading and loading ships.

Sean stacked boxes of freight in warehouses, and loaded the cargo bays of the empty ships with freight to be shipped out. The work was hard, exhausting, but most importantly to Sean, the work was unfulfilling. Molly supplemented the family's income, by taking in laundry.

After six months of attempting to adjust to his newly adopted country, thus far, as far as Sean could surmise, the sole improvement in the family's plight, following their exodus from Ireland, was the fact that in America, they no longer occupied the bottom rung of the social ladder.

The ubiquitous signs and slurs proclaiming that "No Irish Need Apply", "Dogs an Irish, Stay Off the Grass", were a constant reminder of Sean's lowly status in America.

When their circumstances seemed hopelessly bleak, Sean and Molly along with most of the residents of the Irish slum communities, would comfort their hungry children, with the frequently heard lament; "It could be a lot worse; at least we ain't niggers."

****

Sean Leary, formerly Sean O'Leary of Downy court Ireland (Sean dropped the'O in an attempt to Americanize the family name), was a farmer. His father, was a farmer, his father's father was a farmer. Sean longed to feel the warmth of fertile soil, coursing through his fingers.

Having managed to accumulate a total of two hundred ninety dollars, the Leary family, as did many of the hoards of immigrants festering in the slums and ghettos of America's over crowded cities, sought to achieve their dreams, of a better life.

The Sean Leary family, pick up lock stock and barrel, and set out to settle the vast wilderness, to seek a better life in the American west.

On February, 6, 1843, Sean Leary, his wife and three children, left New York, determined to claim their piece of cheap, if not "free", fertile, frontier farmland.

In April of 1843, the Leary family joined a wagon train of more then 1,000 men, women and children, moving westward, seeking a better way of life for their families.

The Leary family joined a wagon train whose ultimate destination was the vast Oregon Territory. The train consisted of 26 families, 32 able bodied men, 26 women, 104 children, 98 oxen, 38 horses. The wagon train left St. Luis Monday May 10, 1843.

****

The oxen that pulled the huge wagons, lumbered along — depending upon the terrain — at a pace of about 10 – 15 miles per day. Progress was exceedingly slow. Three weeks after leaving civilization, the Leary family's the wagon train entered Indian Territory.

Anxiety amongst the settlers was noticeably heightened. Scouts, men who as trappers and traders, had some first-hand knowledge of the land west of the Mississippi River, routinely scouted some 15 – 20 miles ahead of the wagon train.

Sporadically, as the wagon- train moved increasingly further and further into the interior of country, the scouts either observed, or detected signs of small groups of Indians, usually the signs were those of small hunting parties.

On each occasion that a scout had reported signs or sightings of Indians, panic would spread throughout the wagon train. Parents would reinforce instructions that they had repeatedly preached to their children, as to exactly what, they should do in the event of an Indian attack.

The practical self-defense and survival instructions, were invariably hammered home, with tales emphasizing, and dehumanizing, the perceived savagery and barbaric nature of the Indian.

Horrific stories of torture, rape, and cannibalism, were graphically described. As a last resort, women and children were encouraged to commit suicide, rather than be captured by the savages.

Sean was becoming more and more apprehensive and fearful for the safety of his vulnerable family. The reports of Indian sightings increased with each mile of westward migration. His little family unit that consisted of one man, two females, one of which was a twelve-year-old girl, and two toddler sons, was almost totally dependent upon others for their safety.

At night when the children were asleep, Sean and Molly, sitting by their campfire, would quietly, in subdued tones, discuss their growing concerns for the family's safety. "God help us if the savages attack…when it comes down to it, we've got but one rifle between us and a massacre".

****

One especially hot, steaming morning, the presence of Indians was confirmed, the entire wagon train awoke to frantic cries of; "Injuns we're been attacked".

The occupants of the Sam Mueller family wagon, three wagons behind the Leary's, ran screaming through the wagon train. Sam was carrying a feathered arrow that he had removed from the neck of his favorite hound.

"Those red devils snuck in here last night; stole two of my horses, and kilt my dog."

The intrusion of savages, a mere three wagons distance from his wife, and sleeping children, convinced Sean that the Leary Family's journey west had come to an end.

Sean informed the wagon train master that his family would be leaving the caravan at civilization's next outpost. He intended to stake a claim for land, clear the land for farming, settle and raise his family on the fringe of the American Frontier.

The sign swinging from two wooden posts, staked into the ground, read; "O'Fallon Nebraska. Sean and Molly, devout Irish Catholics, and true believers did indeed, believe in miracles.

The Leary family, formerly the O'Leary family of Cork County Ireland, devoid of contact with Catholic Clergy for the past three months, literally interpreted the roadside sign, O'Fallon Nebraska, as an omen, a religious sign.

Sean Leary planted his family's roots. He laid claim to a nineteen-acre tract of land in O'Fallon, Nebraska-Territory.

The Leary's, formerly the O'Leary's, were home.

****

Living on the edge of the American frontier, was an incredibly dangerous, yet satisfying, way of life. Untilled, unclaimed fertile land, ideal for raising crops, was there for the taking. The Leary family, no strangers to hard work, immediately set out to convert the wilderness into livable farmland.

Sean toiled in the fields, while Molly and Eleanor, totally tended to the domestic chores, which included the rearing of the two boys, Patrick and Timothy.

To the Leary family, time just seemed to fly by. During their first three years, the family would rarely, on occasion, catch glimpses of small groups of Indians.

The few white families attempting to settle in O'Fallon were spread thinly. The Leary's closest neighbors, the Stewart's farm was nearly ten miles away.

The two families rarely met. On the rare occasions when they did meet, the number one topic of conversation was invariably, the always-present danger and threat of an Indian attack.

Sean Leary and Adam Stewart, would incessantly drill into their respective families, defensive, escape, and survival plans in the event of an Indian attack. Mutual aid plans between the families, were formulated, modified and either accepted or rejected.

Reports of atrocities supposedly perpetrated by the Indians, some real, most imagined, were drummed into the minds of the children.

Sean and Molly both, constantly, and relentlessly, vilified the "barbaric; savage; inhuman", nature of those "Red Devils."

On a daily bases, they drummed into the heads of Eleanor, Patrick, and Timothy, what would befall them if they were attacked, and overrun by "the godless heathens".

****

One particularly gloomy evening, during their fifth year on the farm, while the family was preparing to sit for their evening meal, Patrick breathlessly ran into the house, having difficulty catching his breath, he excitedly blurted; "Pa, the Indians are coming…there's a whole war party crossing the creek!"

Sean, spoke to the family in calm measured words; "Okay, we've talked about this hundreds of times, you all know what to do."

Sean calmly grabbed his rifle, which hung on a rack above the fireplace. Molly dropped the spoon that she had been vigorously stirring the large pot of stew. She hurried to the windows, let down and secured the wooden slates that covered the cabin's three windows.

Eighteen-year-old Eleanor, slide the table to the side, and removed the rug which covered and concealed a trapdoor. The door opened to a small ladder that descended to the escape tunnel, which lead to a copse of tress that lined the brook.

Eleanor hastily, but calmly took Timothy's hand, and led him into the escape tunnel. Molly replaced the rug, and replaced the table. She then retrieved an unloaded rifle from the far corner of the room, she handed the gun, and a box of shells, to Patrick.

Patrick was peering through the peephole of the wooden slate that covered one of the two windows, surrounding the front door. After placing a box of ammunition, on the floor beside the then unmanned window, Molly retrieved Sean's heavy Navy Colt pistol, and took up station at the window which overlooked the rear of the farmhouse.

Three Indian warriors, slowly, cautiously approached the farmhouse. The three riders each had quivers of arrows on their backs, bows held in their left hands. They each extended their empty right hands, palms forward.

Sean, rifle in hand, barrel pointed towards the ground, stepped out onto the porch. The tall, wiry warrior, obvious the leader, rotated his right hand, palm out facing Sean, and gestured towards his mouth as if he were drinking.

Sean smiled at the trio, mimicked the drinking, pantomime, with his left hand, affirmatively nodded his head, and pointed to the water trough.

The warriors turned their horses, dismounted, and drank from the trough. They allowed their animals to drink, then wordlessly remounted and rode off.

****

For ten years, living on the rapidly changing American frontier, Eleanor, along with her mother Molly, raised her two brothers into stripping, relatively literate young men.

Eleanor's innate intelligence, was fed, nurtured, and blossomed in large part, due to her astute awareness and her appreciation for, her natural environment.

During the family's six months living in the squalor of the Irish slums of New York, Eleanor had attempted to quench her thirst for knowledge, by reading any, and all of the various pamphlets that were readily available in the bustling city.

The Leary Farm prospered. In addition to providing more then sufficient food to feed the family, each year's crop yielded a surplus that Sean was able to sell at market.

At age twenty-three, Eleanor felt a well-earned sense of satisfaction, in her role in having raised, and tutored her brothers.

Patrick and Timothy had turned out to be fine well-spoken, young men, pillars of the O'Fallon Community.

Sean and Molly, Eleanor's parents, boasted to anyone who would listen, that Eleanor's contribution, to the family's success, especially the tutoring of the, by the local standards, well educated boys, Patrick and Timothy, in Sean's words, was "a job well done."

Sean and Molly were content. In their minds, and rightfully so, what they had accomplished was remarkable. They were well on the way to achieving the American Dream. A comfortable living and a home for the family, and the promise of security for the future. For Sean and Molly Leary, life was good.
****

Eleanor Leary was bored. Eleanor was one of those few, rare people who, was truly born to teach. For ten years, as a member of the family, she had labored with the rest, to clear the land, to till the soil, plant, tend to and harvest the crops.

Additionally, Eleanor was responsible for the boys, Patrick and Timothy's home schooling. Eleanor had reached the proverbial "the end of the line". She loved teaching the boys. The boys were eager to learn, they were good students.

Eleanor had simply exhausted her wealth of knowledge. She longed for the opportunity to gain a formal liberal arts education. Eleanor wanted to learn. Her goal was to earn a degree from a well-respected American College.

Eleanor asked her father and mother for, and was given their permission to attend college in the East. In January 1854, Eleanor arrived in Oberlin Ohio.

Eleanor Leary of O'Fallon Nebraska, formerly Eleanor O'Leary of Cork County, Ireland, was accepted as a first-year student, at Oberlin College.

****

Eleanor Leary - Rosewood Plantation - 1859

Eleanor insisted that Rebecca and Jesse's lessons begin promptly each weekday morning, at 8:00 AM.

In order to prepare relevant lesson plans, her first task, was to ascertain the academic level of her two students. It quickly became crystal clear to Eleanor, that a huge chasm — acquired and retained knowledge of English grammar, history, and the arts — separated Rebecca, from her older brother Jesse. Rebecca's interest, and knowledge in these disciplines, by far exceeded that held by Jesse'.

After having held classes for a week, Eleanor, was genuinely impressed with Rebecca's aptitude and mastery of English grammar. Though heavily accented, the girl's enunciation and pronunciation, especially in light of her having been raised as a Southern-Belle, was remarkable.

Not surprisingly, Rebecca's grasp of the concepts and the power of mathematics, and science were average at best.

While Jesse, on the other hand, had poor English language skills. Jesse's command of, and utilization of the rules of English grammar, was barely, slightly superior to that of Lucas Prentiss, the plantation's white overseer. And Jesse's knowledge and appreciation of history, appeared to be confined to what appeared to be, the anecdotal recounting of events, of the history of Essex County, Virginia, with a scanty sprinkling of knowledge, or interest in Virginia's neighboring states.

On the other hand, Jesse's grasp of mathematics, or more precisely, his knowledge and skill of fundamental, of applied arithmetic, was superb.

Jesse was accomplished and comfortable with the utility and the practicality of the application and handling of numbers. He appeared to be remarkably proficient working with weights and measures.

Eleanor concluded that Jesse was well suited for his perceived, eventual life's work, that of becoming, a successful, wealthy, influential, Southern Planter.

****

When Eleanor's lesson plan called for the teaching of English or European Literature, Jesse would sit, fidgeting, squirming in his seat, looking bored, uninterested, and distracted.

Rebecca in contrast would, with obvious keen interest, listen intently, pose intelligent, insightful questions, and enthusiastically participate in the resulting discussion, and analysis of a particular classic.

Over the course of several months, Eleanor quickly came to realize that the Billings children were definitely both, of above average intelligence.

Rebecca absorbed ideas, theories, and facts like a sponge. She seemed to have an unquenchable thirst for knowledge. Rebecca was hands-down, Eleanor's all-time favorite student.

What impressed Eleanor most about her star student, was Rebecca's determination, her childish insistence that the session continue until she comprehended and absolutely understood, the subject matter.

Rebecca would stubbornly refuse to let a session end, until she could articulate, to Eleanor's satisfaction, that she fully and thoroughly understood that particular session's, subject matter.

Jesse would often leave these prolonged, lengthy, sessions prematurely. He would ask permission to leave muttering under his breath, "for heaven's sake Becky...enough is enough."

On those days when extended sessions occurred, Eleanor and Rebecca, would continue their dialogue, until they were called to dinner.

At noon, teacher, and pupils would take a two-hour break for lunch. Eleanor noticed, that Rebecca would invariably be immediately met, by her constantly, attentive, beautiful, slave-companion, Mandy.

Mandy, hands and arms scratched, from her work, weeding in the garden, lunch basket in hand, would be sitting on the floor in the hall, dutifully waiting, for Rebecca. The two girls would bolt from the house, laughing and giggling, as they hurriedly ran, skipped, on their way, to one of their favorite retreats.

While Mandy laid out their lunch, Rebecca would briefly outline the topic of the morning's lesson with Miss Leary. While Rebecca spoke, Mandy would sit mesmerized, concentrating on the subject matter. With quill and paper in her lap, the black slave girl took copious notes.

When Mandy did not fully understand a phrase, a sentence or a concept, she would raise her hand, just as she had seen Becky do, over and over again, in Eleanor's class.

If she could, Rebecca would answer Mandy's question. If she was not able to, or felt unsure of the answer, Becky would have Mandy write down the question. Rebecca would in turn, before the next session commenced, ask Miss Leary the question, and then share the answer with Mandy.

Eleanor usually spent Saturdays and Sundays, reading in her room. On a particularly balmy Saturday morning, Eleanor decided to forego her reading, and to instead conduct some "'in the field" research. She asked Mr. Billings for, and was given his permission to explore the grounds of Rosewood.

Rosewood Plantation was Eleanor's first, real-life, first-hand visit to the South. Her life in America, first briefly in New York, and subsequently in the "Free Soil" Territory of Nebraska, had been in sections of the country that by law did not condone or permit slavery.

Though Eleanor's father, was not a supporter of slavery, he was far being an abolitionist — he truly believed that blacks and for that matter, that Indians, were inferior to the White Race — his reasons for being anti-slavery, were based strictly on economic considerations.

As a farmer who raised crops to sell in the market place, he felt that his slave-holding competitors had an unfair "free-labor" advantage.

Farmers who owned slaves, because of their source of "free-labor", could therefore raise more crops, and afford to sell their produce at cheaper prices.

Eleanor's father had, for his children's safety and for their survival living on the frontier, for their own protection, had repeatedly told his children tales of barbarianism, savagery, and cannibalism, attributed to the red man, and told them of the indolent, slovenly, lazy, stupidity, of the black man.

At that point and time in her life, Eleanor had no reason, or inclination to doubt her father's words, or his opinions.

At Oberlin College, Eleanor entered into a whole new world. A diverse student body community, that consisted of bright educated white men, a sprinkling of white women, and to her complete and total astonishment, four black students, two men and two women.

She had chosen to attend Oberlin College, because of its' proximity to her home, and most importantly, because of Oberlin's willingness to accept female students.

Eleanor was both surprised and amazed, when she first encountered black students, men and women who could read and write, and most astonishingly, blacks, who could reason, could present, and who could defend and prove hypothesis. Their defense and the prove, based upon observable, and/or derived, and deduced facts.

Initially, intellectually, Eleanor had had difficulty reconciling the difference between the dogma — Indians are cannibalistic savages; black people are inherently stupid and inferior — repeatedly drummed into her head, taught to her by her parents, with her own observations of the four black students who were her classmates.

A whole new world had been laid open, for the brilliant, receptive mind of Eleanor Leary.

The diverse, integrated world of Oberlin College was fertile ground for the intellectual maturing, and growth of the mind of Miss Eleanor Leary.

****

The Oberlin campus was far from being apolitical. The overwhelming majority of students were from northern free-states.

The vast majority of the student population, if not themselves abolitionists, were definitely sympathetic and receptive, to the abolitionist message.

And more importantly, the majority of students were ardent supporters of the abolitionists cause, that being total eradication of slavery in America.

This private tutoring position that she had obtained, on an actual Southern cotton plantation, where 99% of the workforce, was slave-labor, afforded an excellent opportunity, for her to see and to evaluate, slavery in America.

Eleanor had come to the South, not only to teach and to help mold young minds, she came with the expressed goal of studying, and documenting, from first hand, objective-observation, the pros and cons, in support of the preservation, or for the abolition of Slavery in America.

****

The previous evening, Eleanor had asked her employer, Henry Billings the Master of Rosewood, for permission to tour the plantation. Henry gave his consent, and had made arrangements to make available for her use, a buggy and a driver.

When Eleanor arrived at the stable, she was greeted by Pee wee, his hat in hand, with a broad smile which extended from ear to ear; *"moaning Missy...I's Pee wee. I's ben tol by Massa Henry, to tak you where you wan ta go on da place."*

Eleanor took the slave's extended hand, as he assisted her at being seated in the buggy. Eleanor smiled; "Good morning...thank you Pee wee. I remember you; you're the driver that met me at the train depot. How are you?"

That simple act, the exchange of pleasantries, between himself and this smart, pretty white woman completely baffled Pee wee.

Once they were both seated in the buggy, Pee wee, eyes staring straight ahead, *"wer you wantta go Mistress."*

Eleanor opened her parasol, sat back in her seat; "Pee wee, I would very much like to see the cotton-fields. Let's start there."

Pee we lightly flicked the horse's reins. The little filly moved away from the house at a trot, towards the cotton-fields.

Eleanor's gaze took in a vast panorama of white. As far as the eye could see, row upon row of snow-white cotton.

Interspaced among the plants, black men and women were picking cotton, removing the fluffy balls of cotton from the plants, depositing the tufts in the bags trailing behind each picker.

Eleanor turned her head, in response to the distinctive sound of the crack of a whip. Two rows to her left, Lucas Prentiss, the overseer leaned down from his saddle, he sat astride a large gray stallion, recoiling his 6-foot long whip.

"Move your black-ass Luther...you bout the laziest nigger there is." "Look at Mabel over there, she's half your size, and picking almost fast as you."

The slave named Luther grunted — lowered his head while ignoring the blood that begin to seep from his shoulder — and continued to pick at the same pace.

Lucas unfurled his whip and once again lashed the slave. "Goddamn it boy…you better speed it up, I ain't got all day ta be watchin you!"

Eleanor was shocked. While she had sat through numerous abolitionist speeches, fiery speeches that graphically described the cruelty, the brutality, the inhumanity of slavery, this was the first time that she had actually witnessed, what appeared to be, the routine, brutal whipping, and the subjugation of one human being, by another.

While her mind was attempting to understand, and to process what she had just witnessed, she heard a commotion emanating three rows over, to the left of the Overseer. There sitting high in his saddle, whip in hand, was one of her students, young Jesse Billings.

Seventeen-year-old Jesse was brandishing and swishing a whip thru the air, he was shouting at a male slave, insisting that the slave quicken his pace, Jesse threatened to; "peel the skin from his lazy black hide."

Eleanor lightly tapped Pee wee's shoulder, and motioned that he should drive-on. Pee wee flicked the reins; the buggy moved forward. Eleanor looked over her shoulder; the slaves were busy rhythmically picking cotton, to the mournful sad refrain:

"I'm gonna ride dat chariot
in da mornin' Lawd
I'm gonna ride dat chariot
in da mornin' Lawd
I'm getting' ready fo da judgmen day
My Lawd, My Lawd!"

"Swing lo – sweet chariot
comin' fo ta carry me home
Swing lo sweet chariot
Comin' fo ta carry me home
I lookd ova yonda an
What did I see
A band of angels comin'afta me
Comin' fa ta carry me home"

The buggy circled one of the cotton fields, which consisted of multiple rows of plants. The white bolls of cotton, stood out in stark contrast to the black hands, of the scores of slave pickers.

Eleanor noted that the vast majority of the slaves working in the fields, were truly, in color black. Skin color not withstanding, the field hands in addition to their black complexions, their facial features were heavily Negroid.

The broad noses, with the flaring nostrils, the thick full lips, and the coarse, matted kinky hair. There before her eyes, were the real-life embodiments, of the classic Negroid phenotypic features, referenced and depicted in the drawings, outlined in her college Anthropology Textbook.

In her mind, Eleanor compared, her thus far, real life unbiased, analytical observations. The slave community, at least in terms of physical appearances, was far from being a homogeneous population.

The complexion of the skin of the majority of Rosewood slaves was dark, bordering on black. The slaves working in the fields were predominantly dark, with broad flat noses, kinky, hair, and thick protruding lips.

In contrast, the slaves working in the "Big House" — with the exception of Rufus the Master's valet, who had for the majority of his life been a field-hand, until arthritis made working in the fields impossible, and the cook Fanny — the rest were "light skinned", differing shades of brown.

Skin complexion varying from caramel brown, to as she had inadvertently heard Fanny refer to some slaves as, "*high yeller*". She noted that the physical facial features of the house-slaves, generally tended to diffuse from Negroid towards Caucasoid, in direct proportion to the variation in skin color, specifically the "lighting" of the slave's complexion.

Eleanor deduced that her personal observations gave credence to the abolitionist's assertions, of widespread and open debauchery, by southern plantation men, perpetrated against black slave women.

To Eleanor, this despicable practice presented for the white slave owner, a win/win scenario. For the plantation owners there was no discernable downside.

The slaveholder was able to sinfully gratify his carnal lust, while at the same time he increased his wealth, through his siring of countless valuable slaves. Slaves who by law, would not and could not be considered his children, but who would by law, must be viewed as his property.

Eleanor, once again lightly tapped Pee wee's shoulder with the handle of her perusal. "Pee wee, how far are we from the "Big House?" Pee wee removed the dilapidated straw hat from his head, scratched his head, hat in hand; "*It not far Missy...it be yonda*", *pointing to his left with his hat, "ova dat der hill Missy."*

Eleanor asked Pee wee to stop the buggy. "I think I'll stretch my legs." Pee wee stopped the buggy, secured the reins, and jumped down to the ground. He helped Eleanor step down from the buggy. "You go on back Pee wee; I'll walk back to the house." Pee wee was about to make a mild protest, then thought it best, that he stay out of *white-folk bizness.*

As Eleanor aimlessly strolled, ambled, lost in thought, away from the cotton fields, towards the creek, she abruptly stopped; she thought that she heard the sounds of girlish laughter. She shielded her eyes with her hand, while turning around in a complete circle, trying to locate the source of the laughter.

Eleanor was surprised to find that she was completely surrounded by trees. She had been so preoccupied with her thoughts that she had lost her bearings, strayed from the footpath, and was, at least at that moment, quite lost.

Mildly annoyed, but still not alarmed, Eleanor walked towards the sound of the laughter. Through the trees, adjacent to the creek, she saw a small clearing.

Rebecca was standing, book in hand, delivering a lecture to her pretty little slave companion, Mandy. Eleanor's curiosity was acutely peeked. She could not quite make out the words being exchanged between the girls. Not wanting to interrupt their dialogue, she quietly, cautiously, moved closer.

Mandy was slowly shaking her head, in exasperation, from side to side; "I'm still confused. It's hard to understand how you can keep saying — in fact why you continue to insist — that that passage — though the words are clearly English words — that the words strung together, make any sense."

Rebecca was affirmatively bobbing her head up and down, "I know...
I know, I had the same reaction when Miss. Leary first read that passage in class, to Jesse and me.

When she was reading, so reverently, from that beautiful, leather bound book, Jesse and I were staring, dumbfounded, at each other. Jesse whispered to me...what's she talking about?"

"While she was reading, from that beautiful book, Miss. Leary's eyes were as bright as I have ever seen them. The look in her eyes reminded me of Reverend Tucker, the look he has in his eyes, as he reads from the bible."

"When Miss Leary finished, as I always do when I don't completely understand, I raised my hand and asked, Miss Leary, what does it mean, what language is that? Neither Jesse, nor do I, speak that language."

Mandy was sitting on a crate; she was staring intently, obviously hanging on to Rebecca's every word. "What did she say Becky?" Rebecca solemnly looked at Mandy. "Miss Leary lowered the book…then she said — that, that was indeed English."

"She said that many say, that those words, are some of the most beautiful, poetic English words ever written. Then as if she was reciting a prayer, or about to quote scripture, Miss Leary said that those words were written, over two hundred and fifty years ago, by an Englishman. By the world's greatest English writer, William Shakespeare."

Eleanor, one hand against a tree, raised her free hand and placed it over her heart. She stared at the girls. Eleanor did not move, she stood transfixed, as if she were frozen in time and space. What was unveiling right before her eyes, was the enactment of every teacher's dream.

Unfolding before her was every dedicated teacher's aspiration, to actually see, to witness the tangible, positive effects of her teachings. Rebecca, her student, was extolling and exchanging with a third party, the teacher's philosophy, the teacher's beliefs, in an actual social interaction.

****

From her vantage point, behind the large tree, she was able to see and hear the girls, without them seeing her.

Mandy looked incredulously at Rebecca; "English, if that's English, I think it's the silliest English I've ever heard…it didn't make sense, I didn't understand any of it. Read it again Becky."

Rebecca inserted a bookmark, and closed the book. Mandy looked quizzically at Rebecca; "I recognize most of the words by themselves. But when put together, to me, they just don't make sense."

Rebecca sat down beside Mandy. Her book was in her lap. Both girls sat facing Eleanor.

Eleanor remained, unseen behind the shrubbery. The slave girl's reaction to Shakespeare's prose, Eleanor mused, was eerily, almost identical, to Rebecca's initial response, when she had first introduced, the young Miss Billings to Elizabethan, English Literature.

Rebecca opened her text book, she handed the book to Mandy; "Read it yourself — read it out loud."

Mandy took the book from Rebecca, and began to read:

Romeo

But, soft! what light through yonder window breaks?
It is the east, and Juliet is the sun.

Arise, fair sun, and kill the envious moon,
Who is already sick and pale with grief,
That thou her maid art far more fair than she:

Mandy closed the book. She then looked up at Rebecca. "I read it…and I still don't understand it. I recognize each of the words. What I don't understand are the phrases, and the sentences, made by the words."

Mandy pronounced each word in a confident clear, voice. She then gave the book back to Rebecca.

Eleanor was duly impressed. She instantly concluded that, either the slave girl had a fantastic memory, or that this slave girl could actually read! Not only could the slave read, she read really, very well.

Rebecca opened the text; "When I first read it, I had the same reaction that you did. After Miss. Leary excused Jesse, she sat with me and explained why at first Mr. Shakespeare's words might not seem to make sense. She said that to understand the words, and subsequently the sentences, they have to be taken in context with the times that they were written."

"William Shakespeare wrote this play, Romeo and Juliet, over two hundred and fifty years ago. And while we recognize the individual words, the meaning of the words then in 1595, may have been different from what, those words mean today."

Mandy listened attentively to Rebecca. She heard Rebecca, she carefully dissected, and analyzed, at length, Miss. Leary and Rebecca's reasoning. Mandy slowly looked up at Rebecca. Mandy definitely did not look convinced.

Rebecca continued; "Miss Leary's explanation was still not clear to me. I told her that I still didn't understand. Miss. Leary then, wrote the passage on the board." Rebecca picked up a small slate black board tablet, from the grass. On the tablet, was written:

Romeo
(Shakespeare)

But, soft! What light through yonder window breaks? It is the east, and Juliet is the sun. Arise, fair sun, and kill the envious moon, Who is already sick and pale with grief, That thou her maid art far more fair than she:

Romeo
(Miss. Leary's - Interpretation)

How soft! What's that light streaming through the window over there? It's the sun rising. Juliet, to me shines like the sun. Rise up beautiful Juliet, obliterate the jealous moon. The moon, your maid is already sick and pale with grief, compared to you, who is more beautiful than is she:

Rebecca slowly closed the book; "Miss. Leary is a Yankee. She lived up North in Ohio, or Nebraska. She said that when she first came to Rosewood, she could barely understand what we were saying.

She said that we, in the South, have a heavy, difficult to understand — at least to non-southerners — Southern accent. Miss. Leary said that, although the English words spoken in the North and South, for the most part, are the same words, it was weeks before she became accustomed to, and began to understand what we were actually saying."

Mandy excitedly rose from her crate, "You know what Becky…that reminds me of when you asked me, why do I speak "nigger talk" when I'm talking to my mother, or for that matter, when I'm talking to any of the slaves."

Rebecca took Mandy's hands in hers. The girls looked gleefully into each other's eyes. It was as if the dam had suddenly broken, and a flood of understanding had washed over them.

Rebecca picked up the slate board from the grass, and wiped the board clean with a rag. Mandy once again, sat down on her crate, her eyes glued to the board. Rebecca wrote on the board, a simple sentence, a sentence recently taught to her and to Jesse, by Eleanor, during a recent civics lesson.

She gave the chalk to Mandy. "How would you write that in "nigger talk."
Mandy rose from her crate, read the sentence, and without a moment's hesitation wrote her response.

Rebecca and Mandy stood side by side. They silently read; the two sentences written on the board. They smiled at each other, and then they hugged. The girls knew that once again, they understood, and were speaking the same language.

102

The girls put the blackboard and chalk on the crates. They covered the crates with a split burlap sack. The girls joined hands, and started to walk and skip — Eleanor presumed— back towards the "Big House."

From her position behind the tree, and the bushes, Eleanor had not been able to make out what the girls had written on the slate-board. She walked over to the crates, removed the burlap sack, she then lifted the slate-board, and read the two simple declarative sentences:

REBECCA: - All white men, who own property, have the right to vote.

MANDY: - *Dem ofay massus, dat got niggers, can vote.*

Tears of joy and of satisfaction, welled in her eyes and begin to flow silently down her cheeks. Eleanor smiled and replaced the blackboard. She turned and, bursting with pride, followed the girls back to the "Big House."

The slave cabins, the stables, the barn, and the "Big House" were now in sight. Eleanor decided to stop at the stables, to retrieve her handkerchief that she thought that she had earlier left in the buggy.

As she entered, the stable, at first, it appeared to be deserted. When she was about to leave, she thought she heard Pee wee, pitching hay in one of the rear stalls.

The sounds of work, seemed to be coming from the last stall. Eleanor peered into the stall, Pee wee, stripped to the waist, pitchfork in hand, was bent over pitching hay.

When Pee we straightened and stood erect, with his back facing Eleanor, she gasped in horror. Pee wee's back was crisscrossed with a multitude of hideous scars. Eleanor stifled a cry, by hastily placing both of her hands over her mouth.

For the second time that day, tears streamed down his cheeks. Her joyful recent tears of pride, had now been transformed into, heart wrenching tears of sorrow, tears of shame.

****

Eleanor sat in the middle of her bed, hugging one of her down-filled pillows. She had been setting in this position of meditation, her brow furrowed, and deep in thought, since her return from her morning tour of the plantation.

Her field trip of the Rosewood plantation, had revealed, in just half a day, far more then she had anticipated, in her quest to gather knowledge, and understanding of the *"South's Peculiar Institution*, Slavery."

During her years as a student at Oberlin College, Eleanor had actually attended classes with Negroes. Eleanor was well aware of the observable fact that members of the Negro race were capable of learning to read and to write.

What was not clear to her, until this morning, was that a Negro, born into slavery, raised as a slave, having never known life, other than that of a slave, was capable of reading, writing, and comprehension at an extremely high level.

And judging from what she had recently witnessed, the apparent results of the tutorial sessions between Rebecca and the slave girl Mandy, slaves were capable of rational thought, and of complex rational problem solving.

Exuberantly, Eleanor reached into her dresser-draw, removed her diary, and began to document, her morning's observations.

She wrote:

September 4, 1852 (Saturday)

"The Fields"

1) Amongst the slave population, by far the darkest slaves, the slaves with the most prominent Negroid facial features, were the field-hands hands.

2) For real and perceived, mostly perceived, low productivity, the slaves were constantly under the lash of the overseer.

3) Young white-males mimicked the behavior of the overseer, in the handling of field-hands.

4) The vast majority of the slaves appeared to be docile; subservient; as if completely, unquestioningly, accepting their fate.

5) The slaves were highly religious; constant singing of songs that foretold of freedom in the hereafter.

September 4, 1852 (Saturday)

"The Education of a slave? (Mandy)"

1) Mandy's displayed superior, reading, writing, and comprehension, skills.

2) Mandy's speech patterns, diction, enunciation, when speaking to Rebecca — (If I had not seen her, I would have thought Rebecca was conversing with a southern white-girl) — impeccable.

3) Mandy's ability to cleverly, superbly, and accurately, translate, and understand Shakespeare's 17th century prose, into what she termed, 19th century "Nigger Talk."

4) Thirteen-year-old Rebecca's courage, or perhaps her naiveté, in her clandestine breaking of a sacred Southern Law; teaching a slave to read and write.

She closed the journal, placed it in the drawer, and then fell into a fitful, restless, sleep.

****

The next day, at the conclusion of class, after Jesse had left, Rebecca as usual, caught the attention of her slave girl Mandy, who had quietly entered the room, five minutes before the end of class. Mandy was dutifully seated on the floor, awaiting her mistress.

Rebecca gathered her books, and prepared to leave. Eleanor called out to Becky, "Rebecca, one moment please." Rebecca stopped, and turned to face Eleanor; "yes Miss. Leary?" Eleanor walked around to the front of her desk. "I think it's time that I met your little friend." Rebecca hesitated. She looked confused, "my little friend? What ever do you mean Miss. Leary?"

Eleanor did not answer. Instead her gaze moved to Mandy. Mandy shrunk in the corner, her body language suggested that, if should could, at that moment, she would have made herself invisible.

Rebecca turned towards Mandy. In a stern, authoritative, tone Rebecca, spoke to her slave; "Mandy, come here!" Mandy scrambled to her feet, and shuffled over to Rebecca. Head bowed, she mumbled; *"yesm mizzy Beka?"* "Miss. Leary would like to meet you."

Eleanor had been intently observing, the interaction between the girls. Amazing, she thought. Their acting! Their body language is stiff, not natural. Yesterday, when I watched them, unobserved behind that tree, those girls where totally comfortable with each other, colleagues, friends, equals.

This "Master-slave" act that they are putting on for my benefit, is just that, it's an act, a charade. Had I not only yesterday, witnessed an entirely different, dynamic, interaction between the two, I would have bought it, I would have been totally fooled.

Eleanor gently placed her fingers under Mandy's chin, and lifted, forcing Mandy to make eye contact. Eleanor saw a look of absolute terror, in the girl's eyes.

"Hello, I'm Miss. Leary…what's your name?" Mandy quickly averted her eyes, she looked down at her feet and in a weak, hesitant, barely audible, subservient voice, responded; *"Ise be Mandy, Missy."*

Eleanor removed her hand from beneath Mandy's chin; "Mandy, what a beautiful name. "How old are you Mandy." Mandy, obviously uncomfortable, looked pleadingly over at Rebecca.

Rebecca placed her hands on her hips, and barked; "Speak up girl, Miss Leary asked you a question. Answer her. You know that we were both born in the same year."

Mandy averted her eyes from Rebecca, and returned her gaze to her feet. She mumbled; *"Missy Beka an me be da same…Ise don'ritely knows dat numba."*

Eleanor was astonished by Mandy's reply. Having only yesterday, seen Mandy effortlessly, with ease and self-assurance, at a remarkably high level, flawlessly read and write.

Eleanor remembered having stood motionless, transfixed; as she listened to Mandy read and speak, unscripted paragraphs, of grammatically perfect English, with flawless pronunciation, and pristine diction.

Today the girl's vocabulary, her diction, her speech pattern, appeared to be that of an illiterate black slave. She glanced at Rebecca. Rebecca's facial expression had not changed. Rebecca had not shown a modicum of surprise at Mandy's response.

Eleanor was taken aback by the girls' blatant, apparent conspiratorial, subterfuge. Instead of right there and then confronting and challenging the girls, Eleanor decided, for the time being, to go along with their charade. To see how far the girls would go to hide the fact that Mandy was highly literate.

Eleanor took Rebecca by the hand; they proceeded to leave the classroom. Mandy followed, three feet behind the two white ladies.

As they left the room, Eleanor abruptly stopped and turned, looking back at her desk; "Oh dear I left my French Text Book on my desk, I'll need it to prepare for tomorrow's French lesson…Mandy would you please get it for me."

"Yessum Ise gwine ta gits it." Mandy turned and hurried back to the desk.

Four, large gray, textbooks were on the desk. The book titles were:

1) Elementary French
2) The History of the United States
3) The History of Western Civilization
4) Fundamentals of Mathematics

Mandy swiftly returned with a large gray textbook, which she held by both hands. She gave the book to Eleanor. Eleanor thanked Mandy, and without a second glance, placed the heavy book into her bag.
****

When Eleanor returned to the privacy of her room, she lay on her bed reflecting on the day's unexpected, bizarre events. She opened her dresser drawer and removed her journal. She began to write:

September 6, 1852 (Monday)

She began to write: After four months of seeing her, but not really seeing her, today I finally, formally met Mandy.

Mandy Billings — the use of the name Billings is not intended to denote familial lineage, in this context, Billings should be more accurately written as Billings', thus correctly denoting, ownership.

Mandy is truly, a beautiful girl, who will soon, along with her Mistress (friend?) Rebecca, are both on the verge to becoming two beautiful young women.

When I spoke today to Mandy, in Rebecca's presence, I gave no indication that I knew, or even suspected, that she was literate. Today, both Rebecca and Mandy skillfully portrayed their assigned, respective roles as residents of the South. The roles that Southern Society mandates, they occupy, that of the Autocratic Southern Slave Master, and that of the illiterate, ignorant, submissive, slave.

Yesterday when I, unbeknownst to them, I observed the girls, interacting in their secluded "Natural Habitat", their relationship was clearly, warm, friendly, collegial, indeed bordering on that of a sisterly, sibling-kinship, relationship.

Sisterly, Rebecca and Mandy, that's a word that, for some reason, has been continuously floating in my head. Skin and eye color aside, Rebecca and Mandy have remarkably similar physical features, and characteristics.

Both girls are approximately 5 feet, five inches tall. And when they smile, each girl's cheeks, displays almost identically, the most gorgeous, symmetrical sets of dimples.

They both possess extraordinarily brilliant, alert, eyes. No matter how hard she tried to project the image of being slow and dim-witted, one deep look into Mandy's eyes, those big brown sparkling, intelligent, eyes, completely dispels that totally false impression.

Today I was really quite amused and impressed with both girls' attempt to hide the fact that Mandy can read and write. In fact, if I had not seen hard evidence, with my own eyes, to the contrary, I would have no reason to believe or suspect otherwise.

Well diary, it's been an especially tiring, busy, and interesting day. I'm really tired; in fact, I'm exhausted.

Oh, one last thing, I deliberately asked Mandy to go back and retrieve my French Text-book from my desk.

I deliberately left four books, with four different titles on my desk. My ruse was to stake the odds against Mandy's randomly retrieving, strictly through luck, the French Text.

Mandy almost immediately, returned with the heavy Textbook.

To have selected the correct book, Mandy would have had to have read the title.

Eleanor closed her journal. And placed it in her dresser. She opened the book bag that she had dropped onto the floor beside the bed. Eleanor lifted the heavy textbook with both hands, from the bag. She eagerly read the book's title.

She shook her head in wonderment, and murmured, "that Mandy is one smart, and a very clever young woman."

Eleanor laid the textbook, face-up on the dresser. She blew out the lamp, and adjusted her pillow.

Moonlight flooded into the room. She one last time, raised her head and glanced at the book. In the bright moonlight, she could clearly make out the book's title:

"The History of Western Civilization"

Following Mandy's retrieval of Miss Leary's textbook, Mandy and Rebecca left the house and hurried to one of their favorite meeting spots, the barn.

Both Rebecca and Mandy, looked flustered and just a little bit frightened. Rebecca closed the barn door, and turned to Mandy. She caught her breath and whispered; "Do you think she knows that you can read?" Mandy was clearly shaken. "I definitely got the same impression, yes I think so. Becky, I'm frightened. Mama says that if the white folks find out that I can read and write, I'd be whipped, and would probably be sold."

Although Rebecca clearly heard Mandy speak the words, "If the white folks find out that I can read and write....", she was one of the so called, white-folks, she flinched at hearing those accusatory words spoken to her by Mandy.

She did not react to the words, because it would never have occurred to her to react. The personal bond that existed between Rebecca and Mandy transcended race. Because neither girl had knowledge of other societies, they had nothing to compare and contrast with their life style.

There was no denying that the polarized society in which they lived, was a divided society, polarized to the extent that the "whites", sanctioned by law, accepted and encouraged, the enslavement of "the blacks".

Rebecca was not offended by Mandy's remarks. It was as if in their own private world, they were immune. The world in which they had intimately shared and inhabited, starting with the forging of a unique bond, a bond not forged from solidified liquid molten iron, but a bond created with their simultaneous suckling of warm, nutritious, human milk.

Milk, mammal's life sustaining liquid, which they had both obtained together, as babies while nursing together. Nursing simultaneously, together, at Ruth, Mandy's mother's, breasts.

The girls sat silently, on bales of hay, contemplating the morning's events. Rebecca broke the silence; "after all this time, why do you think she asked to be introduced to you?" Mandy, raised both hands into the air; "I have no Idea, she totally took me by surprise."

Rebecca grasped Mandy's hands and gently lowered them. "What were you thinking when she asked you all of those questions? I held my breath, praying that when you spoke, you would speak to her in nigger talk."

"Thank God you did." Mandy shifted her position on the hay; "I didn't give it a thought. Nigger talk is my natural language. The only time I feel comfortable speaking "white," is when I'm with you."

* *

For the rest of the week, Miss Leary's classes were uneventful. However, the day following her being introduced to Mandy, she did apologize to Rebecca and to Jesse, for deviating from their lesson plan.

Her explanation for the change from "Elementary French Grammar, to the study of The History of Western Civilization, was that the previous day, she had inadvertently left her French Textbook in the classroom. Therefore, that night, she was unable to properly prepare for today's scheduled, French Grammar lesson.

As the days passed, it increasingly appeared to Rebecca and to Mandy, that their suspicions and apprehensions may have been misplaced. At the conclusion of class, when Mandy arrived to assist Rebecca, Miss Leary either offered a perfunctory, but pleasant, "Hello, Mandy", or if she was preoccupied, she simply did not acknowledge the slave girl's presence.

* *

As usual Sunday, the slaves day off — *"Da Lawd's Day"* — was a special, festive day in the slave-community. Six days of hard labor, Sun-up to Sundown then; "Hallelujah", one whole day off.

Come Sunday morning, the women would bath and scrub the children, until they practically shone. *"Sunday go ta Meetin'"* clothes were carefully laid-out.

Mothers would sit for hours, brushing, combing, braiding the little girls' "nappy" hair. The manual dexterity required to "plait", to gather and to cross-link tiny tufts of "nappy" hair into intricate braids, was a skill learned, honed, and possessed by most of the female slaves.

"Jughaid, Jughaid, who let you out da side?" *"Gal ya betta git yo skinny black ass bak in here"; "Stop dat act'n lik you got good hair lik dat high yeller gal Mandy...let me plait dem naps"*, were typical sounds heard in the slave quarters, as the mothers prepared their children for Sunday Services.

The slave preacher was usually an intelligent loquacious man, with an innate or acquired, oratory gift, that rivaled that of white politicians, and the professional stage actors.

110

The preacher was a well-respected, member of the slave community. His slave -societal status was on par with that of the slave-artisans, those slaves who possessed unique skills; the blacksmith, the conjure-medicine woman.

The preacher officiated at baptisms, at weddings *(Jump da broom),* and at funerals. He ministered to the sick and infirmed. He shepherded the souls of the oppressed slaves.

The slave preacher was of immense value to the slave owners. His sermons and preaching validated and justified the enslavement of his people, the black slave.

His constant admonitions to the slaves to have patience, to be obedient, to be passive, his predilection for, and emphasis of quoting selected biblical passages such as "the meek shall inherit the earth", were messages that in affect, justified slavery, and that encouraged the slaves to accept their plight.

After all, typically at the end of his sermon, the preacher would proclaim words to the effect; "Be patient, suffer in silence, for all would be well in the afterlife".

"On dat Great Getting' up Mounin";

"In de uppa room wid my Lawd."

These melodious, jubilant, words would boisterously, reverberate as sounds, songs, music heard all the way up at the "Big House" and beyond. As scores of voices, men and women; boys and girls, gave full-throated reverence and praise, to the faith that sustained their very being.

In addition to Sunday being a day of rest for the slaves, the Billings family also recognized Sunday, as the Sabbath.

Sunday mornings, Pee wee would drive the family to town for church services. After, what to Henry usually considered, a bland service, the family would return to Rosewood for a day of relaxation.

Henry had, on several occasions, invited Eleanor to attend church services in town with the family. She invariably, declined.

The reason that she gave Henry, for not attending church with the family, was that she was of the Roman Catholic faith, and therefore — respectfully — she declined the family's invitation to attend Southern Baptist services.

In point of fact, her initial reason for not accompanying the family, was because she had an intellectual need to witness, as she titled her journal entry; "The Religious Practices of American Slaves".

Now after having satisfied and documented her intellectual curiosity, Eleanor confessed that she simply now, preferred to listen to the uplifting, joyous, spirited, Slave Church Services.

As usual, when Rebecca returned from Sunday services, she changed her cloths, gathered up her books, and bolted from the house, the screen door banging behind her, as she hastened to her and Mandy's classroom by the creek.

When she breathlessly arrived, she saw Mandy sitting perfectly still. Eyes downcast, hands in her lap, staring at the grass. Rebecca shouted out to her friend; "Mandy what's wrong…why are sitting like that?" Mandy turned at the sound of Rebecca's voice, and responded; "*I'se alrite Missy Bekka; I'se jus sitn' here wid Mizstres Lee ree.*"

Rebecca stopped in her tracks she looked to Mandy's right, then to her left. Seated on a crate, a discreet mirthful smile on her face was her teacher, Miss Eleanor Leary.

Rebecca quickly regained her composure; "Mandy you lazy black wench, why haven't you set-up the blackboard, where are my books?" "Honestly girl, you're the laziest nigger on the place!" Mandy jumped up; "*I'se sawry Missey, I be sho nuff getin' dem books rite now.*"

Eleanor, attempting to suppress a smile, put her handkerchief over her mouth. She coughed, and motioned for Rebecca to be seated. When both girls were seated, side-by-side, Eleanor stood and with a stern expression on her face, scrutinized each girl.

Her frown slowly morphed into a broad smile. "You two are by far, two of the best actresses that I've had the privilege of seeing perform, since the last performance that I attended, at the Chicago Theater".

Rebecca looked directly at Eleanor, with an apprehensive, worried look. Mandy stared at the ground. When she sheepishly raised her head, Eleanor saw what she interpreted as fright and stark terror, in the slave girl's eyes.

Eleanor turned to Rebecca, "Well Rebecca, what do you have to say for yourself? And before you answer, you both should know that I stood behind that tree last Sunday, and witnessed a remarkable scene. I saw you and Mandy taking turns reading, and then each of you independently translating, Shakespeare's Romeo and Juliet."

Rebecca sat stunned. Eleanor shifted her gaze from Rebecca to Mandy.
"Mandy, do you have something to say?" Mandy, eyes still fixed on the grass at her feet, in a barely audible whisper, replied; "*I'se don ritely nos Miztres.*"

Eleanor lowered herself to the grass she looked up at Rebecca, then at Mandy. "Mandy, I heard you conversing with Rebecca, using precise and might I add, correct flawless English grammar.

"I was amazed to hear your impeccable, reading of old English prose. Your diction and your pronunciation of the old English words, was most impressive."

She silently looked at each girl. After a long moment of awkward silence, Eleanor broke the silence; "Do you girls know that you are breaking the law? I've been told that here in Virginia, teaching a slave to read and write, is a crime. A serious offense, with very serious consequences."

Both girls remained silent. They exchanged furtive glances. Rebecca was the first to speak. "Miss Leary, please, please don't tell. This is all, my fault."

"I made Mandy learn. Mandy was just doing what I ordered her to do. Oh please, *"I beseech thee"*, please don't tell my father."

Mandy had not moved. She continued to sit, staring at her feet, in miserable, abject silence."

Eleanor was impressed. For the entire week, she had continuously thought of her serendipitous discovery, that Mandy was highly literate.

That undeniable fact was constantly on her mind. She had lain in bed, sleepless, for hours pondering the significance, the importance of last Sunday's discovery.

Should she believe what she thought she saw? Was this living proof that a black person, born into slavery, reared amongst a totally illiterate population, and culture, was capable of being educated.

Not merely trained to regurgitate words and sentences like a pet parrot, but to actually be able to read, to comprehend and to understand complex thoughts and ideas.

During the course of the discussion following their being exposed, Eleanor had come to the conclusion that, these are two highly intelligent, resourceful, clever, young women. She based her assessment on:

1)   The fact that Mandy had cleverly attempted to warn Rebecca; to alert her to the fact, that all was not well, — *"I'se alrite Missy Bekka; I'se sitn' here wid Mizstres Lee ree."* — by answering Rebecca's greeting in the dialect that the girl's had called "nigger talk", was an excellent example of creative improvisation.

2)   Rebecca, being aware of her admiration and fascination with Shakespeare, pleading that she not tell her father. The fact that her plea, implored the use of the olde English phrase — *"I beseech thee"*, was, by Rebecca a clever, calculated ploy.

Eleanor stood she methodically smoothed the wrinkles from her dress. "Mandy, please place your crate next to Rebecca's."

Mandy did as she was told. After she placed the crate beside Rebecca, she wordlessly, took-up station, standing behind Rebecca, her Mistress.

Eleanor's immediate impulse was to have Mandy take a seat next to Rebecca. However instinctively, she refrained.

Eleanor looked first at Rebecca, and then her eyes locked onto Mandy. She began to speak; "First, young ladies, I want to assure you both, I do not intend to castigate nor do I intend to criticize either of you."

"For the past seven days, including today, I have given a great deal of thought to you two." She looked directly at Rebecca. "To borrow a phrase, no more accurately, to paraphrase from Shakespeare, *"I have come to praise you; not to bury you."*

"Based upon what I observed, Mandy's level of reading and comprehension, is remarkably high, and well developed. Having said that... Mandy, I want you to sit down — on that crate — right next to Rebecca."

Mandy, head bowed, slowly shuffled from behind Rebecca, and eyes staring at the ground, sat down on the vacant crate. Eleanor waited until Mandy was seated. "Mandy...Mandy, please look at me."

Mandy slowly lifted her head, and in a soft unsteady voice mumbled, *"Yessum Miztres?"* Eleanor continued; "I'm not going to hurt you. I am not going to report to anyone, that you can read and write. What I would like to do is...I want to help you."

Mandy again looked down at the ground. "Mandy, do you understand what I'm saying?" Mandy looked up at Eleanor and again mumbled, *"Yessum Miztres."* For the first time, Eleanor looked genuinely annoyed.

Eleanor took a deep breath, "Mandy, last Sunday, when you both thought that you two were alone, I heard you speaking absolutely impeccable English when you were speaking to Rebecca. I am now asking that, here and now, in this setting, that you speak to me utilizing grammatically correct English. Mandy do you understand?"

Mandy looked at Rebecca, almost imperceptibly, Rebecca's head swiftly, nodded. Mandy looked directly at Eleanor; "Yes Miss Leary, I understand you perfectly."

****

Seated on the grass, Eleanor, Rebecca, and Mandy, began to eagerly open up the lines of communication.

Eleanor was sitting with her back against a tree, Rebecca and Mandy, were lying in the grass, casually supporting their weight on their elbows. The girls, individually, took turns giving Eleanor a detailed synopsis of their personal history, of their unique relationship since the girl's births, at Rosewood.

Eleanor sat intrigued, mesmerized, as Rebecca and Mandy detailed for her, the 15-year history, of their shared lives at Rosewood. Rebecca told of her lifelong friendship with Mandy. A friendship that flourished, despite the fact that the society in which they lived, condoned slavery and, therefore by extension, condemned their friendship.

Rebecca told of her early home schooling, of being taught her ABC's by her mother. She told of learning to read, while sitting on her mother's lap. Of she, and her mother sitting for hours on end, reading numerous, fascinating, imaginative, fairy tales.

She told of playing school with Mandy. Of how, she and Mandy spent countless hours; hours playing school, reading writing together, some times changing the plot and the outcome of their favorite fairy tales.

Rebecca told of how excited she and Mandy had been, when they heard that she (Miss Leary), was coming to Rosewood, to further the education of the Billings children.

Rebecca explained why she took such copious, detailed notes during Eleanor's classes. Why during and after class, she asked so many questions, often seemingly endless, repetitive, questions. Questions that she needed to thoroughly understand, so that she could in-turn, be fully prepared to teach Mandy, at their all day, Sunday sessions.

Eleanor sat silently listening intently to Rebecca's recitation. When Rebecca finally paused to take a breath, and to gather her thoughts, Eleanor, turned her attention to Mandy.

"Mandy, a little while ago, Becky asked that I not blame you for your breaking the law. She said that in essence, you were forced to participate in the commission of a crime, because you, being her slave, that you must follow and obey her directives. Is that true? Were you aware that the two of you were in fact, breaking the law? Do you understand that law?"

Mandy had listened quietly, not interrupting Rebecca, as she capsulized for Eleanor, her and Rebecca's life long relationship. She explained that when she — Eleanor — had asked her to answer several explicit questions, her initial survival instinct was to avoid answering, by feigning ignorance, to respond by employing that tried and true "slave" tactic of shucking and jiving, when speaking to white-folk.

Instead, she intellectually realized that, at this juncture, with this particular white lady, she knew that the "jig" was up.

Mandy confessed that in truth, she had felt relieved, she felt as though a great weight had been lifted, that the secret that she and Rebecca had kept for so long, was finally no longer theirs to bear alone.

****

Mandy glanced at Rebecca, then she shifted her gaze to Eleanor, her face took on an expression of relief and resignation; "Miss Leary, I will, answer your questions, to the best of my ability. Before I do, I would like to thank you for affording me, my first opportunity to honestly express my thoughts to someone, other than to Becky…in what Becky and I call, my second language, proper English."

Eleanor was speechless, stunned. Although she had previously, last Sunday heard Mandy and Rebecca talking together; it wasn't until this very minute, that she fully grasped the extent of Mandy's literacy.

Eleanor was in a word, flabbergasted by Mandy's intelligence, by what she perceived was the potential of this 15-year-old female slave. Eleanor returned her full attention, and her concentration, to Mandy's recitation.

Mandy continued to speak; "It is to me, an undeniable fact that I am a slave. That I am legally, the property of the Billings family. As such, by law, I must be obedient, to the directives of my owner, and by custom, if not by law, slaves must obey the directives of all white people".

"These facts were confirmed and reinforced by you Miss Leary, I believe in one of the first civics lesson that you taught, shortly after your arrival, to Becky and to Master Jesse".

"Truthfully, while all of that civics stuff — the fact that we were breaking the law — did give me momentary pause, it in no way dissuaded me, nor did it deter me from my willingness and eagerness to learn".

"Becky and I have been playing school, learning together, since we were little kids. If Becky had chosen not to share her increasing knowledge with me, it would have hurt me, far more then if they had lain a hundred lashes on my back, with the whip."

Eleanor stood. "Amazing…you two young ladies are simply amazing!"
She looked directly into Rebecca's eyes; "I have no intention of telling your father, or for that matter, of telling anyone else, of your extra curricular activities. To say that I am impressed would be a gross understatement."

"I have a million questions to ask you girls. It's getting late. We had better get back before they come looking for us. If you will allow me to, I would be honored to join your Sunday classes."

The three young ladies, the two in front white and free, with the black slave, respectfully walking behind, cheerfully made their way back to the Big House.

****

That night, as Eleanor sat up in her bed, she eagerly began to write in her journal:

September 12, 1852 (Sunday)

Today I confronted, no that's not accurate at all. There was absolutely nothing confrontational about this day. This day, to me, was a day of absolute enlightenment.

I came to the South, not only to teach and to help mold young minds, I came with the expressed goal of studying, and documenting, first hand knowledge of, Slavery in America.

As I rack my brain attempting to put into words my elation at stumbling across these two remarkable girls, one girl white-Rebecca and the other black-Mandy, I confess, I am at a loss for words.

An apropos analogy would be to think of the prospectors, traveling to California, clear across the continent, hoping to find gold. It's being reported that, for the most part, their quest to find gold, usually ends in failure.

Oh a few individuals will find a gold nugget, here and there. But by and large, the vast majority find only disappointment.

Well today diary, metaphorically speaking, today I feel as though, in my quest to study first hand, Slavery in America, today I shout;

"Eureka"!

Today — I've struck the Mother-Load!"

****

The next day, while Rebecca and Eleanor were in class, exploring the world of academia, Mandy was busy performing her routine household tasks, making beds, cleaning, dusting, scrubbing floors.

Mandy, and her friend, a 15-year old slave girl named Lena, were the two young female slaves, who today were responsible for "light housework", in the Big House.

Amongst the slaves, Lena was by far Mandy's closest friend. Lena was tall, easily 5'10". Her skin was ebony, as dark as a star-less, moon-less night. Her full head of close-cropped hair could best be described as frizzy, wiry, and nappy.

To any esteemed professor of anthropology, or for that matter, to any serious student of anthropology, Lena was the epitome, the very embodiment of a beautiful, young, black African female.

Unfortunately for Lena, in the slave community, over time, with each succeeding generation, the slave social structure had adopted a propensity to denigrate, to hold in low esteem, her pronounced, classic, Negroid features. This was due in large part to the influence of the dominant, ruling, white culture.

The fact that in a multiracial environment, that societal standards would be set by the dominant, ruling faction is perfectly understandable, it is in fact, to be expected. However, the almost universal acceptance and adoption, by the slaves, the oppressed population, of these artificially imposed standards, had definite quality of life, implications for the slaves.

A parody often heard, and almost always adhered to in the slave community was:

> If yo's white, yo's allrite
> If yo's brown, yo's can stik aroun
> If yo's black, yo's git back

The lighter the slave's complexion, the narrower the nose; the thinner the lips, the less course the hair, the more likely that the slave would have an easier, less strenuous job on the plantation.

Occasionally, a "high yella" buck would be found working in the fields. In those instances, it was more then likely that the undesirable assignment was punishment, imposed by the whites for some real or imagined infraction, or possibly a perceived affront, or insult to the ruling family.

A high yella slave, that too closely, physically resembled the white Master, could be an embarrassment to the plantation's Mistress

House slaves were almost universally, "light-skinned" slaves, with markedly Caucasoid facial features.

* *

Mandy and Lena were busy, jointly making up Henry and Peggy's huge four-poster bed. Lena was gently, lovingly, caressing, one of the two matching satin pillows.

Mandy paused, straightened, and admonished her friend; *"Lena, gal, yose bes stop dat playn' roun wid dat der pilo! Ifin Missy Margaret, or wors, ifin Fannie cutches yose putn' yo haid on dat pilo…yose sur nuff git yose black ass whiped' and sent bak ta da feels."*

Lena gently placed the pillow onto the bed. She straightened, and sighed; *"dees white fok sho nuff liv'n goood."*

"Mandy, Ise wonts ta thank yose fo telin Fannie ta let me help ya at da Big Hous, til Jennie gits bac from haben ha baby."

Mandy smiled. *"Das alrite Lena, I nos it hard…but yose gotta stop actin' likes a feelhan. Com on now…we gotta finis dees beds. It be lunch time soon an Ise gotta go meets up wid Missy Becca."*

Mandy and Lena's friendship, was a slave community, anomaly. It was rare to find a genuine friendship between, "light-skinned and "dark-skinned" slaves.

The typical discourse when either group referred to the other, would typically be; *"dat high yella nigger; think she be white"*; or *"luka dat dum black, nappy head, liber lip nigger, she be dum as a mule"*.

Mandy, though tolerated, by the adult slaves, was not well treated by the slave children, or by her teenage peers. Lena was the exception.

When they were kids, Lena then a skinny, dark-skinned, tall, awkward ten-year-old, had rescued six-year-old Mandy, following Mandy's being beaten by, as Lena described them to Mandy's mother, *"three nappy headed, liver-lipped gals"*.

Lena had picked the little girl up, lifted her out of the mud, a bruised and battered, pretty little brown-skinned girl, Mandy.

After walking the crying child to Ruth's cabin, and describing to Ruth what had occurred, Lena quietly closed the cabin door behind her.

Mandy lay crying in her mother's arms. *"Mama I won't doing' noting'."* Why dem gals beat me?' Ruth comforting her daughter, soothed; *"der der chile, daz jus jellose caus yose ain't black lik dey is; yose gotcha self good hair; don haz wooly naps lik daz doz"*.

"Hush hush chile." As Ruth gently rocked to and fro, Mandy's sobs began to subside. Lena who had been standing on the other side of the closed door, turned to leave. The last words that she heard from the cabin was a broken, sobbing, whimper from Mandy;

"Why Mama, Why?"

The societal structure of the slave community was that of a distinct, stratified, caste system. Numerically, the vast majority the slave population consisted of slaves who worked in the fields (predominantly, the dark complexioned, blacks).

The remainder of the slave population consisted of the house-slaves (the light and brown complexioned), and the skilled artisans (a variety of complexions; talent being color blind).

Despite their numerical superiority, in general, the darker the slave, the lower was his or her ranking in the societal structure of the slave community.

****

This curious societal caste system evolved, over the course of two centuries, and more then fifteen generations of black slaves in America.

The first generation of African Slaves, snatched from their homeland, and forced into perpetual bondage, was a homogeneous group of black men and women.

At that time, prejudice in the slave community, based upon the slave's skin complexion did not exist. It did not exist simply because the entire slave population was dark-skinned (black or blackish).

Each succeeding generation of slaves born in captivity, saw the birth of a small number of infants, whose skin color was lighter than that of the previous generation.

In addition to a gradual lightening of the skin, there was a distinct alteration of Negroid features; course frizzy hair, gradually tended towards becoming straighter; the African's broad, flat nose, with flaring nostrils, narrowed; thick lips, thinned.

The introduction of these genetically, morphologically altered slaves into the community, was the direct result of the mating of the white ruling class (males), with the enslaved females.

The reasons for these mating ran the gambit, from that of the white men's seeking to satisfy his carnal lust, to —by the second generation — the obvious monetary incentive, of increasing the slave owner's wealth by increasing his real property.

In many instances, his reason(s) were a combination of both, the white men's seeking to satisfy their carnal lust, while increasing his wealth, through the siring of offspring.

Offspring that by law, were not considered to be his biological children, but by law, were legally considered his slaves, his property.

These slaves would be worked or sold; or if female, destined to repeat the cycle, to be violated for the same reasons, as were their mothers, frequently violated by, their own biologic fathers, white uncles, and even their white brothers.

The slave owners, and the Southern Culture itself, contributed and encouraged the creation and the sustaining of the slave caste system. Dissention, jealousy and animosity amongst the slaves, served to divide the slave population.

The strategy of "Divide and Conquer" was encouraged and employed, by the white Masters.

****

The subtle actions, as well as the overt signals, put forth by the whites, such as the giving of the less strenuous jobs to those slaves that were light-skinned, and thin-lipped, gave credence, buttressed, and reinforced, the slave communities, system of internal social discrimination.

By far the most effective means used to control the African slave was not the lash, or the brutal, inhumane treatment inflected upon them, the most effective means of control, was the conversion of the "savage heathen", to Christianity.

In order to control the rapidly growing slave population, it was soon realized that it was essential, that the enslaved maintained at least, a sliver of hope.

Although implying the hope of freedom in the slave's lifetime was totally unthinkable, hope in the form of the promise of freedom in the after-life, became the prevailing message.

The means of delivering the message was first, the eradication of the slave's "pagan" religion, to be replaced with Christianity.

While the slaves were denied by law, access to all reading materials, including the Christian Bible, drawings, vivid images of the Messiah and of a heavenly host of chubby, little, pink, cherubic angels, as envisioned by the ruling white society, were generously distributed, by their Masters, to the slaves.

Colorful drawings of Jesus, the Messiah, hung in nearly every slave cabin. Each and every day, the slaves would awake to stare at the image of the Prince of Peace, the epitome of hope, of their salvation.

The face of hope, the face of righteousness, and deliverance, was that of a white man. The implicit message was that all that is good, all that is to be desired, is embodied in the white man.

Ergo the gradual acceptance, over time, of the white man's standards that is, that people with physical traits that were, or that approximate his; white skin, straight hair, straight nose, thin lips, were universally preferable.

The face of hope, the face of righteousness, was the face of a white man.
A white man with long straight, blond hair; blue-eyes; a high-bridged nose, with narrow nostril, and thin lips, would shepherd his flock, of docile obedient black slaves, into paradise.

****

These subliminal messages, as well as the overt signals, put forth by the whites, such as the giving of the less strenuous jobs, to those slaves that were light-skinned, and thin-lipped.

White's favoring those slaves whose physical appearance conformed to the white man's standards. These actions gave credence to, buttressed, and reinforced, the slave communities, stratified, internal system of social discrimination.

The entire slave community was aware and cognizant of Mandy, and her mother Ruth's, special relationship with Master Henry, and Mistress Margaret.

This special relationship engendered in the majority of the slaves, a controlled, but sustained, resentment against Mandy, her brother Jason, and the Master's sweet "*Brown Sugah*", Mandy's mother Ruth.

The slave community was definitely not, an en**lightened** democracy.
****

Mandy would arrive five minutes before the scheduled end of class. She would noiselessly enter the room, and unobtrusively, sit quietly on the floor, in the corner, awaiting Rebecca.

After the conclusion of each day's class, Eleanor would politely acknowledge Mandy; "Hello Mandy, how are you today?"

Mandy, head down staring at the floor, would respond, with an almost inaudible; *"Ise fin Mistress."*

At the conclusion of Friday's lesson, long after Jesse had hurriedly departed, as Rebecca was gathering her books, instead of her daily greeting to Mandy, Eleanor paused, and asked both girls to approach her desk.

Rebecca stood before her teacher, confidently, hands behind her back, Mandy stood timidly, eyes staring at the floor, holding Rebecca's books.

Eleanor looked from one girl to the other. Although Mandy had assumed her usual head-bowed, submissive posture, Eleanor began to speak; "ladies, as I flippantly stated last week, with your permission, I repeat, with your permission, I would very much like to join you at your Sunday gatherings.

A satisfied expression, spread across Rebecca's face. Mandy, after a quick furtive glance at Rebecca, quickly averted her eyes, and once again reverted to staring at the floor.

Rebecca opened her mouth to speak. Eleanor raised her hand, palm up towards Rebecca, indicating that she should remain silent. "I would like you to jointly consider my request."

Rebecca did not hesitate; Miss Leary, all week long, Mandy and I, have been trying to work up the nerve to speak to you about last Sunday. We would both be ever so appreciative, and would be thrilled to have you monitor our sessions."

Eleanor, smiled, she gently placed her hand under Mandy's chin; "Mandy?" Mandy raised her head, she looked Eleanor in the eye, and mumbled; *"yesm dat be fin"*, she immediately broke-off eye contact, and once again, stared down at the floor.

Eleanor beamed; "then it's settled, I'll join you, Sunday at the creek." Eleanor began to straighten her desk. Neither Rebecca, nor Mandy moved.

Eleanor looked-up; "Is there something else?" Rebecca blurted; Miss Leary, Mandy and I go to the creek, Saturdays and Sundays." Eleanor did not answer immediately, after a few seconds, seconds that seemed to the girls to be "forever", Eleanor said emphatically, I'll be there, I'll see you both, at the creek, tomorrow.

Saturday morning, following breakfast, Rebecca and Mandy hurried to their "classroom", at their shady little alcove, beside the creek. Fifteen minutes later, Eleanor arrived.

Eleanor noticed that now, instead of two crates, there were three. On each crate was a fluffy down pillow. Rebecca and Mandy rose when Eleanor arrived. Eleanor motioned for the girls to be seated.

Eleanor sat on the unoccupied crate. Ladies before we proceed, we need to have a serious talk. She looked directly at Rebecca; "Rebecca, how old are you? Please state your age?"

Rebecca replied; "We are both…" Eleanor held up her hand; "Stop!" "Rebecca, I want you to speak for yourself, only."

I ask you again, "Rebecca, how old are you? Please state your age?" Obviously confused, Rebecca and Mandy looked at each other. Rebecca answered; "I am fourteen years old." Eleanor turned her attention to Mandy.

And you Mandy, how old are you?" Mandy, who during the exchange between Rebecca and Eleanor, had been staring at the grass, responded; *"Ise be foteen."*

Although she had expected it, Eleanor for a brief instant, frowned at the "slave dialect".

"Mandy, please raise your head. Mandy complied. Eleanor looked solemnly, at each girl. She was momentarily lost in thought, as she compared and contrasted the striking facial similarities between the girls.

She thought; If one were to discount, skin color, these two could be sisters. She had a sudden revelation. They are sisters. In that instant, Eleanor was absolutely certain, Rebecca and Mandy are half-sisters. They are both — almost certainly — the biological daughters of her employer, Mr. Henry Billings, Master of Rosewood.

Mandy and Rebecca sat silently, confused, looking at Eleanor, then at each other. Eleanor, as if awakening from a trance, cleared her throat. "The reason that I asked you both separately, to state your age, was to emphasis to you both, that you are no longer children.

You are young women who, I have no doubt, are aware that what you're doing, what you implicitly, and we all realize, what you explicitly want me to be a party to, is in the state of Virginia, is in the South, illegal.

That each of you, have been breaking the law. It is against the law to teach a slave to read and to write, period. Rebecca, what you have been doing, and what I am about to agree to do, goes far beyond; teaching a slave to read and write."

"Mandy, if we are discovered, Rebecca and I, will be legally culpable for breaking the law. Paradoxically, while Rebecca and I will be the named as "criminals", undoubtedly you Mandy, will suffer the severest penalties."

"If discovered, Rebecca will in all likelihood, will be scolded. I on the other hand, being an ignorant Yankee, unaccustomed Southern ways and Southern Law, will at worse, probably be discharged."

"You Mandy, the only real non-law breaker in this "criminal" enterprise, will be the recipient of the harshest punishment. Mandy, do you understand?" Mandy nodded her head, indicating that she understood.

"Mandy, please answer, do you understand?" Mandy stared straight ahead at Eleanor, she hesitated, then she lifted her head, arched her back and replied; **"Yes Miss Leary, I understand perfectly. Not only do I understand what you are saying, I fully understand, and I am aware of the many nasty, brutal, horrible things that they, the law can do to me."**

Eleanor looked directly into Mandy's eyes, she turned, looked at Rebecca, stood and said; "Shall we begin?"

****

Eleanor asked; "What are you girls currently studying. What would you like to study?" Rebecca raised her hand; "Yes Becky." "Mandy and I agreed that if by some miracle, we were lucky enough to have you teach us, we would first ask that you tell us about your experiences, your life growing up in the North."

Eleanor took a seat. "Okay, but first, I have a question for Mandy. I'm fairly sure that I know the answer, however I would like to have my assumption verified." "Mandy, I surmised that the reason you speak in that slave dialect, is to conceal the fact that you can not only read and write, but that you are in fact, highly literate."

Mandy shifted her position on the crate; "Becky and I have been constantly together, since we were babies. My Mom tills me that Becky's mother was experiencing difficulty nursing Becky. Master Henry and the doctor sent for my Mom, who at that time was nursing me."

"When we were infants, my mama nursed both Becky and me. When mama talks about those days, she always smiles and chuckles. Mama's fond of saying;" *"I be sittn' dere, a rockn', widda lil white baby suckin' away on my rite titty, an my lil brown baby a suckin' on da leff."*

"Becky and I have been playing together since we were little kids. When Mistress Margaret started to teach Becky her ABC's, I guess it was only natural that when Becky and I were together, which was all of the time, that Becky would teach me everything that her mom had taught her."

"Becky would teach me at our daily "play-school" session. As you saw last Sunday, Becky is a fabulous, wonderful teacher. I guess she found out early on, that for a kid to effectively, teach a little pick-a-ninny, to read and write, she as the teacher had to really, really, understand the subject material."

Eleanor sat listening intently. She suppressed a smile, and thought, well that certainly explains Rebecca's never-ending, stream of questions. Apparently, continuously asking questions, until she fully understood the subject matter, is a laudable trait, that Rebecca developed long before she became my student.

Eleanor refocused on Mandy who after taking a momentary pause, continued to speak; "During our formative years, from birth through age five or six, at Mistress Margaret's request, I spent most of my waking hours, with Becky, and her family."

"The only time that Becky and I were apart, was when she was asleep, or the few hours, just before dawn, when mama was at our cabin, getting us ready to go to the Big House. As a kid, the vast majority of the English, that I was exposed to, were the verbal communications, the conversations, which I heard, spoken by Becky, and by her family."

"I vividly recall the first time I spoke to mother speaking what she called "white-folk talk". That was the first time that I was actually afraid of my mother. I must have been around three or four at the time."

"Mama shook me so hard, I remember thinking that my teeth rattled. With tears copiously flowing down her cheeks, she screamed; *"Yose stop dat white tawk rite now...you har me gal!" "Lawd help us chile, yo got ta stop dat white tawk!"*

"Niggers hear dat tawk, dey says you uppity, puttin' on airs, thnk you betta den da res of us." "White fok hear dat tawk —you an me be whipped and sold 'way frm here licky de split!" "Baby dey thnk yose be learn' ta reed or ta rite! White-folk kills a nigger dat can reed!"

So finally, Miss Leary, in response to your question, the answer is yes. The reason that I speak "nigger talk" to white people, or as you put it, speak with a "slave dialect", is most definitely to conceal the fact that I can read and write."

To put it mildly, Eleanor was impressed. She looked with unconcealed admiration at the two possibly — dare I say, she thought — brilliant young ladies. This opportunity, is an educator's dream come true.

Two thoughts, almost simultaneously, flashed through her mind. Rebecca, a white girl born into privilege, into the lap of luxury, a Southern Aristocrat, was undoubtedly, a natural teacher. Rebecca displays communication teaching skills, one might have expected to find in ancient Greece, skills embodied in a teenage Socrates.

And Mandy, a slave girl, was apparently, actually, successfully leading a double life. On the one hand, Mandy was an ignorant, subservient; slave, completely dedicated to dutifully serving her teenage mistress. Yet when alone with said teenage Mistress, Mandy is her peer, a well-spoken, inquisitive, intelligent, young woman.

Eleanor, Rebecca and Mandy were seated on their respective crates. The three young ladies were now seated in roughly, the configuration of a triangle.

Eleanor at the apex; Rebecca and Mandy comprising the base. Eleanor addressed her current, and future student. "I think we should spend the rest of the day, my getting to know you, and conversely, your getting to know a little bit more, about me."

"I'll get us started. Rebecca, shortly after I begin teaching you and Jesse, I began to marvel at the academic level that you two had attained. When I responded to your father's advertisement for a tutor, when I learned that neither of you had had any formal schooling, I was somewhat put off, and reluctant to accept the position."

"My intellectual curiosity was aroused. In this censored, controlled society, a society that bans publications that differ from, or criticizes Southern beliefs, and political doctrine, where did you and Jesse, and by extension, Mandy develop such extensive vocabularies?"

Rebecca began to speak; "When we were growing up, Jesse developed an addiction for Dime Novels. When Jesse was ten, and Mandy and I were about five or six, papa took him, on a business trip to Richmond.

When Papa and Jesse returned to Rosewood, Jesse had in his possession, a dozen, "Frontier Western", Dime Novels. Mr. Frasier, Papa's lawyer, gave the books to Jesse.

"When Mandy and I were little girls, forced by my parents, to play together, by far our favorite childhood pursuit was playing school. Naturally I played the role of the teacher, Mandy the student.

From the very beginning, I used the same teaching materials that my mother used, when she taught me my ABC's and how to read and write. The very first teaching aid that I used in our play school, were those little wooden blocks, with the letters of alphabet on each side. Do you remember those blocks Mandy?"

Mandy smiled; "I certainly do. How could I forget? I still have most of those blocks. We where eleven, practically grown, when you gave those blocks to me as a Christmas present. By then, I had completely forgotten that they existed. I still have them."

Rebecca returned her attention to Eleanor; "The first time that I used those blocks at our play school session, I distinctly remember my demeanor; A six year old white child, the teacher, haughtily insisting that my little black pick-a-ninny pupil, when talking to me, the teacher, speak only proper "white-folk talk".

"In the beginning, I secretly taught my single student Mandy, from reference materials and teaching aids that my mother used to teach me my ABC's. We practiced reading and writing, by together reading and re-reading children's stories. The same bedtime stories that my mother, and my father each night, would read to me."

"We read over and over the stories of; Snow White and The Seven Dwarfs", the tale of "Hansel & Gretel", and the childhood imprisonment of "Rapunzel", and others".

It soon became obvious, to both of us, me the teacher and Mandy the student that we were gradually, beginning to lose interest. We were becoming bored. The boredom, began to dissipate when, I quite innocently, by accident, discovered a new source of material, my brother Jesse's "Dime Novels"."

Rebecca paused and asked; "Miss Leary, are you familiar with "Dime Novels?" Eleanor's cheeks expanded with the beginnings of a smile.

She looked as if she where pleased, at having been asked that particular question. "Yes, as a matter of fact, I am familiar with Dime Novels.

In college, I wrote a report on the phenomena. Just one moment please, I think I might have a copy of the paper that I submitted." Eleanor retrieved her book-bag from the ground; she rummaged through the bag, and then she triumphantly, pulled out a sheaf of papers. Ladies, if I may"; she began to read.

"The "Dime-Novel", is a cheap paperback publication, usually depicting the writer's perspective of life on the Wild, Wild, American-Western Frontier."

"The Dime Novels format consisted of highly exaggerated, flamboyant, hyperbolic, writing. A writings style which embellished and romanticized the dangers, the trials and tribulations, encountered by the mountain-men, the "Westward Ho" pathfinders, and by the subsequent vast numbers of families crossing and eventually bringing civilization, to the North American Continent".

Eleanor paused. She looked at the girls, their response thus far to her paper, appeared to coincide with their assessment of the genre.

She continued; "The novels tell stories of heroic, courageous, mountain-men, pushing the boundaries of civilization. Blazing a trail for tens of thousands of men, women, and children to follow. The pioneer families, mostly people of European ancestry, continue to steadily move westward across the continent".

"Pioneers taming and cultivating the land, putting down roots, and hopefully, eventually, fulfilling the United States often stated expansionist policy, Manifest Destiny, the extension of the borders of the United States, from the Atlantic to the Pacific Ocean."

Both girls were definitely giving her their undivided attention. Eleanor deliberately stopped, folded her papers and looked at the girls faces. Both Rebecca's and Mandy's expressions were definitely those of listeners expecting and wanting to hear more.

Pleased with their reaction, Eleanor unfolded the papers, and continued; "The plots or story lines of these widely popular cheap paperbacks, was actually quite simple:

The Heroes — The white mountain-men and/or the homesteaders, the settlers.

The Villains — The Native Americans (The Indians).

Almost each and every edition of the paperbacks, would present the portrayal of courageous white frontiersmen and white settlers, heroically defending themselves and their families, by either killing or, alas being killed by those barbaric, bloodthirsty, vermin that terrorized the west, the American Indian.

Eleanor would later discover, that the characters and situations depicted in the Dime Novels, was the girls first exposure to a world other than the world in which they lived, the Southern Plantation Society.

When Rebecca resumed, Eleanor learned that the seven-year old, Rebecca and Mandy, would spend hours, honing and strengthening their fledgling reading skills, anxiously awaiting, with keen anticipation, the opportunity to read the latest edition of how; "Buckskin Bob, Conquers and Subdues, the Hated Redskins".

The cheap publications had the effect of greatly expanding the girl's vocabularies. They were inundated with new words. Unfortunately, many of the new words, were vicious racist, slurs and epithets. Words, flowing from the lips of their new heroes, "Buckskin Bob", and numerous other mythical, all-powerful, white men.

The publication's conspicuous, enthusiastic, use of these denigrating words, these vindictive terms describing the Indian, especially because they were words appearing in books — in print, in the minds of the children, validated and lent an aura of truth, to these denigrating descriptions of the American Indian.

Eleanor was told that ten-year-old Jesse would spend hours playing, "Woodsman and Indians". He would of course be the "Hero", the brave White Frontiers-man, who protected his family, and fought and killed the savage Indians (Indians were portrayed by young, enslaved black boys).

Rebecca, as do most little sisters the world over, would constantly, and persistently, beg her big brother Jesse, to let her play. At first Jesse refused. But as the plots of the novels gradually changed to include Indian attacks on settler families, he relented. Jesse allowed Rebecca, and her little pick-a-ninny playmate Mandy, to participate as the helpless, settler "women-folk".

When reenacting the latest Dime Novel episode, young Jesse when "under attack", by the marauding redskins, would unleash a litany of epithets directed at the bloodthirsty heathens. The words and phrases shouted verbatim — dripping with vitriol — were words and phrases, as they appeared in his weekly pamphlets.

"Shoot that dirty Redskin; The only good Injun is a dead Injun; Don't let em take the women-folk alive; Them savage cannibals scalp, rape, torture and eat white women; Injuns cut out and eat the hearts and liver of their captives; **The only good Injun is a dead Injun.**

It didn't take long before the two impressionable little girls, joined in and heartily, boisterously, repeated, and shouted-out these, and many other contemptuous refrains.

****

The Sun was now directly overhead. The ladies were no longer, totally in the shade. Eleanor placed her right hand over her eyes; she squinted as she gazed up at the heavens. "My my, it's already past noon." Let's find some shade, relocate, and have lunch."

They each picked up their crates, and moved them under the leafy branches of a neighboring poplar tree. Mandy immediately began to place plates in front of Rebecca, and then she placed a plate in front of Eleanor.

Mandy placed, fried chicken, fresh baked corn bread, and potato salad on each plate. She gave both ladies napkins, which contained cutlery. Mandy stood to the side as Eleanor and Rebecca began to eat.

Eleanor looked up at Mandy; "Aren't you hungry Mandy...why aren't you eating?" Mandy, eyes fixed on the ground replied; *"yesm, Mistress Leery...Ise rite hungry."*

Eleanor looked genuinely mystified; she looked at Rebecca, who was busily devouring a piece of cornbread. Rebecca was apparently unperturbed, totally comfortable with Mandy's response.

Eleanor was delicately holding a drumstick between her thumb and forefinger. She slowly returned the chicken to her plate. She picked up her napkin, dabbed at her mouth. "Rebecca, I truly don't understand." Rebecca stopped eating, and with a quizzical, perplexed look, responded, "what do you mean Miss Leary? What don't you understand?"

Eleanor made an all encompassing, circular motion with her arm; "this, I don't understand this. This morning the three of us laterally had substantive, intelligent, conversations. Yet here we are having lunch.

Rebecca, you and I seated, eating a delicious meal, while our friend and colleague, Mandy, serves us, stands behind us, hungry, watching as we eat. Don't you see the hypocrisy?" "How can you, how can we treat her this way?"

Rebecca looked at Mandy, and then she looked at Eleanor. She spoke in a slow modulated voice. "How can I treat her this way? Miss Leary, I love Mandy. I could not love her more, if she was my sister, my own flesh and blood. How can I treat her this way? I treat her this way because I don't want her to be hurt, whipped, tortured, or sold.

I treat her this way because; we're here, because we live here on Rosewood Plantation. I know that in the eyes of the law, and of course the laws of nature, we are not related.

In every other meaning of the word sister, Mandy to me is my sister. Mandy could not be closer to me, if she were my biological sister. Yes, it hurts me to treat Mandy this way. Miss Leary, you ask how can I treat her this way? I treat her this way, because I love her."

131

Eleanor looked from Rebecca, then at Mandy, then back to Rebecca. She cleared her throat and softly, reverently said; "I understand, of course I truly do understand. Please forgive me." Her eyes, now overflowing with tears, momentarily rested separately, on each teenage girl. "Rebecca, Mandy, please accept my apology."

Mandy looked at Rebecca and winked. *"Yesm, Mistress Lee-ree "Ise sho do cepts yo pology, an rite now, Ise sho wod cept one ah dem drumstiks.*

Eleanor was taken by surprise by Mandy's remarks. She looked at Rebecca, and then at Mandy, the two girls burst out into squeals of laughter. Eleanor grinned, and joined in.

The rest of the meal was consumed in silence. Instead of resuming their discussions after lunch, Eleanor wisely concluded that, all in all, for an introductory session, they had accomplished a great deal. They packed up, and with Mandy carrying the bulk of the paraphernalia, bringing up the rear, began to trudge back to the Big House.

****

That night, Eleanor lay across her bed; multiple textbooks were sprawled before her. After shifting through the books, she selected two of her favorites, "The Collective Works of William Shakespeare, and The Origin of Species, by Charles Darwin".

She assumed her now familiar writing position, two pillows propped behind her head, and once again opened her journal. She began to record her recollection of the day's events.

September 18, 1859 (Saturday)

Today I attended and participated in one of the most enlightening, educational seminars of my career. This seminar did not take place in the hallowed halls, of President Jefferson's University of Virginia. These pearls of wisdom did not flow forth from the mouths of college professors, nor did they emanate from world-renowned scholars.

The old cliché, "from the mouths of babes", for me today, became a reality. Two young girls, children barely into their teens, one girl a black slave, the other, the slave girl's white slave owner, opened my eyes, at times my literally teary eyes, to the absolute wickedness, and the moral absurdity, of slavery.

Prior to today, I had witnessed — on multiple occasions — the physical brutality of slavery. Human beings being whipped for what the white Masters considered infractions, whether the infractions were real or imagined.

Mandy, the slave girl, is an exceptionally intelligent, resourceful, possibly brilliant young lady. She has thus far, successfully walked a tightrope between her clandestinely acquired literacy, and the frank projection of a convincing facade of utter ignorance.

Ignorance that for her safety, and her survival, she is forced to continually display. Mandy must constantly, and convincingly, projects an image of ignorant, passive servitude. A role she is forced to diligently, work at maintaining, as if her very life depended upon it. Rebecca so elegantly, and passionately pointed out to me, it does!

Rebecca is conflicted. On one hand she is a true daughter of the Southern Aristocracy. She was born to privilege. She along with her peers, accepts, without question the institutionalized enslavement of the blacks. Yet, because of her personal feelings for Mandy, her attachment, and love for Mandy, she detests the fact that Mandy, is subject to the implementation of the "white-supremacy" code.

Paradoxically, Rebecca's destine for the implementation of the white supremacist doctrine, in order to maintain the enslavement of blacks, thus making possible the Southern way of life, does not extend to Mandy's mother Ruth, nor to any one of the other Rosewood Plantation slaves.

Rebecca thought of and treated Ruth, the woman at whose breast, she had hungrily suckled, in the same manner as she treated any slave. With the notable exception of Mandy, Rebecca regarded and treated, all slaves as if they were merely property.

I have absolutely no doubt that Rebecca is a thoughtful, compassionate, kind human being. Having acknowledged that, and truly believing that, I have to ask myself, how can this warm kindhearted, intelligent, young lady, be so blind to the evilness of slavery.

Could the answer be that she simply is not aware, not cognizant of the base immorality, of the South's "Peculiar Institution".

Both Rebecca and Mandy, have led isolated, sheltered lives. They have each spent their entire life, albeit a scant thirteen years, living in a cocoon.

Living in a world where the societal norm accepts, human bondage. Where if you're a slave, you can be subjected to arbitrary beatings; if you're a slave, you live knowing that at any time, you can be sold, thus being separated from love ones, wrenched from your family.

Is it possible that they simply are not aware that in most of the world's civilized societies, these things do not occur? They seem to be unaware that in half of the current states and territories of this country, their country, the United States of America, that the commission of these atrocities are against the law.

Does Mandy know that through out history, and even now, today, there are black men who have achieved remarkable accomplishments?

If this is the case, I feel that it is my duty, my responsibility, as an educator, to open their eyes. Open Mandy's beautiful brown eyes, as well as the beautiful blue eyes of Miss Rebecca Billings, to the "big wide glorious world".

I see in both of these girls, enormous potential, and real intelligence. At the same time, I see in them, a real, and profound ignorance.

Ignorance that will evaporate with their exposure to knowledge. Ignorance that will evaporate, dissipate, vanish, as surely and as quickly, as the dew evaporates from the grass, with the rising of the hot summer Sun.

****

The next day, following the family's return from Sunday services, Rebecca hurried to join Mandy and Eleanor in the clearing, beside the creek.

"Good morning ladies." Rebecca and Mandy, who had been in the midst of an animated conversation, turned at Eleanor's greeting.

Rebecca spoke first; "Good Morning Miss Leary." Mandy, head bowed, remained silent. Eleanor looked directly at Mandy. Mandy's eyes were fixed on the ground.

Eleanor seated herself on the vacant crate; "good morning Mandy." Mandy raised her head and mumbled, *"Monin' Mistress."* Eleanor was about to ask Mandy to address her as Miss Leary, she instinctively thought better of it. She decided not to push. She reasoned that it would take time for Mandy, to begin to feel comfortable in her presence.

Eleanor lifted her arms towards the heavens, and then begin to twirl around and around in a circle; "What a gloriously beautiful day. Yesterday too, was a splendid day. Yesterday was a marvelously enlightening, and revealing day. I spent most of last night, thinking about your collective past, the past that yesterday, you shared with me.

You shared with me the environment, the atmosphere that you have thus far, encountered, throughout your short lives. The life experiences that molded your character, the way that you look at, and how you perceive the world. I think I now, know and understand you both, just a little bit better."

134

"I've given a great deal of thought to how I think that we should proceed. Then I remembered something that my grandfather use to say to me, and to my brothers;" "If it ain't broke; don't fix it!"

Rebecca and Mandy looked   confused. They looked curiously at each other, then they turned their attention to Eleanor.

Eleanor continued; "I remembered how impressed I was last Sunday, when I stood behind that tree, and listened to Rebecca teaching Mandy, Romeo and Juliet. How you Rebecca, were so succinctly, meticulously, going over, explaining the material".

How you Mandy, gradually came to understand, and how once you understood, were easily able to translate 17th century Elizabethan English, into modern day, Southern, as you called it, "nigger-talk."

"Obviously, Rebecca, what you and Mandy have been doing is working. I think we should follow the same format, except now I'll be there to contribute. I think my Grandfather would approve "If it ain't broke; don't fix it!"

"So, if you'd like, for the rest of the afternoon, I will answer any questions that you may have about my past. After all, turn-about is fair play, Okay?"

Rebecca and Mandy continued to sit quietly. They quizzically, glanced at one another, but they both remained silent. As the seconds turned in to minutes, the silence was beginning to become somewhat awkward.

Eleanor was first to speak; "Since the cat seems to have taken your tongues, I'll just begin by telling you a little about myself. Please feel free to interrupt, and ask questions, at any time."

****

"Though I am a proud citizen of the United States, I was not born in this country. I was born in Ireland." Mandy could no longer contain her innate curiosity, she timidly mumbled; *"whas dat mistress; whas eyeland?"*

Eleanor continued; "Ireland Mandy, that's spelled, IRELAND. That's my homeland, the birthplace of my ancestors, and the place of my birth. Ireland, the Emerald Isle, Ireland is a beautiful, green island, within one of the groups of islands called the British Isles."

A humongous body of water, the Atlantic Ocean, separates Ireland from America. England is the principle province of a collection of island countries, which includes Ireland. The various island nations together, is known as the United Kingdom."

Rebecca asked; "Is that the same England, that we fought in 1776 for our independence?" Eleanor answered; "Indeed it is the same country. England is an Imperialistic Country, that has a long history of colonizing, or annexing by conquest, other lands. Our country, yours, Mandy's, and now mine, the United States of America, was indeed a former colony of England's".

Eleanor paused for a moment to give the girls a chance to ask questions. Hearing none, she continued; "Ireland, the land of my birth was a sovereign, democratic country, for more than 500 years, before being conquered in war, and then annexed by Imperialistic England."

Eleanor took a deep breath and paused; "but I digress, today is not a day for a history lesson, at least not for a formal, history of the world lesson."

"For the remainder of our time together today, the only history that will be discussed will be a brief history of me, an abbreviated history of my life. the life of Eleanor Leary".

"Now where was I…Umm, now that I think about it, it would be impossible for me to tell you my history, without at least referring to a bit of world history as it relates to me. I want you to remember this very important fact; We are all the products, of those that came before us."

****

"To understand me, you need to understand my parents, and their parents, my ancestors, "those that came before me."

"Mandy, please look at me. Tell us, Rebecca and me, when you look at me, what do you see?"

Mandy fidgeted and squirmed uncomfortably, she felt intimidated, extremely vulnerable at having been singled out. She hung her head and did not speak.

Eleanor spoke; "Mandy do you want me to continue? Do you want to participate in our teaching sessions?"

Mandy, head bowed, nodded her head. Eleanor lifted Mandy's head; their eyes made direct contact; "Mandy the key word is participate. I have a great deal of knowledge that I have accumulated over the years, through formal schooling, and through life's experiences, knowledge that I very much wish to share with you and with Rebecca. That, my dears is the truth."

"However, I want you both to understand that in return for my educating you, it is my intention that you, that the both of you, educate me. In order for that to happen we, the three of us, have to communicate, we have to talk to each other — Understood?" Mandy replied; *"yesm' Ise unnastan'."*

Eleanor removed her hand; "Once again Mandy, I ask that you please look at me. Describe for us, for Rebecca and for me, when you look at me, Mandy what do you see?"

Mandy hesitated, then she began to speak; *"Ise sees a rite preddy smart white Miztress."*

Eleanor was momentarily, disappointed that Mandy had reverted to answering, her in that colloquial southern dialect that, she and Rebecca called, "nigger talk."

Eleanor quickly regained her composure. She realized that for Mandy to change thirteen years of behavior in two weeks, to fully trust this white person, would be expecting a lot. Give her time, I have to gain…I have to earn her trust.

"Ladies, Rebecca and Mandy, when I was about your age, I was thirteen at the time, my father decided that we, the O'Leary family, my father, my mother, my two brothers, and me, that the family, in order to survive, should immigrate to America."

Both Rebecca and Mandy sat mesmerized, fascinated at Eleanor's revelations. Rebecca asked; "Wow Miss Leary, your family just up and left Ireland, sailed across the Atlantic Ocean when you were only thirteen. How exciting!"

"What caused your father to make that decision? My father says that people all over the world want to come to America, because it's the land of opportunity. Was that why your father decided to move your family to America?"

Eleanor gave a little chuckle; "I guess that's partially true. However, the real unvarnished truth, the reason for my father's uprooting the family from his beloved Ireland, subjecting the five of us to six horrible weeks in steerage, at sea, was because, in our beloved Ireland, we were starving! In Ireland, the O'Leary family occupied the very bottom rung, on the economic and the social ladder."

"We were white. So what? Everyone was white. We were Catholics, in a country where 96% of the land, and therefore all of the power, was in the hands of the Protestants. As a group, in Ireland, we were firmly entrenched with the poorest of the poor."

"It's often said that when you're to close to something, when you don't know any better, you just may "not be able to see the forest, because of the trees". I guess what I'm trying to say is that if it were not for the fact that we were starving, because of my surroundings, my environment, I would have never known, that being poor, being constantly hungry, being ignorant, was not just a manifestation of the norm. How its' always been, and how its' always supposed to be."

"It was during my second year in college, during a Sociology Class, that I read some of the writings of a renowned French sociologist, Gustave de Beaumont."

"Professor Beaumont wrote extensively, about Ireland. I'm paraphrasing his words; "After he visited Ireland in 1835, he wrote that; "I have seen the Indian in his forests, and the Negro in his chains, and thought about their pitiable condition." What he then called examples of, "the very extreme of human wretchedness. He went on to say that and then he visited Ireland."

"Professor Beaumont stated as fact, that in all countries, you'll find the poor, a percentage of the people will be paupers. In Ireland, the entire country is a country of paupers."

"When we arrived in New York, my father would rise before daybreak, each morning, trudge down to the docks, and hope that he would be picked for work as a longshoreman, loading and unloading cargo from ships."

"Prejudice against immigrants, especially Irish immigrants, was widespread and almost universally, strictly adhered to. Father learned to ignore the many signs that he encountered, such as "No Irish Need Apply"; "Irish and niggers Need Not Apply".

Most evenings father would return home, pockets empty, not having been picked that day for work. Father soon became discouraged, and depressed. One of the few things that would bring a derisive smile to his face, was that when things were really bad, he would smile and say; "well, at least we ain't niggers!"

Eleanor was intently studying the faces of the girls. She wanted to gauge their reactions, thus far to her biography.

Rebecca was listening respectfully and politely. She was taking in, absorbing Eleanor's recounting and descriptions of the world, beyond Rosewood. She was piecing together facts put forth by Eleanor, with anecdotal information that she had heard; tidbits about a world that she vaguely knew existed.

Her prior knowledge of the world beyond Rosewood, had come from conversations that she had overheard over the years. Conversations held between her father and mother; her father and his various business associates; and most often conversations between her father and Mr. Luis Fraiser, his lawyer.

Mandy's reaction differed distinctly, from Rebecca's. Mandy's listened with rapt unwavering attention. She seemed to be hanging on to each and every word, spoken by Eleanor. Mandy appeared to be digesting Eleanor's words, her sentences, as if they were scripture, being spoken by a prophet.

Eleanor's discourse was literally exposing Mandy to a new world. A world that she did not know really existed. A world beyond the geographical and the societal, boundaries of her world, Rosewood, the Virginia Slave Plantation.

During the course of Eleanor's oration, Mandy's facial expression had continually changed. At the beginning, when Eleanor was describing her homeland Ireland, and her Irish heritage, Mandy's expression gradually changed from that of polite interest, to that of wonder and excitement.

As Eleanor described the beauty of the land of her ancestors, Mandy reflected upon her lack of knowledge of her ancestor's homeland.

In the slave community, any reference to Africa was met with suspicion, and contempt. Those who spoke of "Afrika" were suspected of being malcontents, trouble- makers.

Any talk of the long gone-bye, life led by their ancestors, was discouraged. Their forbearer's freedom to hunt, freedom to move about their vast lands, any talk that mentioned or even implied FREEDOM, even talk by the old folks, was considered subversive.

If talk of "Afrika", is either heard by, or reported to the white-folk, severe repercussions would soon follow. For a brief fleeting moment, Mandy thought, wouldn't it be wonderful to know who my ancestors were. To know who I am.

When Eleanor was describing her family's daily encounters in New York, with widespread racial prejudice. Mandy's facial expression was transformed into that of intense concentration. She had never known of or imagined, generalized, racial prejudice amongst whites, towards other white-folk. This was a concept that she found fascinating, and difficult to believe.

Mandy as did everyone at Rosewood, had heard of and even encountered "poor white trash". Mandy had heard these words used by slaves, and by white-folks, even by Rebecca. She herself had frequently used the derogatory term. Mandy had internalized that term, "poor white trash, as being descriptive of an illiterate, low economic, ill mannered, group of white people.

A group of people, who though being poor and illiterate, and ill mannered, still possessed a distinct advantage. Bottom line, they are white. People who carried the "poor white-trash" label, in terms of social status, and having the opportunity for upward mobility, are literally, *light* years above the status of any black man, in the American South.

When Eleanor spoke of ethnic prejudice being practiced on an economic level up North towards white men, that was marginally analogous to that being imposed against blacks in the South, Mandy stared incredulously at Eleanor, in frank disbelief. Her disbelief was soon dissipated, when Eleanor shared with them, her father's conciliatory comment;

"Well, at least we ain't niggers!"

As if she were reading Mandy's mind, Eleanor spoke directly to Mandy; "well, at least we ain't niggers!" "Mandy, the reason that I shared with you, that flippant, insensitive, racist comment, made by my father, so many years ago, was not intended to hurt you. To the contrary, I deliberately shared that comment, because I want to enlighten you, I want to educate you."

"Mandy, please feel free to correct me if I misspeak. I'm under the distinct impression that for your entire life, you've been sheltered from the rest of the world. I believe that your only exposure to the world, outside of the slave community here at Rosewood, is the result of the extraordinary, special bond that exists between you and Rebecca."

"Mandy all of us, we all have at least one thing in common. Each and every one of us is a human being. We're human beings with a variety of differences, and interestingly enough, a whole bunch of things in common."

"The color of ones' skin, white, black, red, or yellow, is the most obvious, observable difference. Conversely, one of the not so obvious things that we have in common, is the societal propensity of a group or groups of men, be they kings or paupers, masters or slaves, each group, tends to smugly identify and then disparage, groups that they deem as being their inferiors."

"I truly think and believe that this tactic is a societal defensive, coping, mechanism".

"Essentially it provides a modicum of group protection. My father's comment was not said by him to hurt blacks; instead his bigoted, racist comment, "Well, at least we ain't niggers", was intended to give comfort to his little group, my family."

"Mandy, as I said before, I was immensely impressed when you translated Elizabethan English, into nigger-talk." Now I would like to translate for you, poor white folks talk, "Well, at least we ain't niggers", into polite acceptable English. The translation is; "No matter how bad things are, they could be worse".

"During the Irish Potato Famine, thousands of Irish immigrants flocked to America. When my family arrived in America, we congregated, as did hordes of immigrants, in the slums of America's port cities".

The poorest of the white, non-Irish laborers, looked down their snooty noses at us. We were called "Irish Trash, Micks, Paddys, Muckers", horrible names. We were the last to be hired, and the first to be fired."

"Do I think that my father's racial slurs were reprehensible? At that time no, I did not. Do I now? Yes, in a way, I do. But I do now also realize that the sentiment behind those ugly words was not malicious; the sentiment was merely "human". Human in the context that I now understand, that his comments, "Well, at least we ain't niggers", were a reflexive human nature, protective, response to misery."

Mandy sat motionless. She found Miss Leary's words to be profound, thought provoking. Her words were like a key, a key that could open a part of her mind that had until now, lain fallow, lain dormant.

Miss Leary was looking intently at Mandy. Mandy looked into the teacher's eyes. She thought, in those eyes, she saw a question. For her a life-altering question. At that moment she decided to throw caution to the wind. She decided to — with this white woman — let down her guard, to emerge from her protective cocoon.

Rebecca was tugging on Mandy's sleeve; "Mandy, what's wrong…are you all right?" Mandy looked at Rebecca. She then looked back to Eleanor and stated in a clear resonant voice; **"Miss Leary, in response to your earlier question…when I look at you I see a beautiful, self assured, refined, well spoken, highly educated, wonderful, white lady, some one that I respect and consider to truly be my friend".**

Eleanor tucked a lock of dark red hair, which had fallen over her eye, behind her ear; she smiled; "Understood…Thank you Mandy. Ladies, our class today, is dismissed."

****

September 19, 1859 (Sunday)

I think that today's session with the girls was enormously successful. I broke through to Mandy. That's right, I didn't equivocate, I broke through. I am beginning to understand Mandy. More importantly, Mandy is beginning to, NO that's to soft. Mandy TRUSTS me.

I will not betray that trust.

Today as I shared a brief look into my past, with the girls, I intently studied Mandy's face. While both girls displayed polite interest, when I spoke of my family, my ancestors, my homeland-Ireland, Mandy was completely, totally, engrossed.

That wistful, longing, envious, look that I saw in her eyes was most reveling.

Mandy has NO sense of self. She has no idea as to who she is, where she comes from. Who were, and are her people? Where did they come from? Oh, she has some vague hand-me-down verbal, awareness of Africa. Yet I am totally convinced that Mandy's entire cultural awareness is that of her present condition of servitude, the Southern slave culture.

Fortunately for the next two weeks, Jesse will be in Richmond, accompanying his father on a business trip. Tomorrow I will introduce Rebecca to Shakespeare's Othello.

We will have five days to read, study and analyze the tale of the Black General in 17th century Venice, before we open Mandy's eyes to the potential, the accomplishments of a Black man.

****

Saturday morning following breakfast, as usual, Rebecca with Mandy trailing behind made their way to their special spot, beside the creek. When they were still a short distance from the clearing, to their surprise, they saw Eleanor, skirt spread out around her, seated on the grass. She was leaning, her back against one of their crates. The crate that lent support to her back, held a large book, and several sheets of unlined paper.

Eleanor remained seated on the grass. As the girls drew near, she smiled warmly and cheerfully said; "Good morning girls." Rebecca was the first to respond "Good morning Miss Leary". Eleanor nodded, then held her breath, anxiously awaiting Mandy's response; Mandy smiled and spoke; "Good morning Miss Leary, both Becky and I were delighted to see you were here so early."

142

Eleanor slowly let out her breath, Mandy's response was even more then she had hoped it would be. The fact that she had not answered in "nigger talk", but instead, had responded in grammatically correct English, and answered with a compound sentence to boot, spoke volumes to Eleanor. Elatedly she thought, "she trusts me — Mandy trusts me!"

When they were all comfortably seated on the grass, Eleanor broke the silence; "Well Mandy, I know that for the past week, you and Becky have been discussing Shakespeare's Othello. I feel confident that Becky has gone over the material that she and I covered in class. "Have you had a chance to actually read any portion of the play?"

"Actually Miss Leary, I haven't had access to the book, or for that matter to any book. Becky and I agreed many years ago, that it was too dangerous for me to have books, except access to her books when we are alone. If I were to be seen reading a book, or merely caught having a book in my possession, I would endanger not only myself, I would be exposing my entire family to serious repercussions."

Rebecca chimed in; "On Monday, I could hardly wait to see Mandy, I could hardly wait for class to end. When I told her that we were studying the Shakespearean play, "Othello", a play about a black General, a General in command of a predominantly white army, she..." Rebecca looked over at Mandy; Mandy with out a second's hesitation, picked up the narrative; "I was stunned... at first I couldn't believe it!"

"My first thoughts were that Becky had some how misunderstood. That a black character in the Shakespeare play, "Othello", was at best the slave, of or a servant of, the white General, who was in charge of a white army."

"Frankly Miss Leary, nothing that had been told to me in the past, by my people, or that I have read for myself in the books that Becky has shared with me, even hints that a black man would have the intelligence, the opportunity, to rise to such a high position."

"I'm sure that Mr. Shakespeare's black General Othello, the hero of the play, is depicted, as most heroes in literature are, as a brave, intelligent, character. And I'm equally confident that I will find the play, as I think you intend for me to, to be inspiring. But Miss Leary, after all is said and done, "Othello" is a play, a work of fiction. A work of fiction, no less fictional than, say; those silly children's stories, "Hansel & Gretel, and "Rapunzel".

"While each tale makes a positive statement, although the message is real, in the end, the characters are fictitious. After all is said and done, the black General Othello remains a black man of statue and achievement that existed only in the vivid imagination of Mr. Shakespeare. General Othello was a figment of a white man's imagination, he was not a real man."

Eleanor looked up from her open textbook. "Mandy, I'd like to tell you of a black man, a real black man, alive today, a former slave. This black man, and many others like him, possesses the intellect and the statue, of Shakespeare's fictional Othello."

Mandy looked with skepticism at Eleanor, she gave a puzzled look towards Becky. Eleanor continued; "His name is Frederick Douglass." Mandy did not look convinced. Eleanor continued, "to paraphrase Mr. Douglass, a former slave; "Slavery is a poor school for the human intellect and heart".

Mandy looked perplexed, shocked; "Miss Leary, I have neither heard, nor have I read of such a man." Rebecca was now becoming increasingly uncomfortable, agitated, and apprehensive. Still, she remained seated.

Eleanor, seeing the sudden disquietude in Rebecca's posture, the concern, on her face, decided to end the conversation. "Perhaps at some future session, I will have the opportunity to tell you about the remarkable, Mister Frederick Douglass.

Mandy was also cognizant of Rebecca's discomfort, she smoothly and deftly attempted to change the subject; "Well one thing is certain, that black man, Frederick Douglass, must be, pardon the expression, "Damn near white".

Eleanor innocently asked; "What makes you say that Mandy". Mandy sighed, as if she was about to shed the weight of the world from her shoulders; "In my community, the slave community, my world, there's a commonly spoken, and religiously followed edict. This little ditty;

> If yo's white, yo's allrite
> If yo's brown, yo's can stik aroun
> If yo's black, yo's git back

Eleanor abruptly closed the heavy book of Shakespearean plays. The sound, the loud thud made by her emphatically closing the large tomb, startled Rebecca and Mandy. The girls did not know how to react. Mandy thought, what did I say? God, I hope I haven't ruined things. She sheepishly addressed Eleanor; "Miss Leary. If I spoke out of turn, if I offended you, I sincerely apologize."

Now it was Eleanor's turn to be confused, puzzled. She quickly regained her composure; "No, no Mandy…there's no need to apologize. What you said made me realize that I might be "putting the cart before the horse." Now the girls were really confused.

Eleanor continued; "That's a cliché, what I mean by that is that, one really needs to learn to crawl before they learn to walk...another cliché, I did it again."

She took a deep breath; "Girls, I made a mistake. I truly believe that in order to really understand Shakespeare's Othello, we need to understand, to know at least a little anthropology."

"Ladies, first I would like to make an emphatic disclaimer. I want to make it absolutely clear that I have no expertise in that particular area, the discipline of Anthropology." "Now having said that, I would like to share with you my exposure to the fledgling rapidly changing, science of Anthropology."

"When I was your age, a girl growing up on a farm on the frontier, the one thing that I wanted more than anything else in the world, was to get as far away from Nebraska, as I possibly could."

"After my brothers were grown men. After O'Fallon Nebraska was deemed civilized, no longer the frontier, my Mom and Dad gave me the greatest gift imaginable; they agreed to send me to college."

"The one thing that I wanted, more than anything else in this world, they had made possible. I desperately yearned for knowledge. I went to college eager to learn, with an insatiable thirst for knowledge."

"As a child, teaching my brothers, I dreamed of someday having access to unlimited quantities of books. My first visit to the college library, I realized that my dream had come true. Hundreds, maybe thousands of books, surrounded me.

"At the end of the day, after a full day of classes, I would sit reading in the library, until they closed, at which time they had to literally throw me out.

It was at the library that I became acquainted with Dorothy Diggs. Dorothy was one of the colleges "Free Negro" students."

"I wish I could say that Dorothy and I became friends. I cannot. I honestly don't know why we were not friends. Dorothy was a shy, black skinned girl. She had rather full-thick lips, a broad nose, and really tight curly, kinky hair."

"Dorothy was a loner. You would invariably find Dorothy at either one of three sites on campus. She would be in class, or in the library, or she would be auditing Professor Oglethorpe's Theoretical Anthropology lectures."

"Professor Oglethorpe's class was a radical departure from the traditional Anthropology curriculum, which was predicated, on strict adherence to creationist, biblical teachings."

"Professor Oglethorpe was a firm believer that all of human kind was descendants from the same single mating. This of course is consistent with the bible, "Genesis", Adam & Eve. Dr. Oglethorpe, however, did not agree with the currently accepted, literal belief, that of Creationism."

"Professor Oglethorpe, along with his friend and colleague Charles Darwin, are proponents of what Darwin calls, Evolution. I want to pause here for a moment, to once again remind you that Anthropology is not my area of expertise. In fact, I am definitely not qualified, nor do I have sufficient knowledge, to speak with authority on the subject."

"My sole purpose for bringing this into this discussion is you, Mandy."

"Mandy, earlier today, you shared with us, that little ditty, the one that you said influences life amongst the slaves. My interpretation of what you said, and the way that you said it, lead me to believe that that saying, is more than just influential.

The way that I interpreted your words, was that the very social structure of the slave community, was more or less, structured around, and based upon that three-line ditty."

"Mandy, this morning was not the first time that I had heard:

> If you're black, get back
> If you're brown, stick around
> If you're white, you're all right

"Dorothy Diggs, my Negro classmate at Oberlin College, recited that same ditty in Professor Oglethorpe's Anthropology class."

"Dr. Oglethorpe's lecture was addressing a new concept, which his friend, and colleague, Charles Darwin will be soon publishing. Darwin's soon to be published book, "The Origin of Species", introduces the concept of "Natural Selection".

"At the conclusion of his lecture, the Professor invited questions. To everyone's surprise, my black classmate, Dorothy Diggs, timidly raised her hand. That was the very first time that Dorothy, had asked a question, or asked for permission to speak in the class."

"That was the first time that I, and I do believe, that it was the first time that my classmates, heard that little ditty."

"Dorothy shared with the class; exactly how that little ditty had affected her life. She spoke elegantly and passionately of her life as a "Free Black, living in a segregated "Free Black" community."

"She spoke of rampant, long seated prejudice by Free Blacks, against Free Blacks. Prejudice based upon an individual's degree of possession of so called "Negroid" features."

> "If you're black, get back"
> "If you're brown, stick around"
> "If you're white, you're all right"

"Dorothy told of how she, for her entire life, had been led to believe that she was innately inferior. Not inferior because of her intellect, or for her personality, not because of her disposition, Dorothy had been judged innately inferior, by blacks, her own people, because she was born with:

>"Very dark skin"
>"Full-thick lips"
>"A broad, flat nose"
>"Kinky hair"

"With Dorothy's permission, Professor Oglethorpe used those, what he called, phenotypic traits that her culture had taught her to despise, the traits that in effect had contributed to Dorothy's self-loathing, to introduce to the class, his friend and colleague, Charles Darwin's theory of Evolution-Natural Selection."

"Professor Oglethorpe postulated that Darwin's extensive research supports his — and many of those scientists, who have dedicated their lives to the study of Anthropology — belief that man originated in Africa."

The professor explained that; "Equatorial Africa is extremely hot. The sun beats down unmercifully on all living creatures. Those life forms that do not adapt to the environment, plant and animal, do not survive to procreate.

The human brain is prone to overheating. Consistent ambient temperatures exceeding 107° F, can lead to heatstroke, to skin cancers. The East African Savannas average temperature is in excess of 107° F.

Over the course of time, millions of years, thousands of generations of humans that inhabited these regions, adapted to the extreme temperatures. They evolved. Natural selection survival, of the fittest, favored dark-skinned human beings.

Those people whose dark skin color, provided protection from the damage caused by constant exposure to the harmful rays of the Equatorial Sun, were the people who lived to procreate.

Professor Oglethorpe, suggested that instead of viewing dark-skin as a curse from God, we should consider dark-skin, gained by Natural Selection, as a blessing from God for those indigenous people living in tropical areas with intense, harmful, sunlight.

As for kinky hair, he asked the students, "Can anyone think of a possible evolutionary adaptation, remember evolution takes place over time, not time measured in years per say, but time measured in eons". The students remained quiet. Dorothy raised her hand. Dr. Oglethorpe indicated that she had the floor.

Dorothy once again reiterated that she had been brought up, to believe that kinky-nappy-woolly hair was "bad" hair. However, based upon the professor's explanation of natural selection, she would like to propose, that they at least consider the following as a feasible explanation;

"In the summer, particularly in July and August, following a severe rain shower, my wet "bad" hair, when drying under the intense summer sun, tended to mat, to form somewhat of a shield, a bonnet protecting my head from the sun".

Dorothy asked the professor, if he thought that kinky-nappy-woolly hair, might also be one of God's evolutionary, survival of the fittest, blessings."

Professor Oglethorpe, after thoughtfully, stroking his neat little goatee, acknowledged that Dorothy's hypothesis — for that is what it was — a theory whose acceptance or rejection, is based upon proven fact, was indeed plausible.

He felt that Dorothy's comments, though not based upon any scientific criteria, such as data accumulated from controlled, or at least observable studies, was certainly worthy of consideration.

Professor Oglethorpe surveyed the expressions on the faces of his young, eager, receptive students. His gaze came to rest on Dorothy; "Mis Diggs, that is indeed a very interesting, thought provoking theory. Very astute, indeed, very astute".

Eleanor now standing, paused, walked over to the creek, and slowly pulled the rope which held a partially submerged, water resistant container of Lemonade.

She walked slowly, over to the picnic basket, removed three cups, and filled the cups with the cool drink. She handed a cup to Rebecca, and a cup to Mandy. Her protracted separation from the girls, was deliberate. She wanted to give them a chance to digest this morning's lesson.

Eleanor's activity, served as a clear signal that it was time for lunch, time for a break.

The three young ladies sat, eating their lunch, on the thick, lush carpet of grass. Rebecca and Mandy were engaged in animated conversation.

Rebecca after a long swallow of the cool lemonade remarked; "Mandy, I had no idea that there was a such a rigid, defined class structure amongst the slaves. I always thought that a slave is a slave. Well at least, thank heavens, you and Ruth are not discriminated against."

Mandy gave her friend, her very best friend Becky, a look of shear, blatant incredulity. Rebecca, was honestly surprised and puzzled by Mandy's reaction to her innocent, sympathetic, comment.

"Becky it's true that in terms of looks, being thought of as pretty or attractive, in the slave community, is judged on skin color; the degree of blackness, and other non-negroid facial features, those of us that differ from the majority, while being envied, are outsiders. We're called horrible names." Rebecca asked; "what do you mean treated as outsiders...what kind of names are you called?"

"We're called *yella-niggers; red-bones; wanna be's*..., it's as if we don't belong. To the black slaves, we're outcasts... Outcasts who happen to be slaves. Ironically, to the whites, we outcasts from the slave community, are considered to be just plain black, nigger slaves."

Eleanor had been sitting quietly, keenly attentive to this frank conversation between these two teenage friends. One a black slave, and the other, her white mistress. From the body language of both girls, Eleanor concluded that this was more than likely, the first such conversation between the two.

Following the meal-break, Eleanor asked; "Do either of you have questions about this morning's, discussion?"

Rebecca raised her hand. "Yes Rebecca, you have a question?" "Miss Leary, to be honest, I had no idea, that women, let alone, black women, were permitted to attend college, and certainly not together. I have loads and loads of questions. At that college, did whites and blacks live together, eat together?"

Before Eleanor could respond, the words continued to rapidly spew forth from Rebecca. "I found your Professor's answers to the black student's questions, fascinating. I've lived with slaves my whole life. I too have wondered why they look the way they do, you know, dark-skin; kinky hair, the flat nose; the thick-full lips."

"When I was a little girl, I asked my mother? She answered that that's the way it is. Niggers are inferior to whites. The physical differences between blacks and whites is God's way of keeping the two groups separate. It's God's will."

"Once, when I was about seven or eight, at Sunday services, I asked Reverend JoshiahWesley, that's our pastor, the same question. His answer was the same as mother's, It's God's will.

Reverend Wesley, said that it's in the Bible. He opened his bible (Genesis 1:27), read, and read, "God created man in his own image...". Reverend Wesley closed his Bible, and picked up a fan from one of the church pews."

The fan bore a picture which was the profile of a white man, with long straight-flowing, brownish-blond hair, clear blue eyes, and a raised bridged nose. Reverend JoshiahWesley said quietly, in a hushed solemn voice, this is the image of Jesus."

"In response to my question, why are black people slaves, he once again opened his Bible. This time to (Genesis 9:25), and read; "Cursed be Canaan. Let him become the lowest slave to his brothers.""

"When I asked what did that mean, the Reverend answered, that the people of Africa are descendants of Ham, Canaan's father. Therefore, the Bible explicitly sanctions the enslavement of black people.""

"I must admit that I found his answers confusing, I just did not understand his explanation. However Reverend Wesley gained my full acceptance of his explanation, by once again holding up for my inspection, a church fan, that we all knew, blacks and whites, that the fan bore the image of Jesus.""

"Miss Leary, after this morning, I thought that Professor Oglethorpe's theories, actually made sense. Did the Professor have an explanation, as to the reason for black people having flat noses, and thick full lips?""

Eleanor, seated on the cushion that she had placed on her crate, made herself reasonably comfortable. She waited until the girls gave her their full attention. "As a matter of fact, those black phenotypic traits, the broad flat nose, and the thick full lips, were discussed."

"Professor Oglethorpe, instead of his putting forth his or his other colleagues' theories, the Professor shifted the task of promulgating a response, to us, his students".

"He asked the students, in the context of the theories of Evolution under discussion; "Would anyone care to venture a theory, as to the origin and prevalence, of the Negro's flat noses, and thick full lips?""

Dorothy Diggs, the lone Negro student, raised her hand. She stood and with what appeared to me, with newfound dignity, and self-esteem, that she had obtained within the last hour, volunteered the following.

"Professor Oglethorpe, I am ashamed to admit that I know very little about Africa. In fact, the very word Africa, has always had a negative connotation in my family. For me that's over done with, I will no longer be ashamed of my Afro features, nor will I deny my African heritage.""

"I will never forget that look of pride, of self-esteem, that Dorothy exuded as she stated, "Forgive me for being emotional. I have no knowledge of the atmosphere, or quality of the air in Africa; therefore, my theory may, or may not be supported by fact".

"In any event, here goes; I hypothesize that the air quality the combination of extremely high temperatures, the heat, and humidity in Africa was such, that the native populations over time, millions of years, through natural selection had to adapt to the climate".

"The adaptation over time, millions of years, thousands of generations, was the flattened and the broadened nose, which made breathing easier."

'Those individuals with flat noses, with wide nostril, that made breathing easier, survived, and mated with others who had flat noses and wide nostrils".

"Those traits were passed on to their children, then to their children's children. Ergo, "Survival of the Fittest, the fittest being those with broad flat noses, with flaring wide nostrils, that facilitated breathing in the sub-equatorial, African Climate."

Professor Oglethorpe applauded. "That's a very interesting hypothesis. It's certainly one worth investigating." "Okay class, that leaves one of the four so called "Negroid Traits" under discussion, yet to be explained in terms of "Natural Selection".

Would anyone else, other than Miss Diggs, care to offer a plausible explanation, consistent with "Natural Selection", for blacks having thick-full lips...Anyone?"

Professor Oglethorpe looked at each student. No one met his gaze. Than to my chagrin, his gaze settled on me; "Miss Leary, consistent with the theory of Evolutionary Natural Selection, can you suggest a reason for blacks having thick-full lips."

Rebecca and Mandy were looking at Eleanor, with intense anticipation. They were obviously intrigued. Eleanor imagined that this was probably how they had reacted as kids, reading about the exploits and adventures of "Bison Bill", or some such "Dime Store Novel hero.

Well, unfortunately if they expected that she (the heroine) would save the day with a pearl of wisdom, packed inside her trusty brain, as Bison Bill always did with bullets fired from his trusty rifle, they were in for disappointment.

Eleanor continued; "I had nothing. I could not think of a single advantage that thick-full lips, would bestow upon the Negro people".

After what seemed to me, to be an eternity, the professor's attention shifted from me.

Professor Oglethorpe proceeded to ask each of my classmates the following question; "taking into consideration, Miss Diggs', and my hypothesis' to explain dark skin, kinky hair, and flat noses in Negroes, would any one of you care to offer a hypothesis, consistent with the theory of Evolutionary Natural Selection, which would explain why blacks have thick-full lips?"

No one responded. Professor Oglethorpe turned to Dorothy, "Miss Diggs, and do you have a theory?" Dorothy, the only black student in the class, for the first time, appeared to be totally self-conscience.

She gathered herself stood, and faced Professor Oglethorpe; "Professor, I am unable to think of a single way that thick-full lips would protect Africans, thereby ensuring their ability to survive, to mate and to produce the next generation."

One of the students, Calvin Jennings, a brash young man, I believe he was from Pennsylvania, spoke up; "I think that the reason for the Negro's bulbous fat lips is explained in the Bible. God placed a curse on Ham. Africans are the descendants of Ham. There is absolutely no advantage to having unattractive, thick ugly fat lips. It's a fact, Negroes are cursed by God".

An uneasy silence fell over the class. Professor Oglethorpe did not immediately respond. Several of the students myself included, stole furtive glances at our one and only Negro classmate. Dorothy, who only minutes earlier had held her head high, was now seated slumped down in her chair. She looked as if she was about to flee from the room.

Professor Oglethorpe walked over to Dorothy, and stood behind the desolate student's desk. He gently, but firmly placed one of his hands on each of her shoulders.

While his hands provided comfort, they also held the girl firmly in place, effectively holding Dorothy in place.

The professor spoke; "Well, Mr. Jennings, your comments were certainly delivered with an authoritative tone of righteous finality. Before I respond to Mr. Jennings' passionate oration, I first want to remind you all, that this course is entitled Anthropology, not Theology."

"I say that because I don't have, nor do I claim expertise, nor credentials to teach, or to debate Theology. Now having said that, I do believe there is a kernel of truth in Mr. Jennings' diatribe."

We could all see Dorothy attempt to rise from her seat. Professor Oglethorpe hands held her in place.

"First, I would like to offer a hypothesis, consistent with the theory of Evolutionary Natural Selection, as to why Negroes have thick-full lips. First, I want to reiterate and emphasize that Evolution - Natural Selection, occurs over the course of time, over millions of years, over eons,"

"Here is my hypothesis, inspired this very day by this young lady, your classmate, Miss Dorothy Diggs."

"The indigenous peoples who populated the savannas of Sub-Saharan Africa were isolated from other populations of people. For reasons that we have hypothesized, fair-skinned people, with straight hair would be at a natural disadvantage for survival, in the climate and the environment of the savannas of Sub-Saharan Africa".

"Therefore, those features that whites consider attractive, fair-skin, straight hair, narrow nostrils, according to our hypothesis, because of natural selection, due to eons of evolutionary natural selection, those features that whites consider attractive, would not be present in the population of peoples who inhabit the savannas of Sub-Saharan Africa."

"Having said that, we all agree that, one anatomic feature, lips, human lips are present in all humans."

"Lips in many cultures are important anatomic features, utilized to attract the opposite sex. This includes our culture. Look around this room. You ladies love your lip rouge".

"In our own culture, lips play an important role in attracting the opposite sex. "I hypothesize that full thick lips, the thicker and the fuller the better, were regarded as attractive by the Negroes who inhabited Sub-Saharan Africa. Those individuals in the African Community, whose lips did not meet the societal standards of beauty, full thick lips, were deemed by society as being unattractive. Unattractive individuals in any society, have difficulty attracting a mate."

"Therefore, those unattractive individuals, by that society's standards, the thin-lipped peoples, would not be able to attract a mate, and would therefore not produce offspring."

"Those individual, who met the prevailing local standards of attractiveness, full thick lips, would be considered attractive. They would have a "Natural Selection" advantage in successfully attracting mates. Their mating with attractive full thick lipped persons of the opposite sex, would produce progeny with full thick lips."

"If I recall correctly, Mr. Jennings stated that; "There is no advantage to having unattractive, thick ugly fat lips."

"I submit that within a population whose standards admire and revere thick, full bulbous lips, there is a distinct advantage to having full bulbous lips. In that society, attractive couples, with full bulbous lips, mate. The mating results in the producing of offspring with full bulbous lips.'

"My hypothesis contends that in the Negro's native habitat Africa, full bulbous lips, instead of being a manifestation of a curse from God, I suggest that full bulbous lips, in Sub-Saharan Africa, may have been is a desirable trait, a blessing, a gift from God."

Eleanor put her palms together, forming a steeple, she continued; "Dorothy turned her head, looked up into Professor Oglethorpe's eyes, and smiled. Professor Oglethorpe almost imperceptibly, squeezed her shoulder, and returned her smile."

Eleanor stood, picked up her copy of "The Collected Works of William Shakespeare". Rebecca and Mandy remained seated. Eleanor spoke; "although we didn't get a chance to discuss Shakespeare's Othello, as I had planned, I do sincerely believe that what we did discuss, will help us to understand Othello, Shakespeare's troubled Moor.

Okay ladies, I suggest we get back to the "Big House."

****

Jesse Billings was a true rarity, among his rich, white, teenage male peers. Seventeen-year-old Jesse, the son of a wealthy, white Southern planter, the owner of nearly one hundred slaves, of which 50% were female, was still, at the advanced age of seventeen, a virgin. Obviously, Jesse's virginity was not due to a lack of available females, nor was it because of a paucity of male hormones, which were coursing through young Jesse's blood stream, stimulating, and filling tote brink of overflowing, his healthy gonads.

Jesse, like his grandfather, his father and his uncle before him, for years had been fully cognizant of the vast number of enslaved females, that were always available, literally at his beck and call. To as Lucas Prentess, the overseer crudely put it, "to haul your ashes".

Jesse however, unlike his familial male forebearers, had morals. Jesse had, for whatever reason, developed a strong sense of respect for females. All females, as far as Jesse was concerned, were deserving of respect, and most importantly, deserving of male protection. Rebecca, his sister, ascribed Jesse's chivalrous inclinations towards females, to his lifelong addiction to the reading of, "Dime Store Novels".

Jesse had over the years, internalized the "Romanticism", lavishly depicted in those cheap publications. Since he was a child of seven, Jesse had read that true men, the heroes in the novels, respected and protected females. On occasion, real men even protected, the heathen, red-skin squaws. And after all, to Jesse, Indian squaws were just red-niggers.

Despite his propensity for, and his practice of chivalry, Jesse was a devout believer and supporter of the South, the Southern way of life, the South's "Peculiar Institution" Slavery, the enslavement and total subjugation of black men and women.

Jesse had always been exceptionally receptive and susceptible, to the power of the written word. He was inclined to believe the published, printed, word.
His mindset was that if it's published, it must be true.

If by chance, Jesse read something that seemed far-fetched, or caused him to question his beliefs, his authoritative arbiter was the Bible.

The notable exception to his proclivity to believe and trust the printed word, was his ardent disbelief of any of that "Yankee Abolitionist garbage". Jesse had been taught from birth, that that Northern claptrap, propaganda, was written and inspired by the Devil and the Devil's minions.

Jesse was able to reconcile his staunch belief in Slavery, with his profound respect for the treatment of all females, through his unquestioned acceptance, of the racist's slanted interpretation of biblical passages.

The passages from the Bible that were used to justify Slavery, had been force-feed to him, by his parents, by his community, and by his spiritual shepherd, the right Reverend Joshiah Wesley, over the course of his entire life.

Yet another reason for Jesse's persistently lingering virginity, was the fact that he was in essence, isolated, physically separated from other white teens. Other than his "book-worm" sister, the closest white teenagers, were Rodney Wooster, and his the pimply faced fifteen-year-old twin sister, Rosalind. Rodney and Rosalind were the children of Mr. Linwood Wooster, the Master of the Sweetwater Plantation, some twenty miles south of Rosewood.

In addition to the scarcity of potential white female sexual partners, a far more important factor contributing to his sustained virginity, was free time.
It seemed to Jesse that every minute of his time was accounted for.

As heir to the Rosewood Plantation, it was absolutely incumbent upon him, mandated that he become familiar with the ins and outs of successfully managing and running, the plantation, and its' holdings.

On top of all of that, Jesse was expected to be, along with his sister Rebecca, a full-time, attentive student of that imported Yankee school marm's Miss Eleanor Leary's, 'Advanced Literature" classes.

Jesse had of course, been exposed to a bevy of attractive slave girls. His white-male role models, his father Henry, and the plantation's overseer, Lucas Prentess, had made no secret of their taste for "dark-meat".

With the exception of Mandy, who along with his sister Rebecca, he considered a constantly underfoot pest, Rebecca's playmate, and now his sister's maid, Lena, Mandy's ebony, statuesque, friend, was the most attractive of the female slaves.

Lucas Prentess, Jesse's mentor and tutor in his practicum, in the learning of the "fine art of handling field-hand niggers", was perplexed and exasperated with Jesse's taste in black wenches.

Lucas and Jesse were riding up and down the rows of cotton plants. Lucas, after watching Jesse casting admiring glances at Lena, would shake his head and comment; "Jesse, what in the hell is wrong with you. You got all of these fine looking, high-yella wenches to choose from, and who do you fancy, Lena, the tallest, nappy headed, liver-lipped wench on the place. What in the hell is wrong with you?!"

At first Jesse, who stood 5' 9", refused to acknowledge, even to himself, that he was attracted to the black, majestic, 5' 11" female slave. Finally, after days, weeks, of relentless nagging by Lucas, Jesse was forced to confront the fact that he did indeed find Lena, to be attractive, alluringly, desirable.

Lena became aware of the young Master's interest in her, from the giggling whispers, and gossip which was being copiously put forth by her fellow female field-hands. Agnes, Lena's picking-partner, for weeks had been commenting to anyone and everyone; *"dat yun Massa, eyes dey ben eatin' Lena up...I tels ya gal dat white boy wanton somma dat giant blac pootang"*.

Lena was flattered by Jessie's obvious attraction for her. If she were to be perfectly honest, as she always was with her mother, in addition to being flattered, Lena was quite frankly surprised.

In the slave community, Lena's classic Negroid features, were not held in high esteem. The young black males were usually, attracted to those female slaves that had features that conformed to the slave's anthem;

> If yo's white, yo's allrite
> If yo's brown, yo's can stik aroun
> If yo's black, yo's git back

In general, those young black men, who possessed prominent Negroid features, were usually rebuffed, by brown and light skinned female slaves. They tended to pursue female slaves with prominent Negroid features. While Lena's features did not exclude her from the majority of male slave suitors, her statuest 5'11" height did.

Jesse's attraction towards Lena was rooted in his obsession with Dime Store Novels. Although Jesse hated the villainous, savage red-skins, depicted in the books, he also took note of, and admired the dignity, the strength and the regal bearings of these native Americans.

In Lena, Jesse imagined that he saw in her, the beauty, the nobility, and the strength, of Africa's native peoples.

When Lena told Mattie, her mother of *"da Massa's smilin', longin' looks"*, her mother face broke into a dazzleing grin. *"Chile is yu seeros? Massa Jesse sho nuff lustin fo yu? Honey chile dis be portant. Ifn he com pester yu we all be mov'n up in des here worl. Ifn he nocs yu up, prety lil brown baby ain gonna hurt dis fmbly none...we be on da way up"*.

Jesse's duties as a young Master in training, necessitated that his afternoons be spent in the fields, riding along with Lucas, overseeing the work of the slaves in the fields.

The vast acreage of cotton covered a little more than five miles. Each fertile mile was made up of multiple rows of plants. It was practically impossible for Jesse and Lucas to monitor each and every row, each and every day. Yet for the past two weeks, it just so happened, that each and every day, Jesse would find himself riding down the row of plants that Lena was working.

Lena, now fully aware of Jesse's presence, looked up from her work, smiled and softly murmured; *"moanin Massa Jesse"*. Jesse stopped his horse, swung his right leg around the saddle horn, and casually, in as masculine a voice that he could muster, spoke; "you're Lena aren't you…haven't I seen you working in the Big House?" Lena stood erect, she held the hoe that she had been wielding, at her side.

The sun was behind Lena's shoulder. Jesse squinting into the sun, momentarily, did not see a docile subservient, slave girl, instead in his vivid imagination, Jesse saw standing before him, framed by the rays of the sun, a majestic, nearly six feet tall, proud, ebony, female warrior.

He quickly regained his composure, cleared his throat and uttered; "come here gal", Jesse reached into his saddle bags, and handed Lena a package. Without another word, he swung his leg over the saddle horn, and at a gallop, rode away.

Mattie, Lena's mother was ecstatic, flabbergasted. She could not contain her excitement. She delicately, reverently held the beautiful jade bracelet, next to the single lite candle on the table. *"Da youn' Massa, jus up an gib yu dis…dis here be da pretist thing dat I done eber seed."*

Lena held her hand out to her mother; *"mama gib me bak my jewry…what do yu think dis mean?* Lena's mother gently placed the bracelet into Lena's palm. *"Chile is yu funnin wid me? How ole is yu gal?"* Mattie shook her head in unconcealed wonder, and continued; *"yu be 17 year ole…yu ain't no baby. Da youn' Massa sho nuff sniffin' round for some blac pootang. An ifn it be yu, an yu got a lick ah sense…yu be spredn yo legs an shoutn' Halelujah thank yu lawd.*

Before Lena could respond, there was a firm series knocks on the cabin door. Mattie annoyed, shouted; *"who dat a bangin' on da doo?"* She opened the door, there hat in hand, stood the future Master of Rosewood, young Jesse Billings.

Mattie's hand flew to her mouth; *"why Massa Jesse, how is yu…please com on in, habba seat."* Before either Jesse or Lena could speak, Mattie was half way out the door. *"I be gwine oba ta see Ruth…Massa yu stay long as yu wants."* Without another word, she left the cabin, firmly closing the door behind her.

Jesse was totally devoid of any real life, sexual experiences. Of course, living on a plantation that kept and raised a few domestic animals, Jesse as a boy had witnessed the matings between animals.

He had found the coupling of horses, and dogs, particularly interesting, in fact comical. The agitated stallion prancing around with his huge member flailing beneath him, mounting the mare, frantically pumping in and out, then sliding off the mares back, his formerly huge member, shrinking to practically nothing.

Jesse himself as do most adolescent boys, had experienced his share of erections, and "wet-dreams". He would sometimes wake-up in the morning, to find that his underwear was encrusted with what he called "ick".

Jesse distinctly remembered the first time that he had masturbated. It was while reading a particularly exciting chapter of "*Buckskin Bob, Conquers and Subdues, the Hated Redskins*".

His hero, Buckskin Bob had been captured, and brutally beaten, by a band of blood-thirsty, savage redskins. With the help of a beautiful Indian Squaw, Bob made his escape. But before he left the heathen's encampment, Buckskin Bob spent one passionate night with his beautiful squaw.

It was while reading of that fictious romantic encounter, that thirteen-year-old Jesse, experienced the most painful erection of his young life. Lying in bed, mesmerized by his hero's adventures, Jesse begin to stroke his erect penis. To his surprise and dismay, he ejaculated. He hastily, frantically wiped the "ick" from himself as well as from the bed sheets.

In contrast, Lena, who was by no means *promiscuous*, was not a virgin. Lena had willingly surrendered her virginity, at the age of fourteen. At the time, her primary reason for allowing Denny, one of the young field hands *"to pleasure her"*, was strictly due to her natural curiosity.

For as long as she could remember, Lena had almost, nightly heard her mother Mattie, and her presumed father Willie, gasping, moaning, whispering, and *"pleasuring"* each other.

Mattie presumed that Willie was Lena's father based solely in the fact that Willie, who stood 6'3", was the biggest, the blackest man that she had slept with. And the fact that Willie was by far, Mattie's most frequent, after dark, visitor.

Besides, Mattie would often pronounce to anyone who would listen; *"if da truff be tol, if Massa 'lowed it, I be hitched up wid dat big, black, nigger when I foist seed him"*.

It had always been Rosewood's policy to prohibit slaves from marrying. This policy served two purposes;

1) In the event that one or both of the mating parties were sold, the separation tended to be less emotional.

2) Having the female slaves mate with multiple partners, resulted in the birth of more slaves, thus increasing the wealth of the Billings family.

****

Lena motioned for Jesse to sit at the table, in one of the cabin's three chairs. She sat down at the table, across from Jesse. They sat for several seconds, awkwardly staring at each other. Jesse broke the silence. "I see you're wearing the bracelet. Do you like it?" Lena demurely smiled; *"Massa Jesse, I luv it. Dis is da pretist thing dat Ise evva had. Is it really mine ta keep?"*

Jesse walked around the table, bent down, and took Lena's hand in his, the bracelet slide on her arm; from her hand, towards her forearm, Jesse holding her hand, was looking deeply, searchingly into Lena's dark brown eyes.

"Lena do you know why I gave you the bracelet, do you know why I'm here?" Lena broke eye contact, she looked down at the table; *"Yessah Massa, I knows."*

Jesse' heart was racing, he felt as if it would burst from his chest. He swallowed twice, then spoke; Lena, I'll leave if you want." Lena raised her head, her eyes met Jesse'; *"Stay, Massa Jesse, I wonts yu to stay."*

Jesse, gently squeezed, Lena's hand, she stood, a full two inches taller than he. Jesse led his ebony princess, to the curtain that bisected the cabin, then ultimately to the cornhusk bed beyond.

Lena instinctively knew that despite Jesse' mature facade, there was a real possibility that this could well be Massa Jesse' first time.

She was absolutely certain that Jesse had not been with any of the plantation's female slaves. If he had, there was absolutely no way, that her mother, and by extension she, would not have heard. The slave-grapevine was that efficient.

Jesse imperceptibly trembling, gently placed his unsteady hand onto Lena's chin. Lena closed her eyes, Jesse and Lena kissed. Jesse's lips felt as if they were enveloped in the warmest, the softest, the sweetest substance on earth.

Lena parted her lips and sucked on Jesse's lower lip. In response to the increasing vacuum exerted by Lena's suction, Jesse parted his lips and extended his tongue, instantaneously, the suction of Lena's mouth transferred from Jesse' lower lip to his tongue.

Jesse had never experienced feelings, sensations like this. He was light headed, close to feeling faint. He felt as if all of the blood in his body, had been redirected and was now centered in is throbbing penis.

To put it in words that Lucas the overseer would probably have used, Jesse had the hardest hard-on, the biggest boner of his entire life.

Lena was assisting Jesse in removing his trousers, Jesse' pulsating manhood sprang into view. Lena stood, and stepped out of her frock. She laid naked, down onto the bed. She stretched her arms out to Jesse. *"Hurry Massa, I wont's yu insides me rel bad."*

Jesse looked at Lena, lying naked, fully exposed before him. She was magnificent. The glow from the single candle on the table, made her black skin glistened, her voluptuous full lips, framed her perfect pearly-white teeth. The ultimate, native warrior princess, was the thought that fleetingly crossed Jesse's mind.

Jesse, now naked knelt down on the bed, between Lena's parted thighs. With her left hand, Lena parted the lips of her vagina. Jesse caught a glimpse of the cherry red inner lining. Lena reached for and grasped Jesse's throbbing penis, with her right hand.

It was then that — to Jesse — the unthinkable happened, as Lena's warm hand encircled Jesse's member, guiding him to her, Jesse begin to tremble, he moaned and exclaimed "Oh no", to his chagrin, Jesse exploded, he ejaculated.

Jesse was mortified. Lena lay totally exposed before him, her left hand wet from contact with her vagina, her right hand, her stomach wet, drenched with Jesse's warm semen.

Jesse's initial reaction was that of shame, failure. That feeling was quickly changing to anger. His image as the all-powerful, always in control southern aristocratic slave master, had been shattered. This black, thick lipped wench had witnessed, and in his mind, caused his humiliation.

Jesse balled his hands into fists. He was about to lash out when Lena, preempted his actions. Lena, still holding Jesse's semi-erect penis, slide to her knees. She wrapped her voluptuous lips around his rapidly deflating organ. Jesse's fingers unfurled. His hands were no longer fists. Instead his hands dug into Lena's nappy, woolly, hair.

Jesse's rage, instantly dissipated. His shame was transformed into wonder. Lena's voluptuous lips were caressing his flaccid flesh in ways that he could never have imagined. Whether due to his youth and vigor, or to his state of downright "hornyness", or due to the exquisite suction, the warmth, of Lena's mouth, Jessie's organ had regained its' vitality. To his amazement and delight, Jesse was again as hard as a rock.

Reluctantly, Jesse withdrew his penis from Lena's moist, succulent, mouth. Lena once again stretched out on the bed. She reached for Jesse, grasped his rock-hard member in her hand, and introduced his eager throbbing penis, to the inviting warmth of her moist, welcoming, vagina.

Lena wrapped her legs around Jesse's back, and raised her hips in synch, with Jesse's inexperienced, rapid, thrusts. She moaned; *"ah, ah, massa, dat feel sooo good. My titties, plees massa, plees suck my titties"*. Jesse eagerly, did as requested.

While a part of Lena's mind was definitely enraptured, experiencing the throes of genuine, real passion, that pragmatic part of her mind that had been keenly honed, through decades of slavery towards survival, was definitely functioning. She remembered her mother's earlier comments; *"Ifn he nocs yu up, prety lil brown baby ain gonna hurt dis fmbly none...we be on da way up"*.

Lena was determined to do everything that she possibly could, to ensure that this *"good lovin"*, with Massa Jesse, was much more than a onetime thing.

Lena had to slow Massa Jesse down. She realized that at the rapid rate that he was plunging in and out of her, and his ragged, heavy breathing, Jesse would climax within seconds.

There were several reasons why Lena did not want that to occur. First and foremost, she wanted to make this — his first time, she was sure — an unforgettable experience.

Thus, hopefully forging a lasting relationship, with the future Master of Rosewood, that would be beneficial to her and to her family. Her second reason, was purely selfish, she was thoroughly aroused, and definitely, not ready to come, and have Massa Jesse, go.

It was long after midnight, well into the early morning. Mattie, was asleep on the corn shuck pallet that she and Ruth had, placed on the floor.

She stirred being awakened from a fitful sleep, by a soft persistent tapping on the cabin's door. Mattie scrambled to open the door.

Lena was standing on the porch. The sun was trying to rise in the pre-dawn eastern sky. Lena, a broad smile on her face, took Mattie's hand and said; *"les go hom mama"*.
****

As Eleanor prepared to start Monday morning's class, she could not help but notice Jesse's cheerful, ebullient, expression. Before she could say a word, Jesse blurted out in a horrible impersonation of an Irish brogue; "Top of the morning to you lasses, ah tis indeed a beautiful morning, a bonnie, bonnie day.

Eleanor, gave Rebecca a quizzical glance, she arched her eyebrow and smiled, "Well Jesse, you're certainly in a festive mood this morning. Anything that you would like share with me and with your sister?"

Jessie responded by stating that; "the cotton's in bloom, the sun is shining, God's in his heaven, and all's right with the world." Eleanor was amused; "Well at the risk of spoiling your effusive mood, I'm compelled to make a small correction to your earlier Irish greeting. "Bonnie" is an adjective used mostly by the Scotch, not by the Irish."

Jesse hugged his sister, lifting her completely off of the floor. He spun her around and exclaimed; "Irish, Scottish, French, whatever. I repeat, tis indeed a bonnie, bonnie, day". He returned Rebecca to the floor, and without another word, seated himself at his desk. Rebecca, stood staring perplexed and flabbergasted, facing her brother. "Jesse, what's come over you, what's gotten into you?" Jesse smirked, and fleetingly thought to himself, wrong question Sis, the right question would be who have I gotten into! Lena! Lena! Lena!

Instead of giving voice to his feelings, Jesse decided that he had said enough. He grinned and opened the thick textbook on his desk, "The Collected Works of William Shakespeare".

Eleanor stepped behind her desk. "Okay young lady and gentleman, let us get started. Jesse, don't let the size of the textbook intimidate you, we won't be studying the entire book. As you recall, our first venture into the works of Shakespeare, was the reading of the romantic tragedy, Romeo and Juliet.

Today we read, yet another Shakespearean Romantic Tragedy, Othello.

****

October 4, 1858 (Monday)

Today for me, was a watershed day. The inclusion of Shakespeare's Othello, into the curriculum of southern education, can be fraught with real political, and physical danger.

That I was treading on thin ice, became immediately apparent, when I answered Jesse's innocent question; "Miss Leary, what's a Moor?"

When I explained that Moors are a group of people from Northern Africa. I went on to state that during an earlier period in history, the Moor's conquered, and ruled vast portions of Spain. I than added that Moors happened to be black.

Jesse's response was complete and utter disbelief. This morning's happy jocular Jesse had vanished, to be replaced by a stunned, suddenly vitriolic, prejudiced Southern white man, adamant, in his complete denial, refusing to believe that an army of black men, had once defeated and conquered white men, even Spanish white men.

As we begin to read the play, Jesse' demeanor went from disbelief, to anger. Disbelief when it was revealed that the heroic main character — this black man, Othello — was the main character in this English Literature Classic, was the commanding general of the white, Venetian Army.

Jesse's demeanor turned to murderous anger, when it became clear that this black man, this military genius, was married to a beautiful, aristocratic, white woman.

It was at that point that Jesse shouted at the top of his lungs; "This is bull-shit!" slammed his book shut, turned his desk over, and stalked out of the room.

Both Eleanor and Rebecca were alarmed and shocked by Jesse's reaction. Eleanor closed her book she looked apologetically at Rebecca, and murmured in a hushed voice;

"I think that it's best that we cancel today's class. Please read Acts I & II of Othello. We will resume tomorrow.

We will dissect and discuss Acts I & II, tomorrow. Hopefully, Jesse will return to class tomorrow, in a better mood." Eleanor picked up her books and left the room.

****

Jesse stormed from the house. He went straight to the stable, and shouted; "Pee wee, were the hell are you…you lazy trifling, no count nigger. Pee wee!

Pee wee, who had been baling hay in the rear of the stable, came running from the rear stall, pitchfork in hand, *"Yessah massa Jesse, Ise here…can I help yu suh?"* Jesse snarled and spit out; "Where the hell were you…get my horse ready…move it boy, move your lazy black ass!"

Pee wee hurried to saddle the young Massa's horse. Pee wee was confused. *"Sumpin reely bothen Massa Jesse… it not lik da youn Massa ta be mad an mean fo no reason."*

Young Massa Jesse, had a reputation among the slaves of being stern, but fair. He didn't hesitate to use the whip in the fields, but when he did it was usually because *"one ah dem field-hand niggers was slacking off, and deserv' ta be "touched-up" a little wid da lash."*

Jesse leapt into the saddle; he savagely kicked his favorite horse in the ribs. The stallion responded by bolting from the stable, running as fast as his four legs would carry horse and rider, destiny unknown.

****

After racing blindly through the woods, for about five minutes, Jesse reigned in the frantic, panting, horse. He dismounted in a clearing resplendent with sweet, lush tall grass. He then tied the horse to a shrub bush.

Jesse sat down in the grass. He was confused. His mind was racing. How could this be? A respected, a revered, world renowned literary classic, Shakespeare's Othello, whose plot revolved around the marriage of a black man, with a white woman.

Jesse had been brought up in a society that pandered to, that celebrated, promoted, and worshipped the pristine, pure goddess-like image, of the white woman. His mother, his grandmothers, even his little sister Rebecca, to him served as examples, which underscored, and further strengthened this glorified image of the pure white woman.

When Jesse was a boy of ten, he vividly remembered, a two-month visit, from Luis Frazier, Esq., his father's lawyer, and Luis' twelve-year-old nephew, Thomas.

Jesse and Thomas, as are most adolescent boys the world over, were obsessed, curious about sex. The boys had had many a heated discussion, as to where babies came from.

Jesse would never forget the fierce, nose - bled rendering, fistfight between himself and Thomas. Thomas had insisted that; "to make a baby, the man had to stick is dick into the woman's pussy". At first, Jesse had no problem accepting that youthful "pearl of wisdom".

Where Jesse took offense, was Tom's insistence that his beloved, mother Margaret, was regularly spreading her thighs, and she was doing the "nasty", being screwed, by his father, Henry.

Jesse would not for an instant entertain, the thought of his beloved mother, his paragon of Southern gentility, would participate in such "nasty" behavior. Jesse, valiantly defending his mother's virtue, inflicted and received a bloody nose, while losing a friend.

****

Jesse's recent initiation into the glorious world of sex, only served to solidify his ideals, and his values. To Jesse, the time that he and Lena were apart was interminable. Jesse counted the minutes until he and Lena would again be together.

He truly loved the "nasty" things that Lena did when they were making love. He loved the way that she bathed his entire body with hot kisses. He shivered at the memory of how she kissed and sucked his rock-hard penis until he exploded, into her mouth, in the throes of sublime ecstasy.

He loved the way that Lena so lovingly kissed and sucked his depleted testicles and his shriveled soft penis, until it once again became his rock-hard lance. Jesse's pulse quickened, his heart raced, when he thought of the way, that Lena guided him into the all encompassing, exquisitely, wet warmth of her succulent vagina.

While these amorous sexual activities performed by Lena, a black female slave was to Jesse, perfectly natural and acceptable, the thought of a white woman, performing these "nasty" acts on a black man, married to him or not, was unthinkable, outrageous, a crime against God and the universe.

When Jesse's fertile, active, imagination pictured the black man Othello, being made love to by his white wife Desdemona, the image that his imagination presented, was to Jesse, vile, filthy, and abhorrent behavior.

After all, black men, black bucks as they were called, were thought of as animals, as beasts.

By extrapolation, a white woman, whether she was married or not to a black man, performing these sexual acts, with a black man, was to Jesse, and to all white Southern men, vile, disgusting, amoral, unthinkable, ungodly bestiality.

The way that Lena made him feel when they were making love was sublime. However, the thought of his mother or sister, performing the same sexual acts on other men, would actually make Jesse, nauseous, physically ill.

Jesse struggled to reconcile his upbringing, with this foreign world that Miss Leary had exposed him to. A world that recognized a black man as an equal to white men, a world where a black man could actually command and lead white men.

To him, the ultimate unthinkable circumstance was that there existed a world that accepted the union of a black man marrying and being the husband of a white woman.

He was forced to fall back on that tried and true Southern bromide; Yankees are Northern racial agitators; whose sole purpose is to destroy the South. They would stoop to anything, to destroy southern values and the Southern way of life.

Their teacher Miss Leary was from up North. Miss Leary was therefore a Yankee. The Yankees sole purpose is to destroy the South.

Jesse lifted himself from the grass. He walked over to his horse, which was contentedly grazing on the tall sweet grass. Jesse swung into the saddle, and gently nudged the horse back towards the "Big House".

Jesse had come to the conclusion that that Yankee, Miss Eleanor Leary should be watched, and watched very carefully. He was now convinced, that she was up to no good.

****

During the week, in their time alone together, Rebecca told Mandy of Jesse's hostile, truculent, response to their studying Shakespeare's Othello. She told of Jesse's blatant, growing obvious suspicions, and distrust of Miss Leary.

On Saturday, Eleanor, Rebecca, and Mandy, as usual gathered in their "classroom", the meadow beside the creek. Rebecca abruptly, stood to speak; "Miss Leary, both Mandy and I love Shakespeare. After all, what girl wouldn't be enthralled to have experienced, through reading, the love between Romeo and his Juliet."

"Jesse, I suppose because he is a boy, Jesse was not as taken with "that old "mushy play", his words, "Romeo and Juliet", as was I, and as unbeknownst to him, was Mandy."

"When we were reading that "mushy" play, Jesse and I would talk about our reaction to the passages. Jesse's reaction to the tragic deaths of Romeo and Juliet, was that he thought that their committing suicide, was stupid. Other than that, Jesse was mostly bored with the play. He characterized the play, Romeo and Juliet, as mushy, stupid, and full of nonsensical language".

Eleanor and Mandy had sat motionless, listening to Rebecca. Occasionally, Eleanor and Mandy smiled as Becky's description of Jesse's assessment of Shakespeare's Classic. Eleanor folded her hands in her lap, and encouraged Rebecca to please continue; "What has been Jesse's response to our reading of Othello?"

Rebecca's expression changed. Her face took on a look of genuine concern. "Jesse is offended by "Othello". He says that the play is malicious fiction. Yankee Abolitionist propaganda. Jesse insists that the premise of the play, a black military general, commanding white troops, is unbelievably absurd."

"Yesterday, after class, Jesse, without knocking, stormed into my bedroom. He held his copy of the play in his hand, his face was flushed. A vein in the middle of his forehead was pulsating."

"My first reaction to his unannounced intrusion into my room was anger. Then after seeing the degree of his agitated state, my initial anger was rapidly replaced with concern."

"I asked Jesse what was wrong. Was he ill? He flung his Othello textbook onto my bed and shouted; "Becky have you read the end of this...this abomination?" "I admitted that I hadn't. I said that I was waiting to read the final scenes of the play in class with Miss Leary."

****

"Jesse, fuming with anger, ripped a page from the book and shouted; "that black nigger bastard, Othello kills his white wife. That nigger kills a white woman!" Before I could say a word, he turned and stormed out of the room."

Rebecca was looking directly at Eleanor; "Miss Leary, I'm afraid that Jesse is going to tell Papa."

Eleanor was flustered, she felt a momentary pang of fear, she stammered; "What will he tell your father? That I am teaching his children English Literature, the Classics? She said in a somewhat shaky voice, Rebecca dear, I think you're overreacting."

For the first time, Mandy spoke. "Believe me Miss Leary, Rebecca is not overreacting. If Master Henry, or for that matter any white man in the South, knew that you had a book that told of a black man being married to a white woman, and then that black man kills the white woman, any white woman, you would be in serious trouble."

Eleanor, was not naive, still she reasoned; "I'm sure that once I explain to Mr. Billings that Shakespeare's Othello is a play that points out that lies, and evil jealous ambition, can led to ultimate tragedy. Tragedy that destroys a noble, General, his innocent wife, and the very perpetrator of the scheme."

Mr. Billings will surely appreciate the invaluable statement that Shakespeare makes about the human condition."

Mandy and Rebecca perplexed, looked at each other, then at Miss Leary. Mandy spoke first, "with all due respect Miss Leary, what Master Henry and any Southern white man will appreciate, or more accurately NOT appreciate, is a black nigger man, being married to a white woman."

At that moment, Jesse was standing, undetected, behind the very tree that Eleanor, had four weeks ago, once stood behind. He witnessed and heard that morning's entire exchange between the three young women.

****

October 9, 1858 (Saturday)

Eleanor's Journal:

I found Rebecca's recounting of Jesse's violent reaction, following his having read the final scenes, the ending of Othello, was upsetting and truly perplexing. Instead of outrage at Othello's killing of his innocent wife, Jesse' rage was fixated upon Othello and Desdemona's marriage.

I thought Mandy's opinion as to the "Master's" reaction, to be serious, quite curious and illuminating. Mandy stated assuredly and with conviction, that to the "Master", Mr. Billings, the most objectionable, criminal aspect in the play "Othello", to Mr. Billings, would not be Othello's killing of his wife Desdemona, the most egregious offence committed by Othello, was his, a the black man, marrying Desdemona, a white woman.

I have always felt that in addition to the obvious economic reasons for the existence and the support of slavery in the South, there existed an underlying deep-rooted racial prejudice. A prejudice based in large part, on the Southern white man's absolute taboo, his sexual obsession, which forbids sexual activity between black men, and white women.

Interestingly enough, when we lived on the frontier, I found similar, albeit far less intense, prejudicial attitudes of white men, towards the mating of Indian men, with white women.

In either society, the slave holding South, or the western frontier, the mating of white men with "Injun squaws", and white men with "black wenches", though frowned upon in polite society, was not looked upon as a sinful abomination.

If Jesse decides to bring to Mr. Billings' attention, the fact that we have been reading Shakespeare's Othello, I must be prepared to explain and justify my choice of that particular classic.

****

Monday morning, at 9:30 AM, Eleanor sat at her desk awaiting the arrival of her students. Class usually began at 9:00 AM. While it was not unusual for Jesse to saunter in 10 minutes, an on occasion, as much as a half an hour late, Rebecca was never late for class.

Eleanor was growing more apprehensive with each passing moment. At 9:35, Eleanor, who had been steadily scribbling notes on a pad, in response to a gentle, but insistent knocking on the open door, looked up.

Rufus, the "Big House" Butler, stood in the open doorway; *"cuse me Miss Leery, Massa Henry ast me ta fetch yu…he in his offis waitin' fo yu."*

"Thank you, Rufus. Please inform Mister Henry that I will be there momentarily."

****

Eleanor walked the short distance that separated Henry Billing's office, from the "Big House".

Eleanor stood in front of Henry's closed door. She nervously patted her hair to ensure that there were no loose strands. She ran both hands down the bodice of her dress, smoothing out the wrinkles. Eleanor took a deep breath, and then firmly knocked on the closed door.

****

Henry seated behind his desk, bellowed, "Enter". Eleanor walked into the spartanly furnished room. She stood rigidly, three feet in front of the desk of her employer, Henry Billings, the Master of Rosewood.

Henry did not greet her, nor did he invite her to sit. Henry was rolling an unlit cigar between his thumb and forefinger. "Miss Leary, I assume you know why I've sent for you."

Eleanor stood her ground. She was now more then ever, certain that she did indeed know why she was here, standing before this despotic, intolerant, bigot.

Henry's lack of civility, his not having invited her to be seated, his failure to extend simple, basic courtesy, convinced Eleanor that she was indeed, about to be dismissed.

"Yes Mr. Billings, I believe I do know why I have been summarily summoned. Before, we go any further, I would like to say a few words." Henry sat back in his chair, and motioned with his cigar, for her to proceed.

"Yesterday, in the meadow, following my teaching session with Rebecca and Mandy, when I went back to the clearing to retrieve my scarf, I saw Jesse departing the area.

Jesse was apparently behind a tree from which he could easily observe and hear, what the three of us were discussing. Since most of our discussion was about Jesse's feelings, his discomfort with "Othello", the play that Rebecca, Jesse, Mandy, and I are currently reading, I believe is your reason for sending for me."

Henry grabbed his cane, and struggled to his feet; "Forgive my manners Madame, please by all means, be seated." Eleanor sat in one of the two chairs, facing Henry's desk.

Henry limped from behind his desk. He stood facing Eleanor, and then he sat on the edge of his desk. "Miss Leary, your assumption is partially correct. Jesse did bring to my attention that you were subjecting him, and Rebecca to pornographic, bestiality, in the guise of, what did he say you called it...an Old English Elizabethan Classic."

Eleanor stammered; "pornography, bestiality, sir I am deeply offended, and take umbrage to that affront to my integrity. I would never, under any circumstance, expose my students to that kind of filth."

Henry leaned his cane against the desk; "Miss Leary have you, or have you not, exposed my children to "Othello", a play written by William Shakespeare?"

Eleanor nodded and softly but firmly, replied; "Yes sir I have include that classic play as a component of our curriculum, but I assure you..." Henry interrupted; "and is this so-called classic play "Othello", a tale about the marriage between a black man and a white woman, which by definition would have resulted in the unthinkable, the commission of two heinous felonies, the breaking of two sacred laws. Laws against man and God, laws banning, the pornographic acts of Miscegenation, and Bestiality."

Eleanor sat stunned, bestiality, what was he talking about. Before she could ask, Henry resumed speaking; "Miss Leary, when Jesse brought this to my attention, the reading of this Othello play, and its' blatant Miscegenation, after my initial reaction of outrage, I calmed down, and was inclined to give you the benefit of the doubt".

"After all you are a Yankee. A foreigner not accustomed to our ways here in the South. It was my intent today, to discuss my displeasure with your selection of reading material, demand that you stop, and presuming that you agreed, wish you a pleasant good morning."

Henry lifted his cane from the floor; he pointed the cane directly at Eleanor; "Now, young lady, and I use the term lady with definite reservation, after hearing from you, this very morning, hearing that you are teaching one of my slaves, that you have brazenly, purposefully, and knowingly, broken one of our fundamental laws, a law, which serves as one of the pillars, that supports the South's economic survival and way of life".

"That you have taught, and as of yesterday, you continue to teach, one of my slaves to read and write. You have not only broken the law of the state of Virginia, you have consciously, and knowingly betrayed my trust."

Henry lowered his cane, limped to and seated himself in his chair behind the desk. "Miss Leary, your services here at Rosewood are terminated. You are to immediately pack your belongings. I will make arrangements for my stable boy Pee wee, to drive you to town in the morning. You are dismissed. Good day, and good bye Madame."

After Eleanor, in tears left his office, though it was barely 10 AM, he poured himself a double shot of bourbon. He gulped down the fiery liquid and shuddered.

Henry, at the top of his lungs, bellowed; "Rufus, Rufus, get your lazy ass here, and I mean right now!" Rufus hurried into the room. *"Yassah Massa Henry, Ise here."* Henry rose from his chair, he pointed his unlit cigar at Rufus; "I want you to find Mistress Margaret, and ask her to join me, here in the office. Tell her that it's an urgent matter. Right now, Rufus!"

Rufus hurried, as fast as his arthritic knees would allow, to Mistress Margaret's chambers. Peggy was with her maid Ruth. She was being fitted for a new evening gown.

Rufus knocked on the door. Without waiting for a response, he burst into room. Ruth jumped up from her knees, where she had been busily pining the hem of Peggy's gown;

"Rufus — nigger is yu done loss yu dum, fool, mine? What fo yu bargin' in Miz Margret rooms?"

Peggy stepped around Ruth, she motioned for Rufus to approach; "What is it Rufus?" Rufus responded; *"Scuse me Mistress, but da Massa send me ta fetch yu. He powerful mad bout stomping. He say pleas, com ta da office, rite away."*

Peggy's face revealed her concern. It was not like Henry to "send" for her. And it certainly was not like old Rufus, to burst into her rooms, without having been given permission to enter.

She quickly regained her composure; "Rufus, please tell Master Henry that I will join him momentarily."

Rufus and Ruth stood behind the Office's closed doors. The Master and the Mistress were inside. Ruth looked at Rufus, with a slight tremor in her voice she asked; *"Rufus wat's goin' on? Wat's wrong?"* Rufus put his finger to his lips, and his ear to the closed door. He whispered; *"don know. Ise thinks it bout dat Yankee teecha."*

****

When Peggy entered his office, she found her husband, smoking a cigar, while sipping on a glass of whiskey. The cigar was not unusual, however the drinking of strong spirits, at ten o'clock in the morning, was highly unusual.

Peggy seated herself in one of the two seats in front of Henry's desk. Peggy, as calmly as she could spoke; "Henry, what's wrong? Why on earth did you send poor old Rufus, with such haste, and urgency for me? When he barged into my rooms, I thought that either the house was on fire, or that war had been declared."

Henry, his head enveloped in a cloud of cigar smoke, sat on the edge of his chair. "My dear, I apologize for the manner in which I requested that you join me."

"This morning, after breakfast, I told Jesse and Rebecca, not to attend class this morning. The reason that I gave was true enough. I told them that I wished to discuss, with Miss Leary, the curriculum that was being taught to our children.

It was during the course of that discussion, that I learned that that Irish-Yankee bitch, had been and was continuing to teach a SLAVE, Mandy, to read and write."

"I dismissed her. She was instructed to pack and to leave Rosewood tomorrow morning. Pee wee will drive her to town in the morning."

Peggy sat transfixed. "Henry what in the world are you talking about?"

172

Henry told in detail of this morning's meeting with Eleanor. He made it clear that it was never his intent to fire Miss Leary.

As he had explained to Jesse, who had brought to his attention that they were reading "Othello", she very well might have been ignorant of Southern standards, when she chose to include that "Miscegenation, nigger loving play", as English Literature."

"It was when she confessed to teaching a slave to read and write, when she blatantly, broke Southern law, that's when I made the decision, right then and there, to discharge her."

****

Ruth was having trouble hearing the conversation between the Master and Mistress. Ruth was tugging on Rufus' shirt; *"What dat day sayin' Rufus...what dis mess all about?"*

Rufus stepped back from the door. His black face was ashen. He looked directly at Ruth. Ruth saw the frightened look in the old man's eyes. Her hand came up to cover her mouth.

She began to plead; *"Oh lawd, Rufus what done happen?"* Rufus, in a trembling, subdued voice, began to speak; *"Ruthy we gots big troubles. Seems dat Yankee-teecha done went and teech yor Mandy ta reed an rite."*

Ruth felt light-headed, she felt faint. Her legs began to buckle. She leaned against Rufus for support. She started to weep, she wiped at her eyes; *"Lawd Jeeesus, pleese help us."* Without another word, she turned from the door and ran to the "Big House".

****

Peggy heard the muffled sounds outside the door. She rose from her chair and walked over, and opened the door. Rufus was standing next to the door. Peggy instructed Rufus to find Miss Rebecca, and to tell her that her father wants her to come — immediately — to his office.

Rufus hurried to the kitchen. He asked Fannie, the "Big House" cook, and her staff if they knew where he could find Miss Rebecca. Fannie informed him that since there was no school today; *"rite afta brekfas, dem two run outta here t'wards da creek."*

Rufus sent one of the young house slaves to the stable, with instructions to have Pee wee send his helper to the creek, with instructions to have Miss Rebecca come right away to the Master's office.

Having done what Mistress Margaret had asked of him, Rufus returned to his listening spot outside of Master Henry's Office.

****

Eleanor, after leaving Mr. Billings' office, went directly to the little classroom. Tears of rage and frustration were streaming down her face.

She began to gather her belongings. She stopped and slumped into the chair at the desk. Eleanor balled both hands into fists, and pounded them on the desk.

Her mind was in turmoil; she felt that she had betrayed Mandy and Rebecca. Eleanor's eyes fondly surveyed the little classroom. She picked up her book bag, and left.

In her room with the door closed, Eleanor gave vent to her emotions. Tears welled up and overflowed from her pale blue eyes. She slammed her small fist onto the soft yielding bed. Eleanor hastily and resolutely wiped the tears from her eyes.

She reached into her nightstand and removed her journal. She opened the book and began to write, the words spilling forth in anguished torrents:

October 9, 1860 (Saturday)

How could I have been so stupid! Today inadvertently, I informed Henry Billing's Master of Rosewood, that one of his slaves had committed, the dastardly crime of literacy.

Today as I sat in the classroom, awaiting the arrival of Rebecca and Jesse, I knew that something was wrong. All of the signs, the clues that something was amiss were there right in front of my eyes. Jesse's reaction to our reading, and discussing "Othello", Rebecca being so very late for class, were definitely obvious clues.

My discovery yesterday that Jesse had been "spying" on us, as I taught Rebecca and Mandy, screamed of danger. My arrogant assumption, that Jesse's deep-seated Southern prejudices, would result in his disclosing to his father the fact that Mandy was literate.

Why didn't he tell his father? Could it be because he knew that knowledge of Mandy's literacy would ultimately result in her separation from Rebecca, separation that would devastate both girls?

Perhaps it was because he knew of the ramifications, that in accordance with Southern law Mandy would surely be punished for the commission of the crime of slave literacy. After all Mandy as his sister's lifetime playmate and companion, had played an integral part in his own childhood.

174

I feel so very guilty that I did not warn the girls, told them that Jesse had witnessed our last session at the creek.

Well, perhaps for me, it's for the best. I have learned a great deal about the South and its' piteous, feeble attempts to justify, and to preserve Slavery.

Even here, on the plantation, secessionist talk is rampant. At the dinner table, the angst against Mr. Lincoln is a frequent topic of conversation.

As a Northerner, I am having been often asked of my opinion of Mr. Lincoln. As an observer, and a chronicler of Southern culture, I had made the conscience decision, not to put forth an opinion.

If Mr. Lincoln is elected president, I fear that there exists a real possibility that the South might actually secede from the union. Mr. Lincoln has made it absolutely crystal clear of his intent to preserve the Union.

In the event of, God forbid, a Civil War, I wish to be home, far north of the Mason and Dixon Line. If there is war, I most assuredly do not want to be residing in the South.

I will miss Rebecca and Mandy, the two of whom act like, and I believe are truly, in every sense of the word, sisters. They are indeed two of the most engaging and intelligent students that I have had the privilege, and the honor to teach.

My hopes and my prayers, for their future, will always be with them.

My time here at Rosewood, is at an end.

****

Rebecca and Mandy were seated on the grass, facing each other, holding hands. They were engaged in frantic conversation. Mandy was agitated and clearly frightened. "Why do you think that today's classes were suspended...do you think that Jesse complained to Master Henry, that Miss Leary had you and Jesse reading "Othello"? Rebecca squeezed Mandy's hands; "I think so. I can't think of any other reason for daddy to have canceled today's class.

Leroy, Pee wee's helper, came running through the meadow, breathing heavily, while shouting; *"Miz Becca, Miz Becca, where is yu?"* Rebecca and Mandy disengaged their hands, and hurriedly stood. Rebecca stood erect, Mandy stood behind Rebecca, head bowed.

Leroy ran into the clearing, gasping for breath; *"Miz Becca, Massa Henry wont's yu, rite away. "Rufus say Massa be awful mad."*

Rebecca, following Leroy, followed by Mandy, hurried to Henry's office.
****

Peggy had finally weaned Henry away from his early morning libation of a "neat" bourbon. Rufus had substituted a pitcher of chilled water, and discreetly, following Peggy's whispered instructions, removed the crystal, bourbon decanter, from which Henry had been gulping.

Henry was seated at his desk, Peggy in one of the chairs facing the desk. Peggy's reaction to Miss Leary's dismissal, and the circumstances that precipitated Henry's action, was mixed.

As a product of the Southern culture, she absolutely understood the implication of slaves knowing how to read and write. This was especially true during these politically turbulent times. She was well aware of the fact that the South was being flooded with, what she thought of and considered, malignant, seditious, abolitionist propaganda.

Intellectually, Peggy knew that it was absolutely imperative for the South's, for her family's economic survival, and for the survival and the spread of slavery, that those being enslaved, not be influenced and corrupted by this scurrilous, vile Yankee, garbage.

After all, the Nat Turner Slave uprising, where hundreds of white men, women, and children were killed, slaughtered, by rampaging slaves, savages, was by no means, ancient history. She agreed with her husband, drastic action had to be taken.

The most obvious action that the Master would usually take under these circumstances would be the inflicting of severe punishment, on the slave, and his family, who had broken the law. They must punish the slave that had acquired the ability to read and write.

Yet, as a mother she was fully aware of the special bond that had been forged, over the years, between her beloved daughter Rebecca, and Rebecca's enslaved, mulatto half-sister, Mandy.

Peggy had long been aware of Henry's dalliances with her lady's maid, Ruth. When Rebecca and Mandy were babies, she on occasion, suspected that Henry might be Mandy's biological father. As the girls grew, so had Peggy's suspicions.

The fact was that on most plantations, there was usually a fraction of the slave population that strongly resembled the male members of the white ruling families. In Southern society, these unspoken occurrences were universally known, universally accepted, and never admitted.

Paternity, conversely, was also almost always universally, never, ever, ever, acknowledged. When ladies and gentlemen, visited a plantation, and had the opportunity to observe these unmistakable familial resemblances, they might wink, and/or behind closed doors, even share whispers.

Peggy was fully aware that the strong bond that existed between Rebecca and Mandy was in large part, her fault. She was not oblivious to the signs that over the years screamed to her, that the two girls were much, too close.

She realized, as Rebecca's mother, that to sell Mandy, which was the routinely imposed remedy for this crime, would crush Rebecca. Yet she knew that if Henry wanted to impose this punishment, she would support his decision. It was the right thing to do. She rationalized; "Rebecca will in time, get over it".

Rebecca softly knocked on the door of her father's office. Peggy whispered to her husband; "Henry, control your temper — this is our little girl you're talking to".

Henry bellowed; "you girls come in here, right now". Rebecca, followed by Mandy entered the room. Rebecca walked directly to the vacant chair next her mother. Without uttering a word, she sat. Mandy stood, slumped in the corner.

Henry remained silent. His steely blue eyes appeared to be boring into Rebecca's very soul. Henry spoke; "I will get straight to the point, Rebecca, did Miss Leary teach Mandy to read and write?"

Rebecca's initial thought was that he called me Rebecca, not Becky; Papa never does that, unless he is really angry with me.

Both her father and her mother were staring at her. Henry broke the silence, "Did you here me young lady? Did Miss Leary teach Mandy to read and write?"

Rebecca raised her head in defiance, and in a clear resonant tone declared; "No father, Miss Leary did not teach Mandy to read and write".

Henry and Peggy were stunned. They sat in silence, shocked surprise. As far as they knew, Rebecca was entirely trustworthy and forth coming, they had never known her to deliberately lie to them.

Henry was frustrated and confused; "Rebecca, this morning I terminated the employment of Miss Leary, because I was led to believe that she had taught Mandy to read and write. Miss Leary did not deny the accusation." I will ask you once again, did Miss Leary teach Mandy to read and write?

"No father, Miss Leary did not teach Mandy to read and write. I taught Mandy to read and to write."

Henry, at a loss for words, sat back in his chair. Now he was completely confused. He quickly recovered; "This morning when I confronted Miss Leary, she confessed to me that she had been teaching, Rebecca, Jesse, and Mandy some Yankee play "Othello"."

"Yes Papa, that's true. She has been teaching us, including Mandy, Shakespeare's "Othello". However, I — and unbeknownst to him Jesse — have been teaching Mandy to read and to write, since we were five or six years old".

"I used the same teaching aides that Mommy used to teach me. Jesse helped, when he read to with me and to Mandy, his vast collection of Dime Novels. Miss Leary and I both agree that Mandy is an excellent, an exceptional, student."

Both Henry and Peggy were momentarily speechless. Peggy was the first to speak; "Becky are you saying that you alone, except with the inadvertent, unintentional assistance of Jesse, were able to teach Mandy to read and write at a level that she could read and interpret Shakespeare's plays?"

Rebecca smiled, beaming with pride, replied; "Yes mother I did, and Mandy most assuredly can". Mandy had not moved. She stood mute and silent, slumped over in the corner.

Henry reached for his whiskey decanter. His hand encountered the pitcher of chilled water. He grunted and poured himself a glass. Henry glanced at Peggy. "Honey do you want some?" Peggy shook her head, "No thank you." Henry replaced the pitcher of water on the desk. He did not offer a Rebecca a drink.

Henry slowly sipped his drink. While his wife and daughter sat silently, he began to shuffle, to look through a pile of papers, correspondence on his desk. He pulled out what appeared to be a handbill.

Henry read the circular, to himself, silently:

SLAVES For SALE

A Passel of Prime Niggers
Will Be Sold

Thursday 12 Noon

August 18, 1859

Steve's Livery Stables

1) Billy Age 35 (Carpenter & Brick Mason)
2)
3) Hanna Age 18 & Judy Age 16 (House Servants)
4)
5) Lou Age 30; Jim Age 34; Al Age 38 (Experienced Field Hands)

J.P. Johnston, Esq.

Essex County, Virginia

He looked up at Peggy, then his gaze shifted to Rebecca, with his and Rebecca's eyes locked, in an authoritative voice, he summoned Mandy; "Mandy, come over here...come here, right now girl".

Mandy, head bowed, slowly shuffled over, and stood silently, before the Master's desk. Henry spoke to all assembled, "You all know that we can't have no nigger that can read and write, on the place. It's against the law!"

Henry turned his full attention to Mandy. "Mandy, I want you to tell me the truth. Do you understand?" Mandy, looked up, tears streaming down her face; *"Yassah Massa Ise unerstan."*

Henry glanced at Peggy, then his gaze returned to the terrified, slave girl. "Can you read and write Mandy? Answer me girl...can you read and write?"

Mandy stood trembling before the Master. Between piteous gasps for air, head bowed, in a soft whisper, she answered; *"Yassah massa...Ise shonuff knows how ta read and rite."*

Henry looked up and exclaimed, to all in attendance, she's obviously lying. If she's so smart, so literate, and such an exceptional student, why does she still talk like, and sound like a dumb, ignorant, nigger"?

Before anyone could answer, Henry picked up the top sheet of paper, on the pile of papers, on his desk. He thrust the paper towards Mandy. "Mandy, I want you to read this piece of paper, and I want you to read it out loud."

Mandy began to read; "Slaves for sale", she hesitated, Henry made a twirling, rotating motion with his finger; "go on girl...continue." Mandy struggled to regain her composure.

She continued; "A passel of prime niggers will be sold...Thursday 12 Noon...Mandy's hand dropped to her side she began to violently tremble.

Rebecca leapt from her chair, "Stop it Papa, how could you be so cruel?" Peggy rose and leaned over her husband's desk; "Henry, how could you? Out of all of those papers on that desk, you had to pick a notice announcing the sale of slaves!?"

Peggy removed the paper from Mandy's hand. Henry slammed his fist on the desk. Rebecca, and Peggy were startled. Mandy was petrified. Henry shouted, "Damn its Rebecca, you know that it's against the law for a slave to know how to read. You could be arrested."

Peggy looked sternly at Henry. "Now Henry, let's not over react. Rebecca, go to your room, I'll be there shortly, we need to talk. Mandy you go home. Go to your mother's cabin. Do not leave the cabin until either Master Henry or I give you permission.

She looked from one girl to the other; "Under no circumstances are you two to talk to, to see each other. Do you both understand me?"

Rebecca, defiantly, without saying a word, whirled around and stomped out of the room. Mandy muttered *"Yessum Mistress, Ise shonuff unnerstans."*

****

After the girls had departed, Henry sat forward in his chair. An exasperated look of annoyance on his face; "Well it's finally happened, I've seen this coming, I've warned you for years, that no good would come from that bosom buddy relationship, that you fostered and encouraged, between our daughter, and that slave."

Henry took a deep breath and then continued his harangue; "I've been saying it for years now, you wouldn't listen, Mandy is Rebecca's slave, she is not her friend, not her pal, and certainly, under no circumstances, should Rebecca be Mandy's, which we both know is against the law, nor should, they be classmates."

Peggy, shocked and obviously irritated and hurt, exclaimed, "For God's sake Henry, I can't believe that you would throw that in my face. Not now! "You, more than anyone, know that there is, a special bond between our daughter Rebecca, and your bastard, slave daughter Mandy."

As soon as those words left her mouth, words spoken in the heat of the moment, Peggy was instantly overcome with regret. She knew that by giving voice, to what before where only her thoughts, she had broken the South's unwritten, unspoken, code of ethics.

Everyone knew of the common and the accepted practice, of white men, having sexual relations, either forced or consensual, with their female slaves. However, Southern Ladies, never spoke of, or acknowledged these activities. And under no circumstance, would a Southern Lady acknowledge the paternity of the many offspring that resulted from these common-place, "sexual dalliances".

Henry sat back, flustered, he was momentarily, speechless. He reached into his pants pocket and pulled out his handkerchief. Henry, with an unsteady hand, wiped his suddenly damp forehead.

Henry regained his composure, lowered his voice and in a controlled, artificially calm voice, asked; "Peggy, what did you say…did you say my bastard slave daughter? Woman, have you taken leave of your senses?"

Peggy's mind raced, okay that was a mistake, even though everything I said is absolutely true, I shouldn't have said it. That was a mistake. Well what's done is done.

"Henry, I'm truly sorry for that outburst. I apologize. What's important is what we do now." Henry was relieved; he welcomed Peggy's apology and the quick change in the tone of the conversation.

He leaned over his desk, reached for the pitcher of water, and began to fill his glass; "We have got to separate those two. Saturday, I'll place an advertisement in the Gazette, for the sale of Mandy, and her mother Ruth.

Peggy did not agree with Henry's proposed solution. However, she decided that for the moment, she would remain silent. She reasoned that this was definitely not the time to object.

Henry retrieved his cane, and began to rise; "It's time for us to have a serious talk with Rebecca".
****

Rebecca was lying across her bed. Henry knocked on her closed door. Rebecca sat up and softly, but firmly answered, "Come in". Peggy sat on the bed next to her daughter. She could see from looking at Rebecca's red-rimmed eyes, that she had been crying.

Henry, leaning on his cane, stood leaning on the closed door for support. Peggy gently tucked a stray lock of Rebecca's hair behind her ear. "Becky, you know that your father and I love you very much".

Rebecca looked pleadingly at her mother, then at her father.

Henry cleared his throat; "Becky what were you thinking? You know that to teach slaves to read and write is against the law. Hell honey, are you aware of that steady stream of Yankee abolitionist, propaganda tripe, that's been circulating? That trash has been flooding the county, calling for slaves to "rise up".

"Becky honey, if them niggers learned to read, every white man, white woman, and child, would be in danger of having their throats slit, while they slept."

  Becky, you know what we have to do, we have to sell Mandy." Rebecca sprang from the bed, she flung herself on the floor at her father's feet, and screeched hysterically; "No, no Papa, please don't sell Mandy! I'm so sorry, so, so sorry. Please Daddy, don't sell her, I'll be good, I'll do anything you say, oh…God please don't, please don't sell my Mandy!"

Henry, angrily bent over and lifted Rebecca to her feet, he held her by her shoulders, shook her violently, and viciously railed; "Rebecca! Get yourself together. What's come over you? Must I remind you …Mandy is my slave my property. She's broken the law, she's put us all, in danger, our way of life, is at stake."

Peggy went to comfort her daughter; Rebecca tore away from Henry's gripe, and sobbing uncontrollably, fell into her mother's arms. "Mother, oh mommy, please, please don't let him do this. This is all my fault; I made Mandy play school with me. Mandy's so much more than a slave, Mandy is my friend, my closest, my dearest friend. Mommy please, don't let him do this, do this to Mandy. Please mama don't let Daddy do this to me."

Peggy stroked her desolate daughter's hair. She gently lifted her chin and looked deeply into her forlorn eyes. She laid Rebecca's head on her shoulder and whispered in her ear, hush baby, I'll try honey, hush, hush baby, I'll try.

Peggy turned to Henry; "Let's let her calm down, get some rest." Henry turned to leave. As he was holding the door for Peggy, he spoke in a stern, steady voice, "Rebecca, I forbid you to see, to be alone with that slave, Mandy. Do you understand me?"

Rebecca lay moaning, on the bed. Peggy tugged the bedspread under Becky's chin. She kissed her brow, and turned towards her husband. Peggy gently, but firmly grasped his left elbow, and ushered Henry from the room.

****

Back in their bedroom, Henry sat down heavily on the bed. "What a mess. You know what we have to do. We've got to sell Mandy as soon as possible. Lord knows what will happen if the rest of the slaves find out that she can read. That we knew and did nothing!"

Henry's brow wrinkled, he exclaimed; "My god, what if she's not the only one? Has she and that Yankee abolitionist, Irish, slut, we welcomed into our home, subverted any other of our niggers?"

"Before we sell Mandy, by god, I'll have Lucas strip her naked, hoist her up in the barn and lay the cat, heavy on her back. I'll force all the niggers to watch. By god, that'll put an end to this nonsense!"

Peggy bristled, "Stop it Henry, just stop this nonsensical talk right now! You will not have Mandy whipped." She placed her hands over her husband's; "Sweetheart, I've been silent about this now for thirteen years. I've been silent because, heaven help us, here in the South, this behavior's common place."

"I know, that you know, that there is at least, a possibility, know let's be honest, that there is the probability, that you are Mandy's father." As Henry opened his mouth to protest, Peggy raised her hand in the universally recognized symbol; STOP.

"Very well Henry, if you object to my use of the word father, in deference to our Southern sensibilities, I'll rephrase. You knew that in all likelihood that you, and please forgive how crudely this is put, that you are Mandy's sire."

"Margaret Martin Billings, I refuse to continue this filthy, inappropriate, conversation." Peggy gave her husband a look of total exasperation; "Henry you know that I love you very much. And I know that that you love me, that you love our children. Together we've raised two wonderful, beautiful, highly intelligent, children, Jesse and Rebecca."

Henry sat on the bed, crestfallen, holding his head in his hands; Peggy went to him and gently took his hands in hers; "My darling, though we never speak of it, you are not Jesse's biologic father, and I honestly, truly believe, that to you, to me, it absolutely does not matter."

"Henry sweetheart, because you, you alone, and no one else, living or dead; you are Jesse's father. You raised him, you played with him, you taught him to ride, you were there to hug and comfort him when he fell from his pony, you read to him, you did all of the things for Jesse that makes a man a father. That Jesse is your son and heir is an undeniable fact".

"Just as I accept that, as fact, I also accept, the evidence seen by my own eyes. For the past thirteen years, watching Rebecca and Mandy grow, from infants, to young adult hood, I have seen, each and every day, physical and mental, similarities, between, Rebecca, Mandy, and yes, my love, and you."

"Henry, I've known for years, about your dalliances with Ruth. Oh, at first, I was hurt, resentful, and even jealous. It wasn't as if I hadn't been prepared."

"When I was a teenager, my mother sat me down to have "the talk". In addition to the birds and the bees, she told of the many "dalliances", to expect, between my future husband, presumably the Master of a fine plantation, and multiple female slaves."

"When it became obvious that, thank god, you appeared to be content with just one bed wench, — Henry looked at her with a look of genuinely surprise — and that one slave just so happened to be Ruth, well to put it bluntly, I was relieved."

"No Henry, I will not let you flog your daughter, Rebecca's sister." Henry, head in his hands, groaned; "what are we going to do. We can't have that slave, Mandy on the place."

Peggy once again, pulled Henry's hands from his face; "I agree, I think it best that we sell both Mandy and Ruth." Henry looked quizzically at his wife; "Ruth, Ruth can't read. Why do we have to sell Ruth?"

Peggy responded; "Ruth is a lady's maid, and a seamstress. She knows nothing else. More importantly, Ruth is Mandy's mother. After having sold her daughter, we could no longer trust Ruth."

****

Luis Frazier, the Billings lawyer and long-time friend of the family, arrived unannounced at Rosewood. Pee wee, the stable man, knocked on the Master's office door. Henry was seated at his desk. He was going over in his mind, the details of that morning's heated, emotional, conversation that he and Peggy had had with Rebecca.

He and Peggy had lain awake for most of the night, trying to construct the right words and the tone, to use when they informed Rebecca of their decision to sell both Mandy, and her mother, Ruth.

After proposing and rejecting several different approaches, that they had been considering, Henry had thrown up his hands, and had bluntly, and forcefully stated; "Let's just sit her down, and tell her. Rebecca's not a baby. She's thirteen, she'll soon be pursued by all of the eligible young men in the region. They'll be in line asking permission to come courting. It's time that she grows up, and acts responsibly."

Peggy, for several moments had remained silent. When she finally spoke, she had said resolutely; "Of course Henry…you're right".

Then in a wistful voice, Peggy had said; "Henry if she were sixty, instead of thirteen, with teen aged grandchildren of her own, and god willing I am still alive, she would still be my baby. She will always be my baby."

****

Henry's reverie was interrupted, by the steady, persistent, knocking on his office door. He brought his mind back to the present; "Come in."

Pee wee, hat in hand, stepped into the office; *"Scuse me massa. Mista Fraza here ta sees yu."*

Luis stepped into the office. He held two boxes, stuffed with documents, under each arm. Henry stared at his, anxious, obviously agitated, friend. "Pee wee, have Rufus fetch us some refreshments." Luis, what on earth brings you all the way out here? What troubling you?"

"Henry, old friend, the "fat's flying from the pan; getting into the fire". "The election of that abolitionist baboon, Lincoln is about to light the fuse of secession. Most of our friends and colleagues, including me, think that a by god, shooting war with the North, is eminent."

"Henry, I rushed here as your friend, and as your lawyer. As your friend, I know that if there is a war, if our beloved South splits from the North, your heart and your allegiance, like mine, will be with the South."

185

"As your lawyer, and your business manager, I have an ethical, and a fiduciary responsibility, to advise you as to your considerable, financial holdings. Holdings in the South, and far more importantly, your holdings up North."

Henry appeared to be confused. Before him, sat his oldest and dearest friend. Not only was he Henry's mentor, he was his best friend. No one knew the character of Henry Billings, better than did Luis Frazier.

Henry thought, if I'm hearing him correctly, he's asking if my loyalty to the South includes, risking my fortune, in its'defense.

"Luis, there are two reasons that I haven't knocked you flat on your ass, number one, because of this blasted dead leg, you'd be to fast for me to catch, and the second reason is that you're my best friend." "Had any other man asked or implied that question to me, I not only would not have answered, I would have, by god laid them out cold."

Henry gathered himself, thrust forward his chin, and proclaimed; "I don't want to sound melodramatic, but in the words of our founding fathers, to the Southern cause; "I Henry Billings, pledge my life, my fortune, and my sacred honor!"

Rufus entered the office. He was carrying a silver tray with a large pitcher of Lemonade, surrounded by an array of quarter cut, sandwiches. He placed the tray on the side table, and left the room.

Luis reached for a sandwich. "Henry, my friend, as your friend, I knew that that would be your response. But as you can appreciate, as your lawyer, it had to be said. Now that we've settled that, how do you want to proceed?"

Henry sat back in his seat, "What are my options...if war is declared, what would happen to my investments and holdings in the North?"

Luis placed his sandwich on the tray, he poured himself a glass of lemonade, Luis took a long gulp; "They could freeze your assets until the conclusion of the war; or they could confiscate your assets; or they can, and this is the most unlikely, scenario, they could allow you free, unfettered, access to your holdings, during the prosecution of the war."

"The safest course of action would be to divest. Withdraw all of your Northern holdings. Convert everything to gold. Find a secluded safe place in the woods, bury your treasure, and dig it up after the war."

"Having said that, and in line with your earlier eloquent, patriotic, statements, my advice is that you divest immediately, secure the funds.
Once that's accomplished, we can plan your future moves."

Henry nodded his agreement. He reached for the pitcher of lemonade, and began to pour himself a drink. "Luis, I'm especially glad that you dropped in this morning. When you arrived, I was preparing to send for Rebecca. I was about to tell her that I would be selling her slave Mandy, and Mandy's mother, Ruth."

Henry than proceeded to tell Luis of yesterday's events. He started with his firing of, "that Irish Yankee bitch". Luis interrupted, "that would explain my seeing your buggy, with Pee wee and Miss Leary, heading towards town. We passed each other this morning, moving in opposite directions."

"I can see why you chose not to turn that Yankee agitator, Miss Leary into the authorities. By her own admission, Rebecca is the person who taught the slave girl to read and to write. I wholeheartedly agree your chosen course of action. You need to get these two slaves, potential troublemakers, away from Rosewood as soon as possible".

Luis finished his first "min-sandwich", and reached for another, he took a long gulp of his lemonade, burped and returned his attention to Henry; "Two things Henry, with talk of war spreading like wildfire, the price of slaves is rapidly dropping. Don't expect to sell those two for what they would ordinarily be worth. Second, whoever purchases the slave girl, should be notified that she is literate. It's an issue in law, of product liability."

Henry pulled out his pocket watch, opened the lid, and looked at the time. He abruptly stood and excused himself, and left Luis alone in the office. Before leaving, Henry had hastily told Luis, that he and Peggy had instructed Rebecca, to not leave the house, until they had spoken to her. Henry assured Luis that he would return shortly, and that in his absence, he should make himself comfortable.

Henry decided to save time, by entering the house through the kitchen door. Fannie and Rufus were seated at the large kitchen table. Fannie was kneading a large slab of dough, every few seconds she would liberally sprinkle flour over the dough.

Rufus held a mug of coffee in his arthritic hands, and was gingerly sipping the steaming hot liquid. Before opening the door, Henry caught a snippet of their conversation.

Fannie was speaking; "*Wats goin' on old man, Ruth ain sayd a word dis moaning. She be a snifin' an cryn' all moanin*".

When Henry entered, both slaves immediately sprang to their feet. In his haste, Rufus splashed hot coffee on the table as well as on his hands. Other than the tightening of his jaw, and a quick grimace, one would not have suspected that he was in pain.

"*Massa Henry suh, can Ise help wid sumpin?*" Henry, limping badly, gave no indication that he had heard the question. Mid way through the large room, he stopped and turned. "Do either of you know were the Mistress is?"

Fannie shook her head and replied; "*Ise don't ritely knos Massa, I a left dis kitchen all Monin'.*" Rufus spoke; "*Mistress Peggy in da study Massa. Can Ise bring yu sumpin?*"

Henry turned and took three labored steps. He stopped and turned to the two slaves. "We' have a guest for lunch and dinner. Mr. Frasier will be spending the night". Henry turned his back to the slaves, and continued to hobble towards his study.

Peggy was sitting on the sofa, sipping coffee from a delicate china cup. When her husband entered, she leisurely carefully placed the cup onto its' matching saucer, then she carefully placed saucer and cup, onto the coffee table.

"Henry, what took you so long, it seems as if I've been sitting here for ages." Henry informed Peggy of Luis Frasier's unexpected visit. He told her that he had confided in Luis, and told him of yesterday's events. He told her that Luis, as their lawyer, ratified the actions that they had already taken, and was in agreement with their proposed solution, the selling of Mandy and Ruth.

Peggy listened attentively, without interrupting. When Henry's silence signaled that he had finished. Peggy spoke; "Please explain once more, why exactly, does Luis think that finding a buyer for Mandy and Ruth, might be difficult?"

Henry paused before responding. "Luis just reinforced what we already know. He said, and I paraphrase; "Teaching slaves to read and to write, has always been a heinous, seriously, grievous crime, in the South. Hell, right here in Virginia, just about a year ago, that lunatic John Brown tried to start a slave uprising."

Henry paused to give Peggy an opportunity digest his last statement. "That Madman attempted to give guns to our slaves, and encouraged them to murder us in our sleep. With all of this abolitionist poppycock, propaganda, nonsense flooding the South, in today's national political climate, the last thing that anyone wants, is slaves who can read, and spread around that vile trash."

Okay honey, it's time we talk to Rebecca".

Henry knocked twice on his daughter's bedroom door, before Rebecca could answer, Peggy speaking softly said; "Becky honey, it's mommy and daddy. May we come in?"

After a very brief silence, Rebecca opened the door. She returned to sit — fully clothed — on her bed. Peggy went to the bed and sat down. She placed her arms around her daughter; "Becky, your father and I spent most of the night, discussing this "Mandy Problem".

"Sweetheart we know how close you are to Mandy. To a large extent, I hold myself responsible for this dilemma. I know how lonely growing up alone, surrounded by scores of people, can be. Not having the companionship of someone your own age, and your gender, can be, to say the less, very disconcerting, and depressing."

"We should have never let this — I don't know exactly what to call it — this close relationship, between you and a slave, Mandy, have developed."

Henry, not wanting Peggy to be perceived of as the "mean parent", spoke up; "Rebecca we have to sell Mandy." Rebecca tore herself from her mother's arms, and sprang from the bed."

She screamed; "No, no, no, please daddy, she turned to look at Peggy, "please, please mommy, don't sell Mandy. Mandy's not to blame. I forced her to play school with me. I forced her to sit while I pretended to be a teacher, and taught her to read and write. It's my fault, please, please don't punish Mandy. Don't sell my best friend. Don't sell my Mandy. Don't sell my sister.

Henry was stunned. Peggy was speechless. They were both simultaneously thinking, what does she mean by "my sister"? Peggy was the first to recover; "What are you saying Becky...what do mean?"

Rebecca, tears streaming down her face, whimpered; "Mandy is like the sister I never had. I know she's black. I know that she's a slave. But she's Mandy. I've never known a day of life without Mandy. Oh God, Oh God Papa, if you love me, if you love your daughter, I'm begging you, please, please, don't sell Mandy."

Henry slowly limped over and stood facing Rebecca; "Becky, Mandy broke the law. One of the most important laws of our society, has been violated. Becky, we have no choice. We have to sell her."

Peggy rose from the bed, she walked over to Rebecca, and gently kissed her on her forehead. She and Henry turned, and quietly left the room.

Rebecca stepped back; she wiped her arm across her eyes. Gradually, as if by magic, her trembling and sobbing, subsided. She walked over to the bed, sat down and reached under the bed. She extracted a small wooden box. Rebecca rummaged through the box, and withdrew a rolled parchment, with a royal blue ribbon tied around its' center.

****

Rebecca sat quietly at the dinner table. Seated at the table were, her father Henry; her mother Peggy; her brother Jesse, and the family's attorney, Luis Frasier.

Dinner went by swiftly. The predominant topics of discussion were the rapidly approaching national presidential election, the increasing talk of secession, and the likelihood of war.

Jesse was particularly vocal in his seemingly endless questioning of Luis, about secession and the prospect of war. "Mr. Frasier, do you really think that that Northern, abolitionist baboon, Abraham Lincoln, will be elected president?"

189

Luis put down his fork; he picked up his napkin and blotted the corners of his mouth. "Jesse, I'm sure that the ladies, find these political subjects to be uninteresting and boring."

Peggy — who during dinner had been unusually quiet — was preoccupied, by Rebecca's stoic demeanor through out the dinner, attempted to draw Rebecca into the conversation; "No, no Luis, Rebecca and I find this intriguing, we two ladies are most interested in world events. Please, go on."

"In answer to your question Jesse, I am afraid that there is a real possibility that Abraham Lincoln might very well win the election. As you know, instead of two candidates for the presidency, which would give the electorate, North and South, a clear-cut choice, say between Lincoln and Senator Douglas, four gentlemen, are running."

"That means that there exists the danger of splitting the South's vote between, Senator Douglas, and Vice President Breckinridge, while Lincoln garners the entirety of the North's." Luis' gaze passed from Jesse, to Peggy, then finally to Rebecca.

Peggy answered, "Oh I see. It's as if you took a whole pie, and cut it in half. One half, of the pie, the total votes cast in the country, goes to Mr. Lincoln, whose views reflect those of the North. The other half of the pie, the total votes cast, goes to Senator Douglas, and to Vice President Breckinridge, whose views are in concert with those of us in the South."

"The Senator and Vice President, in turn must cut their half of the pie, the total votes cast, in half. Thereby leaving Mr. Lincoln with ½ of the votes, and Senator Douglas, and to Vice President Breckinridge, each with ¼ of the votes."

Luis had been nodding affirmatively throughout Peggy's analysis. He grinned broadly and declared; "Exactly! Henry, you are indeed a most fortunate, and lucky man. To be married to one possessing such extraordinary beauty, and unbridled intelligence."

Peggy noticed that Rebecca had shown no reaction to her mother's attempt to defend their gender. To dispel the all to frequent male stereotypic assessment, that is when it came to politics, women were naïve, uninformed, and uninterested.

Rebecca had remained solemn, placid. Rebecca folded her napkin, placed it in her lap, and asked to be excused. She left the table, and went directly to her room. Shortly after Rebecca left the table, Peggy excused herself, and left the dining room.

Henry pulled back his chair, and said; "Luis shall we retire to the study? I'm dying for a brandy and a cigar." Before the two men could rise, Jesse began speaking; "Father before you leave, I would like to discuss, something with you."

Luis began to rise, preparing to leave father and son alone. Jesse held up his hand; "Please stay Mr. Frasier, I would very much appreciate your thoughts." Intrigued, Luis looked over at Henry for his approval. Henry nodded in the affirmative. Luis returned to his seat.

Both Henry and Luis looked, expectantly, at Jesse. Jesse stood, then thought better of it, and reclaimed his seat. He addressed his father; "My visits with you to Richmond, along with Mr., Frasier's comments, have convinced me that war with the North is coming, and coming soon."

Father other than you, mother and Rebecca, I love no one, nor anything more than I love Virginia. When war comes and come it will, I intend to enlist and fight for the South, for my state Virginia, for my home.

Henry was not entirely surprised. After all Jesse was a 19-year-old, healthy, patriotic young man. If he were Jesse, he too would be prepared, and eager to defend their way of life. Yet while immensely proud of his son, as Jesse's father, Henry was afraid. After all, it was his responsibility to protect his family.

After searching his father's face, looking for a reaction, Jesse continued, "I am a Southern Planter. All of my life I've strived to learn all that I could to be a great planter. I hope to — when you retire Dad — to continue what you and grandfather started. I want to be Master of Rosewood. For that to happen, we have to defeat the North."

Jesse took a breath, "like I said, I'm a planter. I think that I have the ability to lead. Dad, I want to ask for yours and Mr. Frazier's help, to gain immediate admission to VMI."

Henry saw a semi-glimmer of hope. Jesse had inadvertently suggested a way to delay his exposure to the battlefield. Henry instantly reasoned that that in the four years that his son would spend at VMI earning a commission the war, if there is a war, would be over.

Henry exclaimed; "You've got it son. I will, strike that, we will, Luis and I, will do everything we can, to gain your expeditious admittance to VMI." He and Jesse looked at Luis. Luis spoke up; "Absolutely, not a problem. I know the Commandant, Colonel Jackson. I'll write a letter of recommendation immediately."

Henry stood and limped over to his son. He put his arm around Jesse's shoulder; "Son, why don't you join me and Luis, in the study. The three of us will have a drink of good whiskey, and a fine cigar."

****

When she returned to her room, Rebecca pulled the box from under her bed. She retrieved the parchment, that her father had given her, a mere two years ago. Henry's birthday gift to her, in celebration of her 15th birthday. She removed the blue ribbon and began to read:

Date: July 19^{th,} 1858

> I, Henry A. Billings, being of sound mind and body, do hereby gift to my beloved daughter, Rebecca Elizabeth Billings, full and unencumbered title and ownership of the Slave legally known as Mandy.
>
> This gift becomes legally valid, when Rebecca Elizabeth Billings reaches her majority, her 18th Birthday in the year of our Lord
> (July 19th 1863)

> *Signed: Henry A. Billings, Master of Rosewood*
>
> Witnessed: Margaret Martin Billings
> July 19^{th,} 1858

Rebecca read and reread the parchment. She placed the document in the box. Hugging the box to her breast, Rebecca lay down on her bed, and fell into a light, yet blissful sleep.

****

Following breakfast, Jesse left to join Lucas, the overseer, to inspect plants, which appeared to have been infested with boll weevil. Peggy retired to her rooms.

Rebecca asked her father if he could please, spare her "a few minutes of your valuable time." Henry's guess was that Rebecca would once again try to dissuade him from selling Mandy. Henry sighed and decided that this was as good a time as any to put an end to this episode. Henry consented to give Rebecca fifteen minutes. He instructed her to come to office at 10:00 AM.

At precisely 9:55 AM, Henry reached into his pocket, pulled out his watch, and checked the time. He asked Luis to please excuse him. He explained that Rebecca had asked for a few minutes of his time.

Henry asked his friend to return at 10:30 AM. At exactly 10:00 AM, Henry heard a knock on the door of the study. Henry arranged his papers on his desk, "Come in Becky." Rebecca entered the room. She walked to one of the chairs facing her father's desk. "Thank you for seeing me father." Henry frowned, she called me father, she never calls me father unless she's angry with me.

Henry decided that it would be best, not to prolong this meeting. He would let her have her say. He would then one last time, once and for all, reaffirm his decision to sell Mandy and Ruth. After all, Rebecca's 13 years old, almost grown. It's time for her to make the transition from a child to a young woman.

Henry pointed to the chair, and in his calmest, firm voice, asked her to, "Please be seated". Rebecca remained standing. Henry thought, Okay, this is not going to be easy; "Rebecca, please let's not argue. We've been over this before. Mandy broke the law."

Henry paused to let the full impact of statement, sink in. "Breaking the law has consequences. Mr. Frasier has consented to deliver an advertisement announcing the sale of Mandy and Ruth, to the Richmond Slave Auctioneer. He braced himself for the expected crying, hysterics, and the anticipated flood of tears.

Instead Rebecca stood oddly calm, and extended to him a document, a vaguely familiar parchment embossed with a blue ribbon. Henry extended his hand. "What's this?" Without uttering a word, Rebecca, turned and left the office.

Henry sat confused, perplexed, curious. He picked up his reading spectacles from the desk, removed the ribbon, unrolled the parchment, and read. Henry placed paperweights on opposite sides of the document.

He removed the spectacles from his face, sat back in his chair and muttered; "Well I'll be damned!"

****

Henry, summoned Rufus, and instructed him to, have Mistress Peggy, and Mr. Frasier, please join him in the office. Rufus hurried off. As he passed through the kitchen, he called to Fannie, who was busily stirring some deliciously smelling concoction, in a large iron kettle; "*Fannie, Ise on da waytogets the Mistress, an Mr. Fraser. Da all metin' up in da Massa's offis. Yu best be makin' som vittles ifn da gets hungry.*"

As Rufus was leaving the kitchen, he heard Fannie exclaim; "*Lawd hav moicy, Ise shonuff be smellin' me som kinda troble. Lawdy...Lawd, help us all.*"

After rereading Rebecca's document, Henry had barely moved, when Peggy entered the office. She sat in one of the chairs facing her husband's desk. Peggy studied her husband's expression. She could not quite interpret what she saw in his face; it was a mixture of, astonishment, shock, and pride. "Henry, what is it…why do you have that funny look on your face?"

Without uttering a word, Henry handed Peggy the parchment, with its' blue ribbon attached. He watched his wife's expression as she read. When she finished reading, Peggy looked up at Henry, "What in the world?"

She handed the document back to Henry. Before Henry could answer, Luis knocked, and without waiting for a response, entered the office. Luis nodded to Henry, then he greeted Peggy; "Good morning Margaret, you're looking as beautiful as ever."

Henry waited until Luis sat in the vacant chair, next to Peggy. Luis looked inquiringly at Henry, then at Peggy. Henry leaned back, and began to speak; "After breakfast, Rebecca requested an appointment to see me. I agreed to the meeting. I correctly guessed that she wanted to once again object to my selling Mandy, and to plead, to beg me to reconsider."

"I was only partially right." Luis was now intrigued; "Henry, what do you mean partially right?" Henry reached across his desk, and handed Luis the parchment. Luis sat back, then swiftly read document. When he finished reading, he looked at Henry.

Henry leaned forward in his chair; "By partially, I meant that my assumption that our little girl wanted to beg and object, was only half right. It appears that Miss Rebecca Elizabeth Billings indeed, wanted to object. This document, signed by me, her father and by her mother, Henry and Margaret Billings, Mistress and Master of Rosewood, is Rebecca's objection."

Luis spoke, "Come now Henry, you know that document does not convey ownership of that slave to Rebecca. How old is Rebecca? Judging from that document she was 13 years old. I'm surprised at you. You one of my best law students. Rebecca was a minor. She, being a minor, cannot legally enter into a contract. And, for the sake of argument, if this was to be deemed a contract, the terms clearly state that transfer of ownership is effective, July 19th, 1863. Almost three years from now."

Henry was clearly put off by Luis' statement. He stood and spoke directly to Luis. "Luis, I did not ask you to sit in on this family conference, for your legal interpretation of this, this … he picked up the parchment, this piece of paper".

"I requested your presence, because I intend to honor this — he waved the document in the air — this pseudo contract. It was our intent to gift Mandy to Rebecca, as one of her 13th birthday presents. That promissory note, that commitment from us, to our daughter is sacred, and will be kept."

Peggy rose from her chair, and walked to stand behind her husband. Henry turned to face his wife, with all of her strength; she hugged Henry to her breast. "Gentlemen, if you will excuse me." Peggy, head held high, and left the office.

Henry, somewhat flustered, and embarrassed, regained his composure, he then continued; "Where was I…oh yes, as my lawyer, I am asking for your assessment of the possible legal ramifications, of my knowingly, failing to report, and subsequently, my harboring, a slave that has violated the state law, which prohibits, slaves from being taught to read and write?"

Luis spoke; "legally if, and I believe only if, for some nefarious, malicious, reason, someone chose to pursue this as it stands, at most you might be accused of obstruction of justice."

"Since that Yankee Teacher, has departed, for northern parts unknown, and if it is as you say, that Mandy's literacy is known only to me, and fortunately "Attorney Client Privilege", removes me from the equation, and to members of the Billing's family, the odds of any sort of legal ramification, is highly unlikely."

Luis began to rummage around in his brief case. After furtive glances at several documents, he withdrew, and handed to Henry, the Advertisement announcing the "For Sale" of Mandy, and of her mother Ruth. Henry glanced at the poster, and then he methodically, meticulously, began to tear it into little pieces.

Luis began to replace the legal papers into his briefcase. While he was attending to this task, he began speaking to his friend and client; "Henry to summarize, I have been instructed — he patted his briefcase — by you, to immediately, divest all of the Billings Family's considerable, investments in Northern businesses and concerns.

It is your intent that we reinvest your fortune, into similar enterprises in the South. Thereby, increasing your support of the noble Southern Cause."

Henry, began to rise; "those Luis, are my wishes, and my instructions." The two friends shook hands. Luis his briefcase in hand, walked from the office.

Pee wee, was standing by the carriage, and holding the horses' reins, waiting to drive Mr. Luis Frasier, Esq., back to town.

****

When Luis returned to his Richmond office, his first item of business was to expeditiously follow his most valued client, and friend, Henry Billings instructions. He immediately dispatched, withdrawal and divestment orders to Northern brokers and businesses, that held Billings Family assets.

Although the sums withdrawn were substantial, the depression of 1857 had reduced the Billings assets by 20% of their pre-depression value.

Within two weeks of issuing correspondence initiating the transactions, Billings Family cash and bonds totaling $245,000, had been received by Luis.

By letter, Luis informed Henry of the completion of the transactions. He also advised his friend, to consider diversifying his investments.

As a loyal, devoted, son of the South, Luis agreed and supported, Henry's decision to remove his assets from the North, and to reinvest in the South. However, as a lawyer and a business man, he strongly advised Henry, against "putting all of his eggs into one basket".

In one of his several missives to Henry, Luis candidly wrote, "Just as the Founding Fathers did, every true Southerner, in support of preserving our way of life, is prepared to; "mutually pledge to each other our Lives our Fortunes and our sacred Honor". Noble sentiments which I dare say were undoubtedly hedged in 1776, by most of the patriotic gentlemen, of substance, with a workable, reliable, Plan "B".

"I submit to you my dear friend, that in addition to loyalty to one's country, one also must maintain loyalty to one's self and to his family. If these currently hot, political conflicting issues, between North and South, cannot be resolved peaceably, then war, no doubt, is inevitable."

"I have every confidence that if a second war of independence is fought in this country, this one between the North and our homeland the South, the South will emerge victorious."

"Still my friend, I will, and I advise you to also; will adhere to the strategy of the great generals throughout the history of the world, I will hold back, and keep, "A Ready Reserve". "I repeat, my advice as your attorney and your friend; Do not put all of your eggs, into one basket!"

****

The new year 1860, in the South started out under a veil of gloom. Most of the South's ruling class, were not optimistic in welcoming in, the new year.

They viewed last year's mid-October, raid by, as Luis referred to him, that "lunatic" abolitionist, John Brown, as a harbinger of bad things to come.

Although the fanatical "lunatic", John Brown's scheme failed, they realized that John Brown's blatant attempt to end slavery through armed insurrection, was to say the least, deeply disturbing, and deeply troubling.

Luis wholeheartedly believed in the South's way of life. He was an avid proponent of "States Rights". Despite his training in Constitutional Law, Luis was a supporter and advocate, of the doctrine of "Nullification".

Luis was adamant in his belief that if a state legislature, and its' governor, were to decide that a federal law was unconstitutional, that the law was contrary to the U.S. Constitution, and not in the best interest of their particular state, that the state could declare that that specific federal law, to be "null and void", within the confines of that particular state.

There was no denying that the political landscape, the political power pendulum was inexorably, swinging towards the North.

Richmond was abuzz with talk of secession. In May the Republicans selected Abraham Lincoln as their Presidential Candidate. Luis, as did his friend Henry Billings, and most of the South's population, saw this as a definite threat to their way of life.

In November 1860, Abraham Lincoln was elected the 16th President of the United States. The results of the election fortified the South's belief that the North intended to abolish slavery, thus destroying the Southern economy, destroying the Southern way of life.

On December 20, 1860, a little more than a month following Lincoln's election. South Carolina seceded from the Union.
****
Secessionist fever ran rampant in the streets of Richmond. The sentiment heard in taverns and gatherings of men on street corners, echoed the theme; "It's about time. Now we'll show them damn yankees a thing or two!" The city's populace was primed, ready and eager, for war.
****

HAPPY NEW YR 1861

The first two months of 1861, saw a rapid succession of southern states, withdrawing from the Union, forming a Southern Confederacy. A wave of Southern patriotic fever, swept through Richmond, and throughout the South.

A string of minor Confederate military victorious, waged in South Carolina against Union forces, elated, encouraged, and unfortunately, emboldened the war-hawks in the various, Southern legislatures.

On April 12, 1861 Confederate Naval forces, bombarded the U.S. Fort Sumter at the mouth of Charleston Harbor, South Carolina.

The Civil War had begun.

****

The April 12th bombardment of Fort Sumter, placed both the North and the South on a war footing. The dye was caste.

On July 21st the first major land battle between the Northern and Southern Armies, occurred in Fairfax County and Prince County, Virginia. The Battle of Bull Run.

The Battle of Bull Run, the first true major clash, between the warring factions, resulted in a decisive clear-cut victory for the South. Morale through-out the Confederacy sky-rocketed.

The South was the clear victor. The Northern invading army, had been literally routed — fleeing in defeat — by the sons of the South.

Confederate battle field killed and wounded were; 387 killed; 1,582 wounded. Union forces suffered, 460 killed and 1,124 wounded.

In the streets and taverns of Richmond, the newly designated capital of the Confederacy, backslapping and rebel yells, could be heard throughout the nights, cascading from the jubilant celebrants.

"By God we gave them Yankees what for…can you beat that, they had the balls to invade Virginia." "We wupt them and wupt them good."

The Battle of Bull Run was a resounding success for the Southern cause.

Rosewood Plantation, Essex County Virginia, was the home of one of the last of the 387 Confederate soldiers, killed in action.

For the Billings family of Essex County Virginia, the Battle of Bull Run resulted in the most devastating tragedy imaginable.

Lieutenant Jesse Robert Billings, of the Army of Virginia, was killed at the Battle of Bull Run.

****

Henry received notification of Jesse's death, from Luis. Luis Frasier was one of Richmond's more prominent citizens. In addition to the city of Richmond, Luis had earned and gained enormous respect as a lawyer and a financier, throughout the South.

Luis' financial skills and acuity, had made him a serious potential candidate for a cabinet post, in the newly formed government, of the Confederate States of America.

When Luis arrived unannounced at Rosewood, Henry was surprised, but not especially alarmed, by the unexpected visit. In the past, his friend and mentor, had occasionally shown up, unannounced at the plantation.

Henry was seated at his desk. He held a cigar in his mouth, and the plantation's financial ledger, in the other. Peewee knocked on the office door.

Henry without looking up from the ledger, grunted; "Come in." Peewee entered; *"Ise sawry ta bartha you suh."* Henry glanced at the slave; "What is it Peewee?" *"Mista Luis, he here suh. He be now drivin' up ta da stabul"*

When Luis entered the office, Henry motioned to him to have a seat. Luis sat. He waited while Henry finished adding the month's expenses in the plantation's accounting ledger.

Henry looked up; he noticed his friend's forlorn, sorrowful expression. "Come now Luis, whatever it is, it can't be that bad. What brings you unexpected, but I assure you, always welcome, to Rosewood, in the middle of the week?"

Luis rubbed his hands over his eyes. "Henry, I know by now you've heard the news of our glorious victory at Bull Run." Henry's face lite up, a broad grin spread across his face.

Henry beaming, reached for the whiskey decanter, he pushed a glass towards Luis, and exclaimed; "Hell of a fight! Our boys really took it to those Yankee Invaders. Bull Run will certainly give that "Black" Republican in the White House, something to think about."

Henry filled both of their glasses, and proposed a toast; "Here's to our brave soldiers, thanks to them the Confederate States of America, lives." Henry emptied his glass. Luis' glass remained, untouched. Henry placed his glass on the desk; "Okay Luis, spit it out. What the hell is going on?"

Luis, squeezing his glass in his hands, his knuckles turning white, spoke softly; "Henry, this is the most difficult news that I have ever delivered. Jesse fought valiantly and courageously at Bull Run."

Henry fell back into his chair, his face became ashen, as the blood drained from his face.

Taking a deep breath, Luis continued; during the Battle of Bull Run, "Lieutenant Jesse Robert Billings, was killed."

****

After Luis had informed Henry of Jesse's death, Henry sent Rufus to fetch Mistress' Margaret and Rebecca. When Henry told Margaret of their son's gallant, and honorable death, fighting to protect and preserve their way of life, Margaret, wringing her hands together, without making a sound, collapsed to the floor, in a dead faint.

Rebecca's hand flew to her mouth, she screamed and ran to Margaret; "Mother, mother, are you alright?" Henry knelt and held his wife's hand. He yelled for Rufus; "Rufus, go fetch Mamie Ester. Tell her that we need her. Tell her that Mistress Margaret fainted."

After Mamie Ester had revived her mother, Rebecca, who had been silently crying in the corner, when she saw that her mother was recovering, ran from the room. She ran upstairs, in search of Mandy. Mandy was seated in the sewing-room, assisting her mother.

Rebecca, tears streaming down her cheeks, burst into the sewing room. Mandy's back was to the door. Ruth looked up from her sewing and exclaimed; *"Mistress Beca, wha's wrong?"* Rebecca, sobbing and moaning, between gulps of air, she lamented, in the most piteous, sorrowful voice; "Oh Mandy, Jesse's dead, the yankees have killed Jesse."

Mandy opened her arms and ran to Becky. Rebecca was inconsolable

****

200

BOOK 2

THE COMANCHES

June 6th Moon –Moon when the hot weather begins

As the summer sun rose in the eastern sky, Little Beaver once again, for the last time —
he vowed — checked the meager implements that he intended taking with him on his
pilgrimage, his sojourn in quest of an inspirational visit by the spirits, a vision that would
result in his obtaining his personal medicine.

Little Beaver at the beginning of his sixteenth summer was a strapping lean, well-
muscled, bronzed youth, eager to assume, what many thought, was Little Beaver's
predestined place as a courageous warrior, and possibly a leader of the People.

The vision that he sought would he hoped, bridge his communication with the spirit
world. He was confident that the vision, sent to him by the spirit world, would lead him
to his own unique medicine. A warrior's personal medicine, would bestow upon him,
protection, power, and wisdom.

Little Beaver was one of the band's — coming of age — privileged, proud boys, on the
threshold of manhood. He was poised to take his place as a hunter, provider, and
protector of the People. Little Beaver eagerly anticipated the time that he would achieve
the coveted status, that of a Comanche Warrior.

The custom that a young man — prior to his elevation, his acceptance, to the warrior
society — should seek his medicine, by going forth alone, to communicate with the
spirits, was an ancient ritual, a rite of passage into manhood, for the sons of the People.

****
As did all of his boyhood companions, Little Beaver, as a male member of the tribe, had
been introduced to toy replicas of the tools and the weapons used for hunting and for war,
when he was still a toddler.

It was during his fourth summer, that Gray Wolf his father, and his uncle Broken Lance,
began Little Beaver's early training in the use of the bow and arrow.

At first, his father had emphasized distance. How far could the boy launch his arrows.

201

It was only after Little Beaver was able to let fly an arrow whose flight either met, or exceeded, the distance, predetermined by his father Grey Wolf, or by his uncle Broken Lance, would the boy be allowed to concentrate on speed and accuracy.

Buffalo chips, the solid waste shed by the buffalo, in addition to being excellent fuel for their fires, dried buffalo chips, which blanketed the plains, were used by the young boys as targets. The buffalo chips were plentiful, round, and made excellent stationary, and moving targets.

Once Little Beaver was able to consistently place four of five arrows into a stationary target, his father or his uncle would roll the chips, thus presenting more difficult to hit, moving targets.

His lessons with bow and arrows, the most important weapon utilized by the People, began, shortly after Little Beaver had successfully experienced his first, solo pony ride.

Grey Wolf and Broken Lance encouraged the boy to respect, to emulate, the actions, the demeanor, and the deeds of the tribe's warriors.

All of the young boys of the tribe were instilled with, and encouraged to embrace the fighting spirit. They were made aware that their lives, and the survival of the People, depended upon their skills to hunt, and to make war.

Little Beaver was taught that there could be no greater honor than that of becoming one of the People's protectors, a Comanche Warrior.

Death was not to be feared, nor was death to be necessarily avoided. For to die with honor, to be killed in the prime of life, while bravely fighting the enemies of the People, was by far preferable to longevity without honor.

Since infancy, Little Beaver had been indoctrinated and had come to embrace the mindset that, courage and bravery were the most honorable and the holiest of attributes.

As a boy, then as a youth, Little Beaver had been relentlessly and constantly trained to become a warrior. He was taught — and he fervently believed — that death was not a thing to be feared; that there was no greater honor for a warrior than to be killed by an enemy, or a beast such as the buffalo, while protecting, or providing sustenance for the People.

For the past seven summers — which seemed to him to comprise the entirety of his life — Little Beaver's primary duties and services to the tribe, was that of tending to and now, guarding the band's most valuable, and prized possession, their huge herd of horses.

At the age of eight, Little Beaver's ability to ride and to control horses was well known, acknowledged, and lauded by the band.

Last summer, when the grass browned, and a chill accompanied the setting of the sun, Little Beaver, who was nearing the end of his fifteenth summer, was allowed to join the buffalo hunt. This was the most important of the annual hunts.

The success or failure of the hunt would determine if the People would be successful in obtaining staples — food; skins for their clothing and teepees; utensils — essentials needed to survive the harsh winter.

****

Riding his favorite mount Scout — loosing torrents of his arrows within the tight confines of the stampeding buffalo herd — arrows that he had made with the guidance of his father, in preparation for the hunt. Little Beaver managed to bring down three cows, and an old bull.

His exploits as a first-time member of the autumn hunting party, served to convince his father, his uncle, and the warrior society, that the teenaged Little Beaver was a skillful, and accomplished hunter.

His family, as was the entire camp, was impressed and proud of his demonstrated ability and prowess as a hunter, as a provider.

Now at last, after having successfully displayed his skills as a hunter, his father Gray Wolf, his uncle Broken Lance, and Little Beaver himself, believed that it was time that he, Little Beaver, son of Gray Wolf, became a Comanche Warrior.

****

It was the belief and the custom of the People, that a young man should not be elevated to the status of warrior, until he possessed his own personal medicine — divine assistance, a talisman, a supernatural, protective guiding force, that would ensure success — which had been bestowed upon the individual, by a benevolent spirit.

The aspiring young man should not be a part of raiding parties; he should not be allowed to join war parties, until he had successfully communicated with the spirit world, and obtained his own personal medicine.

To the tribe, a man had no real stature, until he had proven himself in combat. He would not be considered a whole man, a warrior until he had counted coup, and had taken the scalps of the People's enemies.

Since the beginning of summer, the time of *the "Moon when the hot weather begins",* Little Beaver had been persistently petitioning the band's Holy Man, He Who Speaks To Ghosts, for counsel, to advise and guide him in his quest to obtain — from the spirits — his own protective medicine.

He Who Speaks To Ghosts, consented to prepare Little Beaver for his vision quest. He streaked Little Beaver's face and torso with red, yellow and blue paint.

The Holy man had then sanctified Little Beaver's body by their mutual smoking of a bone-pipe, puffing while first facing East, then, South, then West, and finally North.

Each offering of smoke was accompanied by chanting to the spirits, asking that they visit, make themselves known to Little Beaver during his vision quest.

****

As he walked from the encampment, clad only in deerskin moccasins, and a brown breechclout, the youth's keen sense of smell was stimulated by the mouth-watering aroma of buffalo meat being cooked by the women, for their family's morning meal.

Little Beaver's stomach growled in anticipation of its customary morning repast. He patted his belly and murmured, "no food today; not tonight; not for four days and nights."

His father Gray Wolf had told his son, that during his vision quest, when he was about Little Beaver's age, the spirits had not made themselves known to him until he had gone four days and nights, without food, or water.

After four hours of non-stop walking in a southwesterly direction, Little Beaver observed that the blistering hot summer sun at his back, was now beginning to send shimmering ripples of heat across the endless swaying waves of grass. His throat was parched and his body was drenched in perspiration.

Little Beaver raised his forearm to blot and remove the sweat that cascaded down from his forehead and stung his bleary eyes. Directly ahead, he saw a clump of Juniper bushes that, with each step he took, seemed to be rising from the deceptively flat-appearing, prairie floor.

The sun cast a sliver of shade on the western side of the bushes. Little Beaver quickened his pace, as he walked towards the only shade insight.

He untied the leather-thong that held the buffalo hide to his back, and spread the hide on the ground. Little Beaver picked up the bone-pipe, and packed it with sumac leaves. He began to smoke. The smoking ritual which had been prescribed by the Holy Man, He Who Speaks To Ghosts, was solemnly, repeated.

At the conclusion of his chant to the spirits, pleading for their assistance, Little Beaver closed his stinging eyelids for a moment, and unwittingly, unceremoniously, dozed off.

Little Beaver was awakened by a loud clasp of thunder. He was annoyed with himself for his apparent lack of discipline, for it had been his intent to merely, briefly rest his eyes. It had not been his intent, to take a nap. To have involuntarily fallen asleep, like an untrained, undisciplined baby was not an attribute of a warrior.

Disgusted and annoyed with himself, he rolled his scant collection of items, into the folds of the buffalo robe, tied the robe with the leather-thong, and slung it across his back.

Stomach growling with hunger pangs, Little Beaver resumed his trek towards the two lone landmass twin mountains, rising above the seemingly endless, flat plains. The two sentinels that served as natural boundaries that enclosed the People's well-established, ancient hunting grounds.

After hours of continuous walking, he began to feel a dull aching sensation in his legs. Little Beaver knew that this long day without water, under the hot sun, was conducive to cramping.

The sun was setting in the western sky. as the sun was setting in the western sky, despite the dull aching in his legs, Little Beaver noticed that as the sun began to set, it appeared to be framed by the twin mountain peaks.

The mountains, though they appeared to the tired youth, to be gradually getting larger, did not seem to be any closer than they had been, at mid-day, when he had first caught sight of the ancient geological projections.

Little Beaver decided to seek out a spot to rest, to smoke, to attempt to communicate with the spirits, and to spend the night. He found a small playa that still contained a few inches of muddy water.

Little Beaver was tempted, but refused to quench his thirst. He removed his buffalo robe from his back, and fifty long strides from the water, spread the robe onto the ground, fifty long strides from the pool of muddy water.

He packed his pipe with sumac, lit the pipe and as he had been instructed to do, by the shaman, and performed the smoke ritual.

At the conclusion of his incantations, Little Beaver concentrated, listening to the wind, listening for a response, a sign, from the spirits. Hearing and seeing none, he rolled himself into his buffalo robe and drifted off into a fitful, restless, dream-filled sleep.

In his exhausted, water and food deprived, state, Little Beaver's exhausted mind, dreamed of his life-experiences. He dreamt of the paths that he had taken. Paths that had now led him to the brink of man-hood.

Little Beaver was familiar with verbal recitations, tales told to him by his father, Gray Wolf, that had been told to Gray Wolf by his father, who in turn had been told by his father, of the hardships the People had endured before they had acquired the horse.

The tribal elders spoke respectfully, reverently of long-ago times — times before the horse — when for generations, following the buffalo was extremely difficult and dangerous.

The People's existence, their survival depended upon their nomadic following of the grazing and migration of the vast herds of buffalo.

The old ones spoke of the limited distances that the People could travel on foot, with the old ones, plodding along in the rear, and if they were not able to keep up, being left to die on the prairie.

They spoke of the long-ago time when the women, the children and the dogs, were tasked with pulling the travoises, ladened with their possessions, including their dwellings, the families teepees, across the endless plains.

Little Beaver remembered asking his grandfather "in the long-ago times before the horse, why did the men not pull the travois?"

The old man puffed on his ever-present pipe. He then after contemplative deliberation, sagely responded; "That is the work of women. The work of men is to hunt to provide meat, and to defend and protect the women and the children."

The People's existence, their survival depended upon their ability to hunt the buffalo. Their nomadic way of life depended upon their ability to follow the grazing and migration of the vast buffalo herds.

Many of the hardships previously associated with the People's frequent treks, following the buffalo across hundreds of miles of prairie, were alleviated, and in large part, had been eradicated with the People's acquisition of the horse.

The horse that expanded the hunter's range; the hose that gave the hunter speed and agility that equaled, and surpassed that of the buffalo, the horse to pull the heavy loads; the horse that made the nomadic lifestyle of the People possible.

Little Beaver found it difficult, nearly impossible, to envision life without the horse. Hunting the buffalo, the People' main source of food, clothing, and shelter, without the aide and assistance of the horse, was to his young mind inconceivable.

In lieu of the women, and the camp's dogs, pulling the heavily laden travois across the continent, the horse, with ease, could now supply the necessary energy, the muscle, thus expanding the People's mobility and range.

The horse was a means of transporting, not only the People's, belongings, it allowed the People to retain an invaluable asset, the old people. The old people were no longer left behind. The horse provided a means to transport their elders across the endless prairie.

Little Beaver remembered, as a child inundating his mother, Little Flower, with endless questions, as she, with his very limited assistance, packed their teepees, their possessions onto the numerous travois utilized to transport the family's dwellings, and belongings, across the vast prairies in pursuit of the buffalo.

Little Beaver recalled his incredulity, when his mother, Little Flower explained that before the horse, during the time of their forebears, the heavily laden travoises, piled high with the People's possessions, were pulled by dogs and by the women and children.

As difficult and ludicrous as it was for him to imagine dogs, instead of horses, dragging their belongings over hundreds of miles of prairie, Little Beaver found it almost beyond belief, that in the past, the warriors had been forced to hunt the easily stampeded buffalo, on foot.

His father Grey Wolf, had explained to the little boy, that the hunting of the Buffalo, without the aid of their swift reliable ponies, had been accomplished by the hunter's creative application of cunning and guile.

Little Beaver would sit wide-eyed, listening with wonder, as his father Grey Wolf, or his uncle Broken Lance, talked of their forefather's ingenious, clever methods of hunting.

They told of the origin of the game Little Beaver and his friends played, the wearing of the animal skins, mimicking the behavior of the animals that they hunted, particularly the buffalo, the elk, and the antelope.

Little Beaver's father, Grey Wolf, as did the fathers of his playmates, smiled at and encouraged these types of activities by the little boys. The tribe's adults viewed these games as helpful preludes, preparing the young boys for their eventual roles as the hunters, and as warriors.

Grey Wolf pointed out to his son that, these games played by children, were merely imitations of some of the methods used by the warriors to hunt, in long- ago-days-gone bye, before the People acquired the horse.

When Grey Wolf explained to Little Beaver that before the horse, Little Beaver's little game was a major ploy utilized by the hunters. Grey Wolf spoke at length of the days before the horse.

He told of the hunters wearing buffalo hides and masks. Of hunters pretending to be members of the herd, pawing the ground, making bleating noises, and leading the herd into traps and frequently over cliffs.

Little Beaver's father, Grey Wolf, as did the fathers of his playmates, smiled at and encouraged these types of activities by the little boys. The tribe's adults viewed these games as helpful preludes, preparing the young boys for their eventual roles as the hunters, and as warriors.

For the entirety of his young life, Little Beaver had been surrounded by a culture that revered, valued, and revolved around the horse. If he were to be asked which of his locomotion skills, walking or riding a horse came first, he would be hard pressed to answer.

For as long as he could remember, Little Beaver had been around horses.
The first kisses of his young life that he remembers, were the kisses from his mother, his aunt, his father, and from his pony.

As a child, Little Beaver was taught by his father, his uncle, and his mother, to respect, to appreciate, and to protect all of nature. Four legged or two-legged, animal or plant, all life had meaning and purpose.

The People, believed that the Great Spirit had rendered all of his creations, round. The Earth, Sun, the Moon, the stalks of plants, the ripples in a stream, were all manifestations of the Sacred Circle.

Little Beaver's faith, and acceptance of the "Circle-Of-Life, was solidified for Little Beaver's through the wise observations of his father Grey Wolf.
During one of his earliest hunting trips with his father, in his haste to break camp, Little Beaver failed to completely extinguish the campfire.

Little Beaver's father, Grey Wolf, as did the fathers of his playmates, smiled at and encouraged these types of activities by the little boys. The tribe's adults viewed these games as helpful preludes, preparing the young boys for their eventual roles as the hunters, and as warriors.

****

It was during the moon of the black cherries, during Little Beaver's eighth summer, that Grey Wolf took his son on his first hunting party. The hunting party was a two man, or more accurately, a one man and a one boy hunting party, Grey Wolf, and his young son, Little Beaver.

Shortly after they broke camp and were riding away, in pursuit of small game, Little Beaver was startled, a bit frightened when his father abruptly turned his mount, and galloped back to their abandoned camp-site.

Little Beaver turned his pony's head and, in a panic, kicked as hard as he could, yelling at his father's rapidly receding back; "father, father, please wait for me".

Grey Wolf dismounted, and sprinted over to the smoldering campfire. He lifted the flap of breechclout, and vigorously sprayed a copious, strong stream of urine onto the glowing embers.

When Little Beaver arrived, he saw his father shifting through the wood ash, with a tree branch. He slid from the back of his pony, and excitedly exclaimed, "My father I thought that I had put the campfire out."

Grey Wolf poked amongst the embers, then satisfied that the fire was dead, threw the stick into the weeds.

He sat down on the grass, crossed his legs, and motioned, for Little Beaver to sit beside him. After the little boy sat down beside his father, he crossing his legs in the exact manner, as had Grey Wolf, Little Beaver raised his eyes to expectantly, to look at his father.

Grey Wolf looked at his only son with the sternest, most solemn face that he could muster. "My son it was your task to see that the fire was cold. It is because of your childish carelessness and negligence, that fire could have destroyed nature's grass."

Little Beaver squirmed under his father's accusatory gaze. "Forgive me, I'm truly sorry. It was my haste to be on the hunting trail with you that made me careless. But as you can see, if we had not returned, the fire would have burned only a small clump of grass."

Grey Wolf frowned. He reached out to touch his son, then before making contact, he hesitated and withdrew his hand. Grey Wolf folded his arms across his chest, and began to speak.

209

"My son we have often spoke of the circle-of-life. You have lived eight summers. By now you know that of all of the four-legged creatures given to us by the Great Spirit, the buffalo is the most essential for the sustaining of the life of the People."

"You know from listening to the stories told by the old ones, that before the Great Spirit gave us the horse, the following and the hunting of the buffalo, was dangerous, and far more difficult, than today.

"Though the buffalo were as plentiful as the stars in the sky, before the horse, the People often spent many winters, with empty bellies, shivering in the cold because they did not have enough buffalo robes. This was so because on foot, without the horse, the hunters could not find the buffalo herds."

"As we depend upon the buffalo and the horse, both the horse and the buffalo depend upon the grass. Without the long green grass to nourish the buffalo, to make them fat, their meat plentiful and juicy, the People would perish.

Without the long green grass to nourish our horses, the horse would not have the strength to support the weight of our warriors, nor the stamina to run down the buffalo."

Little Beaver recalled his father's ending the conversation; "Remember the Circle-Of-Life my son, for without the grass, there would be no horse, without the grass, there would be no buffalo, without the buffalo, the People would cease to exist."

****

As a man-child of the People, Little Beaver had for all of his life — in some manner or form — been constantly trained to eventually assume the status and the mantle of a Comanche Warrior.

Even as infants, before they could crawl or speak, the babies of the People were taught not to cry. The sound of babies crying could stampede the buffalo, or could alert enemies as to the People's location.

Little Beaver and his playmates, as toddlers, while still crawling, learning to walk, were given toys that were miniature versions of the weapons, and tools that they would need — decades later — to have mastered, in order that they, as warriors, could fulfill their roles as the providers and protectors of the People.

As long as he could remember, Little Beaver and his friends, Stone Fist, Crooked Arrow, and Frogs Legs, were practically inseparable.

The four boys had played together, wrestled one another, had mock battles, and together, developed proficiency with the short-bow and arrow, the lance and shield.

During their formative years the boys had each experienced numerous falls, sprains and even broken bones, in their efforts to become expert horsemen.

Over time the four boys' efforts to truly master the horse, had borne fruit. It was generally recognized by all that, of the band's prepubescent boys, the foursome of Little Beaver, Crooked Arrow, Stone Fist, and Frogs Legs, were considered to be the most skilled, and accomplished, of the young horsemen.

****

The ominous, hiss and the distinctive buzzing sound of a rattlesnake awakened Little Beaver. Three feet from Little Beaver was a large snake. Despite his initial impulse to flee, Little Beaver remained seated, motionless. His knife lay along side his pipe, just out of reach of his hand.

Little Beaver knew that any movement, especially sudden movement would cause the snake to strike. While he sat frozen, contemplating his dilemma, two running birds, in unison, swiftly attacked the snake.

Little Beaver grabbed his knife and jumped from the ground. One of the birds struck the snake's head a swift vicious blow with its beak, to the base of the snake's head. The other bird darted in and clamped down on the snake above the head. While one bird held the snake immobile, the other administered rapid punishing blows to the viper's head.

Within seconds, the sound of rattling ceased, the rattlesnake lay motionless. The two birds that run, both held the snake between their beaks.

The predominantly terrestrial birds, in unison, scampered away. Almost immediately they were no longer visible. The birds were loss in a sea of gently swaying, prairie-grass.

****

Little Beaver looked eastward towards the rising sun. He gathered his possessions, and then turned towards the still distant twin mountain peaks.

Finally, when the sun had reached its' high point in the azure blue summer sky, Little Beaver reached the foot of the mountain. Before attempting to ascend the mountain, he once again unfurled his buffalo robe, and spread it upon the ground.

Once again, the smoking ritual that had been told to him by the medicine man, was repeated. Little Beaver blew smoke to the East, to the South, to the West, then to the North.

Each offering of smoke was accompanied by Little Beaver's heart-felt request, to communicate with the spirits.

His ultimate goal was to communicate with the spirits, this he reasoned would be more easily accomplished if he were to climb the mountain, for it was well known and accepted that the spirits, hovered above the earth. Climbing the mountain would bring him that much closer to those powerful, supernatural beings that he sought.

Little Beaver decided to make camp at the base of the mountain. He reasoned that it would be foolish to risk injury, possibly a debilitating injury, by attempting to climb the mountain in the rapidly waning daylight.

Little Beaver's legs began to involuntarily quiver; he recognized that his thus far, two-day fast, and the lengthy walk across the plains, had sapped his strength.

The muscles in his legs, were experiencing painful cramps. Little Beaver shakily gathered dried grass and twigs, and made a small campfire.

Ignoring his grumbling stomach, he gathered his buffalo robe about him, closed his eyes, and quickly drifted into a dream filled sleep.

* *

The buffalo hunt, along with raids and war against their enemies, was for the men of the People, the most exciting and rewarding aspect of life on the plains.

The hunt was a practical and a religious rite. It served to revitalize both the body and the spirit, of the hunters.

The buffalo's hide sheltered, clothed, and warmed the People's bodies. The flesh and blood of the ubiquitous animal fed and nourished the People.

The wild primordial chase, of horseman and stead, against the massive bulk, and the dangerously sharp, often lethal horns of the buffalo, served to stimulate the spirit, providing the opportunity for each man to test his skill and his courage.

Last autumn, when the grass took on a pronounced, vermilion hue, and a chill accompanied the setting of the sun, Little Beaver, who was nearing the end of his fifteenth summer, and his childhood friends, Stone Fist, Crooked Arrow, and Frog Legs — Frog Legs, Little Beaver's childhood, best friend, had come by his name as a child, because of his pronounced, exaggerated, bowed legs — were allowed to join the buffalo hunt.

The scouts from the hunting party had located a vast herd of buffalo, grazing contently, in a recessed valley. Little Beaver counted on the fingers of both hands. He estimated that the number of beasts was at least one hundred times the number of his combined fingers.

The sight was breathtaking. The men slowly, in order to not cause a stampede, walked their horses down the slight slope, towards the herd.
The hunters slowly enveloped the herd, in a loose semicircle

One of the large bulls on the outer edge of the herd, raised his huge head, and stared at the slowly approaching men. Despite the bull's poor vision, with the aid of a sudden shift in the wind, the huge animal detected the presence of the advancing hunters.

The sentinel bull swung his heavy head from side to side; a long strand of mucus flew from his nostrils into the air. The bull turned, and with a series of bleats, sounded the alarm.

When Strong Man, the leader of the hunting party, gave the signal to charge, the trio of neophyte hunters, Little Beaver, Crooked Arrow, and Frog Legs, with the enthusiasm and recklessness of youth, grabbed their ponies, manes and leapt upon their backs.

They burst from the group of hunters, and with blood curdling war whoops, that they had been practicing for years, the trio kneed their ponies into the midst of the beasts.

The frightened animals panicked and began to run. However, the semicircle of mounted hunters forced them into a circle. For the buffalo, it was a circle of death, for the hunters, it was yet another manifestation of their Sacred Circle of Life.

Little Beaver and Crooked Arrow's first hunt was a huge success. Together their arrows brought down five buffalo. Frog Leg's initial headlong charge into the herd landed him in the center of the stampeding, frightened animals.

Frog Legs found himself surrounded, and pinned in by a sea of wild, red-eyed, panicked beasts. On each of his flanks, in front, to his left, behind him, to his right, thousand-pound beasts, pinned him in.

Frog legs loosed an arrow into the right flank of the cow on his left, she stumbled and fell, clipping the left hind leg of the beast running directly in front of Frog Legs' pony. That animal was thrown off stride, and fell amidst an enormous, blinding cloud of dirt.

Frog Legs' pony tripped and fell, throwing his rider — Frog Legs — who landed among the stampeding buffalo. Little Beaver, Crooked Arrow, and Frog Legs, during the excitement and the confusion of the hunt, had lost sight of one another.

At the conclusion of the slaughter, the hunters assembled and began to exchange tales of their daring exploits. The women and children, who had been watching the slaughter, leading their horse drawn travois, descended from the hill to the floor of the valley.

The women swiftly and adeptly began skinning the fallen buffalo. Little Beaver's mother Little Flower, and his younger sister Spring Blossom, were among the first to touch the buffalo.

Little Flower with Spring Blossom's help, examined and attempted to remove the arrow protruding from between the hip bone and last rib of a fallen cow. The arrow clearly bore Grey Wolf's markings.

The women of Grey Wolf's lodge, each grabbed the buffalo's horns, they were startled by the sound of moaning. They stepped back from the animal. On occasion women had received nasty wounds from the sharp horns of presumed dead, wounded, buffalo.

Grey Wolf, seated on his horse, had been watching Little Flower. He rode over to his wife, and dispatched an additional arrow into the cow.

Little Flower stepped up to the cow, prepared to commence the skinning. Once again, she heard a moan, that she again thought had been made by the slain cow.

Grey Wolf dismounted and joined his wife. Frog Legs lay beneath the dead animal, wide-eyed gasping for air.

Miraculously, the bulk of the animal covered but was not directly on the Frog Legs torso. As the spirits would have it, Frog Legs had fallen into a shallow depression in the turf.

The huge buffalo covered him as if it were a blanket, a wrap casually drawn over him for his warmth and comfort. Miraculously none of the beast's half-ton weight was actually on the boy.

Grey Wolf, with the aid of two of his fellow hunters, dragged the slain animal covering Frog Legs to the side.

Little Flower peered into the depression. Frog Legs gasping for air, was attempting to catch his breath. He tried, unsuccessfully, to climb out of the depression.

Frog Legs, though visibly shaken, with no visible injuries, appeared to be unscathed. Grey Wolf and Spotted Elk attempted to help the youth to his feet.

Frog Legs winched in pain. It was then that the warriors noticed that the boy's foot had been slightly twisted beneath him. Frog Legs gingerly sat on the carcass of his "guardian" buffalo.

Little Beaver and Crooked Arrow, both flush with excitement, rode up and dismounted. Little Beaver looked first at his friend, then to his father and nervously inquired; "father, how badly is he injured...will he live?"

Grey Wolf looked up; "Frog Legs is truly smiled upon by the spirits. Having fallen under the hooves of many buffalo, and the weight of a mature buffalo cow, he should be dead or at best severely injured. Your friend Frog Legs, appears to have twisted his foot, to have suffered at worst, a sprained ankle."

Henceforth the boy called Frog Legs, would be for the remainder of his time on Mother Earth, be known as "Twisted Foot".

****

Little Beaver's sleep was disturbed by the haunting howl of a solitary coyote, baying at the full moon. Little Beaver stirred, he sluggishly threw some dried grass onto the dying fire, he readjusted his buffalo-robe, and once again drifted off to sleep.

None of the seasoned hunters, including the elders — who do to the dulling of their senses; the stiffness that now lived in their joints, and the diminishing of their skills, with the passage of many summers, no longer rode the hunting trail — who could no longer chase down the fleeing buffalo, had witnessed a hunter, having been trampled in a stampede of buffalo, fallen on by multiple full grown beasts, who had walked away practically unscathed. That Frog Legs, now known as Twisted Foot, had acquired powerful medicine could not be denied.

The trio's first tribal buffalo hunt had been a huge success. Little Beaver and Crooked Arrow had in the past, each slain multiple buffalo. Their families would have an abundance of fresh meat and pemmican, for most of the summer.

Their friend — no longer called Frog Legs, now known as Twisted Foot — though his single arrow brought down but one buffalo, gained enormous status due to his obvious favor with the benevolent spirits, those who watched over the People.

The three teen-aged boys, and their friend Stone Fist, all on the brink of manhood, were now by far, perceived of, by the unmarried females, but more importantly by the girl's fathers, as the band's most eligible bachelors.

****

With the first rays of the rising sun, illuminating the sparse vegetation that struggled to survive along the mountain, Little Beaver emerged from his warm buffalo robe.

His head ached and his throat was dry. To him, Little Beaver's tongue felt swollen, felt as if it occupied his entire mouth.

He placed dried twigs on the cold campfire. Little Beaver strategically placed combustible kindling at the base, and struck his flint stone against the rock that he held in his hand.

The kindling glowed. He picked up his pipe, then performed the now familiar ritual, blowing smoke to each of the four directions, while he once again, asked the spirits for their assistance, to give him strong medicine, to send him a vision.

Little Beaver rolled his few possessions into the buffalo hide. He tied the leather-thong around the robe and slipped the loop over his shoulder, and began his climb up the mountain.

At mid-morning Little Beaver, stomach growling with the pangs of hunger, head aching, stopped climbing. The temple on the side of his head was throbbing, pulsating.

He attempted — but was unable — to breath through his mouth. As if in a trance, Little Beaver stuck out his tongue. With his left hand, he gingerly felt his tongue. He looked curiously at the yellowish-white substance that covered his hand. Little Beaver lifted his head, and looked up towards the mountain's summit.

In his physically weakened, near mentally delirious state, Little Beaver decided that he had climbed far enough. He rationalized that his climb thus far up the mountain, would serve to convince, to satisfy the spirits that Little Beaver, son of Grey Wolf, was more than willing to meet the spirits halfway.

For the remainder of the blistering hot day, Little Beaver smoked and chanted, chanted and smoked. Exhaustion, hunger and thirst were beginning negatively affect Little Beaver's coordination, and his depth perception.

As the sun slowly, relentlessly, moved East to West across the cloudless, azure blue sky, Little Beaver was becoming increasingly disoriented. His mind began to wander. The more he tried to concentrate, the more jumbled and confused were his thoughts. Inexplicably, he was finding it more and more difficult to focus, to concentrate.

****

Once again, he spread his buffalo robe onto the ground. Little Beaver picked up the bone-pipe, packed it with sumac leaves, and began to smoke.

As he sat smoking, he thought he glimpsed an eagle, swoop down and pluck a jack rabbit from ground, ten feet from where he sat. The eagle, with the rabbit held firmly, trapped in his talons, turned his head towards Little Beaver.

Astonishingly, the bird's head was not that of an eagle, instead it was the head of the running land bird, the birds that had saved him from the rattlesnake's bite.

Smoke from his pipe was irritating his eyes. He blinked, and rubbed his eyes. He opened his eyes. The eagle, with the head of the running bird, had vanished.

Little Beaver pulled his robe tightly around his shoulders. He smoked, he chanted, he smoked, he chanted, he closed his eyes to contemplate that which he had just witnessed, and involuntarily, again Little Beaver slept.

****

Little Beaver lay, twisted in the folds of the buffalo robe, drifting in and out of sleep.

His mind adrift in the spirit-world, Little Beaver, was soaring high in the sky, gliding on the gentle warm southerly winds. As he rode the winds, he looked down, surveying the vast expansive plains.

Little Beaver's sight was enhanced, amplified, magnified. It was as though he was looking through his spirit eyes, the eyes of the eagle.

The scene before him was shrouded in a blue haze, he saw a line of great white-tented wagons, being drawn across the plains by pairs of huge hairless buffalo.

White men, and white women, the women with tent like head coverings similar to those covering the wagons, walked besides, and rode in the wagons.

As he dipped his wings to change direction, Little Beaver saw a war party of the People, attacking four wagons that had separated from the long line.

The wagons were overturned and ablaze. The People's warriors rode off triumphantly, with many scalps, and many horses.

Little Beaver woke in a cold sweat. He rapidly struggled to his feet, and experienced a momentary wave of dizziness. The sun was rising, peeking over the distant eastern horizon.

Little Beaver gathered his belonging, he lit his pipe, blew smoke towards the east, towards the south, towards the west, then towards the north. He ended the ritual by thanking the spirits for opening his eyes, for giving him his medicine that would guide and protect him.

He stepped off ten paces to the east. There laying on the ground, he saw the freshly killed rabbit. Under one of the rabbit's paws was an eagle's white tail feather. Little Beaver picked up the feather, and clutched it to his heart.

He folded the feather and with trembling fingers, placed it into his medicine pouch. He then skinned the rabbit, and hardly able to contain the fluids that filled his salivating mouth, he roasted, and feasted on the meat. A gift sent to him by his benevolent spirit.

As he retraced his journey, Little Beaver stopped at the shady spot that he had rested during his first day. He walked slowly around the periphery of the site of the cold, dead, campfire.

Five times, he circled the site. Each time he expanded the circle. It was on his fifth trip around the site, that he stumbled upon it.

In the grass were the undeniable scaly cones from a rattlesnake. The cones that created the paralyzing death sound — the warning sound of the rattlesnake. Little Beaver picked up the cones and added them to his medicine bag.

Little Beaver was satisfied. He was now at peace; he had communicated with the spirit world. For him, his benevolent spirits had interwoven dreams and visions from the spirit world, dreams and visions that had led to his acquisition of his own, personal, powerful-medicine.

During the course of this journey, this quest, Little Beaver had come to make the distinction between a dream and a vision. In his dreams were events of past times, people and events that he remembered, that he had experienced. Visions were symbolic messages, guidance from the spirit world.

He was convinced that the visions were truly messages sent by the spirits. Eagles with the head of the land running bird, vast numbers of white men, with great wagons drawn by huge hairless buffalo, invading the People's hunting grounds. These were truly visions. Visions sent to him by the spirits.

He had left on his quest as Little Beaver, the boy, soon to be a man. He would return to the People as a man, the Warrior forever to be known as Running Eagle.

****

The death of her son Jesse, her first born, totally devastated Peggy. To her family, and to most of the slaves, the weight of Margaret's grief permeated the air. A veil of gloom hung over the plantation.

Margaret was totally devastated, inconsolable with grief. Slowly, inexorably, she began to withdraw from the world.

Margaret remained in her room. Getting out of the bed briefly, only to answer the call of nature.

After two weeks of constant crying, Henry made the mistake of trying to console his wife, by stating that; "Jesse was a hero. He died heroically, fighting to protect his home from Yankee aggression."

Margaret's response was to throw the contents of her chamber pot into his face. She screamed at her shocked, surprised, flabbergasted husband; "Don't you dare spout that empty, meaningless, dribble to me. My baby, our son, is died. You sanctimonious, flag waving, hypocrites! You sit at home, beating the drums of war, drinking your bourbon, screwing your black wenches, while our babies lay dying in the mud. You so called Southern Gentlemen; you all make me sick."

At Margaret's request, Henry removed himself from their bedroom. Henry and Margaret sleeping together, was over. Although neither Margaret nor Henry realized, in point of fact, their marriage, was over.

****

Henry became increasingly alarmed at his wife's deepening melancholy and depression. Initially, Dr. Sawyer advised Henry to give Margaret time to grieve, to be caring, to be solicitous and to be patient.

Dr. Sawyer assured Henry, that in time, Margaret would come around and would regain her sweet, cheerful, disposition. The good doctor was wrong.

Unfortunately, Dr. Sawyer's presumptive diagnosis, and his subsequent prognosis, did not prove to be accurate. With the passage of time, weeks, then months, following Jesse's death, Margaret had not regained her sweet,

cheerful disposition. Instead she had become moody, withdrawn. She rarely left her bed, and she never ventured from her bedroom.

Her muscles, after months of inactivity, had begun to atrophy. Ruth, at Henry's insistence, was now constantly at Margaret's side.

With each passing day, each passing week, Margaret's health continued to worsen.
****

In contrast, Rebecca's handling of the grief that she experienced following her brother Jesse's death, was totally consistent with the diagnosis and the prognosis that Dr. Sawyer had given Henry concerning his wife.

Rebecca was worried about her mother's health. Each day she would look-in on Margaret. At first her mother had been sullen, moody, and constantly prone to fits of crying. As time passed, as the weeks turned to months, Margaret had become, combative, belligerent, and at times incoherent.

In order to "calm her down", Dr. Sawyer instructed Henry, to have Ruth give Margaret, to help her sleep, two tablespoons of laudanum, each night.

On July 21, 1862 the anniversary of her beloved son Jesse's death, Margaret Billings, while her slave Ruth slept on a pallet, on the floor, reached for the bottle of laudanum on her night stand.

She opened the bottle, and proceeded to swallow the entire bottle of its contents. Margaret slipped the laudanum bottle under the covers.

She closed her eyes and for the first time since Jesse's death, Margaret drifted into a blissful sleep.

****

As had become her habit, Mandy arrived at the Big House shortly before sunrise.

Since the beginning of the war, most notably since Jesse's death, in addition to her regular duties, Mandy had been assisting her mother in caring for Mistress Margaret.

Mandy opened the kitchen door. She was greeted by the smell of sweet dough, as biscuits and rolls sat, covered by a kitchen towels, "rising" on the table.

Fannie, the cook, was seated at the table, grinding coffee beans. *"Monin' Fannie".* Mandy grabbed an apple from the barrel, as she ran through the kitchen.

Fannie shook her head and muttered; *"Dat chile neva waks, she be always inna hurry."*

Mandy hurried up the flight of stairs. She gently opened the bedroom door. Her mother Ruth was on the pallet at the foot of Margaret's bed.

Ruth was asleep, softly snoring. Mandy tiptoed over to her mother, and gently, lovingly squeezed her shoulder.

"Wak up mama. Da sun be up inna minute. Time ta start a new day". Ruth staggered up from the pallet. In a hushed voice she greeted Mandy. *"Monin' sugah...I bes be usin' da pot befo we wake up da Mistress.*

Mandy opened the curtains, sunlight poured into the room. She reached under the bed and removed Margaret's chamber pot.

Ruth went to the bed and gently nudged her Mistress, *"Mistress Margaret, time ta wak up...time ta relief yo sef".*

Margaret did not respond. Ruth increased the pressure, still Margaret did not respond.

Ruth placed both of her hand's on Margaret's shoulders, and began to vigorous shake. *"Wak up Mistress Margaret, oh lawd-god, pleas Mistress Margaret, wak up!"*

Mandy ran over to the bed. She pulled her mother away from the unresponsive, lifeless form on the bed. She placed her hand on Margaret's forehead. *"Mama, she dead. Go get Master Henry."*

****

Ruth, sobbing openly, wringing her hands together, hurried from the room. Mandy gently, folded Margaret's arms across her breast.

She was straightening the sheet, when she noticed the empty bottle of laudanum, entangled in the sheets.

Mandy's intellect immediately, concluded that Mistress Margaret, had *self-medicated. She had* either accidentally or intentionally overdosed.

Mandy reasoned that her mother Ruth, would most likely be held responsible and accountable, for Margaret's death.

After all, Master Henry had given explicit orders that Ruth should care for, and that she should monitor Margaret's actions.

Instinctively, Mandy removed the empty bottle, and placed it on the nightstand. She looked for the cork used to contain the bottle's contents.

The cork was no were to be found. Mandy turned Margaret onto her left side. No cork. Frantically, she turned Margaret onto her right side.

221

The cork was now visible. Mandy picked up the cork and placed it into the mouth of the empty bottle. She replaced the bottle onto the nightstand. Mandy once again, folded Margaret's arms across her Mistress' breasts, and neatly folded the sheets under her arms.

Mandy surveyed the room, her gaze stopped when her eyes again fell upon the empty brown bottle, the vessel that had held the opiate.

Mandy grabbed the pitcher of water sitting beside the empty bottle, she removed the cork, she half filled the bottle with water and sloshed the liquid around in the bottle.

Just then Master Henry, followed by Ruth, were entering the room, Mandy replaced the bottle.

Mandy left the room and went directly to Rebecca's bedroom. She softly knocked on the door. Rebecca answered in a sleepy, slurred, half-awake voice, "Go away…I'm sleeping."

Mandy turned the doorknob and entered the room. Rebecca peeked out from beneath the sheet, and groaned. Mandy walked over and sat on the bed.

She took Rebecca's hand into hers, "Becky, your mother, Mistress Margaret, passed away in her sleep last night."

"Becky, I am so very, very sorry." Rebecca sat up in bed a solitary tear trickled down her cheek.

While hugging Mandy, she mumbled, my mother died a year ago. "Mother died when Jesse died.

****

In the two years following Henry's divestiture of Rosewood's assets from Northern banks and financial institutions, Henry and his Lawyer/Business Manager, Luis Frazier, invested heavily in the Confederacy.

At Henry's insistence, Luis on his behalf had purchased for Rosewood, approximately, $250,000 worth of Confederate War Bonds.

The bonds were backed and guaranteed, by the full faith and credit of the Confederate States of America.

In addition to the war bonds, Henry was actively and vigorously supporting the Confederate cause, through multiple, myriad, investments in various Southern manufacturing and munitions plants.

By the fall of 1862, Henry's patriotic investments in "The Confederacy and the Cause" were being considered, in "neutral" financial circles, as investment, financial, failures.

Although the Confederate Treasury, continued to taut the strength and solvency of its' bonds and currency, it had become increasingly clear that the South's predicted short war, with the North suing for peace, was not in fact, realistic.

Unfortunately for Henry and for Rosewood, not all of those who made up the South's business communities, were blind zealots, apostles, and unwavering, orthodox believers in the "South's eventual victory, and the survival of the Confederate States of America.

When it came to the attention of a cadre of opportunistic scalawags, that the extremely profitable, Rosewood Plantation, had an outstanding mortgage of $80,000 dollars, the unscrupulous southern "businessmen", quickly and quietly, purchased the Rosewood mortgage.

It was well known, amongst the business community that the bulk of Henry Billings fortune was invested in Confederate Bonds. It was also common knowledge, to those in a position to know, that at this time, the Confederate Treasury would not — and most likely could not — redeem the bonds that Henry had so enthusiastically purchased, in his patriotic support of the Confederacy.

Henry received notification that the Rosewood mortgage, had been sold. Presumably sold to unprincipled, speculators. Shortly thereafter, Henry received a letter, demanding payment, in full, of the Rosewood Mortgage.

Failure to pay in full, the sum of $110,000, in gold, on or before, 4:00 PM, June 13, 1862, would result in his immediate eviction, and the confiscation of all of Rosewood's lands and assets.

The letter was signed;

Sincerely yours,

J. Ashton

Theodore Ashton, Esq.,

Chief Financial Officer,
Old Dominion Reality, Inc.

****

Henry and Luis sat in Luis' Richmond Office. Despite the office door being shut, Luis's assistant James Evans, could hear practically every word, at least every word shouted by Mr. Billings, being said behind the closed doors.

Henry's voice was loud, in pitch, it sounded as if it had raised at least an octave. "Luis, how in hell did this happen? Who is this character, Theodore Ashton? What the hell is Old Dominion Reality? I've never heard of them!" How did this outfit gain possession of my mortgage, the Rosewood mortgage? The questions were being put forth — without a pause — in rapid succession.

As Mr. Evans strained to hear his employer's response, the office door opened, Luis, in a calm measured voice, spoke to his assistant; "James, you are dismissed for the day. I'll see you in the morning."

When Mr. Evans had left the outer office, Luis while reading the letter, walked over to his desk. He removed his reading glasses, and reached for the decanter of bourbon on his sideboard. Luis poured two fingers of whiskey into each of two glasses, and handed one to Henry.

"Calm down Henry." Henry began to sputter he almost choked as he tried to swallowed his drink, "Calm down, calm down, are you insane? How can you expect me to be calm when some slimy bastard, that I've never heard of, threatens to take Rosewood away from me!"

"Henry, I know that for the past two decades you've not practiced the law. I am aware of the fact that you've been functioning as a Southern, Gentleman Planter. But I ask you now, in all sincerity, have you forgotten everything that you learned about the law?" "I can't believe the extent of your apparent naiveté. Again, my friend, I am asking you to sit down, to calm down."

Henry, chastened, and slightly mollified, sat. Luis sipping his drink, and gesturing to Henry that he should follow suit, reread the letter. "Okay let's discuss this".

"In answer to your questions; Theodore Ashton is an Essex County, Democrat scalawag, I suspect that he's a Yankee sympathizer.

Shortly, following the commencement of hostilities, Ashton and a few of his associates, sit up this company, Old Dominion Reality. They began to buy up mortgages, call in the loans, and then to foreclose on the properties."

"As to how they came to acquire your mortgage, which as I recall now sits at about $110,000, is due to the rampant speculation that's sweeping the county."

"The financial boys feel that the longer the war goes on, the more unlikely it is that the Confederacy, will be able to honor its' debts. Many of our local merchants, are beginning to refuse, to accept Confederate Script.

I suspect that Ashton's group, offered to pay Richmond Savings, in gold, 75% of your outstanding mortgage. That's been that bunch's usual tactic."

"From a business perspective, as far as Richmond Savings is concerned, the $82,500 — which Ashton's group would have paid in gold — is preferable to $110,000 in potentially, worthless Confederate Script."

Henry slumped in his chair, "Luis, what am I to do? You, of all people, know that I've invested all of my money, everything in the Confederacy."

Henry reached for the decanter, and with a trembling hand, filled his empty glass with whiskey. "There's no way that I could raise $110,000 dollars, in gold by the 13th.

Even if I had time to sell some of, or more than likely most of my niggers, with Lincoln threatening to declare that they're not property, but free people, who would buy them?" Henry threw his head back, put both of his hands over his face, and in abject despair muttered, "Oh shit".

Luis stood, walked from behind his desk and placed his hand on his friend's shoulder. "Henry, I have a confession to make. Old friend, despite our mutual love and support of the South, despite your explicit instructions, to invest everything in support of the South's war effort, I could not bring myself to invest it all, everything, in the risky prospect of the success of the Confederacy".

Henry slowly lifted his head from his hands, "what are you saying Luis?" Henry's expression was undeniably that of hope. Luis returned to his desk.

Instead of setting, he turned to the large oil painting of Jefferson Davis, President of the Confederacy. Luis removed the painting from the wall. An iron safe was recessed into the wall. Luis removed a key from his desk draw, and inserted it into the lock.

****

Henry Billings, and Luis Frasier, were true supporters and believers, in the Confederacy. However, Luis in addition to genuine, enthusiastic, patriotic zeal for the Southern cause was at his core, a pragmatic businessman.

Unbeknownst to Henry, Luis had converted $50,000 of Rosewood's assets, into gold. As Luis would later explain to his friend Henry in a series of clichés; "You should never put all of your eggs into one basket. And always have a solid Plan "B".

Luis was fond of reminding Henry of his oft quoted, favorite axiom. "Henry by all means, you should hope for the best outcome, but more importantly my friend, you should always, always have a contingency plan, for the worst."

Luis removed a manila envelope from the safe, and handed it to Henry.

Henry read;

"Investments and Holdings of Henry Billings,
Rosewood Plantation, Essex County, Virginia"

Henry broke the seal. He empted the envelopes contents onto the coffee table. Four large packets of "Confederate States of America, bearer bonds, and a single sheet of paper, lay sprawled on the table.

Henry thumbed through the impressive looking stacks of bonds. They appeared to all be of the same denomination, $500.00. Henry put the bonds back into the envelope. He read the single sheet of paper.

The Law Office of Luis Fraiser, Esq.

Inventory: Holdings of Henry Billings, Rosewood Plantation, Essex County, Virginia:

1)   Confederate War Bonds;   Quantity = 1,000; Denomination = $500.00.

        Total Value = $500,000

2)   Gold Coins = Quantity = 2,500; Denomination = $20.00

        Total Value = $50,000

****

Henry reread the inventory account. He placed the sheet on the desk. "Luis did I, or did I not instruct you to divest Rosewood of all Yankee investments?

You deliberately disobeyed my instructions?" He fixed Luis with a stern stare…that as if by magic, slowly turned into a broad grin.

"Thank God, you didn't listen. Thank you, my friend,".

Luis, who had been holding his breath, slowly exhaled. "Actually Henry, I did not disobey your instructions. Your instructions were to divest Rosewood of Yankee investments, which I did.

The $50,000 that I moved into gold just happens to be in U.S. $20-dollar gold coins. Gold Coins whose value is impervious to who wins the war."

"That-not-withstanding my friend, you still have a problem. The notice demands payment in full of $110,000 in gold, in two weeks. Other than the $50,000 in gold coins, and the $10,000 in gold that I have…"

Henry struggled to his feet, he leaned heavily on his cane; "Wait a minute Luis, I appreciate it, but I can't let you risk…", Luis frowned, "Come on Henry, you'd do the same for me.

Tell you what, if you won't accept the loan, consider it an investment, my chance to invest, to be a silent minority partner, in the finest Plantation in Virginia, okay?"

Henry sat down, waved his hand gesturing that Luis should continue; "Okay Henry, that brings us up to $60,000. We're still short $50,000". Henry leaned forward; "Other than the cotton-crop, which is not nearly ready to harvest, the slaves are my most valuable assets."

Luis, replaced the quill held in his hand, into the inkwell; "Henry, for all intents and purposes the sale of slaves, in light of Lincoln's threat to free the niggers, is not a viable option."

Henry slumped back into his chair; "Realistically, I guess there's nothing that can be done. Well at least, thanks to you, Rebecca and I won't be penniless."

Luis drained his glass; he then refilled his and Henry's with the bourbon. Luis momentarily turned his attention to the manila envelope on his desk. Wordlessly Luis replaced the documents into the envelope.

He then walked over to the still open safe. Luis methodically replaced the envelope, closed the safe, and replaced the picture of Jefferson Davis. He stood silently studying the image of the President of "The Confederate States of America". Luis turned to look at his friend;

"Unfortunately, Henry, I'm inclined to agree. I can't think of a way for us to raise $50,000 in gold, in less than two weeks".

"My friend I think it's time for us to devise and put into place, a "Plan B". It's time for us to seriously plan for the worst.

Let's say it, get it out there, put it on the table. As it looks now, in less than two weeks, Henry you're going to lose Rosewood. Henry, do you agree?"

Reluctantly Henry nodded his concurrence. Henry took a deep breath, firmly sit his jaw, and with a look of steely determination asked his friend, "what's this "Plan B", what do you have in mind?"

Luis picked up the newspaper. The Richmond Gazette bore the date, May 22, 1862. Luis began to rapidly, scan and then, to turn the pages. He stopped at page seven.

Luis removed his quill from the inkwell, and circled a single sentence, two lines of print, at the bottom of the page. Luis handed the paper to Henry. Henry began to read:

"Abraham Lincoln, that black-hearted baboon in the Yankee White House, signed into law, the Homestead Act.

Henry raised his head with an inquisitive expression covering his face. He arched an eyebrow. He dropped his gaze back to the paper, and read out loud;

"Abraham Lincoln, that black-hearted baboon in the Yankee White House, signed into law, the Homestead Act.

Henry handed the paper back to Luis. "Okay Lewis, I'll bite. What the devil is the Homestead Act, and why exactly should I care about a new Yankee Law?

Luis placed the paper on his desk. Pointed the index finger of his right hand at his best friend; That my friend is "Plan B Henry, that's your Plan B."

Luis, unceremoniously, lifted his legs, and placed them on his desk. He crossed them at the ankles, and leaned back in his chair. "Free land Henry' acres upon acres of free, virgin, fertile, land."

Henry continued to stare, slack jawed, at his friend. He began to rotate the forefinger of his right hand in the universal gesture, of "please continue; tell me more".

Luis instantly, correctly interpreted Henry's hand signal. He took a deep breath, and enthusiastically plunged ahead. "In a nutshell, the Homestead Act gives applicants free land in the West." Before Henry could speak, Luis continued. "I know what you're thinking, what's the catch…what's in it for Lincoln?"

Henry sat transfixed. For more than a quarter century, Henry had known, admired, respected, and trusted this man, Luis Frasier. His trust began when Luis was his teacher, then his mentor and as his employer.

Henry trusted Luis as his lawyer/business manager, and now, most importantly, Henry trusted Luis as his best friend.

"Okay Luis, I'll bite, what's the catch? What's in it for Lincoln…we both know that there's no such thing as a free lunch!"

Luis sat back in his chair. His face took on that professorial demeanor, that Henry remembered when he was Luis' law student. He sat with his hands clasped across his belly.

"Lincoln is attempting to achieve multiple short and long-term objectives. His immediate objective, is to have the farmers own and work the land, themselves. This is in opposition to perpetuating the Southern Planter slaveholder society.

As Lincoln sees it, speaking strictly in terms of economics, legalized Negro slavery is an economic system, that uses slaves as free labor, creating an unfair economic advantage for the Southern Planters, the slave-holders".

"Long term, Lincoln is seeking to placate his political cronies by fulfilling Andrew Jackson's expansionist ambitions of extending the borders of the United States from the Atlantic Ocean, to the Pacific Ocean, Jackson's "Manifest Destiny".

To make that happen, Lincoln needs to recruit an army of white settlers, emigrant farmers who will ultimately supplant the Indians, and populate the west".

Henry had been listening intently, concentrating, while digesting, each word, each sentence, and phrase that Luis was saying.

Luis paused to take a sip from his drink. "Luis, did I understand you correctly? You're saying the Yankees are actually giving away free land? To whom, who's eligible? How much of the Indian's land per applicant, are those Yankee scoundrels giving away?"

Luis placed his glass on the desk; "Got your attention did I. Henry I've had a chance to actually read the law."

"To be eligible to get free land; 1) One must have not ever, taken up arms against the U.S. government; 2) You must be a man or woman (including freed slaves), at least 21 years of age; 3) You must agree to live on and farm the land for at least five contiguous years."

"Come on Luis, there's no way that I could possibly be approved for a land grant. My god man, the very first criteria that you mentioned; "One must have not ever, taken up arms against the U.S. government", disqualifies me".

"Sure, I've never personally, fired a gun at a Yankee, but my purchase of $500,000 of CSA war bonds, have sure as hell made available many a gun, that by god has killed many a Yankee. You can't possibly believe that they don't know, or at least suspect that I have been a fervent supporter of the Southern cause."

Henry was leaning over Luis' desk, an incredulous, exasperated expression covered his face.

Luis put up his hand in protest. "Henry, I totally agree with your assessment.
There is absolutely no way that Henry Billings, slave owner, Master of Rosewood Plantation, a vociferous, advocate and spokesman for Slavery, would ever receive a U.S. land grant."

Henry was puzzled, that Luis agreed with the obvious, that there was no way that he would get a land grant, what was the point. Why had Luis even mentioned this new law?

Henry, I think we both agree that we're backed into a corner. Raising $50,000 dollars within a month, during these times, with your principal assets being tied up in Confederate Bonds, and slaves, would be practically impossible.

My friend, these are disparate times that indeed, call for disparate measures. Would you agree that now is the time for plain talk...especially plain talk between you and me?

Now Henry was absolutely totally confused. Over the past three decades, his friendship with Luis had developed into a solid bond. He had no idea as to what his friend could be so carefully eluding to.

"Spit it out Luis, as far as I'm concerned, there's nothing that we can't talk about. If you have an idea, a solution for this dilemma, and you're afraid of damaging our friendship, because of hurting my feelings, forget it."

Luis took a deep breath. "Okay, here goes. If you recall, two of the criteria to be eligible for a land-grant were; 1) Must be 21 years of age; 2) Be a freed slave, male or female."
Once again Henry rotated the forefinger of his right hand, indicating that Luis should continue.

"Henry it's been well known, but never spoken of, at least in my presence, common knowledge that for the past twenty years, you've been having, shall we say amongst your slaves, more or less monogamous relations with one of your female slaves. I believe her name is Ruth, she has two children a boy and a girl. And that the slave girl, is your daughter Rebecca's, personal slave."

Henry, blustering began to rise from his chair; "Sir I find your tone and your inference, nay your accusations, both to be repugnant and offensive."

Luis shot back; "Come off it Henry. Everyone knows, including the Yankees, that it's common practice for white slave-holders to have sexual relations with their female slaves. Get off your high horse. If you're going to spout that righteous, hypocritical, "Southern Gentleman", crap with me, me your closest friend, we might as well stop, just quit right now. At least we'll remain friends."

Henry somewhat placated, mollified, sat back down. He mumbled; "sorry you're right…besides now that Peggy's gone, who the hell am I protecting?"

"Let me see, I was about seventeen, when I first began visiting Ruth. Can you believe it, twenty-two years?" Luis sighed; "twenty-two years, a quarter of a century, that's a very long time. Henry during that time, your relationship with Ruth — this is important, I want you to be honest with me, put your pride aside, — do you think she's had sexual relations with anyone other than with you?

Henry was silent for a moment, then he shook his head; "No I honestly don't think she did or has." Luis stared at his friend; "Never, let me remind you, your words Henry, twenty-two years is an awful long time. Why do you think that Ruth, that is her name correct?" Henry nodded in the affirmative. Luis continued; "why would Ruth, a healthy, pretty young wench, hold herself exclusively for you?"

Henry was obviously becoming increasingly uncomfortable, and annoyed. Despite his annoyance he answered; "I was about seventeen when I begin to visit Ruth. Ruth, according to Plantation records, was fourteen. She was the prettiest girl, black or white that I had ever seen. Ruth at fourteen had just had a baby, a boy that she named Jason."

"By the way, Ruth's boy Jason was the slave-boy that went as valet, off to VMI with Jesse. After Jesse's death, Ruth's boy, our slave Jason just vanished. Probably headed North probably a runaway.

"That's all very interesting Henry, but you haven't answered my question. What makes you think that Ruth's sexual activity, was exclusively with you?"

Henry continued, "I'll give you two, possibly three reasons. First just as you said, the fact that my slave Ruth and I were, as you put it, sexually active, was pretty much common knowledge. Once I made it clear to our overseer, Lucas Prentess, that Ruth was to be for my use only, Prentess put the word out."

"None of the Rosewood black bucks, would dare touch Ruth. They were in fear of the Master's wrath. Second the only other white male on the place was Prentess, and Lucas Prentess wanted to keep his job.

Luis made a fist. He placed his elbow on the desk and extended his forefinger from the fist; "Okay let me see if I understand; one, the overseer Mr. Prentess, to the slaves represented a deterrent, that of corporal punishment or worst. Two, as his middle-finger emerged from the fist, Prentess was hands-off Ruth, for fear of losing his job."

"If I may ask, what's the third possibility?" Henry looked sheepishly at his friend, "Luis I must admit that I surprise myself by thinking this, let alone saying it. In my mind I've convinced myself that Ruth wanted it that way."

"Henry you do realize that you've just acknowledged that you're Mandy's father?" Henry remained silent. The silence was becoming uncomfortable.
Luis spoke first. "Henry did you hear me. I said that you are in all likelihood, Ruth's daughter Mandy's father.

Henry stirred as if he were waking from a trance; "I freely admit that I am Mandy's sire; However, I am not Mandy's father! A father holds, rocks and coos his baby; A father plays with his baby, comforts her when she has a "*bobo*", when she scraps her knee".

"Mandy and my relationship is, and will always be, that of master and slave. I am merely the source of the sperm. I am not, and have never have been, Mandy's father".

Luis realized that he had inadvertently and most unintentionally, "struck a raw nerve". He quickly changed the subject. "Henry the reason that I asked these uncomfortable, very personal questions, is for me to get a feel, for the following proposal."

"I propose that in the time that we have left before foreclosure, that we sell as many of the Rosewood's assets as we can. We should sell, insisting on payment in gold, the horses the mules, the tools, the cotton gins, all of the tools and machines."

"We'll attempt to sell the slaves, but for the reasons we've just discussed, I don't feel that in this political climate, in terms of payment in gold, I don't feel that the slaves have any real value".

"Then you, Henry Billings, former Master of Rosewood, Plantation, Essex County Virginia, your daughter Rebecca, your slave Ruth and her daughter Mandy, traveling as

Rebecca's governess and companion, should pack your belongings, and join the westward immigration".

"Emigrate, move to Kansas. When you arrive in Kansas, settle and began to build on your 160 acres of land. At your request, I will send to you, your $50,000 thousand in gold".

"With your experience, your knowledge of farming, and your resources, depending upon the outcome of the war, I have no doubt that you will either be Henry Billings, Master of the New Rosewood, Plantation, Lost Springs, Kansas, or Henry Billings, distinguished Owner, Rosewood Farms, Lost Springs, Kansas."

Henry was looking at Luis with naked, frank disbelief. "Obviously this plan is contingent upon my getting 160 acres of free, fertile, Kansas land. How in hell do you think we can accomplish that?"

Luis smiled, "that my dear friend, is indeed the sixty-four-dollar question. Ruth is the answer. Ruth meets the Yankee's criteria for receiving free land under the new Homestead Act".

"Let me remind you, of the stipulations. Second only to the prohibition of not having borne arms against the United States Government, is eligibility if an applicant is a "freed slave, at least 21 years of age".

"If we pursue this, the applicant Ruth, will meet the criteria of being a "freed slave, at least 21 years of age; willing to live on and farm the land for at least five contiguous years".

He paused in order to give Henry time to gather his thoughts. "I still have contacts in Washington who — for a price — would expedite Ruth's application".

"Do you think that Ruth would agree to go along? Do you think that she would accompany and live with you and Rebecca in Kansas?"

Henry was intrigued by the prospect. Damn Yankees, invading his beloved South. Invading Virginia. Threatening his home. Wouldn't it be ironic if he used Lincoln's law, this Homestead Act, to relocate, to resurrect Rosewood?

Rosewood, he loved Rosewood with every fiber of his being. The thought of his losing Rosewood was repugnant, abhorrent.

His initial impulsive thoughts after receiving the notice of foreclosure, was to hang on. To fight, to fight the scoundrels to the bitter end. To exhaust every penny that he had, or could raise, if need be, to retain his ancestral home.

It was this damn war. First it had taken his son. Then, as if it were an insatiable monster, feeding on the Billings' Family, it had taken his beloved Peggy.

Taken her life, not with shot and lead, the cold hard elements that had snuffed out Jesse's young life, instead the war had infected Peggy with a pernicious, mind-crippling grief, which caused her to despise and to blame him, for the death of their son.

His beloved wife, the mother of his children, had been afflicted with an all-consuming melancholy that had ultimately, driven her out of her mind with grief, this damn war had caused her death.

"Henry shrugged his shoulders; "Luis to be honest, I really don't know if Ruth would cooperate."

"If Ruth and my twenty plus years…I don't know what to call it, I guess arrangement is as good a word as any."

"If our more than two-decade arrangement has told me anything about Ruth, it's that although she is undeniably illiterate, she can't read or write, and she is ignorant of life, other than that of being a slave, Ruth is an extremely clever, and highly intelligent person".

"I'll speak to her, explain the situation, and ask for her cooperation, her help."

Luis clasped his hands together, they formed a steeple, he brought them to his mouth, and spoke; "Fair enough; I accept that. Henry, I guess what I'm asking you for, I admit is sheer speculation. What do you think Ruth's answer will be?"

Henry rose, gathered his hat and his cane. He limped to the door, placed his hand on the knob, and opened the door.

Henry turned and spoke to his friend; "Luis please prepare the manumission papers, for my signature. Specifically, the contracts are to make the slaves owned by Henry Billings, known as Ruth and her daughter, the slave known as Mandy, free women.

Oh, and in answer to your question Luis, I believe that Ruth will say yes".

****

Henry sat gazing, listlessly poking with a crooked tree limb, the kindling being consumed in the crackling campfire. He surveyed his immediate surroundings, and mused in silent reflection, "how in hell did I get here?"

"How did I descend from Henry Billings, respected member, and paragon of Southern Aristocracy, Master of Rosewood Plantation, owner of scores of slaves, to this an emigrant, vagabond traipsing across the American Frontier.

Transporting what's left of the powerful Billing's family, now reduced to myself and Rebecca, to parts unknown."

Henry, Rebecca, Ruth and Mandy, had signed up for the wagon train in Saint Luis. Now having traveled, by steam boat to New Franklin, Missouri.

Henry's newly purchased wagon was the 11th wagon — amidships as the wagon-master, Captain Jeremiah Smith, former sea Captain's had declared — in the 27 wagons that made up the Captain Samuel Smith wagon train, whose ultimate destination was, San Diego California.

****

While it was true that Samuel Smith had spent 10 years at sea, as a member of a ship' company, the pinnacle of his ascent in the ship's chain of command authority, was that of a first rate bosun's, deck hand.

In 1826, at the tender age of eight, young Sam Smith, was orphaned and left alone in the world. His mother Lilly, one of New York City's many water front prostitutes, had been killed by a drunken sailor, that she had been servicing.

For four years, following his mother's death, young Sam had survived on the docks, living by his wits.

Sam begged, he stole, and frequently to survive, he was force to sell the only thing of value that he owned, he sold his body.

It was one of Sam's sexual patrons, a handsomely rugged looking midshipman that suggested that Sam join him at sea as a cabin boy.

After three months at sea, during their first voyage as shipmates, Sam's benefactor, his former client, mysteriously while fulfilling his turn at the mid-watch, lost his balance, and fell overboard.

Sam's benefactor, his former client, was officially listed in the ship's log as, "Man overboard - Lost at sea".

Sam's ship had docked for a week, in the beautiful Mexican Seaport of San Diego California. The year was 1840.

San Francisco was the ship's next scheduled port of call. Sam recalled standing at the ship's starboard railing, taking in the panorama of the lush, pristine California coastline, as the ship plied the Pacific, destination San Francisco.

He remembered being speechless, overwhelmed, dumb-founded by the panoply of dense vegetation. Sam thought to himself, 'Oh my God, so this is what heaven looks like". It was then and there that Sam decided to end his seafaring life. He intended to live his life exploring and enjoying this vast untamed land.

Sam, with his seabag, containing all of his worldly possessions, thrown over his shoulder and his Seaman's cap rakishly cocked on his head, left the ship in San Francisco. Sam purchased a horse, a rifle, minimal supplies, and set his course for the distant mountains.

For the next 16 years, Sam along with Mountain men, such as Jim *"Old Gabe"* Bridger, Thomas *"Broken Hand"* Fitzpatrick, and Christopher *"Kit"* Carson, lived his life, as a mountain man, trapping beaver, and living off the land, with and amongst the Indians.

It was following the massacre and mutilation of his Cheyenne wife and two sons, during a raid by a Pawnee war party, while Sam a member of a protracted Cheyenne a hunting party, that Sam — known to the Cheyenne as "Big Canoe Chief" — left the world of the Indian, to return to the world of the "Hair-mouths" as Captain Sam Smith, Santa Fe Trail — Wagon-Master.

* *

Following an uneventful trek of some 20 miles across the prairie, today's progress by the wagon train, had been by all, veterans and novices alike, been deemed excellent. Henry's wagon was a medium sized, modified freight wagon pulled by four mules, with two spare mules, and two horses hitched to the rear.

Henry today, as he did most days, had been crossing the country, alternating riding on horseback, and walking.

Now seated in the relative comfort and security of the "corralled", encircled wagons, the warmth of the fire and the low murmuring conversations of the families that occupied the adjacent wagons, was beginning to act as sedatives, lulling Henry into a semi-conscience state, dominated by his recollection of the flurry of recent, life-changing, events.

* * * * * * * * * * * * * * * * * * *

When Henry had returned from Richmond and Luis Frazier, his attorney's office, he sat at his desk, sipping a tall glass of lemonade. Henry was examining the two manumission documents, the legal documents setting free from bondage, two of his female slaves, Ruth and Ruth's daughter, Mandy.

During the journey returning him to Rosewood, Henry had been pondering just how and when he would share his plans to sell Rosewood, and to remake his and Rebecca's lives, by relocating, via their emigrating to the west.

Henry had sent Rufus to find Mistress Rebecca, and ask her to please join him in his office. He recalled, looking dismayed and nostalgic, at the bright eyed, intelligent, young lady, his daughter, sitting across from him. He remembered thinking, "where's my baby? where's my little girl?".

Henry remembered the awkward prolonged, silence, as he sat speechless, staring at the young lady seated across from him. He remembered that Rebecca, with concern clearly evident on her face, breaking the silence, "Papa, what's wrong? Are you ill?"

After regaining his composure, Henry had calmly explained to his, "Becky", his only surviving child, Rosewood's financial plight. He told Rebecca of his lengthy conversations and planning, with Luis Frasier.

Talks in which he and Luis had formulated and concocted what they hoped, was a viable escape plan.

Henry recalled his expressing to Rebecca, his humiliation and his guilt, in having "recklessly", invested practically all of their fortune, in support of the Confederacy.

He explained to Rebecca, how the failure of the South to force a swift conclusion to the war, had led to the subsequent devaluation of their assets, Confederate Bonds and currency.

Henry told of Luis' and his plan to paradoxically, obtain free, 160 acres of prime fertile, virgin land, utilizing Lincoln's own law, this new Homestead Act.

He also told of his friend's cautious wisdom, contrary to his explicit instructions.

He of Luis' decision to disregard, his instructions, issued by him during a moment of patriotic zeal, his adamant instructions, to invest all of their holdings in support of the Confederacy.

Henry told of Luis' action to conservatively withhold $50,000 of their money, and to convert that $50,000 into gold.

Henry recalled during that meeting, how his heart had swelled with love, and with pride, when instead of words of dismay and disappointment, Rebecca had responded with words of love and encouragement, "I'm not worried daddy, if Grandfather Artimas could create Rosewood in Virginia, I have absolutely no doubt that you'll build a bigger and grander Rosewood in Kansas".

****

Henry was jolted from his reverie, when out on the prairie, a coyote, began to yelp, and to howl at the rising moon. Instinctively he reached for his rifle, then he sheepishly, after observing the nonchalant reactions of his neighbors, the Hadley family, who occupied the

10th wagon in the train, Henry replaced the rifle in its' previous spot, leaning against the wagon wheel.

Henry relaxed, and once again gave in to the drowsiness undoubtedly engendered by his sore tired muscles, muscles not yet accustomed to strenuous exercise, and the warm waves of heat, emanating from the crackling, campfire

His thoughts returned to that pivotal meeting, the last moments that he and Rebecca would share in the office that had been built and occupied by his father, then by his brother, and finally by himself.

After Rebecca's utterance, her proclamation, enunciating those words of love and confidence, Henry had assumed that Rebecca would excuse herself, and leave him to plan their move, their future.

Instead, Rebecca had remained seated in her chair. She looked up expectantly at her father. "Sweetheart why don't you run along now. As you can imagine, I've got a million details to attend to".

"Daddy this plan to acquire free land, that you spoke of, how exactly does that work?" Henry had waved his hand dismissively, "don't worry about it honey, it's complicated. I'll take care of it."

Henry began to shuffle the papers on his desk. He picked up a document and began to read. Rebecca unflappably, remained seated. Henry recalled thinking, "by god she really has changed, she's grown-up".

He put down the document, sat back in his chair, and with a submissive sigh of resignation explained to her, the text of the Homestead Act Law, the law's intent, and the eligibility requirements one must meet, in order to apply for a land grant, under the Homestead Act.

Rebecca sat silently, brow furrowed, concentrating on her father's discourse. When he had finished, Henry recalled that he had politely asked if she had any questions. Becky's response had been, "As a matter of fact I have several questions".

"I'm confused. From what you've said thus far, neither you nor I are eligible for a land grant under this new law. Exactly how do we gain access to the free land?" Henry smiled, he reached into his desk drawer and withdrew what was obviously a legal document.

Without a word, he reached across his desk, and handed the document to Rebecca. She accepted the single page, and began to read. After she read and then reread the document, a broad smile lit up her face. "Does this paper, this Manumission document really free Ruth? Does this mean that she is no longer a slave?"

Before he could answer, she gushed on; the words had seemed to be just pouring from her mouth; "Papa this is wonderful, you're giving Ruth her freedom. I have always planned to do the same for Mandy."

Henry had asked Rebecca to please, calm down. "Rebecca, I plan to take Ruth with us to Kansas." Momentarily Rebecca had looked at him in confusion, then her eyes widened and her expression changed to wonderment.

"Daddy you're planning to use Ruth, a free woman of color, a former slave, to apply for the land grant, aren't you? Henry once again had been amazed by his daughter's perception, her intelligence, by her insight.

"This grand plan, this scheme to acquire 160 acres of free land, that you and Uncle Luis, have concocted, is dependent upon Ruth". Rebecca's smile had disappeared. In its place was the unmistakable look of disappointment."

"Father, — he remembered thinking, why is she upset with me, she only calls me father when she's angry — Rebecca held the manumission paper above her head, please correct me if I am mistaken, this legal document means that you can't take Ruth to Kansas, or for that matter, you can't take her any place that she does not want to go."

Ruth is no longer a slave, she's a free woman. "Does Ruth know that she is, or is about to be free? Have you asked her, as a free woman, if she would be willing to leave Rosewood, and come with us to Kansas?"

Henry had bristled at her, albeit accurate interpretation of the law; "of course she'll want to go with us. Ruth's been with our family her entire life. When we reach Kansas and she gets title to the land, I'll buy the land from her at a fair price. We'll even offer her employment as your lady's maid".

"What about Mandy? What will happen to the other slaves, Fannie, Peewee, Mammy Ester, and the rest?

Henry once again reached into his desk draw. He withdrew, what appeared to Rebecca to be, a duplicate of the Manumission document that she held in her hand.

Again, wordlessly he handed the document to Rebecca. Confused, but curious, she began to read. As she read, she quickly concluded that this legal document, was indeed, a word for word duplicate of the paper that she held in her left hand. She was about to speak, when Henry stopped her and instructed her to continue reading. She did as instructed, until she came to the phrase "the fourteen-year-old female slave, known as Mandy".

As she read Mandy's name, tears began to stream from her eyes. Rebecca left her chair, skipped over to her father, threw her arms around his neck, and whispered, "I love you Daddy. Thank you".

****

Henry had dozed off. Someone was shaking him, attempting to gain his attention. "Capn…Capn Billings, are you awake." Henry snapped out of his stupor.

His bleary eyes focused on the face of Bruce Logan, the man he had hired to drive the wagon, and serve as a trail hand, during their western migration.

Logan was a short, stocky man, in his late forties, or possibly his early fifties. He had decades of experience as a teamster, hauling freight, up and down the Santa Fe Trail.

When his little party arrived in the little town of New Franklin Missouri, one of the first tasks that Henry set out to accomplish, was to find and to hire a competent, experienced driver and guide.

He was in search of a trustworthy, competent, responsible man, who would lead the Billings party safely overland, possibly through hostile Indian country, to their planned destination, the town of Lost Springs Kansas.

Henry had spent the majority of his second day in New Franklin, visiting wagon trains, and commercial freighting outfits, and consortiums. Henry attributed his success in finding and hiring Bruce Logan, to be a stroke of blind luck, and sublime serendipity.

Henry had methodically made the rounds of supply depots and the wagon train staging sites, searching for an experienced, competent guide, and for an experienced driver/muleskinner. Apparently, the men with the skills that Henry sought, had either lift with earlier outfits, or their services had already been committed.

Tired, thirsty and disappointed, Henry decided before returning to his hotel, to stop for rest and refreshment, at one of the local taverns.

He took a seat at a vacant table and ordered a bourbon and water. When the waiter returned with his drink, Henry paid and in a dispirited voice asked; "you wouldn't happen to know were I might find a guide and a driver for my wagon, would you?"

The waiter smiled and nodded towards the bar, "Mister I do believe that this just might be your lucky day. That gent at the bar is Bruce Logan. Nobody in New Franklin knows the Santa Fe Trail better then ole Bruce Logan. Do you want me to send him over?"

Bruce Logan had been working as a bullwhacker and muleskinner *for* the Majors, Waddell, and Russell Freighting Company, since the firm's inception in 1848.

The unexpected collapse of the MW&R freighting in 1862, had left Bruce Logan, for the first time in 14 years, unemployed, without work, and with no immediate prospects.

With each passing year, of his employment with MW&R, Logan had been gradually come to the realization and the conclusion, that his days of traversing back and forth on the Santa Fe Trail, were numbered.

Logan had begun to gradually realize that his body was beginning to tell him, that men of his age should probably, not be engaged in the bullwhacker/mule skinner, occupation.

Logan had thought, when he was first informed that the company had gone bust, was an ironic, exasperated, utterance; "damn, just my luck".

Logan had already decided that his next scheduled haul — New Franklin, Missouri to Santa Fe, New Mexico — would be his last.

He had come to the conclusion that he would return to, and would remain in Santa Fe. Beautiful warm Santé Fe, were the climate was much more forgiving to the constant soreness and discomfort, that he was beginning to experience daily, in his aching, arthritic joints.

****

When Henry offered him the job of driver and guide, at a fee that was double that of his yearly salary at the now defunct M,W & R Freighting Co., Logan jumped at the offer.

He reasoned while Capn Billings', as he had come to address Henry, Kansas destination wasn't his ultimate goal, which was Santa Fe, the trip would at least take him half way to his new home.

After a brief interview, in which Henry described to his perspective employee, the size and composition of his party, Henry became instantly impressed when Logan interrupted, by listing the supplies and provisions that would be needed for the trip.

"Three women, yourself Cap'n, and me, five of us, all adults. I'm thinking we'll have to provision the wagon with;

1) 1,00 lbs of flour; 2)
2) 250 lbs of lard;
3) 250 lbs of beans;
4) 850 lbs of bacon;
5) 125 lbs of dried fruit and rice;

241

6) 100 lbs of coffee;
7) 50 lbs of salt & pepper.

"Cap'n, I recommend we take, in addition to my personal weapons, at least three rifles with plenty ammunition.

Logan's weather-beaten face vividly showed the effects of his many years of laboring, under the merciless sun that relentlessly beat down on the plains.

The lines that crisscrossed his face, made Henry think of the deep wagon-wheel ruts, embedded in the trail.

"I am indeed awake Mr. Logan. Thank you for your concern." Logan, with his tongue, shifting his ever-present wad of chewing tobacco, from the left cheek, to his right cheek spat a stream of tobacco juice into the dying fire. He wiped the tobacco dribble from his mouth with his dirty shirt sleeve.

Henry turned his head in disgust. In the past he had asked Logan to please refrain from expectorating in his, or in his daughter's presence.

Logan's response had been a lusty "beg pardon Cap'n, I don't rightly know zackly what you mean". Henry had repeated his request, this time substituting the word spitting for his previous use of the word expectorating.

Logan had beamed, and nodded his head signifying that now, he understood.

"Why certainly Cap'n, I'll do that." He had then turned his head ever so slightly, and spat a stream of dark brown tobacco juice into the dirt.

Henry decided that tolerating Logan's tobacco chewing habit, was a very small price to pay for gaining his services. Henry had shrewdly decided not to repeat his objection. He had remained silent.

"I've watered and hobbled the stock. Secured the mules and horses to the picket line. It's our turn for guard duty tonight Cap'n. I'll be taking up station over yonder."

Henry, now wide-awake and alert, slowly scanned the campsite. At first, other than the retreating back of his muleskinner, no one was in sight. Then to his right he heard the sound of female voices.

Henry rose and ambled towards the lyrical sound of the voices. He recognized the familiar sweet, throaty, voice of Ruth. "C-A-T, cat, D-O-G, dog, H-O-R-S-E, spells horse."

Ruth was standing. Seated before her, each holding alphabet flash cards were his daughter Rebecca, and Ruth's daughter Mandy.

Mandy was beaming, "that's wonderful mother. You're doing great. Isn't she doing great Becky?" Rebecca clapped her hands. "Remarkable!"

Rebecca placed the cards that she was holding into a box. Mandy placed her cards into the box. Rebecca picked up the box and gave it a number of vigorous shakes. She then faced Ruth, "Okay Ruth, now I would like you to take the words out of the box, place them on the ground and form three complete sentences.

With a look of apprehension, Ruth tentatively took the box. She walked over to the campfire, and began to rummage through the flash-cards.

****

Henry could not quite believe what he had just heard and witnessed. His mind flashed back to his conversation with Ruth, just before they had departed Rosewood for Saint Luis.

As he knew she would, Ruth had agreed to his plan to have her move, to travel, with him and Rebecca, to start over, to rebuild Rosewood in the west.

He was mildly surprised, at her reaction when he asked to use her name to apply for the 160 acres of frontier land.

Meek, docile Ruth, had placed a condition on her participation. *"Massa Henry, Ise wanna go wid yu an Mistress Bekka. Ise luv dat chile lik she be my own. Mandy be my chile Massa an if Ise truly free, I aint gone no wer wid out her"*.

Henry's initial, conditioned, knee-jerk, reaction to Ruth's "ultimatum", after a lifetime of her unquestioned obedience to his wishes, was that of anger and disbelieve. He thought to himself, "how dare she". His slave had given him an ultimatum.

Ruth cringed. She saw the color drain from Henry's face. Her instincts were that she should immediately prostrate herself at his feet, and to beg, for his forgiveness.

Instead, remembering his words when he gave her that fancy lawyer-paper; "Ruth, you are now a free woman", she meekly bowed her head, but stood her ground.

Henry relaxed. As a pragmatist, he knew that to obtain the Yankee land grant, Ruth's cooperation was essential. After all, Ruth his former slave now stood before him as, Ruth a free woman.

As a man, not as a Master, but as a man, who had been in a continuous,

On-going, more than 20-year physical relationship with this woman, to his surprise, Henry experienced an unmistakable, momentary feeling of pride.

After a protracted moment of silence, Henry placed his hand on Ruth's chin, and gently lifted. Her eyes met his. Where just a few moments ago she had seen rage, she now saw something different in eyes, she saw compassion.

Henry withdrew his hand and stepped back. He spoke in a blunt, subdued, matter-of-fact voice; "I have no objection to Mandy's joining us. However, Ruth, I believe that, as we speak, Rebecca is giving Mandy her own, what did you call it… pretty lawyer-paper". Mandy is now free, and can make her own choices."

Ruth smiled. She was certain Mandy would, at least for now, stay with her and with Rebecca.

Henry could not, and would not, attempt to interpret the reason for Ruth's smile. Instead turned and wondered at how his world, and the world at large, was so very rapidly changing.

****

With her face set in determined concentration, Ruth was diligently, and studiously reaching into the box that contained the letters of the alphabet, as well as cards that spelled, a number of simple words.

Ruth would arrange a series of cards on the ground, then she would step back and examine her effort. If not satisfied, she would shuffle, remove and replace, some of the cards.

In an effort to provide Ruth with space, room to concentrate, and to work, Rebecca and Mandy moved to the opposite side of the campfire, where they were joined by Henry.

Mandy turned to face Rebecca. "Becky do you recall what Ms. Leary said about the difficulties of teaching adults who are illiterate. Adults who don't have a rudimentary familiarity with the written language, as compared to teaching children?"

Rebecca was enthusiastically nodding. "As I recall her rational was that babies, more specifically toddlers, learn to speak, long before they learn to read and write.

That by listening to, and then imitating the sounds that they hear, if that environment consists of words spoken and pronounced, phonetically, correctly, children can more easily associate the written alphabet and words, with the sounds that permeate their environment.

Rebecca continued; "Ms. Leary compared the babies and toddlers' brains to empty slate boards, ready and eagerly waiting to receive proffered, *"pearls of wisdom."*

Mandy picked up the narrative; "Ms. Leary's point was that if you were constantly exposed to the sounds made by the letters of the alphabet as a baby, the ah sound of the letter "A" is easily comprehended when you first encounter the written word "Apple". The sound made with the combination of "t" and "h", when you put your tongue behind your teeth, is much easier to understand, if all of your life you've heard the word *this*, as opposed to the same word being pronounced, by all around you, as *dis*.

Believe me, from having lived it, I can personally attest to the validity of Miss Leary's postulation.

During their weeks of travel, Henry had at first marveled at, then gradually grown accustomed to Mandy's "perfect diction, enunciation, vocabulary and extensive command of English grammar. Even more impressive to Henry was Mandy's undeniable, superior intelligence.

He had often, unwittingly found himself looking at and comparing the strikingly stark, physical similarities between Rebecca and Mandy. Henry had long ago, intellectually accepted as fact, that Rebecca and Mandy, were biologically, sisters.

Now with the specter of legalized slavery having been removed from their relationship, despite his long held, and difficult to overcome prejudices, Henry continued to find himself surreptitiously, stealing glances at these two obviously, intelligent, intellectually matched, close friends.

No matter how hard he tried to avoid making comparisons between the girls, his eyes and his mind, like a tongue involuntarily returning to an aching tooth, seemed to be inextricably drawn to their similarities.

Ruth called to Mandy. "Mandy, Miz…beg pardon, Becky, I'm done.

The three of them, Henry, Rebecca and Mandy hurried over to Ruth. There on the ground before them, were three simple declarative sentences:

1) The cat is little.
2) The dog is big.
3) The horse is bigger than the dog and the cat.

Henry looked in wonder at Rebecca, then at Mandy. He then spoke to Ruth, "Ruth that is simply, most impressive".

He then turned and walked back to the wagon. The ladies heard him mumble, "I would not have believed it, if I had not witnessed it for myself".

To him, the facts were undeniable. In a few short weeks, an illiterate adult Negro, 35 years of age, had been taught to read and write.

Grudgingly, Henry had to reluctantly acknowledge to himself, if not yet to fully appreciate, the absolute brilliance, and the potentially far reaching impact, of one Miss Eleanor Leary, that meddling, Yankee teacher, that he had unceremoniously discharged.

* *

The night sky was a pitch-black blanket, encrusted and illuminated, by millions of sparkling stars. Henry reached for his pocket watch, flipped the lid open, and tilting the watch's face towards the faint glow of his neighbor's campfire, read the time. Ten past Two O'clock. "Damn…I overslept." He hastily pulled on his boots, grabbed his rifle, and hastened to relieve Mr. Logan.

As he approached the site where he expected to find, Logan, he was momentarily, annoyed, the man was not at his post.

Before he could whisper Logan's name, an incredibly strong hand clamped over his mouth.

Henry felt the dull edge of a knife at his throat. Henry knew that he had, but seconds to live. With a hopeless feeling of dread, and forlorn resignation, he thought, what's to become of Rebecca.

Bruce Logan relaxed his grip, spit a stream of tobacco juice at Henry's feet, and in a flat desultory voice stated, "you're late, oh if I was a Redskin, you're dead".

Henry's terror instantly changed to rage. He spun around to confront Logan. The muleskinner had vanished; he was nowhere to be seen.

* *

Moments before the eastern sky began to change from dark blue to purple, the wagon trains last shift sentries, along with the help of men from the individual wagons, began to move the animals into the inner sanctum of the protective corral, of the circled wagons.

Mules were re-hitched to the wagons. Bedding, blankets, were rolled tied up and thrown into waiting wagons. A few scattered utensils, coffeepots, stakes and tethers, used to restrict the over night grazing of the stock, were stowed. Before the sun appeared on the eastern horizon, the wagons were moving.

Henry mounted his large chestnut stallion. He spurred his horse towards the front of his wagon. Logan was seated on the raised high spring seat. Rebecca was seated to his right. Ruth and Mandy were walking towards the rear of the wagon.

Henry gave Logan the most reproachful, intense look of displeasure, and disapproval, that he could muster. Logan grinned, spit his customary stream of tobacco juice, in Henry's direction and politely greeted his employer; "Morning Cap'n…looks like a fine day for traveling".

Henry did not respond. Instead he looked at Rebecca, and smiled, "Good -morning princess…I hoped you slept well." Rebecca beamed at her father; "Morning Daddy. I had a wonderful rest. I slept like a baby. For some reason I'm famished. How long before we stop to eat?"

Henry rolled his eyes in exasperation. "Honey every day for the past two weeks, you've asked that question. Every day I give you the same answer. We should be "nooning" in two to three hours.

Remember when we first heard the Wagon master use that word "nooning"? We stopped at 10:15 AM to "noon". We were both confused. Noon as we knew it 12:00 O'clock, would not arrive for another two hours".

Logan who had sat silent during this morning's father-daughter dialogue, chuckled; "I remember that morning. The lot of you four were confused, green pilgrims."

He spat tobacco juice, then continued; "I thought that I did a pretty decent job of splaining. Wagon masters like to get an early start, usually a little after six. So as not to wear out the stock, dependent on the weather, he usually sets his mind to gaining 15 to 20 miles a day, for no more than four or five hours at a stretch. That means we most likely to stop at 10 or 11, we call it "nooning".

"We corral the wagons, he looked over at Rebecca and smiled, I remember Missy you asked me what did corralling mean".

Rebecca returned Logan's smile. Logan continued, "It was my pleasure to explain; Corralling is when the wagons are circled for protection, and the animals are turned out. In any rate, that first break of the day was often depending on the weather. It gives us a chance to eat breakfast, and rest in the shade of wagons or trees if we happen to see any. Sides, the men get a chance to do some chores".

The wagon train was moving at a slow, steady, predictable pace. The terrain was monotonously flat. This morning, the wagons had made good time.

At 10:20 AM, Homer Dickson, the Wagon train's principal scout, galloped up to the Wagon Master. Briefly the two men rode side-by-side, the scout then turned his horse's head, and rode off in a northwesterly direction.

Captain Smith, the Wagon master, passed the word. The scout had reported that approximately ¾ of a mile, was a small creek, surrounded by a few scraggily tress, with drinkable water.

The train veered to the right. When they were within 50 yards of the creek, Captain Smith fired his rifle in the air and shouted; "Wagons Nooning".

The number 1 Wagon, the lead wagon made a "U" turn, followed by the number 2, through the number 10 wagons. The 11th wagon, through the 26th stopped, and stood in place. The lead wagon closed the "circle" with wagon number 27.

Rebecca and Mandy, stood beside their stationary wagon, number 11. Once again, the girls collectively marveled at the speed and the precision of the wagon train's "nooning" maneuver.

The "nooning" encampment maneuver was accomplished with military precision. The wagons were pulled up close together, forming an enclosed circle. The mules remained hitched to the wagons.

The word was quickly passed throughout the train. Captain Smith, the Wagon Master decided that this was the end of the day's journey, that the 21 miles that they had covered today was sufficient. The wagon train would spend the night at this campsite.

Logan unhitched the mules and untied the horse from the rear of the wagon. After the people had obtained water from the creek, the animals were led by their driver's, down stream, to water at the creek. The animals were "picketed" tied by long ropes to stakes driven into the ground, outside the circle of wagons.

Ruth and Mandy went about the task of preparing the meal, "*breakfast*".
Rebecca was earnestly attempting to assist in the preparation of the meal.

In her eagerness to be helpful, Rebecca dropped, and stepped on a prime rack of beef ribs. In her haste to pick up the meat, she knocked over, and spilled onto the ground, the huge pot of coffee that had been heating on the hot coals.

Rebecca was horrified. Ruth placed her arm around Rebecca's shoulder, and in a soft soothing voice; "*Miss Becca we be needin som kindlin for the fire. I'd preciate if yo don't mine pickn' up some twigs, an som of dem dried-up bufla turds dat we seen.*"

With her pride somewhat mollified, Rebecca put on the large apron with the huge pouch in front, that she had seen Mandy wear, and walked towards the creek.

She began picking up twigs and bundling them together. When her bundle had grown to a respectable size, Rebecca decided that she had gathered enough twigs. It was now time to gather those "dried-up *bufla turds*", the buffalo chips that Ruth had requested.

Ruth and Mandy were busy preparing the meal. Mandy left the cooking pit and was walking back to the wagon to retrieve some meat seasoning.

She looked out towards the creek. There she saw Becky attempting to pick-up the buffalo manure. A broad grin began to spread across her face. Then when she could no longer control herself, she began to chuckle then, she began to laugh out loud.

Ruth looked up from the kettle that she was stirring. She saw Mandy at the wagon doubled over in laughter. Ruth, spoon in hand, walked over to her daughter. *"Gal wat's so funny...wat dun gotcha giglin lik a hyena?"*

Mandy attempted, unsuccessfully, to regain her composure. Instead of speaking, she extended her arm and pointed her finger towards Rebecca.

Rebecca was attempting to pick-up a large "chip", approximately 7 inches in diameter, by placing a twig beneath opposite sides of the chip, and slowly lifting, and dropping it into her apron-pouch.

Each time that she would lift the chip a few inches from the ground, try as she might to hold the two twigs level, invariably one or the other of the twigs would rise or fall below the level of the other, causing the chip to fall to the ground.

Each time the chip fell to the ground, Rebecca would — wipe the perspiration from her brow, and diligently — repeat the process.

Ruth despite her valiant attempts to maintain her composure began to chuckle, then she too gave way to unbridled laughter. With tears of mirth streaming down her cheeks, speaking between gasps; *"Stop dat laffin' gal...an don yo dare tease dat chile. Po thing she ain neva doon dis kindda wok befo. Gawd bliss ha she ain neva had to."*

"Now yu git bac ta spicin up dat meat."

****

After the meal, following the post-breakfast clean-up, Logan and Henry inspected the wagon, checking for wear and tear, thus far accrued due to the journey.

The most serious and dreaded accident to befall a wagon on the plains was the damage done to the woodwork in the wheels. Damage due to the dryness of the atmosphere encountered on the plains.

The extreme dryness often resulted in shrinkage, and contracting of the woodwork in the wheels. The metal tires under these atmospheric conditions were at increased risk of working loose from the wheel.

The wheels, in constantly passing, frequently sideways over uneven ground, oftentimes collapsed. The spokes had a tendency to break where they entered the hub of the wheel.

After thoroughly examining the left rear wheel, Logan stood up, spat out his customary stream of tobacco juice, whistled, and exclaimed; "Looks like we bout to have us a loose tire here."

Henry hurried over to the driver. Twice, Henry ran his hands over the wheel in question. He straightened and faced the muleskinner, "I don't see or feel anything. What makes you think the tire's loose?"

Logan bent down to the wheel, placed his finger midway down on the metal tire; "Feel' er right here." Henry placed his finger were Logan had indicated. He turned with a look of confusion on his face, "Mr. Logan, I don't feel anything unusual."

Logan reached into his shirt pocket, pulled out and bit off, a chaw of chewing tobacco. Henry — anticipating that a stream of tobacco juice would be forthcoming — stepped back. Predictably, Logan spat. This stream contained flakes of particulate matter.

Logan wiped his mouth with his sleeve. He pointed at the wheel; "I suggest we pull'er off and replace it with the spare." Henry pondered, Logan's suggestion. He then asked, how far do we have to go before we reach Lost Springs Kansas?"

Logan gave Henry a look of amusement; "Well Cap'n I reckon we done come about a quarter of the way." Once again Henry ran his hand over the wheel.

He stood and spoke, apparently to himself as well as to Logan; "We've got one spare wheel and we're not even halfway there. I tell you what Mr. Logan, we'll keep our eye on that wheel. If it holds up fine, but in any case, we'll change the wheel, when we've covered half the distance to Lost Springs."

Logan spat; "Okay Cap'n... I'd change that wheel now. But it's your wagon, you're the boss".

Ruth, Mandy and Rebecca were seated around the dying cooking fire. Ruth's hands were caressing a large black book. The spine of the book was facing Ruth. The pages of the unopened book collectively appeared to be the color of gold. Ruth reverently handed the book to Mandy.

Mandy read the title aloud; "The Holy Bible". She handed the book back to her mother. Ruth quietly began to speak, "dis book was gived ta me by my mammy, your grandma, Matilda. She neva could read what it say. But she pray wid it, with me an yo dead ant Sadie, every night."

Tears were welling up in her eyes, she opened the book turned the page, and began to read; "In the beginning..." Mandy left her seat and embraced her mother. Mother and daughter, both former slaves, held each other, and unashamedly wept together.

Rebecca, silently, respectfully, rose, and returned to the wagon.

****

When Little Beaver, now known as Running Eagle, returned from his spiritually uplifting vision quest, he eagerly shared his vision with the holy man, He Who Speaks To Ghosts.

Running Eagle's name change was accepted, by his family, his friends, and by the entire band, without question. It was well known that to share the details of your quest to obtain one's personal protection, his medicine, would surely result in the weakening of that medicine.

Running Eagle, his two closest friends Twisted Foot, and Stone Fist, in addition to being considered amongst the band's most eligible bachelors, had definitely emerged as future leaders of the People.

Of the three young braves, Stone Fist was by far, the swiftest, the stronger, and when facing an enemy in battle, the most ferocious of the three.

Despite his obvious physical prowess, or perhaps because of it, amongst the band, Stone Fist was one of the most gentle of men.

Even as a boy, when wrestling with his friends, or with the other boys of the band, Stone fist was aware of, and fastidious in the amount of strength and brawn that he would extend. He never lost a match, yet Stone Fist never seriously hurt or injured a member of the band.

Unfortunately for the enemies of the People, during battle, all of the innate power and strength possessed by Stone Fist was unleashed.

During raids, or defensive battles with other tribes, especially the hated Pawnee, Stone Fist, was fearless, and lethal. He neither asked for himself, nor extended to his enemies, any semblance of mercy.

The taking of many scalps, particularly those of the hated Pawnee, had gained Stone Fist much honor, and enormous respect among the People.

Growing up, Frog Legs, now Twisted Foot, was by far, the most mischievous, the impish member of the trio.

The multitude of pranks that Frog Legs had dreamed up and played on the band's little girls, either with or without the aid and complicity of his two friends, had somehow, during the trio's teen-age years, propelled Frog Legs/Twisted Foot, into his currently held status, that of being a ladies man.

Of the three, it did not come as a surprise to anyone, that Twisted Foot, was the first of the trio, to actively experience the inevitable, joys of mating.

Twisted Foot was the first of the three to partake of, and to enjoy the ecstasy — who knew — to be found in the arms of, and between the thighs, of the same girls that he and his friends, in the name of fun, had growing-up persistently, teased and tormented.

Twisted Foot, being the loyal friend that he was, felt that it was his sacred duty, to as swiftly as possible, open the eyes of his compardres.

To introduce his closest friends, Running Eagle, and Stone Fist, to the magical, mystical wonders awaiting them, nestled so sweetly and moistly beneath that silky, furry mound, at the apex of the young maidens soft thighs.

Running Eagle, on the other hand, Running Eagle possessed and instinctively employed, an amalgamation of the more desirable traits held by the three young braves

Additionally Running Eagle brought to their little enclave, something uniquely his, a trait held in short supply by both Stone Fist and Twisted Foot.

Running Eagle was not an impetuous person. Instead, if circumstances allowed, Running Eagle possessed an intelligent, analytical mind. And a disposition that was prudent, thoughtful, and wise far beyond his years.

In combat, Running Eagle was a courageous and fearless warrior. His strength, skill and stamina in battle, was extraordinary.

Anyone of the People's warriors would consider himself favored by the Great Spirit, to be possessed of the strength, skill, stamina, and wisdom in battle, that the Great Spirit had bestowed upon Running Eagle.

Shortly following one of the band's council meetings, Thunder Cloud, the band's recognized War Chief, was asked by the band's Shaman/Holy Man, "He Who Speaks To Ghosts", if he thought that, as a warrior, Running Eagle, matched the ferocity, the strength, and the lethality of Running Eagle's friend, Stone Fist.

Thunder Cloud, without hesitation, with complete candor, answered, that no man that he had encountered matched or exceeds as a warrior, the strength of Stone Fist.

Thunder Cloud then declared that as a leader, and as a man of wisdom, Running Eagle stood above all of the young men who had recently entered the warrior society.

Running Eagle's father Gray Wolf, overheard that conversation. When he told his son of the War Chief's words, Running Eagle, was silent, contemplating, then smiled and he eagerly, enthusiastically, agreed.

"Father, I do not know of there being a warrior more admired for his strength, ferocity his feats in battle, or of one held in awe by his friends, or more feared by our enemies, than is Stone Fist".

The truth of these sentiments had been vividly displayed during, the trio's actions during their first participation as members of a war party.

****

The Comanche raiding party was comprised of twenty five warriors. The purpose of the planned raid was to weaken the hated Pawnee's ability to make war, by stealing as many of their horses as possible, while increasing the wealth of the People.

The raiding party was lead by Thunder Cloud, the People's most respected, and revered War-Chief.

Twenty members of the group were experienced warriors, who had traveled the warpath on many occasions. Five of the braves were novices, taking to the warpath for the first time.

Running Eagle, Twisted Foot, and Stone Fist rode at the very end of the column of braves. The dust raised by the raiding party's ponies was thick, choking, and irritated the trio's eyes.

For the last two weeks, the three young braves, after being notified that they would be a part of the raiding-party, had been anxiously preparing for their great adventure, their true initiation into the Warrior-Society.

Although the village being raided would be that of the hated Pawnee, the raid was in large part, an opportunity for the warriors to gain individual, honor, respect, and glory, and for the young braves to experience the feel and the thrill of the warpath.

Thunder Cloud, being fully cognizant of the "hot blood" coursing through the veins of his first time raiders, their desire to count coup, tactically assigned, Running Eagle, Twisted Foot, and Stone Fist, to the group of warriors that he would personally lead.

The braves given the usually sanguine, benign assignment of holding the horses during the actual raid was assigned to one of the first-time would-be warriors, and two warriors that had participated in many such raids.

Following two days and eight nights of travel — after the first two days of traveling by day and resting at night, upon entering Pawnee territory, the war-party switched to traveling by night, and sleeping under concealment during the daylight.

Thunder Cloud's forward scouts, trotted up to the slowly advancing, raiding party. They reported that a small Pawnee village, consisting of 21 teepees, was ten miles to the northeast.

The scouts reported that removed from, but within ten minutes walking distance of the village, was the Pawnee's herd of horses.

The scouts reported that they had counted ten times the fingers of two hands, the number of horses in the remuda. Eight young Pawnee braves, were guarding the horses.

Thunder Cloud announced that they would make camp below the rise that they had recently climbed. They would make a no-fire camp, and plan the raid, which would take place that night, before the sun rose.

Thunder Cloud called into council, his four most experienced, battle tested warriors. Additionally the War-Chief invited the five first time, raiders to listen, but not speak, at the council.

The plan was to divide the warriors into three groups. Long Bow, Buffalo Hump, and Thunder Cloud, would each lead a group of seven.

Swift Arrow, whose speed and accuracy, in rapidly nocking and loosing arrows was well known and celebrated by his fellow warriors, was to conceal himself between the remuda and the village. His task was to prevent any of the Pawnee watching the herd, from escaping and alerting the village.

The plan was brilliant in its' simplicity. Kill the guards and steal the horses. Long Bow with his six warriors, would move in from the West. Buffalo Hump's group would approach from the East. Thunder Cloud's group, from the North.

Upon hearing Thunder Cloud's signal, the hoot of the Great Horned Owl, the three groups of warriors would advance as one, and begin the attack.

Running Eagle, Twisted Foot, and Stone Fist, would be a part of Thunder Cloud's contingent of warriors.

When Thunder Cloud's group was in place, he motioned for his warriors to remain silent and undetected. The War Chief waited. He slowly counted three times the fingers of both hands. He then touched the thumb of his right hand with his right index finger, folded the remaining fingers and made the sound of the night hunting, bird of prey, the hoot of the Great Horned Owl.

****

Prior to hearing the signal to advance, Running Eagle along with his fellow warriors had been lying motionless, flat on their bellies. As long as he could remember, he had been preparing for this moment.

When a little boy he had "crawled" stealthily and silently on his belly, intent on killing or counting coup, on the enemies of the People.

As he advanced towards the hated Pawnee, Running Eagle felt completely confident, justified, in his actions, and at ease.

The fact that he was on a mission to steal horses from his enemies, that he was about to take his enemy's life was, Running Eagle felt, literally his purpose for being. He was Comanche.

With his long knife in his right hand, and his tomahawk tucked into his breechclout, Running Eagle noiselessly crept up to within a foot of the Pawnee sentry.

He sprang forth and clasped his left hand around the man's mouth. Before the startled man could utter a sound, Running Eagle, with one swift sure stroke, cut his throat. Bright red blood gushed from the sentry's throat.

With his hand still around the Pawnee's mouth, Running Eagle lowered the lifeless body to the ground, and as Thunder Cloud had instructed, sprinted towards the horses.

Stone Fist, as had the rest of his group of warriors, had quietly advanced, undetected by the Pawnee sentries. As he was about to strike, his intended victim, turned, saw Stone Fist and yelled.

Stone Fist swung his heavy solid oak wood, war club. The weapon impacted the Pawnee across his nose, between his eyes. The force of the blow collapsed the man's face, crushing is skull.

The Pawnee's skull was split wide open. Grey brain matter spewed forth, like the meat from a crushed nut. His nose was shattered, one of his eyes was completely dislodged from its' socket, and rolled on the ground.

Stone Fist, no longer concerned with maintaining the element of surprise, let out a blood-curdling battle cry. A bone-chilling primordial exclamation, that had the intended effect of striking terror in the hearts of the People's enemies.

Before Twisted Foot could engage in hand-to-hand combat, his intended target was alerted by his comrade's yell of alarm. Momentarily frozen in fear by the sound of the Comanche war cry, the Pawnee, quickly reached for his knife and turned towards his still unseen stalker.

Twisted Foot dropped his knife to the ground and unslung his short-bow from around his shoulders. In rapid session he nocked, and let fly three arrows. The first struck the Pawnee in the eye, the second in the throat and the third, in his chest.

The sentry was dead, before the third arrow thumped into his chest.

Thunder Cloud, and a short muscular, athletic warrior, called Turd, with tomahawks and arrows, killed one and gravely injured two of three Pawnee braves, who while carelessly dozing, had been abruptly awakened by Stone Fists' blood-curdling battle cry.

Two of the Pawnee brandishing tomahawks and knifes, rushed towards Stone Fist. Thunder Cloud saw that Stone Fist, who was triumphantly scalping the dead brave, seemed to be oblivious to the two warriors bearing down on him.

Before Thunder Cloud could shout a warning, just as the first Pawnee's tomahawk was about to split Stone Fist's head, Stone Fist, still holding the dead Pawnee by the hair, without looking, but sensing the danger, dropped his right hand, the hand holding his knife to his side, he spun around and drove the knife into the chest of the Pawnee, and simultaneously, with tremendous force and ferocity, the fist of his left hand, smashed into the throat of the second brave.

Three Pawnee warriors, lay died at Stone Fist's feet.

One mortally wounded sentry lay moaning on the ground. The two Comanche warriors that had not directly slain the enemy ran towards the now agitated horses.

As they ran past the fallen, dying Pawnee writhing on the ground, the warriors counted coup, by quirting the dying man's slumped shoulder with their bows.

One of the Pawnee sentries, included in the group attacked by Buffalo Hump, managed to escape the Comanche ambush.

****

Just prior to the attack, a solitary sentry had mounted his horse and was leisurely about to circle the herd. When he heard the terrifying sound of Stone Fist's war cry he knew instantly, "Comanche war-party".

The Pawnee brave also knew that his life, and more importantly, possibly the lives of his clan, were in imminent danger.

To ride to the aid of his fellow sentries, did not enter his mind. The warrior, not knowing the size of the Comanche war-party instantly made the correct decision. Alert the village of the attack.

He turned his horse towards the village, and raced off to sound the alarm.

Swift Arrow lay flat, below a ridge on the seemingly flat prairie. Swift Arrow's strategic place of concealment was midway between the Pawnee village and the herd of Pawnee horses.

The Pawnee warrior's mount was at a full gallop. It's rider, was leaning over his pony's neck. He had eluded the Comanche war party.

His solitary thought was to warn the village of the presence of the hated Comanche in Pawnee territory, and to join the Pawnee war party that would mutilate, torture, kill, and avenge the deaths of friends.

Not hearing pursuit by the treacherous Comanche dogs, he momentarily set upright to catch his breath. It was his last breath.

The instant that the Pawnee passed, Swift Arrow stood and let fly six arrows in rapid succession. Three of his arrows struck the rider. One arrow lodged in the warrior's neck and two in his back. The dead Pawnee brave, fell from his pony.

Swift Arrow trotted over to the fallen Pawnee, who lay face down on the ground. Swift Arrow placed his moccasined foot on the Pawnee rump, and with both hands, pulled each of his arrows from the dead braves back.

Swift Arrow wiped the traces of blood and flesh from the arrows, and replaced them into his quiver.

Swift Arrow lifted the warrior's head by the hair, and with three quick strokes of his knife, removed the Pawnee's scalp.

Swift Arrow walked over to the now rider less pony. One of Swift Arrows shafts had grazed the pony's shoulder. Swift arrow, swung up onto the pony's back. He was depressed, disappointed, and disconsolate with remorse. Two of his arrows had completely missed their intended mark.

Swift Arrow had not been able to retrieve all of his arrows.

****

Once the four warriors that Thunder Cloud had assigned the duty of rear guard, to protect against, Pawnee pursuit, reported that there was no sign of enemy pursuit, the raiding-party slowed to an almost leisurely pace.

Thunder Cloud, Buffalo Hump, Long Bow, and two of the novice warriors, Running Eagle, and Stone Fist, rode ahead of the warriors who were driving the herd of captured horses.

Far off just before the horizon, Running Eagle saw what to his keen eyes, appeared to be a flock of eagles, normally solitary hunters, soaring in circling flight in the clear azure blue sky.

Ordinarily the sighting of an eagle, one of the birds that had bestowed Running Eagle with the protection of his powerful personal medicine, would bring joy to his heart.

This time instead of joy, a feeling of foreboding of dread, swept over the young brave. He turned his pony's head, lightly with his knees he applied pressure to the pony's ribs, and trotted back to speak with Thunder Cloud.

 Running Eagle reined in beside the war chief. And respectfully remained silent, not interrupting the Thunder Cloud and Buffalo Humps conversation.

Thunder Cloud had been recounting to Buffalo Hump, the sound, and the aftermath of Stone Fists blow with his war club, upon the Pawnee's skull.

Both of the mighty, veteran warriors laughed, and shook their heads in obvious wonder and admiration. "Running Eagle, you would speak with me?"

With his left hand gently squeezing the small leather pouch tied around his neck, his medicine bag, Running Eagle pointed to the far distant horizon. "Evil lays beyond those hills."

Thunder Cloud, with out questioning, turned his pony and at a gallop, lead the group back to the main body of the raiding-party. Buffalo Hump and Long Bow were told of Running Eagle's premonition of danger ahead.

Buffalo Hump was to lead half of the braves and half of the horses back to the their village, by moving towards were the sun sets, for one day's travel. Then they were to resume the trail straight to the village.

Long Bow was to lead his group of the braves and his half of the horse herd by one day's travel towards were the sun rose. Then they were to resume the trail straight to their village.

Thunder Cloud and Running Eagle, would scout ahead to see the danger. They would rejoin the raiding-party along the trail.

****

Thunder Cloud and Running Eagle dismounted a mile before the lip of the ridge that surrounded the valley. As they closed the distance to the ridge, it soon became apparent that what Running Eagle had thought was a flock of soaring Eagles, was instead a flock of circling vultures.

It seemed that each step that their ponies took, was met with an increasing smell of decay. A distant sound of buzzing, with each cautious step that they took, was gradually, steadily, intensifying.

Thunder Cloud and Running Eagle crawled to the edge of the ridge, and looked down into the valley. At first neither man could interpret, nor could they comprehend the surreal, images before them.

Hundreds of denuded buffalo carcasses lye haphazardly, strewn in the lush cured grass of the valley.

The remains of the animals, the meat, the organs, the sinew, the horns, the hooves, all gifts sent by the Great Spirit, to sustain and enrich the life of the People, lay rotting, covered with flies, being torn apart by vultures, on the prairie.

Thunder Cloud and Running Eagle, silently slowly descended to the floor of the valley. The putrid smell of rotting, decaying flesh was overwhelming. Running Eagle felt nauseous. He felt the bile rising in his throat. Horrified, he attempted to suppress the overwhelming, involuntary reflex. He failed. Running Eagle vomited.

Running Eagle's stomach spewed forth its' contents. Mortified at his self- perceived weakness, he sheepishly looked towards his leader, the mighty War-Chief, Thunder Cloud.

Thunder Cloud stood motionless. With his head bowed, silent tears were streaming down his cheeks.

****

Thunder Cloud's raiding party, the warriors still bedecked in their ominous black and yellow war paint — war paint that they had "touched-up" during their brief stop at the band's pony herd — rode triumphantly towards the village.

News of their return had been given to the village earlier, by two of the young boys that constantly tended to the band's pony herd.

Thunder Cloud's raiding party had, without a word, simply co-mingled the hundred forty-six stolen Pawnee ponies, with the People's herd.

Each of the twenty-five members of the raiding party, could identify the ponies that belonged to them. Those ponies that Thunder Cloud had awarded, to each member of the raiding party.

As the leader of the war party, Thunder Cloud claimed twenty ponies. The remaining ponies were awarded to warriors based upon their standing. Past honors, enemies killed, scalps taken coup counted.

Running Eagle, Twisted Foot, and Stone Fist, as first time raiders, were entitled to five ponies. Stone Fist, for his individual outstanding display of courage and valor, was allowed first pick of the ponies, that remained after Thunder Cloud's had selected.

As the raiding party neared the village, they were greeted with the rhythmic sound of beating drums. Men, women and children were dancing and singing songs in their honor.

A large fire was burning in an earthen pit. Buffalo, and Elk ribs were being roasted.

The wives and families of the returning warriors, weeping with joy, and singing, rushed to their warrior's ponies. The jubilant women literally pulled the warriors, these expert horsemen from their mounts.

Old Wise One, the venerable warrior/statesman-chief, the band's Head Man, who was now in his sixty-third summer, was at the head of the procession of men, women, and children that had turned out to welcome the returning heroes.

Running Eagles father, Gray Wolf did not speak instead he thrust out his chest, and solemnly with pride filled eyes, nodded to his son

The band's leaders, Old Wise One, He Who Speaks To Ghosts, Grey Wolf, and the elders, welcomed the safe return of the raiding-party.

He Who Speaks To Ghosts, thanked the Great Spirits for protecting the Peoples warriors. Old Wise One spoke of the rarity of such a successful raid, not having a single casualty or an injured warrior.

Thunder Cloud spoke for the group. He told of the many captured ponies that now swelled the People's pony herd. He spoke of the taking of the fresh scalps, which hung from the triumphant warriors, lances, shields and belts.

Old Wise One, called for a council meeting, to be held following the reverie, and the festivities. It was at the council that Thunder Cloud would relate to the band's leaders, the details of his successful horse stealing-raid against the Pawnee.

Gray Wolf had requested of Old Wise One, and He Who Speaks To Ghosts, that his son Running Eagle, be allowed to attend this, his first council. His request was agreed to.

Upon learning that the novice warrior, Running Eagle would be attending the council, Thunder Cloud suggested that the entire group of young first time warrior-raiders be allowed to attend the council.

Both Old Wise One, and He Who Speaks To Ghosts saw the wisdom of Thunder Cloud's suggestion. Old Wise One, Head Man of his people for more than two times the fingers on both hands, realized that the time for new leadership was rapidly approaching, the old warrior/statesman grunted and stated emphatically; "It should be so".

****

Old Wise One's lodge was large and roomy. The red embers of a small fire in the center of the teepee were still smoldering. Those warriors in attendance were seated in two concentric rings.

Old Wise One, He Who Speaks To Ghosts, Thunder Cloud, Grey Wolf, and two additional elders, Dull Knife, and Thoughtful Man, made up the inner circle. Six feet behind, was the outer circle, which was comprised of respected warriors that had distinguished themselves in battle.

Old Wise One packed the band's ceremonial pipe with tobacco and prairie grass. He tamped down the blend, removed a glowing twig from the pit, and lit the pipe. The old man puffed several times, the bowl of the pipe glowed.

Old Wise One blew a stream of smoke to the East. He then passed the pipe to the warrior to sitting to his left, He Who Speaks To Ghosts, who in turn repeated the ritual, passing the pipe to, Thunder Cloud, then to Grey Wolf, then Dull Knife, and finally the pipe was passed to Thoughtful Man.

After Thoughtful Man repeated the ritual, the circle of warriors had blown smoke to all corners of the wind.

Thoughtful man turned, and passed the ceremonial pipe to the warriors that comprised the outer circle. After each warrior had puffed the sacred pipe, it was returned to the Head Man, Old Wise One.

Old Wise One spoke; "Our War-Chief, Thunder Cloud, has returned with much honor and horses. He has lead twenty-five of our warriors against our hated enemies, the Pawnee. Thunder Cloud once again has earned the gratitude of the People".

Thunder Cloud proudly received and acknowledged the praise of the assembled warriors. When he raised his hands, the conversation ceased.

Thunder Cloud looked to his right and addressed the Head Man; "I would speak?" Old Wise One nodded his permission. "I have rode the warpath, and I have lead many raids against the enemies of the People. The accursed Pawnee, the treacherous Kickapoo, and at times, I have even battled the Cheyenne.

"It is true that this raid was good, it brought to us many horses and Pawnee scalps. Yet the thing of greatest importance to the People, the raid brought to my eyes, is the presence of white men having invaded our hunting grounds, the hunting grounds of the Comanche".

Immediately there was confusion amongst the gathered warriors. Several of those assembled, rose from their seated positions, and at the same time, attempted to speak.

Old Wise One raised his hand. Where seconds ago there had been noisy confusion, questions from many of those present, now there was absolute silence.

Old Wise One spoke; "Did your path cross that of the white-man?" Thunder Cloud told of his and Running Eagle's discovery of the hundreds of buffalo carcasses left, rotting in the sun.

During Thunder Clouds report, the occupants of the large teepee were eerily quiet. At the conclusion, the old Head Man, Old Wise One spoke; "who would speak?"

Bear Claw a warrior who had counted many coup, asked; "was this sea of skinned buffalo real? Or — now directing his words to the shaman, He Who Speaks To Ghosts — perhaps Thunder Cloud and Running Eagle, experienced a dream, or a vision?"

Once again there was murmuring amongst the council of warriors. The Holy-man, He Who Speaks To Ghosts spoke; "It is not often that the same vision is seen at the same time by two. I will think on this."

Running Eagle, seated legs crossed in the second circle of warriors, rose; "I would speak. All of the warriors, 1st and 2nd circle alike, were astonished. Warriors seated in the 2nd circle rarely spoke at council meetings. Novice warriors never spoke unless requested to, by the Head Man or by some other warrior of high status.

Running Eagle's father, Gray Wolf was mortified at his son's lack of decorum. Gray Wolf was about to rebuke his son, when Old Wise One frowning at Running Eagle, remarked; "Running Eagle, son of Gray Wolf, wishes to speak."

"These things that the mighty warrior Chief Thunder Cloud spoke of, I too have seen. Our's was not a vision sent from the spirit world. I, as have many of you, have been visited by the spirits visions. Visions do not smell as if all of the earth's animals are rotting.

He bent down and pulled several items from a leather pouch, and held them over his head.

Running Eagle brandished above his head, the chewed-up stub of a cigar; the broken half of a bottle, that still reeked with the lingering odor of cheap whiskey; a torn page from a newspaper.

Visions do not smoke the white man's tobacco sticks, drink the white man's firewater, look for sign or speak from the white man's paper.

Running Eagle replaced the white-man's litter into the pouch. He handed the pouch to his father, Grey Wolf. Grey Wolf, without opining the pouch, handed it to Old Wise One.

The Head Man examined the contents of the pouch. He then passed the pouch to the shaman, He Who Speaks To Ghosts, who after looking at the items handed the pouch to the warrior on his left.

After the last warrior in the 2nd circle had examined the white-man's garbage, He Who Speaks To Ghosts, rose to speak; "I believe in the truth of what Thunder Cloud and Running Eagle say. The white-man has invaded the land of the Comanche. He slaughters our animal brother the buffalo."

"Do the white-men hunt and kill the buffalo for food, do they kill the buffalo for clothing and shelter to keep his people and his lodges warm? No? As told by Thunder Cloud and Running Eagle, the white-man kills our animal brother the buffalo, and leaves the meat to rot."

"Then why? Why does the white-man slaughter the buffalo leaving the carcass to rot in the summer sun. Food that should nourish the People, now and through the coming harsh winter, is left for the scavengers. Rotten meat now only fit for the vultures, and the coyotes."

"The white-man with their wagons, their cattle, their plows, their sheep, have come to take the Comanche's land. Their cattle and sheep eat the grass that the Great Spirit intended to feed the buffalo…the buffalo who are food for the People".

Thunder Cloud stood; "the white-man has come with his long guns. Guns that smoke and kill, before you hear their thunder. They have come to kill all of the buffalo. By killing our buffalo, the white-man is killing the People."

"Our women and children sleep with empty bellies. Instead of warm buffalo robes, the women and children will shiver and die from the cold."

"Others have tried and failed to take the People's hunting grounds. The Apache, have tried and failed; the Pawnee have tried and failed; the Arapaho and the Utes. All have tried, non have succeeded."

"We must fight and kill these filthy hair-mouths. We must drive them from the land of the Comanche."

Numerous council meetings had followed Thunder Cloud and Running Eagles's report of the wanton, indiscriminate, wasteful, slaughter of hundreds, of thousands of buffalo, by the white man.

It was decided that the decision to make war against the hair-mouths — not to just conduct random raids for scalps and horses — was a matter to be discussed by the Head Men and war-chiefs of the many bands and clans, that would gather for the tribes annual spring buffalo hunt.

Wise One and Thunder Cloud would tell of Thunder Cloud and Running Eagle's recent discovery of the overwhelming evidence of the malevolent encroachment, of the white-man on the People's hunting grounds.

Until a decision of the combined tribal leaders, assembled at a mass tribal council, was rendered, it was decided that if hunting and/or raiding parties encountered the white-hunters, or white-settlers, the leaders of the hunting or raiding party, could access the white-man's strength and make the decision whether to attack, or to avoid the hair-mouths.

****

For the past two days, Captain Smith's twenty-seven wagons, wagon train was being constantly scouted, by Comanche warriors.

The wagon train was making good time. In the last week, with good weather, and relatively flat terrain, they were averaging almost twenty miles a day.

Henry was gently jostling along, seated next to Logan on the raised front seat of the wagon. Logan held his plug of chewing tobacco in his left hand, his huge Bowie knife in the left. He was attempting to cut a fresh chaw of chewing tobacco. Logan was holding the leather reins between his teeth.

Henry reached over and removed the reins from Logan's mouth. "Here let me hold those a minute for you. Ruth, who had been feeling out of sorts for the past few days, was resting on folded bedding in the rear of the wagon.

Rebecca and Mandy were walking on the right hand side of the wagon. They were engaged in mirthful chatter.

Suddenly without warning, Jasper their lead mule let out a strident bawl, reared in his harness, and lurched to the left. The mule's front right hoof struck, and decapitated the head from the snake that had struck the mule's left foreleg.

As the lead mule Jasper, frantically pulled to the left, the entire mule team followed. Henry pulled on the reins, attempting to control the team. The tongue of the wagon swiveled 45 degrees to the left. The mules and the wagon lurched from the trail.

The left rear wheel sunk into a prairie-dog hole. The metal tire flew from the wheel. The wheel collapsed, splintered into multiple fragments of shattered spokes and rim.

With the remnants of the wheel plowing up dirt, Logan, who had grabbed the reins from Henry, was able to stop the mule team.

Henry jumped down from the crippled wagon, and ran around the tailgate to inspect what remained of the left rear wheel.

Lars Olson, the huge, blonde, Swedish emigrant whose wagon was the 12th, in line immediately behind Henry's, came running intending to render assistance. "By Gawd Billings, are you alright...is anyone hurt"?

Without looking up from the wheel, Henry waved his hand at the lumbering Swede; "We're fine Lars". Then turning towards Logan; "This wheel is completely shattered. Oh well, we were going to replace it in a couple days anyhow.

Captain Smith rode up in a cloud of dust, dismounting before his horse had come to a complete stop. The Wagon Master shouted; "Is anyone hurt!"

The three men jumped, startled by the loud report of Bruce Logan's Navy Colt revolver. Logan joined Henry, Capn' Smith, and the Swede. "Had to put Jasper down. Rattler. Poor ole Jasper was real bad snake bit".

Mandy and Rebecca were running towards the group. Mandy was sprinting, well ahead of Rebecca. She was shouting; "Mama, Mama...oh my God...Mama are you alright?"

Henry heard Mandy's screams. Then in panic, he ran to the back of the wagon, and pulled down the tailgate.

Henry had completely forgotten that Ruth had been riding in the rear of the wagon. Logan stepped onto the seat, and made his way into the interior of the wagon.

Ruth lay motionless, unconscious on the floorboard. An iron cooking pot was lying beside her. Henry grabbed her under her shoulders, Logan lifted her by her ankles. The two men lowered Ruth to the ground.

Mandy ran to her mother, and gently cradled Ruth's head in her lap. "Mama are you alright...are you hurt?" Ruth slowly opened her eyes; *"Yeh baby, I'se alrite. Whew dat dere be da craziest ride I don eva tok."*

Mandy, looked from her mother's smiling face to the concerned face of Rebecca. Mandy overcome with relief, began to laugh. Rebecca joined in.

The wagon master bent down to examine the shattered wheel. "Well all things considered, it coulda been a lot worse. Looks like the axle's still intact." He looked directly at the muleskinner; "Mr. Logan how long do you think it will take to replace the wheel?"

Logan spat a stream of dark brown tobacco juice; "I reckon me and Mr. Billings, can have it changed and moving in about a half hour or so."

Captain Smith turned his head and spoke to Henry; "Mr. Billings I had planned to keep the outfit moving today for about another five miles."

"Our scout Mr. Dickson, says that five miles or so, as the crow-flys, there's an arroyo with a fast flowing stream of good clean water, and with some thick grazing grass for the animals. That's were I had planned to camp, to corral for the night."

Captain, there's no need to change your plans. There's no need for the train to camp here. Keep the train moving. We'll catch up at the arroyo. We'll be along before you know it."

Captain Smith was about to dismiss Henry's words, his instincts and experience completely rejected the thought of leaving a single wagon with two men and two women, alone for 30 minutes, on the prairie, when Lars Olson chimed in; "by Yimminee Henry, I'll stay to help with the wheel. Between the three of us, we'll be finished in 15 maybe, 10 minutes, By-Yimminee."

Henry shaking his head responded; "I thank you Mr, Olson, but there's no need. Mr. Logan and I can handle it. You go along with the train, with your family."

Lars placed his hands on his hips; "My boy Bjorn, is eighteen, almost a man by golly. He can drive my wagon for five miles."

The wagon master commented; "Mr. Billings, I'd feel a lot better if you'd accept Mr, Olson's offer of help." It's true that we haven't run across any sign of Indians in any significant numbers, but there has been occasional sightings of solitary heathens."

"Two or three bucks, aren't likely to strike a wagon defended with three well armed men."

****

The days of the time that the People called the; "Moon when the ponies shed their shaggy hair", were rapidly dwindling.

The band would soon be leaving for the annual Summer Hunt. They would be but one of the many bands consisting of their friends and distant relatives, that comprised the tribe, the "Lords of the Plains", the Comanche.

It would be at this annual gathering of the People, that the fate of the whites that had invaded the Comanche's ancestral hunting grounds would be decided.

Prior to breaking camp, a small hunting party, lead by Thunder Cloud was organized to obtain fresh meat for the trek. Because of the success of his recent raid on the Pawnee, Thunder Cloud asked the members of that recent successful expedition, to join his hunting party.

Each and every member of that raid was eager to join yet another excursion lead by Thunder Cloud. The fact that the Pawnee raid had yielded many horses and many scalps, without injury or the loss of any of the People's warriors, proved that not only was Thunder Cloud a great leader, Thunder Cloud's medicine was indeed, strong medicine.

Thunder Cloud decided to limit the hunting party to 15 warriors. The ten warriors that were not selected, though disappointed, understood Thunder Cloud's decision.

The hunting party would be required to move stealthily and move rapidly, for the quarry that they pursued, elk and pronghorns, relied upon speed to elude predators.

Thunder Cloud's decision to include the less experienced warriors in the hunting party, was intended for them, the young protectors, and young hunters of the band, to hone their martial skills. The rapid, accurate, loosing of arrows and the firing of rifles, while riding all out on the backs of, or crouching beneath the necks, of their charging mustangs.

****

From the beginning, the hunt had been hugely successful. The first day out, the hunting party spotted a large herd of elk. The party was able to bring down twenty-three animals. The hunters fired not a single rifle shot.

Prior to leaving the village for the hunt, Thunder Cloud's instructions to the members of the hunting party, were to hunt solely with bows and arrows.

Rifles were only to be used in the event of conflict with an armed enemy. The bands limited supply of rifle ammunition, cartridges, was to be conserved, not to be used, expended against "unarmed elk and antelope".

Thunder Cloud decided to send back to the village, the bountiful supply of fresh meat. The meat would be butchered and processed by the women.

Running Eagle, Stone Fist, Twisted Foot, and Crooked Arrow were detailed to take the fresh kills to the village. They were given permission to remain in the encampment overnight, and to rejoin the hunting party in the morning, with fresh horses.

After delivering the meat and making arrangements for fresh mounts and packhorses, Running Eagle and his fellow warriors, dutifully avoided the festivities that accompanied their return. Instead they went to their lodges and rested.

Just before dawn, the four young warriors left to rejoin Thunder Cloud and the rest of the hunting party.

Instead of retracing the path that the entire hunting party had taken the previous day, in order to expeditiously reach the site that they expected the hunting party to be, the four braves took a southeasterly route.

Crooked Arrow, who had been scouting, riding ahead of the other three, was heading back to the group, at a full gallop. As soon as Running Eagle heard the rapidly approaching pony, he signaled for the others to stop, and to take cover.

The only available cover was a slight depression in the otherwise flat terrain. Stone Fist and Twisted Foot held the horses, while Running Eagle slithered to the top of the ridge. His eyes were scanning, focused well beyond the Crooked Arrow, onrushing warrior.

Running Eagle immediately surmised that Crooked Arrow was not being pursued. Running Eagle stood and waved his arms in an attempt to attract the warrior's attention.

Crooked Arrow saw Running Eagle, and reigned in his panting, sweating, pony. He jumped from his pony's back, and ran towards his three companions.

Running Eagle spoke first; "My brother, you ride as if the evilest of the evil spirits are chasing you. What is wrong…what have you seen that causes you such anxiety?"

Stone Fist gave crooked Arrow, who was gasping for breath, his water pouch. Crooked Arrow thirstily drank, then he began to speak; "Many wagons; many guns, many hair mouths, white men, are on our land".

Crooked Arrow went on to describe what he had observed. He had been scouting ahead of the group, constantly alert to the ever-present possibility of discovering Pawnee, or Ute raiding, or war parties.

Five miles out in front of Running Eagle's group, Crooked Arrow had heard, a cacophony of noise. Sounds, noises so loud and diverse, that he could only ascribe them to the sounds made by the mass migration of hundreds of persons, moving their belongings across the plains.

The sounds of the many travois' ladened with their belongings, being dragged by their horses, over the prairie. The sounds of the children, of families, including the old ones and of the sounds of the community's domesticated animals, filled the air.

Crooked Arrow had tied a long rope around his pony's neck, and staked the mustang out to graze. He had then, on foot, cautiously moved towards the source of the loud noises.

Crooked Arrow was determined, to at all cost, avoid being detected. As he cautiously peeked over the rise, down into the valley, he had been astounded by the tableau that sprawled out before him.

Crooked arrow had counted 27 covered wagons, at least 60 white men, 40 women, 50 children — boys and girls — between 2 to 10 summers.

Teams of mules were drawing the wagons. Most of the white men were mounted on large, clumsy looking horses, with long guns attached to their saddles.

At least one unsaddled horse, was tethered to the rear of each wagon. Crooked Arrow remembered thinking as a warrior, that the hair-mouths clumsy horses, in battle, would be no match for the People's fast agile ponies.

There was very little discussion following Crooked Arrows report. Running Eagle declared; "We must make this at once, known to Thunder Cloud."

****

Thunder Cloud stoically received Crooked Arrows news of white men, in significant numbers in Comanche hunting grounds. He called together a council of the hunting party's senior warriors.

Crooked Arrow and Running Eagle were asked to repeat to the assembled warrior, Crooked Arrows observations.

Consistent with Comanche etiquette, Crooked Arrow was not interrupted during his recitation. At the completion of his report, Crooked Arrow sat, he did not speak again.

Thunder Cloud rose and began to speak; "I do not believe that the white men of this long line of wagons, were those who slaughtered the buffalo and left the carcasses to rot in the sun. Yet I do believe that these whites that Crooked Arrow saw and those that are sure to follow, will take our land".

"They will ruin the Earth Mother's grass with their cattle, and sheep. With no grass, there will be no buffalo. Without the buffalo, the People will perish".

"The white men must be stopped. We must let the white man know that those who invade our lands, will be killed"

"The warriors of our hunting party are not enough to attack and to kill these many hair mouths with their many long guns."

"We will return now to the village and will tell Old Wise One, He Who Speaks To Ghost, and the others, of the presence of so many white men on our hunting grounds. We have enough meat for our journey to the People's gathering".

"Running Eagle, you with Crooked Arrow, Stone Fist, and Twisted Foot, are to follow these whites. Watch their habits, look for their strengths and for their weaknesses"

****

Although Running Eagle' was the titular leader of the small contingent of Thunder Clouds hunting party, each member of the group retained the autonomy to act upon his own individual initiative. The warriors followed Running Eagles directives because they respected him as warrior, and as a leader.

Running Eagle's plan was to divide the four of them into two pair. Running Eagle and Stone Fist; Crooked Arrow and Twisted Foot.

They were told by Running Eagle, to if at all possible, avoid being seen, or of leaving sign of their presence to be found by the white men's scouts.

For three days and nights, the braves kept the wagon train under constant surveillance. The warriors identified the wagon master, the trains "chief".

They noted, that while the bulk of the white men could hardly be considered warriors, the few that were, had so disciplined the rest, with their circling of the wagons maneuver, and their long guns, to effectively mount a formidable defense.

A defense that ensured a successful attack on the train, would require surprise, and an overwhelming number of warriors. A defense that would undoubtedly cost the lives of many of the Peoples warriors."

Running Eagle decided that the four warriors had completed their mission, and that they should return to report their findings to the council.

It was decided that before returning to their encampment, the warriors would scout the wagon train, one last time.

As they looked down into the valley, the young warriors, as they had expected, observed the wagon train, steadily plodding along in a southwesterly direction.

Just as they were about to turn for home, Running Eagle abruptly reigned in his pony and dismounted. Twisted Foot's pony was trotting ahead of his three companions. Twisted Foot was anxious to return to the waiting arms of his many female admirers.

Twisted Foot looked back over his shoulder and saw his best friend, Running Eagle, standing on the ground counting the wagons.

Confused, Twisted Foot turned his pony and trotted back, past Stone Fist and Crooked Arrow. He dismounted and walked over to his friend.

"Running Eagle, what is wrong? Why do you not ride with us?" Stone Fist and Cooked Arrow, turned their mounts and joined the two braves, who were standing in quite conversation.

Running Eagle spoke directly to Crooked Arrow; "the number of wagons, how many did you count?" Crooked Arrow, without hesitation, answered; "twenty-seven wagons".

While Running Eagle and Crooked Arrow were talking, Twisted Foot had been pointing to, and counting the wagons. Twisted Foot, with a curious perplexed, look in his eyes, spoke; "twenty-six wagons."

Wordlessly, the warriors swung onto the backs of their ponies, and began to backtrack the trail of the wagon train.

****

That point in time when Henry's wagon lost a mule, and more importantly, one of their wheels, was the only time during the past two days, that the wagon train was not being watched by at least one of Running Eagle's group of warriors.

Bruce Logan and Lars Olson had unhitched the mules. With Henry's help the three men managed to move the wagon a short distance, clear of the dead mule.

In order to reduce the weight that would have to be jacked-up off of the ground to facilitate the changing of the wheel, Henry and Lars had removed various heavy items, including a large trunk, from the wagon.

The front legs of the mules and the saddle horses had been hobbled, to prevent them from wandering off.

Ruth, Mandy and Rebecca were off to the side of the laboring men, sorting through the "Billings' Family Heirlooms", that were stored in the large trunk.

Henry, his shirtsleeves rolled up, displaying ghostly pale white arms, spoke to Rebecca, "Becky why don't you and Mandy take the stock down to that little mud hole." He jerked his head, indicating the direction, over his right shoulder. "Let them graze and get some water. We'll come get you when we're finished repairing and repacking the wagon."

Rebecca and Mandy, each leading a horse, dutifully did as Henry had requested.

As Mandy and Rebecca sat in the puny shade afforded by a solitary juniper bush, talking, gossiping and fantasizing about their new life in the new state of Kansas, their whole world came crashing down.

Both girls froze when they heard one of the most horrific, frightening sounds, to course across the plains. The strident primal battle cries of attacking Indians.

****

When Running Eagle, and his fellow warriors, first heard the distinctive battle cry of the Tonkawa trumpeted in the valley, they quickly dismounted.

Running Eagle, Stone Fist, and Crooked Arrow, noiselessly climbed to the top of the rise. The braves lay flat on the ground, looking down at the battle being waged between their ancient enemies, the hated Tonkawa, and the three white men who had repaired, and were now defending their solitary, crippled wagon.

Five Tonkawa warriors, armed with war clubs, bows and arrows, and an old Springfield rifle, were amongst the white defenders.

****

Bruce Logan was just about finished tightening the *lugs* on the new wheel, when he heard the primordial scream the battle cry of the attacking Indians.

Logan dropped the wrench that he had been welding, and grabbed his rifle. The rifle had been within his reach, leaning against the wagon, directly behind the left rear wheel.

Henry was momentarily stunned. Then he quickly regained his composure. Henry was under no illusion; he realized that with his wagon alone, separated from the train, he would be fighting for his life, and for the life of his daughter, Rebecca.

Henry's rifle was in the scabbard attached to his horse's saddle. Rebecca, at his direction, had removed the saddled horse some quarter of a mile away, in order to water and graze the animal.

Henry dragged himself up into the wagon. On his hands and knees, he began to frantically search within the confines of the wagon, desperately groping for one of the two rifles that he kept in the wagon.

Logan raised his weapon and fired. At the very instant that his rifle discharged, one the several arrows, shot in rapid succession by the Tonkawa warrior, leading the charge, thudded into Logan's chest.

The shot that Logan had managed to fire was intended for and aimed at the maniacal warrior leading the attack. The path of Logan's bullet was altered by the almost simultaneous impact of the two Tonkawa arrows that rapidly passed through Logan's chest.

The heads of the two arrows protruded from Logan's back, the shafts were not visible, embedded within Logan's body. The feathered ends of the arrows, seemed to be vibrating in front of the dying man.

The misdirected bullet, Logan's solitary rifle shot, in essence a stray bullet, struck the Tonkawa warrior who was bringing up the rear, in the forehead.

The impact of the bullet violently snapped the brave's head backward. The Tonkawa warrior was dead before his lifeless body hit the ground.

****

Henry's frantic search, ended when he found the two extra rifles, lying on the wagon's floorboards. The rifle were covered by a heavy quilt.

Henry threw one of the guns through the opening in the rear of the wagon, in the general direction of the unarmed, the panic stricken, Lars Olson.

Before Henry could fire a shot, a strong bronzed hand, pulled the rifle from his hands. The rifle fell to the ground. Henry jumped to the ground. His crippled leg collapsed beneath him.

He was attempting to pick the gun up from the dirt, when the Tanaka warrior's war club smashed against his head. Henry's head literally exploded.

Every tooth in Henry's mouth were dislodged. One of Henry's eyes was knocked from its' socket. His nose was crushed and fragmented. Henry's right eye was dangling, suspended below his nose, by a sheath of muscle, and ligament.

The leader of the Tonkawa's leaped from his pony, grasped Henry's head by the hair, and with three quick strokes of his hunting knife, removed Henry's scalp.

Henry's lifeless form dropped to the ground. The Tonkawa held the scalp in the air, and screeched his triumphant war cry.

****

Ruth had been frozen in terror and fear. She witnessed the Indian warrior's' skirmish with Henry. Ruth stood almost motionless, hands to her mouth, suppressing the silent screams that were trying to escape from her lips.

The awful, bone-crunching sound of the Tonkawa's war club against Henry's, head, released her from her temporary paralysis. Ruth ran to the spot where Henry's rifle lay on the ground.

Although she had absolutely no knowledge of the workings of a firearm, she pointed the gun towards the savage standing over daughter's father, her former Master, Henry Billings.

As Ruth in vain was attempting to fire the weapon, her arms were violently thrust upward. For an agonizing second her eyes met those of an enraged savage.

The lethal warrior, without any display of outward expression, plunged his eight-inch hunting knife into Ruth's chest. The knife thrust was just below her rib cage, traveling upward into Ruth's heart.

In one swift motion, the warrior withdrew his knife. Ruth lay mortally wounded, convulsing at his feet. The heavily muscled, powerful warrior lifted Ruth's unconscious, mortally wounded body by her hair. With three quick strokes of his hunting knife, he removed her scalp.

As the Tonkawa warrior was triumphantly waving the somewhat coarse, wavy haired, scalp in the air, he sensed danger, and quickly turned his head.

Instinctively the Tanaka hunched his shoulders and averted his head. The blow from the wooden stock of a rifle, crashed down on his back and his left shoulder.

For an instant, the warrior's left arm went completely numb. He looked to his left and saw the petrified face of a tall white man with yellow hair. The man's hair was the color of ripe maze. The yellow hair covered the man's head, as well as covering his face.

Within seconds sensation had returned to warrior's left arm, he parried, the white man's blow and stabbed viciously with the knife that he welded in his right hand.

The lethal eight-inch blade, ripped through Lars Olson's abdomen, perforating his intestines.

The Tanaka sat upon the dying white man's legs, and with several deep-scooping motions of his hunting knife, eviscerated, disemboweled, the big Swede.

The smell of fecal matter, of death, pervaded the air. The Tanaka warrior, deftly severed and removed the heart from the body of the dead man.

The Tanaka brought the heart to his mouth, and bit, chewed, and swallowed a chunk of the warm, still pulsating, organ.

With Lars's blood dripping down from his lips, the Tanaka contemptuously stood over the dead man, with the yellow hair. He lifted Lar's head by the hair, and with his minatory, lethal knife, collected the yellow haired-scalp.

The warrior waved the scalp, dripping with blood, over his head and screamed his war cry.

****

The four Comanche watched as their enemies, the cannibalistic Tanaka, slaughtered the three white men, and the helpless woman.

Crooked Arrow was the first to speak; "Look at those puny white men. They are not warriors. They invade our land, slaughter the buffalo, yet do not eat the meat; they kill just to kill."

"The hair-mouths do not respect the land or the People. They come here, and destroy our land, without fear. They and the white women that spawn them should all be killed."

Running Eagle spoke; "The Great Spirit has provided buffalo and antelope, more meat than stars in the sky."

"He Who Speaks To Ghosts, has said that men, who eat men, while surrounded by the buffalo, are led by evil spirits. The Tanaka dogs, the eaters of men, are now four. They are careless."

"Let us kill these followers of evil spirits, these Tanaka dogs."

Stone Fist grunted his concurrence with Running Eagle's words. "We must strike quickly. Kill them all, take their scalps, and their horses."

The two braves turned towards Twisted Foot, who held their ponies. Running Eagle joined the three braves.

Running Eagle, pointing to the two young women who separated from the wagon, had witnessed the Tonkawa's' attack, spoke, before mounting his pony, "Do not kill the women.

The women will be useful to the People. They will work for, and along side our women. The women will give birth to future Comanche warriors. The women will increase the wealth of the People."

Twisted Foot, who had been holding the ponies, galloped forth, shrieking his war cry at the top of his lungs. He was the last of the four charging Comanche warriors to mount his pony.

****

Mandy and Rebecca were seated in the sparse shade of a scraggily Juniper bush, idly watching the horses graze.

The two teenage girls were giggling. Mandy had been teasing Rebecca about the ever more frequent, surreptitious, admiring, sidelong glances that eighteen year old Bjorn Olson, their strapping young blond neighbor, in the wagon just ahead of them, had been increasingly sending in Becky's direction.

Suddenly a horrific aberration, seeming to have just arisen from the pits of hell, four; no five wild half naked savages, demons whose bodies were painted from head to foot, in black and red paint were attacking the wagon.

Rebecca began to scream, "Daddy". Mandy instinctively, reflexively, put her hand over Rebecca's mouth, muffling her screams. They stood frozen in place as three arrows, in rapid succession, burrowed into Mr. Logan's chest.

The two horses whinnied in panic, and were pulling at the reins that held them to the stakes, the stakes that the girls had pounded into the ground, that prevented the horses from bolting.

Henry's huge stallion, with a violent jerk of his head, pulled the stake to which he was tied, from the ground. The big stallion galloped onto the open prairie.

Mandy instinctively realized that she and Rebecca could do nothing that would assist the men fighting for their lives. She grabbed Rebecca's hand and shouted; "Run Becky, run!"

They ran to the remaining horse that was straining to free himself. Mandy forced Rebecca, to place her foot in the stirrup, and to swing into the saddle. Mandy slid the horse's rein over the stake, placed her foot in the left stirrup and swung up behind Rebecca. She dug her heels into the animals flank.

The frightened horse, with the wind carrying the smell of blood to his quivering nostrils, did not need encouragement; he sprang forward in a gallop, following the path that Henry's stallion had taken

Rebecca was sobbing uncontrollably. Mandy looked over her shoulder. To her horror, two of the half-naked savages were in pursuit.

Despite Mandy frantically kicking the horse, pleading that he run faster, their pursuers were rapidly closing the gap.

Just as Mandy had given up hope of outrunning the two demons that were rapidly overtaking them, both of their pursuers, at a full gallop, raced past her laboring horse.

The savages in their hideous black and red war paint, were frantically whipping their ponies.

For a second Mandy experienced first relief, which was then quickly replaced with confusion.

Mandy's confusion turned to dismay when she saw that the painted savages that had killed and butchered her mother and father, were now being chased by three well armed, shouting, whooping, young Indians.

When the two groups of Indians had galloped past them, Mandy turned her horse back towards the wagon. Rebecca, who had been continuously crying, was making an attempt to control herself.

In a halting voice, gulping for air, she asked Mandy; "where are we going?" Mandy kicking the horse as hard as she could, gritting her teeth breathlessly responded; "to the wagon train, we've got to get help from the wagon train".

****

Running Eagle's pony overtook the girl's fleeing horse. He grabbed the horse's bridle.

As Running Eagle was halting the horse, Stone Fist's pony drew even with the two girls, who were riding double on the exhausted horse. With one effortless swipe of his muscular arm, Stone Fist knocked both Mandy and Rebecca from the spent horse's back.

Mandy and Rebecca fell to the ground. Rebecca uninjured, got to her feet screaming, and began to run. Crooked Arrow still astride his pony easily ran her down. Rebecca lay on the ground, sobbing at his pony's feet.

When Mandy fell from the horse, she felt a sharp pain in her right ankle. As she attempted to rise, to run, when she put weight on the injured leg, she collapsed.

Mandy realizing the futility of trying to escape quietly managed to stand tall, her head held high. Mandy awaited her, and Rebecca's deaths.

****

Running Eagle tied Mandy's hands together. Crooked Arrow did the same with Rebecca. The two girls, hands tied, were forced to face each other. Rebecca, seeing Mandy's composure tried to stop crying. She instead began to involuntarily emit occasional, involuntary whimpers.

Running Eagle looped a single strand of rawhide between both girls' bound wrists. He then attached a twelve-foot rope to the strand of rawhide that linked the girls.

Crooked Arrow and Stone Fist, swung up onto the backs of their ponies, and without a word, they galloped back to wagon.

Running Eagle, rope in hand, swung up onto the back of his pony. He too, at a trot, turned his pony in the direction of the wagon.

Mandy and Rebecca staggering, stumbling, and yet managing to remain on their feet, were being dragged behind Running Eagle's pony.

As they neared the Billings' wagon, the girls looked in horror at the human carnage. Henry Billings, Ruth Billings, Bruce Logan, and Lars Olson, all lay on the ground, their bodies scalped and mutilated.

Upon seeing the carnage, both girls almost in unison, began to uncontrollably retch.

The slain men were naked. They had been placed on their backs. The men's genitals had been hacked from their scrotums.

Each man's mouth had been crammed with his penis, with his attached testicles grotesquely, hanging from his chin.

Ruth, as were the men, was lying on her back. Both of her breasts had been hacked off, and been removed from her torso.

The contents of Rebecca's stomach spewed forth its'contents, in torrents. She could not stop the spasmodic, dry convulsions that racked her body.

Mandy, who had been raised and lived in a culture that condoned, and in fact encouraged, the practice of men (white-men), inflicting heinous brutality on their fellow man (black-men), closed her eyes and gritted her teeth. Somehow she managed to overcome the overwhelming, insistent urge to vomit.

Separate from the bodies of their families and friends, were the bodies of two Indian braves. Both of the warriors, had large hunting knifes, lodged in their chests.

The brave that wore black and red war paint, had been scalped, his body mutilated. Attached loosely to the lance held in his left hand, were two bloody human scalps.

One of the scalps consisted of long straight, stringy yellow-hair; the texture of the hair of the other scalp was that of short, curly-kinky, black hair.

Stone Fist and Crooked Arrow were reverently wrapping the warrior devoid of war paint, a young brave, clad in leggings, moccasins, and a simple breechclout, in one of the Billings' family's blankets.

Stone Fist and Crooked Arrow carefully bound the body of Twisted Foot to his favorite war pony.

****

Twisted Foot had arrived at the massacre, as the three Comanche warriors were giving chase to the three fleeing Tanaka's. Twisted Foot had dismounted from his pony, and climbed up on to the seat of the wagon.

He heard movement in the interior of the wagon. He placed his hand on the hilt of his hunting knife. As he moved to enter the wagon, a Tanaka warrior brandishing a bloody knife, leapt upon Twisted Foot's chest.

Both warriors fell to the ground. Neither man moved. Both warriors had delivered and sustained fatal knife wounds.

****

On their belts, Stone Fist, and Running Eagle, had attached the fresh scalps of two of the Tanaka warriors.

Running Eagle had attached the scalp of the third Tanaka, to his friend Twisted Foot' breechclout.

Stone Fist and Crooked Arrow set the Billing's Wagon aflame.

Mandy averted her eyes. When she finally looked up, her gaze fell upon the grieving, somber, stoic, faces, of Running Eagle, Stone Fist, and Crooked Arrow.

Stone Fist, Mandy remembered thinking, looked right through her. It was as if to him, she did not exist.

****

As Running Eagle's group neared the village, two of the young boys who had been watching the band's pony herd, rode ahead and alerted the village of the group's approach.

The boys spread the word, that the warriors were returning with; two captured horses; five mules, and two female captives.

They told of the slain warrior, Twisted Foot, whose lifeless body was draped across his pony.

Stone Fist was leading the little procession. He was followed by Crooked Arrow, who held the reins of Twisted Foot' pony, and then by Running Eagle, with the two captured females, stumbling behind his pony.

Twisted Foot mother and sister took the reins and the bridle of Twisted Foot' pony from Crooked Arrow.

Three shapely attractive young girls, all known to have spent frequent, albeit mostly sleepless nights, snuggled with Twisted Foot, under his blanket, in the young warrior's lodge, were keening shrill, tremolos, death songs. Their ululant choruses dominated the sounds of the village.

Running Eagle threw the ropes that bound Mandy and Rebecca, in the direction of the three grieving girls.

The taller of the three picked up the rope tied to Rebecca, and with all of her strength, yanked Rebecca to the ground. The three young mourners pounced upon the exhausted, helpless white girl, knocking her to the ground, and began to mercilessly, pummel and to kick the prostrate captive.

Rebecca defenseless lay on the ground, in the fetal position. With her hands she was attempting to cover her head.

Mandy as fast as she could move, hobbled over to join the melee. She looped the rawhide-rope that Running Eagle had used to pull her behind his pony, around the neck of the tall Comanche girl, and attempted to pull the Indian girl off of Rebecca.

The two girls that had been beating and kicking Rebecca, turned their attention to Mandy, this snarling demonic creature, the dark version of the cringing white girl.

Mandy seemingly impervious to the multiple blows being rained down upon her by the two Comanche girls, continued to tighten the rawhide around the tall girl's neck.

Just as the girl was about to loose conscientiousness, one of the women spectators, picked up a thick piece of fire-wood and slammed it against the back of Mandy's head.

Mandy fell to her knees, and collapsed. Her limp body fell directed, over Rebecca.

Running Eagle was impressed. Even after being knocked senseless, the little dark one, lay protectively over the helpless, cowering white-girl, lying beneath her.

****

Mandy awoke disoriented, and confused. She lay motionless, looking up at the light streaming through the smoke hole at the top of the tepee. She was lying on some kind of soft animal skin.

As she attempted to rise, she experienced a dull pain at the base of her head. Mandy gingerly, with her right hand, reached for the back of her head and felt a huge lump. She looked at her hand. There was no sign of blood; the skin had not been broken.

Mandy sat up and surveyed her surroundings. As she had suspected she was inside one of the tepees. To her surprise she found the interior of the tepee to be spacious, cool, well ventilated.

The tepee's floor, the ground, was entirely covered with overlapping buffalo robes. Incredibly, Mandy remembered thinking that the tepee's floor of overlapping buffalo robes, reminded her of the rich wall-to-wall carpeting of the Rosewood Plantation's library.

At the center of the lodge was a cooking-pit containing ashes, encircled by rocks.

Rolled buffalo robes, used as couches and bedding, lay along the periphery, the base of the tepee. Cooking utensils and hunting weapons were neatly stacked in the opposite side of the lodge.

As Mandy began to sit-up, her eyes frantically searched her immediate surroundings, looking for Rebecca.

A strikingly handsome Indian woman, Mandy guessed to be about her mother Ruth's age, placed a bowl of corn-gruel at her feet.

The woman was incessantly repeating in a severely agitated tone, That Mandy found to be completely incomprehensible, strange noises and a torrent of alien words, rapidly spewed forth from her mouth.

When it became obvious that this black one, darker than a Mexican, girl did not understand the People's language, Little Flower, Wife of Gray Wolf, Mother of Running Eagle, resorted to pantomiming with her hands and mouth, what she imagined that even an idiot, would interpret as the command to eat.

Although she was not hungry, Mandy instinctively decided to placate the increasingly agitated woman, by complying. She dipped her fingers into the bowl, scooped up the mixture, and following the Indian woman's example, placed her fingers into her mouth.

When Running Eagle had presented the girl to her as a gift to aid his mother in performing the never-ending work, that is daily accomplished by a woman of the People, Little Flower's initial impulsive reaction was to reject the gift that her son's offered.

Despite his mother's protestations, Running Eagle had enlisted Gray Wolf, his father's intervention. "Father, our holy man, He Who Speaks To Ghosts, and all of the signs that we have thus far seen, say that for this summer's hunt, our animal brother, the buffalo will be as many as stars in the sky".

"Father I fear that your many kills, and my kills will be far to many for my mother, and my sister Spring Blossom to skin; to butcher; to cure; to tan, and work the many hides."

My mother, Little Flower, will never complain. As a woman of the People, without complaint, she will do what is expected of her".

"Without an additional woman to share the work, your wife, my mother, Little Flower, as do the wildflowers that thrive on the plains, will soon wither and wilt before our eyes".

Although she would never admit it, not even to herself, Little Flower was gradually, increasingly, beginning to become overwhelmed with maintaining the home of two of the People's most prolific warrior-hunters.

The women of the band frequently spoke with envy, of how even after forty summers —
thirty of which consisted of never ending tedious labor, four pregnancies, two live births
and one surviving son, Running Eagle — Little Flower had remarkably, retained most of
her youthful beauty.

Five summers ago, when Gray Wolf and Running Eagle were participating in a hunting
party, the cowardly Ute's had attacked the camp, killing her first born, her beloved
daughter, Wenona.

In addition to the overwhelming grief of losing her daughter, Little Flower had to adjust
to the pragmatic reality of the debilitating loss of her then, sole domestic helpmate.

Survival of the People was dependant upon the men, the warriors, devoting their time to
providing for, and defending the band.

The duties of the Comanche women, in addition to bearing strong healthy children, were
difficult, tedious, and never ending.

In camp the women, for hours on end, scraped and cured buffalo hides. The tribe's
women fashioned the hides into clothing, bedding, robes, rawhide utensils, carrying bags,
and tepee covers.

Although the man of the lodge owned the tepee, the women made it. They set it up;
maintained it; following the buffalo herds, sometimes as frequently as every few days,
the woman took the tepee down; hauled the dwelling across the plains, by horse or dog
drawn travois, ten to fifteen miles to new encampments.

The women converted the buffalo's horns into spoons and ladles; they cooked the
animal's hooves to produce glue. Other mundane female duties included the collecting of
all kinds of herbs, roots, berries, and usable plants and shrubbery, fetching the firewood,
and the preparation of the meals.

Little Flower was under no illusion. Despite her uncompromising work- ethic, and her
devotion to her duties, it was becoming physically impossible for two females herself and
her youngest daughter, Spring Blossom, to adequately maintain a lodge occupied by two
of the tribes most prolific hunters.

As do all mothers at some point, Little Flower had come to realize that it was time for her
young warrior-son Running Eagle, to marry and to move to his own lodge.

Until such time as Running Eagle moved out, married and established his own lodge, with his own wife, or wives, while Running Eagle remained in the lodge of Gray Wolf, in order for her to perform her duties, Gray Wolf could take a second wife, or she Little Flower, could acquire the labor of at least one female captive, a slave.

Though initially hesitant, Little Flower decided that the second alternative was by far to her, the more preferable.

****

To her surprise, once she began to eat, Mandy discovered that not only was she hungry, she was famished. Though the food was surprisingly tasty and filling, it did nothing to dispel Mandy's apprehension, as to the safety and the whereabouts of Rebecca

Little Flower sat silently watching the pretty black girl, wolf-down her food. This was the first time that she had actually seen one of the blacks.

As far back as she could remember, Little Flower had heard of the existence of the black tribe.

Little Flower studiously, with open undisguised, curiosity, stared at the first living black, that she had encountered.

It was well known among the People, that the whites that wear the blue- coats were now at war with the whites who wear the gray coats.

It was said that the whites that wore the blue coats were fighting to free the blacks; that the blacks, and their children, and their children's children, for their entire lives, are the slaves of the whites that wear the gray coats.

Apparently in the white man's world, no white man could be a slave. All of the slaves of the white man, from cradle to grave, were the blacks.

To Little Flower, the rationale that only blacks could be enslaved, she found to be confusing, impractical, and ridiculous, it did not make sense.

As one of the People, Little Flower's concept of slavery, that is how she viewed the practice of involuntary servitude, was rationale, well established and accepted.

In her world, the world that the Great Spirit had given to the Comanche, any man, woman, or child; Red, White, or Black, who was captured or stolen from the enemies of the People, were subject to enslavement.

It had always been the practice of the People to, if the slave's actions and character proved worthy, accept them as full-fledged members of the tribe.

When Mandy's had finished the bowl of gruel, Little Flower spoke in an authoritative, commanding voice; "Stand so that I may examine this scrawny gift to me, from my son."

Mandy not understanding the language of the Comanche, remained seated. Her reaction was a look of puzzlement, of utter confusion.

Little Flower repeated her demand. This time, in addition to speaking the words, Little Flower rapidly gestured with her hands, thus conveying her directive concurrently in two mediums, in the spoken word, as well as in sign, the universal language of the plains.

****

Mandy not understanding the language of the Comanche, remained seated. Little Flower repeated her demand. This time, in addition to speaking the words, Little Flower was rapidly gesturing with her hands, thus conveying her directive in the spoken word, as well as in sign, the universal language of the plains.

Mandy's frustration at not being able to understand this strikingly handsome Indian woman's alien words, was now being compounded by confusion, and her utter despair at her madding slow progress, in trying to decipher the woman's obvious attempt to communicate, using hand gestures.

Mandy shook her head and slowly, in a firm voice spoke, "I don't understand what you are saying. I do not know what you want."

Little Flower clearly not understanding the "gibberish" coming from the girl's mouth — the words, if they were words, that she perceived must be of the black man language — walked over to the still seated girl, and firmly grabbed her by the elbows, and while lifting, simultaneously once again, repeated her command; "Stand".

Mandy rose to her full height of 5 feet 4 inches. Little Flower, a full grown, mature woman of the People, stood 5 feet 5 inches, an inch taller then the beautiful young girl standing before her.

Little Flower decided this time, to try to bridge the communications gap, by resorting to the use of a combination of simple words and gestures. She looked directly into the black girl's eyes.

Little Flower made a fist. Mandy reflexively recoiled. Little Flower, realizing that her action had been misconstrued as threatening, quickly opened her fist and pointed her index finger towards her chest; "Little Flower", she again pointed to her chest and repeated her name, "Little Flower".

Mandy enthusiastically imitated Little Flower's actions. Mandy pointed to her chest, and proclaimed "Mandy".

Mandy then pointed her finger towards Little Flower and attempted to repeat the odd sounding words that were obviously the Indian woman's name; "Little Flower?"

Little Flower was pleased. She smiled and pointed her finger at the black girl, her new possession, and stated in a clear resonant voice; "Man-dee".

Mandy uttered a guarded sigh of relief. She thought that at last she and this Indian had finally communicated.

Mandy, now her eyes pleading, slowly and deliberately, spoke; "Becky, where is Becky?"

Little Flower ignored the unpleasant, harsh guttural sounds spoken by the girl called "Man-dee". She assumed that the sounds assailing her ears were the words of the Blackman's talk. Little Flower continued with her examination of her slave.

She was fascinated with the texture and the body of "Man-dee's" hair. Little Flower had heard of the "buffalo hair" of the few black mountain men and black soldiers that had come to the land of the Comanche.

This girl's hair, while thicker then that of the Indians, or of the Mexicans, or of the whites, was certainly not the coarse woolly hair of the buffalo's mane.

Mandy tentatively, cautiously touched the Indian woman's arm; "Becky the white girl who was captured with me. Where is Becky?"

Little Flower's reaction to the black girl's unexpected contact was to soundly cuff her, with the open palms of her hands, about the ears.

Mandy staggered backwards, rubbing her ringing ears. Little Flower immediately regretted having struck the girl. She fully expected that the black girl would now cower and cringe like a punished cur.

If the girl withdrew and began to cry, Little Flower feared that her impulsive, reflexive reaction, may have negated, and setback their recent progress in communicating.

Instead of sulking, the girl, who had obviously been taken by surprise, held her ground and defiantly once again slowly and deliberately repeated her lament; "Becky, where is Becky?"

Mandy was stunned. More surprised than hurt, by the blow, she staggered backwards. Almost immediately she regained her composure. With her head held high and her ears ringing, Mandy looked directly, defiantly into the eyes of Little Flower, and once again asked; "Where is Becky…what have you done with Becky?"

While Little Flower did not understand the girl's words, she fully understood the black girl's determination and intensity. Little Flower decided to temporarily suspend her inspection of her property. She instead sat on one of the buffalo robe couches, and motioned that the girl, "Man-dee" should be seated.

Mandy obediently, slowly sat down beside, this Indian woman. The person that she, at least for the time being, was the person that she now perceived to be her new female "Massa".

Little Flower picked up a stick of wood lying beside the cooking pit. She then lifted the edge of a buffalo hide, exposing the bare ground. Hard packed dirt was where the grass, because of the lack of sunshine, had browned and died.

Little Flower drew two stick figures into the dirt. One of the figures was noticeably taller, than the other.

Little Flower pointed her stick at the shorter of the two stick figures. She turned to look at the girl. "Man-dee", she then pointed to the taller stick figure, "Little Flower".

In her attempt to make her point, Little Flower, with her free hand, pointed to her chest and repeated; "Little Flower". She then handed the stick to the black girl seated beside her.

Mandy took the stick and drew a third stick figure in the dirt, hand in hand with the smaller figure. She pointed the stick at the taller figure, and imitating the handsome Indian lady seated beside her, she proclaimed; "Little Flower".

She then pointed to the shorter stick figure that Little Flower had drawn; "Mandy…Mandy". Mandy then pointed to the stick figure that she had just drawn. She looked at Little Flower and said, "Becky, Becky! Where is Becky?".

As soon as "Man-Dee" drew the stick figure linked to the figure that they both identified as "Man-Dee", Little Flower knew why the black girl had been so agitated. She was genuinely concerned and worried about, the fate of the white girl that she had been tied to.

Little Flower found "Man-Dee's concern to be somewhat confusing. Based upon what she had heard about white/black relationships, she had assumed that between the two girls, one white, the other black, their relationship would be that of Master and Slave.

Judging from the obvious depth of this black girl's concern for the whimpering white girl, Little Flower concluded that, what she had heard and had been led to believe about white/black relations in the white man's world, was at least in this case, more complex.

Little Flower pointed to the third stick figure; she said emphatically; "Bee-Kee"? Mandy nodded, "yes Becky. Where is Becky? Is Becky all right?"

Little Flower once again pointed to the drawing that they both had just agreed, represented the white girl, "Bee-Kee". "Bee-Kee was given to Stone Fist. She is his property. "Bee-Kee belongs to Stone Fist."

Mandy's face, the girl's reaction, was that of complete bewilderment. Little Flower could see by "Man-Dee's perplexed expression, that she clearly did understand.

Once again Little Flower choose to communicate by resorting to the combination of her words, sign, and now through the use of props.

She again pointed to the stick figure drawn in the dirt; "Bee-Kee", then she reached for empty bowl that Mandy had discarded; she thrust the empty bowl towards Mandy. She began to repeat a single unintelligible word, over and over; "give…give".

Mandy was confused. Her mind was reeling. What was the Indian woman saying? What was she doing with the bowl. She keeps saying "Bee-Kee", obviously, she means Becky. Then she thrusts the bowl at me. Pointing to Becky and giving me the bowl. That's it, the word means give. "Bee-Kee give?

Little Flower picked up one of the stones that circled the cooking pit. She began to repeat the word "stone…stone". She then held the stone in one hand, and made a fist with the other.

Little Flower pointed to the stick figure. Mandy said the name "Becky". The Indian woman then repeated the new word, "Bee-Kee". Little Flower then held up the stone and pointed to her clenched hand. She repeated the word "fist...fist".

Mandy laboriously pieced together, and spewed forth and understood, her first Comanche sentence. "Bee-Keee give Stone- Fist". In her mind, she converted her rudimentary Comanche, to English.

Becky was given to Stone Fist. Instead of being enlightened, Mandy was confused. Who or what is a Stone Fist?!

Little Flower saw the black girl, "Man-Dee's" expression, rapidly change, once again, from understanding to confusion. Before she could speak, she noticed that the buffalo hide, on which the girl was standing, was stained with fresh blood.

Little Flower rigidly, extended her arm straight out in front of herself. She raised her palm forward in the universal signal to stop.

Mandy stood as if frozen, in place. She stood perfectly still, immobile, like a statue. Little Flower walked over to the petrified girl. Without uttering a word, she unceremoniously lifted Mandy's skirt and petticoat.

Mandy's thighs, and legs were streaked with blood. Little Flower's first thought was that the black girl had been wounded during her capture. Then at closer inspection, not seeing a wound or a bruise, the reason and source of the blood became obvious, Man-dee was in the midst of the woman's moon cycle bleed.

Both of the females, for entirely different reasons, were horrified. Mandy because she had no idea as to the source of the blood. That this was the onset of her first monthly period of menstruation, did not immediately enter her mind.

Little Flower was horrified because Mandy's moon cycle blood, had contaminated her husband, Gray Wolf's buffalo hide.

It was well known by the People, that for a warrior, it was bad medicine, if he or any of his possessions were to come in contact, with a woman's moon cycle blood.

Little Flower hastily grabbed Mandy by the arm, and pulled her from Gray Wolf's tepee. With Mandy standing befuddled at the entrance, Little Flower rushed back into the tepee.

Mandy sat tentatively on the ground. She thrust her hand beneath her dress, and carefully, gently examined her legs and her thighs.

Her fingers did not encounter any sort of wound or injury. However, when she withdrew her hand from beneath her clothing, her fingers were sticky, covered with blood.

Mandy recalled the time, just before they had left Rosewood, that she and Rebecca had sat down with Ruth, Mandy's mother, and were told; "Yu gals at dat age now dat yu be startin ta bled. When it hapen don't be scairt. It jus mean ya now be a womin. Ya kin hav babies. Ya dun got da wimmen's monthly curse."

Little Flower emerged from the tepee. She held the stained buffalo hide, snugly under her arm. She took Mandy by the arm. They hurried towards a large tepee on the fringe of the camp.

The tepee was set conspicuously apart from the tepees that comprised the main groupings, of the community dwellings.

Little Flower opened the flap of the isolated tepee, and firmly pushed Mandy through the entrance hole. She raised her hands, as if to block any effort to retreat, that the black girl might make.

And with a very effective combination of words, sign, and gestures, Little Flower clearly and succinctly, communicated with her slave; " You stay - until no more blood".

****

Mandy's eyes slowly adjusted to the dimly lit roomy, interior of the tepee. She noticed that the kindling in the cooking-pit was cold and dormant. With the entrance flap closed, the sole source of illumination in the tepee, was the sunlight that filtered down through the tepee's smoke hole.

When Little Flower pushed Mandy through the tepee's entrance flap, the conversation and light-hearted chatter within the dwelling, momentarily ceased, then when Little Flower departed, just as abruptly, the chatter resumed.

To Mandy's right, three Indian women were seated on buffalo robe couches. Each of the women was busily engaged in sewing various items of clothing.

To her left, almost directly opposite the three women, she noticed, a figure softly whimpering, huddled on the floor. Unlike the three Indian women dressed in garments made of animal skins and hides, the lone prostrate figure in the opposite side of the tepee, was dressed in what Mandy considered, white people' clothing.

Mandy shouted; "Becky", and hurried to the side of her life-long friend.

When Rebecca heard the sound of Mandy's voice, heard her name,
Rebecca's tears of despair, of abject hopelessness, were instantly transformed to tears of joy.

Rebecca lifted her head. She wiped her eyes with the sleeve of her dress and softly, in a whispered mumbled; "Mandy"? Then in a much stronger voice, filled with hope and conviction, Rebecca exclaimed; "It's you...Oh Mandy...it is you."

As the black girl and the white girl sat hugging one another, Song Bird turned to her friend, Precious, and spoke; "Those two are soiling our lodge.

Do they not know how to contain the moon cycle blood"? Without waiting for an answer, Song Bird put her sewing aside, walked over to a pile of items, neatly stacked to her right of the cooking pit.

Song Bird picked up two garments. Each garment consisted of what appeared to be two triangular shaped flaps. The triangular flaps were separated by an approximate 3 x 6 inch, contiguous length of deerskin.

Slits were cut at the points of the two triangles.

Song Bird thrust the garment at the startled white girl. "You are despoiling the lodge. Put this on". She thrust one of the garments towards Rebecca.

Rebecca tentatively reached for and accepted the offering. At first, both she and Mandy were confused.

Song Bird lifted her buckskin dress, to her waist. She was wearing one of the triangular garments. The flaps were tied together, at her waist, with two strips of rawhide. The front flap was distended. It protruded, it "bulged".

One of Song Birds companions joined the group. She handed Rebecca a small porous bag. The bag was filled with leaves, absorbent fern leaves.

Almost simultaneously, Mandy and Rebecca understood. Mandy accepted the paraphernalia. She assisted Rebecca, then Rebecca in-turn, assisted her.

Song Bird picked up the girls' soiled dresses. She placed the soiled clothing in the furthest recesses of the tepee.

Song Bird gave each girl a simple buckskin dress. As Mandy slid the dress over her head, she marveled at the soft texture of the material. Rebecca followed Mandy's example.

Like most teenaged girls, who were surrounded by "more-mature", teenage girls, Mandy and Rebecca had been eagerly anticipating, the beginning of menstruation, the arrival of their period. The biological event, the rite of passage, that would herald their ascendancy into womanhood.

Strangely, probably because of their recently horrifying experiences, the Indian attack, the massacres, and their subsequent capture, neither of the girls mentioned the event that found them here together, in this tepee, at this time in their young lives, experiencing together, their menarche.

****

After they had cleaned-up, Mandy and Rebecca sat alone together on one of the three buffalo hide couches, positioned about the tepee.

Rebecca breathlessly, between tears told Mandy of the horrible woman, the apparent wife of the huge barbaric savage called, Rebecca tried to remember the words, she made sounds that Mandy's remarkable memory interpreted as the name Stone Fist.

Rebecca asked why did she believe that these unintelligible words, these incoherent sounds, were the name Stone Fist. Mandy explained her previous "*lesson*" with her apparent new female Master, the woman whose name is Little Flower, the woman that had brought her to, what she and Rebecca had just recently decided to call the "*Menses*" tent.

At the beginning of their second day at the "*Menses*" tent, the woman called Song Bird, interrupted the girl's incessant, annoying chatter. Her annoyance was not so much due to the frequency or to the volume of the talk, she as did the other occupants of the tent, were annoyed at what they perceived of as meaningless, harsh noises, foreign words emanating from the mouths of the two captives.

It was clear to Song Bird that the black girl, and the white girl were speaking a tongue that they both understood. For captives this was not all together unusual.

Neither the Utes nor the Pawnee, spoke the tongue of the People. Yet both of these enemies, though inferior to the tongue of the people, understood the meanings of the silent sign talk.

Song Bird had appointed her self as spokesperson for the group. She simultaneously spoke and signed; "It is time for you two lazy girls to do some of the work. To do your share of the work that needs to done".

"Come with me, we need wood, and chips for the cooking fire.
Song Bird then threw two sacks, identical to the one that was slung over her shoulder, one towards Mandy, and the other pouch towards Rebecca.

At Song Bird's approach, the two girls ceased their conversation, and gave their full attention to the Indian woman standing before them.

When Song Bird began to talk, her hands began to rapidly move. The cadence of her words was in sync with the movement of her hands.

Unfortunately, while it was obvious to both girls that the words and the gestures were related, neither girl could understand Song Bird.

When Song Bird threw the tumpline at her feet, Mandy alertly recognized the word and the hand movement; "Stand". Mandy stood. Rebecca followed Mandy's lead.

Encouraged, Song Bird spoke and signed again; "Put the tumpline over your shoulder". Both girls stood in place, a confused look on their face. Song Bird repeated her instruction.

However this time instead of signing words, she pulled the rawhide strap which was attached to the ends of her tumpline, over her head, then she re-slung the pouch over her shoulder.

When they left the "Menses" tepee, Song Bird, head down, walked, eyes darting to and fro, obviously searching the waving grass.

She bent over and picked up a piece of dry wood, the branch from a shrub, and placed it into her pouch. Mandy spoke to Rebecca; "Becky she wants us to gather fuel for the fire. Look, she's picking up some buffalo chips"

Rebecca now clearly noticeably calmer, suggested that in order to cover more ground, that she and Mandy should split-up. Mandy agreed, but cautioned Rebecca, to make their separation from each other and from the Indian woman, slowly and gradual. "We don't want them to think that we're trying to escape".

The three women, walking together — each with their pouches' full — returned to the tepee. When Song Bird pulled aside the flap of the tepee, the delicious aroma of a spicy hot, bubbling stew, assailed their sense of smell.

After breakfast, the women drifted into small groups. One group was busy designing and sewing dresses, leggings and moccasins. Each woman would start and would finish each article of apparel.

A group of women were busily making utensils, knives, bowls, spoons, awls, from the hooves and the horns of slain buffalo.

To Mandy, each group of women appeared to be happy, content, in perfect harmony with their surroundings, with their world.

A constant cacophony of female voices, resulted in an atmosphere of joviality, and sisterhood.

Laughter and giggles were at the forefront of what Mandy quickly realized was, eerily reminiscent, similar to the gatherings that Rosewood's female slaves would hold, during their infrequent periods of free time.

At first Mandy and Rebecca sat alone, isolated, segregated, from the inhabitants of the "*Menses*" tent's, little community.

Song Bird, who appeared to be a leader of the little sewing circle, the group designing and sewing basic articles of clothing, motioned for Mandy, and for Rebecca to join her group.

Mandy almost instantly, fit right into, and was accepted by the group of seamstresses.

Since she was a child, Mandy had sat at the feet of, and informally trained and apprenticed as a seamstress, under the tutelage of her mother Ruth.

Ruth, that Billings' slave-girl, who amongst the ladies of Essex County Virginia, was recognized as one of Virginia's most accomplished seamstresses.

Mandy's wielding of the buffalo bone needle, and her swift accurate, cutting of animal skins, seemed with her, to have come naturally.

All of the Indian women marveled at Mandy's speed, her dexterity, and though at first grudgingly, they all came to acknowledge her extraordinary skill.

Rebecca was the complete opposite. By definition, Rebecca's role in life, as a female member of the Southern Aristocracy, had been to be cared for, to be pampered, to be revered.

This upbringing, this philosophy had precluded the need for Rebecca to have ever acquired skill at sewing, or for that matter, for her to have become acquainted with the simplest tools of the trade.

Both Mandy and Rebecca were given two soft matching doe skin hides. Mandy swiftly aligned and juxtaposed the skins intended for the front and back of the dress.

Mandy threaded a dried, elongated, strand of buffalo sinew into the eye of a large needle. The needle had been crafted from a splinter of buffalo-bone.

Mandy's hands, deftly and expertly united the two pieces of hide into one. Her stitching was immaculate.

Delicate Hands, the youngest of the Indian women, snatched the dress from Mandy's hands. The young woman critically examined the garment. With a look of amazement in her eyes, she handed the dress to Song Bird.

Song Bird, smiled; "Running Eagle is a most fortunate young brave. This one, the dark one is truly gifted. The skill that produced this dress — she held up the dress — rivals the finest work of our best seamstress, Weeping Willow".

"If this one makes babies — Song Bird stood and began to rapidly thrust and gyrate her pelvis — as well as she makes dresses, Running Eagle is indeed one lucky warrior".

With the exception of Mandy and Rebecca, who did not understand a word that had been said, all of the women in the tepee, doubled over with peels and spasms, of uncontrolled laughter.

Rebecca was not nearly as adept at sewing as was Mandy. Her initial thought as she watched Indian women and Mandy was, "how difficult can this be?"

Rebecca picked up two pieces of previously cut, deerskin-hide. She lay the deerskin, one piece upon the other. Rebecca reached for a needle and attempted to pass the thread, as the others had done, through the needle's tiny opening.

Despite Rebecca's excellent vision, threading the needle, holding the needle perfectly still in one hand, while passing the limp thread through its' tiny aperture, was frustrating. It certainly wasn't nearly as simple as it had looked.

Finally the needle was threaded. Rebecca, as she had seen Mandy do, then attempted to sew the two deerskin hides together. For some reason, Rebecca could not force her needle through the deerskin-hides.

As she exerted pressure on the needle, trying to penetrate the hides, her fingers would merely slide down the body of the needle. Exasperated, she looked in Mandy's direction for help.
Mandy was absorbed in watching one of the Indian women decorate a dress. The woman was weaving bright red and green bird quills, into the neckline of the dress.

Not wanting to disturb Mandy, and not wanting to appear to be completely useless, Rebecca doubled over the needle, the material at the bottom of her dress, and after taking a deep breath, pushed down on the needle.

The needle did not puncture the deerskin, however it did puncture the material of Recca's dress, as well as piercing Rebecca's thumb.

Rebecca cried out in pain; "Shit; damn; hell."

When Mandy heard Rebecca's exclamation, and the stream of epithets, she dropped the dress that she had been working on and ran to her friend.

"Becky what's wrong? Are you okay…are you all right?" Rebecca was rocking back and forth, she was holding the hem of her freshly washed petticoat, which she had torn into shreds and tightly wrapped around her thumb.

Mandy gently took her friend's injured hand, and unfurled the temporary bandage. It was immediately apparent that the needle had penetrated Rebecca's thumb. Blood began to again, gush from the wound.

Mandy tore a strip of fabric from Rebecca's petticoat, and fashioned a bandage, which she tightly wrapped around the bleeding finger.

Rebecca had remained quite while Mandy administered to her thumb. After she had securely tied the bandage, Mandy took both of Rebecca's hands in her own, "Becky, what did you do…how did this happen?"

Rebecca stoiccally looked int her friend's eyes. "It was a stupid accident. I was trying to sew that — she nodded towards the dress, lying on the floor, that she had been working on — dress together. I couldn't get the needle through the material."

Mandy picked up the dress that Rebecca had been attempting to sew. She Mandy quickly assessed Rebecca's problem. "Becky, you can't force that needle through a deerskin, let alone through two deerskins at one time.
Rebecca sheepishly looked at Mandy; "You did. Just now I watched you do it."

Wordlessly, Mandy bent over and picked up a tapered pick-like bone-tool. Mandy held the tool up, she gently, gingerly touched the instruments sharp tip.

"Before I began sewing the front and the back of the dress together, I had made holes with this awl, in both pieces of material. The holes on both pieces, the front and the back of the dress, are aligned.

In this case, because I used the awl, the needle did not make the holes. Because the material is so coarse, not easily punctured, I used the awl to make the holes. The needle is merely a carrier, that transports the thread that binds the two hides together".

Rebecca's face was crestfallen. She looked as if she was ashamed, humbled by her ignorance. Mandy put her arm around her life-long friend's shoulders.

"Becky in the world that we grew up in, by law I was kept illiterate, ignorant. Despite the law you, and to a lesser extent Miss Leary, saw to it that I did not remain illiterate, ignorant of so, so many wonderful things."

"Oddly enough that same society that by law attempted to keep me ignorant, and illiterate, in a way, did the same to you. Becky, sweet Becky, my dearest friend, who I truly love, as I would love my own sister, you through no fault of your own, are a ignorant".

"You were raised as a pampered, spoiled southern white girl, you are truly lacking and ignorant in, and of the skills and the work experience, that we will both need if we are to survive this time in captivity".

Mandy held Rebecca face in her hands. She looked deeply into Becky's eyes. "It's my turn Becky. I'll teach you what you need to know to survive enslavement. We'll get through this. Together, we will survive".

****

Towards the end of their fourth day at the "*Menses*" tent, a silver-haired stately looking woman known to the People as Birthing Woman, entered the tent.

Both Mandy and Rebecca noticed the deference and the obvious respect that the Indian women gave the new arrival.

Birthing Woman immediately sought out, and conferred with, one of the more loquacious of the Indian women.

After the two Indian women concluded a brief animated conversation, Birthing Woman turned to face Mandy and Rebecca, and spoke; "You two, come to me." Neither girl moved. Birthing Woman realized that neither the white girl, nor had the black girl, understood her words.

Birthing Woman turned and spoke to the two Indian women who were standing nearest to Rebecca and Mandy. Pointing her finger first at Mandy, then at Rebecca, she commanded in an authoritative voice; "Bring those two to me".

Although Mandy and Rebecca did not understand her words, Birthing Woman's authoritative delivery and her emphatic demonstrative gestures, were easily understood.

Rebecca and Mandy joined hands, and stood. They walked, unassisted to the imposing woman.

Birthing Woman, knowing that her words would not be understood by these young girls, who were not of the People, instead of speaking, stepped up to Rebecca, who to her credit remained perfectly still, and pulled up the girl's dress.

The woman called Birthing Woman reached into the pocket of Rebecca's doe-skin undergarment and pulled out the bloodless, clean, unstained pad. She dropped the unsoiled pad to the floor. She then moved to Mandy and repeated her actions.

Without emitting a sound, Birthing Woman turned and pointed to the tent's entrance. Mandy and Rebecca walked over to the flap, and exited the tent known to the People as the Unclean Woman's tepee.

Mandy and Rebecca stood silently in the sun, next to the tepee. They could hear the faint sounds of the village, stirring to life.

They had no idea as to what would happen next. Birthing Woman emerged from the tepee. Without speaking, she began to walk back to the village.

At this point, having no idea as to what they were now expected to do, Mandy and Rebecca followed Birthing Woman.

****

As the little procession entered the village, Mandy began to vaguely recognize the myriad assemblage of dwellings.

When she and Rebecca had been dragged, hands bound at the wrist, stumbling behind the ponies of the two young warriors, her first impression of the camp, had been that all of the tepees were identical.

The similarity of the tepees one to another, reminded Mandy of the bushels of "cookie-cutter", sugar-cookies that Fannie, the Billing's family cook, use to bake for Christmas.

Closer scrutiny of the tepee of Gray Wolf, his wife Little Flower, their daughter Spring Blossom, and their warrior son, Running Eagle, and now the tepee where she lived, at first glance had appeared to have been identical to that of its' neighbors. Upon closer inspection it became obvious that this dwelling was uniquely different.

The pole arrangement of the majority of the tepees consisted of a three-pole base. Gray Wolf's lodge was larger. Instead of three poles at its' base, there were four. The number of poles, including non support poles, totaled eighteen.

The entry flap to the structure had been reinforced with criss-crossed, hacked tree branches that gave the flap heft and stability.

Intricate designs had been meticulously painted vertically and horizontal, framed the entrance.

As the three women approached a neat basic three-pole tepee, a short, stocky muscular warrior pushed through the structures entrance flap. A old toothless hag of a woman, followed the warrior.

Rebecca instantly recognized the old woman. She, along with an a younger woman, had been the ones preparing her for, who knows what, when they discovered that she was menstruating.

The old hag grabbed Rebecca roughly by the hair, and with an amazing display of strength, literally threw her into the tepee. Mandy was about to go to Rebecca's aide, when Birthing Woman shouted an unintelligible, loud shrill command, "Do not interfere!"

Though Mandy did not understand the words, she absolutely did understand the message. Before she could react, Rebecca shouted, "Mandy don't…I'm all right."

Mandy hesitated. The stocky warrior had not moved. He was standing nonchalantly, apparently disinterested, between Mandy and the entrance to the tepee.

Mandy recognized the warrior as being one of the three that had interrupted the massacre at their wagon, and had subsequently become their captures. His rock-hard countenance, and his muscular physique, exuded an aura of primal strength and masculinity.

Stone Fist turned his head. Stone Fist had not acknowledged the presence of the females.

Birthing Woman pushed Mandy. Mandy staggered forward and reflexively looked back over her shoulder at the older woman. A withering stare from the silver haired woman abruptly ended their brief, momentary short-lived confrontation.

Two tepees behind the home that Rebecca had been thrown into, was the impressive imposing tepee of Gray Wolf.

Birthing Woman stopped at the tepee. Mandy, walking behind the older woman stopped. Birthing Woman wrapped upon the entrance flap, and called out; "Little Flower, it is I Birthing Woman. I have returned to you, the black one."

****

303

The tepee's flap was flung open. Little Flower emerged, and motioned that Mandy should enter. Mandy complied. Little Flower followed Mandy, and closed the flap.

As Mandy's eyes slowly adjusted to the ambient lighting in the tepee, she once again noticed the thick buffalo hides covering the floor, the couches, creatively, tastefully placed around the periphery of the tepee.

As she scanned the interior, her eyes came to a jolting stop when they encountered what she would later, breathlessly describe to Becky as, the most beautiful man that she had ever seen.

Running Eagle, son of Gray Wolf, stood by the cooking fire, stretching his lean muscular frame.

Mandy remembers thinking to her self, how tall is he? The vast majority of the warriors that she had seen were only a few inches taller than was she. Running Eagle was an anomaly. His height, 5' 11", though not especially tall in many cultures, was imposing for a Comanche warrior.

The bronze, supple, muscular man, that was unwittingly and unabashedly preening before her, literally took her breath away.

He was easily six or seven inches taller than was she. His complexion was an unblemished ruddy, reddish, brown. The definition of the muscles in his lean hard, smooth, hairless, powerful chest was remarkably sharp.

His long legs were encased in fringed, buckskin leggings. A simple brown buckskin breechclout, hung from the rawhide belt tied around his narrow waist.

At the conclusion of his stretch, the young man sat on the couch, and jammed his feet into buffalo hide moccasins.

Running Eagle looked up when the little black girl, followed by his mother, entered the tepee. His first thoughts upon seeing her, face washed, cleaned up and wearing the proper clothing of the People was this one, this creature, is truly beautiful.

However, as befits a Comanche warrior, Running Eagle's furtive, dismissive glance gave no indication to Mandy or as he mistakenly thought, to Little Flower, that he had even seen the black girl.

When their eyes briefly met, Mandy felt queasiness in the pit of her stomach. The man seated on the couch had the most penetrating pitch-black eyes that she had ever seen. She would later — when confiding with Becky — describe his eyes, as being similar to the color of the hard obsidian rock that the warriors used for the making of arrowheads.

His straight long black hair was braided into two thick braids that symmetrically, framed the classically chiseled features of his ruggedly, handsome face.

Little Flower observed and sensed, the fleeting moment between the two youths. The emotion that had instantaneously, spontaneously flared. The effect of the eye contact between the two was as sudden and as explosive as a random bolt of lightening, striking the dry parie grass, and igniting an out of control prairie fire.

The silent exchange passed swiftly. Experienced, but not understood nor appreciated, by either the young warrior, or by the captive girl.

The one person present who understood, and who correctly interpreted the exchange, that moment sent by the Great Spirit, was Little Flower.

****

Running Eagle, without looking at his mother or at the captive girl, hurriedly gathered his weapons, his bow, his quiver of arrows, his lance, and left the tepee.

Little Flower motioned for Mandy to be seated. She needed time to think. Little Flower pointed to the stew pot suspended over the cooking fire. She began to speak while slowly, deliberately moving her hands. "Are you hungry? Do you wish to eat?"

Mandy still, after a week in the Comanche encampment, did not understand Little Flower's words. However the woman's gestures were easily interpreted.

Mandy shook her head from side to side, and though she knew that her words would not be understood, she slowly, in a soft modulated voice replied; "No I have already eaten".

Mandy rose and prepared to clean the soiled utensils scattered around the hearth. Little Flower instead, took the dirty bowl from Mandy's hand, and wrapped an empty pouch, the type used to collect firewood, over the black girl's shoulder.

Little Flower escorted the captive girl to the outside. She waved her hand and pointed towards the little stream. "Go — collect fuel for the cooking pit".

Little Flower wanted time to think. She wanted to take her time to analyze that fleeting, brief, moment that she had observed, that transpire between the two young people.

What was the meaning of that, that which she had just witnessed? Little Flower wanted to think on this. After all, Running Eagle was her son, her only son. And was thought by all, to be a future leader of the People.

****

With trepidation, Rebecca entered the tepee of the young warrior Stone Fist.

Four days ago, when she and Mandy had entered the village, stumbling behind the tall Indian's pony, they had been derisively greeted by a crowd of shouting, chanting, women and children. Several young teenage girls were moaning and crying.

Rebecca remembered being pushed, prodded, and hit, by an old crone. The old woman had a full head of stark white hair, and huge ugly hands. Her left hand was missing two fingers.

The old woman had grabbed her by the hair, and had roughly shoved her into one of the tepees.

Rebecca would later learn that the old hag was the grandmother of Stone Fist, the burly warrior that had hung the scalp of her father, on to his war lance.

The old woman while persistently prodding and jabbing, had been spewing forth a constant relentless, loud, non-stop stream of curses and insults, at the frightened captive white girl.

The old toothless woman, was called, "Hen's Teeth". After the death of her only son, Stone Fist's father, five summers past, during a raid for Pawnee ponies, Hen's Teeth and her daughter in law, Quite One, had cared for and raised young Stone Fist.

The family's status and fortune had dramatically changed, with the coming of age of Stone Fist. Stone Fist's transformation from dependent-child, to that of an efficient hunter/warrior, had dramatically changed the family's standing in the community.

Although Rebecca had not understood a single word that the old woman had been shouting at her, she had absolutely understood and comprehended the hostile tone, and the threatening intent of her rantings.

It was Hen's teeth that had dragged the white girl to the tepee that she and Mandy had so cogently named, the"*Menses*" Tepee.

Now upon her return to the Tepee of Stone Fist, Rebecca quickly scanned the interior of the tepee. She took note of the two women of the lodge, Hen's Teeth and Quite One, busily preparing the morning meal.

Stone Fist, a young heavily muscled warrior, was lying on the floor, directly across from the tepee's entrance flap. He was asleep, wrapped in a huge buffalo robe. The burly young warrior was softly snoring.

As Rebecca tentatively entered, both Hen's Teeth and Quite One stopped what they were doing, and looked up at the trembling girl. Hen's Teeth placed a wrinkled, arthritic finger to her lips. Rebecca knew that she was being told to remain silent.

Rebecca did not move. She stood immobile, frozen in place. The old woman rose, took her elbow, and escorted the girl back through the entrance flap. The old woman, Hen's Teeth, picked up the hem of Rebecca's dress, and conducted a swift, cursory inspection.

"So you no longer have the moon bleed. It is time for you to work. There is much work to be done. Stone Fist is asleep. He is not to be disturbed."

Quite One emerged from the tepee. She had in her hand a fuel-carrying pouch. She handed the pouch to Rebecca. "Go gather wood". She pointed in the direction of a little stream several hundred yards from the village.
"I will call you when my son awakens."

Rebecca not understanding the words, but understanding the woman's gestures, took the sack, slung it around her shoulder and began to quickly walk towards the stream.

****

As Mandy was picking up twigs and limbs, worked her way, towards the stream, she spotted Rebecca, sitting on the ground, hands covering her face, softly crying.

Her heart went out to her friend, who was sitting looking completely forlorn, consumed by hopeless self-pity. That helpless image caused Mandy's back to stiffen. She picked up a twig, and resolutely with deliberate steps, marched over to her friend.

Rebecca was unaware of Mandy's approach. She heard a noise behind her and turned her head to look. She was looking directly into the sun, and saw the outline of someone with a raised arm, about to strike her.

Rebecca raised her arm to protect her face. Instead of experiencing the shock of anticipated pain, Rebecca felt the twig lightly brush her shoulder. She then heard the familiar voice of Mandy.

Rebecca stood on woobly legs. She wrapped her arms around Mandy's neck, and continued to sob. Her silent tears of despair had changed to tears of joy.

Mandy was here. Mandy her lifelong friend was here. Mandy her last link between civilization, and this nightmarish world of half-naked savages.

She clung to Mandy with a surprising strength. Strength whose origin rose from her fleeting momentary hope, of in Mandy, finding deliverance from these Indians, these red men, these primitive savages.

"Becky, stand up. Stop crying…get back to work. You've got to get control of yourself."

* * * * * * * * * * * * * * * * * * * *

Mandy gently but firmly removed Rebecca's arms from around her neck. "Becky I don't understand. Why are you falling apart now? We're okay…we're all right. We've been here now, for five days".

Rebecca wiping the tears from her eyes, asserted; "Four days of working amongst the women at the "*menses*" tepee.

That was totally different. Mandy, this morning I was shoved into the tent of a half naked man, a heathen. A wild-man, a bloodthirsty savage who I think, I now belong to. Mandy, we're their slaves."

For the first time that she could remember, over a lifetime of conversations between herself and Rebecca, Mandy was speechless. She thought does she not realize the incredulity of her words… "Mandy we're slaves".

How can she…Becky my dearest friend, now my only friend, so blithely, with a complete lack of sensitivity, say those words to me, "we're slaves".

Mandy quickly recovered from her momentary loss of focus, how do they survive.

The fact that Rebecca would undoubtedly, soon be forced to face, to experience, and to deal with first hand, the reality of the brutal, dehumanizing, fact of human bondage, was something that Mandy realized was inevitable and beyond her control.

As Mandy saw it, their immediate challenge and the objective that they faced was simple, they had to survive. She realized and understood that the achieving of that objective, as a slave, especially for Rebecca, would not be easy.

****

Rebecca's pampered life as a Southern Belle, had not only precluded her from working, learning to perform any type of domestic labor, the lifestyle of the white Southern Belle, had shielded her from assisting, even in witnessing the simplest of biological activities amongst their domestic animals.

Intellectually, thanks to the rudimentary biology teachings of Miss Leary, Rebecca was aware of the necessity of coupling between male and female animals, in order to produce "babies". Babies, be they colts, puppies, chicks, or for that matter, human babies.

As curious eight-year olds, Rebecca and Mandy had on several occasions, witnessed animals coupling and husbandry, while peeking through the space between the slates in the plantation's barn.

Of particular interest and fascination to the girls was that time when Rebecca's father Henry, and the stable boy, Pee Wee, had lead "*Satan*", Henry's huge stallion, to "service", mount one of the mares, that they said was in heat.

Mandy recalled both Rebecca and her astonishment and disbelief, when they saw that long pendulous thing, that huge appendage that was swinging below Satan's legs, plunge into the rear of the mare.

Rebecca and Mandy had breathlessly discussed mating of the horses. "Could you believe that Mandy? Could you believe the size of Satan's pee pee?"

I've seen papa riding that horse hundreds of times. Satan's pee pee was never like that. It was as long as and as thick as a fence post. When he stuffed his pee pee into Daisy, I thought it would split her wide open".

Mandy was pretty sure that that experience was the extent of Rebecca's real life exposure to male female sexuality. While Mandy, as was Rebecca, was still at fifteen, still a virgin.

Mandy's virginity was most likely due to her close relationship with the Massa's precious little daughter.

Neither black nor white males of Rosewood, would chance incurring the wrath of the Master by upsetting his daughter Rebecca, by deflowering her playmate, the pretty little nigger wench, Mandy.

As a slave living in the slave community, Mandy unlike Rebecca was cognizant and well aware of the sexual activities, that were constantly taking place between the sexes.

****

Sex between black men and black women; sex between white men (Massas), and their black female slaves, sometimes, consensual, more often forced.

In large part her knowledge stemmed from her mother's, a female slave's continuous, more than twenty-years of regular sexual encounters with the Master of Rosewood.

In addition to that which she had seen with her own eye; heard with her own ears, Mandy had heard whispered stories and rumors of sexual atrocities, committed in the past, against female members of her family, by the white Massas.

Mandy was under no illusions as to the probability that sexual assaults would be committed against herself, and against Rebecca, by these new Masters, the red man.

Mandy reasoned that since she and Becky had not thus far been killed, their continued survival would in all likelihood, include beatings, forced labor, and that she and Rebecca, would be at best, forced to marry, at worse if not married, they would surely be raped.

It was time for Becky to come to grips with reality, to face the harsh facts of life, in their new world.

****

When Running Eagle left his father's tepee, he walked directly to the tepee of the band's venerable leader, Chief "Old Wise One".

Though still sufficient, the band's supply of meat needed replenishment. A small hunting party, to be lead by Running Eagle, had been chosen to conduct an early hunt for elk and antelope.

It was anticipated that the band would consume the extra meat, during their journey to join their cousins for the great summer buffalo hunt.

The hides and their by-products, the clothing and utensils to be made by the women, would increase the band's stock of goods to be traded, at the summer gathering of the clans.

The great summer buffalo hunt, was an annual event, when most of the nomadic bands of the People, joined for two weeks of combined hunting, celebrations, and games.

The People's bands usually assembled during the first week of June. The time of the *Moon when the hot weather begins.*

Running Eagle, his best friend Stone Fist, and four other hunter-warriors, were to meet at the lodge of Chief Old Wise One. Old Wise One and the band's Holy Man, He Who Speak To Ghosts, for counsel, and to have the power of their medicine, sanctioned, and sanctified by the holy man.

As the ceremonial pipe was being past amongst the assembled men, Swift Arrow, one of the two braves that had been dispatched to scout for game, burst into the tepee.

In his enthusiasm and exuberance, Swift Arrow had either forgotten, or he had chosen to ignore custom. Seeing the men seated around Chief Old Wise One's cooking-pit, solemnly smoking the pipe, Swift Arrow immediately regretted his impetuous action. He stopped and stood respectfully in place, at the tepee's entrance.

When the ceremonial pipe had moved full-circle, Chief Old Wise Man, pipe in hand, looked scornfully directly, at Swift Arrow. "Who is this brave that rudely, without respect, invades my lodge. Does this one follow the peyote path?"

Running Eagle hurriedly stood and walked towards his friend. "Swift Arrow my friend what news do you bring?" Running Eagle was in fact actually thinking; is Swift Arrow under the influence of the "peyote"?

What could be so important that he would show such discourteous behavior towards our leader, Chief Old Wise One?

Swift Arrow spoke; "Forgive me my Chief, forgive my thoughtless actions. My thumping heart, overcame my manners".

Old Wise One being somewhat mollified by the young man's genuinely contrite apology, remained silent. The elderly chief choose wisely, not to pursue the breech of protocol.

Swift Arrow breathlessly reported that he and his fellow scout Dull Knife, while scouting for antelope, had been startled by an increasing rumbling of the ground, the shaking, the rumbling of the ground on which they sat.

Swift Arrow said that it had felt as though Mother Earth, herself, was violently, vibrating.

The two braves had mounted their ponies and rode towards the disturbance. As they crested a ridge, just as the sun was rising in the east, the two hunter-warriors saw below them, buffalo, hundreds maybe thousands of buffalo.

A panorama of dark forms that seemed to move as one continuous, rippling dark wave, undulating in the faint light of dawn, with the waving grass of the prairie.

The Holy Man, "He Who Speaks To Ghosts", rose to speak. "I have walked the path of the peyote. I have seen the People, during the coming Moon when the snow blows like spirits in the wind I have seen the People with their bellies full, warm with many buffalo robes, laughing, happy. It is good. "

Old Wise One stood, "We must break camp and track this vast herd. We will hunt and feast until the time of the Moon when the ponies shed their shaggy hair". "Then we will send word of this vast buffalo herd to all of the clans".

"During the winter snows, the great summer buffalo hunt will fed and nourish all of the People".

****

Mandy and Rebecca were slowly walking together, searching for and picking up kindling. Mandy spoke; "Becky do you remember when Miss Leary was teaching us about the ancient Romans and Greeks."

"How, as they conquered territories and distant countries, how it was common practice to make slaves of the conquered people. Becky, you and I are the conquered people. We are these people's slaves".

Rebecca recoiled. For the first time since their captivity, Mandy saw in Becky's blue eyes, a flicker of defiance. Rebecca stubbornly stuck out her chin, "I'm nobody's slave. I won't be anybody's slave."

In a voice heavily laden with frustration and exasperation, Mandy sighed; "Becky you…we have nothing to say about it. We have no rights. If we want to stay alive, we simply have to…we have to obey the Massas."

"Becky we have to hang on, we've got to survive until we're either rescued or we can mange to escape".

"Well at least so far, the work is really not all that difficult. Gathering wood and chips for the fires…making clothes, sewing, probably we'll have to do the cooking. If that's the extent of the work that we will have to do, we should have plenty of time and energy to plan our escape".

Just then the intensity and the volume of noise coming from the village, rose precipitously. Mandy and Rebecca turned to look back towards the Indian encampment.

From their vantage point, the tepees appeared to be collapsing. The women and the adolescent children were scurrying about.

Upon closer observation, it became obvious that the women and children were dismantling the structures, and they were busily packing their belongings.

Mandy had no idea as to what or why this sudden surge of activity. However she did conclude that in the confusion, this was an opportunity for them to escape.

Mandy did not hesitate she grabbed Rebecca's hand and shouted, "Becky, come on run, let's go." Becky shouted, "What's happening…what's going on."

As they turned to run from the village, four young boys on horseback were suddenly blocking their path of escape. The boys had small bows in their left hands. Each boy had slung upon his back, a quiver that contained three arrows.

The larger boy, presumably the oldest of the four, began to rapidly speak and to gesture; "Spring Blossom and Hen's Teeth, want you to return. They need your help with the move."

The leader of the little group, motioned towards the village with his bow. He then turned his pony's head, and slowly trotted back toward the village.

Mandy and Rebecca, followed the young leader of the group. The remaining three boys dutifully, brought up the rear.

****

That the camp was making an unexpected move, was obvious. Mandy began to be caught up by the infectious atmosphere and the urgency that permeated the village.

The leader of the little procession left Mandy at the site that was formerly the lodge of Gray Wolf. Rebecca was led to the lodge of the Quite One, mother of Stone Fist.

Little Flower and Spring Blossom were busy disassembling Gray Wolf's tepee. The mainframe, the four central poles that served as the base, were lying side by side on the ground.

The tepee's huge buffalo-hide outer coverings were stretched on the ground. The hides were sewn together with thick cords of buffalo sinew.

When Mandy reached the area that had formerly been occupied by Gray Wolf's lodge, she saw Little Flower and Spring Blossom shading their eyes with their hands, looking up at the captive black girl.

Little Flower stopped what she was doing, and motioned for Mandy to follow her. Little Flower walked over to the tepee's heavy buffalo-hide coverings.

From her belt she produced a stone tool similar to the awl that Mandy had used earlier. The tip of the tool instead of being straight was curved. The tip formed a hook.

Little Flower, starting at the top of the buffalo-hide coverings, tool in hand, deftly undid the first three loops that joined two of the hides. She stopped and handed the tool to Mandy. Little Flower indicated that Mandy should complete the separating of the buffalo-hides.

Mandy accepted the instrument, and began the tedious task of attempting to loosen, to undo the meticulously placed lacing.

To her surprise and dismay, removing the bulky threads that held the huge buffalo-hide outer coverings together was proving to be extremely difficult.

Little Flower's demonstration had been so swift, with such little expenditure of energy. Little Flower's fingers had literally flown, separating the heavy buffalo-hides.

Despite having over the years, helped her mother sew and alter innumerable garments, alterations that included countless adjustments of hems, Mandy to her chagrin, was having difficulty trying to pull the cord-like thread through the relatively small holes.

Spring Blossom, seeing the difficulty that the black girl was having, grabbed the hook-like tool, from Mandy, and almost as easily as had Little Flower, she began to remove the coarse sinew that joined the buffalo-hides.

Once the tough buffalo-hides were separated, each individual hide was tightly rolled up, and placed on the ground ready to be placed on a as of yet, unassembled travois.

Mandy noticed that the four central poles which served as the base of the tepee, were now being used as the frame work for two of the family's travois.

Little Flower and Spring Blossom, working independently, yet together as a team, each secured a separate tepee pole to opposite sides of the saddle of a docile mare. The bridle of the mare was being held by one of the camp's young boys.

Little Flower and Spring Blossom attached two nets, made of interlaced- rawhide webbing, to the opposing parallel poles of the travois.

Mandy, having studiously observed the procedure, of her own volition and initiative, attempted to construct a travois.

As she was scurrying through the rawhide bindings lying on the ground, Spring Blossom grabbed her by the forearm; "Leave the making of the travois to me and to Little Flower. Fill the carriers and the cases with our possessions. Hurry we are lagging behind the other families."

The quizzical expression in Mandy eyes, and her body language, told Little Flower that this ignorant black one had absolutely no idea as to what was being said.

As Mandy stood in place, motionless, not moving, Spring Blossom raised her hand, prepared to strike the disobedient girl, thus eliciting her compliance.

Little Flower caught Spring Blossom's hand in mid-flight. "My daughter the black one is not being disobedient; she does not yet understand the language of the People." "Show her what you want done. She will respond."

Spring Blossom lowered her hand. "As you wish mother. I will do as you say."

Spring Blossom began to pack the family's meager possessions, into several of the carrying raw hide cases sprawled out on the ground.

She stood and pointed, first to Mandy, then at the parfleche cases. Spring Blossom in a commanding voice, shouted "Fill".

****

In less than two hours, the entire village, that consisted of 46 tepees; 212 persons; of whom 136 were women and children, and 75 hunter-warriors, were on the move.

Forty warriors would be actually participating in the hunt. Due to the change in the scope and subsequent expansion of this hunting party, the promising young, relatively inexperienced, warrior, Running Eagle, was replaced.

The new leader of the expanded hunting party was, the immensely respected war chief, Thunder Cloud.

Thunder Cloud assigned ten of his senior warriors, all veterans of multiple hunting and raiding parties, the task of controlling the main body of hunters, as they approached, downwind of the vast herd of buffalo.

Chief Thunder Cloud had personally authorized these proven, senior hunters, to knock any eager hunters, who might be showing signs of prematurely charging the herd, off of their ponies.

The hunters were instructed to encircle the herd. And in a constricting, ever tightening counterclockwise circling movements, slowly force the buffalo to pack in towards the center of the circle. The women, whose responsibility would be to butcher slain beasts, was to quietly on-foot, bring up the rear.

When the moment was right, Chief Thunder Cloud, as he had done so many times in battle, would then shout out, for all to hear; "Hoka hey!" "CHARGE"!

****

Mandy was astonished and impressed by the speed and the efficiency of the women and children, in the dismantling and the moving of the entire village.

Barely two hours had passed from the time that she and Rebecca, had first heard the sounds of heightened activity in the village, and they had seen what they had initially thought to have been the collapse of the tepees.

Although a small contingent of braves had remained in the camp, they did very little to help with the move. After all the constructing, the maintaining, and the dismantling of the tepees was women's work. The transporting of the band's belongings across the vast expanse of the plains, was women's work

The role of the men left behind, those who would not be participating in the hunt was to protect the women, the children, and the elderly.

The entire population of the band, those that were not members of the hunting party, was now on the move.

The line of travois, most being pulled by horses or mules, a few hitched to and pulled by dogs, stretched for a quarter mile across the prairie.

The bulk of the women and children were on foot. The braves that had remained behind, were fully armed, and slowly rode their war ponies, in front, abreast of, and behind the steadily moving caravan.

Little Flower and Spring Blossom were leading the ponies that held the belongings of the family of Gray Wolf. Mandy was walking beside the matriarch.

She glanced to her right and saw Rebecca trudging along, with a rawhide carrying case, slung over her shoulder. The old woman she had heard called Hen's Teeth, was urging Rebecca along, by periodically striking the white girl's legs, with a short whip.

The light blows of the little whip, across the girl's legs were clearly not intended to inflict pain, Mandy surmised that the flicks of the whip, that she would later learn was made from the buffalo's tail, were to encourage Becky to keep up the pace.

Mandy felt a pang of guilt. During the past two hours she had been so totally consumed by, and absorbed in the frantic, yet controlled activities of moving the camp that she had not once thought of Rebecca.

The procession had been moving at an uninterrupted steady pace, for the entire afternoon. The people had been judiciously taking sips of water from the deer paunches. The deer paunch was the vessel in which the people carried their drinking water.

The water bags were either hanging over their shoulders, or hanging from the saddles of their ponies. As the hours passed, they would take occasional bites of pemmican; dried buffalo meat mixed with wild berries and chokecherries.

After five hours of continuous walking, Old Wise One signaled that the procession should stop. A brave sent with a message from Chief Thunder Cloud, met with Old Wise One, the band's political chief.

The message from Thunder Cloud, the War chief was that the huge herd had stopped to graze. The signs — interpreted by He Who speaks To Ghosts, the Holy Man, — suggested that the herd would spend the night, foraging and resting, in a little valley, about a mile to the northwest of the hunting party's current position.

The band was instructed to spend the night at this spot, to refrain from making loud noises, and to make a smokeless camp.

In the morning, when the sun had traveled half way, across the sky, the hunting of the buffalo would begin.

****

The hunt was a huge success. Two hundred forty-six buffalo were slain. None of the hunters were killed. Seven of the hunters were injured. Five with broken bones, two with nasty, serious gore wounds, inflected by enraged, wounded buffalo.

Little Flower and her daughter Spring Blossom, with Mandy in toll, butcher knives in hand, hurried into the valley. The grass was crimson, covered and matted with the blood of the dead and wounded buffalo.

Little Flower and Spring Blossom separated. They were each looking for dead and or dying animals that had been brought down by the arrows and the lance of Gray Wolf and/or by Running Eagle.

Their kinsmen's arrows were readily recognized, because of the pattern of their distinctive red and black markings, painted on the shifts of the missles.

Gray Wolf and Running Eagle had emerged from the hunt, unscathed. Between father and son, a total of twelve adult buffalo and two unborn calves, in the womb of two of the slain cows, were killed.

Little Flower and Spring Blossom were scurrying across the valley, pulling Running Eagle's and Gray Wolf's arrows from downed buffalo.

Little Flower held up for Mandy's close visual inspection, two arrows that she had just pulled from between the ribs, just below the left shoulder of a massive bull.

As Little Flower was pointing to the distinctive red and black markings on the shaft of the arrows, markings that clearly identified them as Running Eagle's, her son Running Eagle rode up and in a shower of dirt, dismounted before his pony had stopped.

Mandy stood stark still, petrified, frozen in place. She could not move. Mandy was totally mesmerized and awed by the sudden unexpected appearance of this magnificent CREATURE, this vision that who to Mandy, epitomized and fulfilled her imagined concept of total masculinity.

Running Eagle sprinted to the fallen bull, and with two strokes of his hunting knife, removed from the chest of the slain beast, the bull's huge, warm heart dripping with blood.

Running Eagle held the slippery organ, still dripping blood, high above his head. Running Eagle gave vent to a throaty, blood curdling primordial scream of conquest. He then moved the buffalo heart to his mouth, and bit into the warm flesh.

Oddly to her surprise, Mandy did not find Running Eagle's actions to be repulsive, revolting or disgusting.

At that moment, seeing the shear unbridled pride, pleasure, and delight on the faces of Running Eagle and Little Flower, Mandy embraced and shared their joy.

Gray Wolf rode up and dismounted. Running Eagle gave the buffalo heart to his father. Gray Wolf took a bite, then handed the buffalo organ to his wife, Little Flower. Little Flower eagerly bit into the heart. Still grinning, Little Flower impulsively thrust the heart towards Mandy.

With just a brief, fleeting, few seconds of hesitation, Mandy accepted the proffered heart. She tentatively took a small bite.

To her surprise, she found the taste to be, as she would later confide to Rebecca, "actually very good, in fact Mandy thought that it was delicious".

Running Eagle, for the first time since he took her captive, actually took a long openly appraising, good look, at the captive black girl.

This time, the time immediately following a highly successful buffalo hunt, a hunt that yielded in excess of two hundred buffalo carcasses, was by far the busiest time for the band's women.

It was critical that the butchering of the meat, and the removal and curing of the hides be accomplished, without delay.

Little Flower and Spring Blossom working together began the tedious, labor-intensive task of removing the hides from the animals. Mandy was intrigued and impressed by the women's skill and dexterity.

As a slave back at the Rosewood Plantation, Mandy had often worked in the kitchen helping Fannie, the plantation's cook, skin, pluck, butcher and cook small animals.

Skinning rabbits, and possums was a far cry from removing the hide from a one to two thousand pound animal. Once the hide was removed from the first animal, Little Flower said a few brief words to her daughter, and motioned that Spring Blossom should proceed to begin the skinning of the next fallen beast.

Little Flower beckoned to Mandy. Mandy joined the older woman who was standing over the now headless, hideless, carcass. Little Flower stood with two large knifes one in each hand, between the front and rear legs of the carcass. She thrust the knife that she was holding in her left hand towards Mandy. Mandy accepted the knife.

Little Flower bent and slit the carcass from rear leg to front. The contents of the abdomen spilled to the ground. Little Flower separated the internal organs.

The heart, the liver, the stomach, the spleen, the intestines, was all detached and strewn onto the ground.

Little Flower looked up at Mandy. " It is time that you work." She then pointed her knife at the animal that Spring Blossom had just completed skinning.

Mandy moved to the carcass, and went to work.

****

By the time that the last of the travois' had transported the last of the buffalo meat to be cut into strips, and dried back to the village; transported the last rack of ribs, and succulent tongue to be roasted and broiled for tonight's feast; transported the last of the scrapped hides; to the new encampment; by that time, the entire village was in the throes of celebration.

The rhythmic sounds of the beating of drums filled the air.

Mandy was exhausted. In terms of physical exhaustion, there was not a single day in her life that she could recall, having ever felt this exhausted.

The muscles in her forearms and shoulders, were experiencing episodic tremors, and spasmodic cramping, from her seemingly endless wielding of the butcher knife.

When the butchering had finally been completed, Mandy, Little Flower, and Spring Blossom, waded into the creek, and washed off of their hands, their arms, their legs, and their faces, dried caked on, as well as fresh sticky, buffalo blood.

Mandy climbed up on the bank of the creek, prepared to welcome what she considered, a well-earned rest.

Little Flower and Spring Blossom, each took one of Mandy's elbows, and urged her to her feet. Little Flower verbally and in sign spoke; "We must now began to work the hides before they stiffen, and become worthless".

Mandy not understanding the words that they were speaking, merely followed the two Indian women.

The buzzing of swarms of flies and the odor of the skins was to Mandy, overpowering. The hides belonging to Gray Wolf and Running Eagle were identified.

Each hide was marked with one of the hunter's arrows. To her credit, the captive black girl, gave no outward indication, of the internal revulsion at the smell, that she was experiencing

With Mandy watching intently, Little Flower and Spring Blossom, mother and daughter, began working smoothly together.

They staked a still wet hide, taut to the ground. After the first hide had been staked to the ground, the duo now having been joined by Mandy, the trio moved to the next hide.

Once all of the Gray Wolf and Running Eagle hides were stretched, taut, flat on the ground, Spring Blossom handed Mandy a scraping knife and a rather oddly, peculiar looking tool, that resembled elk antlers.

The three females of the Gray Wolf, Running Eagle lodge, in an effort to remove all of the flesh, meat, fat, connective tissue, and muscle, began to thoroughly scrape the inner side of the hide.

After five continuous hours, of the most labor-intensive work that she had ever experience, at last with her knuckles raw and covered with blood (her blood), her knees and back aching, Little Flower stopped the work.

The twelve adult buffalo hides, and the hides of two calves, the hides belonging to Gray Wolf and Running Eagle, free of any visible sign of flesh, meat, fat, connective tissue, and muscle, lay neatly, head to hoof, staked to the ground.

****

When they returned to the newly erected village, Mandy lay down totally exhausted. She lay in Gray Wolf's tepee — the tepee that she, Little Flower, and Spring Blossom had constructed earlier in the day.

Admittedly since her skill at assembling a tepee was negligible, she had been assigned the parochial, mundane, task of chopping sod, and laying it around the base of the structure.

Mandy lay, motionless, totally exhausted, physically drained, in a state of semi-conscientiousness, on one of the soft buffalo robes that served as bedding.

She was on the edge of being awake, or of drifting off to sleep, Mandy suddenly sat bolt upright. Her mind began to race.

Mandy was fully aware of the fact that she was once again a slave. And that she today had been truly, as Grandma Tilda use to lament, "dem fok don wok'd us lik slaves".

While today's back breaking work, which was beyond a doubt, the hardest physical labor that she had ever done, there was a distinct difference.

Her Indian slave Massas had worked — side by side with her — Little Flower and Spring Blossom had worked as hard, if not harder, then had she.

There was no denying the fact that she, once again was a slave. Though she was a slave, held in bondage by her Indian Massas, she was not being treated as a non-person as she had been treated on the Virginia Cotton Plantation.

Mandy was being treated — at least in the division of labor — as an equal.

What a revelation!

Mandy layback down on her soft buffalo hide bed, and fell into an exhausted, dreamless sleep.

* * * * * * * * * * * * * * * * * * * *

The entire village was celebrating the successful hunt. A communal cooking pit had been dug at the edge of the village. Scores of people were congregating at the pit.

Buffalo ribs were being continuously roasted over the flames. The racks of ribs were being consumed as soon as they were removed from the spits.

The women served horn dishes filled with rich meat stew and wild onions. Among the revelers, buffalo tongue was a popular choice of meat.

Braves were dancing and singing. It seemed as if each tepee was hosting some form of light-hearted gambling. Games of chance frequently employing the throwing of dice were prevalent.

Wrestling among the young braves, was a popular means of expelling pent-up energy, as well as providing an excellent opportunity for gambling.

Games with dice and wrestling matches, with very heavy falls, were taking place, with heavy betting on any and every turn.

The winners were exuberant, exultant. The disappointed losers of the matches could often be heard shouting, pleading with anyone who would listen, for a rematch.

* * * * * * * * * * * * * * * * * * * *

Rebecca's day had been a nightmare. Rebecca Billings, formerly the Mistress of Rosewood, one of the state of Virginia's largest Cotton Plantations, the owner of more than one hundred and fifty slaves, was now herself, a slave.

In the world of the Comanche, the Great Plains of the Southwestern United States, Rebecca Billings, soon to be known by the People as "Blue Wolf Eyes", was a slave. Rebecca was the property of Stone Fist, a Comanche Warrior.

When the three young warriors took possession of Henry Billings property, his horses, his mules, his daughter Rebecca, and his mistress' daughter Mandy, Running Eagle, the leader of the scouting party, wisely divided the white man's property including, the two teen-age girls, according to the needs of the three braves.

Swift Arrow had recently married and had established his own lodge.

When the hated, Pawnee killed Swift Arrow's bride's father, who had been defending the village during, a surprise attack by the Pawnee, Swift Arrow had assumed responsibility for his bride's younger sister. He had taken her for his second wife.

Swift Arrow, having no need for an additional female presence in his tepee was pleased when Running Eagle rewarded him with a horse and two mules.

Both Running Eagle and Stone Fist were bachelors living with their parents. The similarity of the two braves went even further. The familial tepees of both Running Eagle and Stone Fist were seriously deficient in the number of available females to sustain the needs of the lodges.

The leader of the group, Running Eagle, would take a horse, and the black girl. The white girl, and a horse, would be the property of Stone Fist.

****

Stone Fist lived with his mother Quite One, and his elderly grandmother, the not so quite, Hens' Teeth. These two were the only female members in the lodge of Stone Fist.

In reality, Stone Fist's mother Quite One, was the only working female in Stone Fist's lodge. Quite One's mother, Stone Fist's grandmother, Hen's Teeth was practically useless.

The old lady was practically crippled with arthritis. Her hands had become useless claws. As if that wasn't enough, now the old woman was beginning to become increasingly confused and forgetful.

Quite One had been, in her own quite way, urging her son to marry. She needed help.

****

Stone Fist's grandmother, Hen's Teeth was not nearly as subtle as was her daughter. She constantly nagged her grandson, insinuating that he was negligent in not providing she and his mother, with additional help.

Stone Fist had earned his reputation as a fearless, deadly warrior. The warriors that rode the plains, be they of the People or enemies of the People, who had faced Stone Face, respected, feared and envied, his prowess as a lethal, courageous warrior.

Stone Fist did not fear, nor did he avoid confrontation with any adversary. That this was not entirely true, was a fact known only to a few members of the band.

Stone Fist feared and avoided contact with the person and the weapons of but one individual. Stone Fist did everything that he could to avoid the acerbic, often cryptic, forever nagging, critical tongue of Hen's Teeth, his beloved grandmother.

Hen's Teeth was to Stone Fist, the single most revered woman — now an old nearly crippled woman — in his life. More so than had anyone, including his mother Quite One, Hen's Teeth had nurtured and raised him.

Whenever she could corner her grandson, Hen's Teeth would verbally assault him by parading before him, all of the village's eligible young girls.

"Stone Fist, Heavy Thighs, the spinster daughter of Black Crow, is the one. You should ask Black Crow, her father, for permission to wed her".

"Quite One, your mother needs help. True to her name, my daughter will not complain, will not speak-up. My son, no Quite One, my daughter's son, your mother, I your grandmother Hen's Teeth, who will soon be walking the trail of those of our departed people, who have gone to the other side, needs help now".

"True Heavy Thighs is not the most beautiful of our girl's yet, her physical strength and the width of her hips, give promise of a good worker, and one who will bear you many sons."

Stone Fist backed down from no man. Stone Fist could not, would not, stand up to, defend himself against, the complaints of his venerated grandmother, Hen's Teeth!

When the two teen-age girls became available, *"spoils of war"*, Stone Fist had leapt at the opportunity to gain possession of at least, one of the slave girls.

They were both young and healthy, and would be seen by Quite One, and Hen's Teeth, as a welcome addition to the work force at the Lodge of Stone Fist.

****

When Rebecca was returned to Stone Fists' mother, after her stay in the *"Unclean Woman's Lodge"*, Quite One indicated by hand gestures, that Rebecca should help the warrior's grandmother, Hen's Teeth.

Hen's Teeth, through grunts, gestures, and the liberal application of blows to Rebecca's bare legs with a switch, helped to dismantle the tepee, to pack the family's belongings, in preparation to transport Stone Fist' lodge, across the prairie.

****

Quite One and Hen's Teeth, with Rebecca in toll, were among the women and children who walked behind the line of hunters into the valley, stalking the herd of buffalo.

Rebecca was intently watching the distinguished looking leader of the hunting party, the savage with the three eagle feathers in his hair.

Although she had expected it, she was startled when the leader yelled, and the savages began to slaughter the hapless, confused buffalo.

****

Rebecca looked around. Dead, wounded, and dying buffalo littered the ground. Two Indian ponies, gored by the buffalo, lay screaming, in their death throes.

The stench of death, dried and drying blood, the distinctive smell of fecal matter, filled the air. Rebecca was horrified.

Standing on wobbly, trembling legs, among the slaughter, Rebecca began to feel lightheaded, her skin became cold and clammy. She began to perspire profusely. The genteel captive white girl was on the verge of fainting.

Rebecca looked to her left and saw Quite One and Hen's Teeth working furiously. They were slicing open the abdomen of a fallen beast.

Quite One reached, with both hands, into the animal's body cavity. With both hands, she removed a large bloody mass of flesh.

A broad toothless grin, spread across the old woman, Hen's Teeth's face. Together, mother and daughter, grinning and laughing, bite into the raw, still bleeding flesh. Rebecca fainted

Hen's Teeth, with buffalo blood dripping from her mouth, walked over to the unconscious girl. With all of the remaining strength in her old frail body, Hen's Teeth kicked the prostrate white girl.

" Get up and get to work you useless, lazy cur." Quite One walked over to her mother and gently pulled her away from Rebecca. The hapless white girl, trying to protect herself, had instinctively curled her body into the fetal position.

The confused, white girl lay moaning, and retching on the ground.

Hen's Teeth looked with contempt at the pitiful, wretched white girl. "All she does is puke and cry. Those cold blue animal's eyes of hers' are always red rimmed and brimming with tears".

"Mother, stop kicking her, leave her alone. She can't work if she's injured". Quite woman removed from her pony's saddle, an old deer paunch that was filled with water.

She held the water vessel directly over the white girl's head, and poured a steady stream of water onto the girl, who was lying on the ground, at her feet.

Rebecca sputtered, and sheepishly looked up at Quite One, the savage that she had sub-conscientiously come to accept as her Indian Massa.

Quite One handed the water paunch to Rebecca. "You must have a name. You will be known as "Blue Wolf Eyes".

Then verbally and in sign, while waving her huge butcher's knife first at the white girl, then at the panorama of slain buffalo, she spoke; "Blue Wolf Eyes, to live, you must work".

Rebecca did not understand the female savage's words. However, she did fully understand the female *Massa's* directive.

Rebecca drank from the deer paunch, she stood and resolutely, butcher knife in her small, soft, smooth, pink hand, walked over to the hide less carcass, of the largest animal that she had ever seen.

****

During that night's feast and celebration, Stone Fist had been one of the most boisterous and jubilant of the celebrants. Stone Fist was anxious and eager to participate in the wrestling matches, and to place wages in the many games of chance.

Due to his well-earned, well-known, and respected reputation, as an athlete, a wrestler, and as a fighter, Stone Fist was having considerable difficulty in finding an opponent.

None of the braves were willing to risk a humiliating defeat, in a contest with the tribes most accomplished athlete, not to mentioned its' renowned fiercest warrior.

Unable to find an opponent, and tiring of betting, and more often than not losing, Stone Fist, tired and frustrated, decided to return to his deserted lodge, for some much needed sleep.

Stone Fist knew that the women of his lodge would be among those women cooking the vast quantities of food for the feast.

Stone Fist entered his lodge and went directly to his bedding. He removed his clothing, flexed his naked, muscular torso, and lowered himself to the soft feel of his buffalo robe bed.

For the entire day Stone Fist had been experiencing the periodic surge and the release, of adrenaline into his body.

First there was the stealthy encircling of the buffalo herd. Then after hearing Chief Thunder Clouds order to charge, there was his headlong rush into the midst of the lethally dangerous, stampeding, herd.

The thrill of galloping at break neck speed, to be within touching distance, from the huge bellowing beasts, was exhilarating. Stone Fist had ridden his pony to be within distance that enabled him to use his spear to bring down the beasts.

Stone Fist saw the fear and the rage in the buffalo's eyes, as they swiveled their massive heads, hooking their twin horns, violently attempting to gore him and his pony.

Following the hunt, Stone Fist had looked forward to enjoying the village's communal feast. He had also anticipated taking part in the sure to come, multiple wrestling matches.

His inability to coax at least one of the many braves, to oppose him in a wrestling match, had been frustrating, and very disappointing.

Stone Fist lay on his bed, restless, frustrated, an over-abundance of testosterone flowing through his body.

****

Rebecca, being totally exhausted, did not stir when Stone Fist entered the lodge. She slept on, completely oblivious to Stone Fist's presence.

Stone Fist, sensing that he was not alone in the tepee, noiselessly, grasped the handle of his ever present, war-club.

Silently he rolled to his left, and stood, crouched on the balls of his feet. His eyes were now completely acclaiminted to the ambient moonlight that filtered down through the tepee's smoke hole.

Stone Fist saw the small figure apparently asleep, several feet to his right. Immediately he recognized the white girl, that his mother had named, "Blue Wolf Eyes".

He walked over to the sleeping figure. Blue Wolf Eyes was fast asleep. In her deep slumber, the white girl's deerskin dress had become bunched up around her thighs.

Stone Fist looked at the exposed, shapely, oddly colored leg. The white girl's leg from her foot to her knee, were the deerskin dress was slit, had been darkened by the sun.

Stone Fist was astonished by the color of her pale thigh. Stone Fist's initial thought was, that" Blue Wolf Eyes", is truly a pale, white woman".

Stone Fist thought to himself, that the true color of the girl, that part that had not been exposed to the sun, was a pale, hideous, sickly, ghostly white.

Just as he was about to turn away in disgust and revulsion, Rebecca whimpered in her sleep, and rolled over onto her back. Doing so the blond hair that covered and framed Rebecca's vagina came into view.

Stone Fist, this man of twenty-three summers, this young man, a young man who at that moment was filled to overflowing with male hormones, a young man at the peak of his physical masculinity, experienced a tremendous erection.

Involuntarily, Stone Fist's left hand surrounded his engorged penis.

It was at that moment that Rebecca opened her eyes. Standing above her was a naked savage. In her confused mind, she saw that in both of his hands, he held a deadly weapon.

In his right hand, he held his horrific war club. In his left hand, in her hysterical state, to the terrified virgin, he was holding, as lethal a weapon, his engorged, deadly penis.

Rebecca screamed. Stone Fist dropped his war club. In an attempt to stifle the girl's screams, he reached, with both hands for the terrified white girl.

****

Just before sunrise, the morning after the celebratory feast, the persistent shouting of Spring Blossom, and the firm hand of Little Flower, urging her to rise, awakened Mandy from a deep, dreamless sleep.

Little Flower handed Mandy the by now familiar tumpline, the sack used to collect and carry wood and buffalo chips for the fire. Mandy, with every bone in her body aching in protest, rose to her feet, and slung the sack across her shoulder.

Little Flower stood in front of the tepee's entrance flap. She motioned for her daughter, Spring Blossom to join them. She began to speak. The words flowed rapidly from her mouth.

Mandy to her delight, recognized and understood many of the words, "Today we must take from our animal brother the buffalo, all of his gifts."

"We will work, we will not stop, until; the meat has been stripped and hung to dry; the hides have been worked; the bones have been drained of their blood; the skulls have been crushed and the brains collected; the sinew, the hoofs, the horns, the tails; have all been removed".

One of the words being repeated and emphasized, Mandy had surmised, literally translated meant work. Instead of dread or despair, Mandy welcomed work. She had come to realize that work was a solid, common bond that she shared with the women of Gray Wolf's tepee.

After the women had cooked and served the meal to Gray Wolf and Running Eagle, together, the three women, tools carried in the parfleche slung over their shoulders, each woman picked up a bowl, of what Mandy thought was the vilest smelling concoction, that she had ever encountered.

The three women hurried to the hides that they had yesterday, staked to the ground.

****
Little Flower and Spring Blossom, with Mandy following their example, as she had done the previous day, began by removing the multiple willow pickets that anchored the hides to the ground.

Once again they vigorously scraped the inside of the hides, with their tools. The scraping continued until the inner surface of the hide had attained an even thickness.

At which point, once again the hides were turned over, this time exposing the outer side. The women then scraped the outside of the hide to remove all traces of hair.

Each hide was yet again turned over, once more exposing the inner surface. A generous mixture of jellied buffalo brains and liver fats was applied to the hides. The concoction was vigorously rubbed into the fleshy side of the hide, until the mixture penetrated the pores.

The entire fourteen buffalo hides, the combined kills of Gray Wolf and Running Eagle, were to be subjected to this process.

Little Flower knew that this meticulous, labor-intensive process, would in all likelihood, consume the entire day. At mid-day, with the sun at its' zenith, Little Flower left, Spring Blossom and Mandy. She returned to the lodge.

Her departure was temporary. Little Flower had left to prepare a meal for her two braves, for her husband Gray Wolf and for son Running Eagle.

The two warriors, father and son, sat next to each other, at the tepee's cooking pit. They were quietly smoking enjoying Gray Wolf's favorite pipe.

The two warriors, two generations of Comanche warriors, were meticulously fashioning new arrows, and repairing their weapons.

After Little Flower completed cleaning up after the warrior's mid-day meal, she packed several strips of pemmican, refilled her water pouch, and rejoined her daughter Spring Blossom, and the hard working, seemingly tireless, black girl, the one who called herself, Man-dee.

The women worked non-stop the entire day, periodically they would nibble at the dried meat.

The three exhausted women of the Gray Wolf Lodge, before returning to the village, to cook and serve the evening meal, welcomed the opportunity wallow in the creek, to wash off the day's accumulated, dirt, blood, and grime.

Little Flower, Spring Blossom, and the black girl Man-dee, walked to the creek, removed and washed their soiled clothing, and lay them across a scrub brush to dry.

They then completely naked and exhausted, walked back to the nearby shallow creek, and waded into the water.

* *

As the sun crossed the sky, and prepared to set in the west, Running Eagle, left the teepee. His intent was to obtain wood for the new bow that he planned to begin making, the next day.

The osage orange trees, growing on the bank of the nearby little creek, were considered by the warriors as trees that produced wood perfect for making sturdy, strong, bows.

As he approached the creek he noticed the three naked women, bathing in the creek. He immediately recognized the three, his mother, his sister, and the black captive.

Running Eagle was about to turn away, but for some inexplicable reason, he did not. As he stared at the image before him, what peaked his interest, and his curiosity, was the difference in color of the three.

The sun was at the backs of the three women. His mother's and his sister's backs had the coppery dark reddish brown hue of the People.

What he found to be oddly curious, and very interesting, was that the back of the black captive girl, was brown and noticeably several shades lighter than the backs of Little Flower and Spring Blossom.

Running Eagle pondered, was not black the darkest of the colors? Of course he mused, black was the darkest of the colors. His thoughts were confused. That being true, he thought, why is the captive girl, who is clearly light brown, of a color lighter than that of the People, was referred to as the black girl?

Each woman splashed water on and under her arms and shoulders. They then submerged their heads under the water. When they raised their heads from beneath the water's surface, Little Flower's and Spring Blossom's long straight black traces, hung in strands, limply cascading down their backs.

Running Eagle's gaze fell on to the captive girl. He was surprised, and astonished at what he saw.

Unlike his mother and sister, the "black" girl's hair was not hanging limply down her back. The hair on her head actually appeared to have thickened.

Droplets of water appeared to be trapped between the hair follicles.
The light of the sitting sun, had the effect of making the water droplets suspended in the girl's hair, sparkle, and twinkle, like the stars in the night sky.

As he watched this captivating, beautiful creature, he was suddenly overwhelmed with the realization of how utterly innocent, attractive and desirable she looked. He experienced a strong, urgent, involuntary stirring in his loins.

Running Eagle stood mesmerized, watching as the "black" girl gracefully, walked up the bank, out of the creek, followed by his mother and his sister.
He was about to turn and leave, when his keen eyes detected movement in the scrub brush on which his mother, Little Flower had lain her dress.

As his mother was approaching the brush, Running Eagle, heard the distinctive rattle of a snake. Before he could react, the captive girl shouted, and hurled one of the butcher knifes towards the brush.

Little Flower jumped back, Spring Blossom, thinking that the black girl was attacking her mother, threw herself onto the girl, and began to pommel her.

"Stop, Spring Blossom, stop"! Little Flower stood over the two, she had the headless body of a six foot snake in her hand. "Man-dee was not trying to hurt me. Man-dee was protecting me."

Running Eagle, relieved, and grateful for his mother's safety, yet confused, without uttering a sound, turned and slowly walked back to the village.

The young warrior's mind was swirling, attempting to process and to understand the myriad of tangled thoughts, and completely unexpected, strong physical and emotional feelings, that he was experiencing.

****

That evening, when Mandy was serving the father and son warriors, their meal, for some unknown reason she sensed a change in the son.

While his demeanor remained, as it had always been, aloft, superior, not acknowledging that she even existed, tonight for some reason it felt different.

With her back to him, she inexplicably felt as if his smoldering black eyes were boring into her back, that her young captor was following her every move.

At one point, Mandy's premonition was so intense, to verify her suspicion, without warning, she quickly spun around, facing the warrior.

Neither the father nor was the son, looking in her direction. Instead the two men were affably enjoying an after meal pipe.

To her surprise the fact that the remarkably attractive young man, seemed not to be showing any interest in her, Mandy found to be both disconcerting and disappointing.

****

333

Throughout the preparation, the serving and his eating of the meal, Running Eagle had indeed, been frequently, surreptitiously, glancing critically, and looking admiring at the captive girl.

Today, when the three women returned to the tepee, Running Eagle had immediately noticed a palpable change, in the relationship between Little Flower, Spring Blossom, and the captive black girl.

The difference, in the way his mother and sister treated the girl, was starkly striking.

While it was true that over the past few days, his mother's and his sister"s treatment of the girl, seemed to have gradually softened, today's change in their attitude, Running Eagle found to be astounding.

Tonight, when the three returned from working the hides, Little Flower and Mandy's relationship appeared to have morphed from that of master and slave, to something akin to a familial, mother/daughter, relationship.

More and more, Running Eagle was coming to the realization that the "black" captive girl was someone special.

****

That night, after Gray Wolf and Little Flower separated after the conclusion of their love making, as usual, Gray Wolf turned his back to his wife, and within minutes, began to snore.

Little Flower lay wide-awake, beside her husband. She nudged Gray Wolf, he did not respond, she then gently blew into his ear. Gray Wolf, still with his back to his wife, mumbled, "Go to sleep woman. Tomorrow will be a long day." Little Flower persisted:"My husband I would speak with you."

"Our children are no longer children. Any day now Stone Fist will present to you, many horses. He will ask permission to marry Spring Blossom."

Gray Wolf sat up; "This is good, Stone Fist is a brave courageous warrior, and an exceptional hunter. He will provide well for our daughter, and he will give us many fine grandchildren."

Now that she had his full attention, and that he was in a good mood, despite being a little grumpy at having his sleep interrupted, Little Flower decided to press on. "Our son Running Eagle is now a man. A respected warrior, already a leader of hunting and raiding parties. It is said by many that he is destined to be a great leader of the People."

"It is time that our son leave the tepee of Gray Wolf, marry and establish the tepee of Running Eagle."

Little Flower's assessment of her husband's attentiveness had been absolutely correct. Gray Wolf gave his wife a quizzical look; "Has Running Eagle made these wishes known to you?"

Little Flower shook her head; "No, his mouth has not said the words. His body, and the longing in his eyes, when he looks at a certain young girl, speaks loudly without the words."

"The sap in our son's loins rises fast, hot and plentiful. Our son no longer wears his breechclout to bed." Gray Wolf's eyebrows rose, he gave his wife an incredulous, questioning, stare. Little Flower answered her husband's unasked question.

"Three moons ago, around the beginning of the *Moon of Ice breaking in the river*, I noticed that Running Eagles breechclouts were no longer available to me for washing. Curious as to where they were, I made a thorough search of his belongings. Rolled up in his favorite buffalo robe, I found two of his soiled breechclouts. They were stained, sticky, and stiff."

Gray Wolf waved his hand indicating that further explanation was not needed. He was not so old that he did not remember his youthful experience with the nightly dreams of lust.

The fact that Running Eagles seed, which he considered to be the future grandsons of Gray Wolf, was being wasted, should not be allowed to continue.

His son, Running Eagle's body was eager, ready to burst, to spew forth, and repopulate the plains and the prairie, with the grandchildren of Gray Wolf, future sons and daughters of the People.

Gray Wolf asked of his wife; "Has Running Eagle selected a woman to be his wife?" Little Flower did not answer. She paused, attempting to transform her suspicions, into words that would be believable to her husband.

"There are many young girls, and women in the village, who desire our son. Running Eagle has been regularly sampling the charms of several. Unknown to our son, I have watched him closely. I do not believe that Running Eagle has strong feelings for any of these women."

"The black captive girl Man-dee, is intelligent, hard working, courageous, and talented. She is making an effort, beginning to understand our talk. In just three days, she learned to gut the buffalo, to butcher meat, to make pemmican, to cure the hides."

"Today the girl who calls herself Mandee, saved my life." Gray Wolf had been only half listening to Little Flower. He was a bit confused. One minute they had been talking about Running Eagle's leaving the lodge and taking a wife, the next minute Little Flower is lauding the talents of the captured black slave girl.

Gray Wolf forced himself to concentrate, to listen to the words, and more importantly, the meaning of Little Flower's words.

"We had just finished washing our bodies in the creek. I was about to reach for my dress, when I heard Man-dee shout, I looked up, and a butcher knife flew past my face. The knife severed the head, from the body of a huge rattlesnake. The snake was using my dress to shade himself from the sun."

"My husband, Man-dee is no longer to be considered my slave. She is now a member of Gray Wolf's Lodge. She is my…she is our daughter."

Gray Wolf had no objection to Little Flower's words. It had long been the People's custom, for captured women and children to, if deserving, to assimilate, to be accepted as members of the band.

Gray Wolf felt an overwhelming sense of debt and gratitude for the girl "Man-dee's", heroic actions, saving her from the fangs of the rattlesanke. He could not imagine life without Little Flower.

He placed his hands on Little Flower's shoulder; "What does it mean, Man-dee? Little Flower gave her husband a blank look. Gray Wolf then declared; "A daughter needs a name with meaning. I have thought on this. Our daughter is to be known as "Pretty Buffalo Hair."

Little Flower smiled. With the naming, Little Flower knew that Gray Wolf had accepted Man-dee…"Pretty Buffalo Hair", as their daughter.

Although it had been her intention to speak to Gray Wolf of the growing attraction between Man-dee and Running Eagle, she decided to at this time, to defer that particular conversation.

****

The following morning Mandy awoke before the other occupants of Gray Wolf's, crowded tepee.

As she lay motionless on her sleeping robe, next to the bedding of Spring Blossom, her mind was filled with the events that had transpired, since the massacre of her mother, and Rebecca's father.

Silent tears welled up in eyes. She attempted to push the horrific image of her mother's scalped and mutilated body, from her mind.

The sight of Henry scalped, with his genitals stuffed into his mouth. She would never forget that look of absolute terror that had swept across Rebecca's face.

Becky, what had happened to her? Since they were forced to leave the isolation tent, for menstruating women, she had only caught occasional glimpses of Becky. How is she being treated? Is she all right? Mandy decided that today, somehow she would find her, and that she would talk with Becky.

Mandy wiped the tears from her eyes. The only sounds in the tepee, were the strident snores that were emanating from the bedding of Gray Wolf and Little Flower.

As she walked towards the entrance flap, she glanced at the sleeping form of Running Eagle. She stopped in mid-stride, she stood frozen, fascinated, unable to move, her eyes were fixated on the magnificent image of naked masculinity before her.

Running Eagle had kicked the buffalo robe from his body. He lay naked, on his side sleeping. Still asleep, the young brave shifted his body his semi-erect penis came into view. Mandy gasped, with renewed effort, she willed herself into motion.

Mandy reached for her wood gathering equipment, and trembling with excitement, quickly, silently left the lodge.

****

After she had assisted Little Flower in the preparation and serving of the morning meal, and after cleaning the utensils, Mandy without any prodding from either Little Flower or Spring Blossom, began cutting strips of meat to be hung on the drying racks.

Mandy heard shouting from the direction of the tepee, that was situated immediately behind Gray Wolf's. She turned and saw Rebecca, cowering, her hands shielding her face, being repeatedly switched with a branch, by an old woman.

Mandy ran towards the old woman shouting, "stop that". The old woman whirled around at the sound of Mandy's approach. She raised the twig to strike Mandy. Mandy easily blocked the blow, and yanked the twig from the old woman's hands.

Little Flower and Spring Blossom were a few steps behind Mandy. Hen's Teeth looked pass Mandy and screamed at Little Flower; "Did you see that? Are you going to let your slave treat a woman of the People this way?

Little Flower walked over to Mandy, she removed the twig from her hand. A satisfied smirk spread across Hen's Teeth face. She confidently waited, anticipating the beating that Little Flower would rain down on this insolent slave girl.

Mandy also expected blows from Little Flower. She stiffened her back, stood tall, she was determined not to shrink away, or to cower.

Little Flower broke the twig across her knee. She then spoke directly to Hen's Teeth; "Pretty Buffalo Hair is not my slave, Pretty Buffalo Hair; she is my daughter."

Shocked and dismayed, Hen's Teeth looked towards Spring Blossom; "What is Little Flower saying…has she loss her mind?"

Spring Blossom looked quizzically, to her mother, she then looked at Hen's Teeth. Spring Blossom strode over to her mother and to the black girl. She spoke with respect and with conviction to Hen's Teeth; "Pretty Buffalo Hair is not my slave, Pretty Buffalo Hair is my sister."

Mandy had no idea as to what was being said between the three women. Instead of receiving the anticipated blow from Little Flower, Little Flower put her hand firmly onto Mandy's right shoulder, and gave a gentle reassuring squeeze.

Spring Blossom, as had her mother Little Flower, placed her hand on the black girl's left shoulder and gently, she squeezed her sister's shoulder.

****

Mandy spoke rapidly to the white slave girl, who remained slumped over, whimpering; "Becky, if you can find a way, an excuse, anything, collect firewood, collect buffalo chips, anything. Try to meet me on the prairie, in an hour if you can."

Little Flower, Spring Blossom, and "Buffalo Hair", holding hands, walked back to Gray Wolf's lodge.

Hen's Teeth picked up the broken twig. She turned, and shook the stick at the cowering white girl.

When they returned to the lodge, Little Flower spoke at length with Spring Blossom, Mandy respectfully, dutifully concentrating, not understanding all of her words, listened intently.

Little Flower told of her and Gray Wolf's decision, to welcome Man-dee into their family. She told Spring Blossom of Gray Wolf's decision to give their new family member a meaningful name.

She told of how she could not answer her husband's fundamental question; "What is a Man-dee...what does it mean?" She told of Gray Wolf's desire to bestow a meaningful name to their new family member.

She told Spring Blossom of her father Gray Wolf's declaration; "Our new daughter's Comanche name will be Pretty Buffalo Hair".

Her name now is one that has meaning; a name that honors her shared courage with our four-legged brother the buffalo, and the shared texture of both of their hair.

Little Flower faced Mandy. She pointed her finger at the former slave; "Man-dee." Mandy pointed her finger at her chest and firmly stated; Man-dee.

Little Flower began to vigorously shake her head; " No no, no more Man-dee," She pointed her finger at the girl and emphatically stated; "Pretty Buffalo Hair...you are Pretty Buffalo Hair."

****

While Mandy was busily cutting and hanging on the drying racks, strips of buffalo meat to dry in the hot sun, out of the corner of her eye she saw Rebecca, picking up twigs and small branches. Rebecca, as Mandy had instructed her to do, was walking towards the creek.

Mandy placed her last strip of meat onto the drying rack. She wiped her hands on a piece of deerskin, and hastily followed Rebecca.

Little Flower, who was separating sinew according to its thickness, saw Pretty Buffalo Hair walk up to the white girl. Pretty Buffalo Hair's actions neither alarmed, or did they concern her.

Little Flower had no reason to doubt that her daughter, Pretty Buffalo Hair, would act responsibly, and would shortly return to finish her work.

****

Rebecca was seated on the ground tears were streaming down her cheeks. Mandy wiped her life-long friend's cheeks with her hands. "Becky you've got to get a hold of yourself".

"The more you cry and whimper, the more harshly they'll treat you. Becky these are strong, hard working people. They respect strength, they do not, and will not, tolerate weakness. Everyone in the village has to do their share."

Rebecca, weeping out of control, threw herself into Mandy's arms; "Oh Mandy he hurt me, he raped me." Mandy took Rebecca by the shoulders and began to shake her. Stop it Becky! Rebecca Elizabeth Billings, you just stop it, stop it right now!"

Rebecca was taken aback. She had expected Mandy to be shocked and horrified, to sympathize with and to comfort her. Instead she, the victim of the unthinkable, was being scolded.

"Becky, you knew, we both knew that this could happen. We discussed it at the menstruation hut. Together we vowed that what ever happened, we would survive. Somehow, someway we would survive, we would escape."

Rebecca had regained control; "That wicked old woman is horrible. She goes out of her way to torment me. She screams at me she beats me, she treats me like a nigger slave".

Rebecca gasped, mortified, at what she had just said. Oh Mandy, I'm so sorry I don't know where that came from. Please, please forgive me".

Mandy walked away from her friend, then turned abruptly; "Forgive you, forgive you for what? Forgive you for being born white? Forgive you for being born into a family that enslaved other human beings?"

"What's to forgive, as Miss Leary said, no one now living, or for that matter, no one who has ever lived, or will ever live, had or has any control over who their parents will be."

"What we can control is who we are inside. No matter what they call you, no matter what that old fool, that we read about, the Chief Justice of the Supreme Court, Roger Taney decreed, although I was born into slavery, and now that we find ourselves, both of us enslaved, we will never be a slave, unless in your mind, you let them make you a slave."

"Although that horrible old woman, and her family, including the man who raped you, think of you as their slave, as a pieces of property, less than human, you know better".

"Now start acting like it. No more crying and sniveling. You've got to work as hard, and if you can, harder then they do. You can gain their respect, by respecting them and their ways".

"Show that old woman and the man that hurt you that, Rebecca Elizabeth Billings, deserves and demands their respect."

"If I am correctly interpreting and understanding Little Flower and Spring Blossom, the remainder of the week is going to be especially difficult and hectic".

"The meat needed for the winter has to be dried. Pemmican has to be made, the buffalo hides have to be finished, made into clothing and into winter coverings for the tepees."

"The two women in the lodge, Little Flower and Spring Blossom, have come to trust me. They trust me because I do the work. I don't cry, I don't wallow in self-pity, I don't wait to be asked, I try to anticipate what needs to be done, and I do it."

"The older man, the husband and father Gray Wolf, I think, loves and listens to his wife Little Flower. Gray Wolf has given me a new name, an Indian name, she than mouthed the Comanche words, which meant "Pretty Buffalo Hair". "I have no idea as to what it means. But believe me, I intend to find out."

Rebecca was giving Mandy a quizzical looking. "Why do you care what it means? Once again Rebecca took Rebecca by the shoulders, and again she shook her, this time harder than she had before, "Why do I care… I don't care because it means anything to me…I do care, because it obviously means something to them."

"I know by now you've noticed that the women do almost all of the work. They need our help. For us to escape, we have to gain their trust."

"Becky this is your opportunity to show your mettle, work hard, win their respect, and gain their trust. Can you do that? I know you're not at all used to this kind of heavy work. I'll help you as much as I can. Together we can survive this."

Rebecca nodded. She was thinking how much Mandy, this Mandy at this moment, reminded her of their former teacher, Miss Leary.

The girls, chins held high, resolutely, hurried back to the Indian village.

****

If anything, "Buffalo Hair's", forecast of a heightened, accelerated workload was an understatement. The third day following the hugely successful buffalo hunt, presented a real challenge to the work ethic, and the ability of the village's women.

Immediately following the morning meal, the three women of Gray Wolf's lodge, arrived at the area where they had previously staked to the ground, their fourteen, partially cured, buffalo hides, and several additional hides from smaller animals killed since the big hunt, two elk and one antelope.

Little Flower and Spring Blossom, with Pretty Buffalo Hair following their example, as she had done the previous day, began what Pretty Buffalo Hair hoped would be the final tanning process, by removing the multiple willow pickets that anchored the hides to the ground.

Once again they vigorously scraped the inside of the hides, with their tools. The scraping continued until the inner surface of the hide had attained the desired even thickness. Then once again the hides were turned over, this time exposing the outer surface. As they had done yesterday, they scraped the outside of the hide, removing all visible traces of the animal's hair.

Each hide was yet again was turned over, once again exposing the inner surface. That smelly mixture of jellied buffalo brains and liver fats was applied to the hides. The three women vigorously rubbed the gooey paste, into the fleshy side of the hide, being sure to penetrate the pores.

Little Flower, Spring Blossom, and Pretty Buffalo Hair, working side by side, subjected all seventeen hides, the combined kills of Gray Wolf and Running Eagle, to the process.

Today instead of Little Flower, Spring Blossom left at mid-day to prepare the second of the day's meals for Gray Wolf and for Running Eagle.

When she returned, the three women of Gray Wolf's lodge, walked to the creek and sat. Little Flower passed around dried meat, fruit and water.

As the women were enjoying their brief meal break, Little Flower spoke to Spring Blossom; "Your sister Pretty Buffalo Hair, is indeed an asset to the lodge of Gray Wolf. We three are well ahead of the others."

Spring Blossom nodded her head in agreement, "I have become very fond of Pretty Buffalo Hair. She has become the little sister that I always wanted."

Mandy was intently listening, straining trying to translate the increasingly not so foreign words that she was hearing. Trying to understand, to learn the language of her captors.

Mandy remembered one of the most important things that Miss Leary had taught to her and to Rebecca. "Girls if you don't understand something, you must never ever be afraid to ask questions".

"And if you don't understand the first explanation, the answer, especially if you believe that the person that you are asking can eventually explain, keep at it be persistent. "Remember ladies, "Knowledge is power". If you have knowledge, you have power."

Mandy tugged on the sleeve of Little Flower. When she had both of their attention she spoke and attempted to repeat and to emphasize her words through rudimentary signs and gestures.

She spoke her name, pronouncing it as Little Flower had, while pointing to her chest; "Man-dee" then she rapidly shook her head, "No no Man-dee" then she repeated the name that Little Flower and Spring Blossom continued to call her, "*nananisuyake tasiwoo tso-yaa*", she then framed her face with her open hands, "*nananisuyake tasiwoo tso-yaa*", what does it mean?"

Neither Little Flower, nor did Spring Blossom understand Pretty Buffalo Hair's words, other than when she repeated her name, they did recognize from the girl's infliction, that she was asking a question.

Spring Blossom asked her mother; "what is she saying...why does she keep repeating her name Pretty Buffalo Hair?"

Little Flower had been watching, listening, concentrating, as her adopted daughter, Pretty Buffalo Hair spoke.

Clearly Pretty Buffalo Hair, understood that her name was no longer Man-dee, that instead it was now Pretty Buffalo Hair, ahh; "Spring Blossom, I think Pretty Buffalo Hair wants to know the meaning of her name".

Spring Blossom stood then she dropped down to her knees. She balled her hands into fists. Then she extended the forefinger and thumb of both hands forming an "L". Spring Blossom placed her thumbs, the bottom of the "L", against her temples, and started bellowing.

Little Flower began to bend over laughing. Mandy though initially confused, caught on quickly, this was charades. Little Flower pointed to her "horned-bellowing daughter", looked at Mand-dee, pointed and said *"tasiwoo"*.

Mandy pointed to herself, and repeated the Comanche word that Little Flower was saying, the word, *"tasiwoo"*. Now she understood. The word that Little flower kept repeating *"tasiwoo"*, in English meant Buffalo.

She mimicked Spring Blossom's impersonation, placed her thumbs, index fingers extended alongside her temples, and began to bellow, *"tasiwoo"*.

Mandy, Little Flower, and Spring Blossom smiled.

Following that simple breakthrough, the interpretation of her Comanche name, her understanding that the Comanche words "*nananisuyake tasiwoo tso-yaa*", in English translated to the name "Pretty and Hair" was easily accomplished.

This little game, that "*Pretty Buffalo Hair*", began to regularly employ with anyone and everyone, coupled with the fact that she was truly a gifted, astute student, was the key to Mandy's rapid ability to understand the language of the People.

****

After completing their meal, the three women of Gray Wolf's lodge, with a vengeance, returned to work.

Half of the processed hides were bundled onto a travois, pulled by a pony to the edge of the creek. The women, as a team, washed the hides in the creek until they became somewhat pliable.

Additional buffalo brains and liver was rubbed in the inner side of the hides.

After several days when the gooey mixture of buffalo brains & liver had been absorbed, two of the women would grab either end of the hide, and draw it back and forth around a tree for hours. The three women of the Gray Wolf lodge would alternate, relieving each other from this extremely, fatiguing, strenuous activity.

When the hide was pliable enough to fold, then and only then, was the cured, folded hide, ready to become a buffalo robe.

****

That evening, following the evening meal, with both Running Eagle and Spring Blossom out presumably socializing with their friends, Little Flower decided that the time was right for her to resume the talk that she had started and postponed, with her husband; the topic, of the growing feelings, between their Son Running Eagle, and their adopted daughter, Pretty Buffalo Hair.

Gray Wolf was seated next to the dying cooking fire, leisurely enjoying an after meal smoke.

Little Flower put down the garment, Gray Wolf's ceremonial shirt that she had been adorning with the addition of dyed porcupine quills.

She seated herself next to Gray Wolf; "My husband, though our lodge is one of the largest in the village, It has become increasingly apparent, that it is not adequate for five grown adults."

Gray Wolf knocked the ashes from his pipe, and lovingly placed it beside him. "Woman we have been married now for more then twenty-four winters. In that time, I have learned when, you are about to skillfully, gain my consent for something that you more then likely have already done, or have decided needs to be done".

"For us to have a larger tepee would be an insult to, Chief Thunder Cloud, He Who Speaks To Ghosts, and to Chief Old Wise One."

Little Flower fanged surprised hurt; "As always, my husband, your wisdom and perception precedes my words. I had not given thought to the political ramifications of our tepee being larger then that of our leaders."

Gray Wolf picked up his pipe, he turned to look for his tobacco pouch.
Little Flower handed the pouch to her husband. A momentary silence filled the lodge. The only sounds were of Gray Wolf rapid puffing, as he attempted to light his pipe.

Gray Wolf broke the silence. "I have heard from He Who Speaks To Ghosts, that shortly, perhaps as early as tonight, Stone Fist will come with horses, asking my permission for him to marry Spring Blossom. If his gift is adequate, and if Spring Blossom consents, I will accept his horses."

Little Flower remained silent. If Gray Wolf had looked at his wife, he would have noticed a slight smile forming at the bottom of her mouth. Inwardly Little Flower thought, one down, two to go.

During Gray Wolf and Little Flower's conversation, Mandy was seated on her sleeping robes, in the rear of the tepee. She was sewing a dress from the soft hide of a doe that Spring Blossom had given her as a gift.

Little Flower looked in the direction of their adopted daughter, Pretty Buffalo Hair, she discreetly pointed; "Pretty Buffalo Hair is a fine daughter. She is an excellent, seamstress, an excellent cook, hard worker, and a truly beautiful girl. She will make a fine wife for some brave. You will receive many horses when she marries." Gray Wolf absently grunted, and continued to puff on his pipe.

Little Flower studied her husbands face, looking to see his reaction to her words of praise of Pretty Buffalo Hair. Seeing none, she continued; "I think that Running Eagle likes Pretty Buffalo Hair." From the corner of her eye, she looked for Gray Wolf's reaction, still no reaction.

"I think that our adopted daughter, Pretty Buffalo Hair, likes our son, Running Eagle." Gray Wolf grunted, "of course Running Eagle likes Pretty Buffalo Hair, after all, she is his little sister."

Little Flower took a deep breath, "the feelings that I see, are not the feelings of a brother's love for his sister, or a sister's love for a brother." Gray Wolf silently knocked the ashes from his pipe into the fire-pit. Holding the pipe by its still warm bowl, he pointed the stem at his wife.

"Little Flower, it is time that you speak openly…what are you trying to tell me?" Little Flower steadied herself, she took a deep breath; "My husband the furtive glances that I see, are not the feelings of a brother's love for his sister, or a sister's love for a brother, I see in Running Eagle, the desire of a man for a woman, and in Pretty Buffalo Hair, I see the desire of a woman for a man."

Gray Wolf gave his wife a look of sheer incredulity. In his most authoritative voice, he stated; "My son has not been brought up to be a pervert. To have sexual desire for his sister."

Little Flower reached for and held her husband's hand in her two hands; "My husband there is no perversion. Running Eagle and Pretty Buffalo Hair, were not raised as brother and sister. They do not have the experiences and the history of growing up together, being raised in the same lodge".

"There is no blood link between the two. That they are attracted to each other, as a man is attracted to a woman, and as I am attracted to you, is not a perversion, it is natural."

"If they should marry, think of the fine young warriors that would result from a union of our son, a Comanche Warrior, and Pretty Buffalo Hair, a proud courageous member of the Black Tribe."

"Did this not occur, the issue of our tribe's man, Quahada Comanche, Chief Peta Nocona, and the white captive girl, Cynthia Ann Parker?"

****

"Is it not said that their teenage son Quanah, is thought by many, especially by He Who Speaks To Ghosts, to be destined to become a great warrior chief, and leader of the People."

Mandy had been quietly sitting, sewing her beautiful doeskin dress. It had become her custom, to listen carefully to the talk between Indians.

Her motivation, her reason for paying close attention to any and all of the conversations, was not to eavesdrop her intent was to help her to improve her knowledge of the language.

While being far from fluent, in fact she was, with Little Flower and Spring Blossom's help, just learning to put together learned jumbles of words, into understandable simple sentences.

As she strained to listen to her adoptive parents, she would hear familiar words. *Pretty Buffalo Hair*, her Comanche name she heard put forth frequently, by both Little Flower and Gray Wolf. She also recognized the names, Spring Blossom, Stone Fist, and Running Eagle.

A new word that she had recently learned through simple "girl-talk", conversations with Spring Blossom was theword *marry*.

Spring Blossom had poured her heart out, and made crystal clear to *Pretty Buffalo Hair*, her desire to marry the warrior, Stone Fist.

The practice of presenting to the father of the potential bride, a gift of *horses*, was a topic frequently discussed between the two sisters, Spring Blossom and *Pretty Buffalo Hair*.

She could hardly wait to tell Spring Blossom of what she thought was Gray Wolf's decision, to accept Stone Fist's gift of horses.

As hard as she tried to concentrate, Mandy could not grasp, or understand the gist of the conversation between Gray Wolf and Little Flower, when the names Running Eagle and *Pretty Buffalo Hair*, were said together.

Little Flower and Gray Wolf were continuing their conversation. Gray Wolf spoke; "I agree Little Flower, it is time that our son, Running Eagle move to his own tepee. I think that this talk about a romance between Running Eagle and *Pretty Buffalo Hair*, is the wishful thinking of a loving mother."

Once again, Mandy heard her Indian name, *Pretty Buffalo Hair*, and that of Running Eagle, mentioned together, in the same sentence, her name and his, mentioned, one right after the other. Mandy continued to listen. The words were flowing much to fast for her to interpret.

When Little Flower rose, and walked over to her sleeping robes, Mandy's last thought, before she too went to bed was, oh how I wish I knew what they were saying about Running Eagle and me.

****

Now that the women had set up the new encampment, and were constantly working, butchering and tanning hides, in the evening and at night, understandably, the young women were too exhausted to fraternize with the braves.

Running Eagle, who was use to being lavished with female attention and sexual favors from the unmarried women, was becoming increasingly frustrated.

Those women who usually eagerly welcomed, or often sought, clandestine rendezvous with the handsome, eligible bachelor, were either too tired, or were being forced by their mothers to get plenty of rest, so that they would be fresh for the next day's hard-labor.

Having repaired their weapons, and replaced those that were beyond repair, Running Eagle and Stone Fist were beginning to become restless, and bored.

Despite the enormous amount of work still to be done, following the successful hunt, the thought of assisting the belabored women was never a consideration.

Butchering, tanning, sewing, cooking, had long ago, been defined as women's work.

The two friends decided to get away, to leave the village for a few days. As they sat preparing for their sojourn, Running Eagle began to speak to Stone Fist, of his four days without female companionship.

"My man's sack is becoming heavy with seed. I am worried that this hiatus, this time when the women seek only sleep and rest, will result in the return of unwanted, embarrassing, dreams that lead to the unwanted, embarrassing spillage of my seed. "My brother Stone Fist, do you not have this problem?"

Stone Fist set down his quiver of arrows; "Running Eagle, I do not understand. Why does your sack retain overflowing seed? I empty mine regularly using my white slave girl as a receptacle. Why don't you do the same with your black slave girl?"

The black girl, "Pretty Buffalo Hair is not my slave. She is my adopted sister." Stone Fist did not question Running Eagle's explanation. Instead he offered what he considered a reasonable, logical solution; "My friend you are welcome to use my slave, the white girl, the one that your sister Pretty Buffalo Hair calls "Bee-kee"."

348

"I thank you for your offer my brother. By the time we return, I hope it will not be necessary. Our young women should be finished with the tanning, and will be eager to share their bodies, with the two of us".

"After all according to my mother Little Flower's assessment, we two are at the top of the list, of the still available, most eligible of the band's bachelors."

Stone Fist stood, "I am afraid my friend, and brother of my soon to be wife, my eligible bachelor days are over". Running Eagle had a confused look on his face. He waited patiently for Stone Fist to continue. "This morning Gray Wolf accepted my gift of horses. When we return, I will marry Spring Blossom, your sister."

Running Eagle was delighted. Grinning from ear to ear, hardly able to suppress a shout of joy, he embraced his boyhood friend, in a warm bearhug.

He held Stone Fist at arms length, stepped back, and in a solemn voice proclaimed, "I welcome you to the family...brother!"

****

On the fifth day following the great buffalo hunt, the trio of the women of Gray Wolf's tepee, after attending to their routine chores, went together down to the creek for what they anticipated, would be the final day of the tanning of the animal hides.

On this the last day, the gooey mixture of buffalo brains and liver had been fully absorbed into the fabric of the hide. Spring Blossom and Pretty Buffalo Hair, each grabbed opposing ends of a dry hide. They then began to draw the hide back and forth around the thick trunk of a tree.

Little Flower first relieved Spring Blossom, who in turn after fifteen minutes of rest, relieved Pretty Buffalo Hair who in turn after resting, relieved Little Flower.

This monotonous process, continued until the last hide, was folded, placed on a travois and taken to the lodge of Gray Wolf.

****

The next day, following Running Eagle and Stone Fist's departure, Little Flower, Spring Blossom and Pretty Buffalo Hair, were joined by the women of Stone Fist's lodge, his mother Quite One, his grandmother, Hen's Teeth, and Stone Fist's white captive, Bee-kee.

The women's task was to construct two new tepees. One to be occupied by Stone Fist and his wife Spring Blossom, the other to ostensibly be the bachelor tepee of Running Eagle.

It was agreed that Quite One, Hen"s Teeth and the white slave Bee-kee, would remain in the old tepee, Stone Fist and his new wife, Spring Blossom would begin their new life in a new tepee.

Sixteen buffalo hides were selected. Eight buffalo hides for each tepee. To bind the hides together, the women divided themselves into to two working groups.

For strategic reasons aimed at establishing future domestic tranquility, Little Flower placed her daughter Spring Blossom with her new in-laws, Quite One, and Hen's teeth. Mandy was elated when she saw that Becky, would be working with her, and with Little Flower.

Rebecca's spirits soared, when Spring Blossom walked over to join Quite One, and Hen's Teeth, Stone Fist's mother, and grandmother.

When Hen's teeth pushed her towards Little Flower and Mandy, Rebecca hastily and willingly complied. The prospect of having the opportunity to talk at length with Mandy was to her, absolutely exhilarating.

Little Flower gave a welcoming smile to the obviously still frightened, shy white girl. She once again noted how much these two girls, physically resembled one another.

Other than the difference in their skin-color and in the texture, and the color of their hair, these two could truly be sisters.

Little Flower tore her eyes away from staring at the white girl, she turned and spoke to her adopted daughter; "Pretty Buffalo Hair, take your friend and together, select enough strong strands of thread to securely join the hides together."

Becky looked on in amazement and incredulity, as Mandy rose. Did Mandy actually understand the gibberish spewing forth from this savage's mouth?

Mandy took Becky by the arm. The black girl, dressed in a soft doeskin, ankle length dress, with thick black braids framing her beautiful face, and her equally beautiful white friend, walked hand in hand, towards the numerous racks of long strands of dried, and drying, buffalo sinew.

Once they were far enough away from the other women, so that they would not be overheard — not that any of the Indian women would have understood English — Becky began talking rapidly; "Mandy, did you really understand what that heathen, ignorant, savage was saying?"

Becky was surprised, Mandy answered in a harsh, reproachful voice. "Little Flower; Her name is Little Flower. Little Flower is not a savage."

"Mandy, what's wrong with you, what are you saying? These people, if you can call them people, are all heathen savages. Mandy, how could you think otherwise?" She wiped at the tears that had welled up in her eyes. "That brutish, huge savage animal, continues to rape me!"

Mandy was visibly moved by the depth, and by the passion and the hurt that she heard in Becky's voice. "I'm so sorry Becky. I didn't mean to sound so, so insensitive. The name of the brave that assaults you is Stone Fist."

"When I told Little Flower of Stone Fist's violating you, she was not at all surprised. In fact she did not regard his actions as an attack, she viewed his actions as Stone Fist's right. The right of any warrior, his prerogative as to how he treats his captive women."

"As heartless as that sounds, the more that I thought about her words, I couldn't help but remember the way that the white masters at Rosewood, your grandfather Artimas, your father Henry, your uncle Robert, and your brother Jesse, abused its' female slaves. How they abused my family."

Rebecca could not believe what she was hearing. Her best friend Mandy, her only link to a sane civilization, seemed to be condoning what that savage beast, what was his name…Stone Fist, what Stone Fist had done to her.

Rebecca thought, while Mandy certainly was not justifying, or condoning what that beast Stone Fist had done to her, it sounded as if based upon her life as a slave, and Mandy's family's history with the Billings' men, their white Masters, she appears to be saying that what Stone Fist did to me, was understandable.

Rebecca stepped back and stared at her friend. She had assumed that Mandy too, had suffered the same degrading experience. That Mandy had been degraded, raped by one, or by both of the male inhabitants, of Gray Wolf's Lodge.

Rebecca asked in a barely audible whisper; "Mandy, have you ever been raped…either at the Rosewood Plantation, or here in this God forsaken wilderness?"

For a moment, Mandy was confused. What was Becky asking? Surely she knew that if such a horrific act had ever occurred, she would have confided in her best friend.

"No Becky, I personally have not been raped. I, as I am sure you were, until Stone Fist— I am still a virgin."

"Back at Rosewood, my mother spoke to me, as did all of the slave mothers did with their daughters, of the more than likely event that the white Massas' would make you lie down with them. Slave girls were told not to resist. That we were the Massas' property and they, the Massas could do whatever they wanted to do to them."

Rebecca asked; "Mandy why weren't you molested? Mandy everyone said that you were, if not the prettiest, you were definitely one of the prettiest slave girls on the plantation."

Mandy took the dried strands of sinew from Rebecca's hands. She looked directly into her friends, innocent, bright blue eyes.

Rebecca with a curious expression on her face, looked into Mandy's soft brown eyes. She was awaiting an answer to what she considered, was her very reasonable question.

"I don't know why I haven't been raped while living as a slave in the lodge of Gray Wolf".

"I suspect that there are two primary reasons. First Gray Wolf is very much in love with his wife, Little Flower. Not only does Gray Wolf love his wife, it's evident to all who see them together, that he both loves and respects Little Flower.

"As far as their son, Running Eagle, is concerned, I honestly don't know why he has not had his way with me".

"At first, I lived in constant fear, wondering if and when he would rape me. Now I admit, I wonder, if I have been spared because he simply does not find me to be an attractive, desirable, woman".

"In any event my being raped by either of the men of Gray Wolf's Lodge is now moot".

"Little Flower asked Gray Wolf to make me a member of their family, to adopt me. Gray Wolf agreed, gave me an Indian name, and welcomed me, as a member of his family."

Mandy hesitated, then, as if she had just this very moment, decided to unburden her mind, she took a deep breath and sighed.

"The reason that I was not molested by the white men, or for that matter, the black men at Rosewood, is because the Master of Rosewood, Henry Billings your father, had threatened to horse-whip, any man that dared to touch my mother Ruth, his mistress, or Ruth's daughter, Mandy".

Rebecca stood stark still, dumbfounded, confused. Mandy took Becky's hands in her own. Once again she looked deeply into her eyes. Tears were welling up in both Becky and Mandy's eyes; "Becky we share the same blood. We have the same father".

"Becky we are really, and truly, in every sense of the word, we are sisters."

****

Little Flower had joined Spring Blossom's group. The four women were sorting out which of the hides, would be best suited to serve as the outer walls, for the two tepees.

Pretty Buffalo Hair and the white slave girl, had returned. The white slave girl was leading a dog drawn travois. The mobile platform was filled with all manner of thread. Thick, buffalo, antelope, and Elk sinew would be used in the construction of the two new tepees.

Both groups of women set about the task of erecting what they envisioned would be two new, magnificent dwellings, the lodge of Running Eagle, and the lodge of Stone Fist.

****

Running Eagle was determined to make this last, bachelor foray with his best friend, memorable. As they sat smoking and reminiscing before their fire, retelling tales of their exploits and adventures as boys, then as young warriors, they turned their heads in unison, at the ferocious growl of a mountain lion.

Running Eagle looked to his friend; "Stone Fist before you settle down into the responsible life of a married man, I would like for the two of us together, to experience one last adventure. Something that will require the courage and the skill of the People's finest hunters."

Stone Fist spoke, his words solidified that he and his best friend Running Eagle, were of the same mind; "We both hear the screams, the shrieks and the sounds of the Puma. Your thoughts and mine as one my brother. Do we finally hunt the Puma hunt the one who hunts so skillfully at night? Hunt the night hunter, not merely track him during daylight, but hunt him when he is the hunter, hunt the Puma at night".

Running Eagle reached for his bow and his quiver of arrows. "We will follow the scream and the sounds of the great cat, as he pursues his dinner".

****

The two new tepees, stood straight and tall among their neighboring structures.

Little Flower and Quite One, the matriarchs of the two respective families, which would through the children of Stone Fist and Spring Blossom, be united by blood, stood together, admiring their work.

In a soft voice, in fitting with her name, Quite One spoke; "We have done well. These dwellings will resist the might and the fury of the whirling wind, and the drenching, soaking wet of the driving rain."

Little Flower smiled, "Ahh, the comforts, the couches and the bedding are so soft and inviting." With a knowing glance and a wink aimed at Quite One, Little Flower smiled and remarked; "Stone Fist and Spring Blossom, will be so comfortable that they will only interrupt their love, long enough to eat, and to answer the call of nature."

Little Flower was delighted and surprised, at the Quite One's words; "Little Flower must be getting old. Do you not remember when comfort was never a consideration, when your man touched you? How your heart skipped at just the thought of his touch?"

Little Flower chuckled, "after the passage of many winters with my husband, Gray Wolf's touch, when I am hard at work, instead of thrilling me, sometimes annoys me."

"That same touch when we are snuggled in our comfortable bedding, under our warm blankets, is still desired and welcomed. Our youthful passion has whined, and has ripened into a steady, sturdy, comfortable, enduring love."

Quite one, who had been widowed for many winters, dropped her head and in a soft reverent voice mumbled; "It is as it should be. It is as the Great Spirit planned. It is the Sacred Circle of Life."

****

The restrictions that had existed on the movement of Man-dee, the black captive girl, in the eyes of the people, did not apply to "Pretty Buffalo Hair', daughter of Gray Wolf and Little Flower.

Other then being restricted by Rebecca's work, tasks assigned by Quite One, and by Hen's Teeth, Mandy was free to visit her friend, Stone Fist's white captive.

Pretty Buffalo Hair, and the white captive, the one you call "Blue Wolf Eyes", were assigned the task of digging the cooking pits in the two tepees.

After they had dug the pits, and gathered the stones for the linings, the two sisters, ironically, the white girl now a slave, and the black girl free, sat in the center of Running Eagle's new home, digging slots around the pit, for the placement of the peripheral stones.

Mandy and Rebecca were eager to use this opportunity, this alone time, to talk, to catch-up. Rebecca looked at Mandy with wonder and admiration in her eyes, "I can't believe it, you actually speak their language. You understand what these savages are saying."

"Since we were little girls, I've always known that you were a gifted, a fantastic student. But this...learning their language in less than two months, is remarkable."

Mandy blushed at the compliment, and the sincere, genuine praise from Rebecca, "Your only partially correct, although I've come to understand most of the conversations, I still can not speak the language fluently. I have to learn...if we are going to escape, and return to civilization, we have to learn to understand and to speak the language."

Rebecca bristled, "I don't want to learn their language. Anything that that horrible, old toothless woman thinks, does, or says is abhorrent to me."

"Becky, I've grown fond of Little Flower and Spring Blossom. I know that they are fond of me. They trust me. Gray Wolf has given me a meaningful Comanche name; "*nananisuyake tasiwoo tso-yaa*". Rebecca was intrigued. She attempted to repeat the three strange sounding, alien words.

"*nananisuyake tasiwoo tso-yaa*, what does it mean?" *nananisuyake* means pretty, beautiful; *tasiwoo* is the word for buffalo, and *tso-yaa* means hair."

"The name *PrettyBuffaloHair* was Gray Wolf's attempt to give me a name with meaning, something that the People could relate to. He said that my thick, but not straight hair reminds him of the woolly hair of the buffalo."

"At Little Flower's request, Gray Wolf made me a member of his family."

"Little Flower, did not petition Gray Wolf on my behalf because she liked my hair, she did it because, through my hard work, and respect that I showed for her way of life, I had gained her trust and her respect."

"Becky, our only hope of escape is to get these people to trust us. We have to show respect for their ways, work hard, make an effort to understand their language."

"Mandy he raped...,Mandy held up her hand, "Stop Becky. What Stone Fist did to you was wrong, it was despicable...but it's done. It can't be undone. Get over it. Our survival is dependant your getting over it!"

"While we're here, don't call me Mandy. While we're here, call me *Pretty Buffalo Hair*. Becky, we have to assimilate. We have to gain their trust. That's our only hope for escape."

Rebecca was dubious, skeptical. For a brief moment Rebecca wondered, was Mandy, no, was *PrettyBuffalo Hair*, siding with these savages? Has her loyalty shifted?

As quickly as these thoughts had entered her mind, they were rejected. Rebecca felt ashamed that she had for a moment, for a second, doubted Mandy's commitment to their escape from this nightmare.

She remembered the speech. The emotional cathartic speech, that flowed, like molten lava, from the lips of her life-long friend, her beloved sister, Mandy. The truth of their shared paternity, the words that her sister had held-in for years, and had dared not utter, even to her, her best friend. "Becky you and I, we are in every sense of the word, truly sisters."

As they lined the pit with the stones, *PrettyBuffalo* Hair nostalgically spoke of the clandestine Sunday sessions that they had held back at the Rosewood Plantation.

"Miss Leary and I would sit and talk at the creek, each Sunday waiting for you to return from town, after the family had attended church. Sunday Services."

"I remember once, after she had repeatedly tried to impress upon me the innate intelligence, the strength, and the accomplishments of blacks through out history, by rehashing "Othello's status as a 16th century, commanding general of a white man's army. I recall pointing out to her that Othello wasn't real".

"That Othello was a fictional character, during another era, long since past, conceived of and created in the mind of William Shakespeare, a white man."

"Undaunted, Miss Leary had continued, by telling me of the activities, the exploits of a Mr. Frederick Douglas, a Negro, a former slave who had escaped to the North, and was now a brilliant orator, a true champion, and spokesman of the Negro cause".

"After chronicling Mr. Douglas' life, Miss Leary asked, was I not impressed with his life, and impressed with what he had thus far accomplished, and was continuing to work for, the abolition of slavery, and the freeing of his people?"

"I remember setting quietly. Miss Leary asked if I had heard her, did I understand. I remember answering in a soft voice, a non-convincing voice."

"I assured Miss Leary that I understood. She could tell by the lack of conviction in my voice, that I had left something unsaid. Miss Leary asked; "Mandy, you say you're impressed by Mr. Douglass, yet your demeanor, your less than enthusiastic response, leaves me to believe that there is something that you are not saying. What is it…what's troubling you?"

"When I sat there in silence, not speaking, Miss Leary insisted, "Mandy what I have told you is the absolute truth, Mr. Frederick Douglass is a great man, a great black man. I have never lied to you…don't you believe me?"

"I will never forget what happened during the next hour." Rebecca stared into the soft brown eyes of her sister, breathlessly she asked; "Mandy what happened? What happened…what did you say…what did she say? What happened between you and Miss Leary?"

"I assured Miss Leary that I believed her. That I trusted and believed everything that she had taught the two of us. I told her that my lack of enthusiasm was not skepticism, but was instead based on reality."

Miss Leary encouraged me to continue. I did. I said that; "Mr. Douglass, despite his brilliance as a orator, having overcome being born a slave, when all is said and done, highly respected, Mr. Frederick Douglass, is still doing what slaves do."

Miss Leary had a genuine puzzeled look on her face. She asked me to go on. I said to her; "Mr. Frederick Douglass, although his English is superb, his diction precise, his vocabulary limitless, Mr. Douglass, when it comes down to it, is just another black man, begging the white man for his freedom".

"The only difference is that Mr. Douglas' begging the white man is done with correct grammar, using hundred-dollar words. Despite his elegance, in fact, Mr. Douglass, as is the most wretched black-slave field-hand, is still asking, pleading, begging, the white man for his dignity, for his freedom."

"Miss Leary, what would excite and inspire me, would be to hear of a black man who didn't just beg and plead to be free. What would excite and inspire me would be, a black man who fought for, and then took and defended his freedom."

For what seemed like forever, Miss Leary sat staring, looking at me in silence. After a few moments of uncomfortable silence, she rose from the grass, walked over to her book bag, rummaged through the bag, and handed me a paper bound volume entitled, "A Recent History of South East Africa".

"Before I could open the book, Miss Leary began to speak, she told me a truly remarkable story. She told me of a black man, Shaka Zulu, who had in the historicsl context, recently died. Shaka Zulu, she explained, was actually the king, the emperor of a large, wealthy country in Africa, Zululand".

"Miss leary shared with me historical accounts of this great Warrior King, Shaka Zulu. She told of how Shaka, by his intellect, his display of skill and his knowledge of military tactics, fought-off and denied the white man's attempt to steal his people's land. Thus preventing the subsequent enslavement of the Zulu People".

Miss Leary told of Shaka's subsequent assassination, September 22, 1828, just thirty-six years ago.

"Becky these Indians remind me of that Warrior King, Shaka Zulu. This culture makes me think of the culture and the lifestyle of my African Ancestors".

"Right here in America, we have white men trying to take the land from the native population, the Indians. It's the same thing that happened in Africa."

"Becky can't you see how I can relate? I see Gray Wolf, Running Eagle and Stone Fist as the Shaka-Zulu's of America".

"Native men of color, rising up, standing up to resist the taking of their ancestral lands by the interloper, the white man".

"The white man is no nobler, no braver than the black men of Africa, no more noble or braver than these red men here in America. What they take, they take by the sheer force of numbers, and through the utilization of modern weaponry, the gun"

Mandy, with one of the most determined, penetrating looks that Becky had ever seen on her face, resolutely, emphatically stated; "Don't you see Becky, I get it. I know what Running Eagle, Stone Fist, and all of these people are fighting for".

"Becky, I'm beginning to develop a real understanding, a bond with these people. They're fighting to retain their land, their freedom, and their dignity."

Rebecca was silent. Once again, as she had just moments ago thought, and then had immediately dismissed, Rebecca wondered, was Mandy…no, was *Pretty Buffalo Hair*, beginning to convert, was she siding with these savages?

****

Running Eagle and Stone Fist, aided only by the meager light provided by the merest sliver of a moon, together moved towards the sounds of the most dangerous of the night hunters, the largest of the continent's great cats, the deadly Puma

The big cat's growl seemed to be emanating from a small stand of scraggily trees. As Running Eagle and Stone Fist neared the tree-line, using hand signals to communicate, Running Eagle veered to the left, Stone Fist looped off to the left; their paths diverged.

Both warriors heard the frantic flight of small game, fleeing for its life in the underbrush. Once more they heard the petrifying growl of the big cat, then the crash as the predator pounced upon his prey, a prong horn antelope.

Running Eagle saw the outline of the puma, sitting on his haunches, with his huge *canine teeth* firmly embedded in its pry throat. The antelope was feebly thrashing about, in its death throes, while suffocating, being held firmly in the death grip of the big cat.

Running Eagle's plan was simple. While the huge predator was in the process of patiently strangling his pry, Running Eagle would drop from an overhanging tree, and plunge his war lance into the distracted beast.

His choice of the lance, instead of his loosing a flurry of arrows into the puma from a distance, he knew would be perceived as courageous, and would bring him great honor.

The exploits of the hunters or the warriors that dispatched, or counted coup on his prey with a hand held weapon, was held in higher esteem by the People, then the exploits of those men who killed by ambush.

Just as Running Eagle dropped from his perch, Stone Fist, who was about to launch his attack, stepped on a twig. The sound alerted the big cat. The puma jumped. Running Eagle's lance ripped into the left shoulder of the puma. The cat shrieked in pain, and swung his huge, lethal right paw at Running Eagle.

The glancing blow from the huge cat's razor-sharp claws gashed Running Eagle's chest, leaving three deep furrows.

Ignoring the shearing pain, Running Eagle, unsheathed his long hunting knife, and plunged it into the heart of the beast.

Stone Fist loosed two arrows into the throat of the huge cat. Running Eagle slumped at the foot of the tree.

Stone Fist pulled Running Eagle's knife from the chest of the slain puma. He wiped the knife in the grass, removing the blood and the clinging tissue. Sheepishly, holding the knife by its blade, Stone Fist handed the weapon to Running Eagle.

"My brother, please forgive my clumsiness. The sound of my approach, my stepping on that twig, alerted the puma, and thwarted the accuracy of your lance thrust. I was at fault for your having to fight for your life with the knife."

Running Eagle accepted the knife; "Unlike the eyes of the owl and the puma, our eyes cannot penetrate the dark. That is why we chose to hunt during the day, with the aid of the light provided by father sun. There is no fault to forgive. Together, we made the decision to hunt the puma at night. If there is fault, it is ours to share."

Stone Fists grabbed the long tail of the big cat, and dragged the dead animal to the feet of Running Eagle; "Our slave women, your black captive, and my white captive, can make two pair of fine moccasins from this hide."

Running Eagle rose and while examining the slain animal spoke, "the black girl Man-dee, is no longer my captive slave. She is no longer Man-dee, she is now Pretty Buffalo Hair, she is the adopted daughter of Gray Wolf and Little Flower. She is my sister. Pretty Buffalo Hair is the adopted sister of Spring Blossom and Running Eagle.

Stone Fist did not question, he accepted without doubt or reservation, Running Eagle's pronouncement as a statement of fact.

"It is good that the black girl has been judged as one who is worthy of becoming one of the People. The white girl has not. The slow dimwitted one that my mother has named, "Blue Wolf Eyes", the white slave girl that I thought would lessen the work of the women of my lodge, barely works enough to justify the food that she eats."

"When I take her to my blankets, she cries, she is as stiff as a fresh buffalo hide that has been left overnight, neglected and untreated." Running Eagle asked, "if she is unpleasant and unskilled at doing those things that a woman does to please a man, why do you take her to your sleeping robes?"

Stone Fist looked with puzzled, confused eyes at his friend, "Running Eagle, you know that it has always been so. When we do battle with our enemies, the Pawnee, the Tonkawa, we occasionally pay a price for our victories, through the loss of valiant Comanche Warriors. Captured children grow up to be strong Comanche Warriors, captive women, serviced by strong Comanche Warriors, give birth to future Comanche Warriors, replacing those who were lost in battle."

"It is the duty of the People's warriors, it is yours as well as it is mine, to have as many sons as the Great Spirit permits." Running Eagle did not respond. Stone Fist asked, "before Gray Wolf adopted Pretty Buffalo Hair, was she as skillful at pleasing a man, as I have heard she is, in performing the many work tasks that make-up a woman's work?"

Running Eagle spoke, "neither I nor did my father, have the opportunity to judge Pretty Buffalo Hair's skills under the sleeping robes."

Although Stone Fist found his friend's statement to be odd, he refrained from commenting.

"How deeply did the puma claw your chest?" Running Eagle gingerly ran his fingers over the tracks of the three parallel fresh scars, the wounds inflicted by the big cat. "Luckily the puma's weight was not behind the blow."

"At first light, let us remove from the puma, his fine pelt. I will also remove his claws and carry them in my medicine bag. The claw will be a constant reminder, not to hunt puma in the dark. Let the coyotes feast upon the carcass."

****

As the sun began to arise on the eastern horizon, Stone Fist left his sleeping robe, and shook the arm of Running Eagle. Running Eagle groaned in pain.

Stone Fist looked at his friend's face. Running Eagle's face was flushed. Stone Fist placed his open hand onto Running Eagle's forehead. Alarmed, he pulled his hand away. His friend's forehead was hot. He removed the buffalo robe from Running Eagles' chest. The grooves, the edges of the claw scars, that the huge cat had inflicted, were swollen. A purplish, foul smelling fluid was oozing from the wounds.

Stone Fist began to shout, "Running Eagle, can you hear me, speak to me."
Running Eagle was looking directly at Stone Fist's face, yet there was not a glimmer of recognition in his eyes.

Pieces of the inner-surface of the buffalo robe, had stuck to the edges of the scars. When Stone Fist attempted to separate the robe from his friend's body, Running Eagle groaned, and in a hushed whisper, attempted to speak.

Stone Fist placed his ear to Running Eagle's parched dry lips, although not certain, he thought he heard Running Eagle mumble some sort of nonsense, gibberish, a sound or a word that he was not familiar with, he thought Running Eagle, in his delirium had mumbled, "*Mahn-dee*".

With his knife, Stone Fist hastily chopped two long branches from the tree from which the puma had pounced upon prong-horned antelope.

Utilizing his sleeping robe as the weight-bearing centerpiece, he fashioned a travois. Stone Fist attached the poles of the travois to Running Eagle's pony.

He carefully placed his delirious friend onto the travois, mounted his pony, and at a steady pace turned towards the village.

The great cat, slain by the thrusts of Running Eagle's lance, and hunting knife, the dead puma surrounded by, and now infested with hordes of flies lay, rotting under the relentless hot sun.

****

Little Flower, Spring Blossom, and Pretty Buffalo Hair, the women of Gray Wolf's Lodge, were seated around the tepee's large cooking pit. Little Flower was delicately embroidering Spring Blossom's, white doeskin wedding dress, with delicate, intricate quillwork.

Mandy was impressed with the dexterity and the seamstress' skill of her adopted mother. Little Flower was using a two-thread sewing technique. The design was that of four dyed green, symmetrical triangles, surrounding a blue sapphire colored stone. The four triangles were all of the same size, two above and two below the beautiful, sparkling stone.

The apex of the triangles immediately below and above the rock, pointed to the gem. The base of the two remaining triangles, sat approximately ⅓ of an inch from the base of the two triangles that pointed to the sparkling blue gem. The hem and the sleeves of the dress were beautifully fringed.

As Mandy watched the dexterity and skill of Little Flower, she thought of her recent conversation with Rebecca. Rebecca had referred to the Indians as "ignorant, heathen, savages". She wished that Rebecca were here, here with these real people, these amiable, innately intelligent, talented people.

She wanted Rebecca to see and to marvel at the four perfectly symmetrical isosceles triangles that Little Flower had created from dyed quills. She wanted to remind Rebecca of how they had both struggled with and complained about those "stupid", really difficult geometry lessons that Miss Leary insisted that they sit through.

Little Flower looked up from her quillwork. A radiant, knowing smile had spread across the face of Pretty Buffalo Hair. "My daughter, what is it that amuses you?"

"It was of no importance mother. I was thinking that the dress that you are creating is truly, the most beautiful dress that I have ever seen. Your creation would impress, and would please both Euclid and Pythagoras."

Little Flower and Spring Blossom exchanged glances, then without uttering a word, they resumed their work. Both women had become accustomed to hearing Pretty Buffalo Hair, on occasion, revert to injecting one or two of those strange sounding words of the black-tribe tongue, into an otherwise perfectly civilized conversation.

Spring Blossom was assembling and sewing together the soft, white doeskin cuts, that when joined together would be her wedding moccasins.

Pretty Buffalo Hair was in the process of dying the crushed bird quills that would decorate the bride's moccasins.

Her head down, peering into the bowl of quills, she asked of no one in particular, in a shy, subdued voice, "when will Running Eagle, then as if it were an afterthought, she quickly added...and Stone Fist return?"

Spring Blossom gave her mother a conspiratorial wink, "aahh, my sister, so there is some truth in our mother's observations. Prior to your becoming his sister, you were looking at Running Eagle with the moon-struck look, that a woman looks upon a man whose sleeping robes she wishes to share".

Pretty Buffalo Hair was flustered, she raised her head and sheepishly stammered, and "I grow anxious for their return I miss my brother's gentle smile."

Pretty Buffalo Hair lowered her head and concentrated on dying the quills. Little Flower gave Spring Blossom a furtive glance; "It is good that your feelings are those concerns of a sister for her brother. The feelings between a man and a woman that Spring Blossom suggests are forbidden between brother and sister."

Mandy gasped, the spoon that she had been stirring the mixture of quills and dye, dropped from her hand. Her face had taken on a look of forlorn despair. She wiped a tear from her eye.

Spring Blossom and Little Flower looked at each other, then to Pretty Buffalo Hair's surprise, they began to giggle and to laugh. "Forgive us my daughter, my words though true, do not apply to you and Running Eagle."

Mandy looked confused; "You are the adopted daughter of Gray Wolf and Little Flower. You are not of Running Eagles blood. You did not play and fight as children growing up." Marriage between Running Eagle and Pretty Buffalo Hair is not forbidden."

Spring Blossom chimed in, "If Running Eagle shares Pretty Buffalo Hair's feelings, our father Gray Wolf's pony herd will soon be greatly increased. Gray Wolf will be pleased."

****

"Talks Too Much", one of the youths assigned to watching the band's herd of ponies, flung open the flap of Stone Fist's new tepee. "Little Flower, Spring Blossom, you must come quickly, hurry."

Little Flower placed Spring Blossom's wedding dress onto one of the adjacent couches, "What is it? Why has Talks Too Much disturbed work?"

The boy, gasping for breath, blurted out, "Stone Fist approaches, pulling a travois. Running Eagle is hurt."

Little Flower spoke firmly and steadily, to the excited boy, "Go bring our holy man, He Who Speaks To Ghosts, to the tepee of Gray Wolf. Hurry!" The three women ran from the tepee.

****

Running Eagle lay moaning, thrashing about on his sleeping robes. Gray Wolf and Little Flower were anxiously standing apart from the Shaman and his patient, their son.

Stone Fist and Spring Blossom stood next to Running Eagle's parents. Stone Fists kept repeating, over and over, "He was fine last night. Three scars, from the claws of the puma. Three scars that neither Running Eagle nor did I, think to be serious".

Three ugly scars ran across Running Eagle's chest. The flesh surrounding the scars was purplish, and swollen. The wounds were suppurating, pus a foul-smelling liquid, was oozing from the wounds.

Mandy stood alone silently, near the entrance of the tepee. She watched as the medicine man, He Who Speaks To Ghosts, was preparing to apply a bulky poultice to the wound.

Mandy watched in horror, as He Who Speaks To Ghosts, removed multiple leaves from his mouth. The "shaman", by chewing the leaves and mixing them with his saliva, had ground the leaves into a paste. He liberally spread the paste onto a poultice, which with Gray Wolf's assistance, he tied around the body of Running Eagle.

It took all of Mandy's self-control, to refrain from rushing over to Running Eagle, and tearing the filthy cloth from his body. She wanted desperately to hold him in her arms, and to nurse him back to good health. Wisely, Mandy did not interfere.

Running Eagle lay upon the robes, he began to shiver, his teeth began to chatter. The "Holy-Man", placed two buffalo robes over Running Eagle, he then pulled a rattle from his parfleche, and began to circle his patient, dancing and chanting in a soft monotone.

After four complete circles, He Who Speaks To Ghosts spoke to Little Flower; "An evil spirit riding on the claws of the puma, entered Running Eagle's body. The fever was the result of the heated battle between the evil spirit, and the courageous spirit within their son."

Little Flower was told by the shaman, that the evil spirit could be weakened, coaxed out of Running Eagle's body, by the changing of the poultice every hour during this first day, the critical day. The paste, applied to the mature pads of the Prickly Pear Cactus, will help to draw out the evil spirit, and will bring down Running Eagle's soaring fever.

He Who Speaks To Ghosts, in order to control the burning fever ordered that Running Eagle's limbs and face be continually bathed with cool water.

Little Flower asked of the shaman, if Running Eagle should be forced to take nourishment. The "Shaman/Holy-Man", gave instructions to force Running Eagle, at frequent intervals, to drink the bitter draughts of the tea made from the bark of the Sassafras Tree. He insisted that this be done, even if she had to pry his clenched teeth apart.

The Shaman-He Who Speaks To Ghosts; The father-Gray Wolf; and Stone Fist, Running Eagle's best friend, left the tepee and the care of Running Eagle, to the Women of Gray Wolf's Lodge.

****

At first Mandy stood silently watching as Little Flower and Spring Blossom bathed Running Eagle's forehead and his arms and legs, with cool water.

"Come my daughter, if Running Eagle is to live, he needs our help". Hearing those words, spoken so succinctly by his mother Little Flower, in a controlled, non-emotional voice, galvanized Mandy into action.

The bowl that held the cool water in which the multiple compresses were immersed, was empty. Although she was reticent to leave Running Eagle, as every nerve and muscle in her body, screamed for her to be by his side, Mandy grabbed the empty water paunches, and hurried to the creek.

When she returned to the lodge, Mandy saw Little Flower about to remove the poultice that the shaman had wrapped around Running Eagle's chest. Little Flower discarded the poultice. Mandy hurriedly refilled the empty bowl with fresh cool water.

Running Eagle's eyelids were half open. Little Flower could feel the heat radiating from her son's feverish body. He groaned. Spring Blossom, who had been bathing her brother's legs and feet, was at the water bowl wringing-out the now warm compress, "What is he saying mother…does his words have meaning?"

Little Flower placed her ear next to her son's lips, attempting to understand his feeble groans … "Mahn-dee". Man-dee, was he calling for his adopted, black sister, instead of for his mother?

Little Flower felt betrayed. She looked over at her adopted daughter. Pretty Buffalo Hair's huge beautiful brown eyes were staring at Running Eagle. Tears were streaming down her cheeks.

When her eyes and the eyes of Little Flower met, Pretty Buffalo Hair, quickly averted her glance, grabbed the now empty water paunches, and fled from the lodge.

Little Flower smiled. Little Flower thought it is as it should be. Her son, the man, the warrior Running Eagle, in his pain and delirium, did not cry out as a child would, for his mother, instead he called for his woman. She cradled her son's feverish head in her hands, and speaking in a soft loving voice, she whispered; "Rest my son. Mahn-dee is near. It is as it should be."

****

Prior to retiring for the night, Little Flower made arrangements with the boy called, "Talks Too Much", for he and for his friends, to bring cool water to the tepee, throughout the long night.

Pretty Buffalo Hair, had insisted on being the first of the three women who would attend to the patient, during the night. She assured Little Flower that she would strictly adhere to the shaman's instructions. That if Running Eagle's condition worsened, Pretty Buffalo Hair would immediately alert Little Flower.

Little Flower, lay restlessly beside her husband. Gray Wolf's staccato snores were the prevailing sounds within the tepee. Spring Blossom and Stone Fist had moved to the new lodge of Stone Fist.

****

Despite her earlier misgiving, the chewing of leaves; the making a paste with leaves and saliva, then placing the concoction into the bandage, Mandy — as she had promised Little Flower — had religiously adhered to the shaman's instructions.

Yesterday, Pretty Buffalo Hair had studiously and meticulously watched Little Flower as she prepared and changed Running Eagle's poultice.

Little Flower had not hesitated when she, with only a moment's hesitation, agreed to place her son's life, into the hands of the black girl. This extraordinary girl that she had grown to love more and more, with each passing day.

It was not until she saw the faint rays of the rising sun, filtering through the smoke hole of the tepee that Little Flower inwardly relaxed. She had watched carefully, as Pretty Buffalo Hair, wiped her son's body with the cooling water. She had watched as Pretty Buffalo Hair, would periodically, gently place her fingers, then her lips on Running Eagle's brow.

Little Flower recalled her son's barely audible, feverish word, "*Mahn-dee*", Little Flower was convinced that the "Great Spirit" had sent "Man-dee...*Pretty Buffalo Hair* to save her son, and to complete Running Eagle's life.

Little Flower snuggled up against her husband and gave thanks. Gray Wolf turned to his wife; "What did you say woman...were you speaking to me?

Little Flower kissed her husband's cheek; "Go back to sleep my husband. I was merely speaking to the Great Spirit".

Gray Wolf asked; "Did the Great Spirit speak to you? Little Flower smiled, snuggled up to Gray Wolf's back and whispered in his ear, the Great Spirit did not speak in words to me. He placed in my head and in my heart, his silent message".

Gray Wolf grunted, "what does that mean?" Little Flower playfully nibbled his ear and whispered…our son will recover. It is, as it should be."

****

It was on the third night, following Running Eagle's injury, that the fever broke. Running Eagle's slow, gradual, return to conscientiousness was reminiscent of what he had experienced, during his vision quest, seven summers ago.

He felt as if he was emerging from a fog. There was the sensation of a cool and gentle hand on his forehead. Long Eagle struggled to open his eyes. As his vision cleared, he saw an apparition, Pretty Buffalo Hair was there. Her back was toward her.

In the dim light given off by the still glowing embers in the cooking pit, Pretty Buffalo Hair appeared to him to be a vision. When she began to turn towards him, Running Eagle quickly closed his eyes.

Pretty Buffalo Hair gently placed her lips on his forehead. Running Eagle's weakened body, betrayed him. Pretty Buffalo Hair's moist full, lips upon his forehead, was to Running Eagle, the most sexually erotic sensation that he had ever experienced.

To his dismay and chagrin, the towel that had been covering his loins, seemed to come alive of its' own accord. The towel draped over Running Eagle's genitals, rose into the air. His sudden, unwanted, involuntary erection, resembled a flag, raised at full staff.

Pretty Buffalo Hair was startled. Her eyes traveled from his mid-section to his face. When their eyes met and held, they both felt a spark, like a sudden bolt of lightning that starts an out of control fire on the dry prairie, had arched between them.

Pretty Buffalo Hair broke the eye contact, "Little Flower, he is awake. Running Eagle has come back to us."

****

One week following the recovery of Running Eagle, Stone Fist and Spring Blossom were married.

Rebecca viewed the marriage of Stone Fist and Spring Blossom, as truly, a God's send. Since his return from that fateful hunting trip with Running Eagle, the hunt where both he and Running Eagle, had thought that the wound inflicted by big cat, to be a minor scratch.

The infected *minor* scratch had almost cost Running Eagle his life, Stone Fist, either because he was worried and concerned for his friend's health, or perhaps because he now spent most of his free time with Spring Blossom, had completely ignored Rebecca.

Rebecca's life amongst the "heathen savages" had become tolerable. She missed Mandy. For the past week, she had not been able to sit and to talk to her friend, her only link to civilization.

Mandy had no time for her. Instead of their spending time together to devise a plan of escape, Mandy was devoting all of her time and energy to nursing Running Eagle.

Without the support of Mandy, Rebecca found herself, day by day, becoming resigned to her status as a captive slave, and to her fractious relationship with her principal tormentor, Hen's Teeth.

Her plight had forced her to come to examine and to appreciate the difference between the form of slavery practiced by the Indians, the slaves were acquired as booty, as the "spoils-of-war", and the slavery that she had, by pure chance of her birth, profited from and supported her entire life.

While lying wide awake on her sleeping robes, Rebecca had prayed and lamented in her mind, over and over again; *"Why, why me...why did this happen to me...why am I a slave?*

One night while she tossed and turned, every muscle in her body aching and sore, as if in answer to her query, Rebecca experienced a simple, yet monumental, moment of clarity.

She reasoned that no one, if it were under his or her control, would choose to be born a slave. The fact that she was born white, a member of the Southern Aristocracy, as opposed to being born a black slave, was something she concluded, that just happened. She as an entity had absolutely no say in the matter.

As Miss Leary had often said, which until now Rebecca had not given too much thought, "There are a lot of choices that we humans are capable of making in our lives, however, in the history of man, no one has ever been, nor will anyone yet to be born, be able to choose who will be their biological parents".

The fact that she had been born, a member of the white Southern Aristocracy was a random event. She had absolutely no control as to who her parents would be. Instead of Master and Mistress of Rosewood, her fate could have just as easily have been, that she be born the daughter of two of Rosewood's black field hands.

For the Indians, while the captive slave was property, the Indian's slaves could at least, look forward to freedom by eventually assimilating, and being accepted as a member of the tribe.

More importantly Rebecca had come to believe that while all forms of slavery are wrong, the South's practice of that "Peculiar Institution", the dehumanizing, legal enslavement of blacks, from cradle to grave, which meant that for all intents and purposes, the enslavement of the blacks, and of their progeny, was forever, was truly barbaric.

After having been a slave, having experienced the humiliation, and the dehumanization, Rebecca had come to the absolute, conclusion, and the realization that all forms of slavery are wrong.

Rebecca vowed that when, not if, but when she and Mandy escaped, and returned to civilization, that she and her sister would do everything that they could to end slavery.

Rebecca was confident that it was just a matter of time before she and Mandy would have time to plan and execute their escape. Her opposition was fueled by her common sense assessment, Running Eagle would either recover or he would die from his wounds.

Rebecca failed to allow for what to her mind, was literally the unthinkable. Rebecca did not consider the possibility that love, the love that a man feels for a woman, would develop between Mandy and Running Eagle.

****

Running Eagle loved Pretty Buffalo Hair. Little Flower knew it. Spring Blossom knew it, even Gray Wolf and Stone Fist, as a result of confidences shared with their wives, while snuggled together in their sleeping robes, knew it. Pretty Buffalo Hair, suspected, and with all of her heart, wanted to believe it.

In fact, for three weeks following his recovery, the two of them Running Eagle and Pretty Buffalo were constantly in each other's company. The village was awash with gossip. The prevailing opinion among the people was, that Pretty Buffalo Hair and Running Eagle were in love.

Excluding Rebecca, the only person in the village that did not know that Running Eagle loved Pretty Buffalo Hair, was Running Eagle.

Pretty Buffalo Hair was delighted when Little Flower asked that she assist Running Eagle, in his move from Gray Wolf's lodge, to his newly constructed bachelor tepee.

Mandy relished with joy and great anticipation, to performing the women's work of Running Eagle's lodge. She took pleasure in gathering the kindling, in cooking his meals, in the sewing and repairing of his few articles of clothing.

Most of all, Pretty Buffalo Hair, looked forward to and enjoyed, the time that she and Running Eagle spent together after the completion of the morning meal. That's when she would lovingly, comb and braid Running Eagle's long flowing pitch-black, ebony tresses.

Running Eagle was confused. He knew without a doubt that he felt a tremendous, almost overwhelming desire for this woman, Pretty Buffalo Hair.

He was certain that the People's taboo forbidding intimate relations between brother and sister, for him and Pretty Buffalo Hair, did not apply.

This he found out, after having asked, and been told by the holy man, "He Who Speaks To Ghosts", that the taboo did not apply.

Before speaking of this with the holy man, Running Eagle had been assured by the shaman, that their conversation would be viewed by him as being sacred, and would not be repeated or be told to anyone.

Running Eagle was not a virgin, in fact he was far, removed from being a virgin. It was during his fifteenth summer, that he had first experienced, and enjoyed the special warmth that washes over one's body, and indeed over the mind, after finding sexual release in the arms of a woman.

Running Eagle, seven summers ago, during his fifteenth summer, had loss his virginity to "Willows Breath", the plain, sad, mournful widow, who at that time, was just about to see the passing of her thirty-second summer.

It was during her twenty-sixth summer, that Willows Breath, the mother of two small children, one who had just completed two summers, and the other still a suckling infant, that Willows Breath's husband had been killed in an unsuccessful raid against the Pawnee.

Since his first coupling, seven long winters ago, when the then boy of fifteen summers, Little Beaver, who later became known as the warrior, Running Eagle, had since on a regular basis, shared his sleeping robes, with a long list of comely females.

Most of that bevy of eager females had one goal in mind they were vying to make the handsome young warrior Running Eagle, their future husband.

When Running Eagle moved from his father's lodge, into his own dwelling, there was an immediate stream of nightly, female-visitors. Running Eagle graciously, politely, rebuffed their advances.

The young women of the village were at first surprised and bewildered by his uncharacteristic, unexpected reaction.

Many of the girls who were now being rejected, had in the past, prior to Running Eagle's recent illness, been enthusiastically, welcomed by him, with open arms.

It didn't take long for the rumor to circulate, that Running Eagle lack of interest, was because he was infatuated with the beautiful black girl, Pretty Buffalo Hair.

Running Eagle was perplexed. The one female that he longed to share his sleeping robes with, Pretty Buffalo Hair, in the night, did not come to him.

****

Mandy was convinced that her intense feelings towards Running Eagle were reciprocated. She knew in her heart, was absolute sure, that the longing, the sexual tension that she felt when she was with him, touching him, was also being felt by Running Eagle.

As hard as she tried, Mandy could not fathom a single reason as to why, Running Eagle, the man of her dreams, had not made a single conscience, attempt to court her, had not held her hand, had not kissed her.

A societal cultural divide was exacerbating Mandy and Running Eagle's mutual frustrations.

Mandy, although black, had been raised to accept and to respect the cultural customs and values, of the white man's culture. She had been taught, and firmly believed, that in matters of love, the male was supposed to make the first overt move, to be the aggressor.

In the society in which Running Eagle was raised, if a woman was interested in a man, it was perfectly acceptable, and expected, that she would make that known to the man.

In the world of the red man, the practice of a single women uninvited, and unannounced, showing up at night at the bachelor's tepee, was not scandalous, it was expected, it was the accepted norm.

After four days of frustrated suffering, Pretty Buffalo Hair sought out for her advice, her adopted sister and friend, Spring Blossom. "My sister, I wish to share with you an intimate secret. I am in love with Running Eagle."

Spring Blossom giggled, "My sister, that you are in love with Running Eagle, and that Running Eagle is in love with you, is no secret. It is a fact that is instantly known to anyone who sees the two of you together."

Pretty Buffalo Hair looked surprised, but definitely neither annoyed nor angry at Spring Blossom's response to her declaration. "If it is true that Running Eagle loves me as I love him, why has he not made that known to me? Why has he not held my hand? Why has he not kissed me? Why has he not told me of his love?"

"My sister, how in such a short time, you have learned of the Comanche tongue, is truly remarkable. In time, just as you have come to know and understand our words, you will come to know and understand our customs."

"It would be a dishonor for a Comanche brave, to court a woman in the manner that a cur pursues a bitch in heat. It is the responsibility of the woman to, as you say, to make the first move. The Warrior will either accept our reject the woman.

For a warrior to be rejected by a woman weakens and can destroy his medicine. It would bring dishonor to the warrior. Without strong medicine, a warrior would be killed in battle."

'Pretty Buffalo Hair, if you love and want Running Eagle as your husband, you must, initiate the romance. You must as you say, move first."

****

That night, after finishing her work, Pretty Buffalo Hair, as usual bathed in the creek. She thought about drying her body with a towel, which had been earlier in the day, submerged in sweet smelling rose water.

As she reached for the towel, she stopped instinctively she decided to refrain from having her body exude artificial scents.

When she returned to the tepee, she noticed the rhythmic movement of Gray Wolf and Little Flower's sleeping robes.

Pretty Buffalo Hair, undid the plaited strands of her two thick braids. She ran her hands through her curly, semi-straight hair.

Her hair, freed of all restraints, framed her face. Her soft brown eyes sparkled in the dwindling light of the fire.

Pretty Buffalo Hair slipped into her prettiest doeskin dress, she stepped into her moccasins, and quietly left the tepee.

Little Flower had inconspicuously watched Pretty Buffalo Hair dress, and leave the tepee. Gray Wolf was snoring softly. He had drifted off into that blissful state of post-sexual release.

Little Flower gently shook her husband's shoulder. Gray Wolf grumbled, "What is it woman…Let me rest." Little Flower responded, "My husband you will soon be the recipient of several fine ponies." Again, Gray Wolf grumbled, "What are you saying? Go to sleep Little Flower, we can talk in the morning."

Little Flower rolled over, before she fell asleep, she whispered, "It is as it should be."

****

Mandy sheepishly, timidly, rapped on the entrance flap of Running Eagle's tepee. Running Eagle who was seated, morosely staring into the dying embers of his cooking fire, in a dejected voice spoke, "Enter". Mandy took three steps into the tepee, and stood silent, immobile, head lowered.

Running Eagle, his heart beat racing, stood, took two steps towards Pretty Buffalo Hair, opened his arms and said, "Welcome to my lodge…welcome to my heart."

****

Mandy lay expectant, trembling in Running Eagle's arms. Running Eagle suppressed a tremble of his own. He recalled how he had felt when, as a boy he had picked up a baby bird that had fallen from its' nest, and injured its' wing.

He remembered the overwhelming protective feeling that had swept over him, as he gazed down at that fragile, defenseless creature, trembling in his hand.

Running Eagle, not a particularly spiritual man, thanked the Great Spirit for this moment, for bringing this beautiful, strong, courageous woman to him.

Running Eagle marveled at his good fortune. He deduced from the way that she was trembling, that she was showing her love, while valiantly trying to hide her apprehension, her fear of the unknown.

Running Eagle gently lowered his head and lightly brushed his lips across Mandy's soft, moist, full lips. Mandy shuddered and threw her arms around the young warrior's neck.

His right hand found the hem of her dress. Both he and Mandy sat up. He pulled the dress over her head. Mandy kicked off her moccasins. Their lips met, and Running Eagle gently lowered her head, to the sleeping robes.

Mandy lay before him, nude. Her pert young mahogany colored breast, round and firm with dark brown nipples, beaconed Running Eagle's hungry lips. His mouth was flitting from each of the perfectly symmetric mounds, like a hungry bee gathering nectar from a field of prairie wild flowers.

Running Eagle's hands slid down her sides to her smooth, slim exquisite waist. An audible gasp escaped his lips, and he swallowed hard when his eyes locked onto the little tuft of brown hair, that sat like a sentry, either guarding, or pointing to the gates of paradise.

Running Eagle's heart was furiously pounding in his chest, pumping hot blood, filling and expanding his throbbing, manhood. He felt his organ expanding it to its full impressive length, beneath his breechclout.

Her breasts felt hot and wonderful pressed against his bare chest.

He began to deliver soft kisses across her lips, and then over her closed eyelids, then upon her nose. He slowly and sensually, moved his lips, his tongue, down the length of her body.

As Running Eagle tenderly kissed and licked her pulsating body, Mandy's body began to shiver with delight and with anticipated ecstasy.

While his tongue explored the crevice encasing her belly button Running Eagle's thumbs and forefingers were gently squeezing and rolling her nipples. Sensual waves of pleasure cascaded up and down Mandy's spine"

"Ah yes…yes", she whispered, as her pelvis gyrated, as her body responded to his tongue, as he licked then, as his lips sucked, the tender bud tucked in at the apex of the entrance to her now wet, pulsating, vagina.

As he had suspected — but to Running Eagle, it certainly did not matter — Pretty Buffalo Hair had never lain with a man. Although his body was crying out for release, he was determined, committed to ensuring that Pretty Buffalo Hair's first time experiencing the joys of sex, would for her, be pleasurable, memorable, and satisfying.

His hands began to slowly move over her thighs. At first, he stroked her flanks, then with the palm of his hand, he applied amazingly gentle, light pressure to the mound of curly soft hair that framed and surrounded her vagina. Mandy's head was swimming. Her only thoughts were of these hitherto unknown, sensual sensations that were flooding through her body.

Running Eagle, gently inserted his finger into her wet opening. Mandy threw her head back and begin to moan, "Please…please…ah." He thrust his finger deep up inside of her, she gasped as she felt a sharp pain, when his finger ruptured the membrane, caused by the deep penetration of his finger.

Mandy's eyes flew open. Running Eagle glimpsed a fleeting look of confusion and fear that briefly flickered in her beautiful brown eyes.

He looked deeply into her eyes, with his finger still inside her body. He lovingly whispered, "shush…shush, that brief pain was the pain of your awakening. It announced that you are open, ready to receive my body. Ready for us both to give to each other the full pleasures of our love.

He slowly withdrew his finger from her body. He held his finger up for her to see. His finger was wet and sticky with blood. Her blood covered his finger.

Running Eagle stood, he brought his bloody finger to his lips, he then gently kissed the front, and then the back of his finger. Running Eagle then placed his wet finger, covered with her blood and secretions, into his mouth, and sucked it clean.

To her surprise, instead of being repulsed by his actions, Mandy found his display to be highly erotic.

She started to ask him why he had withdrawn his finger, when before she could speak, Running Eagle suddenly dropped his breechclout to the floor, and kicked it away from his body. He stood before her, the embodiment of masculinity.

Running Eagle's body was magnificent. Not an ounce of extraneous fat was visible on his lean, athletic, bronzed frame. His well-defined, understated muscled rib cage, tapered down into a narrow waist. His stomach was flat and hard. His legs were long, well-muscled, and firm.

When he turned to face her, the sight that burned in her retina, took her breath away. His male member was thick and long. A fleeting thought flashed across Mandy's mind.

The way that his sex organ protruded from his body, the angle of the turgid staff, reminded her of the length, and the rigidity of the horn, that extended from the mythical Unicorn's head.

Running Eagle held his manhood in his right hand, and advanced towards the recumbent girl.

He leaned over, and as if her hand had a mind of its own, Mandy, shyly tentatively took him in her hand. She gently squeezed and caressed his pulsating manhood.

As she had seen him do to his finger, Mandy lovingly, tenderly kissed his organ, and then she took him into her mouth. Into the sweet wet, warm cavern of her mouth.

With her full, perfect red lips surrounding his manhood, she gently sucked and caressed with her tongue, his pulsating, engorged organ.

Her uninhibited, unexpected, bold aggressive gesture almost caused Running Eagle to prematurely shoot his seed into her mouth, down her throat, into the very center of her being.

Instead, he gritted his teeth and disengaged himself from her mouth. In a hoarse voice he managed to whisper; "Not now my love, we will have a lifetime to satisfy all of our needs. Now is my time, the time for me to make you my love. My woman, my Pretty Buffalo Hair…my *Mahn-dee*."

Running Eagle knelled beside her, she was cognizant of one of his knees spreading her legs apart he leaned over and kissed her passionately.

His tongue explored the warm wet haven of her mouth. Their eager tongues met and intertwined. Running Eagle sucked her tongue into his mouth.

Mandy with all of her heart and soul, wanted this man, this viral, strong, aboriginal warrior. She desperately wanted to feel his essence, his strength throbbing within the deepest recesses of her body.

Yet when she felt his hardness pressed against her stomach, her body tensed.

Involuntarily she had anticipated pain. Pain that she had felt, when he had inserted his finger into her body.

Running Eagle with his left hand gently separated the lips of her vagina. With his right hand, he guided his engorged, throbbing organ to its target. Still passionately sucking her tongue, he plunged his organ into Mandy's quivering, eager, receptive, body.

She gasped, instead of pain she was filled with a sensual shock when she felt Running Eagle enter her. As he began to rhythmically move within her, the sensation that she felt was ecstatic, euphoria. Once again with his tongue, he probed between her lips, flicking in and out.

As he plunged deeper and deeper inside her, her gasps became muted whimpers. Running Eagle placed his hands under her buttocks and lifted her closer his body. Mandy locked her legs around his waist, she thrust her pelvis towards his pounding member.

His hands swept around her hips to her buttocks, and lifted her even closer, the two lover's bellies were colliding, slapping together noisily, like hands beating a drum.

Running Eagle's ears were roaring now as his heartbeat quickened. He was overwhelmed with pleasure, yet he still held back, wanting to make Pretty Buffalo Hair's first time, unforgettable.

Their mouths, as was their bodies, was locked in a desperate, hungry kiss. Running Eagle's body stilled for just a moment, their lips separated.

Mandy's breath was stolen away as the most ultimate of pleasures coursed through her. She clung to him as his body quivered against hers.

"I love you Mahn-dee," he whispered against Mandy's lips, then he plunged deep inside her as she arched toward him.

As one, they released their pent-up emotions, the two lovers reached the peak of sexual release, together.

Overcome with emotion, physically, and spiritually, too spent and exhausted to move or to speak, they lay together, locked in each other's arms.

Reluctantly, Running Eagle withdrew his deflating manhood, from the warmest, most comforting portal, that he had ever visited or had imagined existed. Totally spent, he collapsed beside Mandy.

To stunned to speak, still basking in the afterglow, brought on by the wondrous feelings resulting from their lovemaking, Mandy snuggled closer to Running Eagle.

"That was wonderful," Mandy murmured as she laid her cheek against his chest. She listened to the rapid pounding of Running Eagle's heart. She was very much aware of how hard his heart was pounding, as was hers.

At that precise moment in time, Mandy knew without doubt, that the synchronized beating of this man's heart with hers, foretold of their future lives together.

She picked up his hand, and placed it between her heaving breasts. She placed her hand over his and whispered, "Me too my love...me too".

****

Pretty Buffalo Hair's nightly visits to the tepee of Running Eagle, were well known and accepted by the People. That these two young people were very much in love was evident to all who saw them together.

The question, the topic of gossip throughout the village, was why did these two not marry?

The day following their first night of blissful sex, Running Eagle had made his wishes to marry Pretty Buffalo Hair, known to Gray Wolf. Gray Wolf neither consented nor, did he deny his son's request.

Three days following the first of Pretty Buffalo Hair's nightly visits to Running Eagle's tepee, the nightly visits, changed. On the fourth day, instead of repeating the pattern of the visit, that ended with Pretty Buffalo Hair, quietly before dawn, returning to the tepee of Gray Wolf, the nocturnal interludes became nightly sleepovers.

To the people, it made sense. It was well known that Little Flower, Pretty Buffalo Hair's adopted mother, had decreed that Pretty Buffalo Hair was to perform the women's work required of Running Eagle's tepee.

The prevailing opinion of the people was, that Pretty Buffalo Hair could get an early start on doing the arduous routine work, if she simply spent the night with Running Eagle, whose dwelling was her responsibility. It made sense.

When Gray Wolf neither voiced approval or disapproval, Running Eagle decided to follow the People's age-old custom. He left two of his finest ponies outside of Gray Wolf's tepee.

The next morning both Running Eagle and Pretty Buffalo Hair, eagerly looked to Gray Wolf's tepee, the two ponies stood were Running Eagle had tethered them, the previous evening.

Gray Wolf had not accepted the gift. He had not given his permission for the marriage of Running Eagle and Pretty Buffalo Hair.

****

Gray Wolf sat at council, leisurely smoking with his peers. The main topic of discussion at the council meeting was planning for the annual summer gathering of the multiple bands, and clans, that comprised the Comanche Nation.

At the conclusion of the meeting, as the council members filed out of Old Wise One's tepee, Old Wise One's, the venerable, titular leader of the band, requested that Gray Wolf and He Who Speaks To Ghosts, remain.

When they had all once again smoked the pipe, Old Wise One spoke; "Gray Wolf my friend, I would speak with you. First, I speak to you as your chief, not as your friend, but as chief of our village."

Each day that you decline to give Running Eagle an answer to his request to marry Pretty Buffalo hair, his offering of ponies increases by two additional ponies each passing of the sun. Three times now the sun has set, since Running Eagle asked you for permission to wed Pretty Buffalo Hair".

"I nor do — nodding his head towards the seated holy man — He Who Speaks To Ghosts, wish to influence or to question your decision. That is not to say that we don't have an opinion. What we do ask is that you make a decision".

"We can no longer tolerate the droppings of a growing herd of ponies in the midst of the village. The people are complaining".

He Who Speaks To Ghosts sat stoically listening; occasionally he would nod his head, indicating his agreement with the Chief's words.

Gray Wolf looked somberly at his two closest friends. "Your speaking to me of your concerns about the cleanliness of the village, needed to be said."

Then with a crinkle at the corners of his eyes that quickly disappeared — but had been noticed by the Shaman —, he resumed speaking, "I do not believe that you my friends, would deny me as much time as needed to make my decision."

Old Wise One wandered if he had gone too far, did Gray Wolf think that he was intruding in his personal affairs? He Who Speaks To Ghosts suppressed a smile. Old Wise One sat in gloomy despair with his head down, trying to think of a diplomatic response.

Before the chief could speak, Gray Wolf placed his hands on his knees and began to laugh uproariously.

"Old Wise One, my lifetime friend I am not at all displeased with your words. It is I who must apologize for my thoughtlessness."

The consequences of leaving eight ponies overnight in the middle of the village, was predictable. Everyone knows that the Great Spirit's design is that, all living things that eat, at some point, have to relieve themselves."

Then as if he smelled a foul odor, Gray Wolf frowned, and pinched his nostril together. The three men laughed.

"Long before he asked, Little Flower and I…Little Flower knew, and told me, that Running Eagle would ask for permission to marry Pretty Buffalo Hair. That is when, his gaze shifted to the holy man, I sought the counsel of He Who Speaks To Ghosts."

"He Who Speaks To Ghosts' words, gave me assurance that Running Eagle and Pretty Buffalo Hair's union was not taboo. The Holy Man's words removed my only concern. When Running Eagle asked, though I did not at the time speak my consent, and have not spoken of this but to Little Flower, my answer was then and has always been, yes.

A look of relief, of satisfaction spread across the faces of both Chief Old Wise One, and the Shaman/Holy Man, He Who Speaks To Ghosts."

For the first time, He Who Speaks To Ghosts spoke; "Gray Wolf, because of my dedication and service to the spirit world, I have never known the love between a man and a woman, a man and his son. I ask, what is the reason that you choose to delay the happiness of these two young people, the children that you love."

Gray Wolf sat silently, puffing the communal pipe. He blew out a thin cloud of pungent blue smoke he then passed the pipe to his friend and chief, Old Wise One.

"I, as do the rest of my family, my wife Little Flower, my daughter, Spring Blossom, and even my new son-in-law, Stone Fist, we all approve of and support the marriage of Running Eagle and Pretty Buffalo Hair."

"I have two reasons for delaying the giving of my permission. The first is too bestowing in my son the knowledge that the prudent man is the man with patience. That something's and especially someone, someone as special as Pretty Buffalo Hair, is worth waiting for."

"Old Wise One passed the pipe to He Who Speaks To Ghosts; "My friend Gray Wolf speaks with the wisdom of a true loving husband and father. The only fault that I find with his words is that I did not speak them first."

He Who Speaks To Ghosts spoke; "I am curious my friend, you say you had two reasons. What is the second?"

Gray Wolf gave Old Wise One conspiratorial glance. "I enjoy teasing my son. I would never knowingly deprive him of any of life's pleasures."

"Now as it is known by the entire village, Running Eagle and Pretty Buffalo Hair, without my permission, are nightly enjoying the pleasures of marriage. Their bodies are satisfied, but still their minds are not quite at ease."

I saw no harm in, for a little while longer, teasing Running Eagle's mind, while strengthening his character."

Old Wise One and He Who Speaks To Ghosts grunted their approval. The three old friends sat in silence, enjoying the smoke from their sacred pipe.

****

Under the omnipresent gaze of her tormentor Hen's Teeth, Rebecca was cleaning the eating utensils from the morning meal. Quite One was busy repairing a loose hem on one of Hen's Teeth's dresses.

Without warning Rebecca experienced a series of short cramps in her stomach. Hen's Teeth noticed that the white girl had stopped working and was doubled over in pain.

She walked over and with her open palm, cuffed Rebecca behind her ear. "You lazy girl, get back to work".

Rebecca fell across one of the buffalo hide couches; her dress parted showing a white thigh, streaked with blood.

Immediately, the old woman realized what was happening. The lazy white girl was starting her moon bleed. She grabbed Rebecca by the arm and pushed her out of the tepee.

Quite One had put down her sewing and asked, "mother what is wrong with the white girl, what is wrong with "*Eebi Tseena Puis*?"

Hen's Teeth turned to her daughter; she is having the moon bleed; her blood is contaminating the tepee.

"Mother are you so old that you do not remember the woman's moon bleed"? "Do you not recall the pleasant time spent in the woman's bleeding lodge?" Without waiting for an answer, she swept past Hen's Teeth. Rebecca was sitting on the ground. Quite One went to her; "Come *Eebi Tseena Puis*", I will walk you to the woman's bleeding lodge.

Despite being a captive for over two months, Rebecca had learned but a few words of the People's language. It was not that she could not have learned, Rebecca had chosen not to learn.

In her mind she equated her gaining knowledge of the heathen language, as losing her identity, of becoming one of them, of becoming "*Eebi Tseena Puis*", whatever that meant, and losing forever, Rebecca Billings, daughter of Henry Billings and Margaret Billings.

As each day stretched into an interminable night, Rebecca's only solace had been the marriage of Stone Fist to Spring Blossom. She had to admit, that that savage Stone Fist seemed to adore his new wife. Since his marriage, Stone Fist had shown absolutely no interest her.

Her only regret that she associated with Stone Fist's marriage, was after he returned from the hunting trip with the gravely ill Running Eagle, she had seen very little of Mandy.

Oh, how she missed Mandy. Mandy who she now unequivocally, wholeheartedly, accepted as truly being her sister, was her only hope to ever return to the civilized world.

Rebecca was convinced that Mandy was being forced to attend to the needs of that tall young, stately savage, her rapist Stone Fist's best friend, Running Eagle.

Rebecca pitied Mandy. Mandy who had been forced to constantly, both day and night, be at that savage's beck and call, tirelessly nursing him back to good health.

Any doubts that Rebecca may have been harboring, about Mandy's commitment to escape, in her mind, had been totally dispelled.

She reasoned that any weakening of Mandy's resolve to escape this hellish nightmare, had to have been totally obliterated when her so called adoptive parents, forced her to work like a slave, a black slave providing continuous, uninterrupted nursing care for their son, Running Eagle.

Rebecca marveled at the way that Mandy had managed to cleverly worm her way into the good graces of these savages. That Mandy, her very own sister Mandy, had ingeniously, somehow, tricked them into adopting her, into trusting her.

At first, Rebecca had found it difficult to believe that Stone Fist's in-laws, his friend, Running Eagle's parents, had welcomed Mandy into their family.

Rebecca took comfort and encouragement from the fact that Mandy had gained the heathen's trust. The hard part was over, the only thing left for them, was to develop and to execute a plan of escape.

All of that "Noble Savage", nonsense that Mandy had been espousing when they had last talked, was just that, pure nonsense. Rebecca attributed Mandy's having said those absurd things, to her need to role-play. Thus, perpetrating a deception that they would use to help them to escape.

Rebecca realized that her being banished to the tepee for females having their period — that's what her mother Peggy had called it her period — was actually a blessing in disguise.

Since they were infants, she and Mandy — of course with the exception of social events when Mandy served her as her slave — had done just about everything together.

The two girls had had measles and chicken pox together. They had examined each other's chests, and seen their fledgling breasts burst forth at practically the same time. As pre-teens, anxious to become grown-ups, they had examined each other "*down there*", to see who would be the first to sprout pubic hair.

They had both matured "*down there*", the growth of pubic hair, at practically the same time. Finally, here, during this nightmarish captivity by these savages, they had experienced the onset of menstruation together.

As she sat mending different items of apparel, Rebecca expectantly watched the entrance to the tepee. Her pulse raced with excitement, and anticipation, each time that someone entered the tepee.

Each time that someone entered, it was someone other than Mandy.

At the end of her first day of her exile at the women's bleeding tepee, Mandy had not arrived. Rebecca was disappointed, but not overly concerned. She was confident that at any moment, Mandy would enter the tepee.

After four days had elapsed, Rebecca's flow had stopped. Still there was no sign of Mandy.

Rebecca began to worry. What had happened to Mandy? What had these heathens done to her sister?

****

When she returned to Quite One's lodge, she was greeted by Hen's Teeth. The old woman scowled, and immediately began to berate the white girl;
"Ah, *Blue Wolf Eyes,* the lazy white one returns."

Hen's Teeth pointed her knarled finger at a huge pile of dirty utensils, stacked in the rear of the tepee. It's about time you returned. Look at what I have managed to save for you."

The old crone shoved Rebecca towards the dirty pottery, and shouted; "*maaitu aitu.*"

Rebecca barely understood the meaning of the plethora of foreign sounding words, being shouted to her. However, one phrase, *maaitu aitu*, the words that she had heard her tormentor relentlessly scream at her since the first day of her captivity, the words *maaitu aitu*, without a doubt she knew that *maaitu aitu*, was a command that she, "get to work"!

After the evening meal, Rebecca, gathered together the soiled eating utensils, and took them to the creek to wash.

As she approached the water her heart began to race. An Indian maiden, was sitting on the bank, washing eating bowls. Her back was to Rebecca. The woman appeared to be loss in her in thoughts, lost to the world. She was softly, sweetly humming a sprightly, faintly, vaguely, familiar tune.

Rebecca, paused to listen, and without thinking, Rebecca started singing, putting words to the tune."

> *Oh she danced all night with a hole in her stockin'*
> *Her knees kept a-knockin'*
> *And her heels kept a-rockin'*
> *She danced all night with a hole in her stockin'*
> *She danced to the light of the moon.*
>
> *Oh Buffalo gal can you come out tonight...*

Rebecca dropped her basket, and ran towards the serene Indian maiden. The woman continued singing; Rebecca began to run towards her shouting, at the top of her lungs; Mandy, Mandy...

****

Mandy turned, and saw Becky running towards her. She jumped to her feet, she stumbled, and then she ran, with open arms, to greet her sister.

Rebecca and Mandy stood together, arms around each other. Both sisters were crying.

Rebecca stepped back; she was reluctant to release her sister's hands. "Mandy I've been so worried. What have they done to you? Why didn't you come to the women's bleeding lodge? I waited for you?"

"Mandy, did that animal, that savage Running Eagle hurt you? Did he rape you?"

"Slow down Becky...take a breath. Give me a chance to answer. I want to answer all of your questions."

"First, I didn't join you at the women's bleeding lodge because I was not having my period. In answer to your second question, what have they done to me; the answer is that they have done nothing to me. They've treated me with dignity and respect, dignity and respect that I worked hard to earn."

"What was your other question...oh yes. Did Running Eagle hurt me? Did he rape me? My answers to those questions are no, he did not rape, me and no he did not hurt."

Mandy took her sister's hands in her own, she smiled and while looking deeply into her sister's bright blue eyes, she smiled and said, "Becky, Running Eagle did do something with me and for me, he married me."

Rebecca withdrew her hands from Mandy's. She stared at Mandy. Shock, disbelief, and incredulity swept across her face, "You're married to that Indian, that craven savage?"

Then, as if she were completely oblivious to the joy and happiness radiating in Mandy's soft brown eyes, Rebecca threw her arms around her sister and began to sob, "Oh Mandy, I'm so very sorry."

Mandy disengaged herself from Rebecca, and held her at arm's length. "Becky, don't be sorry for me, be happy. I am so very, very happy. In fact I have never in my life been as happy as I am right here, right now."

"Running Eagle is the kindest, the most considerate, the most loving man, that I have ever met."

Rebecca recoiled; she turned her back to Mandy. She felt betrayed, abandoned, and completely alone. It had happened. What she had feared, but had stubbornly refused to acknowledge, had really happened. Mandy, her blood, her black sister had become, one of them.

"Mandy, what are you saying? You can't possibly think that these savages are capable of feeling love, like white people do."

"When you told me that Gray Wolf had adopted you, that they had given you some heathen Indian name, I told myself that you were merely, cleverly trying to gain their trust in order to help us escape, to return to civilization.'

Rebecca's sparkling blue eyes were now red rimmed. Tears of hopeless frustration were streaming down her cheeks.

Mandy walked over to the distraught girl. She put her arms around Rebecca's trembling shoulders. Mandy gently wiped the tears from her sister's cheeks. She placed Rebecca's head onto her shoulder.

She then in a hushed but firm voice spoke; "Becky, I love Running Eagle with all my heart and soul. I love everything about him. I love his humor; I love his strength, his courage, and his indomitable spirit. I love the way he looks at me, the way he makes me feel."

"Running Eagle is my man, my husband, and hopefully, soon he will be the father of our children. Becky I will not go back to your world. This is my world, here with these people, here with my noble warrior, here with my man."

"I love you Becky, not just because we share the same blood, I love you in spite of the fact, that we share the same blood."

"I love you because, for whatever reason you may have had, you plucked me out of a world of ignorance. You shared with me on an equal footing, next to my mother, the most important adult of my formative years, Miss Eleanor Leary."

"As you know, Little Flower asked Gray Wolf to make me a member of their family, to adopt me. Gray Wolf agreed, gave me an Indian name, and welcomed me, as a member of his family."

"I have grown to love my new mother and father Little Flower, and Gray Wolf. I love my sisters, *Blue Wolf Eyes* and Spring Blossom. But most of all, I love Running Eagle. Running Eagle is the love of my life. Running Eagle makes me whole, Running Eagle is my husband, my man."

Breathlessly the words continued to pour out of Mandy's mouth. "To me, Running Eagle is my Hercules, my Othello, and my Sahka Zulu, all rolled into one."

"He is what a man should be, brave, courageous, honorable and most of all, he walks with pride and dignity. Running Eagle, is my hero, my confidant, and my lover, Running Eagle is to me the embodiment of what a man should be."

"Becky let's be honest with each other. I love you and you love me. Even before my mother and our father acknowledged that we are sisters, we loved each other as though we were sisters. Unfortunately for most of our lives, our relationship has been spent adhering to the segregationist laws and standards of Southern Society."

"At Rosewood, at first your love for me was that of a child for a pet, or for a favorite toy."

As Rebecca was about to protest, Mandy held up her hand, "I don't blame you, … mine for you, was influenced by a slave's love for a benevolent master who kept me out of the fields; for a master who defied the law who taught me to read and to write. I loved you for violating a law whose sole intent and purpose was to keep an entire race of enslaved people, from learning that their enslavement was based upon a lie".

"I love you because you gave me Miss Leary, who opened my eyes. Who showed me that the wretched condition of perpetual bondage was not as they the Southern Slave Holding Society would have us believe; that our own people the black preacher taught, every Sunday that slavery was ordained and in accordance with the word, and the will of their blond, blue eyed, white God."

"You remember Becky, one of the most enlightening things that Miss Leary taught us was that "Knowledge is Power". Remember that?" A perfect example in support of what I just said was that mathematical model that she taught us."

"I'll probably get this wrong, we both know that math was never one of my strong subjects. Let's see, I think she called it an inverse function, relationship. As one variable factor increases, that same variable causes another related factor or event, to decrease."

She picked up a stick and drew a graph in the clearing.

"Mandy saw that same bored, confused, expression on Rebecca's face, that she had seen when as children, Miss Leary had forced them to sit through tedious hours of mathematics lessons.

"I forgot; you were even worse at math than was I. What I'm trying to say and point-out is that we both intuitively, and intellectually knew, that the social structure of the South mandates, that when it comes to white kids and black kids growing-up together, that that particular mathematical principal, the inverse function, is certainly valid. The older we became, she plotted on the "y" axis of the crude graph, the farther, she plotted on the "x" axis, especially in our early teens, the farther the Southern Society, forced us apart."

"I belong here. With my husband Running Eagle, the man I love, with these people, the Comanche, this is where I belong, this is where I want to be."

"Becky, I'm not naïve. Despite my profound personal feelings, my love for Running Eagle, I realize that my decision to stay with these people, to become Comanche, is in part influenced by my being black, living in America's white society. I would like to believe that if I were white, my decision would still be the same."

"But I am not white, and none of what I just said applies to you. You Rebecca, my sister, my only living blood relative, you are white. And you have every right and every reason to want to return to your white world."

"I believe that if I ask, my husband Running Eagle, will help me return you, to your white world."

Rebecca had no intention of just accepting, unchallenged, Mandy's words, and her conclusions. "Mandy you're no longer a slave. You're free. We're no longer in the South; we're in a free-soil state. We were well on our way to a new life. The four of us, together, you and me, and Ruth, and our father, together, were about start a new life as a family in Kansas, a free state."

"That all ended when we were attacked by these savage animals. Mandy how could you even consider living amongst these beasts who killed and mutilated your mother, and our father."

"*Eebi Tseena Puis*, the Indians that attacked our wagon…, Rebecca interrupted, "that's the second time that you spoke that gibberish to me, *Eebi Tseena Puis*, what does it mean. Mandy smiled, "*Eebi Tseena Puis*" is the name given to you by Quite One, Stone Fist's mother. It means, "Blue Wolf Eyes". Comanche names often reflect the deeds, the visions, or the physical appearance of the person."

"My Indian name is much longer than yours. It's a real mouth full, *Nananisuyake Ta?Si?Woo? Tso?Yaa*, it means Pretty Buffalo Hair."

"Running Eagle explained that that was the name that Gray Wolf and Little Flower gave me. He said that it was because the texture of my hair vaguely, reminded Gray Wolf of the wooly hair of the buffalo. Although my hair is thicker than the People's or the whites, it was just slightly less coarse then the hair of the buffalo."

"Little Flower thinks that my slightly-woolly hair is pretty."

"You and I know that we can thank, or blame Henry Billings for the texture of my hair, for the dimples in our cheeks."

"As I was saying, the Indians that attacked our wagon, and killed my mother and our father, were Pawnee, not Comanche." Rebecca looked doubtful.

Mandy quickly added, "Oh don't misunderstand, Running Eagle, assured me that…what were his words, oh yes; "The cowardly Pawnee had arrived at the disabled wagon first, otherwise it would have been Running Eagle's raiding party that would have attacked and killed our people."

"I honestly can't say, I really don't know if the fact that the Indians who killed our people were not Comanche per se, though believe me I am grateful it was not the Comanche, I can't in all honesty say that that mitigated in any way, my decision to stay with these people."

"Becky I am in total support of the Indians, all of the Indians, the Comanche, the Cheyenne, the Apaches, the Utes, all of this continent's aboriginal peoples, resisting the stealing of their land, the subjugation of their people, and the ultimate destruction of their culture. Becky, I know that I can be of help."

****

Rebecca was frantic, wringing her hands, shaking her head from side to side.

"Mandy please…please don't do this. You're not making any sense. We need to stay together. Come with me, we've been together all of our lives. Let's escape from this hellish place together."

"You're no fighter. What do you know about fighting? How can you help these backward, primitive people?"

"You're right Becky, I cannot fight nor, do I have the military planning skills of a Napoleon, of a Robert E. Lee, or a Ulysses S. Grant. What I do have though is knowledge, I know that no matter how courageous and fierce their warriors are in battle, that in the end they can never win. I know that if all of the Indian nations allied themselves into one, their combined number would be but a fraction of that of the whites. I know that the white's killing technology is vastly superior, then that of those you refer to as these 'backward, primitive people".

"You know Becky, back at Rosewood, in the slave community, behind closed doors, and drawn curtains, people would wonder and ask each other, "why dint da white massas wont da niggas to reed and rite. *Why wud da massas whup da hide offa a nigga cauht wid a bok?"*

"The prevailing thought was that a black slave that could write, might be able to forge a pass and escape to freedom, and that the ability to read would come in handy when trying to make his way to the North".

"I, as did most of the slaves, accepted that. After all, it sounded logical it made sense. Now thanks to you Becky, I know that that simple explanation while not a lie, is only a partly true. I know without a doubt that it is at best, only partially true, it's basically a lie." Rebecca looked confused. "I don't understand, why do you say thanks to me? What did I do?"

A solemn, almost reverent expression crossed Mandy's face. "Becky you remember hearing and reading, "Knowledge Is Power"? What you did for me, what you gave me, you gave me access to Miss Eleanor Leary."

Miss Leary opened my eyes and my mind. She taught, and we learned. We gained knowledge. Miss Leary gave me, an illiterate black slave girl, knowledge, she gave me power."

"That's what I can bring to these people. Knowledge of the outside world."

"Come *Eebi Tseena Puis*, it's getting dark. We had better be getting back, before Running Eagle sends out a search and rescue party.

****

Anyone who saw Running Eagle and his new wife Pretty Buffalo Hair together, within a very short period of time, within minutes, was struck by the "rightness" of these two people being together.

That they loved each other was evident and expected. The village, the world was full of young men and young women who were in love. That the Great Spirit breathed love, and even lust into the young, was as accepted as was the rising of the sun.

To the amusement of the camp still — after the passing of many sunsets following their marriage — Running Eagle and Pretty Buffalo Hair, spent most of their time, day and night, together in their tepee. One would only catch glimpses of either of the newlyweds when the call of nature, forced them to abandon their love nest.

When the couple finally emerged — their fire-making and food supplies, as well as their bodies, exhausted —, they joined a jocular, teasing and amused community.

Running Eagle and Pretty Buffalo Hair heard and graciously endured, the usual jokes and innuendoes, that are heaped upon newlyweds.

Little Flower watched as the women good-naturedly teased the new bride. Sweet Willow, one of the many attractive unwed women, who had actively pursued Running Eagle as a potential husband, smiling, walked over and handed Pretty Buffalo Hair, a large bowl filled with scented bear grease.

"It was my intention to give this to you before your wedding night. Before your arrival, when I shared Running Eagle's sleeping robes, I found that a generous application of this, down there, before and after made life much more comfortable."

****

The women that were within listening distance, chuckled. White Fawn, a strikingly attractive girl, with whom, when he was a bachelor, Running Eagle had on occasion also, shared his sleeping robes, laughed loudly.

She continued laughing after the others had ceased. White Fawn's laughter was not the laughter of good-hearted amusement; instead it was the laugh of bitter distain.

White Fawn knew when she was pursuing the handsome young warrior, that she had lots of competition. She, as did they all, thought that Running Eagle would choose as his mate, from many of the People's beautiful young unwed women. White Fawn thought it an insult, a sign of disrespect, that Running Eagle would choose as his woman, this black captive. This slave.

Pretty Buffalo Hair accepted the bowl of bear grease. "I thank you Sweet Willow for her most thoughtful gift. I will use it when I comb and braid my husband's beautiful, flowing hair. Although I know that it can be used to prepare a woman to receive her man, for that use, I have no need."

The touch of my husband's hand in mine, when he looks at me, and smiles, my heart melts, filling my body with warm juices that make unnecessary, the use of artificial lubricants.

Little Flower, who had been unobserved, in the background listening, smiled.

That night after having enjoyed a hardy meal, Gray Wolf sat alone, smoking his pipe. Little Flower, picked up a pair of her husband's favorite leggings, sat beside him, and began the process of repairing the torn garment. Gray Wolf, lost in thought, did not acknowledge his wife's presence.

The only sounds were the crackle of the fire, and the rhythmic puffing of a contented man, smoking his pipe.

Little Flower accidentally pricked her finger with the needle. "Ouch, I guess that I'm either getting clumsy, or getting old".

Gray Wolf looked fondly, lovingly at his wife, "Maybe it is both." Little Flower gave her husband a quizzical stare.

Gray Wolf was smiling, his face half hidden in the shadows; "My beautiful, graceful Little Flower, is now an old clumsy woman." He ducked his head just in time, as the leggings that she had been sewing, sailed above his head.

"Old and clumsy? I'll show you who is far from being old and clumsy." She jumped into his lap, Gray Wolf, in anticipation of her advance, had laid his pipe aside, and opened his arms to meet the charge of his not so old, not so clumsy wife.

They rolled, locked in mock battle, onto their sleeping robes. Gray Wolf held his wife's arms, pinned to the robe, stretched above her head. He looked down into her laughing beautiful back eyes. "I believe that my Little Flower still has plenty nectar for this old Gray Wolf."

He released her arms, and gently kissed her lips. Little Flower held his face between her hands. She returned his all so familiar kiss. Happy and as always, amazed at how, after all this time together, his searching probing tongue, thrilled and aroused her.

Almost as though in the absence of conscientious effort, they joined in the age-old familiar embrace of lovers.

Their love making, was deep, unhurried, and complete. They both knew what the other wanted, what they each needed. His body was as familiar to her, as hers was to him.

Instead of it being dull from countless repetitions of how they expressed their love, each thrust of his manhood, each reciprocating arching of her pelvis, was a reaffirmation, of

Gray Wolf and Little Flower's feelings for each other. Each thrust, each moan, served as punctuation, certification of their love, their timeless, endless love.

After more than twenty-five winters together, after having given life to three beautiful babies, the first dying three months after her birth. After a lifetime of shared joy and suffering, Little Flower marveled and rejoiced at the fact that she still, was madly in love with this man.

As they lay in each other's arms enjoying that familiar, relaxing after-glow that inexorably followed their love making, Little Flower sat up, and began to, with her finger, trace circles onto Gray Wolf's broad, practically hairless chest.

"I had forgotten how wonderful it felt, for us to have time alone together. It seems like forever since it was just Gray Wolf and Little Flower, sleeping together alone, in the same lodge. She sat up, wrapped her arms tightly around her body, and exclaimed; "It is truly a wonderful feeling".

Gray Wolf grunted, and rolled over onto his side. "My husband, now that our children have married and left our lodge, do you think as I do, of their happiness?

Gray Wolf sleepily replied; "To me they all, Running Eagle and Pretty Buffalo Hair appear to be happy. Spring Blossom and her husband Stone Fist appear to be happy. You're happy. Go to sleep Little Flower and Gray Wolf your husband too, will be happy."

Little Flower persisted. "Spring Blossom and Stone Fist obviously think that they are in love. Their being in love at this point in their relationship, is based mostly on their lust. It would be more accurate to say at this moment, right now, as in most young marriages, what they think is being in love, is in reality, could be more correctly defined as their being in lust."

Gray Wolf grumbled; "In love, in lust, it is all the same. Whatever it is, we agree, they all appear to be happy…go to sleep Little Flower.

Unperturbed, Little Flower continued, it was as though she had not heard a single word that Gray Wolf had spoken; "I understand that at their age, especially in the boys, the sap is rising. Love is not the driving force that leads the men to seek the warmth found between the thighs of an available female. I admit for most who marry, as happened between us, falling in love eventually, leads to falling in love."

"Running Eagle and Pretty Buffalo Hair are rare. Anyone who looks at them can plainly see that they are deeply in love."

"What I have seen in them is something special, something that is essential to a good marriage. If the marriage is to good, both the man and the woman have to like each other. To like each other, not necessarily as lovers, but should like each other as a person."

There is no doubt that Running Eagle and Pretty Buffalo Hair, as are Spring Blossom and Stone Fist, are deeply in love. What I have seen of Running Eagle and Pretty Buffalo Hair, in addition to having fallen in love, those two are among those fortunate few, who before they fell in love, were fortunate and lucky to have first "*fallen in like*".

Little Flower nudged her husband; Gray Wolf, do you agree…are you listening?

Instead of hearing an answer, she heard the even breathing and the steady snore, coming from her husband, the man she loved, and liked, above all others.

Little Flower kissed Gray Wolf's ear. She wrapped her arms around him, and snuggled her belly up to his back, her knees, pressed against his. They lay together, their bodies in repose, forming a perfect pair of spoons.

****

To Running Eagle, his beautiful wife seemed to excel in everything. He was amazed at how rapidly she learned and the way that she so easily, acclimated herself to an entirely new way of life.

Often Indian women, women from other tribes, women captured in raids, found it difficult to adjust to the People's language, to the People's way of doing things. Difficulty in doing things, the Comanche way, that they had essentially been doing, with only minor variations, all of their lives.

Running Eagle was especially pleased and impressed with how rapidly, and easily Pretty Buffalo Hair, learned the People's language.

"She Plucks Flowers", a young Pawnee woman, captured more than three winters ago, after three winters living amongst the People, could now understand what was being said, but still could not speak, in coherent sentences, the words of the People.

Running Eagle had wondered, were the people living in the white man's culture, the culture that Pretty Buffalo Hair, and her white *master/sister*, Blue Wolf Eyes, came from, of superior intelligence?

After speaking to his friend Stone Fist, who spoke only negative, derisive words about the clumsy, stupidity, of the frail white girl, Running Eagle had quickly dismissed those thoughts. The idea that the whites, and their black slaves, lived in a superior intellectual culture, where even the downtrodden slaves, possessed intelligence, and had the innate ability to learn, superior to that of the Comanche, was ridiculous.

Running Eagle instead, came to embrace the more reasonable, and logical reality, that "Pretty Buffalo Hair", or "Mahn-dee", as she was known by the whites, "Pretty Buffalo Hair, his wife was a singularly gifted, a child blessed by the Great Spirit.

Not only had he captured, and fallen in love with this remarkable young woman, he knew with absolute certainty, that "Pretty Buffalo Hair/*Mahn-dee*", loved him.

Running Eagle sat smoking his pipe, his eyes riveted on his wife, as she scraped the remnants of their meal into a waste bowl. He watched the movement of her firm shapely, supple, buttocks, as the muscles quivered under her dress.

He resisted the temptation to rise, —his manhood had a mind of its own, —and to take those now so familiar firm ripe melons into his eager hands. Instead he forced his mind to think of more mundane things; His favorite pony needed brushing, he would soon need to refill his pipe, he concentrated on these tasks, trying to deflate, and to deflect the seemingly, independent mind of his insatiable organ.

"Pretty Buffalo Hair, *Mahn-dee*, come sit with me. Your husband would talk with you. Mandy neatly folded the towel that she had been using to wipe the bowls. She placed the folded towel beside the clean utensils, and walked over to the cooking pit, and sat beside her husband.

Running Eagle was having difficulty finding the words to express himself. He settled for a feeble; "Are you happy?" Mandy took the pipe from his hand, placed it onto the edge of the pit.

She took his hands into hers; "My husband, at this time, our marriage, is the happiest time of my life. I would be content and deliriously happy, if we remained as we are now, never having to leave our sleeping robes, never having to leave this lodge."

Once again, Running Eagle felt the familiar stirring, the beginning of stiffening activity beneath his breechclout. He drooped her hands and looked away. Mandy thinking that she may have said something inappropriate, something that had offended him, spoke; "Forgive me my husband. Running Eagle, have I offended you? That was not my intent.

Running Eagle rose and stepped back. He realized that if he was going to have a non-sex related encounter with his wife, it would require that there be actual, physical separation, distance between them. With an effort, he managed to shift his gaze from her moist, succulent, full lips.

"*Mahn-dee*", the way that you have mastered the People's tongue in such a short time, in less than three moons, has impressed all of the people."

"I would like to give you a gift." Mandy, her curiosity pecking, remained seated, followed him with her eyes, as he paced around the circular interior of the tepee. "My gift to you, requires that you give a gift to me."

Misinterpreting his intent, thinking that Running Eagle, at that moment was saying that he wanted her, as much as she wanted him, smiled and began to remove her dress.

Running Eagle dashed over to his wife and grasped her hands. "No, no my love, if you take off your dress, he pointed down at his breechclout, now standing out at a 45-degree angle, "his mind, will overpower, pointing to his head, this mind."

"I will forget what I was about to ask of you." "*Mahn-dee*", I want to be able to speak to you in your tongue, the black man's language."

Running Eagle held his wife's petite, strong hands in his. He looked into her soft brown eyes. "That is the gift, that I want to give to you."

"To be able to give you that gift, the gift that you must give me, is to teach me language, the black man's tongue. Will you do this for me, so that I can do that for you?"

Mandy was overcome with emotion, she was filled with love, and appreciation for this man. She had noticed during the past week, that on occasion, Running Eagle he attempted to use her Christian name "Mandy", when addressing her.

Undoubtedly Little Flower had told him that her name was Man-dee. Running Eagle had evidently practiced the, to him, odd sounding word. She had rather liked the way that he pronounced her name, "*Mahn-dee*".

No Mandy decided, she would not teach him her tongue, the black man's language. She would instead teach him a far more valuable tongue, the language of the white man. The white man who, with his greed, his lust for land, his guns, and by sheer force of numbers, loomed as an eminent deadly threat, to his…to their way of life.

Mandy agreed to teach Running Eagle the white man's language. There and then, she began her lesson by explaining, "Though "*quid-pro-quo*", is not a part of the language currently being spoken by the white man, non the less, it will be the first phrase that you will be taught."

Running Eagle repeated the phrase, "*quid-pro-quo*", "what does it mean?"
Mandy smiled, then in a stern no nonsense voice she said, "my gift to you is not given freely, I expect something from you in return."

Running Eagle's face broke into a broad grin, "I like this phrase. It is the bases of all trade. Tell me Mahn-dee, an amused twinkle in his black, obsidian, colored eyes, what is it from me, that you expect in return?"

"I want you to teach me to ride like a Comanche."

****

The next day, amidst hoots and hollers, the newlyweds, Running Eagle and Pretty Buffalo Hair, finally, together emerged from their tepee.

Running Eagle squeezed Pretty Buffalo Hair's hand, and trotted towards the band's pony herd.

Pretty Buffalo Hair rapped on the entrance flap of Gray Wolf's tepee. Little Flower pushed the flap open and stepped out to greet her daughter; unable to resist, Little Flower teased, "Ah, at last, my daughter, you have decided to come up for air".

"On behalf of our village, I welcome the presence of Running Eagle, and his beautiful wife, Pretty Buffalo Hair."

Mandy at first blushed, at the light-hearted, well-intentioned insinuations. She then, with genuine reverence accepted Little Flower's recognition of the Running Eagle and her status as a family unit.

"I thank you my mother, for all that you have given me. First, I thank you your kindness, then your patience, then your love, and finally, I thank you and my father Gray Wolf, for Running Eagle."

Little Flower held her hand over her eyes as if she was shading them from the sun. Mandy noticed tears welling-up in her adopted mother/mother-in-law' eyes. Little Flower motioned for Mandy to precede her, as they both entered the dwelling.

Mandy sat on a familiar couch. Little Flower handed her a bowl filled with steaming, herbal tea. Mandy waited until Little Flower, filled a bowl for her own consumption, and joined Mandy on the couch.

"I come to ask for your help." Little Flower sat quietly, waiting for Pretty Buffalo Hair to continue." "Running Eagle, my husband — Little Flower noted that the words "my husband", were spoken as though in wondrous disbelief —, Pretty Buffalo Hair repeated — my husband has asked that I teach him the white man's language."

Seeing the puzzled expression on Little Flower's face, Mandy explained; "My husband, your son Running Eagle, knows that we must deal with the coming of the white man into the land of the Comanche. Running Eagle wisely feels that as a warrior, he would be better prepared to fight for our land, if he understood the words of the whites." I will teach him those words."

"In return, Running Eagle has agreed to teach me to ride like a Comanche."

Little Flower immediately understood the logic, and the wisdom of her son's reasoning. "Has Running Eagle spoke of this to Gray Wolf, or to Chief Thunder Cloud, or to Chief Old Wise One?"

"Although I disagree, and have told him so, my husband thinks that he may not be capable of learning the white man's language. If he cannot learn the words and their meaning, he does not want to disappoint our leaders."

"My daughter my son...your husband is wise beyond his winters. What is it that I can do to assist you?"

"As a black slave in the world of the white man, my white sister Rebecca, "*Eebi tseena puis*", "Blue Wolf Eyes", taught me to read and to write. She did this against the white man's taboo, forbidding the teaching and the learning of black slaves, to read and to write the white man's words."

"Rebecca...Blue Wolf Eyes" and I would sit, secluded, away from everyone with Miss Leary, the most wonderful white woman I have ever known. We would sit until the sun sat, learning from her."

"I believe that if we are alone, secluded, uninterrupted, I can teach Running Eagle, and he will learn the language of the white man."

"Little Flower saw the wisdom in Pretty Buffalo Hair's reasoning. She did not however, mention the obvious distraction afforded by of their solitude.

Little Flower's thoughts were that Running Eagle, and Pretty Buffalo Hair's seemingly unquenchable lust for each other's bodies, just might reduce their time to study the white talk."

Suppressing a chuckle at her thoughts she asked, "How can I help?"
Mandy sipped her tea; "I would like your assistance in my first attempt to take down, and to relocate our lodge, on the north bank of the creek."

"Pretty Buffalo Hair, though you have learned many of the Comanche ways and learned to speak our language, in a very short time, you have still more to learn. It is our duty, Spring Blossom and I, as your closest female relatives, to help you relocate, and reconstruct your lodge."

As they rose to begin the process of dismantling and moving Running Eagle and Pretty Buffalo Hair's tepee, Little Flower placed a restraining hand on Pretty Buffalo Hair's elbow; "My daughter, in your condition, I think you should delay learning, anything more than the fundamental ways to sit a pony."

With a quizzical expression on her face, what had Little Flower meant by, "in your condition", Mandy dismissed the thought, stood and followed Little Flower from the tepee.

When Running Eagle returned to the village, riding his favorite pony and leading two older horses by their reins. Pretty Buffalo Hair, Little Flower, and Spring Blossom had taken down the tepee, and were in the process of packing the couple's belongings.

Little Flower accepted the reins of one of the ponies. She steadied the animal, while Pretty Buffalo Hair, and Spring Blossom attached the poles of the travois, on opposite sides of the animals.

When all was ready, Running Eagle lifted his wife onto his pony, clutched the animal's mane in his left hand, and swung himself up onto the pony's back, firmly seated behind Pretty Buffalo Hair. Little Flower handed the reins of the pony pulling the travois, to her son.

Running Eagle spoke to his mother; "Our tepee will join the others, when we move to join the summer meetings. Until then we will be camped there, he pointed towards the creek. Tell my father, Gray Wolf, Stone Fist, and our leaders that my wife "*Mahn-dee*", will be teaching me the white man's talk.

As the slowly rode from the encampment, Running Eagle reined in his pony. He lifted his wife to the ground.

Mandy ran to the entrance of the tepee that Quite One, Hen's Teeth, and their white captive, "Pale Wolf's Eyes lived.

Rebecca had been standing by the tepee, she had anxiously watched as the three women dismantled Mandy and Running Eagle's tepee. She was nearly in a state of panic, not knowing where Mandy was going, if she would return.

Mandy, breathlessly ran up to and embraced Rebecca. "Becky, my husband and I are temporarily moving about twenty yards from the creek. I will ask him to help you escape, to help return you to your civilized world.

"When Running Eagle, hunts, I will come to visit you, Little Flower, and Spring Blossom. Becky, I love you. I have not, and never will, abandoned you."

Mandy turned, and ran back to Running Eagle, who had been patiently waiting.

Once Running Eagle and Pretty Buffalo Hair reached their destination, the site where they intended to erect their tepee, the couple began the daunting task of putting the structure together.

Running Eagle had very little experience in performing this "women's work". Mandy's experience at pitching the elaborate tent, consisted of once having assisted Little Flower and Spring Blossom.

Their energetic, but feeble, efforts had resulted in a comedy of errors. Twice the four poles forming the base of the tepee, were raised and latched together, by Running Eagle with broad, rawhide bindings.

When Running Eagle and Pretty Buffalo Hair, began to wrap the heavy buffalo hides around the poles, the poles collapsed, crumbled to the ground.

When Little Flower and Spring Blossom arrived, they found Running Eagle and Little Flower, laughing and struggling under the weight of the heavy hides.

Little Flower and Spring Blossom called out; "Running Eagle, Pretty Buffalo Hair, we bring meat and bread for your meal.

Mandy, still laughing peaked out from beneath the heavy hides that enveloped them. "Little Flower, Spring Blossom, my mother and sister, you are always, and always will be welcome in our lodge."

"As you can see, neither my husband nor do I, have the requisite skill to erect a sturdy dwelling." Little Flower, who had anticipated and suspected that these two, during their surreal period of being "*totally, blindly, madly in love*", would not be up to the real challenge of setting up a tepee.

"The three of us working together, a mother and her two daughters, will have your tepee firmly standing, very shortly".

After the four family members, comfortably seated in the solidly constructed, majestically standing tepee, had eaten a hardy meal, Pretty Buffalo Hair, once again thanked Spring Blossom, and Little Flower for their help.

Spring Blossom, spoke; "It is I, my sister who thanks you". Confused, Pretty Buffalo Hair asked; "Why does my sister thank me, when it is clearly I who should thank you and our mother for your help."

Spring Blossom sat in silence for a moment, as if gathering her thoughts, "With my husband, Stone Fist, away leading a raiding party against the Utes, keeping busy, frees my mind from constantly worrying about his safety. For that, I thank both you and my brother Running Eagle, for your inexperience, and his clumsy, tepee set-up, ineptitude."

Running Eagle in a mock display of machismo, pointed his finger at his expanded chest and proclaimed, "I Running Eagle, son of Gray Wolf, am a fierce Comanche Warrior."

Running Eagle bent at the waist, balled up his hands into fists and growled. "Grrrr...grrr. It would be unseemly for such a mighty warrior as I, to be proficient in women's work. The making of tepees, is after all, the work of women."

Spring Blossom, followed by Pretty Buffalo Hair, threw pillows, at the mighty Comanche Warrior's head.

Little Flower, smiled at the antics of her children, as her grown up adult children, "played".

****

After Little Flower and Spring Blossom returned to the village, Running Eagle and Pretty Buffalo Hair, despite their fatigue, the newlyweds, as they had been doing at each and every opportunity, day and night, made mad passionate love.

As they lay pressed together, entwined on their sleeping robes, basking in the afterglow of their lovemaking, Mandy whispered, "Tomorrow, if it pleases my husband, I think will be a good day for us to begin our lessons".

"Each day, until the sun is directly over our heads, I will teach you the white man's words. This we will do."

"After our second meal, until the sun sets, we will review what was taught during the morning hours".

Running Eagle murmured, "*Mahn-dee,* as they had discussed, as the lessons progressed, they would speak the white talk whenever possible, *Mahn-dee,* you have not left time for me to teach you to ride like a Comanche."

"That time will come. My husband now is not the right time for those lessons."

Without further explanation, Pretty Buffalo Hair pressed her body against the back of Running Eagle. Within minutes her breathing became rhythmic, and regular.

Pulling her arms tightly around his waist, Running Eagle, looking forward to tomorrow, began to drift off into sleep. Before crossing the threshold, he remembered his wife's declaration, "now is not the right time for those lessons", with sleep rapidly approaching, he wondered, what did "*Mahn-dee*", mean, when she said, "Now is not the right time for those lessons".

****

Running Eagle proved to be a determined, energetic student. Mandy had insisted that during them time away from the village that they speak only the white man's talk. When Running Eagle was having difficulty with an English word, phrase or concept, and seemed ready to abandon the project, he had asked "*Mahn-dee*" how she had managed, in such a short time, to learn Comanche. Mandy had resounded; "I simply had no choice, and I was fortunate to have been under the tutelage of Little Flower".

"Everyone around me spoke nothing but Comanche. Becky and I are the only ones in the village that speak the white man's talk. Becky and I were separated. There was no one that I could communicate with".

Initially, Little Flower and I communicated using sign. After a week of pantomime, Little Flower would no longer acknowledge my crude gestures, my signs. Instead she interpreted the gestures, and translated them into Comanche words, phrases and sentences."

"Little Flower insisted that Spring Blossom, when communicating with me follow her example."

"If I wanted food, Little Flower would not give me food, until and unless I asked for it in the language of the People. "If I wanted a blanket, I had to make my need known by speaking Comanche". in the words of the people". "In addition to my sincere desire to learn the People's language, Little Flower made it absolutely clear, that my every day survival, my acceptance by the People, was in large part dependent upon my learning the language of the People".

"I think it worked, therefore while we are here, once I have taught you a white man's word, a phrase a sentence, we will talk to each other using, only the white man's words."

She smiled mischievously, "Running Eagle, I want you to listen closely to these white man's words; "I want you", repeat them to me." Running Eagle slowly repeated the strange alien words; "*I wont you.*" A stern expression crossed over Mandy face.

"No that is not correct, that is not what I said. In fact, what you just said, my love, has the opposite meaning of what you intended to say."

Running Eagle concentrated; He tried again, "*I wont you...* that is what I heard that is what you said. "Listen carefully, I said "I want you. That is what I want to hear you say to me, each and every day of our lives."

Instead my love, the white man's words that you are saying, "*I wont you*", has an entirely different meaning. "I want you; I will always want you. I will never not, want you. The words you said "*I wont you*", is the opposite of what you meant to say, "I want you".

"As much as it pains me my love, until you say what you mean, our love making is in serious jeopardy."

With Mandy's guidance, Running Eagle immediately corrected his miss use of the white man's words "want and wont". To Mandy this little episode served as an effective example of English antonyms. To Running Eagle, his correctly stating this phrase, "I want you", whenever he was with her, was essential for the survival of his love life.

****

After their meal, the three women of Gray Wolf's lodge, returned to work.

Half of the processed hides were bundled onto a travois, pulled by a pony to the edge of the creek. The women, as a team, washed the hides in the creek until they became somewhat pliable.

Additional buffalo brains and liver was rubbed in the inner side of the hides.

After several days when the gooey mixture of buffalo brains & liver have been absorbed, two of the women would grab either end of the hide, and draw it back and forth around a tree for hours. The third of the Gray Wolf lodge women would relieve one of the other two.

When the hide was pliable enough to fold, then and only then, was the cured, folded hide, ready to become a buffalo robe.

That evening, following the evening meal, with both Running Eagle and Spring Blossom out presumably socializing with their friends, Little Flower decided that the time was right for her to resume the talk that she had started and postponed, with her husband; the topic, the growing feelings, between their Son Running Eagle, and their adopted daughter, *nananisuyake ta?si?woo? tso?yaa* (Pretty Buffalo Hair).

Gray Wolf was seated next to the dying cooking fire, leisurely enjoying an after-meal smoke.

Little Flower put down Gray Wolf's ceremonial shirt. She had been adorning the shirt with the addition of dyed porcupine quills. She sat down next to Gray Wolf; "My husband, though our lodge is one of the largest in the village, it has become increasingly apparent, that the space is not adequate for five grown adults."

Gray Wolf knocked the ashes from his pipe, and carefully placed the pipe st his side. "Woman we have been married now for more then twenty-four winters. In that time, I have learned that, you are about to skillfully, gain my consent for something that you more then likely have already done, or have decided needs to be done. For us to build a larger tepee would be an insult to, Chief Thunder Cloud, He Who Speaks To Ghosts, and to Chief Old Wise One."

Little Flower fanged surprised hurt; "As always, my husband, your wisdom and perception precede my words. I had not given thought to the political ramifications of our tepee being the larger than that of our leaders."

Gray Wolf picked up his pipe, he turned to look for his tobacco pouch, Little Flower handed the pouch to her husband. A momentary silence filled the lodge. The only sounds were of Gray Wolf puffing, attempting to light his pipe.

Gray Wolf broke the silence. "I have heard from He Who Speaks to Ghosts, that shortly, perhaps as early as tonight, Stone Fist will·come with horses, asking my permission for him to marry Spring Blossom. If his gift is adequate, and if Spring Blossom consents, I will accept his horses."

Little Flower remained silent. If Gray Wolf had looked at his wife, he would have noticed a slight smile forming at the bottom of her mouth. Inwardly she thought, one down, two to go.

During Gray Wolf and Little Flower's conversation, Mandy was seated on her sleeping robes, in the rear of the tepee. She was sewing a dress from the soft hide of a doe that Spring Blossom had given her as a gift.

Little Flower looked at her adopted daughter, Pretty Buffalo Hair, she discreetly pointed; "Pretty Buffalo Hair is a fine daughter. She is an excellent, seamstress, an excellent cook, hard worker, and a truly beautiful girl. She will make a fine wife for some brave. You will receive many horses when she marries." Gray Wolf absently grunted, and continued to puff on his pipe.

Little Flower studied her husbands face, looking to see his reaction to her words of praise of Pretty Buffalo Hair. Seeing none, she continued; "I think that Running Eagle likes Pretty Buffalo Hair." From the corner of her eye, she looked for Gray Wolf's reaction, still no reaction.

"I think that our adopted daughter, Pretty Buffalo Hair, likes our son, Running Eagle." Gray Wolf grunted, "of course Running Eagle likes Pretty Buffalo Hair, after all, she is his little sister."

Little Flower took a deep breath, "the feelings that I see, are not the feelings of a brother's love for his sister, or a sister's love for a brother." Gray Wolf silently knocked the ashes from his pipe into the fire-pit. Holding the pipe by its still warm bowl, he pointed the stem at his wife.

"Little Flower, it is time that you speak openly…what are you trying to tell me?" Little Flower steadied herself, she took a deep breath; "My husband the furtive glances that I see, are not the feelings of a brother's love for his sister, or a sister's love for a brother, I see in Running Eagle, the desire of a man for a woman, and in Pretty Buffalo Hair, I see the desire of a woman for a man."

Gray Wolf gave his wife a look of sheer incredulity. In his most authoritative voice, he stated; "My son has not been brought up to be a pervert. To have sexual desire for his sister."

Little Flower reached for and held her husband's hand in her two hands; "My husband there is no perversion. Running Eagle and Pretty Buffalo Hair were not raised as brother and sister".

"They have not experienced the history of growing up together. There is no blood link between the two. That they are attracted to each other, as a man is attracted to a woman, and as I am attracted to you, is not a perversion, it is natural."

If they should marry, think of the fine young warriors that would result from a union of our son, a strong Comanche Warrior, and Pretty Buffalo Hair, a proud courageous member of the Black Tribe."

"Did this not occur, the issue of our tribe's man, Kwahadi Comanche, Chief Peta Nocona, and the white captive girl, Cynthia Ann Parker.

Is it not said that the child of their union, their teenage son Quanah, is thought by many, especially by He Who Speaks To Ghosts, to be destined to become a great warrior chief, and a leader of the People."

Mandy had been quietly sitting, sewing her beautiful doeskin dress. It had become her custom, to listen carefully to the talk between the Indians. Her primary reason for paying close attention to the conversations was to help her to improve her knowledge of the language.

While being far from fluent, she was, with Little Flower and Spring Blossom's help, just learning to put together a learned jumble of words, into understandable simple sentences.

As she strained to listen to her adoptive parents, she would catch familiar words. *Pretty Buffalo Hair*, her Comanche name she heard put forth frequently, by both Little Flower and Gray Wolf. She also now recognized, and could distinguish, the names, Spring Blossom, Stone Fist, and Running Eagle.

One of the new words that she had recently learned through numerous, simple conversations with Spring Blossom, was the word *marry*. Spring Blossom had poured her heart out, and made crystal clear to Pretty Buffalo Hair, her desire to marry the warrior, Stone Fist.

The practice of presenting to the father of the potential bride, a gift of *horses*, was a topic frequently discussed between the two sisters, Spring Blossom and *Pretty Buffalo Hair*.

She could hardly wait to tell Spring Blossom of what she thought was Gray Wolf's decision, to accept Stone Fist's gift of horses.

As hard as she tried to concentrate, Mandy could not grasp, or understand the gist of the conversation between Gray Wolf and Little Flower, when the names Running Eagle and *Pretty Buffalo Hair*, were said together.

Little Flower and Gray Wolf were continuing their conversation. Gray Wolf spoke; "I agree Little Flower, it is time that our son, Running Eagle move to his own tepee. I think that this talk about a romance between Running Eagle and *Pretty Buffalo Hair*, is the wishful thinking of a loving mother."

Once again, Mandy heard her Indian name, *Pretty Buffalo Hair*, and that of Running Eagle, mentioned together, in the same sentence, her name and his, mentioned, one right after the other. Mandy continued to listen. The words were flowing much too fast for her to interpret.

When Little Flower rose, and walked over to her sleeping robes, Mandy's last thought, before she too went to bed, oh how I wish I knew what they were saying about Running Eagle and me.

****

Now that the women had set up the new encampment, and were constantly working, butchering and tanning hides, in the evening and at night, the young women were too exhausted to fraternize with the braves.

Running Eagle, who was used to being lavished with female attention and sexual favors from the unmarried women, was becoming increasingly frustrated. Those women who usually eagerly welcomed, or often sought, clandestine rendezvous with the handsome, eligible bachelor, were either too tired, or were forced by their mothers to get plenty of rest, so that they would be fresh for the next day's hard-labor.

Having repaired their weapons, and replaced those that were beyond repair, Running Eagle and Stone Fist were beginning to become restless, and bored.

Despite the enormous amount of work still to be done, following the successful hunt, the thought of assisting the belabored women was never a consideration. Butchering, tanning, sewing, cooking, was women's work.

The two friends decided to get away, to leave the village for a few days. As they sat preparing for their sojourn, Running Eagle began to speak to Stone Fist, of his four days without female companionship; "My sack is becoming heavy with seed, I am worried that this hiatus, this time when the women seek only sleep and rest, will result in the return of unwanted, embarrassing, dreams that lead to the unwanted, embarrassing spillage of my seed. Do you not have this problem?"

Stone Fist set down his quiver of arrows; "Running Eagle, I do not understand. Why does your sack retain overflowing seed? I empty mine regularly using my white slave girl as a receptacle. Why don't you do the same with your black slave girl?"

The black girl, "Pretty Buffalo Hair is not my slave. She is my sister." Stone Fist did not question Running Eagle's explanation. Instead he offered what he considered a reasonable, logical solution; "My friend you are welcome to use my slave, the white girl that your sister Pretty Buffalo Hair calls "Bee-kee"."

"I thank you for your offer my brother. By the time we return, I hope it will not be necessary. Our young women should be finished with the tanning, and will be eager to share their bodies, with the two of us. After all, according to my mother's assessment, we two are at the top of the list, of the still available, most eligible of the band's bachelors."

Stone Fist stood, "I am afraid my friend, and brother of my soon to be wife, my eligible bachelor days are over". Running Eagle had a confused look on his face. He waited patiently for Stone Fist to continue. "This morning Gray Wolf accepted my gift of horses. When we return, I will marry Spring Blossom, your sister."

Running Eagle was delighted. Grinning from ear to ear, hardly able to suppress a shout of joy, he embraced his boyhood friend, in a warm bear-hug. He held Stone Fist at arm's length, stepped back, and in a solemn voice proclaimed, "I welcome you to the family...brother!"

****

On the fifth day following the great buffalo hunt, the trio of the women of Gray Wolf's tepee, after attending to their routine chores, went together down to the creek for what they anticipated, would be the final day of tanning the animal hides.

On this the last day, the gooey mixture of buffalo brains and liver had been fully absorbed into the fabric of the hide. Little Flower and Spring Blossom, each grabbed opposing ends of a dry hide. They then began to draw the hide back and forth around the thick trunk of a tree.

Pretty Buffalo Hair, first relieved Little Flower, who in turn after fifteen minutes of rest, relieved Spring Blossom, who in turn after resting, relieved Pretty Buffalo Hair.

This monotonous process, continued until the last hide, was folded, placed on a travois and taken to Gray Wolf's tepee.

****

The next day, following Running Eagle and Stone Fists departure, Little Flower, Spring Blossom and Pretty Buffalo Hair, were joined by the women of Stone Fist's lodge, his mother Quite One, his grandmother, Hen's Teeth, and Stone Fist's white captive, Bee-kee.

The women's task was to construct two new tepees. One to be occupied by Stone Fist and his wife Spring Blossom, the other to ostensibly be the bachelor tepee of Running Eagle.

It was agreed that Quite One, Hen" s Teeth and the white slave Bee-keep, would remain in the old tepee, Stone Fist and his new wife, Spring Blossom would begin their new life in a new tepee.

Sixteen buffalo hides were selected. Eight buffalo hides for each tepee. To bind the hides together, the women divided themselves into to two working groups.

For strategic reasons aimed at establishing future domestic tranquility, Little Flower placed her daughter Spring Blossom with her new in-laws, Quite One, and Hen's teeth. Mandy was elated when she saw that Becky would be working with her, and with Little Flower.

Rebecca's spirits soared, when Spring Blossom walked over to join Quite One, and Hen's Teeth, Stone Fist's mother, and grandmother. When Hen's teeth pushed her towards Little Flower and Mandy, Rebecca hastily and willingly complied. The prospect of having the opportunity to talk at length with Mandy was to her, absolutely exhilarating.

Little Flower gave a welcoming smile to the obviously still frightened, shy white girl. She once again noted how much these two girls, physically resembled one another. Other than the difference in their skin-color and in the texture, and the color of their hair, these two could truly be sisters.

Little Flower tore her eyes away from staring at the white girl, she turned and spoke to her adopted daughter; "Pretty Buffalo Hair, take your friend and together, select enough strong strands of thread to securely join the hides together."

****

Becky looked on in amazement and incredulity, as Mandy rose. Did Mandy actually understand the gibberish spewing forth from this savage's mouth?

Mandy took Becky by the arm. The black girl, dressed in a soft doeskin, ankle length dress, with thick black braids framing her beautiful face, and her equally beautiful white friend, walked hand in hand, towards the numerous racks of long strands of dried, and drying, buffalo sinew.

Once they were far enough away from the other women, so that they would not be overheard — not that any of the Indian women would have understood English — Becky began talking rapidly; "Mandy, did you really understand what that heathen, ignorant, savage was saying? To her surprise, Mandy answered in a harsh, reproachful voice. "Little Flower; Her name is Little Flower. Little Flower is not a savage."

"Mandy, what's wrong with you, what are you saying? These people, if you can call them people, are all heathen savages. Mandy, how could you think otherwise?" She wiped away the tears that had welled up in her eyes. "That huge savage animal, raped me!"

Mandy was visibly moved by the depth, and by the passion and hurt, that she heard in Becky's voice. "I'm so sorry Becky. I didn't mean to sound so, so insensitive. The name of the brave that raped you is Stone Fist."

"When I told Little Flower of Stone Fist's violating you, she was not at all surprised. In fact, she did not regard his actions as an attack, she viewed his actions as Stone Fist's right. The right of any warrior, his prerogative as to how he treats his captive women."

"As heartless as that sounds, the more that I thought about her words, I couldn't help but remember the way that the white masters at Rosewood, your grandfather Artimas, your father Henry, your uncle *Robert*, and your brother Jesse, abused its' female slaves. How they abused my family."

Rebecca could not believe what she was hearing. Her best friend Mandy, her only link to a sane civilization, seemed to be condoning what that savage beast, what was his name…Stone Fist, what Stone Fist had done to her.

While Mandy certainly was not justifying, or condoning what that savage did to her, it sounded as if based upon her life as a slave, and Mandy's family's history with the Billings' men, their white Masters, she appears to be saying that what Stone Fist did to me, was understandable.

Rebecca stepped back and stared at her friend. She had assumed that Mandy too, had suffered the same degrading experience. That Mandy had been degraded, raped by one, or by both of the male inhabitants, of Gray Wolf's Lodge.

Rebecca asked in a barely audible whisper; "Mandy, have you ever been raped…either at the Rosewood Plantation, or here in this God forsaken wilderness?"

For a moment, Mandy was confused. What was Becky asking? Surely, she knew that if such a horrific act had ever occurred, she would have confided in her best friend.

"No Becky, I personally have not been raped. I, as I am sure you were, until Stone Fists, I am still a virgin."

"Back at Rosewood, my mother spoke to me, as did all of the slave mothers did with their daughters, of the more than likely event that the white Massas' would make you lie down with them. Slave girls were told not to resist. That we were the Massas' property and they could do whatever they wanted to do."

Rebecca asked; "Mandy why weren't you molested? Mandy everyone said that you were, if not the prettiest, you were one of the prettiest slave girls on the plantation."

Mandy took the dried strands of sinew from Rebecca's hands. She looked directly into her friends, innocent, bright blue eyes.

Rebecca with a curious expression on her face, looked into Mandy's eyes. She was awaiting an answer to what she considered, her very reasonable question.

"I don't know why I haven't been raped while living as a slave in the lodge of Gray Wolf".

"I suspect that there are two primary reasons. First Gray Wolf is very much in love with his wife, Little Flower. Not only does Gray Wolf love his wife, it is evident to all who see them together, that he respects Little Flower.

"As far as their son, Running Eagle, is concerned, I honestly don't know why he has not had his way with me".

"At first, I lived in constant fear, wondering if and when he would rape me. Now I admit, I wonder, if I have been spared because he simply does not find me to be an attractive, desirable, woman".

"In any event my being raped by either of the men of Gray Wolf's Lodge is now moot".

"Little Flower asked Gray Wolf to make me a member of their family, to adopt me. Gray Wolf agreed, gave me an Indian name, and welcomed me, as a member of his family."

Mandy hesitated, then, as if she had just this very moment, decided to unburden her mind, she took a deep breath and sighed.

"The reason that I was not molested by the white men, or for that matter, the black men at Rosewood, is because the Master of Rosewood, Henry Billings your father, had threatened to horse-whip, any man that dared to touch my mother Ruth, his mistress, or Ruth's daughter, Mandy".

"And although he never acknowledged it, everyone, including your mother Margaret, knew that Ruth my mother, and Henry's mistress', that Ruth's daughter Mandy, was the biological daughter of your father, Henry Billings".

Rebecca stood stark still, dumbfounded, confused. Mandy took Becky's hands in her own. Once again, she looked deeply into her eyes. Tears were welling up in both Becky and Mandy's eyes; "Becky we share the same blood. We have the same father".

"Becky we are really, and truly, in every sense of the word, we are sisters."

****

Little Flower had joined Spring Blossom's group. The four women were sorting out which of the hides, would be best suited to serve as the outer walls, for the two tepees.

Pretty Buffalo Head and the white slave girl, had returned. The white slave girl was leading a dog drawn travois. The mobile platform was filled with all manner of thread. Thick, buffalo, antelope, and Elk sinew would be used in the construction of the two new tepees.

Both groups of women set about the task of erecting what they envisioned would be two new, magnificent dwellings, the lodge of Running Eagle, and the lodge of Stone Fist.

****

Running Eagle was determined to make this last, bachelor foray with his best friend, memorable. As they sat smoking and reminiscing before their fire, retelling tales of their exploits and adventures as boys, then as young warriors, they turned their heads in unison, at the ferocious growl of a mountain lion.

Running Eagle looked to his friend; "Stone Fist before you settle down into the responsible life of a married man, I would like for the two of us together, to experience one last adventure. Something that will require the courage and the skill of the People's finest hunters."

Stone Fist spoke, his words solidified that he and his best friend Running Eagle, were of the same mind; "We both hear the screams, the shrieks and the sounds of the Puma. Your thoughts and mine as one my brother. Do we finally hunt the Puma; hunt the one who hunts so skillfully at night? Hunt the night hunter, not merely track him during daylight, but hunt him when he is the hunter, hunt the Puma at night".

Running Eagle reached for his bow and his quiver of arrows. "We will follow the scream and the sounds of the great cat, as he pursues his dinner".

****

The two tepees stood straight, and tall among their neighboring structures. Little Flower and Quite One, the matriarchs of the two respective families, which would through the children of Stone Fist and Spring Blossom, be united by blood, stood together, admiring their work.

In a soft voice, in fitting with her name, Quite One spoke; "We have done well. These dwellings will resist the might and the fury of the whirling wind, and the drenching, soaking wet of the driving rain."

Little Flower smiled, "Ahh, the comforts, the couches and the bedding are so soft and inviting." With a knowing glance and a wink aimed at Quite One, Little Flower smiled and remarked; "Stone Fist and Spring Blossom, will be so comfortable that they will only interrupt their love, long enough to eat, and to answer the call of nature."

Little Flower was delighted and surprised, at the Quite One's words; "Little Flower must be getting old. Do you not remember when comfort was never a consideration, when your man touched you? How your heart skipped at just the thought of his touch?"

Little Flower chuckled, "after the passage of many winters with my husband, Gray Wolf's touch, when I am working, instead of thrilling me, sometimes annoys me." That same touch when we are snuggled in our comfortable bedding, under our warm blankets, is still desired and welcomed. Our youthful passion has whined, and has ripened into a steady, sturdy, comfortable, enduring love."

Quite one, who had been widowed for many winters, dropped her head and in a soft reverent voice mumbled; "It is as it should be. It is as the Great Spirit planned. It is the Sacred Circle of Life."

The restrictions that had existed on the movement of Man-dee, the black captive girl, in the eyes of the people, did not apply to "Pretty Buffalo Hair', daughter of Gray Wolf and Little Flower.

Other than being restricted by Rebecca's work, tasks assigned by Quite One, and by Hen's Teeth, Mandy was free to visit her friend, Stone Fist's white captive.

Pretty Buffalo Hair, and the white captive, the one you call "Eebi tseena puis", were assigned the task of digging the cooking pits in the two tepees.

After they had dug the pits, and gathered the stones for the linings, the two sisters, ironically, the white girl now a slave, and the black girl free, sat in the center of Running Eagle's new home, digging slots around the pit, for the placement of the peripheral stones.

Mandy and Rebecca were eager to use this opportunity, this alone time, to talk, to catch-up. Rebecca looked at Mandy with wonder and admiration in her eyes, "I can't believe it, you actually speak their language. You understand what these savages are saying."

"Since we were little girls, I've always known that you were a gifted, a fantastic student. But this…learning their language in less than two months, is remarkable."

Mandy blushed at the compliment, and the sincere, genuine praise from Rebecca, "Your only partially correct, although I've come to understand most of the conversations, I still cannot speak the language. I have to learn…if we are going to escape, and return to civilization, we have to learn to understand and speak the language."

Rebecca bristled, "I don't want to learn their language. Anything that that horrible, old toothless woman thinks, does, or says is abhorrent to me."

"Becky, I've grown fond of Little Flower and Spring Blossom. I know that they are fond of me. They trust me. Gray Wolf has given me a meaningful Comanche name; "*Pretty Buffalo Hair*". Rebecca was intrigued. She attempted to repeat the three strange alien sounding words.

"*Pretty Buffalo Hair*, what does it mean?" *pretty* means pretty, beautiful; *buffalo* is the word for buffalo, and *hair means* hair."

"The name *Pretty Buffalo Hair* was Gray Wolf's attempt to give me a name with meaning, something that the People could relate to. He said that my thick, but not straight hair reminds him of the woolly hair of the buffalo."

"At Little Flower's request, Gray Wolf made me a member of his family."

"Little Flower, did not petition Gray Wolf on my behalf because she liked my hair, she did it because, through my hard work, and respect that I showed for her way of life, I had gained her trust and her respect."

"Becky, our only hope of escape is to get these people to trust us. We have to show respect for their ways, work hard, make an effort to understand their language."

"Mandy, he raped… Mandy held up her hand, "Stop Becky. What Stone Fist did to you was wrong, it was despicable…but it's done. It can't be undone. Get over it. Our survival is dependent upon it"

"While we're here, don't call me Mandy. While we're here, call me *Pretty Buffalo Hair.* Becky, we have to assimilate. We have to gain their trust. That's our only hope for escape."

Rebecca was dubious, skeptical. For a brief moment Rebecca wondered, was Mandy, no, was *Pretty Buffalo Hair*, siding with these savages? Has her loyalty shifted?

As quickly as these thoughts had entered her mind, they were rejected. Rebecca felt ashamed that she had for a moment, for a second, doubted Mandy's commitment to their escape from this nightmare.

She remembered the speech. The emotional cathartic speech, that flowed, like molten lava, from the lips of her life-long friend, her beloved sister, Mandy. The truth of their shared paternity, the words that her sister had held-in for years, and had dared not utter, even to her, her best friend. "Becky you and I, we are in every sense of the word, truly sisters."

As they lined the pit with the stones, Pretty Buffalo Hair nostalgically spoke of the clandestine Sunday sessions that they had held back at the Rosewood Plantation.

"Miss Leary and I would sit and talk at the creek, each Sunday waiting for you to return from town, after the family had attended church.

I remember once, after she had repeatedly tried to impress upon me the innate intelligence, the strength, and the accomplishments of blacks throughout history, by rehashing "Othello's status as a 16th century, commanding general of a white man's army.

I recall pointing out to her that Othello wasn't real. That he was a fictional character, during another era, long since past, conceived of and created in the mind of William Shakespeare, a white man."

"Undaunted, Miss Leary continued, by telling me of the activities, the exploits of a Mr. Frederick Douglass, a Negro, a former slave who had escaped to the North, and was now a brilliant orator, a true champion of the Negro cause".

After chronicling Mr. Douglass' life, she asked, was I not impressed with his life, and with what he had thus far accomplished, and was continuing to work for, the abolition of slavery, and the freeing of his people?"

"I remember setting quietly. Miss Leary asked if I had heard her, did I understand. In a soft voice, non-convincing voice, I assured Miss Leary that I understood. She could tell by the lack of conviction in my voice, that I had left something unsaid. Miss Leary asked; "Mandy, you say you're impressed by Mr. Douglass, yet your demeanor, your less than enthusiastic response, leaves me to believe that there is something that you are not saying. What is it…what's troubling you?"

When I sat there in silence, not speaking, Miss Leary insisted, "Mandy what I have told you is the absolute truth, Mr. Frederick Douglass is a great man, a great black man. I have never lied to you...don't you believe me?"

"I will never forget what happened during the next hour." Rebecca stared into the soft brown eyes of her sister, breathlessly she asked; "Mandy what happened? What happened...what did you say...what did she say? What happened between you and Miss Leary?"

"I assured Miss Leary that I believed her. That I trusted and believed everything that she had taught the two of us. My lack of enthusiasm was not skepticism, but was indeed based on reality. Mr. Douglass, despite his brilliance as an orator, overcoming being born a slave, when all is said and done, he is still doing what slaves do." Miss Leary looked puzzled.

"Mr. Frederick Douglass, although his English is superb, his diction precise, his vocabulary limitless, Mr. Douglass, when it comes down to it, is just another black man, begging the white man for his freedom".

"The only difference is that Mr. Douglass' begging the white man is done with correct grammar, using hundred-dollar words". I truly respect and admire Mr. Douglass' accomplishments".

"But when all is said and done, Mr. Douglass, as is the most wretched black-slave field-hand, is still asking, pleading, begging, the white man for his dignity, for his freedom."

"Miss Leary, what would excite and inspire me, would be to hear of a black man who didn't just beg and plead to be free. What would excite and inspire me would be, a black man who fought for, and then took and defended his freedom."

It was then Miss Leary's turn to be silent. After a few moments of uncomfortable silence, she rose from the grass, walked over to her book bag, and handed me a volume entitled, "A Recent History of South East Africa".

Before I could open the book, Miss Leary began to speak, she told me a truly remarkable story. She told me of a black man, Shaka Zulu, who had in the historical context, recently died. Shaka Zulu, she explained, was actually the king, the emperor of a large, wealthy country in Africa, Zululand.

Miss Leary shared with me historical accounts of this great Warrior King, Shaka Zulu. Of how Shaka, by his intellect, his display of skill and his knowledge of military tactics, denied the white man's attempt to steal his people's land, and the subsequent enslavement of the Zulu People.

Miss Leary told of Shaka's subsequent assassination, September 22, 1828, just thirty-six years ago.

"Becky these Indians remind me of that Warrior King, Shaka Zulu. This culture makes me think of the culture and the lifestyle of my African Ancestors. Right here in America, we have white men trying to take the land from the indigenous population, the Indians. Don't you see Becky, it's the same thing that happened in Africa."

"Becky can't you see how I can relate? I see Gray Wolf, Running Eagle and Stone Fist as the Shaka-Zulus of America. Native men of color, rising up, standing up to resist the taking of their ancestral lands by the interloper, the white man. The white man is no nobler, no braver than the black men of Africa, no more noble or braver than these red men here in America. What they take, they take by the sheer force of numbers, and through their access to and utilization of modern weaponry, the gun"

"I get it Becky, I know what Running Eagle, Stone Fist, and all of these people are fighting for. Becky, I'm beginning to develop a real understanding, a bond with these noble people. They're fighting to retain their land, their dignity, and their freedom."

Rebecca was silent. Once again, as she had just moments ago thought, and then had immediately dismissed, Rebecca wondered, was Man...no, was *Pretty Buffalo Hair*, beginning to convert, was she siding with these savages?

****

Stone Fist loosed two arrows into the throat of the huge cat. Running Eagle slumped at the foot of the tree.

Stone Fist pulled Running Eagle's knife from the chest of the slain puma. He wiped the knife in the grass, removing the blood and the clinging tissue. Sheepishly, holding the knife by its blade, Stone Fist handed the weapon to Running Eagle.

"My brother, please forgive my clumsiness. The sound of my approach, my stepping on that twig, alerted the puma, and thwarted the accuracy of your lance thrust. I was at fault for your having to fight for your life with the knife."

Running Eagle accepted the knife; "Unlike the eyes of the owl and the puma, our eyes cannot penetrate the dark. That is why we choose to hunt during the day, with the aid of light provided by father sun. There is no fault to forgive. Together, we made the decision to hunt the puma at night. If there is fault, it is ours to share."

Stone Fists grabbed the long tail of the big cat, and dragged the dead animal to the feet of Running Eagle; "Our slave women, your black captive, and my white captive, can make two pair of fine moccasins from this hide."

Running Eagle rose and while examining the slain animal spoke, "the black girl Man-dee, is no longer my captive slave. She is no longer Man-dee, she is now Pretty Buffalo Hair, she is the adopted daughter of Gray Wolf and Little Flower. She is my sister. Pretty Buffalo Hair is the adopted sister of Spring Blossom and Running Eagle.

Stone Fist did not question, he accepted without doubt or reservation, Running Eagle's pronouncement as a statement of fact.

"It is good that the black girl has been judged as one who is worthy of becoming one of the People. The white girl has not. The slow dimwitted one that my grandmother has named, *"Eebi tseenapuis"*, the white slave girl that I thought would lessen the work of the women of my lodge, barely works enough to justify the food that she eats."

"When I take her to my blankets, she cries, she is as stiff as a fresh buffalo hide that has been left overnight, neglected and untreated." Running Eagle asked, "if she is unpleasant and unskilled at doing those things that a woman does to please a man, why do you take her to your sleeping robes?"

Stone Fist looked with puzzled, confused eyes at his friend, "Running Eagle, you know that it has always been so. When we do battle with our enemies, the Pawnee, the Tonkawa, we occasionally pay a price for our victories, through the loss of valiant Comanche Warriors. Captured children grow up to be strong Comanche Warriors, captive women, serviced by strong Comanche Warriors, give birth to future Comanche Warriors, replacing those who were lost in battle."

"It is the duty of the People's warriors, it is yours as well as it is mine, to have as many sons as the Great Spirit permits." Running Eagle did not respond. Stone Fist asked, "before Gray Wolf adopted Pretty Buffalo Hair, was she as skillful at pleasing a man, as I have heard she is, in performing the many work tasks that make-up a woman's work?"

Running Eagle spoke, "neither I nor did my father, have the opportunity to judge Pretty Buffalo Hair's skills under the sleeping robes."

Although Stone Fist found his friend's statement to be odd, he refrained from commenting.

"How deeply did the puma claw your chest?" Running Eagle gingerly ran his fingers over the tracks of the three parallel fresh scars, the wounds inflicted by the big cat. "Luckily the puma's weight was not behind the blow."

"At first light, let us remove from the puma, his fine pelt. I will also remove his claws and carry them in my medicine bag. The claw will be a constant reminder, not to hunt puma in the dark. Let the coyotes feast upon the carcass."

As the sun began to arise on the eastern horizon, Stone Fist left his sleeping robe, and shook the arm of Running Eagle. Running Eagle groaned in pain.

Stone Fist looked at his friend's face. Running Eagle's face was flushed. Stone Fist placed his open hand onto Running Eagle's forehead. Alarmed, he pulled his hand away. His friend's forehead was hot. He removed the buffalo robe from Running Eagles' chest. The grooves, the edges of the claw scars, that the huge cat had inflicted, were swollen. A purplish, foul smelling fluid was oozing from the wounds.

Stone Fist began to shout, "Running Eagle, can you hear me, speak to me."
Running Eagle was looking directly at Stone Fist's face, yet there was not a glimmer of recognition in his eyes.

Pieces of the inner-surface of the buffalo robe, had stuck to the edges of the scars. When Stone Fist attempted to separate the robe from his friend's body, Running Eagle groaned, and in a hushed whisper, attempted to speak.

Stone Fist placed his ear to Running Eagle's parched dry lips, although not certain, he thought he heard Running Eagle mumble some sort of nonsense, gibberish, a sound or a word that he was not familiar with, he thought Running Eagle, in his delirium had mumbled, "*Man-dee*".

With his knife, Stone Fist hastily chopped two long branches from the tree from which the puma had pounced upon prong-horned antelope.

Utilizing his sleeping robe as the weight-bearing centerpiece, he fashioned a travois. Stone Fist attached the poles of the travois to Running Eagle's pony.
He carefully placed his delirious friend onto the travois, mounted his pony, and at a steady pace turned towards the village.

The great cat, slain by the thrusts of Running Eagle's lance, and hunting knife, the dead puma surrounded by, and now infested with hordes of flies lay, rotting under the relentless hot sun.

****

Little Flower, Spring Blossom, and Pretty Buffalo Hair, the women of Gray Wolf's Lodge, were seated around the tepee's large cooking pit. Little Flower was delicately embroidering Spring Blossom's, white doeskin wedding dress, with delicate, intricate quillwork.

Mandy was impressed with the dexterity and the seamstress' skill of her adopted mother. Little Flower was using a two-thread sewing technique. The design was that of four dyed green, symmetrical triangles, surrounding a blue sapphire colored stone. The four triangles were all of the same size, two above and two below the beautiful, sparkling stone.

The apex of the triangles immediately below and above the rock, pointed to the gem. The base of the two remaining triangles, sat approximately ⅓ of an inch from the base of the two triangles that pointed to the sparkling blue gem. The hem and the sleeves of the dress were beautifully fringed.

As Mandy watched the dexterity and skill of Little Flower, she thought of her recent conversation with Rebecca. Rebecca had referred to the Indians as "ignorant, heathen, savages". She wished that Rebecca were here, here with these real people. These real, amiable, innately intelligent, talented people.

She wanted Rebecca to see and to marvel at the four perfectly symmetrical isosceles triangles that Little Flower had created from dyed quills. She wanted to remind Rebecca of how they had both struggled with and complained about those "stupid", really difficult geometry lessons that Miss Leary insisted that they sit through.

Little Flower looked up from her quillwork. A radiant, knowing smile had spread across the face of Pretty Buffalo Hair. "My daughter, what is it that amuses you?"

"It was of no importance mother. I was thinking that the dress that you are creating is truly, the most beautiful dress that I have ever seen. Your creation would impress, and would please both Euclid and Pythagoras."

Little Flower and Spring Blossom exchanged glances, then without uttering a word, they resumed their work. Both women had become accustomed to hearing Pretty Buffalo Hair, on occasion, revert to injecting one or two of those strange sounding words of the black-tribe tongue, into an otherwise perfectly civilized conversation.

Spring Blossom was assembling and sewing together the soft, white doeskin cuts, that when joined together would be her wedding moccasins. Pretty Buffalo Hair was in the process of dying the crushed bird quills that would decorate the bride's moccasins. Head down, peering into the bowl of quills, she asked of no one in particular, in a shy, subdued voice, "when will Running Eagle, then as if it were an afterthought, she quickly added…and Stone Fist return?"

Spring Blossom gave her mother a conspiratorial wink, aahh, my sister, so there is some truth in our mother's observations. Prior to your becoming his sister, you were looking at Running Eagle with the moon-struck look, that a woman looks upon a man whose sleeping robes she wishes to share.

Pretty Buffalo Hair was flustered, she raised her head and sheepishly stammered, "I grow anxious for their return. I miss my brother's gentle smile."

Pretty Buffalo Hair lowered her head and concentrated on dying the quills. Little Flower gave Spring Blossom a furtive glance; "It is good that your feelings are those concerns of a sister for her brother. The feelings between a man and a woman that Spring Blossom suggests are forbidden between brother and sister."

Mandy gasped, the spoon that she had been stirring the mixture of quills and dye, dropped from her hand. Her face had taken on a look of forlorn despair. She wiped a tear from her eye.

Spring Blossom and Little Flower looked at each other, and then to Pretty Buffalo Hair's surprise, they began to giggle and to laugh. "Forgive us my daughter, my words though true, do not apply to you and Running Eagle."

Mandy looked confused; "You are the adoptive daughter of Gray Wolf and Little Flower. You are not of Running Eagles blood. You did not play and fight as children growing up." Marriage between Running Eagle and Pretty Buffalo Hair is not forbidden."

Spring Blossom chimed in, "If Running Eagle shares Pretty Buffalo Hair's feelings, our father Gray Wolf's pony herd will be greatly increased. He will be pleased."

****

"Talks Too Much", one of the youths assigned to watching the band's herd of ponies, flung open the flap of Stone Fist's new tepee. "Little Flower, Spring Blossom, you must come quickly, hurry."

Little Flower placed Spring Blossom's wedding dress onto one of the adjacent couches, "What is it? Why has Talks Too Much disturbed work?"

The boy, gasping for breath, blurted out, "Stone Fist approaches, pulling a travois. Running Eagle is hurt."

Little Flower spoke firmly and steadily, to the excited boy, "Go bring our holy man, He Who Speaks to Ghosts, to the tepee of Gray Wolf. Hurry!" The three women ran from the tepee.

****

Running Eagle lay moaning, thrashing about on his sleeping robes. Gray Wolf and Little Flower were anxiously standing apart from the Shaman and his patient, their son.

Stone Fist and Spring Blossom stood next to Running Eagle's parents. Stone Fists kept repeating, over and over, "He was fine last night. Three scars, from the claws of the puma. Three scars that neither Running Eagle nor did I, think to be serious.

Three ugly scars ran across Running Eagle's chest. The flesh surrounding the scars was purplish, and swollen. The wounds were suppurating, pus a foul smelling erudite, was oozing from the wounds.

Mandy stood alone silently, near the entrance of the tepee. She watched as the medicine man, He Who Speaks to Ghosts, was preparing to apply a bulky poultice to the wound.

Mandy watched in horror, as He Who Speaks to Ghosts, removed multiple leaves from his mouth. The "shaman", by chewing the leaves and mixing them with his saliva, had ground the leaves into a paste. He liberally spread the paste onto a poultice, which with Gray Wolf's assistance, he tied around the body of Running Eagle.

It took all of Mandy's self control, to refrain from rushing over to Running Eagle, and tearing the filthy cloth from his body. She wanted desperately to hold him in her arms, and to nurse him back to good health. Wisely, Mandy did not interfere.

Running Eagle lay upon the robes, he began to shiver, his teeth began to chatter. The "Holy-Man", placed two buffalo robes over Running Eagle, he then pulled a rattle from his parfleche, and began to circle his patient, dancing and chanting in a soft monotone.

After four complete circles, He Who Speaks To Ghosts spoke to Little Flower; "An evil spirit riding on the claws of the puma, entered Running Eagle's body. The fever was the result of the heated battle between the evil spirit, and the courageous spirit within their son."

Little Flower was told by the shaman, that the evil spirit could be weakened, coaxed out of Running Eagle's body, by the changing of the poultice every hour during this first day, the critical day. The paste, applied to the mature pads of the Prickly Pear Cactus, will help to draw out the evil spirit, and will bring down Running Eagle's soaring fever.

He Who Speaks To Ghosts, in order to control the burning fever ordered that Running Eagle's limbs and face be continually bathed with cool water.

Little Flower asked of the shaman, if Running Eagle should be forced to take nourishment. The "Shaman/Holy-Man", gave instructions to force Running Eagle, at frequent intervals, to drink the bitter draughts of the tea made from the bark of the Sassafras Tree. He insisted that this be done, even if she had to pry his clenched teeth apart.

The Shaman-He Who Speaks To Ghosts; The Father-Gray Wolf; and Stone Fist, Running Eagle's best friend, left the tepee and the care of Running Eagle, to the Women of Gray Wolf's Lodge.

****

At first Mandy stood silently watching as Little Flower and Spring Blossom bathed Running Eagle's forehead and his arms and legs, with cool water.

"Come my daughter, if Running Eagle is to live, he needs our help". Hearing those words, spoken so succinctly by his mother Little Flower, in a controlled, non-emotional voice, galvanized Mandy into action.

The bowl that held the cool water in which the multiple compresses were immersed, was empty. Although she was reticent to leave Running Eagle, as every nerve and muscle in her body, screamed for her to be by his side, Mandy grabbed the empty water paunches, and hurried to the creek.

****

When she returned to the lodge, Mandy saw Little Flower about to remove the poultice that the shaman had wrapped around Running Eagle's chest. Little Flower discarded the soiled poultice. Mandy hurriedly refilled the empty bowl with fresh cool water.

Running Eagle's eyelids were half open. Little Flower could feel the heat radiating from her son's feverish body. He groaned.

Spring Blossom, who had been bathing her brother's legs and feet, was at the water bowl, wringing-out her now warm compress, "What is he saying mother…does his words have meaning?"

Little Flower placed her ear next to her son's lips, attempting to understand his feeble groans … *"Mahn-dee". Man-dee*, was he calling for his adopted, black sister, instead of for his mother?

For a fleeting instant, Little Flower felt betrayed. She looked over at her adopted daughter. Pretty Buffalo Hair's huge beautiful brown eyes were staring at Running Eagle. Tears were streaming down her cheeks.

When her eyes and the eyes of Little Flower met, Pretty Buffalo Hair, quickly averted her glance, grabbed the now empty water paunches, and fled from the lodge.

Little Flower smiled. Little Flower thought it is as it should be. Her son, the man, the warrior Running Eagle, in his pain and delirium, did not cry out as a child would, for his mother, he called for his woman.

The distraught mother cradled her son's feverish head in her hands, and speaking in a soft loving voice to her son, she whispered; "It is as it should be."

Prior to retiring for the night, Little Flower made arrangements with the boy called, "Talks Too Much", for he and his friends, to bring cool water to the tepee continuously, throughout the long night.

Pretty Buffalo Hair, had insisted on being the first of the three women who would attend to the patient, during the night. She assured Little Flower that she would strictly adhere to the shaman's instructions. And that if Running Eagle's condition worsened, Pretty Buffalo Hair would immediately alert Little Flower.

Little Flower, lay restlessly beside her husband. Gray Wolf's staccato snores were the prevailing sounds within the tepee. Spring Blossom and Stone Fist had moved to the new lodge of Stone Fist.

Despite her earlier misgiving, the chewing of leaves; the making of a paste with leaves and saliva, then placing the concoction into the bandage, Pretty Buffalo Hair — as she had promised Little Flower — had religiously adhered to the shaman's instructions.

Yesterday, Pretty Buffalo Hair had studiously and meticulously watched Little Flower as she prepared and changed Running Eagle's poultice.

Little Flower had not hesitated when she relinquished his care and placed her son's life, into the hands of the black girl. This extraordinary girl that she had grown to love more and more, with each passing day.

It was not until she saw the faint rays of the rising sun, filtering through the smoke hole of the tepee that Little Flower inwardly relaxed.

She had watched as Pretty Buffalo Hair, wiped her son's body with the cooling water. She had watched as Pretty Buffalo Hair, would periodically, gently place her fingers, then her lips on Running Eagle's brow.

Little Flower recalled her son's barely audible, feverish word, "*Mahn-dee*", though not being an overly religious Little Flower was convinced that the "Great Spirit", had sent "Man-dee…Pretty Buffalo Hair to save her son, and to fill the void in Running Eagle's life.

Little Flower snuggled up against her husband and gave thanks. Gray Wolf turned to his wife; "What did you say woman…were you speaking to me?"

Little Flower kissed her husband's cheek; "Go back to sleep my husband. I was merely speaking to the Great Spirit. Gray Wolf asked; "Did the Great Spirit speak to you? Little Flower smiled, snuggled up to Gray Wolf's back and whispered in his ear, "No the Great Spirit did not speak in words to me. The Great Spirit placed in my head and in my heart, his silent message."

Gray Wolf grunted, "what does that mean?" Little Flower playfully nibbled his ear and whispered…our son will recover. It is, as it should be."
****

It was on the third night, following Running Eagle's injury, that the fever broke. Running Eagle's slow, gradual, return to conscientiousness was reminiscent of what he had experienced, during his vision quest, seven summers ago.

He felt as if he was emerging from a fog. There was the sensation of a cool and gentle hand on his forehead. Long Eagle struggled to open his eyes. As his vision cleared, he saw an apparition, Pretty Buffalo Hair was there. Her back was towards her.

In the dim light given off by the still glowing embers in the cooking pit, Pretty Buffalo Hair appeared to him to be a vision. When she began to turn towards him, Running Eagle quickly shut his eyes.

Pretty Buffalo Hair gently placed her lips on his forehead. Running Eagle's weakened body, betrayed him. Pretty Buffalo Hair's moist full, lips upon his forehead, was to Running Eagle, the most sexually erotic sensation that he had ever experienced.

To his dismay and chagrin, the towel that had been covering his loins, seemed to come alive of its' own accord. The towel draped over Running Eagle's genitals, rose into the air. His sudden, unwanted, involuntary erection, resembled a flag, raised at full staff.

Pretty Buffalo Hair was startled. Her eyes traveled from his mid-section to his face. When their eyes met and held, they both felt a spark, like a sudden bolt of lightning that starts an out of control fire on the dry prairie, had arched between them.

Pretty Buffalo Hair broke the eye contact, "Little Flower, he is awake. Running Eagle has come back to us."
****

One week following the recovery of Running Eagle, Stone Fist and Spring Blossom were married.

Rebecca viewed the marriage of Stone Fist and Spring Blossom, as truly, a God's send. Since his return from that fateful hunting trip with Running Eagle, the hunt where both he and Running Eagle, had thought that the wound inflicted by big cat, to be a minor scratch. The *minor* scratch had almost cost Running Eagle his life.

Stone Fist, either because he was worried and concerned for his friend's health, or perhaps because he now spent most of his free time with Spring Blossom, had completely ignored Rebecca.

Rebecca's life amongst the "heathen savages" had become tolerable. She missed Mandy. For the past week, she had not been able to sit and to talk to her friend, her only link to civilization.

Mandy had no time for her. Instead of their spending time together to devise a plan of escape, Mandy was devoting all of her time and energy to nursing Running Eagle.

Without the support of Mandy, Rebecca found herself, day by day, becoming resigned to her status as a captive slave, and to her fractious relationship with her principal tormentor, Hen's Teeth.

Her plight had forced her to come to examine and to appreciate the difference between the form of slavery practiced by the Indians, the slaves were acquired as booty, as the "spoils-of-war", and the slavery that she had, by pure chance of her birth, profited from and supported her entire life.

While lying wide awake on her sleeping robes, Rebecca had prayed and lamented in her mind, over and over again; "Why, why me...why did this happen to me...why am I a slave?

****

One night while she tossed and turned, every muscle in her body aching and sore, as if in answer to her question, Rebecca experienced a simple, yet monumental, moment of clarity.

She reasoned that no one, if it were under his or her control, would choose to be born a slave. The fact that she was born white, a member of the Southern Aristocracy, as opposed to being born a black slave, was something she concluded, that just happened. She as an entity had absolutely no say in the matter.

As Miss Leary had often said, which until now Rebecca had not given too much thought, "There are a lot of choices that we humans are capable of making in our lives, however, in the history of man, no one has ever been, nor will anyone yet to be born ever be, able to choose who will be their biological parents".

The fact that she had been born, a member of the white Southern Aristocracy was a random event. She had absolutely no control as to who, or what, her parents would be.

Instead of her parents being the Master and Mistress of Rosewood, fate could have deemed that she be born the daughter of two of Rosewood's black field hands.

For the Indians, while their captive slaves were property, the Indian's slaves could look forward to freedom by eventually assimilating, and being accepted as a member of the tribe.

After having been a slave, Rebecca had come to the conclusion, the realization that all forms of slavery are wrong.

More importantly Rebecca had come to believe that while all forms of slavery are wrong, the South's practice of that "Peculiar Institution", the dehumanizing, legal enslavement of blacks, from cradle to grave, which meant that for all intents and purposes, the enslavement of the blacks, and of their progeny, was forever, was not only wrong, it was truly barbaric.

Rebecca vowed that when, not if, but when she and Mandy escaped, and returned to civilization, that she and her sister would do everything that they could to end slavery.

****

Rebecca was confident that it was just a matter of time before she and Mandy would have time to plan and execute their escape. Her optimism was fueled by her common sense assessment, Running Eagle would either recover or he would die from his wounds.

Rebecca failed to allow for what to her was literally the unthinkable. Rebecca did not consider the possibility that love, the deep enduring love felt between a man and a woman, would develop between Mandy and Running Eagle.

****

Running Eagle loved Pretty Buffalo Hair. Little Flower knew it, Spring Blossom knew it, even Gray Wolf and Stone Fist, as a result of confidences shared with their wives, while snuggled together in their sleeping robes, knew it. Pretty Buffalo Hair suspected.

In fact, for three weeks following his recovery, the two of them Running Eagle and Pretty Buffalo were constantly in each other's company. The village was awash with gossip. The prevailing opinion amongst the people was, that Pretty Buffalo Hair and Running Eagle were in love.

Excluding Rebecca, the only person in the village that did not know that Running Eagle loved Pretty Buffalo Hair, was Running Eagle.

Pretty Buffalo Hair was delighted when Little Flower asked that she assist Running Eagle, in his move from Gray Wolf's lodge, to his newly constructed bachelor tepee.

Pretty Buffalo Hair relished with joy and with great anticipation, looked forward to performing the women's work of Running Eagle's lodge. She took pleasure in gathering the kindling, in cooking his meals, in the sewing and repairing of his few articles of clothing.

Most of all, Pretty Buffalo Hair, looked forward to and enjoyed, the time that she and Running Eagle spent together after the completion of the morning meal. That's when she would lovingly, comb and braid Running Eagle's long flowing pitch-black, ebony tresses.

Running Eagle was confused. He knew without a doubt that he felt a tremendous, almost overwhelming desire for this woman, Pretty Buffalo Hair.

He was certain that the People's taboo forbidding intimate relations between brother and sister, for him and Pretty Buffalo Hair, did not apply.

This he found out, after having asked, and been told by the holy man, "He Who Speaks To Ghosts", that it was so.

Before speaking of this with the holy man, Running Eagle had been assured by the holy man, that their conversation would be viewed by him as being sacred, and would not be repeated or be told to anyone.

Running Eagle was not a virgin, in fact he was far from it. It was during his fifteenth summer, that he had first experienced, and enjoyed the special warmth that washes over one's body, and indeed over the mind, after finding sexual release in the arms of a woman.

Running Eagle, seven summers ago, during his fifteenth summer, had loss his virginity to "Willows Breath", the plain, sad, mournful widow, who at that time, was just about to see the passing of her thirty-second summer.

It was during her twenty-sixth summer, that Willows Breath, the mother of two small children — one who had just completed two summers, and the other still a suckling infant — that Willows Breath's husband had been killed while on an unsuccessful raid against the Pawnee.

Since his first coupling, seven long winters ago, when the then boy of fifteen summers, Little Beaver, who after his vision became known as the warrior, Running Eagle, had since on a regular basis, shared his sleeping robes, with a long list of comely females.

Most of that bevy of eager females had one goal in mind; they were vying to make the handsome young warrior Running Eagle, their future husband.

When Running Eagle moved from his father's lodge, into his own dwelling, there was an immediate stream of nightly, female-visitors. Running Eagle graciously, politely, rebuffed their advances.

The young women of the village were at first surprised and bewildered by his uncharacteristic, unexpected reaction to their overtures.

Many of the girls who were now being rejected, had in the past, prior to Running Eagle's recent illness, been enthusiastically, literally welcomed by him, with open arms.

It didn't take long for the rumor to circulate, that Running Eagle was infatuated with the beautiful black girl, Pretty Buffalo Hair.

Running Eagle was perplexed. The one female that he longed to share his sleeping robes with, Pretty Buffalo Hair, in the night, did not come to him.

****

Mandy was convinced that her intense feelings towards Running Eagle were reciprocated. She knew in her heart, she was absolutely sure, that the longing, the sexual tension that she felt when she was with him, touching him, was also being felt by Running Eagle.

As hard as she tried, Mandy could not fathom a single reason as to why, Running Eagle, the man of her dreams, had not made a single conscience, attempt to court her, had not held her hand, had not kissed her.

A societal cultural divide was exacerbating Mandy and Running Eagle's mutual frustrations.

Mandy, although being black, had been raised to accept and to respect the cultural customs and values, of the white man's culture.

Mandy had been taught, and firmly believed, that in matters of love, the male was supposed to make the first overt move, the man should be the aggressor.

Conversely, in the society in which Running Eagle was raised, if a woman was interested in a man, it was perfectly acceptable, and expected, that she would make that known to the man.

In the world of the red man, the practice of a single women uninvited, and unannounced, showing up at night at the bachelor's tepee, and her discreet departure before daybreak, was not scandalous, it was expected, it was the culture's accepted norm.

After four days of frustrated suffering, Pretty Buffalo Hair sought out for her advice, her adopted sister and friend, Spring Blossom. "My sister, I wish to share with you an intimate secret. I am in love with Running Eagle."

Spring Blossom smiled, "My sister, that you are in love with Running Eagle, and that Running Eagle is in love with you, is no secret. It is a fact that is instantly known to anyone who sees the two of you together."

Pretty Buffalo Hair looked surprised, but definitely neither annoyed nor angry at Spring Blossom's response to her declaration. "If it is true that Running Eagle loves me as I love him, why has he not made that known to me? Why has he not held my hand? Why has he not kissed me? Why has he not told me of his love? Why has he not made the first move?"

"My sister, how in such a short time, you have learned the Comanche tongue, is truly remarkable. In time, just as you have come to know and understand our words, you will come to know and understand our customs."

"It would be a dishonor for a Comanche brave, to court a woman in the manner that a cur pursues a bitch in heat. It is the responsibility of the woman to, as you say, to move first."

"The Warrior will either accept our reject the woman. For a warrior to be rejected by a woman weakens and can destroy his medicine. It would bring dishonor to the warrior. Without strong medicine, a warrior will be killed in battle."

'Pretty Buffalo Hair, if you love and want Running Eagle as your husband, you must, initiate the romance. You must, as you say, move first."

That night, after finishing her work, Pretty Buffalo Hair, as usual bathed in the creek. She thought about drying her body with a towel, which had been earlier in the day, submerged in sweet smelling rose water.

As she reached for the towel, she stopped instinctively she decided to refrain from having her body exude artificial scents.

When she returned to the tepee, she noticed the rhythmic movement of Gray Wolf and Little Flower's sleeping robes.

Pretty Buffalo Hair, undid the plaited strands of her two thick braids. She ran her hands through her curly, semi-straight hair. Her hair, freed of all restraints, framed her face. Her soft brown eyes sparkled in the dwindling light of the fire.

Pretty Buffalo Hair slipped into her prettiest doeskin dress, she stepped into her moccasins, and quietly left the tepee.

Little Flower had inconspicuously watched Pretty Buffalo Hair dress, and leave the tepee. Gray Wolf was snoring softly. He had drifted off into that blissful state of post-sexual release.

Little Flower gently shook her husband's shoulder. Gray Wolf grumbled, "What is it woman…Go to sleep…Let me rest." Little Flower responded, "My husband you will soon be the recipient of several fine ponies, but it will cost you the loss of yet another daughter."

Gray Wolf grumbled, "What are you saying? Go to sleep Little Flower, we can talk in the morning."

Little Flower rolled over, before she fell asleep, she whispered, "It is as it should be."

****

Mandy sheepishly, timidly, rapped on the entrance flap of Running Eagle's tepee. Running Eagle who was seated, morosely staring into the dying embers of his cooking fire, in a dejected voice spoke, "Enter". Mandy took three steps into the tepee, and stood silent, immobile, head lowered.

Running Eagle, his heart beat racing, stood, took two steps towards Pretty Buffalo Hair, opened his arms and said, "Welcome to my lodge...welcome to my heart."

Mandy lay expectant, trembling in Running Eagle's arms. Running Eagle suppressed a tremble of his own. He recalled how he had felt when, as a boy he had picked up a baby bird that had fallen from its' nest, and injured its' wing.

He remembered the overwhelming protective feeling that had swept over him, as he gazed down at that fragile, defenseless creature, trembling in his hand.

Running Eagle, not a particularly spiritual man, thanked the Great Spirit for this moment, for bringing this beautiful, strong, courageous woman to him.

Running Eagle marveled at his good fortune. He deduced from the way that she was trembling, that she was showing her love, while valiantly trying to hide her apprehension, her fear of the unknown.

Running Eagle gently lowered his head and lightly brushed his lips across Mandy's soft, moist, full lips. Mandy shuddered and threw her arms around the young warrior's neck.

His right hand found the hem of her dress. Both he and Mandy sat up. He pulled the dress over her head. Mandy kicked off her moccasins. Their lips met, and Running Eagle gently lowered her head, to the sleeping robes.

Mandy lay before him, nude. Her pert young mahogany colored breast, round and firm with dark brown nipples, beaconed Running Eagle's hungry lips. His mouth was flitting from each of the perfectly symmetrical mounds, like a hungry bee gathering nectar from a field of prairie wild flowers.

Running Eagle's hands slid down Pretty Buffalo Hair's sides to her smooth, slim exquisite waist. An audible gasp escaped his lips, and he swallowed hard when his eyes locked onto the little tuft of brown hair, that sat like a sentry, either guarding, or pointing to the gates of paradise.

Running Eagle's heart was furiously pounding, pumping hot blood, blood that filled and expanded his throbbing, manhood. He felt his organ expanding beneath his breechclout, to its full impressive length, and width.

Her breasts felt hot and wonderful pressed against his bare chest.

He began to deliver soft kisses across her lips, and then over her closed eyelids, then upon her nose. He slowly and sensually, moved his lips, his tongue, down the length of her body.

As Running Eagle tenderly kissed and licked her pulsating body, Mandy's body began to shiver with delight and with anticipated ecstasy.

While his tongue explored the crevice encasing her belly button Running Eagle's thumbs and forefingers were gently squeezing and rolling her nipples. Sensual waves of pleasure cascaded up and down Mandy's spine"

"Ah yes...yes", she whispered, as her pelvis gyrated, as her body responded to his tongue, as he licked then, as his lips sucked, the tender bud tucked in at the apex of the entrance to her now wet, pulsating, vagina.

As he had suspected — but to Running Eagle, it certainly did not matter — Pretty Buffalo Hair had never lain with a man. Although his body was crying out for release, he was determined, committed to ensuring that Pretty Buffalo Hair's first time experiencing the joys of sex, would for her, be pleasurable, memorable, and satisfying.

His hands began to slowly move over her thighs. At first, he stroked her flanks, then with the palm of his hand, he applied amazingly gentle, light pressure to the mound of curly soft hair that framed and surrounded her vagina. Mandy's head was swimming. Her only thoughts were of these hitherto unknown, sensual sensations that were flooding through her body.

Running Eagle, gently inserted his finger into her wet opening. Mandy threw her head back and begin to moan, "Please...please...ah." He thrust his finger deep up inside of her, she gasped as she felt a sharp pain, when his finger ruptured the membrane, caused by the deep penetration of his finger.

Mandy's eyes flew open. Running Eagle glimpsed a fleeting look of confusion and fear that briefly flickered in her beautiful brown eyes.

He looked deeply into her eyes, with his finger still inside her body. He lovingly whispered, "shush…shush, that brief pain was the pain of your awakening. It announced that you are open, ready to receive my body. Ready for us both to give to each other the full pleasures of our love.

He slowly withdrew his finger from her body. He held his finger up for her to see. His finger was wet and sticky with blood. Her blood covered his finger. Running Eagle stood, he brought his bloody finger to his lips, he then gently kissed the front, and then the back of his finger. Running Eagle then placed his wet finger, covered with her blood and secretions, into his mouth, and sucked it clean.

To her surprise, instead of being repulsed by his actions, Mandy found his display to be highly erotic.

She started to ask him why he had withdrawn his finger, when before she could speak, Running Eagle suddenly dropped his breechclout to the floor, and kicked it away from his body. He stood before her, the embodiment of masculinity.

Running Eagle's body was magnificent. Not an ounce of extraneous fat was visible on his lean, athletic, bronzed frame. His well-defined, understated muscled rib cage, tapered down into a narrow waist. His stomach was flat and hard. His legs were long, well-muscled, and firm.

When he turned to face her, the sight that burned in her retina, took her breath away. His male member was thick and long. A fleeting thought flashed across Mandy's mind. The way that his sex organ protruded from his body, the angle of the turgid staff, reminded her of the length, and the rigidity of the horn, that extended from the mythical Unicorn's head.

Running Eagle held his manhood in his right hand, and advanced towards the recumbent girl.

He leaned over, and as if her hand had a mind of its own, Mandy, shyly tentatively took him in her hand. She gently squeezed and caressed his pulsating manhood.

As she had seen him do to his finger, Mandy lovingly, tenderly kissed his organ, and then she took him into her mouth. Into the sweet wet, warm cavern of her mouth. With her full, perfect red lips surrounding his manhood, she gently sucked and caressed with her tongue, his pulsating, engorged organ.

Her uninhibited, unexpected, bold aggressive gesture almost caused Running Eagle to prematurely shoot his seed into her mouth, down her throat, into the very center of her being.

Instead, he gritted his teeth and disengaged himself from her mouth. In a hoarse voice he managed to whisper; "Not now my love, we will have a lifetime to satisfy all of our needs. Now is my time, the time for me to make you my love. My woman, my Pretty Buffalo Hair…my *Mahn-dee*."

Running Eagle knelled beside her, she was cognizant of one of his knees spreading her legs apart, he leaned over and kissed her passionately.

His tongue explored the warm wet haven of her mouth. Their eager tongues met and intertwined. Running Eagle sucked her tongue into his mouth.

Mandy with all of her heart and soul, wanted this man, this viral, strong, aboriginal warrior. She desperately wanted to feel his essence, his strength throbbing within the deepest recesses of her body.

Yet when she felt his hardness pressed against her stomach, her body tensed. Involuntarily she had anticipated pain. Pain that she had felt, when he had inserted his finger into her body.

Running Eagle with his left hand gently separated the lips of her vagina. With his right hand, he guided his engorged, throbbing organ to its target. Still passionately sucking her tongue, he plunged his organ into Mandy's quivering, eager, receptive, body.

She gasped, instead of pain she was filled with a sensual shock when she felt Running Eagle enter her. As he began to rhythmically move within her, the sensation that she felt was ecstatic, euphoria. Once again with his tongue, he probed between her lips, flicking in and out.

As he plunged deeper and deeper inside her, her gasps became muted whimpers. Running Eagle placed his hands under her buttocks and lifted her closer his body. Mandy locked her legs around his waist, she thrust her pelvis towards his pounding member.

His hands swept around her hips to her buttocks, and lifted her even closer, the two lover's bellies were colliding, slapping together rhythmically, like hands beating a drum.

Running Eagle's ears were roaring now as his heartbeat quickened. He was overwhelmed with pleasure, yet he still held back, wanting to make Pretty Buffalo Hair's first time, unforgettable.

Their mouths, as was their bodies, was locked in a desperate, hungry kiss. Running Eagle's body stilled for just a moment, their lips separated.

Mandy's breath was stolen away as the most ultimate of pleasures coursed through her. She clung to him as his body quivered against hers.

"I love you Mahn-dee," he whispered against Mandy's lips, then he plunged deep inside her as she arched toward him.

As one, they released their pent-up emotions, the two lovers reached the peak of sexual release, together.

Overcome with emotion, physically, and spiritually, too spent and exhausted to move or to speak, they lay together, locked in each other's arms.

Reluctantly, Running Eagle withdrew his deflating manhood, from the warmest, most comforting portal, that he had ever visited or had imagined existed. Totally spent, he collapsed beside Mandy.

To stunned to speak, still basking in the afterglow, brought on by the wondrous feelings resulting from their lovemaking, Mandy snuggled closer to Running Eagle.

"That was wonderful," Mandy murmured as she laid her cheek against his chest. She listened to the rapid pounding of Running Eagle's heart. She was very much aware of how hard his heart was pounding, as was hers.

At that precise moment in time, Mandy knew without doubt, that the synchronized beating of this man's heart with hers, foretold of their future lives together.

She picked up his hand, and placed it between her heaving breasts. She placed her hand over his and whispered, "Me too my love…me too".

****

Pretty Buffalo Hair's nightly visits to the tepee of Running Eagle, were well known and accepted by the People. That these two young people were very much in love was evident to all who saw them together.

The question, the topic of gossip throughout the village, was why did these two not marry?

The day following their first night of blissful sex, Running Eagle had made his wishes to marry Pretty Buffalo Hair, known to Gray Wolf. Gray Wolf neither consented nor, did he deny his son's request.

Three days following the first of Pretty Buffalo Hair's nightly visits to Running Eagle's tepee, the nightly visits, changed. On the fourth day, instead of repeating the pattern of the visit, that ended with Pretty Buffalo Hair, quietly before dawn, returning to the tepee of Gray Wolf, the nocturnal interludes became nightly sleepovers.

To the people, it made sense. It was well known that Little Flower, Pretty Buffalo Hair's adopted mother, had decreed that Pretty Buffalo Hair was to perform the women's work required of Running Eagle's tepee.

The prevailing opinion of the people was, that Pretty Buffalo Hair could get an early start on doing the arduous routine work, if she simply spent the night with Running Eagle, whose dwelling was her responsibility. It made sense.

When Gray Wolf neither voiced approval or disapproval, Running Eagle decided to follow the People's age-old custom. He left two of his finest ponies outside of Gray Wolf's tepee.

The next morning both Running Eagle and Pretty Buffalo Hair, eagerly looked to Gray Wolf's tepee, the two ponies stood were Running Eagle had tethered them, the previous evening.

Gray Wolf had not accepted the gift. He had not given his permission for the marriage of Running Eagle and Pretty Buffalo Hair.

****

Gray Wolf sat at council, leisurely smoking with his peers. The main topic of discussion at the council meeting was planning for the annual summer gathering of the multiple bands, and clans, that comprised the Comanche Nation.

At the conclusion of the meeting, as the council members filed out of Old Wise One's tepee, Old Wise One's, the venerable, titular leader of the band, requested that Gray Wolf and He Who Speaks To Ghosts, remain.

When they had all once again smoked the pipe, Old Wise One spoke; "Gray Wolf my friend, I would speak with you. First, I speak to you as your chief, not as your friend, but as chief of our village.

Each day that you decline to give Running Eagle an answer to his request to marry Pretty Buffalo hair, his offering of ponies increases by two additional ponies each passing of the sun. Three times now the sun has set, since Running Eagle asked you for permission to wed Pretty Buffalo Hair".

"I nor do — nodding his head towards the seated holy man — He Who Speaks To Ghosts, wish to influence or to question your decision. That is not to say that we don't have an opinion. What we do ask is that you make a decision".

"We can no longer tolerate the droppings of a growing herd of ponies in the midst of the village. The people are complaining".

He Who Speaks To Ghosts sat stoically listening; occasionally he would nod his head, indicating his agreement with the Chief's words.

Gray Wolf looked somberly at his two closest friends. "Your speaking to me of your concerns about the cleanliness of the village, needed to be said."

Then with a crinkle at the corners of his eyes that quickly disappeared — but had been noticed by the Shaman —, he resumed speaking, "I do not believe that you my friends, would deny me as much time as needed to make my decision."

Old Wise One wandered if he had gone too far did Gray Wolf think that he was intruding in his personal affairs? He Who Speaks To Ghosts suppressed a smile. Old Wise One sat in gloomy despair with his head down, trying to think of a diplomatic response.

Before the chief could speak, Gray Wolf placed his hands on his knees and began to laugh uproariously.

"Old Wise One, my lifetime friend I am not at all displeased with your words. It is I who must apologize for my thoughtlessness."

The consequences of leaving eight ponies overnight in the middle of the village, was predictable. Everyone knows that the Great Spirit's design is that, all living things that eat, at some point, have to relieve themselves."

Then as if he smelled a foul odor, Gray Wolf frowned, and pinched his nostril together. The three men laughed.

"Long before he asked, Little Flower and I…Little Flower knew, and told me, that Running Eagle would ask for permission to marry Pretty Buffalo Hair. That is when, his gaze shifted to the holy man, I sought the counsel of He Who Speaks To Ghosts."

"He Who Speaks To Ghosts' words, gave me assurance that Running Eagle and Pretty Buffalo Hair's union was not taboo. The Holy Man's words removed my only concern. When Running Eagle asked, though I did not at the time speak my consent, and have not spoken of this but to Little Flower, my answer was then and has always been, yes".

A look of relief, of satisfaction spread across the faces of both Chief Old Wise One, and the Shaman/Holy Man, He Who Speaks To Ghosts."

For the first time, He Who Speaks To Ghosts spoke; "Gray Wolf, because of my dedication and service to the spirit world, I have never known the love between a man and a woman, a man and his son. I ask, what is the reason that you choose to delay the happiness of these two young people, the children that you love."

Gray Wolf sat silently, puffing the communal pipe. He blew out a thin cloud of pungent blue smoke he then passed the pipe to his friend and chief, Old Wise One.

"I, as do the rest of my family, my wife Little Flower, my daughter, Spring Blossom, and even my new son-in-law, Stone Fist, we all approve of and support the marriage of Running Eagle and Pretty Buffalo Hair."

"I have two reasons for delaying the giving of my permission. The first is too bestowing in my son the knowledge that the prudent man is the man with patience. That something's and especially someone, someone as special as Pretty Buffalo Hair, is worth waiting for."

"Old Wise One passed the pipe to He Who Speaks To Ghosts; "My friend Gray Wolf speaks with the wisdom of a true loving husband and father. The only fault that I find with his words is that I did not speak them first."

He Who Speaks To Ghosts spoke; "I am curious my friend, you say you had two reasons. What is the second?"

Gray Wolf gave Old Wise One conspiratorial glance. "I enjoy teasing my son. I would never knowingly deprive him of any of life's pleasures."

"Now as it is known by the entire village, Running Eagle and Pretty Buffalo Hair, without my permission, are nightly enjoying the pleasures of marriage. Their bodies are satisfied, but still their minds are not quite at ease."

I saw no harm in, for a little while longer, teasing Running Eagle's mind, while strengthening his character."

Old Wise One and He Who Speaks To Ghosts, grunted their approval. The three old friends sat in silence, enjoying the smoke from their sacred pipe.

****

Under the omnipresent gaze of her tormentor Hen's Teeth, Rebecca was cleaning the eating utensils from the morning meal. Quite One was busy repairing a loose hem on one of Hen's Teeth's dresses.

Without warning Rebecca experienced a series of short cramps in her stomach. Hen's Teeth noticed that the white girl had stopped working and was doubled over in pain.

She walked over and with her open palm, cuffed Rebecca behind her ear. "You lazy girl, get back to work".

Rebecca fell across one of the buffalo hide couches; her dress parted showing a white thigh, streaked with blood.

Immediately, the old woman realized what was happening. The lazy white girl was starting her moon bleed. She grabbed Rebecca by the arm and pushed her out of the tepee.

Quite One had put down her sewing and asked, "mother what is wrong with the white girl, what is wrong with "*Eebi tseena puis*?"

Hen's Teeth turned to her daughter; she is having the moon bleed; her blood is contaminating the tepee. "Mother are you so old that you do not remember the woman's moon bleed"? "Do you not recall the pleasant time spent in the woman's bleeding lodge?" Without waiting for an answer swept past Hen's Teeth. Rebecca was sitting on the ground. Quite One went to her; "Come *Eebi tseena puis*, I will walk you to the woman's bleeding lodge.

Despite being a captive for over two months, Rebecca had learned but a few words of the People's language. It was not that she could not have learned, Rebecca had chosen not to learn. In her mind she equated her gaining knowledge of the heathen language, as losing her identity, of becoming one of them, of becoming "*Eebi tseena puis*, and losing forever, Rebecca Billings, daughter of Henry Billings and Margaret Billings.

As each day stretched into an interminable night, Rebecca's only solace had been the marriage of Stone Fist to Spring Blossom. She had to admit, that that savage Stone Fist seemed to adore his new wife. Since his marriage, Stone Fist had shown absolutely no interest her.

Her only regret that she associated with Stone Fist's marriage, was after he returned from the hunting trip with the gravely ill Running Eagle, she had seen very little of Mandy.

Oh, how she missed Mandy. Mandy who she now unequivocally, wholeheartedly, accepted as truly being her sister, *was* her only hope to ever return to the civilized world.

Rebecca was convinced that Mandy was being forced to attend to the needs of that tall young, stately savage, Stone Fist's best friend, Running Eagle.

Mandy had been forced to constantly, both day and night, be at that savage's beck and call, tirelessly nursing him back to good health.

Any doubts that Rebecca may have been harboring, about Mandy's commitment to escape, in her mind, had been totally dispelled.

She reasoned that any weakening of Mandy's resolve to escape this hellish nightmare, had to have been totally obliterated when her so called adoptive parents, forced her to work like a slave, a black slave providing continuous, uninterrupted nursing care for their son, Running Eagle.

Rebecca marveled at the way that Mandy had managed to cleverly worm her way into the good graces of these savages. That Mandy, her very own sister Mandy, had ingeniously, somehow, tricked them into adopting her, into trusting her.

At first, Rebecca had found it difficult to believe that Stone Fist's in-laws, his friend, Running Eagle's parents, had welcomed Mandy into their family.

Rebecca took comfort and encouragement from the fact that Mandy had gained the heathen's trust. The hard part was over, the only thing left for them, was to develop and to execute a plan of escape.

All of that "Noble Savage", nonsense that Mandy had been espousing when they had last talked, was just that, pure nonsense. Rebecca attributed Mandy having said those absurd things to her need to role-play. Thus, perpetrating a deception that they would use to allow them to escape.

Rebecca realized that her being banished to the tepee for females having their period — that's what her mother Peggy had called it her period —, was actually a blessing in disguise.

Since they were infants, she and Mandy — of course with the exception of social events when Mandy served her as her slave — had done just about everything together.

The two girls had had measles and chicken pox together. They had examined and saw their fledgling breasts burst forth at practically the same time. As pre-teens, anxious to become grown-ups, they had examined each other "down there", to see who would be the first to sprout pubic hair.

They had both matured *"down there"*, the growth of pubic hair, at practically the same time. Finally, here, during this nightmarish captivity by these savages, they had experienced the onset of menstruation together.

As she sat mending different items of apparel, Rebecca expectantly watched the entrance to the tepee. Her pulse raced with excitement, and anticipation, each time that someone entered the tepee. Each time that someone entered, it was someone other than Mandy.

At the end of her first day of her exile at the women's bleeding tepee, Mandy had not arrived. Rebecca was disappointed, but not overly concerned. She was confident that at any moment, Mandy would enter the tepee.

After four days had elapsed, Rebecca's flow had stopped. Still there was no sign of Mandy.

Rebecca began to worry. What had happened to Mandy? What had these heathens done to her sister?

When she returned to Quite One's lodge, she was greeted by Hen's Teeth. The old woman scowled, and immediately began to berate the white girl;
"Ah, *Eebi tseena puis,* the lazy white one returns." She pointed her finger at a huge pile of dirty utensils, stacked in the rear of the tepee. It's about time you returned. Look at what I have managed to save for you."

The old crone shoved Rebecca towards the dirty pottery, and shouted; *maaitu aitu.*"

Rebecca barely understood the meaning of the plethora of foreign sounding words, being shouted to her. However, one phrase, *maaitu aitu,* the words that she had heard her tormentor relentlessly scream at her since the first day of her captivity, the words *maaitu aitu,* without a doubt she knew that *maaitu aitu,* was a command that she, "get to work"!

****

After the evening meal, Rebecca, gathered together the soiled eating utensils, and took them to the creek to wash.

As she approached the water her heart began to race. An Indian maiden, was sitting on the bank, washing eating bowls. Her back was to Rebecca. She appeared to be loss in her in thoughts, lost to the world. She was softly, sweetly humming a sprightly, faintly familiar tune.

Rebecca, paused to listen, and without thinking, Rebecca started singing, putting words to the tune."

> *Oh she danced all night with a hole in her stockin'*
> *Her knees kept a-knockin'*
> *And her heels kept a-rockin'*
> *She danced all night with a hole in her stockin'*
> *She danced to the light of the moon.*
>
> *Oh Buffalo gal can you come out tonight...*

Rebecca dropped her basket, and ran towards the serene Indian woman. She stopped singing and shouted, as she began to run, Mandy...Mandy!

****

Mandy turned, and saw Becky running towards her. She jumped to her feet, she stumbled, then she ran, with open arms, towards her sister.

Rebecca and Mandy stood together, arms around each other. Both sisters were crying.

Rebecca stepped back; she was reluctant to release her sister's hands. "Mandy I've been so worried. What have they done to you? Why didn't you come to the women's bleeding lodge? I waited for you?

Mandy, did that animal, that savage Running Eagle hurt you? Did he rape you?

"Slow down Becky…take a breath. Give me a chance to answer. I want to answer all of your questions."

"First, I didn't join you at the women's bleeding lodge because I was not having my period. In answer to your question, what have they done to me, the answer is that they have done nothing to me.

They've treated me with dignity and respect, dignity and respect that I worked hard to earn."

"What was your other question…oh yes. Did Running Eagle hurt me? Did he rape me? My answers to those questions are no, he did not rape, me and no he did not hurt."

Mandy took her sister's hands in her own, she smiled and while looking deeply into her sister's bright blue eyes, she smiled and said, "Becky, Running Eagle did do something for me, he married me."

Rebecca withdrew her hands from Mandy's. She stared at Mandy. Shock, disbelief, and incredulity swept across her face, "You're married to that Indian, that craven savage?"

Then, as if she were completely oblivious to the joy and happiness radiating in Mandy's soft brown eyes, Rebecca threw her arms around her sister and began to sob, "Oh Mandy, I'm so very sorry."

Mandy disengaged herself from Rebecca, and held her at arm's length. "Becky, don't be sorry for me, be happy. I am so very, very happy. In fact, I have never in my life been as happy as I am right here, right now."

Running Eagle is the kindest, the most considerate, the most loving man, that I have ever met."

Rebecca recoiled; she turned her back to Mandy. She felt betrayed, abandoned, and completely alone. It had happened. What she had feared, but had stubbornly refused to acknowledge, had really happened. Mandy, her blood, her black sister had become, one of them.

"Mandy, what are you saying? You can't possibly think that these savages are capable of feeling love, like white people do."

"When you told me that Gray Wolf had adopted you, that they had given you some heathen Indian name, I told myself that you were merely, cleverly trying to gain their trust in order to help us escape, to return to civilization.'

Rebecca's sparkling blue eyes were now red rimmed. Tears of hopeless frustration were streaming down her cheeks.

Mandy walked over to the distraught girl. She put her arms around Rebecca's trembling shoulders. Mandy gently wiped the tears from her sister's cheeks. She placed Rebecca's head onto her shoulder. Then in a hushed but firm voice she spoke; "Becky, I love Running Eagle with all my heart and soul. I love every thing about him. I love his humor; I love his strength, his courage, and his indomitable spirit. I love the way he looks at me, the way he makes me feel."

"Running Eagle is my man, my husband, and hopefully, soon he will be the father of our children. Becky I will not go back to your world. This is my world, here with these people, here with my noble warrior, here with my man."

"I love you Becky, not just because we share the same blood, I love you in spite of the fact, that we share the same blood."

"I love you because, for whatever reason you may have had, you plucked me out of a world of ignorance. You shared with me on equal footing, next to my mother, the most important adult of my formative years, Miss Eleanor Leary."

"Little Flower asked Gray Wolf to make me a member of their family, to adopt me. Gray Wolf agreed, gave me an Indian name, and welcomed me, as a member of his family."

"I have grown to love my new mother and father Little Flower, and Gray Wolf. I love my sisters, *Eebi Tseena Puis* and Spring Blossom. But most of all, I love Running Eagle. Running Eagle is the love of my life. Running Eagle is my man."

Breathlessly the words continued to pour out of Mandy's mouth. "To me, Running Eagle is my Hercules, my Othello, and my Sahka Zulu, all combined. He is what a man should be, brave, courageous, honorable and most of all, he walks with pride and dignity. Running Eagle, is my hero, my confidant, and my lover, Running Eagle is to me the embodiment of what a man should be."

"Becky let's be honest with each other. I love you and you love me. Even before my mother and our father acknowledged that we are sisters, we loved each other as if we were sisters. Unfortunately for most of our lives, our relationship has been spent adhering to the segregationist laws and standards of Southern Society."

"At Rosewood, your love for me was that of a child for a pet, or for a favorite toy." As Rebecca was about to protest, Mandy held up her hand,
"I don't blame you, … mine for you, was influenced by a slave's love for a benevolent master who kept me out of the fields, for a master who taught me to read and to write, in violation of the law".

"A law whose sole intent and purpose was to keep an entire race of enslaved people, from learning that their enslavement was based upon a lie".

"That their wretched condition of perpetual bondage was not as they were taught, every Sunday by the black preacher, ordained and in accordance with the word, and the will of their blond, blue eyed, white God."

"You remember Becky, one of the most enlightening things that Miss Leary taught us was that "Knowledge is Power". Remember that?" A perfect example in support of what I just said was that mathematical model that she taught us."

"I'll probably get this wrong, we both know that math was never one of my strong subjects. Let's see, I think she called it an inverse function, relationship. As one variable factor increases, that same variable causes another related factor or event, to decrease."

She picked up a stick and drew a graph in the clearing.

Mandy saw that same bored, confused, expression on Rebecca's face, that she had seen when as children, Miss Leary had forced them to sit through tedious hours of mathematics lessons.

"I forgot; you were even worse at math than was I. What I'm trying to say and point-out is that we both intuitively, and intellectually knew, that the social structure of the South mandates, that when it comes to white kids and black kids growing-up together, that that particular mathematical principal, the inverse function, is certainly valid. The older we became, especially in our early teens, the farther the Southern Society, forced us apart."

"I belong here. With my husband Running Eagle, the man I love, with these people, the Comanche, this is where I belong, this is where I want to be."

"Becky, I'm not naïve. Despite my profound personal feelings, my love for Running Eagle, I realize that my decision to stay with these people, to become Comanche, is in part influenced by my being black, living in America's white society. I would like to believe that if I were white, my decision would still be the same."

"But I am not white, and none of what I just said applies to you. You Rebecca, my sister, my only living blood relative, you are white. And you have every right and every reason to want to return to your white world."

"I believe that if I ask, my husband Running Eagle, will help me return you, to your white world."

Rebecca had no intention of just accepting, unchallenged, Mandy's words, and her conclusions. "Mandy you're no longer a slave. You're free. We're no longer in the South; we're in a free-soil state. We were well on our way to a new life. The four of us, together, you and me, and Ruth, and our father, together, were about start a new life as a family in Kansas, a free state."

"That all ended when we were attacked by these savage animals. Mandy how could you even consider living amongst these beasts who killed and mutilated your mother, and our father."

"*Eebi Tseena Puis*, the Indians that attacked our wagon…, Rebecca interrupted, "that's the second time you spoke that gibberish to me, *Eebi Tseena Puis*, what does it mean. Mandy smiled, "*Eebi Tseena Puis*" is the name given to you by Hen's Teeth. It means, "Blue Wolf Eyes". Comanche names often reflect the deeds, the visions, or the physical appearance of the person."

"My Indian name is much longer than yours. It's a real mouth full, *Nananisuyake Ta?Si?Woo? Tso?Yaa*, it means Pretty Buffalo Hair."

"Running Eagle explained that that was the name that Little Flower gave me. He said that it was because the texture of my hair vaguely reminded Little Flower of the wooly hair of the buffalo. Although my hair is thicker than the People's or the whites, it was less coarse then the hair of the buffalo."

"Little Flower thinks that my slightly-woolly hair is pretty."

"You and I know that we can thank, or blame Henry Billings for the texture of my hair."

"As I was saying, the Indians that attacked our wagon, and killed my mother and our father, were Pawnee, not Comanche." Rebecca looked doubtful.

Mandy quickly added, "Oh don't misunderstand, Running Eagle, assured me that…what were his words, oh yes; "The cowardly Pawnee had arrived at the disabled wagon first, otherwise it would have been Running Eagle's raiding party that attacked and killed our people."

"I honestly can't say, I really don't know if the fact that the Indians who killed our people were not Comanche per se, that that mitigated in any way, my decision to stay with these people."

"Becky I am in total support of the Indians, all of the Indians, the Comanche, the Cheyenne, the Apaches, the Utes, all of this continent's aboriginal peoples, resist the stealing of their land, the subjugation of their people, and the ultimate destruction of their culture. Becky, I know that I can be of help."

Rebecca was frantic, wringing her hands, shaking her head from side to side.

"Mandy please…please don't do this. You're not making any sense. We need to stay together. Come with me, we've been together all of our lives. Let's escape from this hellish place together."

"You're no fighter. What do you know about fighting? How can you help these backward, primitive people?"

"You're right Becky, I can not fight nor, do I have the military planning skills of a Napoleon, of a Robert E. Lee, a Ulysses S. Grant. What I do have is knowledge, I know that no matter how courageous and fierce their warriors are in battle, that in the end they can never win".

"I know that if all of the Indian nations allied themselves into one, their combined number would be but a fraction of that of the whites. I know that the white's killing technology is vastly superior, that that who you refer to as these backward, primitive people".

"You know Becky, back at Rosewood, in the slave community, behind closed doors, and drawn curtains, people would wonder and ask each other, *"why dint da white massas wont da niggas to reed and rite. Why wud da massas whup da hide offa a nigga cauht wid a bok?"*

"The prevailing thought was that a black slave that could write, might be able to forge a pass and escape to freedom, and that the ability to read would come in handy when trying to make his way to the North".

"I, as did most of the slaves, accepted that. After all it sounded logical, it made sense. Now thanks to you Becky, I know that that explanation is a lie. I know without a doubt that it is at best, only partially true, it's basically a lie." Rebecca looked confused. "I don't understand, why thanks to me? What did I do?"

A solemn, almost reverent expression crossed Mandy's face. "Becky you remember hearing and reading, "Knowledge Is Power"? What you did for me, what you gave me, you gave me access to Miss Eleanor Leary."

Miss Leary opened my eyes and my mind. She taught, and we learned. We gained knowledge. Miss Leary gave me, an illiterate black slave girl, knowledge, she gave me power."

"That's what I can bring to these people. Knowledge of the outside world."

"Come *Eebi Tseena Puis*, it's getting dark. We had better be getting back, before Running Eagle sends out a search and rescue party.

****

Anyone who saw Running Eagle and his new wife Pretty Buffalo Hair together, within a very short period of time, within minutes, was struck by the "rightness" of these two people being together.

That they loved each other was evident and expected. The village, the world was full of young men and young women who were in love. That the Great Spirit breathed love, and even lust into the young, was as accepted as was the rising of the sun.

To the amusement of the camp still — after the passing of many sunsets following their marriage — Running Eagle and Pretty Buffalo Hair, spent most of their time, day and night, together in their tepee. One would only catch glimpses of either of the newlyweds when the call of nature, forced them to abandon their love nest.

When the couple finally emerged — their fire-making and food supplies, as well as their bodies, exhausted — they joined a jocular, teasing and amused community.

Running Eagle and Pretty Buffalo Hair heard and graciously endured, the usual jokes and innuendoes, that are heaped upon newly weds.

Little Flower watched as the women good-naturedly teased the new bride. Sweet Willow, one of the many attractive unwed women, who had actively pursued Running Eagle as a potential husband, smiling, walked over and handed Pretty Buffalo Hair, a large bowl filled with scented bear grease.

"It was my intention to give this to you before your wedding night. Before your arrival, when I shared Running Eagle's sleeping robes, I found that a generous application of this, down there, before and after made life much more comfortable."

The women that were within listening distance, chuckled. White Fawn, a strikingly attractive girl, with whom, when he was a bachelor, Running Eagle had on occasion also, shared his sleeping robes, laughed loudly.

White Fawn continued laughing after the others had ceased. Her laughter was not the laughter of good-hearted amusement; instead it was the laugh of bitter distain.

White Fawn knew when she was pursuing the handsome young warrior, that she had lots of competition.

She, as did they all, thought that Running Eagle would choose as his mate, from many of the People's beautiful young unwed women. White Fawn thought it an insult, a sign of disrespect, that Running Eagle would choose as his woman, this black captive. This slave.

Pretty Buffalo Hair accepted the bowl of bear grease. "I thank you White Fawn for your most thoughtful gift. I will use it when I comb and braid my husband's beautiful, flowing hair. Although I know that it can be used to prepare a woman to receive her man, for that use, I have no need."

The touch of my husband's hand in mine, when he looks at me, and smiles, my heart melts, filling my body with warm juices that make unnecessary, the use of artificial lubricants.

Little Flower, who had been unobserved, in the background listening, smiled.

****

That night after having enjoyed a hardy meal, Gray Wolf sat alone, smoking his pipe. Little Flower, picked up a pair of her husband's favorite leggings, sat beside him, and began the process of repairing the torn garment. Gray Wolf, lost in thought, did not acknowledge his wife's presence.

The only sounds were the crackle of the fire, and the rhythmic puffing of the contented man, smoking his pipe.

Little Flower accidentally pricked her finger with the needle. "Ouch, I guess that I'm either getting clumsy, or I'm getting old".

Gray Wolf looked fondly, lovingly at his wife, "Maybe it is both." Little Flower gave her husband a reproachful stare.

Gray Wolf was smiling, his face half hidden in the shadows; "My beautiful, graceful Little Flower, is now an old clumsy woman." He ducked his head just in time, as the leggings that she had been sewing, sailed above his head.

"Old and clumsy? I'll show you who is far from being old and clumsy." She jumped into his lap, Gray Wolf, in anticipation of her advance, had laid his pipe aside, and opened his arms to meet the charge of his not so old, not so clumsy wife.

They rolled, locked in mock battle, onto their sleeping robes. Gray Wolf held his wife's arms, pinned to the robe, stretched above her head. He looked down into her laughing beautiful black eyes. "I believe that my Little Flower still has plenty nectar for this old Gray Wolf."

He released her arms, and gently kissed her lips. Little Flower held his face between her hands. She returned his all so familiar kiss. Happy and as always, amazed at how, after all this time together, his searching probing tongue, thrilled and aroused her.

Almost as though in the absence of conscientious effort, they joined in the age-old familiar embrace of lovers.

Their love making, was deep, unhurried, and complete. They both knew what the other wanted, what they each needed. His body was as familiar to her, as hers was to him.

Instead of it being dull from countless repetitions of how they expressed their love, each thrust of his manhood, each reciprocating arching of her pelvis, was a reaffirmation, of Gray Wolf and Little Flower's feelings for each other. Each thrust, each moan, served as punctuation, certification of their love, their timeless, endless love.

After more than twenty-five winters together, after having given life to three beautiful babies, the first dying three months after her birth. After a lifetime of shared joy and suffering, Little Flower marveled and rejoiced at the fact that she still, was solidly and madly in love with this man.

****

As they lay in each other's arms enjoying that familiar, relaxing after-glow that inexorably followed their love making, Little Flower sat up, and began to, with her finger, trace circles onto Gray Wolf's broad, practically hairless chest.

"I had forgotten how wonderful it felt, for us to have time alone together. It seems like forever since it was just Gray Wolf and Little Flower, sleeping together alone, in the same lodge. She sat up, wrapped her arms tightly around her knees, and exclaimed; "It is truly a wonderful feeling".

Gray Wolf grunted, and rolled over onto his side. "My husband, now that our children have married and left our lodge, do you think as I do, of their happiness?

Gray Wolf sleepily replied; "To me they all, Running Eagle and Pretty Buffalo Hair appear to be happy. Spring Blossom and her husband Stone Fist appear to be happy. You're happy. Go to sleep Little Flower and Gray Wolf your husband too, will be happy."

Little Flower persisted. "Spring Blossom and Stone Fist obviously think that they are in love. Their being in love at this point in their relationship, is based mostly on their lust. It would be more accurate to say at this moment, right now, as in most young marriages, what they think is being in love, is in reality, could be more correctly defined as their being in lust."

Gray Wolf grumbled; "In love, in lust, it is all the same. What ever it is, we agree, they all appear to be happy…go to sleep Little Flower".

Unperturbed, Little Flower continued, it was as though she had not heard a single word that Gray Wolf had spoken; "I understand that at their age, especially in the boys, the sap is rising. Love is not the driving force that leads the men to seek the warmth found between the thighs of an available female. I admit for most who marry, as happened between us, falling in lust eventually, leads to falling in love."

"Running Eagle and Pretty Buffalo Hair are rare. Anyone who looks at them can plainly see that they are deeply in love."

"What I have seen in them is something special, something that is essential to a good marriage. If the marriage is to be good, both the man and the woman have to like each other. To like each other, not necessarily as lovers, but should like Ione another as a person."

There is no doubt that Running Eagle and Pretty Buffalo Hair, as are Spring Blossom and Stone Fist, are deeply in love. What I have seen of Running Eagle and Pretty Buffalo Hair, in addition to having fallen in love, those two are among those fortunate few, who before they fell in love, were fortunate and lucky to have first *"fallen in like"*.

Little Flower nudged her husband; Gray Wolf, do you agree…are you listening?

Instead of hearing an answer, she heard the even breathing and the steady snore, coming from her husband, the man she loved, and liked, above all others.

Little Flower kissed Gray Wolf's ear. She wrapped her arms around him, and snuggled her belly up to his back, her knees, pressed against his. They lay together, their bodies in repose, forming a perfect pair of spoons.

****

To Running Eagle, his beautiful wife seemed to excel in everything. He was amazed at how rapidly she learned and the way that she so easily, acclimated herself to an entirely new way of life.

Often Indian women, not of the People, women from other tribes, women captured in raids, found it difficult to adjust to the People's language, to the People's way of doing things.

Difficulty in doing things, the Comanche way, that they had essentially been doing, with only minor variations, all of their lives.

Running Eagle was especially pleased and impressed with how rapidly, and easily Pretty Buffalo Hair, learned the People's language.

"She Plucks Flowers", a young Pawnee woman, captured more than three winters ago, after three winters living amongst the People, could now understand what was being said, but still could not speak, in coherent sentences, the words of the People.

Running Eagle had wondered, were the people living in the white man's culture, the culture that Pretty Buffalo Hair, and her white *master/sister*, Blue Wolf Eyes came from, people of superior intelligence?

After speaking to his friend Stone Fist, who spoke only negative, derisive words about the clumsy, stupidity, of the frail white girl, Running Eagle had quickly dismissed those thoughts.

The idea that the whites, and their black slaves, lived in a superior intellectual culture, where even the downtrodden slaves, possessed superior intelligence, and had the innate ability to learn, superior to that of the Comanche, was ridiculous.

Running Eagle instead, came to embrace the more reasonable, and logical reality, that "Pretty Buffalo Hair", or "Mahn-dee", as she was known by the whites, "Pretty Buffalo Hair, his wife was a singularly gifted individual, a child blessed by the Great Spirit.

Not only had he captured, and fallen in love with this remarkable young woman, he knew with absolute certainty, that "Pretty Buffalo Hair/*Mahn-dee*", truly loved him.

Running Eagle sat smoking his pipe, his eyes riveted on his wife, as she scraped the remnants of their meal into a waste bowl. He watched the movement of her firm shapely, supple, buttocks, as the muscles quivered under her dress.

He resisted the temptation to rise, —his manhood had a mind of its own —and to take those now so familiar firm ripe melons into his eager hands.

Instead he forced his mind to think of more mundane things; His favorite pony needed brushing, he would soon need to refill his pipe, he concentrated on these tasks, trying to deflate, and to deflect the seemingly, independent mind of his insatiable organ.

"Pretty Buffalo Hair, *Mahn-dee*, come sit with me. Your husband would talk with you. Mandy neatly folded the towel that she had been using to wipe the bowls. She placed the folded towel beside the clean utensils, and walked over to the cooking pit, and sat beside her husband.

Running Eagle was having difficulty finding the words to express himself. He settled for a feeble; "Are you happy?" Mandy took the pipe from his hand, placed it onto the edge of the pit.

She took his hands into hers; "My husband, at this time, our marriage, is the happiest time of my life. I would be content and deliriously happy, if we remained as we are now, never having to leave our sleeping robes, never having to leave this lodge."

Once again, Running Eagle felt the familiar stirring, the beginning of stiffening activity beneath his breechclout. He drooped her hands and looked away.

Mandy thinking that she may have said something inappropriate — *after all the language and its' nuances were new to her* — something that had offended him, apologetically spoke; "Forgive me my husband. Running Eagle, if I have offended you… that was not my intent.

Running Eagle rose and stepped back. He realized that if he were going to have a non-sex related encounter with his wife, it would require that there be actual, physical separation, distance between them. With an effort, he managed to shift his gaze from her moist, succulent, full lips.

"*Mahn-dee*", the way that you have mastered the tongue of the Comanche, in such a short time, in less than three moons, has impressed all of the people."

"I would like to give you a gift." Mandy, her curiosity peaking, remained seated, followed him with her eyes, as he paced around the circular interior of the tepee. "My gift to you, requires that you give a gift to me."

Misinterpreting his intent, thinking that Running Eagle, at that moment was saying that he wanted her, as much as she wanted him, smiled and began to remove her dress.

Running Eagle dashed over to his wife and grasped her hands. "No, no my love, if you take off your dress, he pointed down at his breechclout, now standing out at a 45-degree angle, "his mind, will overpower, pointing to his head, this mind."

"I will forget what I was about to ask of you." "*Mahn-dee*", I want to be able to speak to you in your tongue, the black man's language."

Running Eagle held his wife's petite, strong hands in his. He looked into her soft brown eyes. "That is the gift, that I want to give to you."

"To be able to give you that gift, the gift that you must give me, is to teach me language, the black man's tongue. Will you do this for me, so that I can do that for you?"

Mandy was overcome with emotion she was filled with love, and appreciation for this man. She had noticed during the past week, that on occasion, Running Eagle he attempted to use her Christian name "Mandy", when addressing her.

Undoubtedly Little Flower had told him that her name was "Man-dee". Running Eagle had evidently practiced the, to him, odd sounding word. She had rather liked the way that he pronounced her name, "*Mahn-dee*".

No Mandy decided, she would not teach him her tongue, the black man's language. She would instead teach him a far more valuable tongue, the language of the white man.

The tongue of the white man who, with his greed, his lust for land, his guns, and by shear force of numbers, loomed as an eminent deadly threat, to his…to their way of life.

Mandy agreed to teach Running Eagle the white man's language. There and then, she began her lesson by explaining, "Though "*quid-pro-quo*", is not a part of the language currently being spoken by the white man, non the less, it will be the first phrase that I will teach to you."

Running Eagle repeated the phrase, "*quid-pro-quo*", "what does it mean?"
Mandy smiled, then in a stern no nonsense voice she said, "it means that my gift to you is not given freely, I expect something from you in return."

Running Eagle face broke into a broad grin, "I like this phrase. It is the bases of all trade".

Tell me Mahn-dee, Running Eagle asked coyly, with an amused twinkle in his obsidian, colored eyes, what is it from me, that you expect in return?"

"I want you to teach me to ride like a Comanche."

This was not the answer that Running Eagle had expected. It took him totally by surprise. His head was confused, but only for a moment.

The "head" under Running Eagles breechclout, which had been steadily rising, had been disappointed but only for a second, as Running Eagle joined Mahn-dee on their sleeping robe.

****

The next day, amid hoots and hollers, the newly weds, Running Eagle and Pretty Buffalo Hair, finally, together emerged from their tepee.

Running Eagle squeezed Pretty Buffalo Hair's hand, and trotted off towards the band's pony herd.

Pretty Buffalo Hair rapped on the entrance flap of Gray Wolf's tepee. Little Flower pushed the flap open and stepped out to greet her daughter; unable to resist, Little Flower teased, "Ah, at last, my daughter, you have decided to come out for air".

On behalf of our village, I welcome the presence amongst us, of Running Eagle, and his beautiful wife, Pretty Buffalo Hair."

Mandy at first blushed, at the light-hearted, well-intentioned insinuations. She then, with genuine reverence accepted Little Flower's recognition, that of Running Eagle and Pretty Buffalo Hair's new status as a family unit.

"I thank you my mother, for all that you have given me. First, I thank you for your kindness, then for your patience, then your love, and finally, I thank you and my father Gray Wolf, for Running Eagle."

Little Flower held her hand over her eyes as if she was shading them from the sun. Mandy noticed tears welling-up in her adopted mother/mother-in-law' eyes. Little Flower motioned for Mandy to precede her, as they both entered the dwelling.

Mandy sat on a familiar couch. Little Flower handed her a bowl filled with steaming, herbal tea. Mandy waited until Little Flower, filled a bowl for her own consumption, and joined Mandy on the couch.

"I come to ask for your help." Little Flower sat quietly, waiting for Pretty Buffalo Hair to continue." "Running Eagle, my husband — Little Flower noted that the words "my husband", were spoken as though in wondrous disbelief —, Pretty Buffalo Hair repeated — my husband has asked that I teach him the white man's language."

Seeing the puzzled expression on Little Flower's face, Mandy explained; "My husband, your son Running Eagle, knows that we must deal with the coming of the white man into the land of the Comanche. Running Eagle wisely feels that as a warrior, he would be better prepared to fight for our land, if he understood the words of the whites." I will teach him those words."

"In return, Running Eagle has agreed to teach me to ride like a Comanche."

Little Flower immediately understood the logic, and the wisdom of her son's reasoning. "Has Running Eagle spoke of this to Gray Wolf, or to Chief Thunder Cloud, or to Chief Old Wise One?"

"Although I disagree, and have told him so, my husband thinks that he may not be capable of learning the white man's language. If he cannot learn the words and their meaning, he does not want to disappoint our leaders."

"My daughter my son…your husband is wise beyond his winters. What is it that I can do to assist you?"

"As a black slave in the world of the white man, my white sister Rebecca, "*Eebi tseena puis*", "Blue Wolf Eyes", taught me to read and to write. She did this against the white man's taboo, forbidding the teaching and the learning of black slaves, to read and to write the white man's words."

"Rebecca…Blue Wolf Eyes" and I would sit, secluded, away from everyone with Miss Leary, the most wonderful white woman I have ever known. We would sit until the sun sat, learning from her."

"I believe that if we are alone, secluded, uninterrupted, I can teach Running Eagle, and he will learn the language of the white man."

"Little Flower saw the wisdom in Pretty Buffalo Hair's reasoning. She did not however, mention the obvious distractions that seclusion afforded the newlyweds.

Little Flower's thoughts were that Running Eagle, and Pretty Buffalo Hair's seemingly unquenchable lust for each other's bodies, just might reduce their time to study the white talk.

Suppressing a chuckle at her thoughts she asked, "How can I help?"
Mandy sipped her tea; "I would like your assistance in my first attempt to take down, and to relocate our lodge, on the north bank of the creek."

"Pretty Buffalo Hair, though you have learned many of the Comanche ways and learned to speak our language, in a very short time, you have still more to learn. It is our duty, Spring Blossom and I, as your closest female relatives, to help you to relocate, and to reconstruct your lodge."

As they rose to began the process of dismantling and moving Running Eagle and Pretty Buffalo Hair's tepee, Little Flower placed a restraining hand on Pretty Buffalo Hair's elbow; "My daughter, in your condition, I think you should delay learning, any thing more than the fundamental ways to sit a pony."

With a quizzical expression on her face, Pretty Buffalo Hair mused, what had Little Flower meant by, "in your condition", Mandy dismissed the thought, stood and followed Little Flower from the tepee.

When Running Eagle returned to the village, riding his favorite pony and leading two older horses by their reins. Pretty Buffalo Hair, Little Flower, and Spring Blossom had taken down the tepee, and were in the process of packing the couple's belongings.

Little Flower accepted the reins of one of the ponies. She steadied the animal, while Pretty Buffalo Hair, and Spring Blossom attached, on opposite sides of the animals, the poles of the travois.

When all was ready, Running Eagle lifted his wife onto his pony, clutched the animal's mane in his left hand, and swung himself up onto the pony's back, firmly seated behind Pretty Buffalo Hair. Little Flower handed the reins of the pony pulling the travois, to her son.

Running Eagle spoke to his mother; "Our tepee will join the others, when we move to join the summer meetings. Until then we will be camped there, he pointed towards the creek. Tell my father, Gray Wolf, Stone Fist, and our leaders that my wife "*Mahn-dee*", will be teaching me the white man's talk.

As they slowly rode from the encampment, Running Eagle reined in his pony. He lifted his wife to the ground.

Mandy ran to the entrance of the tepee that Quite One, Hen's Teeth, and their white captive, "Pale Wolf's Eyes lived.

Rebecca had been standing by the tepee, she had anxiously watched as the three women dismantled Mandy and Running Eagle's tepee. She was nearly in a state of panic, not knowing where Mandy was going, or if she would return.

Mandy, breathlessly ran up to and embraced Rebecca. "Becky, my husband and I are temporarily moving about twenty yards from the creek. I will ask him to help you escape, to help return you to your civilized world".

"When Running Eagle, hunts, I will come to visit you, Little Flower, and Spring Blossom. Becky, I love you. I have not, and never will, abandon you."

Mandy turned, and ran back to Running Eagle, who had been patiently waiting.

Once Running Eagle and Pretty Buffalo Hair reached their destination, the site where they intended to erect their tepee, the couple began the daunting task of putting the structure together.

Running Eagle had very little experience in performing this "women's work". Mandy's experience at pitching the elaborate tent consisted of her once having assisted Little Flower and Spring Blossom.

Their energetic, but feeble, efforts had resulted in a comedy of errors. Twice the four poles forming the base of the tepee, were raised and latched together, by Running Eagle with broad, rawhide bindings.

When Running Eagle and Pretty Buffalo Hair, began to wrap the heavy buffalo hides around the poles, the poles collapsed, crumbled to the ground.

When Little Flower and Spring Blossom arrived, they found Running Eagle and Little Flower, laughing and struggling under the weight of the heavy hides.

Little Flower and Spring Blossom called out; "Running Eagle, Pretty Buffalo Hair, we bring meat and bread for your meal".

Mandy, still laughing peaked out from beneath the heavy hides that enveloped them. "Little Flower, Spring Blossom, my mother and my sister, you are always, and always will be welcome in our lodge."

"As you can see, neither my husband nor do I, have the requisite skill to erect a sturdy dwelling." Little Flower, had anticipated and suspected that these two, during their surreal period of being "*totally, blindly, madly in love*", would not be up to the real challenge of setting up a tepee.

"The three of us working together, a mother and her two daughters, will have your tepee firmly standing, very shortly".

After the four family members, were comfortably seated in the solidly constructed, majestically standing tepee, and had eaten a hardy meal, Pretty Buffalo Hair, once again thanked Spring Blossom, and Little Flower for their help.

Spring Blossom, spoke; "It is I, my sister who thanks you". Confused, Pretty Buffalo Hair asked; "Why does my sister thank me, when it is clearly I who should thank you and our mother for your help."

Spring Blossom sat in silence for a moment, as if gathering her thoughts, "With my husband, Stone Fist, away leading a raiding party against the Utes, keeping busy, frees my mind from constantly worrying about his safety".

"For that, I thank both you and my brother Running Eagle, for your inexperience, and his clumsy, tepee set-up, ineptitude."

Running Eagle in a mock display of machismo, pointed his finger at his expanded chest and proclaimed, "I Running Eagle, son of Gray Wolf, am a fierce Comanche Warrior."

He bent at the waist, balled up his hands into fists and growled. "Grrrr...grrr. It would be unseemly for such a mighty warrior as I, to be proficient at women's work. The making of tepees, is after all, the work of women."

Spring Blossom, followed by Pretty Buffalo Hair, threw pillows, at the mighty Comanche Warrior's head".

Little Flower, smiled at the antics of her children, as her three grown up adult children, "played".

After Little Flower and Spring Blossom returned to the village, Running Eagle and Pretty Buffalo Hair, despite their fatigue, the newly weds, as they had been doing at each and every opportunity, day and night, made mad passionate love.

As they lay pressed together, entwined on their sleeping robes, basking in the afterglow of their lovemaking, Mandy whispered, "Tomorrow, if it pleases my husband, I think will be a good day for us to began our lessons".

"Each day, until the sun is directly over our heads, I will teach you the white man's words. This we will do."

"After our second meal, until the sun sets, we will review what was taught during the morning hours".

Running Eagle murmured, "*Mahn-dee,* as they had discussed, as the lessons progressed, they would speak the white talk whenever possible, *Mahn-dee,* you have not left time for me to teach you to ride like a Comanche."

"That time will come. My husband now is not the right time for those lessons."

Without further explanation, Pretty Buffalo Hair, pressed her body against the back of Running Eagle. Within minutes her breathing became rhythmic, and regular.

Pulling her arms tightly around his waist, Running Eagle, looking forward to tomorrow, began to drift off into sleep. Before crossing the sleep threshold, he remembered his wife's declaration, "now is not the right time for those lessons", with sleep rapidly approaching, he wondered, what had "*Mahn-dee*", meant, when she said, "Now is not the right time for those lessons".

****

Running Eagle proved to be a determined, energetic student. Mandy had insisted that during their time away from the village that they speak only the white man's talk.

When Running Eagle was having difficulty with an English word, phrase or concept, and seemed ready to abandon the project, he had asked "*Mahn-dee*" how she had managed, in such a short time, to learn Comanche. Mandy had resounded; "I simply had no choice, and I was fortunate to have been under the tutelage of Little Flower".

"Everyone around me spoke nothing but Comanche. Becky and I are the only ones in the village that speak the white man's talk. Becky and I were separated. There was no one that I could communicate with".

Initially, Little Flower and I communicated using sign. After a week of pantomime, Little Flower would no longer acknowledge my crude gestures, my signs. Instead she interpreted the gestures, and translated them into Comanche words, phrases and sentences."

"Little Flower insisted that Spring Blossom, when communicating with me follow her example."

"If I wanted food, Little Flower would not give me food, until and unless I asked for it in the language of the People. If I wanted a blanket, I had to make my need known by speaking the words of the People".

"In addition to my sincere desire to learn the People's language, Little Flower made it absolutely clear, that my every day survival, my acceptance by the People, was in large part dependent upon my learning the language of the People".

"I think it worked well, therefore while we are here, once I have taught you a white man's word, a phrase a sentence, we will talk to each other using, only the white man's words."

She smiled mischievously, "Running Eagle, I want you to listen closely to these white man's words; "I want you", repeat them to me." Running Eagle slowly repeated the strange alien words; "*I wont you.*" A stern expression crossed over Mandy face.

"No that is not correct, that is not what I said. In fact, what you just said, my love has the opposite meaning of what you intended to say."

Running Eagle concentrated; He tried again, "*I wont you...*that is what I heard that is what you said. "Listen again carefully, I said "I want you. That is what I want to hear you say to me, each and every day of our lives."

Instead my love, the white man's words that you are saying, "*I won't you*", has an entirely different meaning. "I want you; I will always want you. I will never not, want you. The words you said "*I wont you*", is the opposite of what you meant to say, "I want you".

"As much as it pains me my love, until you say what you mean, using the white man's words, our love making is in serious jeopardy."

With Mandy's guidance, Running Eagle immediately corrected his miss use of the two white man words "want" and "**won't**".

To Mandy this little episode served as an effective example of "English-grammar antonyms". To Running Eagle, his correctly stating of this phrase, "I want you", to *Mahn-dee*, was essential for the continuation of his love life.

****

Their days and nights passed quickly. At first Running Eagle found it difficult, and frustrating to speak only the white man's words. His initial objection, to him was perfectly logical. On the tenth day of their intense lessons, he asked, in Comanche; *Mahn-dee*; "How am I to know if I speak the right word, if you do not permit me to ask, in the tongue of the People?"

Mandy did not answer. She ignored his question. Thinking that she had not heard, Running Eagle, once again repeated his question. Mandy, who was sitting within arm's reach of her husband, stared at him with a blank look on her face.

Running Eagle, realizing that she had heard, but true to her word, was not responding to words from him, other then the white man's words, turned his back to her and muttered, in perfect English," Navah mine". Mandy smiled, and continued with that day's vocabulary lesson.

Mandy was extremely pleased with Running Eagle's progress. She was so immersed in their lessons, that she completely loss track of time.

While her world now revolved almost exclusively around her husband, Running Eagle, Mandy missed Becky. She was fully aware of the difficulty that Becky was having. Difficulty adjusting to this sudden, drastic, unexpected, change in their lives.

Mandy realized that Becky's failure to adjust, was in large part due to her determination to resist. To not cooperate with her captors, and her desire to escape to, return to her white-world.

It was the beginning of their third week alone, away from the camp, that Mandy began to have bouts of early morning nausea.

Mandy had noticed that her breasts, which were routinely undergoing daily and nightly, caresses, kisses and the ardent-sucking, from her husband's eager mouth, were now becoming increasingly, tender.

Oddly her tender breasts, inexplicably caused Mandy to recall the last conversation between herself and Rebecca.

Becky had been worried when her friend, her sister, the person whom she had shared so many of life's experiences and events with, when Mandy had not come to the women's bleeding lodge.

Mandy had explained to Rebecca, that she had not gone to the women's bleeding lodge, because she was not having her period. To this day, she still had not had her period.

As her hands unconscientiously touched her tender breasts, she recalled Little Flower's recent comments to her.

Her reaction when she told Little Flower that Running Eagle had agreed to teach her to ride like a Comanche; "My daughter, in your condition, I think you should delay learning, anything more strenuous, than the fundamental way to sit a pony."

Mandy slapped her palm against her forehead. "I'm pregnant"! She wrapped her arms around her belly and whispered, "I'm pregnant?"

Mandy looked around; she was completely alone. She could see the cooking fires from the village. Running Eagle had left early that morning, to hunt for fresh meat.

Mandy threw her arms up towards the bright blue cloudless sky, and shouted; "I'm pregnant…I am going to have a baby, Running Eagle and I are going to have a baby."

Mandy was elated. She could hardly contain her joy as she tidied up the lodge, anxiously awaiting Running Eagles return.

When she heard the sounds of a pony rapidly approaching. Mandy burst through the entrance of the tepee, eager to greet her husband. Instead of her husband, Stone Fist, Running Eagle's best friend, was dismounting from his exhausted, spent pony.

"Pretty Buffalo Hair, I return to inform my brother, Running Eagle, of our glorious raid against the Utes. We counted many coup, and brought back many ponies, with no loss of life for our warriors."

Mandy quickly concealed her disappointment that the rider was not her husband, she smiled and as cheerfully as she could manage, she greeted her brother-in-law.

"My brother Stone Fist, you are welcome at our lodge. Running Eagle should be returning from the hunt shortly."

"May I offer you food and drink? Stone Fist was visibly disappointed that Running Eagle was not at the lodge.

Following his hugely successful raid, Stone Fist's had been anxiously anticipating the retelling to his best friend Running Eagle, the details of his first mission as the leader of a major Comanche raiding party.

As Mandy and Stone Fist sat awaiting Running Eagle's return, Mandy could not help but notice Stone Fist's uncomfortable anxiety. It was apparent to her that Stone Fist was uneasy when alone in her presence.

Unlike his wife, Spring Blossom, or his best friend, Running Eagle, Stone Fist was not at all enamored with the two captive women. The dull lazy, stupid, white girl that Stone Fist had used, discarded, and dismissed, and the clever, black girl, that had somehow, in such a short time, gained the respect of Gray Wolf's family, most of the village, and the love of his best friend, Running Eagle.

Stone Fist did not like, nor did he trust, *Pretty Buffalo Hair*, Running Wolf's black wife. He felt that her attitude, her intelligence, industry, and most of all, her professed love for Running Eagle, was unnatural, was a facade.

True enough, in the past some captives had come to embrace the ways of the Comanche. These were usually very young captives, who were essentially raised as a Comanche. On occasion pre-teens, and a few adolescents converted to the Comanche way of life.

Never had Stone Fist seen or heard told of such a rapid conversion, as had apparently happened with this captive black young woman, Pretty Buffalo Hair.

Stone Fist was pleased that his best friend Running Eagle had found happiness. However, he could not rid his mind of his suspicions, that the black girl, Running Eagle's wife, was manipulating his friend, and would eventually betray Running Eagle. That she would betray the People.

Stone Fist was about to leave, when they both heard Running Eagle's voice. Stone Fist recognized the voice of his friend, yet he did not comprehend, did not understand, the strange words, that came spewing forth from Running Eagle's mouth; " *Mahn-dee I have returned with four fat rabbits.* "

To Running Eagle's surprise, Mandy answered him, not in the white man's tongue that the two of them had agreed to exclusively use during Running Eagle's lessons, she answered in the language of the People.

"My husband, our brother Stone Fist is here. He has returned in honor from the land of the Ute's".

Stone Fist hurried past Mandy, and embraced his friend. Pointed to and laughed at the four rabbits lying at his friend's feet.

"Running Eagle, this is what you do while, I fight and count coups against the Utes? You hunt the ferocious rabbit?" The two friends laughed.

"We bring back many Ute ponies, and much honor."

Running Eagle, with a huge grin on his face, clutched his friend in a huge bear hug. "The mighty warrior Stone Fist has indeed returned".

****

"My brother, the women of our village are preparing a feast in celebration of the successful raid against the Utes. It would please me if you, my best friend, were there with me to share this triumphant moment."

Running Eagle placed his arm around Mandy's shoulders; My wife *Mahn-dee*, and I will gladly return to the village, and join in the festivities, the honoring of the mighty warrior Stone Fist, and the brave warriors you lead against the Utes."

Stone Fist's reaction to his friend's acceptance of his invitation, and to the words that Running Eagle used, was mixed. He was pleased that Running Eagle would attend the celebration. However, he had found it surprising and curious to witness Running Eagle's overt public display of affection, for his wife.

Stone fist was lost in thought as he slowly rode back to the village. "What was the language that Running Eagle spoke when greeting his wife before he was aware of my presence? What was the odd name that Running Eagle called his wife Pretty Buffalo Hair, "*Mahn-dee*"?

He abruptly stopped his pony, Stone Fist had come to the realization that, what he had heard his friend, Running Eagle speak, was the white man's tongue.

Stone Fist entered the village. The expression on his face was a look of worried concern.

****

Mandy took the four rabbits from Running Eagle. We will take these rabbits to the village. Although they are but a small contribution, they will be an addition to the feast."

"My husband, in honor of Stone Fist's triumphant return, and our attendance at tonight's feast, being given in his honor, I think, if you agree, that for the remainder of the day, and until we return, that we suspend speaking the white talk."

"Besides my husband, what I have to say ought to be said, should be said in the tongue of the Comanche." Running Eagle, with a puzzled expression on his face, waited for Pretty Buffalo Hair, to continue.

Pretty **B**uffalo Hair wrapped her arms around her as yet, still slender waist, she smiled, hugged herself; "Running Eagle, my beloved husband, I am with child. We are going to have a baby."

Running Eagle swept his wife into his arms and swung her around. And then as has been repeated the world over by first-time expectant fathers, he abruptly stopped and gently returned the expectant mother to the ground.

Regaining his composure and displaying the dignity one expects from the head of a Comanche family, Running Eagle spoke; "Pretty Buffalo Hair, your news brings me great joy. In words often spoken to me by our mother, Little Flower, "It is as it should be.""

****

Mandy was eager and excited at the prospect of seeing, her family. Of seeing her mother, Little Flower, her father, Gray Wolf, and her two sisters, her Comanche sister Spring Blossom, and her white sister, Becky.

To Mandy, it had become obvious, that Rebecca was miserable. That she would not survive if she were not, somehow returned soon to her white world.

During the past two weeks, in those few moments in the day that she was not with Running Eagle, when she was gathering kindling for their cooking fire, or preparing their meals, Mandy's thoughts were frequently, thoughts of Becky.

Mandy thought that the time to ask for her husband's help was now. Stone Fist, who in the eyes of the Comanche, owned Rebecca, had returned in triumph. Running Eagle, Stone Fist's closest friend, had just been told by Pretty Buffalo Hair, that he was to become a father. Mandy reasoned that if ever there was a right time to ask Running Eagle to help her, to help Becky, that time was now.

As they were preparing to leave for the feast, Mandy approached her husband. She spoke to him in the language of the Comanche. "My husband, I would speak to you."

Running Eagle smiling answered, "Why does my wife speak to me in the tone and manner of a warrior's wife?" He saw that his wife was not returning his smile.

Running Eagle, realizing that something was troubling his wife, no longer smiling, asked; "Pretty Buffalo Hair, you wish to make talk?" She nodded. "Then you must speak".

"It is about my sister. I fear for the health, and the life of my sister." A look of concern settled over Running Eagle's face. "Is Spring Blossom ill? Does Stone Fist know?

"No, my husband, please forgive me. It is not my sister Spring Blossom of whom I speak." Running Eagle's face relaxed. His previous look of concern, changed to a look of total confusion.

Before he could ask for clarification, Mandy continued; "I fear for the health, and the life of my sister, Becky, the white girl" who was with me when we were captured. I speak of my sister Becky, the captive that Hen's Teeth calls, "*eebi tseena puis*", "Blue Wolf Eyes".

"Pretty Buffalo Hair, I am confused. Where you not the slave of the white girl? Why do you call your oppressor, your former slave-master, sister?"

Mandy acknowledged that Becky, in the white man's world had indeed been her slave-master. She talked of her life as a slave on the cotton plantation. She told of the multi-generations of abuse that had been inflicted on the women of her family, by the white men, the white men of the Billings Family.

She told of Becky's father, Henry Billings', decades long, extra-marital affair with her mother. She told of how everyone on the plantation, blacks and whites, knew but never dared say that the white master of the plantation Henry Billings, was her father.

She told of how she and Becky had been together all of their lives. Rebecca as the white mistress, she as the docile, presumed ignorant, 'nigga slave".

She told of how Becky had allowed and encourage, her to learn to read and to write. She spoke with reverence of her and Becky's relationship with their white tutor, Miss Eleanor Leary.

She talked for an hour, with only infrequent brief interruptions, to clarify a point, telling the story of her life, the life she had led before her life began, her life with Running Eagle.

474

"The reason that I found it easy to adapt to the life of the Comanche, and why Becky is having so much difficulty, is because I can relate to the Comanche." I too desire to live free. Until now, I've never known true freedom."

"Becky's life has always been a life of privilege. "I have to help her get away, if she is to escape, if she is to live, Becky needs my help."

"I am asking that you my husband, help me, help my sister, escape."

Running Eagle had been listening in silence. Pretty Buffalo Hair, was staring at him, pleading with those oh so beautiful, soft, doe like brown eyes.

Running Eagle spoke, "Your history with the pitifully, weak white girl, answers many of my unasked questions. I am curious at the word escape, which you speak. It is true that the white girl, as you were, is a captive. You and the white girl, were never prisoners."

"It is true, for the Comanche, captives taken in battle, are the property their captors. Captives are not guarded, if they chose to "escape", to leave the village, no one is obligated to chase them, to return them to their captors".

"I believe that if the white girl walked away from the lodge of Stone Fist's mother and grandmother, Old "Hen's Teeth", would not be disturbed by her departure.

"If you wish, I will trade my finest breast-plate to Stone Fist for the white girl. I will give the white girl to you."

"You would do that for me…Running Eagle, I thank you. I truly love you."
Running Eagle asked, "If Stone Fist agrees to trade, and you own the white girl, what will you do with her?"

Without hesitation, and as Running Eagle would later remind her, without thought Mandy replied; "I will give her, her freedom."

"And what do you think the white girl will do with her freedom. You say she does not want to remain with the People. If she chooses to leave, the white girl will not survive, she will die on the prairie."

"My husband speaks with the wisdom of a seasoned, knowledgeable warrior. Becky will not choose to live with the Comanche. Her proposal, her plan is that she and I, escape together, and return together, home to the white man's world."

"I have told Becky that this is my home, with you my husband. That Little Flower, Gray Wolf, Spring Blossom, and yes, even Stone Fist, who she despises and hates, are my family. I have told Becky that my place is with you, Running Eagle. You are my man, my husband, the one who I love beyond all others."

"Becky knows that my wish is to live my life, as a Comanche. And that I, intend to eventually die as a Comanche, in the land of the Comanche."

"If Stone Fist agrees to the trade, I ask one more thing from you. I ask that you take the two us to one of the wagon trains that cross the land of the Comanche. I will then deliver Becky to the Wagon Master, and then I will return to you."

Running Eagle remained silent for several minutes. Mandy sat silently awaiting his answer. Running Eagle rose; "I will discuss this with my father Gray Wolf and with the leaders of the village."

Pretty Buffalo Hair was elated. Although Running Eagle had not agreed to take them, herself and Becky to one of the wagon trains, he had not refused.

After having lived five months amongst the Comanche, she knew that in this matter, the thing for her to do was to now, do nothing. She must wait for her husband's decision.

****

When Running Eagle and Pretty Buffalo Hair entered the village, they immediately noticed that the level of morning activity was heightened.

In addition to the everyday, routine activities that the women performed daily, the women were busily preparing for that evening's feast, a feast to celebrate Stone Fist's successful raid.

Pretty Buffalo Hair went directly to Gray Wolf's lodge. Running Eagle stopped his pony at the lodge of Stone Fist. As he dismounted, "Limping Boy", one of the village's pre-teen boys, took the reins of his pony.

That the boy was in awe at being in the presence of the well-respected, young warrior, Running Eagle, was evident in the boy's demeanor.

Running Eagle gave the awe struck boy a nod. Limping Boy lead Running Eagle's pony towards the band's pony herd. He could not wait to tell his friends and peers that the warrior Running Eagle, who everyone says is a future leader of the Comanche, had smiled at him.

Before Running Eagle could announce his presence, Stone Fist strode from the tepee. He greeted his friend, and ushered him into his lodge.

"Forgive me my friend for not having the women bring you meat and drink. I am alone, most of the women, including Spring Blossom, are working together, preparing for the evening's feast."

Stone Fist and his guest Running Eagle sat across from each other. Stone Fist reached for his pipe. He removed a flaming twig from the cooking pit, and lit the pipe.

Silently the two friends sat smoking. Stone Fist did not speak. It was obvious to him that his friend Running Eagle had something on his mind.

After the pipe was passed three times between them, Running Eagle spoke; "My friend there is something that you own, that I would like to give to my wife."

Stone Fist was intrigued, what could this be? What did he posses that could possibly be of interest to the black girl, Pretty Buffalo Hair, the wife of his best friend, Running Eagle? He did not speak. He knew when he was ready, that Running Eagle would make known to him, the answers to his question.

Stone Fist reached for his pipe, puffed two streams of smoke into the air, and passed the pipe to his friend. Running Eagle smoked the pipe. The two friends sat in silence, watching the blue smoke rise and disappear through the smoke hole, at the top of the tepee.

Running Eagle, broke the silence. Pretty Buffalo Hair wishes to own "Blue Wolf Eyes", the white girl that we captured more than five moons ago

"The breastplate that Stone Fist has admired; I will trade the breastplate for the white girl."

To Stone Fist, the offer by Running Eagle, to trade his priceless breastplate for the lazy, worthless, white girl, was an unexpected, welcome opportunity.

In addition to the ponies captured in the raid against the Utes, Stone Fist's raiding party had captured three women, and two children.

As the leader of the raid, he had chosen one of the adult captives. The Ute captive woman would be an excellent replacement for the inept, petulant white girl.

Stone Fist had been intending to attempt to trade "Blue Wolf Eyes", the worthless white captive. Had he not been able to trade the white girl, Stone Fist would have killed her. Captive slaves who could not, or would not work, continued to eat. They were a burden to their owners and to the band.

Non-productive slaves were worthless. Non-productive slaves were liabilities.

Stone Fist would have gladly, freely given the white girl to Running Eagle. However, to do so now, without receiving recompense, would have been an insult to Running Eagle.

To tell Running Eagle that the white girl was not worth the breastplate that he had offered in trade, would have insulted his friend.

Stone Fist was facing a dilemma. He intended to trade the white girl, yet he did not want to take advantage of his friend.

"Running Eagle, my grandmother, Hen's Teeth tells me that the white girl, is lazy and stupid. She has no skills, she does not learn, she is worthless".

Running Eagle listened to and appreciated the honesty of his friend. He explained; "My wife, Pretty Buffalo Hair, and the white girl are of the same father, they are sisters. Though they were carried in different wombs, they have the same white father.

Stone Fist commented, "ahh mixed blood, that is why your wife, Pretty Buffalo Hair, the black girl, is not really black."

"Pretty Buffalo Hair explained that in the world of the white man, to be considered a member of the white tribe, both your mother and father must be white".

If your father is white, and your mother is black, you the child, are considered to be black, a black slave. The whites treat with respect, the white fathers of the black slaves. He has increased his property by producing a valuable slave."

Stone Fist found Running Eagle's words to be confusing, he asked his friend for clarification, "In the white man's world, if the child is born of a black father and a white mother, to which tribe, white or black, does he belong?"

Running Eagle remarked, "I asked Pretty Buffalo Hair that question. Her answer to me, was at first logical, but then it became illogical.

Pretty Buffalo Hair said that in the white man's world, if the father is black, and the mother is white, the child is considered to be of the black tribe, a black slave. This I found to be consistent, logical"

"I found her next statement to be illogical and confusing. She said that if the father is black, and the mother is white, the child's black father, is tortured, then, killed by the white men."

"The black child's white mother, is considered by the whites, as an abomination. This I found to be inconsistent, not logical"

"Although the white man's law does not call for the white woman to be tortured and put to death, the white woman is banished, shunned".

"The white woman, who gives birth to the black slave, becomes dead to the white world."

"This too, I find to be puzzling, since the white woman's mating with the black man, produced valuable property, as did the mating of the white man with the black woman."

"Pretty Buffalo Hair, wishes to return the white girl, her sister, to the white world. She has asked for my help in doing this."

"I, as do my mother and grandmother, find no value in the white girl. You because of your love for Pretty Buffalo Hair, the black sister of the white girl, find her valuable. At least her value to you is the value to you, of your breastplate. I will trade." Running Eagle and Stone Fist nodded and grasped each other's forearm.

"I would ask of my brother, two additional favors. In seven settings of the sun, the band will be moving to join our tribesmen for the last buffalo hunt, before we move to our winter encampments. I would ask that you deliver the white girl to me at that time, when Pretty Buffalo Hair and I will join the trek south".

"Before the feast I will speak to the council of my plan to return the white girl to the world of the whites. I would like you, my friend to sit with me at the meeting of the council."

Stone Fist nodded his assent to Running Eagle's request. Running Eagle removed the parfleche bag, which had been slung over his left shoulder. He unwrapped a beautiful white buffalo bone breastplate.

Running Eagle presented the garment to Stone Fist. Once again, the two warriors grasped each other's forearm.

****

Mandy handed the four rabbits to one of the women who were skinning, and preparing small game for the feast. She located and greeted Little Flower and Spring Blossom. "My mother and sister look well. Running Eagle and I could contribute but four rabbits to this feast."

Little Flower, who had been mixing a large vat of a most delicious smelling concoction, smacked Spring Blossom's hand with the spoon, as her daughter stuck her finger into sauce, attempting to sneak a taste the aromatic mixture.

"We welcome you my daughter. As Spring Blossom and I had surmised, it would take an event of great significance, to get you and Running Eagle to,
how did Hen's Teeth put it", Spring Blossom chuckled, and completed her mother's thought, "I believe she said it would take the quacking of mother Earth, to interrupt those two's coupling."

Mandy felt the blood rushing to her cheeks. "My mother and sister, other than my husband should be the first to know that…I am with child."

Spring Blossom began to laugh; Little Flower quickly joined her in laughter. Mandy was confused and surprised. Of all of the reactions that she had thought might greet the news of her pregnancy, joy, wonder, even surprise, she would have understood. She had not considered laughter as a likely response.

When Little Flower and Spring Blossom saw the confusion and the disappointment in Pretty Buffalo Hair's face, their peels of laughter, instead of abating, intensified.

"Forgive us my daughter, Spring Blossom and I are not laughing at your announcement, we are laughing because we knew you were with child. We knew before you and Running Eagle left camp. We are laughing because it took you so long to know."

Mandy stared at the two women with a look of wonder, amusement, and love shining from her eyes. Pretty Buffalo hair joined the two, in ruckus laughter.

When their laughter finally subsided, Mandy asked, "I would like to speak to my white sister, "Blue Wolf Eyes". Do you know where she is working?"

Spring Blossom answered, "Hen's Teeth sent the white girl, to help dig a large roasting pit." She pointed towards the northern end of the village.

"Mother, it is important that I speak with her. After we have talked, I will return to assist you and the women of the village, in the preparations for the feast."

Mandy walked in the direction that Spring Blossom had indicated that Becky had been put to work.

****

Pretty Buffalo Hair approached Hen's Teeth, who was supervising the digging of the roasting pit. "Good morning Grandmother. I am Pretty Buffalo Hair, wife of Running Eagle. I would like your permission to speak to my sister, "Blue Wolf Eyes"."

Hen's Teeth scrutinized the black girl standing before her. She uttered a non-committal grunt. Shifting her gaze from Pretty Buffalo Hair, she called out to "Blue Wolf Eyes", "stupid, lazy, white girl, come here, speak with your black sister."

Becky heard the shrill irritating voice of Hen's Teeth, her nemesis. She looked up warily, and saw the face of Mandy. Although she had not understood Hen's Teeth's words, Becky instinctively moved towards Mandy.

Hen's Teeth looked with suspicion, first at her white captive slave, then at the former black captive slave, who was now a member of the band. The white girl climbed out of the pit. Pretty Buffalo Hair stood in place.

Becky raced towards Mandy. Despite her attempt to refrain from public displays of emotions, as a woman of the People should, Mandy took two steps, opened her arms and tearfully embraced her sister.

481

Tears streaming down her cheeks, Becky threw her arms around Mandy's neck, and clung to her as if she were a life preserver, a rope thrown to a drowning woman, her last hope.

Pretty Buffalo Hair lead the weeping distraught girl away from the eyes of the curious women. Pretty Buffalo Hair looked over her shoulder, she spoke directly to Hen's Teeth; "We will be but a moment grandmother."

Mandy held Rebecca's hands in hers; "Becky Running Eagle has agreed to help us. He has agreed to help me, help you return to your world."

For a second, Becky was overjoyed. Then after having had a few seconds to think about what Mandy had just said, she looked at Mandy with alarm, "What do you mean, help you, help me. Mandy, we have to, together get away from here. We've both, got to escape from these heathens."

"Becky, I won't be going back to the white world with you. I have found my home. It's here…here with these people. These are my people."

"Running Eagle, the noble Comanche warrior, is my husband, he is my man. Becky, I'm pregnant. I want to be free, really free. Not just legally free. Free because I'm in possession of some document that my former Master signed. I want to be free because just as I believe, everyone around me believes, and lives by the words in the white man's founding documents; "That All Men are Created Equal".

"I want my son to know and to feel that freedom. To be born free, not to be born and raised in a world that treats him as an inferior being."

"Not to be judged by the white world as inferior due to a lack of intellect or the lack of talent, but to be automatically classified as inferior because of something that he had absolutely no control over, the color of his skin. Becky, I want my son, your nephew, to be truly free."

"Born and raised as a Comanche, my son will be an exceptional human being. He will be taught by his father Running Eagle, and by the members of our community, the ways of the Comanche. His father will teach him to respect and to appreciate, the animals, the plants, to respect all of nature. Running Eagle will teach our son to thrive and survive, in the world of the Comanche."

"I will teach him the language and the ways of the white man. I will tell him of the white man's greed, their believe and commitment too achieving their doctrine of "Manifest Destiny". The ultimate goal of taking all of the land from the Atlantic to the Pacific for themselves, by destroying the culture of the Red Man."

"I will also speak to my son, your nephew, of the kindness, the goodness, the generosity of some of the white people. I will tell him of his white aunt, Rebecca. I will tell him of our time growing up together. I will tell him of our teacher, Miss Leary."

"He will know that without the teachings, the love and respect of his aunt "Becky", and the white woman, Eleanor Leary, his mother would not be who she is. She would not know of these worldly things, that she now passes on to him, the poetry of Shakespeare, the genius of Isaac Newton, the majesty of Shaka Zulu."

"These things are but a few of the worldly things that I can teach my son, that his father cannot. These are the things that will help him and his children, to survive if, — no not if, — but when the white man steals the land of the Comanche."

"Becky, we both know, from Miss Leary's world history lectures, what happens when the white man finds new lands, rich in myriad, abundant, natural resources. They take what they want. Often at the expense of, and sometimes the annihilation, the destruction of the aboriginal native population."

"Here in America, history will surely repeat itself. It won't be the first time, and it certainly want be the last time, that by the shear force of their numbers, and with the advantages of the power of their modern weapons, the white man will in time, most assuredly, eventually take this land from the Indians."

Pretty Buffalo Hair stood with all of the dignity and bearing that she had seen displayed at important moments by her Comanche mother, Little Flower. "Blue Wolf Eyes, in five sleeps, when Running Eagle and I rejoin the band, my husband, Running Eagle will take possession of the white captive girl."

"The white captive girl, you "Blue Wolf Eyes". Have been purchased from Stone Fist, by my husband Running Eagle."

"When the time is right, Running Eagle and I will deliver you to the white man's wagon train. "Blue Wolf Eyes", I will not go with you back to your so-called, civilization."

"I will return with my husband, to his world, now my world, the land of the Comanche."

****

Running Eagle, his father Gray Wolf, and his best friend Stone Fist, walked to the lodge of Old Wise One, the band's civil Chief. The flap covering the entry to the tepee was pinned back, to the exterior of the lodge, capturing a cool breeze wafting off of the creek.

Gray Wolf announced before entering, "Old Wise One, it is I Gray Wolf with two of our fine young warriors, Running Eagle and Stone Fist. The young warriors wish to make talk, to gain the counsel, the advice and the wisdom of their elders."

Old Wise One gave his permission to enter. The three recognized leaders of the band, Old Wise One, He Who Speaks To Ghosts, and Thundercloud, were seated around the cooking-pit.

Old Wise One, the band's venerated civil chief, was flanked by his two most trusted advisers, the band's holy man, He Who Speaks To Ghosts, sat to his right, and Chief Thundercloud, the band's war chief, sat to his left.

The three leaders of the band were smoking, talking, and making preliminary plans for the band's upcoming move to join their cousins, for the big buffalo hunt.

Old Wise One motioned that the three warriors, be seated. The six men, five warriors and the band's holy man sat in a circle, around the rock-rimmed fire-pit.

They sat in silence as Old Wise One packed his red-stone pipe with tobacco. He lit the pipe with a burning stick that Stone Fist removed from the fire. Old Wise One puffed on his pipe, then blew three puffs of smoke up towards the tepee's smoke hole.

Chief Old Wise One passed the pipe to the holy man, He Who Speaks To Ghosts.

The holy man repeated the ritual, and then he passed the pipe to Gray Wolf, who was seated to the right of the holy man. The pipe was then in turn passed to Running Eagle, to Stone Fist, and finally the pipe was passed to Thundercloud, the band's war chief.

Old Wise One looked at the faces of Gray Wolf, Running Eagle, and Stone Fist. The Chief remained silent. Gray Wolf spoke; "My son Running Eagle has a problem with his wife, that he wishes to gain your advice, and your counsel."

Thundercloud chuckled, "Running Eagle you have been married for less than two moons, already you have a problem with your woman? I am surprised that your father Gray Wolf has not given you the advice that a father should give his son before he takes a wife. It will solve all such problems. Chief Thundercloud leaned back against the couch; "beat her."

He Who Speaks To Ghosts nodded his head in agreement. "It is the duty and the responsibility of the husband to beat his wife, when she is in his eyes, deserving of a beating."

Running Eagle quickly spoke. "Pretty Buffalo Hair has done nothing for which she should be beaten. He told of his wife's request that he assist her in returning Stone Fist's former white captive slave, to the white man's world.

He told of the blood bond between his black wife, Pretty Buffalo Hair, and her white sister, the captive slave girl, Blue Wolf Eyes. Running Eagle explained that the sisters, one black and one white, sprang from the seed of the same white man, their father.

After Running Eagle had finished, the holy man was the first to speak; "Does your wife, Pretty Buffalo Hair, wish to return to the white man's world with her sister?"

"No, Holy One, Pretty Buffalo Hair does not whish to return to the white man's world. Pretty Buffalo Hair is my wife, she is Comanche."

Chief Old Wise One, turned and spoke to Stone Fist; "The white slave, before you traded her to Running Eagle, what was she to you…what were her duties? Was the white captive your slave wife?

"My grandmother, Hen's Teeth, gives the slave girl work. Hen's Teeth says that the white girl is lazy and stupid. I coupled once with the white girl. She was my slave. She was not a wife to me."

Old Wise One shifted his attention to Thundercloud; "What of Running Eagle's plan to take the white girl, to the whites as they pass through our country? Would delivering the white girl endanger the People?"

Thundercloud sat silently, contemplatively, lost in thought. No one spoke. Finally, the war chief turned and spoke to Running Eagle. "I do not approve of this plan. I do not think the white men would allow you to approach their camp, with a white woman. If the white men did allow you to approach, they would not let you leave. The white men would kill you."

Running Eagle responded. "Chief Thundercloud speaks with wisdom, with the straight tongue of a proven war-chief. I ask for your forgiveness. I did not clearly make known to you the details of my plan to return the white girl."

"My plan was to have three of our warriors, locate, and scout a wagon train of the whites. Once we have located the whites, at a time that I chose, Pretty Buffalo Hair will deliver the white girl to her people."

Old Wise One spoke; "Will Pretty Buffalo Hair stay with her sister. Will she stay with the whites?"

Running Eagle answered; "Pretty Buffalo Hair is my wife. She is Comanche. She will return with me. To live with me in the land of the Comanche."

Old Wise One looked, in turn, intently at each of the men seated around the fire-pit. When his eyes fell upon Stone Fist, he stopped.

"Stone Fist, you as have Running Eagle, have had intimate contact with one of these sisters, one black, the other white, since their coming to the People. What are your thoughts?"

That Stone Fist was uncomfortable was obvious to everyone. At last Stone Fist began to speak. "I am a warrior. I am not a leader, I am not a chief, I am not a holy-man, in touch with the spirit world."

"I am a warrior; I kill the enemies of our people. I am the friend of Running Eagle. There is no man or warrior that I respect more than Running Eagle.

"I do not respect, nor do I trust the captive white slave girl, Blue Wolf Eyes. I respect my brother Running Eagle's wife, Pretty Buffalo Hair, because she is the wife of Running Eagle."

"I too as have most of the People, marveled at her skills, her industry, and the way she so quickly, became fluent, in our tongue."

"I trust Running Eagle with my life, with the lives of my family. I do not know Pretty Buffalo Hair well enough to trust her. I do know that the white man, and the black slaves that depend upon the white man, cannot be trusted."

"Pretty Buffalo Hair was a slave of the white man. She was the black slave, of her white sister. The white captive slave girl that my brother Running Eagle, wishes to return to the white-eyes."

Gray Wolf gave a furtive glance towards his son. Running Eagle sat perfectly still. His face was expressionless, impassive.

Thundercloud waited patiently for Stone Fist to continue. Stone Fist, one of his fiercest warriors, a man renowned and respected for his proficiency with the weapons of war, and not known for his mastery of words, paused.

Stone Fist looked directly at Running Eagle, his life-long friend; "I suspect and I fear that since the day of her arrival, in our village, Running Eagle's wife, my sister-in-law, Pretty Buffalo Hair, has been plotting her, and her white sister, Blue Wolf Eyes' escape."

The Holy Man, "He Who Speaks To Ghosts", spoke to Gray Wolf. "Gray Wolf, my brother, it is understandable, and honorable, that Running Buffalo trusts his Sits-Besides-Wife, the wife that carries his shield when we move camp."

"You my friend have not been, since you were wise enough and lucky enough to marry Little Flower, it is safe to say that, you have not been   influenced by the charms of this beautiful woman. Yet you Gray Wolf, consented to Little Flower's request that you adopt Pretty Buffalo Hair as your daughter. Do you trust Pretty Buffalo Hair, your son's wife?"

Without a second's hesitation, Gray Wolf answered, "I trust Pretty Buffalo Hair. Pretty Buffalo Hair is truly an exceptional human. I am honored and proud to be her father. I do not share Stone Fist's belief that she plots against the Comanche. Pretty Buffalo Hair is Comanche."

Old Wise One repacked his pipe with tobacco. He removed a burning twig from the fire-pit, held it to the bowl of the pipe and began to slowly draw on the steam of the pipe.

The chief blew three puffs of smoke towards the tepee's smoke hole. He passed the pipe to the man on his right. When the pipe had completed the circle, Chief Old Wise One spoke; "Running Eagle, what is your opinion of the character of the white girl?"

Running Eagle's brow wrinkled as he gave thought to Old Wise One's question. "I do not know the white girl. She has not lived in my lodge, under my control. I have listened to the words of my brother Stone Fist. I do not doubt that he speaks the truth as he has been told by his grandmother, Hen's Teeth."

"I too have heard words of this white girl's character. Words told to me by a woman that I love, and respect, my wife, Pretty Buffalo Hair".

"My wife, blood sister of the white girl, tells me that Blue Wolf Eyes, is intelligent, and loving. Pretty Buffalo Hair told me of the pampered life of the white women in the village of their birth, a place she called Rosewood."

"Pretty Buffalo Hair told that before being captured, the white girl had never cooked a meal, made a fire, raised a tepee, made clothing or moccasins. Pretty Buffalo Hair has told me that Blue Wolf Eyes, tries, but is not familiar with or accustomed to work. As a slave, at the white man village called Rosewood, Pretty Buffalo Hair, did the work of, and for her white-sister."

"The white girl known as Blue Wolf Eyes is too old to learn the work and the ways of Comanche women. She will not survive. Pretty Buffalo Hair wants to return her white-sister to the world of the white man".

"My wife, soon to be the mother of my son, embraces the life and the ways of the Comanche".

"Pretty Buffalo Hair says that the life of the Comanche, is the life, that her black grandparents, parents, lived in hunting grounds, four moons distant, across the big waters".

"Her black ancestors as free men, roamed the big land, that she calls Africa. They hunted the four-legged; buffalo, antelope, and the zebra, our ponies' cousins. These free black warriors hunted with lances, with war-clubs, and with the bows and arrows".

"As do the Comanche, Pretty Buffalo Hair's ancestors raided, and made war, on the villages of their enemies."

"Pretty Buffalo Hair's black ancestors, who now wait for her in the Shadow World, had great chiefs and holy men. Pretty Buffalo Hair says that for her, to live the life of the Comanche is to live the life of her ancestors".

"Pretty Buffalo Hair is true, she will not deceive or betray us, Pretty Buffalo Hair is Comanche."

After more than twenty minutes of silent meditation, Old Wise One spoke; "I have heard, and I have decided. Based upon his and his grandmother, Hen's Teeth's experience with the white captive girl, the girl who is blood sister, to Pretty Buffalo Hair, Stone Fist's suspicions are reasonable."

"Based upon the words of Gray Wolf, and most importantly, those of Running Eagle, husband of Pretty Buffalo Hair, our Comanche sister Pretty Buffalo Hair, and Running Eagle, with two warriors, will take Pretty Buffalo Hair, and her white sister, to the white wagon train".

"Pretty Buffalo Hair under the white flag, will deliver the white girl, Blue Wolf Eyes to the whites."

"Running Eagle will lead the party. If you have not crossed the trail, or seen the whites within three sleeps travel, you are to abandon the search. If the white girl wishes to continue alone, that is your choice to make.

"Running Eagle, the party that you lead is a party of peace. You are not to raid or steal animals from the white man's wagon train. No warrior is to enter the circled of the white man's wagons".

"If either Running Eagle, Gray Wolf, Little Flower or I, have misjudged Pretty Buffalo Hair's heart, and she decides to stay with the white eyes, she is to be allowed to do so."

"Running Eagle, you will only fight the white man, to protect Comanches. If Pretty Buffalo Hair decides to stay with the white eyes, she is no longer Comanche"

Old Wise One rose, folded his arms across his chest, and proclaimed;
"I am "Old Wise One", I have spoken"

****

After the passage of three sleeps, Running Eagle and Pretty Buffalo Hair, joined the band's trek, as it moved towards the southwest.

Their band would rendezvous with the other bands of Comanches, for the last large buffalo hunt, before the bands would separate, and travel to their winter camps.

When Pretty Buffalo Hair spotted her mother, Little Flower's pony-drags, followed by those of her sister, Spring Blossom, a satisfied smile, of satisfaction spread across her face. She was especially proud that she had disassembled, the tepee, and packed Running Eagle and her belongings, by herself.

Pretty Buffalo Hair was briskly walking, leading an aged pony, and a mule. Two of her lodge poles were attached to either side of both animals. The poles were the foundation of the travois, which bore the young couples' possessions.

As she approached Spring Blossom's pony-drags, she noticed that Becky was walking, leading the pony pulling the trailing travois. When Becky, relieved when she saw Mandy, was about to speak.

Mandy shaking her head from side to side, put her finger to her lips, walked past Becky. Becky did not speak.

"Greetings Spring Blossom, greetings mother, what a fine beautiful day."

Little Flower, was being assisted in her move, by two of the village's adolescent girls. The arrangement between Little Flower and the girl's mothers was symbiotic.

Little Flower gained four additional hands to help her with the move, while the young girls received the opportunity to hone their skills.

The girls gained valuable experience in one of a Comanche wife's most important tasks, the rapid and efficient art, of moving the lodge and all of the family's possessions.

"Ahh my beautiful daughter, it is indeed a beautiful morning. I see that you have managed to gather Running Eagle's lodge." She turned to speak to one of the girls, "Fragrant Willow, take the reins of Pretty Buffalo Hair's mule."

The young girl instantly complied. Pretty Buffalo Hair handed the reins to the shy young girl. Pretty Buffalo Hair smiled; "I thank you Fragrant Willow, you are as kind as you are beautiful."

Just then, two little boys ran up to Pretty Buffalo Hair. One of the boys thrust out his hands, which held an iron kettle. Although the pot was covered by dirt, Pretty Buffalo Hair immediately recognized the utensil as being hers.

She looked at the kettle, surprised and confused. The little boy who had stood in the background, began pointing towards the rear of the caravan. Pretty Buffalo Hair understood. She concluded that the kettle must have fallen off of the travois being drawn by the mule.

"I thank you both. It is wonderful to know that we are guarded by two such alert, watchful future-warriors."

The boys beamed at having been referred to as warriors, turned in unison, and scampered away.

Little Flower smiling exclaimed, my son Running Eagle had best be vigilante, Pretty Buffalo Hair, his beautiful wife, is admired by two young, very young men.

"This is my first move with the entire band. Where are the men, where are our warriors?" Little Flower waved her arm, "Look amongst and around you. The grandparents, and the lame are carried by their families on the pony-drags. Our warriors ride in front and behind us. They are there to protect us from attacks by our enemies."

Mandy found her mother's answer to be both logical and reassuring, "How far, before the sun sets, do we travel?" Little Flower replied simply, "We travel until Old Wise One says to stop."

The first day's travel under the hot summer sun proceeded smoothly, without interruption.

The caravan approached a stand of mesquite trees, surrounding a streambed that held water in pools that their animals could drink.

Old Wise Man sent a courier along the caravan, notifying the people that they would make camp at this spot. A substantial number of warriors, returned to guard the transient camp.

Each day, one after the other, followed this familiar routine. Until finally, after having traveled during the day, sun-up, to sun-set, for six sleeps, of travel, Old Wise One, instead of saying stop, stated instead; "We have arrived".

The women began and completed; what Mandy regarded as the awesome, miraculous construction of an entire village. The village, consisting of fifty-three tepees, was completed in what she estimated to be, little more than two hours' time.

****

Old Wise One's band was the first of the Comanche bands to arrive for the widely anticipated communal buffalo hunt. The location that had been pre-selected by the elders of the various bands was ideally suited for the life-style of the Comanche.

The terrain consisted of flat plains with intermittent stands of mesquite and cedar trees. Fuel for the many campfires was readily available. There was a flowing stream of clear sweet water, and an abundance of nutritious grass for their animals to graze.

Pretty Buffalo Hair, with help from Little Flower and Spring Blossom, set up Running Eagle's tepee. The tepee was some twenty feet behind the tepee of Gray Wolf. Running Eagle's lode was within twenty feet of the tepee of friend and brother-in-law, Stone Fist.

That evening, after all of the village's tepees were standing, Little Flower told her anxious daughter, Pretty Buffalo Hair, that she expected Gray Wolf, and Running Eagle to return, before the rising of the moon.

When she heard the voice of her husband and that of Stone Fist, his closest friend, Pretty Buffalo Hair, Pretty Buffalo Hair, busy preparing a special meal to celebrate her husband's return, rushed to the entrance of the tepee.

Stone Fist opened the flap of the tepee. Becky tentatively entered, closely followed by Stone Fist, and finally by Running Eagle. Stone Fist lightly pushed Becky towards Mandy.

Although the night was warm, Rebecca was shivering. Any time that Rebecca heard Stone Fist's voice she became frightened, and withdrawn. Mandy wrapped her arms around her trembling, white sister.

The last time that Rebecca and Mandy had spoken, was when the village was preparing the feast to celebrate Stone Fist's successful raid against the Utes.

Becky had not had an opportunity tell Mandy of the Stone Fist's recent assault.

Five days ago, when Spring Blossom begin to experience the uncomfortable cramps that presided her monthly menstruation,

Hen's Teeth had, in her usual bullying manner, told Rebecca, that until Spring Blossom returned from her stint at the unclean women's lodge, the workload of Pale Wolf Eyes would be increased.

It was the second night of Spring Blossom's absence from his sleeping robe, that Stone Fist had his grandmother; Hen's Teeth bring the white girl to his tepee. Stone Fist without uttering a single word to the frightened girl, raped Rebecca.

After he had "made her good" with his seed, Stone Fist had roughly pushed Rebecca from his tepee.

Now Stone Fist was gazing, without outward expression, at Pretty Buffalo Hair, the wife of his Best friend, Running Eagle.

Stone faced spoke directly to Pretty Buffalo Hair; "I have brought the white slave girl to you. I, along with Crooked Arrow, will go with you, and Running Eagle, to find the white man's wagon train."

Pretty Buffalo Hair, still comforting the trembling girl, spoke; "Stone Fist, I welcome you the lodge of Running Eagle. You honor our home with your presence. Please be seated. I will bring food and drink".

Mandy hastily ushered Becky to the rear of the tepee, out of the line of sight of the intimidating warrior. Running Eagle and Stone Fist sat.

Pretty Buffalo Hair, handed her husband, his tobacco-filled pipe. She sat a platter stacked with freshly cooked buffalo steaks, and a gourd of sweet fresh water, between the two boyhood friends, now two imposing Comanche warriors.

Pretty Buffalo Hair took Becky by the hand, and quietly, the two sisters left the tepee.

After the two sisters, one white, the other black, had left the lodge, and after the two warriors had completed their pipe smoking ritual, Running Eagle opened the conversation. "Once again my friend, I thank you and our brother Crooked Arrow, who will join us on the trail tomorrow, for helping me to find the white man's wagons."

"Stone Fist, hearing your words spoken at council, when you doubt Pretty Buffalo Hair's sincerity and her commitment to becoming a "True Human, a Comanche, distressed me".

"I have no doubt that you feel that your words are true. They are not. When we find the white man's wagons, Pretty Buffalo Hair's actions will remove your doubts".

****

Mandy and Rebecca walked, hand-in-hand, towards the babbling stream. Rebecca with frightened eyes, was taking furtive looks back over her shoulder. Mandy could not recall having ever seen Becky so skittish, dejected, so forlorn.

The sisters sat on the ground, staring into each other's eyes. Before Mandy could speak, Becky began to softly whimper. "Oh, Mandy it's been horrible. Just when I thought that I was beginning to learn a few words of their gibberish, and the beatings by Hen's Teeth were becoming less frequent, that old hag Hen's Teeth dragged me over to Stone Fist's tepee."

"Spring Blossom was staying at the menstruation lodge, without his uttering a single word, Stone Fist raped me."

"Mandy we've got to escape. I'll die if I don't get away from these savage heathens."

"Either Stone Fist or that wicked old hag, Hen's Teeth, is going to kill me, or I'll kill myself."

Mandy wiped the tears from Rebecca's cheeks. "Becky, it won't be long. You've got to hold it together. Running Eagle has purchased you from Stone Fist."

"Chief Old Wise One has agreed to letting a scouting party, led by Running Eagle, search for a wagon train. The chief has given us three days. If we have not located a train in three days, Running Eagle will abandon the search, and return to the village.

"Tomorrow you and I, Running Eagle, Stone Fist, and Crooked Arrow, will go in search of a wagon train."

"When we find a wagon train, Running Eagle has agreed to turn you over to the train's Wagon Master."

****

As the sun began to peak over the horizon, the scouting party, Running Eagle, Stone Fist, mounted on their war ponies, followed by Mandy astride her gentle mare, and Rebecca, riding an old mule, pulling a short pole-drag, started moving towards the trail, the most frequently used trail by the white wagon trains.

Crooked Arrow had left earlier, to scout ahead of the party.

Shortly after Father Sun had passed his highest point in the sky, Running Eagle, who had been riding in front of the two women, protected by Stone Fist, rode back to the group and stopped the advancing scouting party.

Running Eagle pointed to several depressions in the ground. The depressions were made by passing buffalo, the depressions contained, pools remarkably clear, water.

Running Eagle announced; "We will rest and eat here. Let the animals animals graze. Crooked Arrow will join us with fresh meat."

Mandy and Rebecca, dismounted and detached the travois from Rebecca's mule. Rebecca took the reins of the animals, and lead them to grass and water.

Mandy began the process of building a fire. Running Eagle and Stone-Fist stood apart, speaking quietly, while sipping water that they carried in their treated buffalo bladders.
After Rebecca had staked out the animals, she searched the area picking up twigs and buffalo chip, for the fires.

Crooked Arrow rode into camp. A slain deer lay in front of his legs, as he straddled his pony.

Stone Fist greeted his friend; "Once again Crooked Arrow, you have shown that you are well named".

With a broad grin covering his face, Stone Fist lifted the head of the deer; "Such a puny deer could have only been slain when the flight of your arrow missed its' intended target, and killed...this."

Their friend, Running Eagle, joined the two warriors. Running Eagle picked up the deer, and tossed the carcass in the direction of his wife, who working beside the white slave girl, was stacking kindling for the fire.

"Pretty Buffalo Hair and the white girl, will skin and roast our dinner." Running Eagle handed Crooked Arrow his container of water, and asked; Did you find sign of the white man's wagons?"

Mandy grasped the deer by its' antlers, and with the long knife that she used for just this purpose, began to skin and butcher the carcass. Rebecca gamely but clumsily, attempted to help.

As she worked, Mandy listened closely as the warriors talked. Crooked - Arrow was speaking; "Two sleeps ride away, I have seen a group of the white man's wagons. The wagons move towards the spot in the sky where the sun rises. They come to us"

Crooked Arrow paused and took another drink of water. "The train numbers seventeen wagons, thirty-two men, twelve women, sixteen children."

Rebecca was throwing dried buffalo chips in to the fire. Mandy expertly, removed the deer's liver. Then as she had seen her adopted mother Little Flower do on multiple occasions, she handed this delicacy, the raw liver, to Crooked Arrow, the warrior that had made the kill.

Crooked Arrow eagerly accepted the raw meat. He took a huge bite from the dark red, slimy organ. Crooked Arrow grunted with satisfaction, and passed the meat to Stone Fist. Stone Fist brought the liver to his lips, and with his gleaming white teeth, ripped off a huge chunk of the tender meat.

Stone Fist appreciatively, smacked his lips together. With dark red blood, and greenish bile dripping down his chin, Stone Fist handed the liver to Running Eagle. Running Eagle took a bite, and handed the remnants of the choice morsel, back to Crooked Arrow.

Pretty Buffalo Hair and Rebecca served delicious venison stew, seasoned with wild onions and wild potatoes, that Mandy had packed in a parfleche bag.

After their meal was completed, without having been asked, Mandy handed Running Eagle, his sacred pipe.

Mandy earlier, during the warrior's meal, had filled the pipe with tobacco. She removed a burning twig from the fire, and held it over the bowl of her husband's pipe.

Running Eagle drew on the pipe until smoke entered his lungs. He blew a puff of smoke towards the sky (*Sun; North*), then the second puff towards the ground (*Earth; South*), he then proceeded to blow smoke to his left (*West*), and then to his right (*East*).

Running Eagle then passed the pipe to Stone Fist, who repeated the ritual. Stone Fist passed the pipe to Crooked Arrow.

After Crooked Arrow had smoked, thus completing the warrior's oath, that what would now be spoken, would be truthful. Crooked Arrow returned the pipe to Running Eagle.

Running Eagle handed the pipe to Pretty Buffalo Hair. His as well as Stone Fist's eyes were riveted on Crooked Arrow. Running Eagle spoke; "What is the strength and the weakness of the white man's wagon train?"

"Ten of the big wagons are each pulled by three teams of the white man's huge cattle. The ten cattle pull wagons, that do not have the high white cloud covers.

The wagons are covered with dark hides, pulled tight and flat behind the seat of the driver. The seats are empty. The white men walk beside the huge cattle that pull the wagons. The white men are constantly lashing the animals with loud cracks from their long snake whips."

"Seven of the wagons are smaller. These have the high white cloud covers stretched over the ribs of the wagons. The seven wagons are pulled by mules, and have a white man in the seat of the driver. The women and children travel with these seven wagons."

After he had given his detailed scouting report, Crooked Arrow sat silently. He looked first at Running Eagle, then to Stone Fist.

Running Eagle spoke; "We will wait for the white man's wagons to appear below that rise. Then, under the white flag, I Running Eagle, and Pretty Buffalo Hair will give the white girl to the hair-mouths. In this we will succeed, for my *puha,* my medicine is strong."

Two of the three warriors returned to their sleeping robes. Stone Fist, Jogged away from the camp, to act as a sentry, to be relieved first by Crooked Arrow, who in-turn, would be relieved by Running Eagle.

Pretty Buffalo Hair and Rebecca, put out the campfire, and cleaned up the debri, and retired to their sleeping robes.

Pretty Buffalo Hair, with a disturbed, worried expression on her face, in a subdued, reserved voice spoke; "My husband Running Eagle is a fearless and a wise leader. Yet I feel that in his love for me, he has placed himself in needless, unnecessary danger".

"If Running Eagle, proud Comanche warrior, were to ride with the white girl, without weapons, into the camp of so many white men, he would be killed."

Running Eagle pulled the robe over his head. "My medicine is strong. It will protect me. The white men will honor the white flag."

"My husband, please believe me, I know the white man. I know how he thinks. I have lived most of my life in his camp. White men are not rational when they see their women with men who are not white."

Running Eagle lifted his head from beneath the robe, he looked confused.

Pretty Buffalo Hair noted his confusion. She explained as she had so often done when teaching him the white man's talk, and the white man's ways.

"When the white man sees you, the most beautiful, virile, man that I have ever seen, you a red man with a white woman, they will assume that you violated her, raped, tortured, and humiliated her".

"To the white man, just the sight of you with Becky, will send the white man into a rage. My husband, the white men will kill you."

Running Eagle, still surprised and confused by his wife's questioning of his plan asked; "does not the white man honor and respect the white flag?"

Mandy gently held her husband's face between her hands, "Usually he does, but again my husband, when he sees a man other than a white man, with a white woman, he becomes enraged. Believe me, my husband, the white men will kill you."

"I believe that if Becky and I were to walk into the white man's camp, and we told them that we had escaped, we would be believed. I will leave Blue Wolf Eyes, with the white men. When everyone sleeps, before father sun rises over the hill. I will slip out of their camp, and I will return to you."

Running Eagle lowered his head, and pulled the robe up. For the first time since he and *Maun-dee* had professed to each other, their mutual love, he began to have doubts.

Could Stone Fist be right? Was Pretty Buffalo Hair plotting to deceive him. Had it all been a lie? Running Eagle raised himself, leaning on his elbow; "if what you say is true, why not have the white girl go to the wagon train alone?

Pretty Buffalo Hair responded; "I don't think that they will believe that she could have escaped and survived on the prairie alone.

"The white man would be cautious, suspicious, thinking she was being used as a trap. It might result in the white men sending out a large number to find and fight the Comanche.

Running Eagle decided to adopt her plan. Pretty Buffalo Hair's (*Maun-dee's*) actions would answer his *burgeoning* questions, for the first time, Running Eagle was no longer convinced of Pretty Buffalo Hair's professed love.

****

Captain Sam Smith, Santa Fe Trail, Wagon-Master, was in the second leg of his last cross-country journey. He was shepherding, this small commercial freight wagon train, and the ten emigrant families that had decided to return to the East.

The hybrid freight-emigrant train, that made up in the town of Santa Fe, New Mexico Territory, destination the city of New Franklin, Missouri.

The former Sea Captain, turned overland Wagon Train Master, had been badly shaken by the tragic loss of life of the Billings and the Johansen families, on his westward bound wagon train, four months ago. Captain Smith felt that tragedy could have been avoided; that it had been his fault.

He should have never left them alone. Left Billings, his driver; Logan, and that big Swede fellow, "Good Samaritan" Johansen, alone to fix that busted wagon wheel. Captain Smith blamed himself for what had transpired on that fateful day. He was responsible for the safety of his charges. He was ridden with guilt and remorse.

Captain Smith would never forgive himself, for what he would forever think of as, his poor decision. The decision to let them — "sod busters-farmers" — fix that damn wheel, then catch up to the main body of the wagon train.

The thought that it shouldn't have happened, that it was his fault, would haunt him for the rest of his life. And for what? To gain an extra hour of travel distance!

In his lifetime, Sam Smith had made many mistakes. Some he regretted, most he regarded as, "couldn't be helped". Captain Smith had convinced himself that the deaths of those four white settlers, and the two black servants, could have and should have been avoided. It was his fault. It "could've been helped". It had been his decision; it was his fault.

To this day, Captain Smith could not rid his mind of the horrific images that he saw at the scene of the massacre. The mutilated bodies, of the men with their genitals stuffed in to their mouths. The disfigurement, the cutting off of her breasts that the Indians had inflicted on the black woman.

But most of all, Captain Smith, could not stop thinking of that pretty little blond white girl, and her servant, the cute little black girl, taken captive by the savages. He was well aware of the cruelties, the humiliations, the frequent torture that the Indians routinely, reigned down upon their captive-slaves.

Captain Smith, from his time living with the Cheyenne, knew what happened to females who were taken captive by the Indians.

Captain Smith knew from personal observation, that female captives —, including white female captives —, were routinely and repeatedly raped by the warriors.

After having buried the slain, butchered victims, people that had placed their lives in his hands, people who had looked to him for protection, Captain Smith, hoping to rescue the two abducted girls, immediately returned to the main body of the wagon train. He recruited ten heavily armed men, and rode out hoping to rescue the girls.

Having lost the trail, and after a full day of trying to reacquire any sign as to the direction taken by the Indians, Captain Smith, taking into account his overall responsibility for the safety of the entire wagon train, grudgingly abandoned the search.

Back at the wagon train, Captain Smith began to frantically rummage through his papers. He discovered the letter of credit, given to him by Henry Billings before the wagon train left New Franklin, Missouri.

The letter was from a lawyer, a Mister Luis Frasier, Esq., of Richmond Virginia. The letter of reference, attested to the character, and to the financial solvency of Henry Billings.

Captain Smith, pulled a piece of blank paper from his make-shift desk. Squinting his eyes in the dim light of one of his two oil lamps, he began to write:

April 4th, 1863

Dear Mr. Frazier,

It is my painful duty to inform you of a tragedy that has befallen the Henry Billings family, traveling, with my wagon train, under my guidance and protection.

Mr. Billings and his daughter's governess, a Negress by the name of Ruth, were attacked and killed by a war party of hostile Indians.

Your friend Mr. Henry Billings, fought and dyed bravely, attempting to protect his daughter, Miss Rebecca Billings.

I truly regret informing you that Miss Rebecca Billings, and her Negress servant, Mandy, were abducted by the heathens.

A posse of men, led by me, followed the Indians, until we lost their trail, and were forced to abandon our search and rescue efforts.

With my deepest sympathy,

Sincerely,

Sam Smith

Captain Samuel A. Smith, Wagon Master

As soon as the wagon train reached the next outpost of civilization, Captain Smith posted the letter.

The Captain viewed his abject failure, his lack of judgment, which lead to the tragic deaths and abductions of the Billings, had led him to his decision to abandon guiding emigrants across the vast sea of prairie grass.

At the end of this return trip back east, sea captain Sam Smith, who had become Captain Sam Smith, Wagon Master, had decided to complete the trilogy. Captain Sam Smith planned to return to the sea.

****

The wagon train had been steadily proceeding east. Captain Smith estimated that they had made at least a dozen miles, following the completion of their afternoon meal.

The sun was about to sit in the western sky, when Homer Dickson, his chief scout, came racing back towards the train; "Capn Smith, look yonder, you won't believe your eyes…two Indian squaws, toting' a white flag on a twig, just popped up, outta nowhere. Liked to make me almost wet my breeches."

Captain Smith spurred his horse towards the two squaws. Reflexively, his right hand reached down to the rifle in its scabbard. As his horse rapidly closed the distance between himself and the apparition that was gradually coming into focus. "Oh my God, it's her. Its' the Billings girl, that was taken by the Indians, the white girl that I lost five months ago".

As he approached the girls, Captain Smith pulled hard on the reins, the intensity of his grip, violently twisted the horse's neck, nearly causing horse and rider, to fall onto the ground. Before his mount could fall, the captain had leaped from the saddle, and ran, stumbling towards Rebecca.

"Oh my God, Miss Billings, is that really you?" Before Rebecca could respond, he swept her into his arms. As the captain lifted Rebecca from the ground, and joyously swung her around, it felt to him that he was lifting, and discarding the terrible weight of guilt, that had been plaguing him, haunting the him, incessantly, day and night, for nearly a half year.

Mandy stood not moving, behind Rebecca. She was holding the reins of both ponies in one hand, and in the other, she held the twig to which was tied the white piece of parchment.

As he was twirling Rebecca, the wagon master finally noticed the dark little squaw, standing meekly off to the side.

The captain reluctantly, put Rebecca on the ground. Rebecca had been both laughing and simultaneously crying with joy. She ran over to Rebecca and exclaimed, "Mandy we did it, we're safe!"

The wagon master stared transfixed, at the girls. They were both wearing Deerskin dresses. Both women's hair was parted down the center of their heads.

Their skirts were made of two pieces of deerskins, reaching down to the women's ankles, sewn together with buckskin thongs.

Their blouse was made in the style of the Mexican poncho, from single animal skins. The sleeves and the hem of the dresses were neatly fringed. On their feet, they each wore soft, deerskin, fringed moccasins.

Captain Smith remembered having thought, when he had first seen them a half a year ago, together on that ill-fated wagon train, how much the Billings girl and her servant, resembled one another.

Now standing side by side, both of their faces deeply tanned by the intense, relentless, effects of the plains sun, the white girl nearly as dark as her black servant, the captain mused, that the resemblance between the two, was now, even more eerily striking.

Dressed in Indian clothing, wearing their hair identically alike, both wearing identical clothing, each woman's skin, deeply tanned by the sun, the wagon master mumbled, "my god, they look like they could be sisters".

Although the color and the texture of their hair, and the color of their eyes, differed drastically, the girl's facial features, including their dimpled cheeks, was undeniable.

Rebecca's hair was sun bleached blond, with two straight golden braids, hanging over her shoulders, framing her sun burnt face. Rebecca's bright blue eyes, stood out in vivid contrast to her deeply tanned face.

The servant girl Mandy, had thick, curly black hair, and soft warm, brown eyes. She too wore her hair in two plaits. Her braids were black, thick, and wavy. They hung over her shoulders, and when she moved, the braids appeared to bounce, to possess independent energy and vitality.

"Where did you girls come from? Were have you been?" Where did you get those horses? Captain Smith, definitely not a pious man nor a religious man religious man, and certainly not a man prone to showing his emotions, exclaimed with tears in his eyes, thank god you're safe."

Rebecca and Mandy now found themselves surrounded by the wagon train's women and children.

Gladys Kinsley led by two of her brood of seven, were the first to arrive. Timmy, Gladys's eight-year-old boy, was running in a circle, around Rebecca and Mandy, he was jabbing a stick at Mandy while shouting, "momma, momma, look, look. Cap'n Smith's caught two wild Injuns."

Gladys, with Annabel, her youngest, clinging to her dress shouted, "Timmy, you stop that talk. Ain't no such thing. They're not two injuns. Can't you see that one of them girls is white".

Timmy ignored his mother and continued to poke Mandy with the stick. Mandy dropped the "truce flag" that she had been holding, and snatched the stick from Timmy's hands. She took a step towards the boy.

Timmy the tormentor, instinctively realized that he might become the one tormented, quickly pivoted, a ran screaming in fright to the protective arms of his mother.

Gladys now with both kids clinging to her apron, approached the wagon-master, "why Cap'n", pointing her finger at Rebecca, "that one's white". "Is she one of those whites that we've heard that's been brought up Injun?"

"Mrs. Kinsley, it is with a great deal of pleasure that I introduce you to Miss Rebecca Billings, formerly the Mistress of Richmond Virginia's, famous Rosewood Plantation".

"Last April, Miss Billings — he paused and pointed to Mandy — and her servant girl Mandy, were abducted, by Indians, from my wagon train. Mrs. Kinsley".

The wagon train master placed his hands onto Rebecca's shoulders, and looking deeply into eyes, ended his conversation with Gladys Kinsley; "I expect that tonight, for the first time, since her abduction, I'll have an uninterrupted night's sleep.

****

Running Eagle, Stone Fist, and Crooked Arrow, well hidden in a dense Stand of cotton wood trees, witnessed Pretty Buffalo Hair, and the white girl "Pale Wolf Eyes'", initial encounter with the white-eyes.

Running Eagle had experienced a fleeting moment of panic, when Pretty Buffalo Hair, instead of handing the white girl to the white man, and immediately riding back to him, had allowed herself to be escorted, with the white girl, back to the wagon train.

Crooked Arrow had whispered, "Pretty Buffalo Hair is wise. To ride away from the white eyes now, could have made them think that she was leading them into a trap.

That our warriors waited in ambush. That we wish for them to follow her so that our warriors could destroy them from ambush. Pretty Buffalo Hair shows great courage, and great wisdom."

Running Eagle glanced at Stone Fist. The fierce face of the mighty warrior, was impassive.

****

When they returned to the wagon train, Captain Smith planned to first take the girls to the Henley family's wagon.

In route, the progress of the trio, endured the gawks and the whispers of the small group of emigrants, who had gathered, curious to know what was causing all the commotion.

"Who are they?" "Looks like two wild Indian Squaws." "Did Capn' Smith capture those two savages?" "What do you think that they're up to?

****

Joseph and Gertrude Henley were newly weds who were traveling to St. Luis. They had *"pulled up stakes"*, to claim a surprise, unexpected inheritance, following the death of Joseph's distant relative.

Gertrude was a young shapely, nineteen-year-old bride. Her figure and frame was very closely that of Rebecca and Mandy's.

Captain Smith remembered that in April, many of the travelers had remarked upon the physical resemblance between the Billings girl and her Negress servant girl. Not only did they have similar facial features, the two girls body build was similar.

Some of the women on that train had been prone to remark on how the servant girl's dresses, obviously hand-me-downs from Miss Billings, fit the black girl. It was as if the dresses had been made for her.

Now as the Captain intently scrutinized the girls, following six months of having been held captive by the Indians, their difference in their demeanor, and their body shape was obvious.

Rebecca's eyes were sunken in their sockets. Though her eyes were still a brilliant crystal blue, after looking closely, the Captain concluded that some of the life, the vitality that had been, was no longer there. Rebecca had definitely loss weight.

On the other hand, the black servant girl Mandy, appeared to have thrived in captivity. Her soft brown eyes were clear, and lively. During her captivity, the girl had actually blossomed. As he recalled, before they were abducted, both girls had had very attractive, slender waistlines.

The servant girl Mandy's waistline had vanished. She even appeared to have gained weight.

Captain Smith, with Rebecca and Mandy trailing behind, walked through the circled wagons. He stopped when they reached the Henley wagon.

"Evenin' Joe, Miss Gerty. Joe and Gertrude nodded, their eyes were riveted on the faces of the two Indian squaws. Captain Smith removed his hat from his head, and with a flourish, with hat in hand, bowed and swept the hat below his knees; "It is my honor to introduce you to Miss Rebecca Billings, and her servant girl, Mandy".

Gertrude covered her mouth with her hand and gasped. Joseph ducked his head, and entered the wagon. Rebecca and Mandy looked quizzically, at each other. They could here Joseph, rummaging around in the wagon.

Gertrude, eyes bulging, asked, "Is she the one that was dragged off your wagon train by wild Indians. Before Captain Smith could respond, Joseph's head emerged from the wagon. He was holding a poster in his hand.

"By golly that's her. That's the girl from this poster. He handed the poster to the wagon master. It seemed to Sam, that he had read that poster at least a million times.

Without looking at the parchment, he handed the poster to Rebecca. Both Rebecca and Mandy, silently read:

REWARD OF $10, 000 DOLLARS

FOR THE SAFE RETURN OF MISS REBECCA BILLINGS

On April 4th, 1863, a white female by the name of Rebecca Billings and her Negress servant, known as Mandy, were abducted, from a wagon train, guided by the famous pathfinder, Captain Sam Smith.

The wagon of the Billings family, having experienced a broken wheel, was temporarily separated from Captain Smith's wagon train. While three men were working to repair the wheel, the Billings' wagon was attacked by a band of marauding savages.

The adults, Mr. Henry Billings, Mr. Bruce Logan, and Mr. *Lars Johannsen*, from a neighboring wagon, were tortured, and butchered.

Miss Rebecca Billings (Becky) is:

Height – 5' 4''
Weight – 98 to 100 pounds
Hair – Blond
Eyes – Blue

CONTACT:

Mr. Luis Frasier, Esq. C/O Central Post Office,
Richmond Virginia

$10, 000 DOLLAR- REWARD

After reading the paper, Rebecca's face beamed. She spoke to the wagon train master; "Captain Smith, I can't begin to tell you how grateful we are. It means a lot to us to see that we were not forgotten, that our people were looking for us."

Mandy was looking down at the ground. She had assumed, to her a remembered, disgusting, familiar, submissive posture. Actions that that she found to be abhorrent, yet she sensed were once again, expected and needed for her survival.

Captain Smith's eyes scrutinized Rebecca and Mandy. He then gave the same swift impartial examination to Gertrude; "Miss Gerty, these ladies look to be about your size. Do you think that you might be able to find a couple of dresses for them? I imagine that they're anxious to get out those Indian clothes. I'll be happy to pay you for your trouble."

Gertrude's eyes ran up and down each girl. "Captain Smith, I'd be pleased to help. I have a couple spare dresses packed in my trunk". She looked directly at Rebecca, "Becky, I think we'll have to take yours in a few inches. She studied Mandy, "Mandy…is that your name honey? For you, looks like we'll have to let a dress out. Not too much mind you, just a smidgen."

"Captain Smith, why don't you take these ladies to the get something to eat. By the time they finish eating I should have a few dresses ready to be altered. Then bring them back here. We'll fix the dresses together."

Captain Smith, now noticeably walking with new spring in his step, led Rebecca towards the chuck wagon. Mandy followed, tightly clutching the rolled-up "Reward Poster", in her hand.

****

Running Eagle grudgingly acknowledged that the location that the wagon train chief had selected to set up his encampment, met the Comanche criteria, for the choosing of an ideal campsite.

The wagon train was framed, east and west, by flat open prairie. With an undulating, waving sea of grass, seen through the eyes of the former sea Captain Sam Smith, in the diminishing light of the setting sun, as being, "fore and aft", of the wagon train.

To the south of the wagon train, stood a small stand of mesquite trees and bushes, surrounding a small stream. Approximately five hundred yards to the north of the wagon train were elevated ridges and bluffs, from which earlier, Rebecca and Mandy had emerged.

Running Eagle lay prone on the ground, on a small hill, looking intently down into the circled wagons. Several small fires could be seen, as the families sat down for their evening meals.

Running Eagle was impressed by the way the wagon train's chief, posted his sentries.

Single guards were positioned to guard the exposed east and west approaches to the wagon train. Two men were actively criss/crossing an area every fifty yards, patrolled north and south. Guarding the avenues that would provide an attacker cover, thus posing the greatest threat of an ambush.

The plan that had been agreed to, was that after the camp went to sleep, in the early morning hours, Pretty Buffalo Hair would quietly, under the cover of darkness, sneak away from the train. Running Eagle, Stone Fist, and Crooked Arrow would be waiting for her, in the copse of mesquite trees.

The three warriors stealthily made their way to the trees. Once there, after observing the guards' movements, Running Eagle immediately saw the flaw in their plan of escape.

The criss/crossing patrol, made it virtually impossible for Pretty Buffalo hair to make it to the trees undetected.

As the hours ticked by, and Pretty Buffalo Hair did not appear, Running Eagle's mind was in a quandary. He very much wanted his wife to return, yet he knew if she attempted to meet him in the trees as planned, they would have to kill the two sentries.

Old Wise One had given explicit instructions to if at all possible, avoid killing the white men.

Running Eagle, did not want to disobey his chief. Old Wise One's medicine had told him, that at this time, during this "party of peace", they should not kill or take horses from the white men.

Running Eagle came to a decision. He instructed Stone Fist and Crooked Arrow, to return to their temporary camp.

So as to minimize the chance of detection by the hair-mouths, the warriors would leave at timed intervals. Running Eagle would wait alone for Pretty Buffalo Hair.

If she did not come before father sun's first light pierced the spot where father sun and mother earth met to start the new day, Running Eagle would return to their temporary camp.

Running Eagle knew that if the sentries stopped Pretty Buffalo Hair, he would kill them, he would not take their scalps, still he would have to kill them.

As the sun crept over the eastern horizon, Running Eagle concluded that Pretty Buffalo Hair, had seen the futility in trying to reach the trees. And had decided to abandon the original plan.

Running Eagle heard the sounds of the wagon train encampment awakening, coming to life. He was both disappointed and relieved.

He knew that he had to leave, before the sun-rise, exposed his place of concealment among the trees. If he remained among these trees, there would be a good chance that he would be discovered by the hair-mouths.

Quietly, after the sentries returned to the wagon train, Running Eagle made his way back to join Stone Fist and Crooked Arrow at their camp.

As Running Eagle rode into camp, and prepared to dismount, Crooked Arrow grabbed his pony's bridle. "You are alone my brother?"

Stone Fist who had been standing guard, came into the clearing. He stood silently awaiting the words of Running Eagle.

Running Eagle once again, repeated the flaw in their original plan. He confessed his shame at underestimating the wisdom of the wagon chief.

The multiple sentries, and the sentry's trail crossing patrols, had made it impossible for Pretty Buffalo Hair to meet them in the trees.

After a breakfast of dried pemmican meat, and cold water, Running Eagle and Stone Fist sat and smoked. Crooked Arrow had left to scout the area.

Running Eagle repeated his previous statement, that Pretty Buffalo Hair, had seen the flaw in their plan, and would escape when she thought that the time was right.

Stone Fist stood as solid, and immovable as the tall mountains; "My brother I believe that that is so. But my brother, I must now speak to you…not as your brother, but as a Comanche warrior."

"Pretty Buffalo Hair, may not have come to you last night, because she choice to stay with Pale Wolf Eye. She may have now chosen to live among the white eyes".

Running Eagle felt ashamed. He felt ashamed because although Stone Fist's words hurt and tore at his soul, Running Eagle felt ashamed because last night, while patiently waiting for the women he loved, Running Eagle had had the same thoughts.

"We will follow the wagon train, no more than two sleeps from this camp. Each day and night, we will watch the white man's camp, and we will receive Pretty Buffalo Hair when she escapes.

If she does not come back to her husband, she will be dead to me and to the People. The name Pretty Buffalo Hair will never again, be spoken by the People.

****

As Running Eagle had surmised, that first night, when Mandy saw the deployment of the sentries, she decided not to attempt leaving the wagon train under the cover of darkness.

She knew that if she had tried to leave, and was caught, she knew that Running Eagle would have rode to her defense, either killing or being killed, by the white men.

She decided to wait. Perhaps, an opportunity to rejoin Running Eagle would present itself.

****

Captain Smith had made arrangements with the Henley's for Rebecca and Mandy to travel with and behind, the Henley wagon.

The Captain had purchased, at a more than generous price, from one of the families, a small spare wagon. Additionally, he purchased two mules and assigned the task of driving the wagon to Wilbur Bailey, one of the teamsters.

Captain Smith promised Joseph and Gertrude, that in return for their help, he would equitably share the "Rebecca Billings", reward money with them.

Rebecca and Mandy, last night, after the evening meal, had assisted "Gerty", in the altering of two of her spare dresses.

Rebecca wore a simple green dress. Gerty had assisted her in "bringing in" the waistline of the dress.

Mandy was clad in a simple, no frills, mousy brown colored, housedress. Gertrude had handed Mandy, a pair of scissors, and a needle and thread. Mandy had slipped the simple frock over her head. She found the fit around her waist to be, as Rebecca put it, "a bit snuck". Mandy had expertly, *"let-out"* the waist.

When the morning meal had been consumed, Captain Smith at the head of the wagon train bellowed out the command; "Wagons Ho!"

The wagon train, like a giant centipede, began to slowly move toward the sun, which had ascended a quarter of the way up, in the brilliant eastern sky.

Rebecca and Mandy were walking together beside the wagon that Captain Smith had purchased. An ex-mule skinning, tobacco-chewing, teamster by the name of Wilbur Bailey, sat up in the driver's seat, spitting and cussing, as he drove the mules.

Both of the girls wore the soft comfortable, doeskin moccasins that they had worn when they had first encountered Captain Smith. The moccasins were far more comfortable for walking, then were the stiff leather shoes that Gerty had given them.

Rebecca was absolutely beaming. "Mandy, we did it. You did it! You said you would and you did."

Mandy smiled. "Becky I was supposed to have met Running Eagle, Stone Fist, and Crooked Arrow earlier this morning, before sunrise. The plan was that I would slip out after everyone was asleep, and join them in the trees. We would, the four of us, then return home to the village of our people".

Rebecca looked at her. A look of genuine astonishment was on her face. "Mandy, it took every bit of strength and will power for me not to tell Captain Smith that there were three Comanche warriors, including that beast, Stone Fist, the animal that repeatedly raped me, lurking in the bushes."

"Every fiber of my being wanted Captain Smith and his men to capture and to torture, and then hang that beast, Stone Fist. I didn't tell, because of you. You made me promise not to. I only promised because I was afraid if I didn't promise, you might not help us to escape."

"Mandy we're free. You can stop pretending that you love that filthy Indian. I know you did it for us, to keep us alive. I'll never be able to repay you. You saved our lives."

Mandy, head bowed, her eyes fixed on the ground, silently continued to walk with Rebecca. She did not speak. Her mind was in turmoil.

How could Becky, the person that she had known all of her life, her best friend, her confidant, the person who knew her better than anyone else did. How could Becky think that she could be so duplicitous?

How could she believe that she had been deceiving Running Eagle, the man that she loved, her husband, the father of her unborn child, the man that she loved above all others.

"Becky, I meant every word that I said to Running Eagle, to Little Flower, to Gray Wolf, and to all of my fellow Comanches. I persuaded Running Eagle to help me to return you to your white world, for one reason only, for the simple reason that I love you, because of my love for you, Becky."

"I never ever needed acknowledgement from Henry Billings, that you and I are sisters. I've known for practically all of my life, that we were sisters. I knew, not because we share the same blood. I knew that we were sisters because between us, we shared our lives."

"From the time that we were babies and we together, suckled at my mother, Ruth's breasts. My mother was fond of telling me about how she used to nurse us together, at the same time when we were babies.

Momma would chuckle as she reminisced; *"Lawdy it be lik dem two havin a contest. Da white one on ma lef tit, da black one on da rite. Seems lik dem two tryn' ta see who could suck da hardest."*

"Remember Becky, when we were little kids and our big brothers, Jesse and Jason, let us play cowboys and Indians with them?"

"Jesse would always be the heroic, courageous, white mountain-man, wagon- train master, or lawman. You and I played the determined white settler, and her loyal, obedient slave, moving west, trying to build a better life for the family."

"My brother Jason would be cast as the villainous, Indian Chief, that treacherous, barbaric, bloodthirsty, savage, who for no good reason, killed and tortured the courageous white settlers, who were merely trying to bring civilization to the west."

"We were told and as kids, we learned and we believed some pretty awful things about the Indians."

Remember when we were told, and believed, that; "Them dirty savages, scalp, rape, torture, and eat white women. That the only good Injun is a dead Injun!"

"We believed those things because they were taught to us. We didn't know any better."

Rebecca's eyes flashed with steely defiance. "What we learned Mandy is true." In a sarcastic, vicious tone she continued; "Did you forget that that brutal savage Stone Fist, raped me? I'll never forget what that animal did to me."

****

Captain Smith had the word passed down the length of the wagon train, that it was time to break for the afternoon meal.

Mr. Wilbur Bailey, their driver, climbed down from his perch on the wagon's seat, and went over to tend to the mules. He was easing the bit from the mouth of his favorite, most trusted animal.

Jasper, his lead mule, stood quietly, as Wilbur began to ease the bit from the animal's mouth.

The constant friction of the leather harness on the mule's back had raised a small welt, which had suppurated, and was oozing a thin stream of pus onto the mule's back.

Two large horse flies, settled on Jasper's hunches and simultaneously, bit into the appetizing pool of pus, on Jasper's back. The mule involuntarily, reflexively, snapped his teeth, and flecked his tail at the feasting flies.

Jasper's teeth nipped Wilbur's finger. Luckily the teamster's fingers were exiting the mule's mouth when the animal snapped his teeth together.

"Ouch... shit...gotdamn it!" Wilbur looked down at his injured finger. The skin had not been broken.

Wilbur shook his hand and deliberately, purposefully, walked over to the wagon, climbed up onto the seat, and reached into the wagon's boot. He jumped down to the ground, wielding a long, lethal looking eight-foot long bullwhip.

Wilbur unhitched Jasper from his harness. He calmly led the mule a short distance from the wagon. Wilbur looped a rope around the animal's neck, played out about four feet of line, and securely stacked the rope into the ground.

The teamster then unfurled the whip; "You long-eared, onary, black son-of-a-bitch, I'll teach you not to bite me, he then began to mercilessly whip the mule.

Jasper bellowed, bucked, tried to break free of the constricting rope around his neck. Loud whip cracking blows, continued to reign down across the mule's back. The mule's screams split the air. The more the mule struggled, the tighter was the constriction of the rope around his neck.

The emigrants stood by stunned, disgusted, appalled, at the inhumane punishment being inflected, by the irate, now profusely sweating, panting, teamster, on the bloody, lacerated back, of the helpless mule.

Captain Smith had been out, ahead of the wagon train, with his scouts. As he rode into the encampment, he heard the torture braying and shrieking of the mule. He rode his horse to the scene of the commotion, dismounted and snatched the whip from Wilbur's hands.

He shouted; "Wilbur, what the hell do you think you're doing? Without waiting for an answer, the wagon master went over to the mule who was now piteously, lying screaming in agony, on the ground.

Captain Smith, unholstered his big navy colt pistol, walked around to face the tormented animal, and with one shot to the forehead, put an end to Jasper's suffering.

He walked over to the winded man, and shoved the whip back into his hands. "The price of that mule is going to come outta your pay. Now get that carcass away from here before it starts to stink."

Captain Smith turned to the gawking crowd. He waved his arms and shouted; "That's it folks, the show's over, get back to your wagons."

After Rebecca and Mandy had completed their meal, and after they had washed their dishes, they sat down together next to their wagon.

They could hear the sounds being made by some of the occupants of the surrounding wagons. The camp was filled with laughter, heated conversations, even the sound of several voices singing, accompanied by the melodious notes of someone playing a harmonica.

"Becky before we witnessed that scene of our driver, that horrible man Wilbur, whipping that poor helpless mule, you in essence asked how could I forget that Stone Fist raped you."

"I haven't and never will forgot that Stone Fist raped you. I haven't and I never will forget that our father Henry, and our uncle Robert Billings, raped my aunt Sadie."

"I'll never forget that my mother, who did gradually come to love him, was in essence because she didn't have a choice, was raped by our father, Henry Billings."

"No, I haven't forgotten that Stone Fist raped you. Stone Fist raping you was barbaric and horrible."

"Nonetheless, Stone Fist's raping you Becky was no different, than the actions of the Billings' brothers, Henry and Robert raping my aunt, and my mother."

Rebecca stood and looked down at Mandy. Her expression was a mixture of shock, surprise, and incredulity.

Mandy continued, "Everyone, the blacks and the whites at Rosewood, knew that it was the white owner's prerogative to, if he wished, to rape his female slaves. That fact was understood, accepted by both master and slave. That was the culture of that society."

"When we were taken captive by the Comanches, we entered into another world, a completely alien society. But in many ways, a not so different society, from the one we had recently left, the Southern Plantation society."

"In the master/slave relationship, especially the female captives, in the Comanche culture, it is the red man's, the slave owner's prerogative to, if he wishes, rape with impunity, his female slaves."

"As horrible and as heinous as the commission of the act of rape is, from a cultural perspective, the so called modern, enlightened, practices of the slave holding South, are identical to the so called, "uncivilized culture of the Comanche".

"In fact, the only difference that I can see is that the Comanches in this regard, are at least honest. In contrast, the southern men, and women, the civilized aristocrats, are all a bunch of outright hypocrites".

"Stone Fist's raping you, in that sterile, clinical, intellectual context, was no different than Henry Billings', Master of Rosewood, rape of Ruth, my mother, and Henry and his brother Robert's, raping of my aunt Sadie."

Rebecca sat; silent tears were trickling down her cheeks. In a soft almost inaudible voice, she whispered, "Mandy, it hurt so much. Each time that he took me, Stone Fist hurt me so badly."

Mandy placed her arms around her sister's shoulders. They sat there, gently rocking, listening to the strains of the soft music, and strengthening their already intense, familial bond.

****

The second day after Pretty Buffalo Hair had returned Blue Wolf Eyes to the white's, Running Eagle, Stone Fist and Crooked Arrow, continued to trail the wagon train, at a discreet distance.

Crooked Arrow, because of his renowned superior eyesight, and expertise with the short bow, was always a welcome member of anyone's hunting or raiding party. The keen-eyed warrior had been scouting ahead of his companions.

Running Eagle and Stone Fist had been riding in the rear, exchanging ideas as to how they should proceed. Stone Fist was in favor of ending the mission, and returning to the village. "Chief Old Wise One has made it clear that he did not wish us to come into contact with the white men. Their wagon train is but three sleeps from our new village. We have done what we intended. We have returned the white girl to her people. Now, we should return to our homes, to our people."

Crooked Arrow rode up to his two friends; "I have seen Pretty Buffalo Hair and Pale Wolf Eyes, walking next to a wagon." Running Eagle asked; "Is Pretty Buffalo Hair bound, is she a prisoner of the hair-lips?"

Crooked Arrow answered; "No my brother, she walks freely with the white girl. Come if we ride to that ridge, the wagons should soon pass below. They will be within our sight. The ridge will keep us unseen by the white eyes."

The three warriors galloped their ponies towards the distant ridge, the hill that Crooked Arrow had pointed to.

The three warriors crawled to the top of the hill, and peered down into the valley. Crooked Arrow pointed to the last wagon in the procession.

Running Eagle saw two women walking next to the wagon. At first, he thought that Crooked Arrow had been mistaken. The two women were leisurely, walking and talking.

They were both dressed in the impractical dress of the white women. Both women wore long dresses that dragged in the dirt. The wide-brimmed, bonnets that they wore, hid the women's, hair, and much of their faces.

Running Eagle was about to inform Crooked Arrow that he was mistaken, that these two were not Pretty Buffalo Hair and Pale Wolf Eyes, when in order to avoid having their garments dragged through the mud, they both lifted the hems of their dresses, and stepped over a mud hole. Both women were wearing Comanche moccasins.

The three Comanche braves, slithered back down the hill. Running Eagle spoke; "Stone Fist, Crooked Arrow, you are to return to the village. Inform my father and Chief Old Wise One, that we have returned the white girl to her people". Tell them that I will return within three sleeps."

Stone Fist asked his life-long friend, "Where do you go my brother? Why do you not return to our village with us?"

"I will return to the village, after I have killed the one who has deceived and dishonored, my family, my chief, and myself. I will return after I have killed *Mahn-dee*."

Stone Fist and Crooked Arrow looked at Running Eagle with a blank expression of confusion.

"I will return to our village either with, or after I have killed Pretty Buffalo Hair".

****

Mandy and Rebecca were about to start preparing their evening meal, Gerty stopped at their unlit campfire. Mandy was strategically spreading buffalo chips and dry twigs in the cleared spot, reserved for their fire.

Gertrude cleared her throat; "Rebecca, some of the women are planning to get together after dinner, for a little sewing, and a whole lot of gossip. Why don't you...and Mandy join us? It's going to be hosted by Maureen Dawson. The Dawson's wagon is the second one, behind the freight wagons."

After they had completed their dinner, while they were washing their eating utensils, Becky turned to Mandy; "Mandy, let's go with Gerty and join the sewing circle. "It's been ages since I've heard a real conversation with English words being spoken, instead of that awful Indian gibberish".

Besides, Gerty said that there would be gossip. I'm dying to hear what's been happening in the world, while we were being held captive by those horrible savages."

Mandy was slowly, deliberating, shaking her head. "Becky you go. As for me, I have no interest, or desire to be ogled and stared at, by a group haughty white woman". Haven't you seen the smirks of derision that passes between them, when they think that we aren't looking?"

Rebecca felt that Mandy was being too sensitive. Of course, she had seen the curious looks from both the women and the men. The furtive, even sly glances that Rebecca, had attributed to that of natural curiosity.

Before giving up, Rebecca decided to try one last approach. She would appeal to Mandy's unquenchable thirst for knowledge. "Mandy, don't you want to know what's going on in the real world? How badly the South has whipped those Yankees?"

Mandy hesitated for a moment. Her mind automatically switched to a mode that she used when faced, with an academic or even a semi-academic question; what would Miss Leary do? Miss Leary had stressed that one should never miss an opportunity to learn. As she had come to expect, Miss Leary's favorite quote popped into her head;

"Remember girls, Knowledge is Power".

Looking into Mandy's eyes, Rebecca could see the look of determination, being gradually replaced by that look that she had become used to seeing, the look of intellectual curiosity.

Mandy placed the last of their dinner plates into the wagon. With her back to Becky, she reluctantly said; "I'll go with you Becky. But I intend to leave, the minute that I begin to feel uncomfortable or not welcome."

As the sun was setting in the western sky, six women gathered, seated around a large, two-foot high fire that Jim Dawson had built, at his wife's request.

Before departing to play poker with some of the teamsters, Jim had left an amble stack of branches, twigs and buffalo chips, beside the roaring fire.

The huge fire served a twofold purpose. In addition, for providing light for the ladies to sew by, the smoke from the fire served to repulse insects.

Three of the six women, who had been invited to join the sewing circle, were seated around the fire. Maureen Dawson the hostess was a twenty-nine-year-old woman, who after having given birth to seven, looked to be in her mid, to late forties.

Maureen was speaking to her neighbor on the train, Sarah Stalin; "Did you hear how that uppity-nigger wench speaks? She talks as good as a white person."

Sarah chuckled; "She's probably one of those educated free blacks. That reminds me of a good riddle that my husband told me…would you ladies like to hear it?"

Two of the three women, nodded in the affirmative. Rachel Bernstein, dropped her eyes, intently concentrating on the wool material in her lap.

Rachel and her Husband Jacob Bernstein, were the only Jewish family in the wagon train. They had come to America to escape the insidious anti-Semitic bigotry, which ran rampant in their native Germany.

The Bernstein's were traveling west to raise their children, to start a new life where they would be free. Free to practice their religion, free from bigotry and religious persecution.

Sarah put down her knitting and grinned; "What's the difference between a good nigger, and a educated nigger? Maureen eyes were locked on Sarah's. Sarah sat impatiently, eagerly anticipating, awaiting, the punch line.

"When a white man tells a good nigger to jump, by god Sambo will grab his hat and say, "yessah, yessah!"

"The only difference with your so-called educated nigger, is when a white man in the South tells an educated nigger to jump, that nigger gonna say, "yessah, boss, **how high?**

The two women were doubled over in laughter. Rachel continued to stare at the ball of yarn in her lap, concentrating on her knitting.

As Rebecca, Mandy and Gerty, approached the huge campfire, they were greeted by the sounds of the women's laughter.

Gertrude was the first to speak, "my, my, my ladies, it sounds like the party started without us. Sorry we're late. What did we miss? What's so funny?"

Maureen stood up, "hello Gerty", then she turned her gaze towards Rebecca and to Mandy, "Welcome ladies. We're all so very glad you could come."

Gerty, followed by Rebecca and Mandy sat opposite the three women. Since no one had answered her question, Gertrude asked again; "When we arrived you all were in such good humor, its' been a hard day's travel for us all, Rebecca, Mandy and I could certainly use some light hearted humor. What was the joke, what was so amusing?"

Maureen, the hostess of the gathering answered; "It was nothing dear, only a little "old married lady humor", which was much to raunchy for these young girls, young innocent ears to hear. Rebecca, other than you're being skin and bones, and land sakes, who wouldn't be? Being forced to eat dog, and rats, and to submit to all sorts, of activities. All in all, you seem to have survived with everything intact."

Rebecca's face under the light of the campfire turned a crimson shade of red. Mandy looked angrily at the corpulent, haggard looking woman. Everyone seated around the fire, had caught the innuendo in Maureen's words.

It was widely believed that the sole reason that white women were taken captive by Indians, was so that the Indian braves could rape and defile them.

While all eyes were focused on Rebecca, Mandy quickly changed the subject; "Rebecca and I have been away for such a long time. We often fantasized that when we escaped, the first thing that we wanted to find out was, what had happened in the civilized world, during our captivity."

Gertrude seeing Rebecca's involuntary reaction to Maureen's jab, and Mandy's immediate attempt to stir the conversation into another direction, jumped right in; "I don't know you ladies' political sympathies, and I certainly don't want to offend anyone, by my telling of the latest war news."

"We all know that Rebecca and Mandy are both from Virginia. Well ladies in early April, ending in early May, there was a major battle that took place in Suffolk Virginia.

A Yankee detachment of soldiers from Connecticut, or was it from New York, captured Fort Huger. The South's Confederate General James Longstreet was able to prevent the Yankees from taking Richmond."

Rebecca had regained her composure; "Speaking of Richmond, do any of you know or if, this dreadful war has affected the city's social life.

Were they able to hold the annual Debutante's Cotillion? I had planned to attend this year, before father decided to capitalize on a tremendous business opportunity for the family in Lost Springs Kansas."

Mandy gave Rebecca a satisfied smile. In three short sentences, Becky had shifted the dynamics of the conversation. Maureen's attempt to shame Becky for events beyond Becky's control, salacious events that may have, or may not have, occurred, had clearly failed.

Rebecca had established, emphatically, reminded those present, that though she had been held captive by Indians for nearly six months, that she Miss Rebecca Elizabeth Billings, former mistress of Rosewood plantation, was a lady, a member of the Southern Aristocracy.

The message was received. All of the white woman seated around the campfire, with the exception of Rebecca, had toiled their entire lives.

Trying disparately to scratch a living from the often unyielding, ground while simultaneously, attempting to raise a brood of kids.

None of the women felt qualified to banter or engage, in a conversation about Southern Society, with Miss Rebecca Elizabeth Billings, former Mistress of Rosewood, one of Richmond Virginia's, wealthiest, most successful Plantations.

Sarah Stalin realizing the futility of pursuing, of bringing into question Rebecca's chastity, decided to attempt to shame the "little harlot", by throwing cold water on her hopes of ever returning to her pampered Southern lifestyle. "Rebecca honey, I believe that it was in July that your General Robert E. Lee's, Army of Virginia, invaded the North. Some little town in Pennsylvania named Gettysburg."

I am certainly no authority on warfare, but all of the papers said that General Lee failed, and that he and his Army of Virginia, their tails between their legs, went slinking back down into Dixie."

Rebecca's showed no outward sign of emotion, upon hearing this news. Mandy on the other hand, could not suppress the smile that was threatening to burst forth, the North was winning, Mr. Lincoln's setting the slaves free just might actually happen.

Rachel Bernstein noticed Mandy's delight at hearing the news of the outcome of the Battle of Gettysburg. Both Rachel and Mandy were having a difficult time not smiling.

Having failed at their malicious attempts to degrade the former captive young women, the conversation drifted into idle gossip about the families in the wagon train. Mandy yawned and excused herself. Rebecca rose, and hastily joined her sister.

After the three women, Mandy, Rebecca, and Gertrude were well out of earshot of the campfire, Maureen remarked; "Did you her the "Princess", Miss Rebecca. Miss high and mighty, Miss SDS.

Sarah Stalin interrupted; "I'm sorry Mo, I'm not familiar with the term SDS. What does it mean?

"SDS is a term I heard my Harvey use when he was talking about, the South's "Upper-class Whites". He told me that they all have their noses in the air. The act as though their "Shit Don't Stink. SDS means, "Shit Don't Stink."

Maureen and Sarah both erupted into spiels of hysterical laughter.

When Maureen caught her breath, she continued; "You would think that it was us instead of her who fornicated with those filthy animals."

"Did you see Miss "High and Mighty's face when I practically confronted her with letting those savages have their way with her? Sarah picked up the conversation; "I surely did. She turned as red as a beet. If she had an ounce of decency, she would have killed herself before letting those bloodthirsty redskins have their way with her.

Rachel thought to herself, as she continued her knitting, "I can't imagine any man — *with the probable exception of her lout of a husband Harvey* — including those wild Indians, who would want to "have their way", with Maureen.

****

As they walked back towards their wagons, Gerty abruptly stopped and began to frantically search her sewing bag. "Oh darn, I think I left my knitting needles at the Dawson's wagon. She turned to go back for her needles. Mandy placed her hand on her new friend's shoulder, "I'll get them for you Gerty. I'll only be a minute.

As she approached the wagon, she heard the strident voice of Sarah Stalin; "Could you believe the nerve, and the tone of that uppity nigger wench, Mandy. The way she just walked in and sat down, just like she was a white woman."

Mandy walked over to where Gertrude had been sitting. She picked up Gertrude's knitting needles. It was obvious that Mandy had heard Sarah's vile, bigoted comments.

"Thank you, ladies, for helping make Rebecca and my return to civilization, so seamless." Mandy turned her back, and walked away.

****

Mandy and Rebecca sat together talking, while they prepared for bed. "Mandy, we're safe now… are you still determined to go back to live with those Indians?"

"Captain Smith says that father's friend and lawyer, Mr. Frasier, has kept in escrow for me, substantial holdings of the Billings estate. You and I are Henry Billings's daughters, his sole survivors. That money rightfully belongs to both of us."

We can settle in the North, live in a free state. We'll be wealthy, and you'll be truly free. Mandy, I'll be there for you and the baby."

"Mandy we're both young, we'll both probably meet someone, and get married. And even if we don't, we're family, we're more than family; we'll have each other. Mandy please, please reconsider. Please, stay with me. Let's stay together."

"Becky, I can't stay. I don't want to live, and raise my black, and white, and red son in the white world."

"Becky face facts, even if we were to go live in the North, if my son, the son of the great Comanche Warrior Running Eagle, the grandson of Henry Billing's, if my son, your nephew, grew up to be the most learned, accomplished man of his time, if he were to become President of the United States, in the white world, in that world, he would just be, in the words of Sarah Stalin, that delightful enlightened woman that we just left, my son would be seen as just another "Uppity Nigger".

"Becky, I love you. I am your sister. I am also "Pretty Buffalo Hair, wife of Running Eagle."

Mandy pulled the blanket up to her shoulders. "Good night my sister, I love you, and I will always hold you dear in my heart."

The sisters lay silently, back to back. At that moment, Rebecca knew that she would soon be losing her best friend, her sister.

Depressed and exhausted, Rebecca rolled over, and almost immediately fell into a sound sleep.

As Mandy lay motionless, quietly, listening to the gentle sounds of Rebecca's steady breathing, Rebecca's words resonated in her head; "we're safe now finally, we're safe". Fitfully she fell into a light state of sleep. Her eyes began to flutter, she began to softly moan, "no, no, don't".

In her dream she was reliving the whipping of that helpless mule, by that horrible white man, the teamster, Wilbur Bailey.

Wilbur continuously laid that long, ugly, thick whip across the animal's back. As she continued to toss and turn, to her horror, the mule's braying turned into human pleas, *"Massa, I'se a good nigger…won't runnin'… plees plees, plees Massa."* The mule's long equine face, slowly morphed into the face of Pee wee, the Rosewood Plantation's stable boy.

The face of the white man whipping Pee-wee, changed from that of the teamster, Wilbur Bailey, to that of her father, Henry Billing.

Mandy woke with a start. She placed her hand over her mouth to stifle the soft moans that were emanating from her throat. Mandy glanced about her. Rebecca was fast asleep. Her sister's deep-slumber had not been disturbed.

With the sleeve of her nightgown, she wiped the beads of perspiration that had formed, from her brow. In the distance, she thought she heard the plaintive call of a Night Owl. She strained her ears, listening, concentrating intently. Nothing.

Mandy quietly so as not to disturb Rebecca, threw back the blanket, and using the light of the full moon, began to rummage, searching the wagon. She found what she had been searching for, stuffed it into the bag that she used to collect firewood.

She returned to pallet and drew the blanket around her shoulders. Her last thought before she fell asleep was, tomorrow, tomorrow.

****

Running Eagle had been discretely following the wagon train. During the daylight he managed to catch glimpses of Pretty Buffalo Hair, dressed in the ridiculous long dirty garb of the white women.

He had meticulously used his skills to remain unseen by the hair-mouths. As an added precaution, to avoid detection, during daylight, he removed the two eagle feathers that he wore in his scalp lock.

At the end of the second day, of watching, and not seeing any indication that Pretty Buffalo Hair intended to escape, Running Eagle had come to the heart-wrenching conclusion, that Stone Fist had been right.

Pretty Buffalo Hair had lied. She had never loved him. She had used his love for her, to trick him into returning her to the white man's world.

She had dishonored his entire family. His heart filled with grief; Running Eagle knew that his medicine had been severely weakened. His only hope of restoring the power and the strength of his, and his father Gray Wolf's medicine, was for him to kill Pretty Buffalo Hair.

His decision to kill the woman that he loved, was not based on either pride nor revenge. His decision was based upon the future survival of his family.

Without strong medicine, neither Running Eagle nor Gray Wolf would be able to protect and to provide food for their families.

Tonight, it must be done. Running Eagle painted the left side of his face black, and the right-side red.

During the early morning hours of day three, he decided to stealthily, infiltrate the sleeping camp of the white man. He would enter through the opening at the rear of the wagon that Pretty Buffalo Hair and the white girl, *Beeky* slept.

He planned to kill Pretty Buffalo Hair. He would not harm *Beeky*, Pretty Buffalo Hair's white sister. Old Wise Man had emphatically said to not kill the whites.

As Running Eagle crept on his belly towards the encampment, he stopped, frozen in place. In front of him to his right, he heard movement.

Then he heard a voice whisper, "Johnny, did you hear that? Someone's out there." Johnny's whispered response was, "shush, be quite I heard it."

Running Eagle was surprised, he actually understood the white man's talk. Running Eagle uttered a perfect imitation of a great Owl hunting.

Johnny stood, the tension no longer in his voice; "shucks, its' just and old hooty-owl, done caught hisself a mouse.

Chief Old Wise One's explicit instructions that his was a party of peace. That he should not kill the whites, was the only reason that these men would live to see another sun-rise.

Running Eagle noiselessly, withdrew. He would wait. A better opportunity to appease the spirits, to strengthen his, and his father's weakened medicine, would present itself.

****

Mandy arose early. She grabbed the bag that was used to collect kindling for the fires. Mandy stepped down and away from the wagon. The encampment was slowly, gradually, coming to life.

The sun was peeking through the eastern sky. Mandy turned away from the rising sun. She began to slowly walk with her back to the sun. Picking up twigs and branches as she walked.

As she stuffed her bag with twigs, she took a tentative glance over her shoulder. Her eyes scanned the wagon train, as far as she could tell no one was paying any particular attention to her.

Mandy saw a small hill directly in front of her. As she began to crest the top of the hill, she turned and silently mouthed, "Good bye, Becky, good bye my sister." She turned and slowly walked down the hill. Then she began to run towards a stand of willow trees.

Mandy disappeared amongst the trees. She stopped to catch her breath. While still panting, Mandy hurriedly stepped out of the dress that Gerty had given her.

She emptied the bag of kindling. At the bottom of the bag, amid the twigs and branches, was the deerskin dress that she had been wearing when she and Becky, three days ago had met Captain Smith, the wagon master.

Mandy quickly donned her deerskin dress she picked up the rolled-up parchment, and ran.

Pretty Buffalo Hair was running, head down, as fast as she could. She looked up at the sound of hoofbeats, riding towards her was an Indian, his face was clearly covered with black and red war paint.

Her first instinct was to turn, and flee back towards the wagon train.

Then she heard it. "Mahn-dee, Pretty Buffalo Hair." Mandy stopped in her tracks, turned and ran towards that, oh so familiar voice.

Mandy stopped. Running Eagle, riding at a full gallop, hung down from his perch astride his war pony, and swept Mandy up into his arms.

With Mandy arms firmly, lovingly wrapped around him, Running Eagle kneed his pony. They rode at a gallop, away from the wagon train, towards their village, towards their people, towards their home.

****

Pretty Buffalo Hair's arms were wrapped tightly around Running Eagles' waist. As they galloped across the prairie, his and her hair blowing in the breeze, Pretty Buffalo Hair buried her face into the small of her man's back.

Running Eagle's musky, masculine scent was like ambrosia to her senses. For the first time since being captured by the Comanche, Pretty Buffalo Hair felt that she was absolutely free.

She had had choices, and she had chosen by her own volition, to be where she was. Racing across a sea of gently waving, sweet grass, clinging to hold on to this strong, noble, warrior, her husband, the father of her unborn son.

Her body was free, her mind was free, Mandy/Pretty Buffalo Hair for the first time in her life, felt that she was at last, truly FREE.

****

After they had ridden hard, double for ten minutes, Running Eagle, slowed the tired, heavily lathered pony. He threw his right leg across the drooping neck of his pony, jumped to the ground, helped his wife to the ground, and sprinted back in the direction that they had just traversed.

Satisfied that they were not being pursued, Running Eagle trotted back to his wife.

Pretty Buffalo Hair ran to meet him. He held her in his arms and covered her face with kisses. They both had tears of joy, streaming down their cheeks.

She because she was back in his arms, he because he loved her and his *PUHA*, had not deserted him. Last night his medicine, his *puha*, had prevented him from killing this wonderful, beautiful woman, Pretty Buffalo Hair, his wife."

"My wonderful husband, I knew you would come for me, you would not abandon me."

Running Eagle examined his wife. Her hair was no longer braided. Instead it sat atop her as if it were a crown, a natural battle helmet. She was dressed as she had been when he had watched her and the white girl, ride into the camp of the hair-mouths.

As he held her at arm's length and gazed into her beautiful brown eyes, Running Eagle began to tremble. He trembled when he thought of how close he had come to killing the only woman that he had ever loved, of killing his unborn son.

Pretty Buffalo Hair felt her husband's shiver. A look of concern, replaced the look of happiness that had spread across her face. She placed the back of her hand against her husband's forehead; "My husband, you tremble... are you ill?"

Running Eagle gently removed her hand from his forehead. He kissed the palm of her hand, and unabashedly, this fearless warrior, this man who feared no man, began to cry.

"My wife, my tears are of joy and happiness. They are the tears of mourning that my soul felt at the thought that I had lost you. The tears of mourning that lay hidden in my heart and soul have burst forth as tears of joy and happiness, because now you are here with me. Now I hold you in my arms."

Hand in hand, the fierce Comanche warrior, he leading his still weary pony, his face painted for battle, and his radiant smiling woman, began walking. They were going home.

****

The couple's approach to the village was first observed by one of the young boys, charged with watching the band's pony herd.

As the couple, riding double, Pretty Buffalo Hair in front, Running Eagle seated behind, entered the village, they were met by what appeared to be a delegation of three, consisting of Gray Wolf, Chief Old Wise One, and Stone Fist.

Leaping Boy, the youth that had first spotted the couple, had rode ahead and alerted Stone Fist, who in turn informed the others of the couples pending arrival.

Stone Fist was the first to speak. "Welcome home my brother." Stone Fist did not acknowledge the presence of Pretty Buffalo Hair.

Running Eagle vaulted down to the ground. He then immediately assisted Pretty Buffalo Hair in dismounting. Gray Wolf clasped his son by his shoulders. "My son, your return has been much too long awaited."

"Tomorrow we join the other bands for the last big hunt of the season. The hunt that will provide the meat needed to fill the bellies of our women and our children during the cold winter that we face."

Little Flower walked over and placed her arms around Pretty Buffalo Hair. She smiled, "welcome home my daughter...we have missed you."

****

Running Eagle had sat patiently answering questions posed by the members of the council. He detailed the white man's vigilance, his tactics, in guarding and protecting his wagons.

Running Eagle was eager to return and share some private moments with his wife. He was slightly annoyed when he heard the sounds of multiple female voices coming from within the confines of his tepee.

Running Eagle hesitated at the entrance. He recognized the distinctive sound of his sister, Spring Blossom's lyrical voice. "What hides do the white women use for their dresses?" Her heard his mother Little Flower chime in; "Do the white women paint their faces?"

Since one of the women that his wife was entertaining was his mother Little Flower, he reasoned that his father Gray Wolf would be returning from the council meeting, to an empty lodge.

Running Eagle decided that this would be a good time for him to visit and seek the counsel of his father.

When Running Eagle entered the lodge of Gray Wolf, he found his father picking chunks of meat from a kettle, resting on the heated stones, still glowing in the fire pit.

"Ah, your presence here at my lodge, confirms my suspicions as to the whereabouts of my wife. My wife Little Flower is with your wife, Pretty Buffalo Hair."

"Come my son sit…join me. When I returned from the council, I found the lodge empty, but the stew was hot, which makes me believe that the women have not been visiting for long."

After they had smoked and passed the pipe twice, Gray Wolf spoke; "Running Eagle, though you are back with Pretty Buffalo Hair, among the people, and your belly is full, something weighs heavy on your heart."

Running Eagle sat silently. Gray Wolf studied his son's face. It was obvious that the younger warrior was struggling.

After taking a deep breath, Running Eagle spoke; "My father I have been less than honest with Pretty Buffalo Hair. I have been deceitful."

Running Eagle repeated a portion of what he had reported at the council meeting. He told of how, during the early morning, just after sunrise, he had seen Pretty Buffalo Hair leave the wagon, collecting wood for the cooking fire.

Running Eagle told of how she appeared, to be aimlessly picking up twigs and putting them into her bag. Running Eagle told of how he had reluctantly, after deep meditation, made plans to kill the woman he loved, his wife, Pretty Buffalo Hair.

Running Eagle told of how Pretty Buffalo Hair had walked slowly over the hill, in her silly white woman's dress, and after several minutes, had emerged at the top of the ridge, running, towards him, dressed as a woman of the People.

He spoke to his father of his vision, the vision when Pretty Buffalo Hair had changed before his eyes. He told of how he knew at that moment, that the spirits had abandoned him that his medicine was strong.

Running Eagle told of how, when she saw him, in full war paint, she had turned to run from him, how she stopped in mid-stride, when he called her name.

Gray Wolf sat silently, concentrating on his son's every word. Running Eagle, in a piteous, anguished voice told of how Pretty Buffalo Hair had turned to him, ran to him, trusting him, loving him.

"My son, it is good that you shared with me your vision. It is good that your spirit protector has made known to you, that your medicine is strong. I ask again, my son, why is your heart troubled?"

Running Eagle took a deep breath and spoke to his father; "during the night, before she left the white man's wagons, Pretty Buffalo Hair said she heard my voice call to her. She said that my voice had come to her in the hoot of the owl. She said she knew then, that I had not abandoned her, that I would come for her."

Running Eagle rose from the couch. He paced back and forth in front of the dying fire. "Pretty Buffalo Hair believed in me; she did not lose faith in me. Pretty *Buffalo Hair* knew that I would come for her".

"Pretty Buffalo Hair, my wife, did not know that I had come to take her life."

Gray Wolf motioned for Running Eagle to be seated. After he had once again seated himself beside his father, Running Eagle head bowed, stared at the thick buffalo robe beneath his feet.

"I have heard your words, still I do not know what troubles you." Running Eagle lowered his eyes, "I have deceived Pretty Buffalo Hair."

"After we fled from the white man's wagons, we stopped to rest the pony. Pretty Buffalo Hair said that she saw me riding towards her, at first, she had turned to run because all that she saw riding towards her, was a fierce warrior in full war paint."

Pretty Buffalo Hair asked if I wore war paint because I had come to fight for her?" Gray Wolf asked; "What were your words to Pretty Buffalo hair?"

Running Eagle, his head lowered, mumbled; "That I wore war paint because I had come for her. I did not tell Pretty Buffalo Hair that I wore war paint, because I had come to kill her. I did not tell Pretty Buffalo Hair that I wore black paint to mourn her death."

Running Eagle sat silently, dejected, his face distorted with guilt.

Gray Wolf relit his pipe. He smoked in silence. The sweet pungent smell of the smoke from his pipe pervaded the lodge. The smoke from his pipe encircled Gray Wolf's head.

After what to Running Eagle, seemed forever, Gray Wolf spoke; "My son do you love this woman, Pretty Buffalo Hair?" "Yes, my father…I love Pretty Buffalo Hair above all others."

Gray Wolf placed the stem of his pipe between his lips, he drew in and blew out two puffs of smoke; "My son…does your love for your wife, the woman who carries your war shield, exceed your love your love for Little Flower, your mother, for Spring Blossom, your sister, does it exceed your love for me, your father?"

Running Eagle, took a moment to collect his thoughts; "My father, all of the people, the members of my family, I love, I would give my life for."

"Pretty Buffalo Hair is my wife; she is my shield carrying wife. She will soon be the mother of my son. I love Pretty Buffalo Hair above all others."

"Pretty Buffalo Hair is my wife; she carries my shield. She carries my child. She will soon be the mother of my son. I love Pretty Buffalo Hair above all others."

"My son, that is as it should be. "Love without commitment is just a word without meaning. When you speak of your love for Pretty Buffalo Hair, what is your commitment?"

"I will provide for her; I will protect her." Gray Wolf sat back on his buffalo couch; "You will protect her from our enemies. But will you protect Pretty Buffalo Hair from being hurt?"

Running Eagle looked confused, "My father, your meaning is unclear to me."

Gray Wolf puffed again on his pipe. "If you tell Pretty Buffalo Hair that the night that you called to her with the voice of the owl, that that night you were coming to kill her, do you think that that knowledge will gladden her heart, or that that knowledge will bring to her heart, hurt?"

Before Running Eagle could speak, Gray Wolf continued; "Pretty Buffalo Hair is new to the ways, the laws, and the customs of the Comanche. Your telling this to Pretty Buffalo Hair would be selfish."

"It would make you feel better. You are an honest and honorable man. The telling of this would hurt Pretty Buffalo Hair. You would needlessly, selfishly, hurt the one you love beyond all others."

Both men heard the unmistakable chatter of Little Flower and Spring Blossom, on the path leading to the lodge.

Gray Wolf rose, walked to the entrance flap of the tepee, and opened the flap; "Go to your wife. I am Gray Wolf, your father. I have spoken."

****

When Running Eagle entered his tepee, he found Pretty Buffalo Hair, busy roasting buffalo ribs over the open flame of a spit that she had placed over the cooking fire. "My husband, I missed you. Where did you go? Have you eaten?" Are you hungry? Her questions were asked in rapid succession, one right after the other.

Running Eagle sensing that Pretty Buffalo Hair may have been feeling guilty for her impromptu entertaining of his mother and his sister, sought quickly to put her at ease. "I have eaten with my father.

Although you were not aware of my mother and sister's surprise visit, our mother left a large meal of antelope stew, for my father, and judging by the quantity of meat, she intended a meal for me."

"It is good that the three women I love, the three most beautiful of all the Comanche women, love each other, and are all three, very good friends. I enjoy sitting and talking with my father. Besides being my father, Gray Wolf is a wise and honorable warrior."

Pretty Buffalo Hair took the wooden stick, on which were skewed charred ribs, their delicious smelling dripping, causing crackling sounds, as they fell into the flame. She handed the aromatic, juicy meat to her husband.

Running Eagle switched the stick from his right to his left hand, licked his fingers of his right hand and bit into the succulent rib. "My stomach makes mockery of my words; this is delicious meat."

Running Eagle caught Pretty Buffalo Hair by her wrist, and gently pulled her down into his lap. "While those buffalo's ribs are tasty, they do not compare with the taste of these "Pretty Buffalo Hair" ribs." He pulled Pretty Buffalo Hair' dress over her head, and he began to gently nozzle Pretty Buffalo Hair's ribs, just above her noticeably expanding waist.

The skewered meat that Pretty Buffalo Hair had cooked, lay burning in the fire, where he had dropped it, as Running Eagle sprayed hot kisses upon his wife's ribs, her stomach, her thighs.

With his knee, he gently parted his thighs. Running Eagle untied his breechclout.

He smiled to himself, as a strange thought fleetingly, crossed his mind, I am about to place the most delicious "*Pretty Buffalo Hair*" meat, on the stiff skewer of Running Eagle.

Running Eagle made tender, slow delicious love with his wife.

****

Pretty Buffalo Hair lay happy, and content in her husband's arms. While she lay there waiting to be overtaken by sleep, her mind began to drift.

She thought of Becky. She thought of Becky, of their lives together. She thought of their childhood. She began to dream.

In her dream, Rebecca was clutching "Patty", her favorite doll, in her left hand, and with her other hand, Becky was holding on to Mandy. Rebecca's big brother Jesse was sitting astride the back of his pretend horse, Mandy's brother Jason.

Twelve-year-old Jessie was kicking the skinny slave boy, in the ribs; "Get up you lazy bag of bones, we've gotta reach Miss Perkins' farm before those murdering redskins do. Get moving you lazy black bastard."

Seven-year-old Rebecca was pleading with her brother, "Jesse, can we play with you and Jason? Please, please, Jesse, let me and Mandy play with you.

Jesse waved his hand dismissively, "Becky you and Mandy get. You're too little. Besides you don't know nothing about wild, Injuns. Jesse lifted the piece of wood that was his rifle, and bellowed; Hold on Miss Perkins, "Buckskin Bob" is on the way, Buckskin Bob will safe you and your little girl, I'm gonna kill every last one of those savage redskins."

Jesse kicked Jason savagely in the ribs, and pulled sharply on the rope that he had forced between the boy's lips. The skinny slave boy grimaced in pain, and then began to crawl, as fast as he could manage, through the mud and the muck of the yard.

* *

Pretty Buffalo Hair awoke with a start. She sat bolt upright. Her sudden movements had startled Running Eagle.

Revenge raids by enemy tribes, though a rarity during these large gatherings of the numerous Comanche clans, did sometimes occur.

Running Eagle sprang to his feet, in a defensive crutch. His weight was centered on the balls of his feet. Running Eagle held his hunting knife, thrust before him, clutched in his hand. He was alert, ready to defend his family.

Running Eagle swiftly surveyed his surroundings. There were no intruders in the tepee. He looked down at his wife. Pretty Buffalo Hair was trembling.

Running Eagle discarded his knife, dropped to his knees, and wrapped his arms around Pretty Buffalo Hair's shoulders. "You are safe, it was only a bad dream. I am here. Nothing will harm you."

Pretty Buffalo Hair slowly relaxed. Her husband's strong arms and his comforting words, enveloped and soothed her.

She realized that Running Eagle was right. It was just a dream. As he gently rocked her, she gradually relaxed, and fell into a dreamless sleep.

****

Before the sun could peek over the eastern horizon, the hunting parties from the various bands left for the big hunt.

Little Flower and Spring Blossom, their butchering equipment packed and loaded onto their pony and mule-drags, were preparing to join the many women, from the many bands, who would be following, close behind the hunters.

Pretty Buffalo Hair walked over to one of Little Flower's travois, she placed her bundled knifes onto the travois.

Little Flower walked up to Pretty Buffalo Hair; "My daughter, since you carry your first child, my first grandchild, and Spring Blossom's first nephew. I do not want you to participate in the butchering on the killing fields."

"Little Flower, my mother, and also you Spring Blossom, my sister, I deeply appreciate your concern. But I have been told that this is the last big buffalo hunt before we move to our winter camp".

The many buffalo said to be in the herd, as reported by our scouts, means that the butchering will require as many women as possible. I want to help."

Little Flower looked at Pretty Buffalo Hair, then at Spring Blossom. "I would speak with Spring Blossom".

After a short conversation, Little Flower turned to speak with her pregnant daughter/daughter-in-law.

"Pretty Buffalo Hair, I will permit you to join Spring Blossom and me on the hunt, if you agree to the following:"

"You will not venture on to the killing field. You will wait to butcher buffalo sections that are sent back to you on the mule-drags. You will stop work when I decide that you should. Do you agree?"

Pretty Buffalo Hair though disappointed, agreed to Little Flowers conditions.

****

The communal buffalo hunt, the last large hunt before the various bands separated and traveled to their winter camps, was a huge success.

Running Eagle, and Gray Wolf managed to bring down between them, twenty-five adult buffalo. Stone Fist's count was eight, and rising, before his pony tripped, sending him to the ground amongst the stampeding, crazed, animals.

When Stone Fist fell, ironically one of the cows that had two of his arrows protruding from her ribs, collapsed on his left leg.

In the midst of the cacophony of noise being made by the hunters and the panicked beasts, Stone Fist claimed that when the weight of the cow landed on his leg, he distinctly heard the bone in his left thigh crack.

Gray Wolf, who was riding abreast of Stone Fist, saw the incident. He and a hunter from the Snake Eaters band were able to pull the crippled hunter from the danger of being trampled by the crazed, stampeding beasts.

****

Little Flower, Spring Blossom, and Pretty Buffalo Hair efficiently accomplished the butchering and processing of the meat, and the tanning of the hides of thirty-three adult buffalo, and seven calves.

Stone Fist's mother, Quite One, and his grandmother, Hen's Teeth, spent most of their time tending to Stone Fist's injuries, nursing their provider back to good health.

For Pretty Buffalo Hair, the three weeks spent at the communal gathering of the bands of Comanches, were busy times. The seemingly never-ending work, was a welcome distraction from her recurring feelings of depression, and the increasingly, troubling dreams.

Pretty Buffalo Hair spoke to Little Flower of her mood swings, and the recurring dreams. Little Flower had assured her that mood swings, cravings and the like, were common when a woman was with child.

Little Flower had attributed the changes to, "the mother spirit", preparing the body to nourish and develop the unborn child". Pretty Buffalo Hair, rather the "*Mandy*" remnant of Pretty Buffalo Hair, reconciled Little Flower's words with those of "*Mandy's*" her former teacher, in her former life, Miss Eleanor Leary.

Miss Leary during her biology lecture, had spoke of theorized hormonal, substance changes in the woman's life span. Changes in her body's chemistry, which brought on; first menstruation, then childbirth, and later menopause.

Mandy, who *was now more and more, coming to think of herself solely* as Pretty Buffalo Hair, would on occasion reflect on the markedly similar wisdom of the two highly intelligent women, living in two entirely different worlds, who had influenced her life. The white Irish woman, Eleanor Leary, and her Comanche mother, Little Flower.

Little Flower was becoming mildly concerned about Pretty Buffalo Hair's recurrent nightmares.

The meaning of visions, and dreams, good or bad, could best be interpreted by their Holy Man, their Shaman, "He Who Speaks To Ghosts".

Little Flower told the Holy Man of her daughter's troubling, recurring dreams.

He Who Speaks To Ghosts promised Little Flower, that he would speak of this to the spirits, and would share the spirit's counsel with Pretty Buffalo Hair, after the band had settled into their winter camp.

****

The site that Chief Old Wise One had chosen for their permanent winter encampment was a beautiful green valley.

The valley was encircled by wooded timber, and buffered by high ridges and bluffs. The valley bordered a large creek, with more than sufficient water for the people and their domesticated animals.

The high ridges provided a natural wall, which afforded the People shelter from the frequent cold chilling winds, and blizzards that swept down from the north, paralyzing the plains in deep frigid white blankets of snow.

The tepees were swiftly erected. Additional layers of buffalo hides were lashed to the structural poles inside the tepees to provide insulation.

All of the lodge entrances, faced east, to allow the dwelling's occupants to be greeted each morning, by the life- giving rays of father sun.

The village was laid out in one large circle, with smaller circles within smaller circles. The innermost circle was comprised of the tepees of Chief Old Wise One, Chief Thundercloud, the Holy Man, He Who Speaks To Ghosts, and three other minor chiefs.

Gray Wolf's tepee was one of the large tepees of the first circle, removed from the innermost circle.

Running Eagle, and Stone Fist's tepees were pitched in the second ring, removed from the innermost circle. This circle was comprised of the tepees of warriors who had counted many coups, and had distinguished themselves in battle.

The mood of the camp's women was relaxed, often jubilant. The pressures associated with supporting their men during war, during the hunt for food, and the constant burden of erecting, dismantling, and moving the household as they followed the trail of the buffalo, were no longer present.

Pretty Buffalo Hair was finding, that in general, life in the winter encampment was for the People, an overall, enjoyable time, a time to relax and to enjoy the company of family and friends.

Occasionally, the men would join small hunting parties, and some, usually the younger braves seeking glory, would participate in small raiding parties.

But for the most part, especially when snow fell, the men and women of the camp enjoyed their time spent around their lodge's warm fires, the men making and repairing their weapons, the women making and repairing the family's clothing.

Little Flower was especially happy and content. Her husband Gray Wolf, her son Running Eagle, and her daughter Spring Blossom's husband, Stone Fist, had provided well. Food would not be a problem this winter.

Little Flower thanked the Great Spirit for her wonderful, growing family. It was two sleeps ago, that Spring Blossom had informed her that she too, was with child.

Little Flower was seated beside the warm glow of her fire. Gray Wolf had gone to smoke and to gamble with friends. Little Flower was busy cutting the soft pliant pelt of doeskin, into two sets of infant moccasins.

She was making one pair of the baby booties, for each of her expected, grandbabies.

Pretty Buffalo Hair entered the tepee. Little Flower looked up from her work. "My daughter, my beautiful daughter, come in, come in."

"Look", she held up the doeskin, "I am making two pairs of moccasins, one for the child of Running Eagle and Pretty Buffalo Hair, and a pair of moccasins for the child of Spring Blossom and Stone Fist."

"Life is good. Is it not wonderful? I will soon have two papooses to love and to spoil."

The fact that Pretty Buffalo Hair was with child was now obvious. She had just entered the fifth moon cycle of her pregnancy.

"Mother, my bad dreams continue. Last night I saw my aunt Sadie, being raped, defiled at the hands of two white men. When she was raped, she was just a girl of eleven summers."

"In my dream, the white men, after they raped my aunt Sadie, would not stop laughing. They threw her into the river. When her head surfaced, instead of Sadie's face, the face was mine. The white men held my head under water."

"I woke up in a panic, gasping for air, as if I had actually been drowning in the river. Instead of river water, I was drenched in my own perspiration. It was fortunate that Running Eagle is away, hunting antelope, and was not sharing our sleeping robes."

Little Flower saw the anguish that was distorting her beautiful daughter's face. She rose from her seat, walked over and put her arms around the piteously, sobbing young woman.

"Tomorrow, I will take you to, He Who Speaks To Ghosts."

****

He Who Speaks To Ghost listened as Pretty Buffalo Hair told of her recent spates of irritability, her sudden mood changes. These things did not alarm the Holy Man.

These things he had seen many times before. He Who Speaks To Ghost, attributed these things to the changes that women went through when they are with child.

The Holy Man was about to dismiss the distraught girl with some sanguine, innocuous advice, when Little Flower, the girl's mother interrupted; "Pretty Buffalo Hair, tell the Holy Man of your frightening visions."

Pretty Buffalo Hair, took a deep, calming breath. She then told He Who Speaks To Ghost, of the rape and the drowning of her aunt Sadie at the hands of the white men.

She told of how in her "*vision*" the drowned, bloated face of her aunt, had become her face, the face of Pretty Buffalo Hair.

She told of the white man on the wagon train, mercilessly whipping the mule. She told of how the tormented, blooded face of the mule had become the face of a black boy, the boy Pee wee. A boy that she had known on the huge farm that the white men called Rosewood Plantation.

He Who Talked To Ghosts asked, "Do these visions come to you only when you sleep? Or do they visit you when you are awake?"

Pretty Buffalo Hair answered; "At first the visions came only when I slept. Recently I have come to see patches of the vision when I am awake. The visions come to me when I am cooking, when I am sewing, when I am engaged in conversation with my friends."

The Shaman's expression, during Pretty Buffalo Hair's telling of her visions, had changed drastically. His first reaction had been that the beautiful young woman was not having true visions. That she was having a series of bad dreams, even possibly dreams that some would call, nightmares.

This he was inclined to attribute an angry stomach, troubling her sleep, as the girl's stomach rebelled at sharing space with the growing papoose.

His opinioned changed when Pretty Buffalo Hair told of having the visions while she was awake. "Pretty Buffalo Hair, when these visions come while you are awake, do they come to you before or after you have eaten? Do you or your husband Running Eagle eat, drink, or smoke the peyote?"

Pretty Buffalo Hair's response was that the visions, when she was awake, first came when she was working alone. Now they came at any time. She looked at the Holy Man, then at Little Flower and asked, "What is this peyote that you speak of?"

Little Flower answered the Shaman; "None of Gray Wolf's family uses the peyote."

He Who Speaks To Ghosts, stood; "I will rid you of your visions. I will rid you of the evil, dark spirits. Tomorrow, after the sun goes to rest in the western sky, Little Flower is to bring you to my tepee."

The Holy Man held up his right fist. He extended his fingers, one at a time. Little Flower, you are to bring Pretty Buffalo Hair to me, one, two, three, for four sleeps."

The morning of her first treatment, Pretty Buffalo Hair, accompanied by Little Flower, went to bathe in the clear, cold, frigid, waters of the stream, adjacent to the encampment.

As Pretty Buffalo Hair pulled her loosely fitting dress over her head, Little Flower's eyes quickly and expertly examined her daughter's ever-changing, pregnant body.

The color of her daughter's beautiful bronzed skin that had been shielded from the rays of father sun was noticeably lighter than that of her face.

Pretty Buffalo Hair's belly protruded from her frame, just slightly more than the distance projected, by her swelling breasts. When her first-time pregnant daughter turned to kick off her moccasins, Little Flower was able to examine her profile.

Little Flower observed that Pretty Buffalo Hair's extended belly and her firm buttocks appeared to extend about the same distance from the midline.

With a thankful sigh of gratitude and appreciation, Little Flower concluded that Pretty Buffalo Hair appeared to be a beautiful, healthy, fertile, young woman of the People. She appeared to be carrying well, Little Flower's first grandchild, the next generation of Comanche.

After Pretty Buffalo Hair had followed, He Who Speaks To Ghost's instructions, by cleansing her body in the frigid waters, she joined Little Flower on the bank of the stream.

As Little Flower was drying her daughter's back with a soft, absorbent, cloth she spoke; "My daughter, wife of my son, you are a beautiful Comanche woman, soon to be the beautiful mother of a strong Comanche warrior."

The two women, mother and daughter walked together, to the lodge of the Shaman, the Holy Man, He Who Speaks To Ghosts.

****

When they entered the lodge of the shaman, they found He Who Speaks To Ghosts, to be in deep meditation.

The two women stood silently, respectfully, outside the entrance of the tepee of the Holy Man. Finally, He Who Speaks To Ghosts swung open the flap to his tepee.

He motioned that the women should enter the tepee. Pretty Buffalo Hair was instructed to lie down on a buffalo robe couch. A ring of eagle talons surrounded the buffalo robe.

He Who Speaks To Ghosts wore a heavy buffalo hide, with the beast's head with horns, intact. The hide extended from the shaman's head to his heels.

The Holy Man had strung around his neck a pouch. The pouch was filled with a black powdery like substance. In his hands he clutched two rattles, the dried tails of rattlesnakes.

As she lay on the robe, Pretty Buffalo Hair closed her eyes. He Who Speaks To Ghosts began to chant and to dance around her. He stopped, bent over Pretty Buffalo Hair, and breathing heavily, he spit on her stomach, and her head.

"Evil, dark spirits, It is I, He Who Speaks To Ghosts. I command that you, leave this woman's body!" The shaman reached into the pouch suspended from his neck, removed a pinch of powder, and threw it into the fire. The fire erupted with a small explosion. He Who Speaks To Ghosts repeated the ritual a total of four times.

He then turned to Little Flower, and indicated that she should assist her daughter. Little Flower went to Pretty Buffalo Hair, extended her hands and helped the pregnant girl rise from the buffalo robe.

He Who Speaks To Ghosts spoke; "You are to come to me a total of four times. After the fourth treatment, the evil, dark spirits will have departed your mind, and your body. I am He Who Speaks To Ghosts. I have spoken."

As much as she wanted to believe, Pretty Buffalo Hair, to her dismay, doubted that the chants, the dancing, blowing of his breath, the spitting on her head and abdomen, that the powerful medicine, the *puha* of the Holy Man, would rid her of her disturbing dreams.

Pretty Buffalo Hair had, in five short months, completely accepted and believed in the lifestyle of the Comanche.

However to her chagrin, her extremely intelligent, educated brain, having been exposed to, and indoctrinated with sixteen years of the white man's perspective, his "scientific method of practicing medicine, her brain would not, could not, accept the feasibility, and the viability of the art of healing, as practiced by the Comanche Holy Man.

Pretty Buffalo Hair realized that this moment might very well be her defining moment. "I must have faith…these are the beliefs of the People. I am of the People. This is not just a whole lot of primitive superstition!"

"I must have faith…I must keep the faith!"

****

Following the third day of the shaman's treatment regime, Pretty Buffalo Hair was once again assailed by a vision. It occurred as she was leaving to visit the lodge of her sister, Spring Blossom. The vision was still yet another, version of the recurring *Sadie* visions.

As she was about to leave her lodge, she experienced a sharp, throbbing, pain in her head, just above her left temple.

Pretty Buffalo Hair placed her hands onto her temples. She slumped onto one of her buffalo robe couches. Pretty Buffalo Hair began to gently message her temples. She closed her eyes, waiting and hoping that the pain would subside.

As she reclined on the couch, eyes closed, she was once again visited by the image of her Aunt Sadie's drowning. Again, the image of Sadie's bloated face morphing into her own was repeated.

However, this time, she saw and recognized the face of the white man, stubbornly, steadily pushing her head under water. The face was that of Henry Billings, the face of her father.

Pretty Buffalo Hair told Little Flower, of the re-occurrence of the visions. She asked for Little Flower's advice; "My mother, I do not think that the Holy Man's treatment is working. Do you think that I should inform him of today's vision? Do you think that I should abandon his treatments?"

Without hesitation, Little Flower responded; "Pretty Flower, do you recall the words of the Holy Man, He Who Speaks To Ghosts?" Little Flower held up four fingers, "His words were that after four treatments, he would drive the evil, dark spirits from you. You have received but three treatments."

Before the commencement of the fourth and final session, Pretty Buffalo Hair told the Holy Man of the sharp pain to her temples, that she had experienced, and the subsequent vision.

The Holy Man, responded by repeating; "After the fourth treatment, the evil, dark spirits will have departed your mind, and your body. I am He Who Speaks To Ghosts. I have spoken."

The first night following the conclusion of the Holy Man's therapy, when Pretty Buffalo Hair retired to her sleeping robes, she was hopeful for a good night's sleep.

She wanted to believe, to have faith in He Who Speaks To Ghosts' definitive proclamation, that she would now be free of bad dreams, nightmares, and visions.

She was apprehensive, her mind still with some residual doubts. She lay restless, afraid to sleep. After a long period of tossing and turning, Pretty Buffalo Hair finally, drifted into sleep.

She dreamt. She dreamed of her husband, Running Eagle. She dreamt of the time, shortly after their marriage, when they had left the village.

She dreamt of the glorious days and nights that she and Running Eagle had shared, alone together, just the two of them, falling deeper and deeper, in love.

She dreamt of her and Running Eagle's passion as they explored each other's bodies.

She dreamt of the ecstasy, she had felt that moment when he exploded within her, his hot seed coursing through her body.

She dreamt of the exact moment, when holding her husband's spent body, locked between her thighs, that she knew beyond a doubt, that that was the moment that she had conceived their son.

The next morning, Pretty Buffalo Hair awoke refreshed, smiling, and happy.

****

While their men were away hunting, Pretty Buffalo Hair and Spring Blossom the two sisters, sisters-in-law, had become best friends.

In addition to their strong familial bonds, they were now sharing the experience of going through their first pregnancy together.

The two women spent most of their time together. To the inhabitants of the village, Pretty Buffalo Hair and Spring Blossom seemed to be inseparable.

They collected wood for their fires together. They took their meals together.
Meals were cooked and consumed at either the lodge of Running Eagle, or at the lodge of Stone Fist.

The one person that they allowed into their inner circle was Little Flower, their mother the exuberant, expectant grandmother of both of their babies.

The three women sat for hours, repairing clothing, making new buckskin shirts and leggings for their men. Making dresses of deer, elk and antelope skins for themselves.

While all three women were adept at each facet of the process, Pretty Buffalo Hair was the first to recognize that within this small group of laborers, each woman appeared to excel in one or two particular crafts.

Little Flower's expertise was the outlining and the cutting of the many patterns. Almost as if by magic, when she lay out and cut hide for the front and the back of a garment, the two pieces fit each other perfectly.

Spring Blossom's nimble fingers made her an ideal seamstress. Her ability to handle an awl would rival her husband, the mighty Stone Fist's skill with his war club.

Pretty Buffalo Hair had become skilled at adorning the garments with beads, shells, quills, and fringes.

It was Little Flower's idea that instead of each woman starting and finishing each garment or pair of moccasins, that it would be much more efficient if they were to divide the labor.

Little Flower drew the patterns, and cut the hides for all of the dresses, shirts, leggings and moccasins.

Spring Blossom expertly, sewed the individual pieces of hide together.

Pretty Buffalo Hair applied the finishing touch to the garments, with patterned arrays of beads, shells, quills, and fringes.

* *

Running Eagle and Stone Fist returned to the encampment. Their hunting trip had not yielded nearly the amount of fresh meat that the two hunters had anticipated.

The hunter-warriors had traveled far beyond the region that the council had deemed advisable. Although the threat of enemy warriors was small, the threat of being caught in an unexpected blizzard, an avalanche of snow, was a real and a constant danger.

* *

Running Eagle and Pretty Buffalo Hair lay together, wrapped in their thick buffalo-sleeping robe. Warm, happy and content, listening to the whistling sound of the chilling wind, and falling snow, cascading down from the north.

The couple had just recently finished their evening meal. Pretty Buffalo Hair had prepared one of her husband's favorite meals. She had made a hearty stew, heavily laced with thick chunks of fresh venison, seasoned with wild onions, and wild potatoes, swirling in the thick, delicious smelling mixture.

Running Eagle and Pretty Buffalo Hair lay facing the still warm, but dying fire. Pretty Buffalo Hair was lying on her side. Running Eagle was snuggled up, pressed tightly against her back, his arms around her, gently stroking her swollen belly.

"It is good to have you home my husband. I have counted the days, and the nights, I asked for, and was granted by the Great Spirit, your safe return."

Running Eagle gently nuzzled her neck, and kissed her ear. He mumbled as his nose burrowed into and beneath his wife's fragrant *"pretty buffalo hair"*; "I too rejoice at being here with you. My beloved wife, I truly love you. I am happiest when I am here with you, here with you where I belong."

Pretty Buffalo Hair sighed she closed her eyes and remained silent for a few brief seconds. When she spoke, she spoke in English, choosing her words carefully; "Together we, you and I, speak the language of the Comanche, as well as the talk of the white man. Despite my having the many words of those two languages, there are not enough words for me to truly express the love that I have in my heart for you."

She abruptly switched from English to the tongue of the Comanche; "I, Pretty Buffalo Hair, truly love you, Running Eagle, my husband."

"I say I love you in two languages, using many words. Before you, I did not believe it possible for anyone to love another, as much as I love you. I exist to be with you. Without your love, I would cease to exist."

"Running Eagle my beloved husband, you have completed me."

Running Eagle felt his wife shiver and tremble in his arms. Thinking that he may have been causing her some sort of physical discomfort, he began to remove his arm.

Pretty Buffalo Hair clasped his hands with hers, and returned them to her stomach. As if on cue, the baby gave a swift, gentle kick to his mother's abdomen.

Running Eagle excitedly exclaimed; "Did you feel that? The little warrior kicked you." Pretty Buffalo Hair smiled, "Of course my husband...I felt it."

"How could I not have felt the energy of the son of Running Eagle, one of the future leaders of the Comanche people, stirring inside my body"?

****

Most of the community looked forward to the time spent at the winter encampment. This was the season when the fast paced, nomadic lifestyle of the People, dramatically, slowed down.

Having had centuries to adapt to and grow accustomed to the harsh frigid temperatures, and the many snowstorms that swept down onto the plains, the People used their time spent at their winter encampment, to rest, to socialize with family and friends.

Life at the winter camp was a welcomed change from the constant pressures of defending their territory from their enemies.

A brief reprieve from the ancient on-going wars, with the hostile tribes of red men, and now the new threat, the white man, with his thunder sticks, determined attempts to steal their land.

Rest from the frequent raiding parties of the young warriors, to acquire honor and horses.

And a more than welcome suspension of the pressures felt by the women, of the continual moves, as the band followed the migration of the buffalo.

For the men, women and children of the band, the winter camp was thought of as the true home of the Comanche.

As the season gradually changed from the "Moon of the falling leaves", to the "Moon when the rivers start to freeze", the days, evenings and nights of Gray Wolf's extended family, settled into a pleasant, predictable, routine.

After they had prepared and served the morning meal to their husbands, Pretty Buffalo Hair and Spring Blossom would visit their mother, at the lodge of Gray Wolf.

Each day, before Pretty Buffalo Hair and Spring Blossom would arrive, Gray Wolf would have usually left, or would be in the process of leaving.

Gray Wolf enjoyed spending his day, smoking and talking, being in the company of his old and trusted friends. Men with whom he had fought many battles, lost many friends, and shared in many honors.

Most of the time, Gray Wolf, Chief Old Wise One, Chief Thunder Cloud, and He Who Speaks To Ghosts, would meet informally, in the village's largest tepee, the lodge of Chief Old Wise One.

Frequently these men, Gray Wolf, Chief Old Wise One, Chief Thunder Cloud, and He Who Speaks To Ghosts, the leaders of the band, would extend their social meetings, by holding council meetings.

The Council meetings were convened to discuss and to mediate civil or spiritual matters that were affecting the community.

Invited senior and respected warriors of the band would join them at council, in the lodge Of Chief Old Wise One.

Running Eagle and Stone Fist, had drifted into the habit of gathering with friends, in the tepee of Stone Fist. The young warriors would smoke, they would gamble, and they would spend countless hours talking of their past acts of individual bravery and courage.

****

Spring Blossom, and Little Flower, were busy sewing, finishing the previous day's batch of dresses. Pretty Buffalo Hair, having completed the task of adding the beautiful 'frills" to the batch of clothing, piled high in the corner of the tepee, was busy making hot tea for the group.

The quality and more importantly, the quantity of the clothing being made by the three women who met each morning in the lodge of Gary Wolf, had been noticed and favorably commented on by the women of the village.

The three women turned in unison, when they heard a persistent wrapping at the flap covering the entrance to the lodge.

Little Flower spoke; "Enter, you are welcome. Please come in." Four of the village women entered the tepee.

Little Flower rose and greeted her visitors. "Snow Bird", "Plucks Flowers", "Precious", and "White Fawn", Little Flower motioned towards a vacant couch of buffalo robes; "please be seated. You are all welcome in the lodge of Gray Wolf."

The four women sat, facing the fire. Without having been asked, Pretty Buffalo Hair, brought cups of hot tea to their visitors. The women eagerly accepted the hot beverages.

Pretty Buffalo Hair returned to the kettle. She placed additional sassafras tree bark into the boiling water. It was her intent to make more hot tea, enough for her family and for their guests.

"Snow Bird", "Plucks Flowers", "Precious", and "White Fawn", sat on the couch, and judging by their loud slurps, were appreciatively, consuming the smoldering beverage, that Pretty Buffalo Hair had previously made for herself, for her mother and for her sister.

Little Flower waited until their visitors relaxed. Little Flower addressed her comments to whom she perceived to be the spokesperson for the group, the woman so appropriately named Snow Bird; "From the snow on your robes, it is apparent that once again, winter's snow has begun to fall."

"What brings you to the lodge of Gray Wolf, during this time of the heavy falling snow?"

Snow Bird stood and placed her cup on to the couch. She turned and began to speak; "Little Flower, the four of us, are but a few of the women of our village, who admire and marvel at the quantity of work of Little Flower and her two beautiful daughters, Pretty Buffalo Hair and Spring Blossom."

"Most of our women make dresses, shirts, leggings and moccasins, that are equal to the quality of these." Snow Bird pointed to the impressive pile of clothing and moccasins in the rear of the tepee. "Yet no three of us, can make such fine clothing in the number, and in the time that you do. All of the women would like to know how this is done?"

Little Flower beamed; "My daughter Pretty Buffalo Hair suggested that instead of having one person start and finish each garment, that we should divide the work, work as a team, and each concentrate a completing a piece of the garment."

Snow Bird and the other visitors, looked at each other in wonderment. White Fawn, the youngest of the visitors stammered; "That is not our way. Each woman has always completed the work that she started."

Spring Blossom chimed in; "My sister Pretty Buffalo Hair was not raised among the People. She was brought up where much of the work was spread between many people. Pretty Buffalo Hair said that the practice that we are using, improves the amount that can be accomplished. My mother, Little Flower and I, have found this to be true."

Snow Bird while listening intently to the words of Little Flower and Spring Blossom rose from the couch. She walked over to inspect and survey the items of clothing piled high, into the corner of the tepee.

Snow Bird concluded that if the items were distributed equally between Little Flower, Spring Blossom, and Pretty Buffalo Hair, each woman's portion significantly exceeded that which the most skillful of the band's women could have made, in the passing of two moons.

Little Flower thought she knew Snow Bird's thoughts. "We have made more clothing then that which you see. Spring Blossom and Pretty Buffalo Hair, have removed some of the cloths to the lodges of Stone Fist, and Running Eagle."

Snow Bird was impressed. "Would Little Flower allow us to come tomorrow to watch a full day of your work?"

Little Flower agreed to the request. A representative group of the band's women would, after the morning meal, come to observe this new way of making clothing.

After the three visitors left, Little Flower spoke to her daughters; "Pretty Buffalo Hair, this method to increase the quantity of finished items of clothing, was yours. Why did you not respond to the questions?"

Pretty Buffalo Hair, was beaming with pride. "It was not necessary for me to answer. Both you and Spring Blossom said the words that I would have said."

"My mother, in my other life, the life I had before this, the life that I have chosen to live with, and as one of the People, I had a great teacher.

She was a white woman. Her name was Eleanor Leary. This white woman was one of the most generous, and the wisest persons, that I have ever known."

"Eleanor Leary taught me many things, some of those things that I hope to teach my husband, my son and the Comanche people."

"One of the wisest things that Miss Leary taught me was to listen to your student. If your students can teach to others, that which you have taught them, your students truly understood your lesson."

Little Flower listened, and in her mind once again gave thanks to the Great Spirit, for giving them this remarkable woman, her daughter Pretty Buffalo Hair.

"Tomorrow will be a day that the three of us, the wife of Gray Wolf, the wife of Running Eagle, and the wife of Stone Fist, will make our husbands step with pride."

"Tomorrow we will, together, as Pretty Buffalo Hair says, as a team, we will show our sisters, how to make huge numbers of finished, shirts, leggings, dresses, and moccasins."

"Spring Blossom was busy laying out materials for tomorrow's demonstration. She was examining her favorite awl, when she noticed a small crack near the tip of the spike.

She turned to Pretty Buffalo Hair, "Sister, I see that you have checked, and are satisfied with your supplies and your tools, that you will need for tomorrow. I ask a favor of you."

Spring Blossom held up the damaged awl. "Would you go to my lodge, the lodge of Stone Fist, and bring to me, my spare awl? I have much to do, to prepare for tomorrow."

Pretty Buffalo Hair rose, "Certainly my sister. "Where in the lodge of Stone Fist, do you keep the awl?" Spring Blossom nonchalantly replied; "I keep my tools in the rear, three steps to the left, from Stone Fist and my sleeping robes."

****

Pretty Buffalo Hair walked briskly through the snow, to the Lodge of Stone Fist. She noticed that the sun was about to end its' journey across the western sky.

The snow was beginning to accumulate as the diminishing rays of the setting sun bounced reflected light through-out the village.

Not expecting an answer, Pretty Buffalo Hair shook the entrance flap of Stone Fist's tepee. "Stone Fist, its' Pretty Buffalo Hair. Spring Blossom sent me for her spare awl."

As she had expected, no one answered. Stone Fist as usual at this time of day would be with Running Eagle. The two friends would be either at tribal council, or they would be engaged in games of chance with their warrior friends.

Pretty Buffalo Hair opened and latched the entrance flap, letting in the cold, but more importantly, also letting in the light. The sunlight reflecting off of the snow illuminated the interior of the tepee.

As Spring Blossom had instructed, Pretty Buffalo Hair walked to the rear of the tepee. Her eyes were drawn to three war lances tied together at their tips, forming the legs of a tripod. Suspended by rawhide thongs, resting upon two of the lances was Stone Fist's battle scarred, war shield.

Three human scalps hung down from the top of the shield. The hair attached to the two scalps surrounding, framing the scalp in the center was straight, black in color, and the texture typical of that of the plains Indians.

The hair of the scalp in the center of the three was different. It was brown. The color of the hair was brown, with a few streaks of gray.

Despite her revulsion at encountering the gruesome trophies, Pretty Buffalo Hair moved closer to the shield. It was then that she noticed that the texture of the scalp in the center was curly, wiry and coarse. The texture was similar to that of the hair of the buffalo.

Her heart began to race, pounding in her chest. Pretty Buffalo Hair was having difficulty catching her breath. A cold clammy sweat covered her forehead.

Pretty Buffalo Hair realized that the curly-haired scalp was from the head of her mother. The scalp hanging in the center of Stone Fist' war shield, was from the head of Ruth, her birth mother.

Pretty Buffalo hair screamed and fainted. The sound of her scream was lost, swallowed, muted by the sound of the howling wind.

****

When Pretty Buffalo Hair regained conscientiousness, she was disoriented, confused. She had a splitting headache. Pretty Buffalo Hair rubbed her temples. It did not help. The throbbing head splitting pain did not subside.

She looked around at her surroundings. The interior of the tepee was vaguely familiar. She knew that it was not the lodge that she shared with Running Eagle, yet she felt that she had been in this place before.

As her eyes settled on the war shield, Pretty Buffalo Hair bolted upright, and ran from the tepee.

The intensity of the wind had increased. Snow was now falling and sticking to the earth, at a steady rate.

Pretty Buffalo Hair stumbled into her lodge. The pain in her head was a steady throbbing ache. Pretty Buffalo Hair as if in a trance, began to build a fire; she began the preparation of the evening meal.

As she sat staring into the crackling fire, her eyelids were growing increasingly heavy. Pretty Buffalo Hair nodded; her head slumped to her chest. She fell asleep. She dreamt.

Little seven-year-old Rebecca and Mandy were happily playing house in the barn.

Jesse, Rebecca's twelve-year-old brother, the future Master of Rosewood Plantation, was astride Mandy's brother, ten-year-old Jason' back. Jesse was enthusiastically kicking Jason in the ribs, "spurring on his trusty steed".

Jesse was shouting to his horse (Jason); "Come on Blacky, you lazy bag of bones, them damn Redskins is getting away".

"We gotta get 'em, gotta catch those savages. Don't let them take our white women folk alive. All those Injuns are savage cannibals, they cook and eat white women; Injuns cut out and eat their hearts and their innards. Those murdering Injuns steals, rapes, tortures, scalps and murders our helpless white women."

"We gotta kill all of those savages. The only good Injun is a dead Injun!"

Pretty Buffalo Hair woke with a start. The delicious, mouth-watering aroma of roasted venison, the last of their fresh meat, wafted into her nostril. She hurried over to the spit and removed the slightly charred, meat.

Pretty Buffalo hair was still experiencing, what was now, a dull persistent headache. Her head continued to throb. Pretty Buffalo Hair decided to lie down while she awaited the arrival of Running Eagle.

****

Running Eagle pulled aside the flap that covered the entrance to his lodge. Both his head and his heavy buffalo robe were covered with snow.

As he removed the heavy robe from his shoulders and shook off the snow, the delicious aroma of roasted meat greeted him.

Running Eagle, to himself admitted, though he enjoyed spending leisure time with his warrior friends, the time that he spent with his wife, his best friend, Pretty Buffalo Hair, was by far, the happiest times of these cold winter days.

Running Eagle quickly scanned the interior of the lodge. He was attempting to locate his wife. The smell of the roasted venison that was stimulating his digestive juices, to him was ample evidence that she had recently been, or was presently in the lodge.

Running Eagle's eyes picked up Pretty Buffalo Hair's outline, lying uncovered, asleep on one of their heavy sleeping robes. His initial impulse was to wake her, to have her join him, to enjoy her company, as they together, consumed their evening meal.

As he approached Pretty Buffalo Hair, Running Eagle marveled at this beautiful, brilliant, loving woman. This wonderful person that the Great Spirit had sent to him, to share his life.

Running Eagle, rather than waking Pretty Buffalo Hair, decided to let his very pregnant, beautiful wife, rest. He lovingly spread a buffalo robe over Pretty Buffalo Hair's body, and returned to his meal.

****

Pretty Buffalo Hair had been vaguely aware of someone's presence in the lodge.

She found herself in that hazy state between being asleep, while attempting to, but not succeeding, at waking up.

She felt the warmth of the heavy buffalo robe being placed over her. The effect of the robe, its' comforting warmth, contributed to her inability to throw off the heavy veil of sleep.

Running Eagle eagerly joined Pretty Buffalo Hair under their warm Buffalo robes. He was cognizant of Pretty Buffalo Hair's restless tossing.

Running Eagle placed his arm around Pretty Buffalo Hair's ever-expanding belly. He snuggled up to her back and kissed the nape of her neck.

For him, it had been an especially long busy day. Within minute, Running Eagle had fallen into a deep sleep.

Pretty Buffalo Hair's fitful, restless, sleep continued. The troubling images, her bad dreams, persisted. Had returned. Returned more vivid and stronger than ever:

Mandy and Rebecca were terrified. They cringed in horror, shock and fear, watching as the Indian, his face painted black and yellow, scalped the white man, Henry Billings, their father.

Mandy watched horrified as yet another savage beast plunged his huge knife into her mother's chest. She watched as that sub-human animal lifted her mother Ruth's unconscious, mortally wounded body by her hair. She watched as he, with three vicious slashes of his huge, long knife, this visage of savagery, ripped her mother's scalp, dripping with blood, from her head.

The gruesome, savage face, covered in black and yellow war paint, turned towards her. He held her mother's scalp in his filthy, dirty hand. The beast's mouth, in a vicious grin, that revealed his fangs, his large yellow teeth.

Pretty Buffalo Hair's eyes sprung open. She sat bolt, upright. She looked at the face of the man lying beside her. In her state of confusion and unbridled terror, the face that she saw was not that of Running Eagle.

The familiar face of Running Eagle was the face of a warrior, wearing black and red warpaint. The face she had seen when Running Eagle had come, face painted half black and half red, for her when she was fleeing from the wagon train.

Pretty Buffalo Hair...Mandy, stood, and as if she were in a trance, walked over to her tools, picked up the large knife that she used to butcher buffalo, and walked back to her sleeping husband.

Running Eagle stirred when Pretty Buffalo Hair left the warmth of their sleeping robes. Her rising during the night was not at all unusual.

Frequently during her state of pregnancy, Pretty Buffalo Hair, during the night, feeling the need to relieve herself had left the warm confines of their sleeping robes.

When he felt the robes once again being lifted from his body, Running Eagle, his eyes closed with sleep, opened his arms to receive and to cuddle, the warm welcoming body of his wife.

Instead of the familiar feel of Pretty Buffalo Hair's warm body, Running Eagle's eyes flew open when he felt a shearing pain in the center of his chest.

He instinctively grabbed for the object that had caused the pain. His hand was wrapped around the hand of his wife, Pretty Buffalo Hair. In her hand she held a large knife, a knife that the women used for the butchering of large game.

Running Eagle's chest was covered with blood. He looked into the dull, lifeless eyes of his wife. Pretty Buffalo Hair pried Running Eagles, rapidly weakening hand from hers.

Wordlessly she rose and slowly walked from the lodge. The wind and snow were swirling. A momentary lull interrupted the storm.

As Mandy, in a daze, trudged through the deepening snow, she clearly heard Running Eagle's voice, coming forth through the open flap of the tepee;

"WHY?"

"WHY *Mahn-dee*?"

"WHY?"

The End

www.ingramcontent.com/pod-product-compliance
Lightning Source LLC
Chambersburg PA
CBHW030347130626
46549CB00004B/1400